THE
Biographical Cyclopaedia
OF
American Women

VOLUME I

COMPILED UNDER THE SUPERVISION OF

MABEL WARD CAMERON

NEW YORK
THE HALVORD PUBLISHING COMPANY, INC.
1924

Republished by Gale Research Company, Book Tower, Detroit, 1974

Library of Cangress Catalog Card Number 24-7615

ISBN 0-8103-3990-0

8-5-80

Preface

BIOGRAPHY is not only the account of the life of an individual; it is, or should be, the study of history as seen through the individual's reaction to the national traditions or to the progress of national events. As a nation is the sum total of its citizens, past and present, so the raw materials for its history should be found in the records of the lives of all these citizens, whether they have been, in the common phrase, "makers of history," or, as in the case of the majority, the products of the forces at work in their day. History, however, in such terms of individual biography, is an impracticable ideal: a selection must be made, and thus there have appeared during the last generation or so several general biographical cyclopaedias in which this selection has been effected on excellent principles, but on principles which have seemed to betray a one-sided appreciation of the elements that constitute a great country. For on turning their pages one would suppose that the work of the world had been performed entirely by men, so few are the articles about women and so lost are they among the material devoted to men. Similarly histories for general reading or for use in the schools have on the whole disregarded the work done by women in forming our civilization side by side with the more conspicuous warriors and statesmen, and to arrive at a just conception of the debt due the women of the United States has necessitated long research through many scattered volumes and columns of magazines and newspapers.

Nevertheless this is an age of women. During these last few years Woman has come, as it were, into her own. No longer is she disregarded in the councils of the nation; no longer does she have to commend her art to the public under a masculine pseudonym; no longer is she told that exclusively her "place is in the home." How has this change come about? Who have been the women, fearless pioneers in public life, who have forced entrenched privilege to admit that "women are people?" Who are the artists and writers whose clear insight into the subtler things of the spirit has brought a consecration to this development? Who are those others, of whom it will never be said that they are of "the weaker sex," who have stood shoulder to shoulder to their brothers in the World War and proved that women can also defend that home which it is her pleasure and privilege to make? And again, who are they, the mothers and grandmothers and great-grandmothers of the women of today, whose noble lives and brilliant thoughts have been the inspiration of the present?

Questions such as these demand an answer, and one in clearer terms than it has been customary to give hitherto. This answer *The Biographical Cyclopaedia of American Women* intends to give by frankly applying the principle of selection and devoting itself consistently to one-half of the nation. For this first volume the Editors have made a further selection and offer to the student of American traditions representative biographies of contemporary women of all professions and every walk of life as well as of the mothers of the leaders of to-day, who, although perhaps not widely known in their own time, are deserving of due recognition for the training in character which they impressed upon their children. In doing so they wish to express their deep gratitude to all those who by advice and unfailing encouragement and by the generous contribution of material or finished articles have made the publication of this volume possible.

WARD GRISWOLD CAMERON, M.A.

Acknowledgments

For kind assistance in the preparation of the First Volume of *The Biographical Cyclopaedia of American Women*, special thanks are due to the following persons who have contributed original articles, supplied valuable material, or made suggestions of value:

Addams, Jane

Beatty, Mary D.

Blatch, Harriet Stanton

Cairns, Mrs. Jasper

Cameron, Ward Griswold

Coleman, Emma L.

Cross, Grace Ella, M.D.

Delevan, David Bryson, M.D.

Hays, Matilda Orr

Locke, Bessie

McComas, Reverend Joseph Patton, D.D.

Milholland, Vida

Miner, Maude E.

Peck, Mary Gray, B.A.

Phelps, Professor William Lyon

Sabin, Ellen C.

Sanger, Elizabeth

Stevens, Harry

Winslow, Erving

Wood, Charles Erskine Scott

Dedicated

TO

THE MEMORY OF

Mabel Ward Cameron

THE
BIOGRAPHICAL CYCLOPAEDIA
OF
AMERICAN WOMEN

ADAMS, ABIGAIL SMITH (Mrs. John Adams), was born at Weymouth, Massachusetts, November 11, 1744, daughter of William and Elizabeth (Quincy) Smith. Her father, who was Pastor of the First (Congregational) Church, maintained his family on a small income, but in an environment of learning and quiet culture, which emphasized the fact that in Colonial New England the clergy and their families represented the gentry of the period. Her mother was a daughter of John and Elizabeth (Morton) Quincy.

The Quincy family in America originated with Edmund of that ilk (born in Wigsthorpe, Northamptonshire, England, in 1602), who came to Massachusetts in 1628, returned to England, and sailed again, with his wife and children in the ship which anchored in Boston Harbor, September 4, 1633. In 1635 a large tract of land was granted to him in the Mt. Wollaston plantation. His son, Edmund Quincy, Junior, born at Achurch, Northamptonshire, England, in 1627, was a magistrate in Braintree and a representative of his town at the General Court, also Lieutenant-Colonel of the Suffolk Regiment. In 1689 he was appointed one of the Committee of Safety, which formed the provisional government of the colony until the arrival of the new charter from William and Mary. The line is traced through his son, Daniel, and his only son, John Quincy, the statesman (born in Wollaston, 1689; died there in 1767), who was graduated at Harvard College in 1708; held the office of Speaker of the House of Representatives longer than any other person in the colonial period, and was for forty suc-

cessive years, a member of the Council. He married Elizabeth, daughter of the Reverend John Norton, of Wollaston, who was descended from Saier de Quincy, Earl of Winchester, a surety of the Magna Charta.

Because of her delicate health, as a child, Abigail Smith was educated at home, her father, mother, and grandmother all uniting in the agreeable task of instructing the bright and intelligent girl. The grandmother, Mrs. John Quincy, possessed a remarkably brilliant mind, and was an excellent teacher. Abigail always held her in the deepest veneration and love. Later in life she wrote of the lessons received from her: "I frequently think they made a more durable impression upon my mind than those I received from my own parents." But her whole environment was one of learning and good breeding, in which the love of God was the paramount teaching, and Abigail made the most of every opportunity that came to her. Her mind was assimilative, and she absorbed a great deal from intercourse with the high type of men and women who frequented her father's house. Much of this culture found expression later in the remarkable letters which she wrote. These documents have been published as *Letters*, *2 Volumes*, and *Familiar Letters*.

However, the life of the beautiful young girl was not all devoted to lessons and household tasks. Her childhood was normal and happy, and she took part in many joyous social gatherings, especially at her grandmother Quincy's hospitable mansion. On October 25, 1764, she was married to the young lawyer, John Adams, Junior, of

Braintree (now Quincy). He was the eldest son of John Adams, a farmer, and was born October 30, 1735, in his father's house at Braintree. He died in his own house, July 4, 1826. Both these quaint old houses which stand side by side, are now (1924) in the care of the Quincy chapter of the Daughters of the American Revolution.

The young couple began their married life in the house built next to the one in which John was born, and as the years passed Mrs. Adams was much alone there with her children. After the manner of the lawyers of that period, her husband journeyed from place to place, following the circuit. He also maintained an office in Boston, coming to Braintree for every Sunday.

On July 11, 1767, was born the son who was destined to be the Sixth President of the United States—the second from Massachusetts. In accordance with the request of Mrs. William Smith the child was named for her father and his great-grandfather, the aged John Quincy, who then was dying at his home at Mt. Wollaston. During his boyhood his mother superintended all his studies, inculcating in him lessons of a lofty, moral character. In John Quincy Adams' diary are numerous references to his mother's care and devotion—"She has been to me more than a mother. She has been a spirit from above watching over me for good, and contributing by my mere consciousness of her existence to the comfort of my life." These early years of association with and care of her family were undoubtedly among her happiest. The serene, lovely woman rose to each emergency that came in the daily domestic round as house-wife, teacher of her children, or overseer, in his absence, of her husband's estate.

In 1774, Mr. Adams went as one of the delegates to the Continental Congress at Philadelphia, and one of the first letters of Abigail Adams that has been made public, dated August 15, 1774, was written to him. From this time the correspondence was continuous, for she was alone through all the distressful period following the bombardment of the nearby city of Boston. Her letters reflect her unselfish and loving spirit, as well as her ardent patriotism. Perhaps the most famous of all is the one which has earned for her the title of the "first woman suffragist" in which she writes: "In the new code of laws which I suppose it will be necessary for you to make, I desire you would remember the ladies and be more generous and favorable to them than your ancestors. Do not put such unlimited power into the hands of the husbands. Remember all men would be tyrants if they could. If particular care and attention is not paid to the ladies we are determined to foment a rebellion, and will not hold ourselves bound by any laws in which we have no voice or representation." But Mrs. Adams did not foment any rebellion. Her vigorous and clear mind continued to show its energy in the practical matters of her simple home and ordinary pursuits.

In the autumn of 1777 John Adams was appointed Minister to France. This further separation came as a cruel blow to his wife, and was augmented by the decision that the ten year old son should accompany his father, as his private secretary. But on her part there was no thought of dissuasion, and in loneliness, but with courage, she passed the eighteen months which followed the departure of father and son from the beach at Mount Wollaston Farm. On August 2, 1779 she welcomed the travelers home, but after only one week with his devoted wife, at their peaceful farm, John Adams was sent to draw up the Constitution of Massachusetts. Soon after this he was appointed to the Court of St. James. His errand of diplomacy was an adventure that, for success, has not a parallel in history, for he settled the questions which established the liberties of the British free colonies.

Mrs. Adams joined her husband in England, where she was the first American woman to be presented at court. Charming in her matronly beauty, she now appears in a background wholly new. From her life of retirement in a quiet New England town she was suddenly obliged to take her position in the ceremonious environment of a large European city, and to assume the requirements of court life. She was perfectly adapted in all ways to share, indeed to augment, her husband's high position, and made for herself a reputation for charm and grace. This was true of her also, when, following their return to America, and the election of John Adams as second president of the United States, she occupied the position of "first lady of the land."

Her character, in its depth and purity is revealed in the letter which she wrote to her husband upon his inauguration: "My feelings are not those of pride or ostentation, upon the occasion. They are solemnized by a sense of the obligations, the important trusts, and numerous duties connected with it. That you may be enabled to discharge them with honor to yourself, with justice and impartiality to your country, and with satisfaction to this great people, shall be the prayer of your A.A."

After her husband's retirement to private life, Mrs. Adams returned with him to their beloved Braintree, there to spend their last years in peace and happiness, honored by their townspeople, and sought out by the great from other lands, who, on coming to America, delighted to make the pilgrimage. They continued to live in the old house, where, it is said, "Independence began." At all times, through the varied, often tragic experiences of their life, Mrs. Adams' influence over her famous husband was evident though always unobtrusive. Her advice was given discreetly, and she surrounded him with an influence of love and tender care. It was one of the examples of a wife so tending her husband and so encouraging him, so lifting all home cares from his shoulders, that he had nothing to distract his attention from his public career.

Abigail Adams died October 28, 1818, and on her tombstone, which she shares with her husband in the cemetery at Quincy, there is inscribed "at his side sleeps, till the trump shall sound, Abigail, his beloved and only wife—in every relation a pattern of filial, conjugal, maternal and social virtues."

ADAMS, LOUISA CATHERINE JOHNSON (Mrs. John Quincy Adams), was born in London, England, in 1775; married in London, July 26, 1797; died in Quincy, Massachusetts, daughter of Joshua and Catherine (Nuth) Johnson. Her father (born June 25, 1744), was a brother of Governor Thomas Johnson of Maryland, and grandson of Thomas Johnson who came to Maryland from England in 1689–1690. He removed to London in early manhood, and was a merchant there for many years. During the War of American Independence, he was agent of Maryland in Nantes, France. Upon the organization of the United States Government, he returned with his family to London, and was the first United States Consul there, 1785–1799.

Louisa's education, begun under the best conditions in France, was continued in England. The family home was a centre of diplomatic life, and among the frequent visitors was John Quincy Adams, who had been appointed by President Washington, in 1794, United States Minister to the Hague and later to Germany. In 1797, Mr. Adams and Miss Johnson were married and thereafter she led the eventful life of a diplomat's wife. In 1801 the overthrow of the Federalist party caused the recall of Mr. Adams to America. He was elected United States Senator in 1803, and the following six years were passed by Mrs. Adams in Washington. In 1809 she accompanied her husband to St. Petersburg, when he was appointed Minister to Russia.

The personal friendliness of Tsar Alexander I, opened to Mr. Adams the brilliant career that ultimately led to the White House. When, in the winter of 1814–1815, it was deemed advisable that Mrs. Adams should leave St. Petersburg, she crossed Europe in her travelling carriage, with her seven-year old son, Charles Francis, as her only travelling companion, passing through the opposing Allied and French armies, and reaching Paris during the *Cent Jours*, after Napoleon's return from Elba. This courageous episode was typical of her dauntless spirit and ability to meet every emergency that arose in her eventful life.

Her husband was next sent as Minister to England, where Mrs. Adams again presided with her well-known charm and grace. In 1817 the couple returned to America on Mr. Adams' recall to be Secretary of State. In 1825 he was elected President of the United States and for the next four years Mrs. Adams, as first lady of the land, was an inspiration and aid to her husband as well as an example, in diplomatic life, of tact with unfailing courtesy. Her life was still passed in Washington after she left the White House, for her husband, after his term of office expired, and after a brief rest as a private citizen, was elected to a seat in Congress, and retained it for fifteen years.

The latter years of Mrs. Adams' life were passed in peaceful retirement in Quincy, Massachusetts, where she was an object of universal deference. The radiant loveliness of her youth merged into the delicate beauty of age, the charm of her sweet face enhanced by the becoming caps that she always wore. She was fragile, an exotic in her surroundings in the small New England town, but after the many turbulent years, passed as mistress of a diplomat's household in many lands, she was contented to live uneventfully in the quiet of the old Massachusetts home, and the town welcomed her and paid her homage.

ADAMS, ABIGAIL BROWN BROOKS (Mrs. Charles Francis Adams) was born April 25, 1808, daughter of Peter Chardon and Ann (Gorham) Brooks. The family consisted of four sons and three daughters.

One daughter, Charlotte, married Edward Everett, and another, Ann, married Nathaniel Frothingham, Minister of the First Church, Boston. Mr. Brooks was born at Yarmouth, in what was then the Province of Maine, January 6, 1767. He was named for his father's friend, Peter Chardon. The family was one of the most distinguished in New England, and many of its members were clergymen. The family ancestry is traced to Sir Richard Saltonstall, of Huntswick, York, England, an original patentee of Massachusetts Bay Colony, who came to New England in April, 1630; was the founder of Watertown, Massachusetts, and after his return to England, was sent as Ambassador to Holland. He married Grace Kaye, who was descended from fourteen Sureties of Magna Charta: William d'Albini, Hugh Bigod, Roger Bigod, Henry de Bohun, Gilbert de Clare, Richard de Clare, John Fitz-Robert, John de Lacy, William de Lanvallie, William Malet, William de Mowbray, Saire de Quincy, Robert de Roos and Robert de Vere.

Richard Saltonstall, Junior, Sir Richard's son (born at Woodesome, Yorkshire, England, 1610), settled at Ipswich, Massachusetts, and married Muriel Gordon, also descended from the Magna Charta barons, Henry de Bohun, William de Mowbray, Robert de Vere and Saire de Quincy. Their son, Colonel Nathaniel Saltonstall (1639–1707) had a daughter, Elizabeth, who married Reverend Roland Cotton of Sandwich, Massachusetts, grandson of the famous Reverend John Cotton, Pastor of the First Church of Boston. Their daughter, Joanna, married Reverend John Brown of Haverhill, Massachusetts. Their daughter, Abigail, married Reverend Edward Brooks, of Medford, Massachusetts, and their son was Peter Chardon Brooks, who married Ann Gorham.

Abigail Brooks, named for her grandmother, was reared at the family home at Medford, where she had every advantage of environment and education. She was married, September 3, 1829, to Charles Francis, son of

John Quincy and Catherine Johnson Adams. Their city home was on Beacon Hill, Boston, a locality filled with historic memories, and Mr. Adams also built, for a summer home, a house on the high ground at Quincy, above the old homestead occupied by his father, with a view eastward over Quincy Bay, and northward over Boston. Mrs. Adams spent much time away from New England, however, for her husband represented his country abroad. His work was especially important during the Civil War, when he was minister to the Court of St. James, a position which both his father and grandfather had filled before him, and which at this time required the highest order of diplomatic ability. Mrs. Adams acquitted herself, through this most trying time, with success, winning a reputation for patriotism and tactful social ability.

The children of Mr. and Mrs. Charles Francis Adams were: Louisa Catherine (born 1830), who married Charles Kuhn of Philadelphia; John Quincy, who married Fannie Crowninshield; Charles Francis, who married Mary Ogden; Henry Brooks (named for a favorite brother of Mrs. Adams), who was a professor at Harvard College, and the author of many books; Mary, who married Henry Parker Quincy; and Brooks, who married Evelyn Davis. Mr. Adams died in Boston, November 21, 1886. Mrs. Adams died in Boston, in June, 1889.

McCORMICK, HARRIET BRADLEY HAMMOND (Mrs. Cyrus Hall McCormick), daughter of Captain George Woodbury and Emma Young Hammond, was born in Newport, Monmouthshire, England, on December 21, 1862, and died in Chicago, Illinois, January 17, 1921. Her father was an American sea captain of English ancestry, a direct descendant of the Woodbury, Hammond, and Bradley families, whose names are intimately connected with the early history of New England. John Woodbury, her first American forefather, was one of the historic founders of the Massachusetts Bay Colony. He emigrated from Somersetshire, England in 1624, and settled in Salem, Massachusetts, where by reason of his service as deputy to the General Court, town treasurer, selectman, and original member of the first meeting house, he became an outstanding figure, and was often referred to as "Father Woodbury." The Hammond family also came from England in the seventeenth century; and Mrs. McCormick's great-great-grandfather, Philip Hammond, a member of the Marblehead branch of the family, fought with the Fourth Massachusetts Regiment in the Revolutionary War. Joseph Bradley, another ancestor, left London, England, to settle in Haverhill, Massachusetts, in 1659. It was through these pioneers, and also through Captain Daniel Hale, John Dodge, and Paul Thorndike, that Mrs. McCormick was eligible to membership in the Society of Colonial Dames.

Captain Hammond, although less than thirty years of age at the time of his marriage, was in command of one of several merchant ships trading between America and India, which he owned jointly with his elder brother. Mrs. McCormick's mother was an Englishwoman, the daughter of James Young, a small Monmouthshire land owner; and she lived in Newport, England, until after her marriage. In 1863 Captain Hammond brought his wife and daughter Harriet, then one year old, to Haverhill, Massachusetts, to live in the old family homestead.

Harriet Hammond lived in Haverhill until she was twelve years old, when, following the death of her father in 1875, she was adopted by her aunt, Mrs. Edward S. Stickney (Elizabeth Hammond) of Chicago. She was educated at Miss Kirkland's school in Chicago, and after completing her course there went abroad for two years of European travel and study. Her training as a child in her grandfather's home in New England, and her education under her aunt's supervision in Chicago and in Europe, further developed those sterling Anglo-Saxon qualities which she had inherited from her English ancestors.

Combined with the sincerity, fairness, and devotion to duty which dominated her life, there was a natural simplicity, an innate kindliness of spirit, and an unfailing graciousness, which made her character even from girlhood singularly fine and beautiful.

Harriet Bradley Hammond was married on March 5, 1889, at Monterey, California, to Cyrus Hall McCormick of Chicago, the eldest son of the inventor of the reaper, who at that time was President of the McCormick Harvesting Machine Company, later the President of the International Harvester Company, and in recent years the chairman of its board of directors. Three children were born to Mr. and Mrs. McCormick, two sons, Cyrus and Gordon, and a daughter, Elizabeth, who died in 1905 at the age of twelve. Mrs. McCormick's supreme interest always centered in her family, and in her home life she created an atmosphere of beauty and distinction.

A ready response to all worth-while movements, and a genuine desire to be of service were always characteristic of Mrs. McCormick. One of her earliest outside interests was in the introduction of welfare work among the employees of the great industry with which her husband's family had long been associated. Her concern was first stimulated by a study of the writings of Jacob Riis, but after visiting the Sociological Exhibits at the Paris Exposition of 1900 her ideas took more definite form, and it was largely through her influence and her understanding insight that welfare work was soon begun in the McCormick Harvesting Machine Company, placing the organization among the pioneers in that branch of industrial development.

After the death of her little daughter, Mrs. McCormick became increasingly occupied with civic and philanthropic movements, particularly those concerned with the needs of childhood. In their desire to help other children in memory of their daughter, Mr. and Mrs. McCormick made a thorough survey of child welfare problems, and in 1908 established the Elizabeth McCormick Memorial

Fund incorporated "to improve the conditions of child life in the United States." Mrs. McCormick followed its work with intense interest, and its far-seeing program was due largely to her own wide and sympathetic vision. Her eagerness to serve the cause of children, and her consciousness of the opportunities for constructive work in this important but neglected field, also prompted her to promote and finance the Child Welfare Exhibit, held in 1911 in the Chicago Coliseum. Under her earnest leadership, and with the coöperation of an able group of men and women, this notable exhibit made a wide appeal, attracting more than 400,000 visitors from all parts of the country and stimulating nation-wide activity in behalf of children.

The improvement of conditions of child life did not, however, absorb all of Mrs. McCormick's time or attention, and her public interests were never limited to those projects which had only a personal appeal. She was for many years an enthusiastic member of the Visiting Nurse Association, and in 1906 assumed a more active part in its work, first as a director, and later as a vice-president. As a constructive leader in the work of the Young Women's Christian Association, she aided effectively in the advancement of its program, both local and national, giving valuable assistance at the time of the formation of the Central Field Committee, taking an active part in bringing about the affiliation of the Chicago organization with the National Board, and holding in her home the first meetings outside of New York in the interests of the Association war-work program. She believed earnestly in equal suffrage, and by her dignified and womanly support was a source of strength to the movement. She gave of herself, as well as of her means, to many other causes; whether it was the Juvenile Protective Association, of which she had been a director, some comparatively unknown philanthropy, or a great movement of national importance, it was always her policy to investigate carefully not only its aim but its business standards.

Mrs. McCormick responded with enthusiasm to literary and artistic, as well as to civic and philanthropic affairs. Her diversified interests included the opera, music, and such important organizations as the Woman's City Club of Chicago, of which she had been a director; The Fortnightly, and the Friday Club, both of which she had served as president; the Society of Colonial Dames; the Chicago Historical Society; the Cordon Club; the Arts Club; and the Colony Club of New York. She was a communicant of St. James Episcopal Church, and following her marriage was closely identified with the Fourth Presbyterian Church and its varied activities.

Shortly after they were married Mr. and Mrs. McCormick purchased the house on Huron Street in which Mrs. McCormick had lived as a girl, and there they established their home. A few years later they built a country house on the bluffs of Lake Michigan in the suburb of Lake Forest. In the development of the woodlands and ravines of "Walden," as this place is called, in the creation of its gardens and its vistas, Mrs. McCormick took constant pleasure. Her study and appreciation of the fundamental principles of landscape gardening made her an ardent member of local and national Garden Clubs, and a valued contributor to their programs and to current landscape literature. She loved the out-of-doors, and found refreshment for mind and body in gardening, walking, camping, and other simple forms of recreation.

Imbued with an intense patriotism, Mrs. McCormick was ready to serve her country eagerly and unsparingly. When the United States entered the World War she was among the first to anticipate the need of organization among women for war-time service, and from its beginning was Treasurer of the Woman's Committee of the National Council of Defense, Illinois Division. As Vice-Chairman of the United War Work Drive for Chicago, she rendered further valuable aid. Through her inspiration the Elizabeth McCormick Memorial Fund became the agency to carry out in Illinois the war-time program of the Children's Year. Always reticent by instinct, it was only because of her unfailing desire to serve that Mrs. McCormick ever spoke in public; but during the war her loyal, patriotic spirit led her on many occasions to make short public addresses in the interests of the Council of Defense, the Young Men's and Young Women's Christian Associations, Conservation, the Children's Year, and other movements to which she gave herself untiringly.

In the philanthropic, civic, and social life of Chicago Mrs. McCormick was a gracious leader, such leadership seldom having been accorded to one whose nobility of soul combined more perfectly with her loveliness of person. But varied and absorbing as were her many interests, she always succeeded in maintaining a true sense of values, keeping for her home and her family the largest share of her energy and devotion. The inspiration of her character shines forth in her eager and sympathetic service for others, in her constant adherence to the highest ideals, and in her steadfast Christian faith.

THE ELIZABETH McCORMICK MEMORIAL FUND

The Elizabeth McCormick Memorial Fund was established in Chicago in 1908 by Mr. and Mrs. Cyrus Hall McCormick in memory of their daughter Elizabeth, "a child whose radiant young life was so marked by deeds of kindness to others that her ministries of love were not allowed to cease, when, at the age of twelve, she was called into the presence of the Great Friend of all the children." Soon after her death in 1905 Mr. and Mrs. McCormick began a careful study of the needs and problems of children, and after consultation with sociologists, philanthropists, and educators from all parts of the country, established the Elizabeth McCormick Memorial Fund, incorporated "to improve the conditions of child life in the United States." By its wise and far-seeing terms no limitations have been placed upon its usefulness, making it a responsive, living memorial, ready to serve the needs of each generation. It is controlled by a self-perpetuating board of trustees, and its activities are carried on by a staff of thirty-four able workers. Every stage of its development, as well as all of the details of its organization, have been matters of the deepest interest and concern to Mr. and Mrs. McCormick, and their vision of its possibilities has been largely responsible for its achievements.

Alert both to the spiritual and physical problems of childhood the trustees have been in touch from the beginning with all constructive projects. As one of its first activities the Fund promoted the baby tents which had been opened by the United Charities as experimental centers of medical and nursing care for the children of the crowded districts of the city during the hot summer months. The great success of this demonstration resulted in the organization of the Infant Welfare Society of Chicago, with its many well-equipped stations and workers. An open-air school for tubercular and anemic children, opened in 1909 by the United Charities on the roof of the Mary Crane Nursery in the congested district near Hull House, was financed by the Memorial Fund. Clothing suitable for out-door life in a rigorous climate, and a regular regime of resting and special feeding were combined with the public-school curriculum in this experiment. The results were so immediate and remarkable that the trustees adopted, as the major activity of the Fund, a program for the promotion and maintenance of open-air and open-window school rooms, until they were not only taken over as a part of the school system of Chicago but were extensively copied in many other cities.

When the United States entered the World War, the trustees placed the entire organization at the service of the Government, and the Fund became the agency through which in 1918 the program of the Children's Year was carried out in the State of Illinois under the direction of the Child Welfare Department of the Woman's Committee of the Council of Defense. The results of this intensive, state-wide program in behalf of children, which extended into more than one thousand communities, were outstanding and far-reaching.

As the principles underlying the earlier experiments became firmly established, the efforts of the Memorial Fund were directed toward problems of nutrition among school children, and, as in its previous work, the Fund again became a pioneer in an important field. The organization is now engaged in extensive studies in malnutrition and underweight, in developing methods to overcome these conditions, and in training workers to conduct nutrition classes. General health education for children has at all times been an important part of the program, and it has been promoted through coöperation with different school systems in experimental work, and through exhibits, lectures, and literature. During the year 1922, 526 lectures were given: exhibits were supplied 220 meetings, including three in foreign countries; and more than 363,000 pieces of literature were distributed in the United States and fourteen foreign countries.

It has always been the policy of the trustees to conduct the Fund as a laboratory center rather than as an agency to carry on any single program over an indefinite period. Through the experiments which it has conducted and the investigations and research in which it has been engaged, new theories and methods have been developed and tested for improving the conditions of child life, and the results made available for practical application by such public and private agencies as are equipped to carry forward the definite projects.

In the fifteen years of its existence the Elizabeth McCormick Memorial Fund has carried on faithfully and well its "ministries" in memory of the child whose name it bears; thousands of young lives have been directly benefited through its experimental programs; and it has been notably instrumental in awakening public interest in the fundamental needs and problems of childhood.

BRENT, MARGARET, was born in England about 1600 and died in Maryland in 1661. She came to Maryland with her brothers in November, 1638, and with them, in 1640, received a grant of land on Kent Island, which was called the "Manor of Kent Fort." Maryland was then the proprietary colony of Cecilius, "Absolute Lord and Proprietary of the Provinces of Maryland and Avalon, Lord Baron of Baltimore" in the peerage of Ireland. His residence was generally in England, and he never visited Maryland. Under the laws of England the colony was administered by Governors, his representatives. Leonard Calvert, brother of Lord Baltimore, was the first Governor. Mistress Margaret Brent enjoyed the confidence of Governor Calvert, for she was a woman of influence and powers in the colony, and held estates in her own right, which were increased by a bequest from Thomas White who had vainly sought her hand in marriage. On various occasions she acted as attorney for her brothers; but interest centres around her principally as the first woman to demand the right to vote in an American colony or state. She also sought a seat in the Colonial Assembly, which she was permitted to address on several occasions. Her claim was based on the fact that she was sole executrix under the will of Governor Calvert, who died June 21, 1647. She entered the General Assembly at Fort St. John's on January 21, 1648, to demand one vote as a planter, along with other planters and a second vote as Lord Baltimore's representative, as executrix of the late Governor's estates, and also of Lord Baltimore's estates, which the Governor had administered, and which she now held in right of executrix. Her claim was refused by the Assembly, which sat as a court, but she was permitted to address it at that time, and frequently thereafter in Lord Baltimore's interests. Upon his sending from England a letter objecting to her course of action, the Assembly formally advised him that she was "the ablest man among them." Notwithstanding her difficulties with Gov-

ernor Thomas Green, Leonard Calvert's successor, he appealed to her to pay the late Governor's indebtedness to some soldiers, which she promptly did. She stands out as a fascinating, brilliant, daring woman, who displayed unusual courage and ability.

AGASSIZ, ELIZABETH CABOT CARY (Mrs. Louis Agassiz), educator, daughter of Thomas Greaves Cary, was born in Boston, Massachusetts, December 5, 1822. In 1850 she was married to Professor Jean Louis Rudolphe Agassiz, the noted Swiss naturalist, who, in 1848, had been appointed to the Chair of Zoology and Geology at the Lawrence Scientific School, Harvard University. During the early years of her married life she conducted at her home in Cambridge a school for young ladies, having among her pupils Pauline Agassiz (later Mrs. Quincy Adams Shaw) and Ida Agassiz, her husband's daughters by his first marriage.

A woman of unusually brilliant mind, she assisted Professor Agassiz with devoted industry in his scientific investigations and accompanied him on his expeditions to Brazil in 1865, and to the Pacific Coast in 1871. In 1868 she published her book, *A Journey to Brazil*, written under her husband's direction, and contributed an account of the Pacific Expedition to the *Atlantic Monthly*. After Professor Agassiz's death in 1873, Mrs. Agassiz was influential in securing the establishment of the Harvard University Annex for Women Students, opened in 1879, and upon its foundation as Radcliffe College, became its first President, serving until 1899, when she resigned with the title of Honorary President.

Mrs. Agassiz was the author of *A First Lesson in Natural History* (1859); and in collaboration with her step-son, Alexander Agassiz, of *Seaside Studies in Natural History* (1865); and *Marine Animals of Massachusetts Bay*. In 1885 she edited the *Life and Correspondence of Louis Agassiz*, and in 1886, *Geological Studies*.

SHAW, PAULINE AGASSIZ (Mrs. Quincy Adams Shaw), philanthropist, daughter of Jean Louis Rodolphe and Cécile (Braun) Agassiz, was born in Neuchâtel, Switzerland, February 6, 1841. Her father came of a long line of Protestant ministers of Motier, Canton Fribourg, Switzerland, where he was born May 28, 1807. After attaining a brilliant reputation for research in medicine and biology, he came to the United States in 1846. In 1848 he was appointed to the Chair of Zoölogy and Geology at the Lawrence Scientific School, of Harvard University. His lectures at Harvard and at other universities and his many scientific explorations won for him the reputation he held at the time of his death (December 14, 1873) as the leading naturalist of his day. His first wife, Cécile Braun Agassiz, died in Neuchâtel in 1848, and in 1850 he married, in Cambridge, Massachusetts, Elizabeth Cabot Cary. Upon establishing a home, he at once sent for his three children by his first marriage, Alexander (afterward his father's associate, and still later his successor in zoölogical studies), Ida (Mrs. Henry Lee Higginson), and Pauline.

The younger daughter, Pauline, who had begun her education in Switzerland, continued her studies in the unique school for girls conducted by her stepmother, Elizabeth Cary Agassiz, in the Agassiz home in Cambridge. The relation between Mrs. Agassiz and Pauline was one of loving sympathy and unusual understanding. To be in daily association with a woman of such high mental calibre was of inestimable advantage to the young girl in the formative period of her life. In Cambridge, Massachusetts, on November 30, 1860, Pauline Agassiz married Quincy Adams Shaw, a financier of Boston, who later was a director of the Calumet and Hecla Mining Company with Pauline's brother, Alexander Agassiz. Pauline (Agassiz) and Quincy Adams Shaw were the parents of five children: Louis, Pauline, Quincy, Marian and Robert. Out of her efforts to determine the best methods of training these children developed her practical interest in education.

Mrs. Shaw's love for the young was an integral part of her nature; when she herself was but a child she found pleasure in giving help and comfort to the children of the poor. From her father she inherited scientific instincts and intuitive powers of reasoning. From her mother, who came of a family of artists and scientists famous in Germany for their achievements, she derived vision and creative imagination. Thus she possessed gifts rarely combined in one individual. She enjoyed the additional advantage, that her own carefully supervised education had differed from current methods. Therefore, in devising a program for her own children's training she became a pioneer, and in the school that she established, at 6 Marlboro Street, Boston, for them and for the children of some of her friends, she demonstrated many of the progressive principles today practised in modern pedagogy. From her keen interest in children and in education developed that devotion to philanthropy and other great causes which filled her life. Possessed of a large income, which she used altogether for purposes of public benefaction, she was able to meet the financial needs of her many educational experiments.

When, in 1877, Mrs. Shaw opened two kindergartens, one in Jamaica Plain, Massachusetts, and one in Brookline, Massachusetts, she initiated the kindergarten movement in the East. Isolated attempts to inaugurate public, private and special charitable kindergartens had previously been made in various cities, but Mrs. Shaw's organized system of model kindergarten work under expert supervision established the kindergarten as a part of a great educational movement. Because of her success in and near Boston, such schools were established in other centres. By the year 1883 Mrs. Shaw was supporting thirty-one free kindergartens, which were a power in the Boston educational system. Many of these were located in public-school buildings, but all the expense of salaries and maintenance was borne by Mrs. Shaw herself. The influence of these kindergartens was far-reaching. They were the first social and educational centres ever connected with schools, and from them went the first social workers and visitors in the homes. Mothers' meetings and parents' clubs also originated in these kindergartens, and Mrs. Shaw provided instruction for grown people in many subjects other than the care and education of children. Eventually she established a kindergarten and a kindergarten training school in connection with her private school on Marlboro Street, Boston. She had in view not only the training of professional kindergartners, but also the education of girls for the vocation of motherhood. Her own motherliness, which would not tolerate distinctions of race, color, or creed, led her to gather into safe shelters forlorn and neglected children deprived of their mothers' care. In 1877, in connection with one of her kindergartens, she started her first day nursery. By 1880 seven others had been established in or near Boston. The day nursery was raised by Mrs. Shaw from the plane of a mere agency for material relief to that of an educational institution. An early report of one of these nurseries, says: "The aim has been not only to provide for the care and training of the children in the kindergarten method, but to reach the homes through the influence of the work and the visiting of the matron in them. . . . Mrs. Shaw regards these nurseries as elementary kindergartens. . . . In connection with the nursery, mothers' classes have been held where instruction in nursing, hygiene, and temperance, has been given. Classes in sewing, cutting, and mending, are held for women and girls. Evening clubs for boys and girls are also a part of the work."

The nurseries prepared the way for the settlement work which followed. The Roxbury Neighborhood House, formerly the Childrens' House, organized in its present form in 1906, the Ruggles Street Neighborhood House, at Roxbury, and the Cambridge Neighborhood House, at Cambridgeport, all developed from kindergartens and day nurseries established by Mrs. Shaw in 1878. In 1901 she opened Social Service House, to be conducted as a model home in the neighborhood of the North Bennett Street Industrial School, and to form a connecting link between that school and the community. This school proved one of her most judicious and fruitful experiments. In the same district, the heart of the Italian quarter, she had for many years maintained a day nursery. Other establishments of hers with similar objects are the Cottage Place Neighborhood House and Day Nursery, which houses the Cottage Place Library; and the Civic Service House, which teaches citizenship to adult immigrant wage-earners, and with which was connected the first night school in Boston.

At Westford, Massachusetts, Mrs. Shaw founded Long-Sought-For Lodge and Children's House, both vacation houses. In 1888 she founded, and from that time supported, in the North End of Boston a school for teaching sloyd and training sloyd teachers. This institution developed into a school of craftsmanship and design, housed since 1909 in the building given by Mrs. Shaw in Harcourt Street. In 1907, as a result of the marked success of the classes that had been held at the Breadwinners' Institute in Civic Service House, and on the advice of Professor Frank Parsons, Mrs. Shaw founded the first Vocation Bureau in the United States. At this time, also, she endowed the course in vocational guidance in the Department of Education at Harvard University.

Mrs. Shaw early became convinced that a recognition of the equality of women before the law was indispensable to social progress. Therefore she continually devoted more and more of her time and her means to the fundamental work of improving the condition of humanity by raising the political and social status of women. For sixteen years she served as President of the Boston Equal Suffrage Association for Good Government, which she founded, and she generously aided every one of the campaigns in the western states. Her desire to improve human society and government led her, moreover, to endorse the efforts to prevent war and assure peace. That her influence might count to the full, she joined the League to Enforce Peace, as well as the World's Court League. She was the first Vice-President of the Massachusetts Branch of the Woman's Peace Party. In 1914 she attended the Conference on International Arbitration at Lake Mohonk.

Mrs. Shaw died on February 10, 1917. In personal appearance she was slight, delicate, and very beautiful, with a singular radiance of expression. Vision, sincerity, sweetness and sympathy, combined with exceptional executive ability, made constructive and enduring her work for education and for the relief of human suffering.

LUKENS, REBECCA WEBB, iron manufacturer, daughter of Isaac and Martha (Webb) Pennock, was born in Chester County, Pennsylvania, January 6, 1794. Her father, founder of the Lukens Iron and Steel Company, was reared a farmer, but in 1793 erected the Federal Slitting Mill at the place now known as Rokeby on Buck Run, Chester County, Pennsylvania, about five miles southwest of Coatesville. From this beginning developed the present mammoth manufactory, which has remained in the possession of his descendants for over 125 years.

In the year 1810, Isaac Pennock, in conjunction with Jesse Kersey, purchased from Moses Coates the Brandywine mill property at Coatesville, which had been used previously as a saw mill, and transformed it into a mill for the rolling of sheet iron. In 1817, he purchased Jesse Kersey's interest in the property and the business, and rented the mill to his son-in-law, Doctor Charles Lukens, who, in 1813, had entered into partnership with Isaac Pennock in the Rokeby mill. Isaac Pennock continued in the conduct of his own business at Rokeby until his death, in 1825.

Doctor Charles Lukens, beginning in 1817, conducted the business at the Brandywine Iron Works on his own account until he died, in 1825. He had practised medicine for a short time before he married Rebecca Webb Pennock, in 1813, but preferred to become a manufacturer. He foresaw that steam boilers, previously very little used, were destined to much more general adoption for power purposes. Further, he realized that the superior qualities of the charcoal iron, which at the time he was manufacturing into sheets, was exceptionally well suited for the conditions of high pressure strains in steam boilers. He therefore proceeded to adapt the Brandywine mill to the work of rolling boiler plates. To that end, he installed a reverberatory furnace for heating the charcoal iron slabs, which prior to that time had been heated in an open charcoal fire. The reverberatory furnace also furnished an excellent means of welding the scrap shearings so that they also could be rolled out into sheets. Thus it was possible to avoid the waste otherwise occurring from the loss of these shearings, which had formerly been used, to some extent, for making nails.

Doctor Lukens had barely completed the alterations to the mill when he was taken ill, and died. At his request, his widow, Rebecca W. Lukens, assumed direction of affairs after his death. She had had little training for the business, except from association with her husband, having been closely occupied with the care of a large family of children. Her large mental capacity, however, as well as her excellent education, enabled her to overcome all difficulties and carry the business to an exceptional success.

In a sketch of this earlier period of her life, which she wrote for her children after her husband's death, Mrs. Lukens says: "My design is not merely to gratify their curiosity, but, if possible, to improve them by an instructive lesson, by warning them of those errors into which my own inexperience and warmth, both of imagination and feelings, too often led me, and, by holding up to their view the bright example of their father, incite them to follow in his steps the path of every noble, every sublime virtue." She continues: "My paternal ancestors were among the most respectable of those who, wearied with the tyranny and oppression of civilized Europe, sought amid the solitudes of America a quiet retreat and a secure home. What is it to me, though pride would whisper their titles designated them of Patrician race? They were willing to forego such petty distinctions and rest their claims to respect in the country of their adoption solely on their actions and rights as men, willing to devote their talents and their fortunes in aiding to civilize and improve this interesting section of the world." She adds that her grandfather, Joseph Pennock, "inherited, with the large patrimony of his father, all his lofty and unbending principles. Devoted to the country of his birth, he served her with fidelity in the Assembly of his native state until the loud tocsin of war sounded through the land to awake her sons from the lethargy in which they were sunk, to vindicate their rights as men and shake off the trammels of despotism. My father was his youngest child and had, until the period of his marriage, always remained under the paternal roof, but long before that event the struggle for freedom had ceased, a new government organized, and the United States declared and acknowledged independent."

Mrs. Lukens writes that her mother, Martha Webb, was a woman of superior understanding and possessed a remarkable mind, but that, occupied with the care of an increasing family, she was able to devote but small time to the life of her eldest daughter who was left to exercise her own will in her childish pursuits. Mrs. Lukens was reared in the companionship of some older cousins. Of her childhood she writes: "With my young friends I have bounded over hill and dell as wild, happy and joyous as youth could make me, when I neither knew nor feared misfortune. At an early period of my life my father, affluent in his circumstances, had spent

a few years in the metropolis of our country to give his family the advantages of education which our residence at that time denied; but a city life, not being congenial to my mother's taste, it was abandoned before I had received any permanent advantages from it, and at the age of twelve I was placed in a boarding school." After about a year a change was decided upon and "I again resumed my studies, but at a different seminary," in Wilmington, Delaware. "Now it was that life began to open new charms for me. I was rapidly improving, a favorite with my teachers and at the head of all my classes, and here I first found that the wealth and respectability of my father made many eagerly seek my favor. I had many friends, and, with them, every beautiful and romantic situation was explored with unabated enthusiasm. The banks of the Brandywine afforded many a delightful view and often were trod over by the elastic steps of youth. My preceptor was the best of men. All pains were taken to instil religious impressions into the minds of his pupils. He was a minister in the religious Society of Friends, and in truth he practised what he preached. When he showed to us the wonderful order of the heavenly bodies he dwelt with energy on the Great Glorious Architect, and with a strength of language and sublimity of expression which still dwells in my memory. And when he opened to our view the book of Nature it was to draw our minds to Nature's God."

At the age of fifteen she returned to her father's house, and assisted with the care of the family, indulging her spare time in reading the best class of literature, which her instructors had led her to select. After about a year at home she returned to the school, which her teacher had very much enlarged. There, she said: "I was happy in devoting my attention to the different branches in which I wished to perfect myself. Chemistry and the French language claimed my attention and I devoted myself with untiring zeal to their acquirement." She left the school with regret, and a few weeks later visited Philadelphia with her father. There she met Doctor Charles Lukens, also a member of the Society of Friends, who had recently begun practice at Abington, a short distance north of Philadelphia. "He bowed," she says, "with a peculiar grace, and for a moment my eyes rested on his interesting face and his tall and commanding figure. The next I bent them with confusion to the ground. After a desultory conversation he rose, and, pleading business, left us." They met several times again on this visit to the city, and, as she says, she could not banish his image from her mind for some length of time, but with strong determination and persistent effort she finally thought that she had succeeded, after she had returned home. Somewhat later, when spring had more fully opened, she was surprised by a visit from a lady and her husband, who had introduced the young physician in the city, and they brought the friend into the country with them. She says: "Mr. W. shook me familiarly by the hand, and I felt my face and neck glow as I turned from him to meet the approach of his friend." She says: "He was in his person above the common height. An air of grace and dignity were blended in his form. His hair was of the deepest shade of black, his eyes hazel, and his other features manly and remarkably handsome. But, although his was the 'glass of fashion and the mould of form', yet it was the expression of his countenance, 'where every good had seemed to set its seal', that most interested me. It spoke of lofty unbending principle, of a mind exalted, and that felt its own power, while the benevolence which beamed from his eye and the suavity of his manner won their way to the heart and fixed his empire there."

On their walks in the neighborhood, he conversed with fluency on the beauties of the view before them. This he did with an animation and strength of expression which plainly showed he fully felt and could appreciate its power. She says: "I had never

before met with a mind so congenial with my own and I listened with delighted attention. From the beauties of the view he turned to the charms of poetry, and here again I was in an element of my own. He quoted with animated expression some of the witching stanzas of 'Marmion.'" The moon had arisen in all her splendor when they reached the wide piazza which fronted their dwelling. "What a glorious view is this," said he, as their eyes rested on the beautiful scenery before them, softened by her rays. They paused to contemplate it and, seating themselves on the bench of the piazza, he expatiated on the beauties and order of the heavenly bodies, of the vast attributes of Him who formed and controlled them, and said that he felt the one who could view them unmoved must possess a mind dead to every noble, every exalted feeling.

As it would be natural to expect, their long walks and talks under God's open sky resulted in a declaration of love and acceptance, and their marriage, when she was yet but eighteen years of age. In addressing himself definitely to her he had said: "I cannot make those unmeaning professions found on the tongue of every trifler, but I can offer thee a heart that has never before felt the witchery of female power, a heart that would love and cherish thee as the first, best gift of heaven." His own personal characteristics and life undoubtedly had a large influence upon her character, as she almost idolized him, and was to the day of her death absolutely devoted to his memory. She continually held him up as a model before her children. In his own relationship with his employees he visited them in his medical capacity, prescribing for their physical ills and oftentimes followed this by kneeling at the bedside of the sick one and offering up a fervent prayer in his behalf. This endeared him to his employees and when their turn came to minister to him in his last illness by sitting up with him by night, two and two, the two earnest Methodists who sat with him the night that he died declared that they plainly heard strains of celestial music around his dying bed.

At her husband's request, Mrs. Lukens assumed control of the business after his death, very much against the wishes of her mother and others of her family. But, with the help of neighbors and friends, she persisted, and built up a reputation for her product, and established the standards of excellence which have been the guide for all subsequent managers of the business. Among the many difficulties which she had to meet with was the competition of others, who, stimulated by her success, proceeded to build similar mills immediately up-stream and, making an error in establishing the level of their mill, failed to make sufficient allowance for the waste water to clear itself from the large water wheel. Consequently it was choked and its power was reduced. Then they brought suit against Mrs. Lukens, claiming that, when repairing her mill dam, she had raised the level and backed the water.

A long controversy, involving a law suit, followed with the result that the matter was finally compromised by the courts and she ordered to lower her mill dam six inches. When this decision was rendered, she turned to the man who had brought the action against her, and with upraised finger said: "Man, I have something to say to you. You have started out in business taking unfair advantage of your neighbor, and, mark my words, you will never prosper." She lived to see her son-in-law the assignee of the property, which was finally sold at sheriff's sale.

Mrs. Lukens' sons did not live to maturity. Their business was handed down to her two sons-in-law, Abram Gibbons and Charles Huston. When Mr. Gibbons retired, the business passed wholly into the possession of the Huston family. Mrs. Lukens died, on December 10, 1854.

BOWEN, LOUISE DeKOVEN (Mrs. Joseph Tilton Bowen), the daughter of John and Helen (Hadduck) deKoven, was born in Chicago, Illinois, February 26, 1859.

Mrs. Bowen, who is one of the most distinguished citizens of Chicago, claims the uncommon distinction of tracing her lineage to Fort Dearborn itself. Her grandfather, Edward H. Hadduck, came to the Fort in the early thirties, as a young government agent, bringing $200,000 in gold for governmental uses. He was so delighted with his impression of the virgin prairie extending south and west from the Fort situated on the Lake at the mouth of the river, and so convinced of the commercial possibilities to be developed from the trading posts already established there, that he returned a year later with his bride, driving from western Ohio in a typical prairie schooner. Like all the other settlers, he was obliged for his own protection, to live within the stockade of the Fort and his daughter, Helen, who was born there, was the third white girl, according to tradition, born on the present site of the great city of Chicago. Mr. Hadduck was a typical pioneer, conspicuous in the city's early history, and amassed a large fortune from the opportunities which Chicago offered him. Mrs. Bowen, in some early recollections which she has indited for the benefit of her children, thus describes him and his house: "My earliest recollections are clustered around an old-fashioned red brick house which belonged to my grandfather, which was set back from the road on the corner of Wabash Avenue and Monroe Street. There were shade trees in front of the house and a broad strip of green sward before the roadway was reached. This road was made of good, black prairie soil. When it was muddy, it was almost impassable, and when it was dry there were huge ruts which shook up everyone who drove over them. In these early days the cattle for the stock yards were unloaded at the Randolph Street Station of the Illinois Central, and were often driven through the streets to the yards.

Michigan Avenue was not much more than a sandy beach and, as Wabash Avenue was a harder and better roadway, the cattle were frequently driven down this avenue. Sometimes the steers would become frightened and would rush from one side of the street to the other, coming up on the sidewalk and imperilling the passersby. Many a day I have quickly climbed over the low iron fence around my grandfather's house, in order to get away from the frightened beasts.

"Almost next door to my grandfather's house was a little hotel, the old Clifton House, where the Lincolns often stopped when they were in town. Tad Lincoln was a great friend of mine, and I remember Mrs. Lincoln talking to us as we played together.

"Sometimes as we slowly drove our horse and buggy through the town, my grandmother would tell me stories of the early days in Chicago, when she lived in the Fort and used to pull herself across the Chicago River on a little flat boat which was propelled by the passenger pulling a rope stretched across the river. She would tell me how she used to go to the North side to pick blackberries; how oftentimes she would hear an Indian coming and would crouch down beside the bushes until he had passed. Then there were thrilling tales of Indian massacres, and of her experience of being shut up in the Fort in one room, with fifty other people, for several days, while the Indians bombarded the place, shooting flaming arrows into the Fort and often attempting to set it on fire, and how happy the beleaguered were when the scout, who had been sent out to get help, returned with some soldiers and the Indians were dispersed.

"She would point out to me, as she drove, the prairie schooner wagons which were often seen in our streets, and recall the lovely drive she had had to early Chicago, although as they drove she always sat with a loaded rifle across her knees."

Dearborn Seminary, where Mrs. Bowen was educated, was at that time situated on the present site of Marshall Field's great store, although, before Mrs. Bowen completed her schooling, it had been moved to Twenty-Second Street and Wabash Avenue, where it remained for many years, a pioneer outpost of education for the young women of Chicago. Mrs. Bowen finished her school life when she was sixteen, but as the graduation exercises were held in a large church her father would not allow her to be "so unwomanly" as to participate. The incident is interesting in view of Mrs. Bowen's later successes as a public speaker.

For some years after this inglorious graduation the active young girl occupied herself with such public work as was allowed her. Naturally it was to be found only in connection with the church. Thus she established a Bible class of one hundred young men at St. James Church, to meet the spiritual needs of the many enterprising youths who had taken Horace Greeley's advice, to "go west." Most of these youths lived in rather uncomfortable boarding houses, and, although many of them evolved later into leading citizens, they were then lonely and forlorn. Their enterprising Bible Class teacher came to know them very well, and finally established a club house for them on Huron Street, which was her first large public philanthropy. Her second venture was a kitchen garden association, which she established with Miss Eleanor Ryerson, and pushed with characteristic energy.

She was married in June, 1886 to Joseph Tilton Bowen, who had come to Chicago from Providence, Rhode Island. During the next decade she was very much absorbed in her four children, and her public activity consisted principally in her work in connection with the Children's Memorial Hospital. She was President of the Board, and built a wing that the Hospital might extend its usefulness. She was also President of the Woman's Board of the Passavant Hospital and Vice-President of the Woman's Board of St. Luke's Hospital during this same period.

In 1896 she became a Trustee and the Treasurer of Hull House, the pioneer Social

Settlement of Chicago, and with characteristic earnestness and devotion identified herself with its manifold activities. Her many generous gifts to the Settlement were in a large measure the outgrowth of her personal knowledge of the neighborhood and its needs. She was for seventeen years a member, and for many years President, of the Hull House Woman's Club, for which she built a spacious hall. This not only housed the Club activities but many other social and educational enterprises carried on at Hull House, notably an open dance once a week, which demonstrated Mrs. Bowen's belief that the public dance may be made a wholesome as well as a popular form of recreation. She also built a large five-story structure to take care of the activities of 2,500 men and boys after she had become familiar with the great need for better recreational facilities in the vicinity and the influence politicians often obtain over young men through the control, not only of saloons but of club and billiard rooms as well.

Mrs. Bowen also gave to Hull House, in memory of her husband, who died in 1911, the Joseph Tilton Bowen Country Club, consisting of seventy-two acres of beautiful land at Waukegan, Illinois. On this site she restored a fine old house and erected a commons building containing a commodious kitchen and dining room. This Club she endowed, so that its woods, ravines and gardens might always be cared for properly. Children and their mothers in groups of two hundred come here every summer from the congested sections of Chicago to enjoy a fortnight's outing amid the beautiful and healthful surroundings.

The first Juvenile Court, not only of America but "in the world," was opened in Chicago in 1899, largely through the influence of a group of women who felt that children were too easily arrested, were confined in wretched quarters, often with debasing companions, and in the end did not receive the care to which they were entitled. The Judiciary of Cook County established the court and coöperated in every way in the new

undertaking. But the group of which Mrs. Bowen was one of the leading spirits were very anxious that the Court should be a model in every respect, and made themselves responsible for a staff of probation officers without whom the whole plan would have been more or less a travesty. They organized themselves as the Juvenile Court Committee, with Miss Julia Lathrop, who afterwards became the first Chief of the Children's Bureau in Washington, as President. She was succeeded, in the following year, by Mrs. Bowen, who for seven years, with the Committee, took not only the responsibility of securing the salaries of the constantly increasing numbers of Probation Officers, but of presiding over the deliberations of the Committee as they carefully considered case after case brought before them by the Probation Officers, sorely in need of help and advice in their new work. Some member of the Committee, especially Mrs. Bowen as President, sat quite regularly in the new Court in a chair beside the Judge, who was always ready to discuss his decisions with her. This same Committee established a home for children who needed to be kept for a few weeks awaiting trial, and under no circumstances did it permit a child to be put in a police station or jail. In 1907 the Juvenile Court Committee secured the legislation which placed the salaries of the Probation Officers, as well as the maintenance of the Juvenile Detention Home, upon Cook County; and while the Juvenile Court Committee was freed of financial responsibility for many years, it continued its interest in dependent and delinquent children, advocating the Mothers Pension Law and other safeguarding measures which became attached to the Juvenile Court. At this time the Committee, with Mrs. Bowen still acting as President, turned its attention to the formation of a Juvenile Protective Association, the purpose of which is to reach the child before he yields to temptation, to influence his parents, to raise the standard of the home, and to keep him from committing the crimes and misdemeanors which take him into the Court. This Association receives every year about six thousand complaints concerning children who are going wrong or concerning conditions demoralizing to children. It prosecutes in the courts when necessary; it labors with parents and guardians, and it endeavours to bring about an enlightened public opinion which will put out of business those places imperilling children and young people. Mrs. Bowen has been President of this Association ever since its inception twenty-two years ago. It has been followed by the formation of Juvenile Protective Associations in many other states, although as yet there is no national body.

Mrs. Bowen has been for twelve years a member of the Executive Committee of the Committee of Fifteen, which has done such valiant work in enforcing the Injunction and Abatement Law, and in suppressing commercialized vice in Chicago. For, although her primary interest was in the children, she realized that children with every possible safeguard and special attention cannot be secure unless decent general conditions surround all citizens, big and little, and unless all laws are fearlessly enforced. This is clearly brought out in a book which Mrs. Bowen wrote out of her long experience with the Juvenile Protective Association, and which was published by The Macmillan Company, entitled, *Safeguards for City Children at Work and at Play*. This book utilized the publications of the Juvenile Protective Association, many of which had been written by Mrs. Bowen herself. Several of these in pamphlet form have had a very large circulation; one of them, *The Straight Girl in the Crooked Path*, having been published in full in the Sunday edition of a Chicago newspaper, and affording a basis for much comment throughout the city and, according to rumor, producing a certain panic in the police department itself. Mrs. Bowen has been for eleven years Vice-President of the United Charities of Chicago; she is greatly interested not only in alleviating

poverty, but in discovering that almost invisible line, so often crossed by the child whom poverty has made a dependent, into the regions of delinquency and crime.

On appointment by the Governor of Illinois, Mrs. Bowen served during the World War on the State Council of Defense, as the only woman member of that body. She was also elected, at the beginning of the War, Chairman of the Woman's Committee, Council of National Defense, Illinois Division. There were serving under her, during the War, 692,229 women, who registered for work in Illinois. This Committee perfected the most complete organization of women ever attempted in Illinois, with 7,700 chairmen throughout the state, every village large enough to have a post-office being represented. The Woman's Committee was divided into eighteen departments.

In February, 1920, Mrs. Bowen, was appointed by the United States Department of Justice the Woman Fair Price Commissioner for Illinois; in June, 1920, she received the degree of Master of Arts from Knox College, Illinois; and in April, 1922, was appointed by President Harding Official Delegate of the United States to the Pan-American Congress of Women held in Baltimore. During the three days of this Congress a constant demand was made upon her for careful information upon child welfare, laws for women and industrial safeguards in the United States with its diversified state laws, and she was obliged to give these reports in practically spontaneous speeches. The occasion brought out to the full her unusual gift for making facts and figures alive and illuminating, dramatizing statistics as it were, and thus driving home her point as can never be done by mere generalizing, however eloquent. This power has always characterized her public speaking which has been singularly direct and forceful and has placed her in the front rank of women speakers in the United States.

Mrs. Bowen did valiant service for the cause of Woman Suffrage, and for two years served as a member of the Executive Board of the American National Woman's Suffrage Association. She realized, however, that the cause could not be won until women actually made good in political life.

Mrs. Bowen has been for eight years, out of the twelve years of its existence, President of the Woman's City Club of Chicago. This Club has thirty-four civic committees and has 5,056 women on its membership roll. It was organized during one of the dark periods of municipal corruption in Chicago, and long before women had the vote. It has constantly interested and educated its members in civic affairs, but it has not hesitated to take a hand from time to time, when occasion seemed to require it, in actual civic reform. The Club has been no small factor in changing the method of garbage disposal in the city, in increasing and regulating bathing beaches on the Lake, in defeating bond issues when it seemed likely that the money would be improperly or foolishly spent, and in many another situation constantly confronting the voters of Chicago. At one time it made a striking contribution by furnishing a program of municipal activity after an overflow meeting held in the largest auditorium in the city, which rather dramatically rallied together the dispersed and discouraged forces for municipal betterment. In another crisis, as is conceded by the political parties themselves, the Club was a determining factor in the defeat of undesirable candidates for Judges of the Municipal Court, who would undoubtedly have placed the courts under political domination. To be President of such a Club requires both courage and unsleeping vigilance, and happily Mrs. Bowen possesses both qualities. She is ready to defend her position with her pen and by spoken word, and often her decision not only influences club policies but also actual civic situations.

Mrs. Bowen brings to her many undertakings a clear and vigorous mind, and in the cause of the helpless and oppressed she shows a tireless devotion which is never affrighted nor dismayed by obstacles. She has become a power for righteousness, not only because of her unnumbered deeds in the field of social service and civic reform, but because of that inner urge which does not allow her to remain indifferent when a public crisis demands vigorous action. Many of her fellow-citizens have come to depend upon the clarity of her mind, the integrity of her purpose and her unfailing energy as among the most valuable moral assets of Chicago. In even the slightest record of Mrs. Bowen's personality it is impossible to overlook her delightful sense of humor, which brightens the dreariest situations, and her deep kindness and understanding, which enable her to get the point of view of the forlornest young delinquent and to sympathize even with those whom life has beaten into distorted and unlovely forms.

Mrs. Bowen is a member of the Executive Committee of the Woman's Roosevelt Republican Club, and a member of the Chicago Woman's Club, the Fortnightly, the Cordon and the Friday Clubs. She is the mother of two sons and two daughters. The elder son, John DeKoven Bowen, educated at Hill School and Yale University, enlisted in the United States Navy at the outbreak of the World War, and saw active service as a lieutenant. He married Elizabeth Winthrop Stevens of New York, and has three children. The second son, Joseph Tilton Bowen, Jr., also educated at Hill School, enlisted in the Army, and served in France with the rank of captain. He married Gwendolyn High of Chicago, and has one child. Her daughter, Helen Hadduck Bowen, married William McCormick Blair of Chicago, and has four children. Her younger daughter, Louise DeKoven Bowen, married Mason Phelps of Chicago, and has one child.

BOISSEVAIN, INEZ MILHOLLAND (Mrs. Eugen Boissevain), the daughter of John E. and Jean (Tory) Milholland and sister of Vida Milholland, was born in Brooklyn, New York. In June, 1913, she was married, in London, England, to Eugen Boissevain, of Holland, son of Charles Boissevain, owner of *Handelsblad*, a Dutch newspaper.

Even when a child, her sense of justice and her democratic sympathies were highly developed. She was educated in London, Paris, and Berlin, and upon her return to America, entered Vassar College, where her studies increased her interest in social and economic problems. There she organized a woman suffrage club, and when refused a meeting-place by the President, who was opposed to the principles advocated by the young radical, rallied her supporters and held an enthusiastic meeting in the local cemetery. Although it was not necessary for her to earn her own living, she preferred to be self-supporting, and entered the Law School of New York University, where she was graduated in 1913. She then became a clerk in the office of James W. Osborne at 115 Broadway, New York, and was admitted to the Bar.

During all this time she had been active as an organizer for labor, especially in connection with the work of the Woman's Trade Union League, of which she was a member. In the winter of 1910 she took a leading part in the shirtwaist makers' strike in New York. She was arrested while doing picket duty, and, when brought into court, acted as her own attorney, taking advantage of the opportunity to make a strong plea for the girls on strike. A deep rooted love of the race made her champion valiantly the rights of the workers. She often said, "I can't be happy while others are not; I can't be free until the others have got at least as much as I have." It was this big, inclusive, universal love that made her enter the struggle for Socialism, for peace, for the rights of the Negro Race, for prison reform, etc. expressed by her work at Sing Sing Prison. Soon after she became associated in law practice with Mr. Osborne, he selected her to assist him in the work of investigating conditions at Sing Sing, to which he had been appointed. As always she welcomed this opportunity to uncover wrong and injustice, and

to make demands for fundamental changes. This investigation took place when conditions at Sing Sing were at the very worst, before Thomas Mott Osborne inaugurated his admirable regime of the Mutual Welfare League. From different sources, from the prisoners and officers at the prison, and above all from Mr. Osborne himself, it has been told how she devoted week after week of that summer to digging down and ferreting out the filth and accumulated wrongs existing in that institution. The whole system of legal procedure seemed to her a travesty on justice; often she urged that there should be a public defender as well as a public prosecutor; but capital punishment seemed to her the climax of cruelty and public callousness. This beautiful girl went alone among the prisoners, where no woman had been allowed to go before, for at that time the authorities had traditional ideas about the lack of restraint to be expected of the men at the presence of a woman. She looked upon such ideas as absurd, and understood that they had all become mesmerized with fear. It was only when her big fearless spirit entered the place that the nonsense was routed, and all began to understand that individuals do not become totally depraved just because they have failed in a part of the problem of human existence. She talked with the men; she unearthed appalling conditions; but she did not flinch. The ensuing official report was practically all her work, and it remains a classic among legal documents. This was her real contribution to prison reform, in spite of the fact that the world heard more of the dramatic Stielow case than it did of this hard, steady, nerve-racking law accomplishment.

On one of her visits to England she became a personal friend of Mrs. Emmeline Pankhurst and her daughters, and joined the Woman's Social and Political Union, the militant suffrage organization of England. Her experience there led her to ally herself on her return to America with the Congressional Union, later the National Woman's Party, and to throw herself with whole-souled enthusiasm into its work. Her radiant personality and great beauty made her a figure to appeal to the popular imagination, and readily led even skeptics and antagonists to give a courteous attention to her advocacy of the cause. When she marched at the head of the first great Suffrage Parade in New York in 1912, her appearance, as she led her fellow-women up Fifth Avenue, made a picture never to be forgotten.

Inez Milholland was a great soul with a great vision, hence everything that she did was related to a fundamental ideal, the ideal which she called Liberty. The impetus of her every action, small or large, was to do all that she could to further this hope of a liberated humanity. Knowing the mighty import of this achievement, being absolutely convinced that this was the supreme task, she threw herself whole heartedly into every sincere struggle having for its object the breaking of chains, seeing clearly, the while, that it was a manifestation of impending upheaval. If woman suffrage had merely implied the use of the ballot it would have received but scant attention from her. But her idealism (in no way connected with sentimentality), showed her that the vote only symbolizes woman's greater struggle for a fuller emancipation from age-long chatteldom. It was a challenge to her Crusader Spirit to help free the imprisoned spirits of other women. Thus, for her clear and luminous vision the drab ballot-box campaign became a glorified battle. To hear her on her last western trip calling to the enfranchised women of those states to realize that "it was women for women now, and will be, until the fight is won," was to understand that the women's struggle had passed out of the field of politics into the higher realm of pure idealism.

It would be difficult to imagine a more inspiring picture than she made as she stood before an audience supposed to be violently hostile, in one of the large western cities, and assured them that "women will stand by women, never fear." One forgot to think of

her as human merely. As one newspaper expressed it, "she was more like a blazing spirit of freedom, than a beautiful girl with a boyish stride." But freedom for women was not her only message that night. As with all the truly great, she had no fear. Consequently the thought that the mob might be violent impressed her in no way, except with a longing to make them understand, for she always felt strongly that "to understand all is to forgive all." When they began to make a disturbance she folded her arms, leaned up against the table with the unconcern of one waiting for his turn at a game, and smiled at the offenders with all the friendliness imaginable. She was perfectly calm, rather amused, and absolutely determined to be heard. Naturally enough she was heard; in fact they would not let her go until her friends dragged her away, pleading that most of the lights had gone out.

When the war broke out in 1914, all she could see was that those in authority had by their stupidity, greed, and callousness brought about the ghastly state of affairs, where man was lined up to kill his fellow. She agonized over the waste and the hatred which it bred, and stood ready in any way to serve the cause of peace. When asked to become a passenger on the Ford Peace Ship, there were countless personal reasons which might have hindered a less ardent warrior, but, after many doubts, she decided to, thinking that, although she did not have much hope, she might be able to help, and that was all that mattered. However, by the time she reached the other side she saw that the effort was, as one viewed it, being undemocratically handled; so she left the expedition. As a sequel to this, she started alone through warring Germany to Berlin, there to talk with the then very powerful Zimmermann, and see what could be done towards peace. No wonder Herr Zimmerman reported to the American Ambassador that "He was very much impressed with Miss Milholland."

Soon after her return to America she decided to go to Italy, and come into closer contact with war conditions. She went as a special correspondent for the New York *Tribune*, and, as her articles show, she was deeply impressed by the misery and apparent hopelessness of conditions then existing. At every opportunity she spoke valiantly for peace. Never would she let convenience or conventionality silence her. An appreciation of her from the *Masses* says: "She never in her life purchased a moment's admiration or happiness for herself, or any other, by observing, or denying, or neglecting, to express the truth. She loved truth better than happiness. She loved it better than love . . . Truth burned in her like a flame and sentimental or hypocritical people were scorched by it . . . She was brave enough to be true."

Inez Milholland was always urged on by her great ideal. She made every activity connect with this central driving force, which was in itself an inspiration, but her intensive work impaired her health, and on November 25, 1916, she died at Los Angeles, California.

MILHOLLAND, VIDA, was born in Brooklyn, New York. Her father, John E. Milholland, was a son of John Henry Milholland, who, came from Ireland with his wife, Mary Moore, a relative of Sir John Moore, and settled in Lewis, Essex County, New York. Miss Milholland's mother, Jean (Tory) Milholland, daughter of John and Mary (Caldwell) Tory, is a descendant of the Highland Tory family originally of Stonehaven and Tory Hill, Scotland.

Miss Milholland began her education at the Comstock School, New York City, but at the age of twelve she was taken to London, England, where she attended the Kensington High School. On her return to America, she was a student at Vassar College for one year. Then, deciding to specialize in music, she came to New York and studied singing, harmony, and piano, as well as languages. In 1913 she returned to England for further study in singing, under Fernando Tanara. She made her début before the Persia Society,

in London, singing Persian songs in the native language, and in 1916 made her first appearance on the American concert stage in Aeolian Hall, New York. She has always felt strongly that a person's art should be closely associated with his or her ideals and activities. Hence she has used her voice as a means for expressing her strong sentiments for freedom, justice, and idealism, and has always included in her programs songs highly appropriate to her purpose. In London she became identified with the militant suffrage movement. In America, with her sister, Inez Milholland Boissevain, she joined the National Woman's Party and exercised a unique influence. Her singing voice, which she employed to excellent advantage, always aroused great enthusiasm, in behalf of the cause. On July 4, 1917, while in Washington engaged in picketing for suffrage, she was arrested for carrying the suffrage banner, and sentenced to three days in the District Jail. There she was allowed to sing for the prisoners and finally, at the Warden's request, sang to an assembly of all the inmates. Her serving of a prison sentence qualified her to tour the country on the "Prison Special," with other women who had been imprisoned as a result of their suffrage activities. This train traveled from coast to coast in 1919, and the women spoke all along the way, urging the passage of the "Susan B. Anthony Amendment." To their arguments Miss Milholland added the persuasive power of her songs. At various times she has also used her musical talent to aid the Socialist Party; the People's Council; the Friends of Irish Freedom; the Emergency Peace Federation; at meetings of protest against injustice to Russia; for the benefit of the Woman Trades Union League; and at various strikers' meetings. She has been an active member of the Advisory Council of the National Woman's Party and of the Executive Committee of the People's Council. In 1920, Miss Milholland said: "For the last three years I have felt that music is one of the greatest mediums for the expression of lofty sentiments. So my one aim is to use my voice to give, insofar as I understand them, the messages of liberty, justice, and true democracy. We are living in too important an era to talk for the sake of talking, or write for the sake of writing, or sing for the sake of singing. The greatest struggle is taking place that the world has ever known. Then, surely it behooves us all to do our part in bringing about the inevitable triumph of right, through whatever instrument we are qualified to use."

HYATT, ANNA VAUGHN (Mrs. Archer M. Huntington), sculptor, the daughter of Alpheus and Audella (Beebe) Hyatt, was born in Cambridge, Massachusetts, in 1876. Her father was a descendant of Charles Hyatt, who came to Maryland from Gloucestershire, England, about 1664. A genius for form and line expressed itself early in childhood, when the future sculptor spent whole days making drawings of the sheep on neighboring farms. Animals, to her, were not only pets but playmates and respected companions that she delighted to follow and observe. From her keen sympathy with them was developed her amazing power over even the wildest—a power which has actually soothed a newly caught jaguar whose keeper dared not go near him, and compelled an escaped and raging bull to come quietly at her call, and stand while she slipped on his nose ring.

Miss Hyatt was educated in private schools in Cambridge and for six years devoted herself to the study of the violin. But the instincts of the artist could not be denied, and she turned her attention to the harmonies of sculpture. Entering the Art Students' League in New York, she studied with Henry H, Kitson and H. A. McNeil, and later became a pupil of Gutzon Borglum.

Though of late her art has dealt with the human form, her early works were entirely of animals. These she studied on her farm at Gloucester, Massachusetts, as well as in zoölogical gardens both in Europe and in the vicinity of New York City, where she has her studio. In 1908 she studied in Naples, where the Aquarium furnished her with suggestions for the forms of those dwellers of the deep, both actual and mythical, which adorn her numerous fountains and sun-dials. In Naples also, she modelled a heroic lion for the school children of Dayton, Ohio, who raised a fund to purchase it, and later had a studio outside of Paris.

Miss Hyatt's masterpiece is the equestrian statue of Joan of Arc, placed on Riverside Drive, New York City, in 1915. The first life-sized model of this statue received honorable mention at the Paris Salon of 1910, and at once attracted attention because of its great realism and spirituality compared with other interpretations of the Maid of Orleans. "By using a Percheron of the type bred in the fifteenth century to carry knights with their heavy suits of armour, by giving his legs a free and forceful action, and by carrying the line of the back through his neck to the head so as to suggest onward and upward motion, the sculptor has given the horse a monumental quality and grandeur of expression that stir the feelings in harmony with the continuous rhythms of the design." In contrast to this foundation of magnificent physical power, rises the slender figure of the Maid, rapt in her vision, her eyes fixed on the uplifted cross of her sword as she sets forth in answer to the divine command. "Jeanne's face and features are alive with a spiritual fervor that bespeaks both her own high purpose and the intuition of her interpreter." The unveiling of this statue was the occasion of the greatest ceremony of the kind ever held in New York City. And whenever any stranger of international note comes to America, he always places a tribute of flowers at the feet of this monument, which is becoming more and more a symbol of the friendship between France and the United States. It has been decorated with wreaths by the Prince of Wales, Cardinal Mercier, General Joffre and General Pershing. Reproductions are now permanently placed in Rome, on the terrace of the Bishop's

Palace at Blois, France, in New Orleans and in Gloucester, Massachusetts, the home of the sculptor, where a large replica has been erected by the American Legion.

During the World War Miss Hyatt divided her time between Red Cross Canteen work and farming—doing all the labour of a seven acre farm, besides the care of cows and chickens. In 1919 she designed the bronze medallion for the Woman's Roosevelt Memorial Association—a strong profile head of Theodore Roosevelt. Since then, her work has been largely devoted to memorials.

In the Spring Exhibition of 1920 the National Academy of Design awarded Miss Hyatt the J. Sanford Saltus Gold Medal of Merit, given for the best work of Art, including painting and sculpture. This medal is the only unrestricted prize in the Academy, everything else being classified according to age, sex, or nationality. The Bronze chosen—an eye-reduction of the Joan of Arc—had just been returned from the Luxembourg Gallery, where it formed a part of the Exhibition of Representative American Art, sent to France as an international exchange of courtesy.

Since 1899, every important exhibition of sculpture in the United States has included some of Miss Hyatt's work, and five of her bronzes are in the permanent collection of the Metropolitan Museum of New York.

It has been said that "a happy differentiation of texture in skin, hair, and bone, a sympathy and insight into all forms of animal life, and a sane sense of clean-cut design make this sculptor's work one to be enjoyed by all lovers of life in art"; and again, "throughout her marbles and bronzes, is seen a joy in free movement and the play of muscles under the control of a severe sense of form." Kingsley Porter, writing of contemporary art, uses the sentence: "Our plastic artists of today, our Rodins, our Anna Hyatts, our Manships, our St. Gaudens!"

Miss Hyatt is Curator of Sculpture at the Institute Francais aux Etats-Unis. She is a member of the National Sculpture Society, the National Academy of Design, the American Numismatic Society, the Federation of Arts, the Art Alliance of America, and the Cosmopolitan Club. Her work has been welcomed by all the principal museums of America and also by the Luxembourg, Paris, the Vatican, Rome, and the Scottish Museum, Edinburgh. She has been awarded the Purple Rosette of Honor by the French Government (1915), the Silver Medal at the Panama Exposition, and the Rodin Gold Medal by the Philadelphia Academy in 1917. In 1922, she was made an officer of the Legion of Honor by the French Government.

HAMMOND, EMILY VANDERBILT (Mrs. John Henry Hammond), was born in New York City, September 16, 1874. Her father, William Douglas Sloane (born February 29, 1845; died March 10, 1915) was descended from an ancient Scottish family. He married Emily Thorn Vanderbilt, daughter of William Henry Vanderbilt.

Mrs. Hammond's early education was obtained in Mrs. Lockwood's School, and after four years there she attended the Spence School, New York. Since her childhood she has studied the piano under such teachers as Albert Ross Parsons, Ulysses Buehler, Francis Moore, and E. Robert Schmitz. On April 5, 1899, she was married in St. Bartholomew's Church, New York, to John Henry Hammond, a partner in the firm of Brown Brothers and Company, bankers. Mr. Hammond is a son of General John Henry and Sophia Vernon (Wolfe) Hammond, and was born in Louisville, Kentucky, October 3, 1871. They have five children: Emily, who married John Merryman Franklin on September 7, 1922, Adéle, Alice Frances, Rachel and John Henry, Junior.

Following the traditions of her family, Mrs. Hammond has always been a patron of the arts, a practical philanthropist, and interested in all forms of civic betterment. This was early manifested, when, as a young woman, in 1894, she founded the Anti-Basement Circle, of which she has since been President. The object of this organization is to form and develop clubs and classes for the people of the poorer districts in New York City. Its earliest practical move was to start and finance a kindergarten on the west side. In conjunction with this, classes have been held for the mothers of the children at the Hudson Guild in cooking, sewing, and civics. The women have responded eagerly, and the Circle has been able to relieve want by means of an early established discretionary fund. The name of the Circle and its progress were inspired by the words of Henry Drummond: "We find in ourselves the residuum of many animals; disposition of the savage is built in the stories. If the bottom story is the animal, on the second story is the savage, on the third story the man. Temptation is the appeal of the animal to the man. It is no sin to be tempted, but it is a sin when a man deliberately walks down from the top floor of his being to the cellar."

Since 1905 Mrs. Hammond has been President of the Three Arts Club of New York City. She is also President of the Home Thrift Association, which was organized in 1911 by Louise Brigham (Mrs. Henry Arnott Chisholm), author of *Box Furniture*. The purposes of the Association, as set forth in its constitution are: to educate and train the community, by illustration, to utilize materials usually burned or considered useless; to develop a sense of order, an understanding of value and economy of space; to put within the reach of the unskilled person a more artistic product than he can purchase with a larger outlay of money; to preserve in the lives of those who came to us from other lands their native arts, crafts, and industries, which are rapidly lost in the tawdry and cheap imitations of less beautiful things; to solve the problem of making homes more possible in the crowded sections of the city; to make more intelligent home-makers and citizens; and satisfactorily to demonstrate its practical,

educational, and economic value in one section of the city, in order to lead to the establishment of similar centres in other sections of the city and elsewhere. At the beginning of Miss Brigham's work, the City of New York granted her the use of the Gracie Mansion in Carl Schurz Park, where she opened her free workshop for boys and developed many of the activities for home thrift. Thanks to the generosity of the Board of Managers, the Association has acquired possession of its own headquarters, Thrift House, 516 East 89th Street, New York, and under the able direction of Miss Mildred Pew and with an enrollment in 1923 of 300 children, the benefits are far-reaching. Each morning the kindergarten meets, and every afternoon and five evenings a week, find the older boys and girls in the various clubs and classes, which include a circulating library, and instruction in cooking, sewing, singing, banking, shopwork, and scouting for both boys and girls. Mrs. I. Chauncey McKeever conducts a very successful class in applied design, and practical thrift is also taught by means of a savings banks and garden classes.

In September, 1913, Mrs. Hammond was elected President of the Froebel League, in which she had been actively interested for many years, and in December of the same year she helped organize the Parents' League of New York, and has since been its President. The Art Alliance of America, of which she is Second Vice-President, had its first meeting at her house in April, 1914. When, in January, 1919, the Woman's Roosevelt Memorial Association was formed to preserve Theodore Roosevelt's birthplace as a shrine for American youth, Mrs. Hammond was among the first to grasp the importance of such a proposed centre of Americanization, and, as the Association's president, she has, together with the other officers, directed the purchase of the site and the original building with adjoining property, the drive for funds, and the development of a program for the house's work.

For several years Mrs. Hammond has been actively interested in the Girl Scouts, and in 1920 was elected commissioner of the newly organized Westchester County Council of Girl Scouts. Other organizations of which she is a member are the League for Political Education, the Women's Municipal League, the Consumers' League, the Republican Neighborhood Association, the Women's Republican Club, the Cosmopolitan Club, and the Women's City Club of New York.

Mrs. Hammond's busy life has been inspired by an idealism which has found expression also in the two books, compiled by her: *Golden Treasury of the Bible* (1900) and *Looking Upward Day by Day* (1909).

THE FROEBEL LEAGUE of New York, was founded in September, 1898, to put into practice the educational theories of Friedrich Froebel, who had demonstrated the connection between the instinctive play of the child and the foundation of an education in the arts and sciences, and also to train those having the care of children in methods of carrying out these theories. It follows Froebel's dictum that "What the natural mother does incidentally and disconnectedly, she may learn to do with conscious intent and in logical sequence. In this way she rises from blind impulse to conscious and spiritual motherhood."

The Froebel League was a pioneer in organizing mothers' classes. Since the beginning of its activities six primary grades have been added to the kindergarten which form a complete cycle of elementary education. In 1909 the Training School for Kindergartners was established and the whole organization incorporated under the University of the State of New York. The League building at 112 East 71st Street, New York, and located in a neighborhood convenient to serve its aims, was especially constructed to meet its needs. Since 1916 the League has been extending the number of its mission kindergartens and its ultimate ideal is to give the privilege of kindergarten training to each of the 22,000 children in the Yorkville district. The Training School courses offer opportunities to study subjects related to the education of children, from infancy through the kindergarten and primary grades. It includes all the studies required by both the State Regents and the City Board of Education, and offers work along such lines of self-culture as will give the student a broad understanding of life. The Normal Course is planned for young women who intend to become kindergartners, the theoretical work being supplemented by directed observation and practice in eight kindergartens under the supervision of the Froebel League. The mothers' and nurses' classes held at the League each winter and the mothers' meetings in the practice kindergartens provide opportunities for the study of childhood in its relation to home life. Conferences with a physician, in weekly clinics for babies and their mothers, afford opportunity for practical observation of the physical care of children. Close to the League's headquarters is a Students' Residence, and the alumnae of the school own a tract of farmland, "Bobolink Field," in Connecticut, where each year the senior class spends a short period combining classwork with outdoor life.

The work of the League is not confined to school instruction, but one of its most far-reaching efforts has been the mothers' circles, held in eight centres, where the women gather informally to do various kinds of handwork and listen to instructive talks upon many subjects from cooking and hygiene to civic instruction for new voters. The attendance figures indicate that parents appreciate the kindergarten and want it for their children, while the diversity of nationalities represented shows how universal are the ideals and teachings of the League which is helping to make American the mass of foreigners who come to New York.

Under the leadership of Mrs. Marion B. B. Langzettel, who has been Director since 1898, the work of the League has expanded to its present proportions. Mrs. R. Burnham Moffat was its first President, and she was succeeded by Mrs. William Jay Schieffelin, who is now its Honorary President. Mrs. John Henry Hammond has been President since 1913. In 1923 the other officers were: First Vice-President, Mrs. Harold A. Hatch; Second Vice-President, Mrs. William H. Truesdale; First Secretary, Mrs. William E. G. Gaillard; Second Secretary, Mrs. Dudley Phelps; Treasurer, Mrs. George E. Wood; Assistant Treasurer, Mrs. John Ross Delafield.

THE THREE ARTS CLUB of New York City is a non-sectarian Christian organization which provides, under the auspices of the Protestant Episcopal Church in the Diocese of New York, a home and a club for young women engaged in the study of music, the drama, and the fine arts (including the arts and crafts). It was founded in 1903 by Deaconess Jane Harriss Hall, who realized that young women students and workers in the arts, especially those from distant hômes, not only found it difficult to obtain suitable board and lodging in the right environment at a reasonable rate but also required the companionship of congenial co-workers.

Mrs. John Henry Hammond has been President of the Club since 1905, and associated with her are twenty-four active members who constitute the Board of Directors. The other officers are Mrs. Franklin W. Robinson, Vice-President, Mrs. Russell H. Hoadley, Secretary, and Mrs. Breck P. Trowbridge, Treasurer. The Very Reverend Howard C. Robbins is the Honorary President.

The young women who avail themselves of the privileges of the Club are classed as associate members, resident and non-resident, and club spirit as well as interest on the part of former and present members are fostered by the Three Arts Club Auxiliary. The clubhouse at 340 West 85th Street, which is

under the able direction of Miss Anna Seaborn, accommodates ninety-two resident members and there is a restaurant which is open also to non-resident members. The rules are simple and are only those which would be formulated in any well regulated home. A spirit of mutual helpfulness, harmony, and coöperation pervades the club, each member exercising an influence over the newer arrivals, and all enjoying the personal guidance of the Board of Managers.

Committees on music, art, and drama, which also unite as a Scholarship Fund Committee, have been formed by the Board. The Committee on Music is a vital force in the Club, each member directing a small group of the music students who are drawn from all parts of the country. In addition to the facilities offered by the Metropolitan Museum of Art, the students of painting and sculpture have, through the Art Committee, the privilege of examining collections in private houses in New York, not otherwise open to the public. An annual exhibition is held of the work of club members at which the students have the benefit of the criticisms of some well-known painter. The Committee on the Drama assists girls studying for the stage and those already playing: first, by friendly contact and sympathetic interest in their work; and second, by superintending series of plays which are usually given first at the club and later in a public performance in some theatre. The Three Arts Club Auxiliary, composed of the resident and non-resident members, holds monthly meetings which have been addressed by such well-known people as Julia Arthur, Elsie Ferguson, Laurette Taylor, John C. Johansen, Robert Henri, and Mrs. Waldo Richards. The members of the club, and all others interested in its activities, are in touch with it through *The Foreword*, a monthly magazine, which, in addition to club notes, contains articles by prominent educators, artists and writers.

THE ART ALLIANCE OF AMERICA is an association of workers in art and users of art in all its branches. It had its inception in the survey of art schools and art organizations made by Mrs. Ripley Hitchcock, who, as President of the Art Workers' Club for Women, had encountered many of the problems confronting both artist and art employer in America. Associated with her in founding the Alliance was Mrs. John Henry Hammond, President of the Three Arts Club, who had had similar experiences. In the course of their investigation these ladies received many letters and reports from teachers, artists, and business men, which indicated especially the need of vocational guidance for young students looking to art as a means of livelihood. They learned that there was a large army of workers in various branches, whose efforts were purely individual, and whose lack of success indicated the constant repetition of misdirected efforts in unprofitable fields. The failure to learn technical requirements, and the lack of knowledge of the needs of many different fields for the work of artists, illustrators, and designers led to a great economic loss. It became apparent, therefore, that there should be some connecting link between art workers and their normal markets.

The Art Alliance of America was publicly started in April, 1914, at a meeting in Mrs. Hammond's house. Among its charter members were public spirited men and women, many of whom were artists and educators. The present officers and directors are as follows: The Honorable Henry White, President; Mrs. Ripley Hitchcock, First Vice-President; Mrs. John Henry Hammond, Second Vice-President; Charles M. Van Kleeck, Treasurer; Mrs. Harriet E. Brewer, Secretary; Helen M. Hilley, Office Secretary.

The following are members of the Board of Directors: Herbert Adams, John P. Adams, Richard F. Bach, Mrs. Harriet E. Brewer, Edward F. Caldwell, Heyworth Campbell, Grace Cornell, Jerry Drew, Fanny P. Goddard, A. J. Graffin, Ray Greenleaf, Elizabeth B. Grimball, Mrs. John H. Hammond, William Laurel Harris, Albert W. Heckman, Mrs. Ripley Hitchcock, Francis C. Jones, George F. Kunz, H. Percy Macomber, Richard L. Marwede, George McGeachin, Mrs. Laurent Oppenheim, John Clyde Oswald, Walter Scott Perry, Mrs. Eleanor C. Slagle, Charles M. Van Kleeck, Harry Wearne, Irene Weir, The Honorable Henry White, Mrs. Harry P. Whitney.

The objects of the Alliance, as set forth in its Constitution are (1) to promote coöperation between artists, art students, and artisans, publishers, manufacturers, advertisers, and all others who are engaged in artistic activities; (2) with the assistance of experts, to aid, direct, and advise artists, art students, and artisans in their studies and pursuits; (3) to provide a general registry for artists, art students, and artisans, and to supply employers with trained art workers; (4) to provide a department of information; (5) to hold exhibitions; (6) to publish information relating to the objects of the Alliance. Since its organization the Alliance has striven to stimulate the public to an appreciation of the economic value of art in both social and industrial life, and to restore.all the arts to a footing where inspired work may be expected again, as in the decorative arts of the fifteenth and sixteenth centuries. In these earlier days workers in metal and textiles ranked beside the great painters and sculptors. During the seventeenth and eighteenth centuries cabinet making was considered a branch of architecture, and the best architects designed furniture. In modern times the memory of William Morris has stood for the beauty possible in the construction and ornamentation of common things for daily use.

Another aim of the Alliance is to move artists to effective coöperation with manufacturers of machine-made articles, in the conviction that there is distinct need for artists trained to incorporate in factory output the spirit that once inspired the handicraftsman. The Alliance has collected examples of work by which the fitness of registered artists may be judged by those desiring to employ them, and it files opinions of experts as to the best methods of promoting American art for the production of beautiful objects "made in America." Since 1914 it has held in its galleries, first at 45 East 42nd Street, and later at 10 East 47th Street, exhibitions of textile designs and hand-decorated textiles, Liberty Loan posters, toys, craft works, illustrations, paintings and sculptures by members, objects designed and executed by high school pupils, War Savings stamps, National Poster Competition, and other practical instruction work. It also has offered prizes for superior designs. Lectures and conferences have constantly been held for the members. The Placement Section is extensive and of great importance. During the last three years it has secured positions for 1,719 art workers. The membership of the Alliance includes 450 Active Professional Members, and 487 of other classes, many being manufacturing firms of high standing who recognize the value of bringing together the artist and the buyer. Its present headquarters are in the Art Center Building, 65–67 East 56th Street, New York City.

WOMAN'S ROOSEVELT MEMORIAL ASSOCIATION: On January 6, 1919, the great American, Theodore Roosevelt, died, and at once a discussion was started throughout the United States, by his admirers, upon the most suitable form for a memorial to him. Two women, Mrs. Henry A. Wise Wood and Mrs. William Curtis Demorest, of New York, planned a memorial that met with instant approval of all who heard of it, and which also received the endorsement of members of his family. This plan contemplated the purchase and restoration of his birthplace, 28 East 20th Street, New York, in order that it might become a shrine to his memory where could be studied the principles and ideals of American patriotism for which Theodore Roosevelt stood. To work for this object the Woman's Roosevelt Memorial Association was founded

early in 1919 by a number of representative New York women. The officers are: Mrs. Leonard Wood, Honorary President, Mrs. Robert Bacon, Mrs. Joseph H. Choate, Mrs. William Bayard Cutting, Mrs. James T. Leavitt, Mrs. Thomas J. Preston, Jr., Mrs. Whitelaw Reid, Mrs. James Roosevelt, Mrs. Elihu Root, Miss Louisa Lee Schuyler, and Mrs. Robert Winthrop, Honorary Vice-Presidents; Mrs. John Henry Hammond, President; Mrs. Henry A. Alexander, Mrs. William Curtis Demorest, Mrs. Henry A. Wise Wood, Mrs. James Russell Parsons, and Mrs. Alexander Lambert, Vice-Presidents; Mrs. Charles A. Bryan, Secretary, and Mrs. A. Barton Hepburn, Treasurer. Through the courtesy of the New York Trust Company headquarters were established at 1 East 57th Street. A Bulletin detailing the progress of the work is published from time to time. Though at first the organization was purely local it soon became necessary to organize along national lines in response to a country-wide desire of his fellow citizens to participate in this memorial to Theodore Roosevelt. In April, 1919, work was started to form committees in the different states under the direction of Mrs. Henry A. Wise Wood as chairman of the National Organization Committee. Kentucky was the first state to organize and the first to send their quota of $7,000, the result of a campaign for funds carried on through the summer. Committees were also formed in Alaska, Brazil, England, France, The Netherlands, Venezuela, Argentina, Uruguay and China; and throughout the United States. In addition to the state committees, others formed in colleges and clubs helped to carry out the purposes of the Association. During 1919 the total income of the Association amounted to $121,344.60. Of this amount $86,177.53 was paid in December, 1919, for the purchase of the Roosevelt birthplace site and the adjoining house, 26 East 20th Street, the residence of Theodore Roosevelt's uncle, Robert Roosevelt, during Theodore's boyhood. Funds were then solicited for the restoration and endowment of this living memorial, the plans and program of the Association calling for the ultimate raising of a total of $1,000,000. A bas-relief portrait medallion of Theodore Roosevelt, designed by Anna Vaughn Hyatt, was struck to commemorate the purchase of the house, and replicas were distributed as follows to members of the Association. Every contributor of one dollar or more received a copy of the medal in the form of a small bronze pin. One hundred dollars entitled the contributor to a three-inch bronze medallion; and one thousand dollars, to a nine-inch bronze medallion. The names of all contributing one dollar or more are inscribed in the Book of Donors to be preserved at Roosevelt House. In order that children might share in the work, boys and girls under sixteen, upon payment of twenty-five cents, were enrolled as Junior members and given the pin. In January, 1920, Theodate Pope (Mrs. John Wallace Riddle) was appointed architect of Roosevelt House, and while her plans restore the birthplace in the style of 1850, she has adapted the adjoining house to her design so that the entire building has a distinctly monumental character. In her work she had the hearty coöperation of Mrs. William Sheffield Cowles and Mrs. Douglas Robinson, the sisters of Colonel Roosevelt, who could remember many of the details of architecture and interior decoration in the Roosevelt home. Roosevelt House has a frontage of fifty feet on 20th Street and a depth of 92 feet. It is a four-story building of brown stone front and brick construction, and that part of the memorial covering the former home of Robert Roosevelt at 26 East 20th Street has been subordinated to enhance the definite character of the birthplace, No. 28. In designing her plan, Theodate Pope has used wing walls on either side of the building, to separate the memorial from commercial structures in the neighborhood. The House is a practical, useful memorial, carrying Theodore Roosevelt's own views on the subject of monuments, when he said: "As for those of us who, with failures and shortcomings, but according to our lights, have striven to lead decent lives, if any friends of ours wish to commemorate us after death the way to do it is by some expression of good deeds to those who are still living." The largest room in the basement is devoted to a museum which contains photographs, letters, manuscripts, and other personal mementos of Roosevelt, the boy, the man, the public servant, the citizen, and the explorer, including even relics of his early interest in natural history. This valuable collection has been permanently installed here by the Roosevelt Memorial Association who will take entire charge of it. Ascending to the first floor, the visitors finds the entrance hall, drawing room, library and dining room restored practically as they were in 1858. To the right of the entrance, in the part that was the Robert Roosevelt house, is a large oval room which is a continuation of the museum in the basement. On the second floor the two bedrooms and the porch of No. 28 are restored with faithful attention to details. In the front bedroom Theodore Roosevelt was born October 27, 1858. The back bedroom became his nursery from which two windows open upon a children's porch. Here his father arranged an outdoor gymnasium to help Theodore overcome physical handicaps and to develop a healthy body for his active mind. Above the museum, on the second floor, is the Roosevelt Library, which belongs to, and is under the direction of, the Roosevelt Memorial Association. It contains the books he wrote, the books he loved, and other works capable of teaching sound American doctrine to young Americans, both native born and newly naturalized. The third floor is devoted to the offices of both Associations, a Board room for meetings and a Club room, and the entire fourth floor has been made into a compact theatre with a seating capacity of over three hundred and a motion picture apparatus, where may be given lectures and plays dealing with history, civics, and other subjects.

Members of the Roosevelt family have restored to the dwelling many articles of furniture formerly there, among them the rosewood and satinwood bedroom furniture, which belonged to Martha Bulloch Roosevelt, Colonel Roosevelt's mother. Following the lead of Colonel Roosevelt's sister, Mrs. Douglas Robinson, who has written articles of intimate reminiscences and has spoken before high schools, libraries, and many different organizations on the life and ideals of her great brother, the Association is extending its work beyond Roosevelt House, through its Educational Board, by means of classes in American and English history, a series of Roosevelt textbooks for the public schools, and three annual Roosevelt scholarships awarded to winners of prizes, offered by each State Committee, for essays on his life. In the words of Mrs. John Henry Hammond: "If sound doctrines are inculcated in our children during their formative years, we are convinced that later in life the children will be impervious to such anti-social, antinational forces as now threaten the established order of society. The present generation can render the future no higher service than to make the American child Roosevelt-minded in its personal and its national relations. This can be accomplished through the teachings of Roosevelt principles and ideals in the schools."

THE PARENTS' LEAGUE OF NEW YORK CITY was founded in December, 1913, with the object of uniting parents in an effort to promote the moral, mental, and physical well-being of their children by establishing wholesome standards in matters affecting their education, amusements, and home life. Mrs. John Henry Hammond was an important factor in the League's organization and has been its President since the beginning. The Council, consisting of the officers and nine active members, meets once a month to direct the various activities of the League. Any parent residing in New York City or vicinity, or having children who attend school in New York, and is in sympathy with the object of the League, and intends by influence and example to further the aims of the League, is eligible for active membership.

Among the recommendations adopted at the first meeting of the League were: (1) that boys and girls of school age refuse all invitations to parties, theatres, and other diversions, during the school term, except occasionally on Fridays and Saturdays, and that parties and theatre-going be limited during the holidays; (2) that parents arrange simple and appropriate forms of recreation for their children, and that they reserve time during the holidays to join them in such recreations; (3) that reasonable hours for the beginning and ending of dances for young people be advocated and stated in all invitations, and that the manner of dancing be carefully supervised; (4) that a theatre committee recommend suitable plays for children and that parents, in sending invitations for the theatre, state the name of the play; (5) that parents confer frequently with the teachers of their children, and cooperate with them in upholding the rules and standards of the schools; and (6) that articles on child-culture be circulated among the members, and that they hold informal meetings for discussion. Other sections of the country were quick to understand the benefits that would accrue from the application of the League's recommendations, and similar groups were organized in Boston, Worcester, Buffalo, Providence, Montclair (New Jersey), Brooklyn, and other cities.

In view of the fact that the drama plays an important part in New York schools, where children of all ages are taught acting as part of their education in literature, diction, self-possession, and imagination, the work done by the Theatre Committee has been of great importance in selecting, often with the coöperation of the Drama League, plays suitable for young people to attend. After investigating the purpose of the Junior

Cinema Club, a committee was also temporarily appointed to pass upon motion pictures.

In 1917, the Home Efficiency School, now the Commonwealth School, was founded, under the auspices of the Parents' League. During the World War it supplied secretarial courses for girls and lessons in cooking and nursing. Thanks largely to the new program adopted by the Junior League of New York, which requires every debutante to do at least six hours of serious work a week, in order to qualify for membership, there were in 1921 14 full-time and 110 part-time students, and the school is self-supporting. The courses are in social and economic problems, practice in budget making and household accounts, cooking, sewing, and home nursing.

The ideals of the Parents' League have been summarized in one of its reports in the following words: "Our aim is to make it fashionable to be sensible and unfashionable to be foolish. The home is the foundation of society, and as we keep it intact and fill it with love and the right kind of comradeship, we shall be preparing our children in the best way possible to take their place in the school as conscientious pupils, in society as young men and women with high standards, and in the nation as citizens realizing their great opportunities for service."

WADSWORTH, ALICE HAY (Mrs. James W. Wadsworth, Jr.), daughter of John and Clara Louise (Stone) Hay, was born, January 6, 1880, in Cleveland, Ohio. Her father (born, Salem, Indiana, October 8, 1838; died, Newbery, New Hampshire, July 1, 1905), was a notable figure in American history. He was Secretary to President Lincoln, whose biography he wrote, in collaboration with John G. Nicolay; served many years in the diplomatic service in Paris, Vienna, and Madrid; was First Assistant Secretary of State, under President Hayes (1879–1881), and was Ambassador to the Court of St. James (1887–1890). He was also a gifted poet and litterateur and the author of "A History of the Administration of Abraham Lincoln" (New York, 10 volumes, 1890), and editor of "Lincoln's Complete Works" (2 volumes, 1894).

Alice Hay was educated in private schools in Washington, District of Columbia; in the Misses Masters' Boarding School at Dobbs Ferry, New York; and later in a French private school. On September 30, 1902, at Newbery, New Hampshire, she was married to James Wolcott Wadsworth, Junior, son of James Wolcott and Louise (Travers) Wadsworth. He was born at Geneseo, New York, August 12, 1877, is by profession a farmer, and has served several terms as United States Senator from New York State. Mr. and Mrs. Wadsworth are the parents of three children: Evelyn Wadsworth (born at Mount Morris, Livingston County, New York, on July 7, 1903); James Jeremiah Wadsworth (born at the same place on June 12, 1905); and Reverdy Wadsworth (born at Washington, District of Columbia, on November 10, 1914).

Mrs. Wadsworth was President of the National Association Opposed to Woman Suffrage, from 1917 to 1920. She is a member of the Executive Committee of the National Playground and Recreation Association of America, and was a member of the Executive Committee of the War Camp Community Service. She is Vice-President of the Ladies' Board of the Children's Hospital at Washington, District of Columbia; President of the National American Women's League, and a leader in the Roosevelt Memorial Association of New York. She is a member of the Colony Club, New York.

SCHUYLER, LOUISA LEE, daughter of George Lee and Eliza (Hamilton) Schuyler (1811–1890) and a great-granddaughter of General Philip Schuyler and of Alexander Hamilton, was born in New York, October 26, 1837. Her early training was of the kind usually given in the best families in the second quarter of the nineteenth century, conservative and intensely patriotic.

When, in April, 1861, came the news that the Confederates had fired on Fort Sumter, thus beginning the Civil War, the shock was felt not only by her parents, but by Miss Schuyler as well. Among the first to volunteer were her father and her brother, Philip, the latter leaving for Washington with the Seventh New York Regiment, on April 19, 1861. To provide funds until Congress could be convened, a group of prominent New York men, including Mr. Schuyler, organized the Union Defense Committee, and, as an auxiliary to furnish necessities and comforts for the soldiers, the Women's Central Association of Relief was formed. The object was to coördinate the efforts of all relief organizations, and to prevent the waste incidental to individual and desultory labors. A preliminary meeting was called at the Infirmary for Women on Second Avenue, conducted by Doctors Emily and Elizabeth Blackwell, and the central agency was started at Cooper Union, New York, on April 29, 1861, when Peter Cooper offered the second floor as a depot for the work. Two thousand women answered the appeal for helpers. Mrs. Hamilton Fish headed the Finance Committee, assisted by Miss Schuyler's aunt, Miss Mary Morris Hamilton. Miss Ellen Collins, a member of the Society of Friends, was Chairman of the Committee on Supplies, and with her worked, Mrs. William B. Rice (then Miss Gertrude Stevens), Mrs. d'Oremieulx, and others.

The first nurses received, on account of the urgency of the need, only a hasty single month's training under Doctor Blackwell and Mrs. William Preston Griffin; but the results justified the confidence of the Committee. Mrs. George Lee Schuyler had been one of the first women chosen on the Executive Committee, but, because of her ill-health, Doctor Bellows, the Vice-President of the Association, asked her young daughter, Miss Louisa Lee Schuyler, to take her place. Miss Schuyler's ability as an organizer soon became evident and she was often left in charge of stabilizing

the work in other cities, after a first meeting to win public interest had been held. Miss Schuyler became Chairman of the Committee on the Diffusion of Information, later called the Committee on Organization, Correspondence, and Publicity.

Miss Schuyler's own description, written in 1865, of the first days of the work in Cooper Union, and of its later developments, is worthy of quotation. "We began life" she writes, "in a little room on the second floor. It contained two tables, one desk, half a dozen chairs and a map on the wall. We had one man who was by turns clerk, carpenter, errand boy and porter. For many days we sent out circulars and looked out of the windows, sometimes hopefully and sometimes in despair. After what seemed an endless time of waiting our first box arrived. It came from Orange, New Jersey. No box ever before or since underwent closer scrutiny. We were jubilant! We told everybody that our first box had come. During the past four years our one little room has expanded into an office ninety-seven feet long, running through the building on the first floor from one street to another, a large storeroom next door, and three lofts for storage across the street. The man of all work has multiplied himself into two clerks, three porters and an errand boy. The one box stands at the head of a list of seventeen thousand boxes. Gradually we found ourselves launched into an enormous business, of a character entirely without precedent, of such a nature that few ordinary business rules could be of service to us. We had to feel our way; we were ignorant and blundered; but we learned by experience and our organization now meets the requirements of our work." With the arrival of supplies in large quantities, came the problem of distribution. "At first the idea of the women was to send things to their own regiments; but we found it quite impossible, for the express companies were not allowed to go inside the lines."

In the face of the many difficulties, Doctor Bellows, with others, went to Washington, and after repeated conferences, the United States Sanitary Commission, at first a mixed board of civilians and army men, authorized to suggest measures for improving the health and comfort of the army, and to represent the people who desired to offer their services for relief during the war, was appointed by the Secretary of War, June 9, 1861, and approved by President Lincoln on June 13th. Its chief duties were: (1) to suggest to the Government the means of preventing the spread of disease among the men of the army; (2) to inspect camps and hospitals and suggest methods of improving their sanitary condition; and (3) to act as an officially approved clearing house for volunteer relief. Its headquarters were in Washington with the Reverend Henry W. Bellows as President and Mr. Frederick Law Olmstead as General Secretary. The latter was the organizing genius of the Commission, for many months laying aside his private practice as landscape architect and devoting himself without remuneration to the service of the enlisted men.

The Commission worked in subordination to the military authorities who were ordered to give its agents the greatest aid possible in the performance of their duties. During the active existence of the United States Sanitary Commission from June, 1861, to January, 1866, it raised and spent about $7,000,000, and received and distributed $15,000,000 worth of supplies, including underwear, blankets, slings, crutches, pillows, tea, coffee, cocoa, sugar, milk, crackers, wine, brandy, writing materials, and tobacco, sent from auxiliary stations throughout the North from coast to coast. Not only was the condition of the sick and wounded improved, but recreational and athletic activities were arranged for the well.

The women of the Commission were attached to hospitals and transports, taking charge of food dispensaries and acting as assistants to the nurses. The Commission not only won the unqualified praise of army officers, but was considered as a model to be copied by army surgeons in Europe. Mr.

Henri Dunant, the Swiss philanthropist, finding the commission a success, summoned the International Sanitary Convention at Geneva in October, 1862, from which resulted the International Sanitary Congress of Geneva held in August, 1863, and, its successor, the International Red Cross Society.

An excellent example of loyalty to the greater needs of the army was set by the Women's Central Relief Association. As soon as the Sanitary Commission was appointed, the Central Association voluntarily gave up its independence and, placing itself under orders from headquarters, became simply the oldest branch of the Commission. Miss Schuyler remembers with satisfaction that it was she who offered the resolution to make the change. The connection between the Commission and the Association were close, the latter was but one division coöperating with other branches in New England, Pennsylvania, and the West, each of which adopted its own policy to secure the needed supplies.

"Each of us," writes Miss Schuyler, "had our merits and our defects, but we were all animated by the same spirit of devotion to the interests of our soldiers and sailors— we were all united by a common love of country." American women in other countries did their share. "The records of the Sanitary Commission show that no absence from home can change the hearts of our American women. To our call of distress they have responded from Italy, from France, from England, from Canada, from every quarter where our appeal has followed them." Miss Schuyler's chief interest lay with the workers who actually made the supplies in the villages and the countryside, the little sewing circles and other groups that sprang up all through the North. She sent patterns, and in her eager and inspiring letters gave brave encouragement. "Let us in the security and happiness of our own homes as good soldiers of Christ, fight the good fight of humanity, fight it through all reverses, knowing no discouragements, no compromises, no defeats."

She formed the Soldiers' Aid Societies and showed the leading women in the different villages, how to summon the neighbors and how to organize and systematize their work. Later Junior Auxiliaries were started, known as *Alert Clubs*, composed of children who collected weekly or monthly contributions of small sums for the support of the Aid Societies. Funds were also raised by means of Sanitary Fairs, the first of which was held in Chicago in the autumn of 1863, while others taking place in Boston, Washington, Philadelphia, New York, and other cities did good work in bringing the members of the city and country relief societies together.

The figures of the New York Branch for the six months preceding November, 1864, give an indication of what was accomplished: 17,000 cotton shirts, 24,000 woolen shirts, 9,000 cotton drawers, 10,000 woolen drawers, 700 socks, 46,000 handkerchiefs, 9,000 sheets, 2,000 blankets, 200 barrels of dried fruit, 2,500 gallons of blackberry cordial and brandy. From time to time delegates from all the branches met in conference in Washington. Miss Schuyler calls them "earnest women, strong in their quiet enthusiasm and deep love for their work, desirous only of gaining information as to the best means of going on with it" conscious of their duty to aid the government by sending supplies to the army, "abundantly, persistently, methodically."

At the close of the Civil War, Miss Schuyler bade farewell to her Aid Societies in words of sincerest emotion and personal gratitude for the inspiration she had received from the true and steadfast patriotism of her co-workers. "As members of this branch of the United States Sanitary Commission, we have been brought into immediate contact on the one hand with the earnest, active minds of the officers of the Commission, and on the other with the most patriotic, the most earnest, the noblest-hearted men and women from among our people. It is impossible to be engaged with such a cause and for so long a

time without feeling one's own nature elevated and deepened."

Toward the end of the war Miss Schuyler took a leading part in calling another large meeting of women at Cooper Union to consider the matter of war economy, especially in the matter of dress, with the result that several hundred women pledged themselves to "abstain from the purchase of foreign luxuries, mirrors, bric-a-brac, laces and jewels during the continuation of the war."

With the conclusion of peace and with relief from the strain under which she had labored, Miss Schuyler's strength gave way and she was obliged to travel for several years in Europe in search of health. Restored to health in 1871, she became interested, through reading the reports of the State Board of Charities, in the conditions in poorhouses and almshouses. As a result of personal observation in Westchester County, New York, she became convinced that much could be done to remedy the deplorable state of affairs by means of volunteer visiting committees. Miss Schuyler formed the first committee in Tarrytown, New York, on January 9, 1872, as a preliminary to the State Charities Aid Association, which she organized on May 11, 1872, at her father's house at 19 West 31st Street, New York, under by-laws which she had drafted in the previous autumn. In the meantime, at the suggestion of General Bowen, President of the Board of New York City Commissioners of Charities and Correction, she had investigated the city public hospitals, and on January 26, 1872, organized the Visiting Committee for Bellevue and Other Hospitals, later expanded into the New York City Visiting Committee of the State Charities Aid Association.

As there was at this time no training school for nurses in the United States, the committee, realizing that the provision for adequate training was a necessity, were led by Miss Schuyler, and former members of the Sanitary Commission, to overcome prejudice against the then radical suggestion, and the

Bellevue Training School for Nurses, modelled on Florence Nightingale's school in London, opened its doors May 1, 1873. This pioneer school was the one from which all other training schools for nurses, in the United States have sprung. From 1889 to 1896, Miss Schuyler led the State Charities Aid Association, in the reform of providing proper care and treatment of the insane in state hospitals, which it accomplished by means of the state care for the Insane Acts of 1890 and 1891; and in 1906 Miss Schuyler organized pioneer work for after-care of the insane.

Between 1898 and 1907 a Joint Committee of the Association and the Association for Improving the Condition of the Poor cared for a thousand foundlings placed in their charge by New York City, and raised over forty thousand dollars for their maintenance. In 1907 Miss Schuyler and Mrs. William B. Rice were appointed by Mrs. Sage, trustees of the Russell Sage Foundation, and in 1908 Miss Schuyler organized the first committee in the United States for the prevention of blindness.

In 1893 she was appointed by the Governor of New York to represent the State at the opening of the World's Columbian Exposition in Chicago, but was unable to attend. In 1901 she was one of two women appointed by President Roosevelt, to represent New York, at the opening of the Pan-American Exposition at Buffalo. The Colony Club of New York elected her an honorary member in 1910, and in 1912 she was made an honorary member of the Society of the Bellevue Training School for Nurses. In 1915 Columbia University at its 161st Commencement conferred upon her the honorary LL.D. degree, the second one given to a woman in the history of the institution. In presenting it, President Butler said:

"Louise Lee Schuyler: A pioneer in the service of noble women to the state; founder of the State Charities Aid Association and of the system of visitation of state institutions by volunteer committee of citizens; originator of the first American Training School for Nurses; initiating and successfully advocating legislation for the care of the insane; powerfully aiding the first public movement for the prevention of blindness in little children; worthy representative of a splendid line of her ancestors; distinguished through two centuries for manifold services to city, state and nation; great-granddaughter of General Philip Schuyler of the American Revolution, great-granddaughter of Alexander Hamilton of the class of 1777, I gladly admit you to the degree of Doctor of Laws."

SCHUYLER, GEORGINA, daughter of George Lee and Eliza (Hamilton) Schuyler and sister of Louisa Lee Schuyler, was born in New York City in 1841, and died December 25, 1923. She was educated in private classes, and in 1858 at Mrs. Louis Agassiz's School for Girls, Cambridge, Massachusetts. During the Civil War she worked with the Soldier's Aid Societies in Westchester County, New York, and was a member of the Hospital Book and Newspaper Society of the United States Sanitary Commission. A collection of fourteen songs composed by her was published in 1886. In 1911 the Governor of New York appointed her a Trustee of the Schuyler Mansion at Albany, New York, of which she has written an historical sketch, *The Schuyler Mansion at Albany*. She has also written other historical articles and has devoted much time to the study of history and genealogy. She was a member of the Society of the Colonial Dames of America.

JENKINS, HELEN HARTLEY, philanthropist, is the daughter of a long line of patriots and philanthropists distinguished for their services to their country and their fellow men. Her father, Marcellus Hartley (1827–1902), of New York, was a member of the firm of Schuyler, Hartley and Graham, manufacturers of firearms, the organizer of the Remington Arms Plant and the Union Metallic Cartridge Company of Bridgeport,

Connecticut, and noted for his many charities, among them the founding, in 1897, of Hartley House, the uniquely efficient settlement in New York City. He was the son of Robert Milham Hartley, who was also a leading philanthropist of New York, the founder in 1829 of the New York Temperance Society, and, in 1844, of the New York Association for Improving the Condition of the Poor. He was also largely instrumental in founding the Presbyterian Hospital, New York, and was a supporter of the Workingmen's Home, the Juvenile Asylum, the Hospital for the Ruptured and Crippled, and other charitable institutions. He started also the first pure milk crusade. The fourth child, and eldest son of his parents, he was born in Cockermouth, Cumberland, England, February 17, 1796, and was brought by his mother, in 1799, to join his father, Isaac Hartley, in New York, where he died March 3, 1881. Isaac Hartley was, like his father and grandfather, a woolen manufacturer, and was born in Cockermouth, December 30, 1765, came to America in 1797, and died in Perth, New York, October 6, 1851. In 1787 he married Isabella, the daughter of Joseph Johnson of Embleton, England. His father, Robert Hartley, who was born in Broughton, England, in 1736 and who died in Cockermouth in 1803, married, in 1754, Martha Smithson, the daughter of Isaac Smithson, granddaughter of Sir Hugh Smithson, Bart., and a cousin of Sir Hugh Smithson (afterwards Percy), 1st Duke of Northumberland, the father of James Smithson, who founded the Smithsonian Institute at Washington, District of Columbia. Robert Hartley's father, James Hartley, was the son of the Reverend Mr. Hartley, vicar of Armley, Yorkshire.

Isabella Johnson, the wife of Isaac Hartley, was the daughter of a man of literary attainments, who, dying early, left the education of his daughter to her mother and an elder brother, by whom she was regarded with peculiar affection, and was instructed with more than ordinary care. She acquired the usual branches of education given to girls with such care and rapidity that an opportunity was allowed her to pursue classical studies. She had the encouragement and aid of her brother and acquired great proficiency. During her twentieth year she married, and became the helpmate of her husband in a very literal sense of the term. When, in 1797, Isaac Hartley sailed for America on a business trip, as well as to investigate the workings of republican institutions, in which he and his wife were both interested, he left the care of his business to his wife and in this new line of duty she acquitted herself admirably. Upon Mr. Hartley's decision to remain in the United States, it devolved upon Mrs. Hartley to bring the business to a close. She collected and adjusted all dues and claims, disposed of a free hold estate, superintended the packing and removal of her furniture and household goods, and, with her four children, embarked on board ship and joined her husband in New York in September, 1799. Mr. Hartley immediately took his family up the Hudson River to a home that was in an almost unbroken wilderness. For the delicately nurtured and cultivated wife the change from the comforts, elegancies, and enjoyments of her English home to the privations and solitude of the new was great indeed, but she rose to the emergency, as she had always done, and found delight in the romance of her surroundings, taking joy in the natural beauty of her environment, and devoting herself to the care and education of her children, whom she aided in all their tasks, and to whom she taught the Greek alphabet, and the hymns and gems of poetry with which her memory was stored.

In 1824, Robert Milham Hartley married Catherine Munson, who was born in 1804, and who died December 7, 1873. She was a woman of marked physical attractiveness, of medium stature, light complexion, blond hair, and an expressive countenance, enlivened by blue eyes at once significant and penetrating. Industry and economy were conspicuous in her care of her family, and conjugal love and tenderness were displayed in a life devoted to the interests of her husband and her children. She was the daughter of Reuben Munson, who served in the War of 1812, and who was born in 1770 and died in Flushing, New York, in 1846. He married Abigail Wilsey (1781–1865), the daughter of Peter Wilsey (1742–1811–1816) of Williamsbridge, New York, and his wife, Margaret Little (1745–1838). The latter was enthusiastic for the. success of the Colonies during the Revolution and was a personal friend of General and Mrs. Washington and of Mrs. James Montgomery. Peter Wilsey was descended from Philippe Maton Wilse who came to this country as a representative of the West India Company, and was murdered by the Indians while on a trip of exploration to one of the outlying forts. Reuben Munson was the son of Peter Munson, grandson of William Munson, great-grandson of Samuel Munson, and great-great-grandson of Ensign Samuel Munson (1643–1693), a founder of Wallingford, Connecticut, and a soldier in King Philip's War (1675). His father was Captain Thomas Munson (1612–1683), who settled in New Haven, Connecticut, served with distinction in the Pequot War (1637), was sergeant of the Train Band in 1642, ensign from 1661 to 1664, lieutenant in King Philip's War, and captain in 1676.

Marcellus Hartley, the father of Mrs. Jenkins, married November 15, 1855, in the Madison Avenue Presbyterian Church, New York, Frances Chester White, who was born in Hudson, New York, March 3, 1833, and who died in New York City, April 22, 1909. Before her death she presented the house in Hudson in which she was born to the Daughters of the American Revolution, putting it in condition for their chapter meetings, and adding a large hall at the rear for public entertainments. She was descended from Elder John White (1605–1683–1684), who came from England in 1632 on the ship *Lion* and, after living in Cambridge, Massachusetts, where he was admitted freeman in 1633 and townsman in 1635, removed to Hartford, Connecticut, in 1636, as one of the original proprietors. He was frequently townsman there as well as at Hadley, Massachusetts, whither he moved in 1659. In 1671 he returned to Hartford and was ordained ruling elder of the Second Church in 1677. In 1622 he married Mary Levitt, the daughter of William and Margaret Levitt. His son, Lieutenant Daniel White (1639 [1634] 1713), settled in Hatfield, Massachusetts. He married, November 1, 1661, Sarah, the daughter of John Crow (1606–1686), a proprietor of Hartford, and his wife, Elizabeth, the only daughter of Elder William Goodwin, an original proprietor of Hartford and a man of great influence there and at Hadley, where he was ruling elder of the church. He died in Farmington, Connecticut, in 1673. The son of Lieutenant Daniel and Sarah (Crow) White was Captain Daniel White (1671–1726), who married, 2d Ann, the daughter of John Bissell of Windsor, Connecticut, and his wife, Isabel, the daughter of Major John Mason of Saybrook, Connecticut, the famous leader in the Pequot War. John Bissell was the son of John Bissell, one of the settlers of Windsor, whose family was of Huguenot origin. The son of Captain Daniel and Ann (Bissell) White was Captain Joel White (1705–1789), who married Ruth Dart. He lived in Bolton where he was Justice of the Peace, Town Treasurer, and representative to the legislature. During the Revolution he lent £3,000 to the State of Connecticut and to the United States. His son, Captain Daniel White (1749–1816), married Sarah Hale, the daughter of Captain Jonathan Hale and his wife, Elizabeth Welles. The latter was the daughter of Captain Thomas and Martha (Pitkin) Welles and Captain Thomas Welles was the great-grandson of Thomas Welles, an original proprietor of Hartford, and governor of the Colony of Connecticut in 1655 and 1658. Jonathan Hale's father, Jonathan Hale, married Sarah, a descendant of the Worshipful Honorable John Talcott, an original proprietor of Hartford. Jonathan Hale was also descended from William Pynchon, a patentee of Massachusetts Bay Colony and a founder of Springfield, Massachusetts, whose book, *The Meritorious Price of our Redemption*, was burned in 1650 in the Boston market-place for heresy, after which he returned to England, where he died. The son of Captain Daniel and Sarah (Hale) White was Samuel White, M.D. (1777–1845), of Coventry, Connecticut, who married Wealthy Pomeroy (1778–1854), the daughter of Eleazar Pomeroy (1752–1811) and his wife, Sibyl, the daughter of Denison Kingsbury. Eleazar Pomeroy was the son of Daniel Pomeroy (1727–1785) and his wife, Naomi, the daughter of Edward Kibbey. Daniel Pomeroy's father, Noah Pomeroy (1700–1779), married Elizabeth, the daughter of Captain Daniel and Mary (Marvin) Sterling, the latter the daughter of Lieutenant Reinold Marvin and granddaughter of Reinold Marvin who died in Saybrook in 1662. Noah Pomeroy was the son of Joseph Pomeroy (1652–1734) and grandson of Eltwed Pomeroy who was born in 1615. Joseph Pomeroy married Hannah (1666–1736), the daughter of Richard Lyman and granddaughter of Richard Lyman. Samuel and Wealthy (Pomeroy) White were the parents of Samuel Pomeroy White, M.D., who was born in Hudson, New York, in 1801 and died in 1867, the father of Frances Chester (White) Hartley. During the Civil War he rendered great service in the hospitals in and about New York City. He married Caroline Mary Jenkins (1803–1883) of Hudson, New York, the daughter of Robert Jenkins, who was born at Nantucket, Massachusetts, in 1772, and died in Hudson in 1819, and granddaughter of Seth Jenkins, who was born in Nantucket in 1735 and died in Hudson, of which he was a founder, in 1793. The latter married Dinah Folger, the daughter of Abisha Folger and his wife, Dinah Coffin, a great-granddaughter of Tristram Coffin, a founder of Nantucket in 1660, and chief magistrate there from 1677 to 1681, and a son of Peter Coffin of Brixton, Devon, England.

Seth Jenkins was the son of Thomas Jenkins (1707–1756) of Nantucket, who in 1728, married Judith Folger (1712–1765), the daughter of Nathan Folger (1678–1747) and granddaughter of Eleazar Folger (1648–1716). The latter married Sarah Gardner, who died in 1729. She was the daughter of Richard Gardner, who was born in Salem, Massachusetts, and who died at Nantucket in 1688, the son of Captain Thomas Gardner, who was born in England and died in 1677 at Nantucket where he was chief magistrate. Eleazar Folger was the son of Peter Folger, who was born in England about 1617, and who died in Nantucket in 1690. He and his father, John Folger, were founders of Edgartown, Martha's Vineyard, where the latter died in 1660. Peter Folger was the author of a poem in defense of liberty of conscience; his daughter, Abiah, was the mother of Benjamin Franklin. Thomas Jenkins was the son of Matthew Jenkins (1681–1758), who in 1706 married Mary Gardner (1686–1761 [1767]), the daughter of Joseph Gardner and granddaughter of Richard Gardner above. Joseph Gardner married Bethiah Macy, the daughter of Thomas Macy (1608–1682), chief magistrate of Nantucket, Matthew Jenkins was the son of Peter Jenkins, who died about 1679 and was a founder of Edgartown.

Mrs. Helen Hartley Jenkins was born in New York City and was married to George Walker Jenkins in Orange, New Jersey, in 1892. They are the parents of Helen Hartley Jenkins Geer and Grace Hartley Jenkins.

From her childhood, Mrs. Jenkins has given herself to philanthropy, carrying on the traditions of her father and grandfather, with a breadth of vision and a large hearted devotion that have placed her in a unique position in the City of New York. Few charitable organizations have been without the benefit of her coöperation and advice, and she has become, as it were, a final court of appeals for the solution of their many problems. Never intruding herself, at the same time she stands always ready quietly but efficaciously to guide and foster. The success of her method is well demonstrated by the remarkable development of Hartley House at 413 West 46th Street as the centre of a large part of the social life of the neighborhood, and as a contributor to community leadership along many lines of social welfare. Founded by her father, Marcellus Hartley, in 1897, it has become one of the best known settlements in New York, and a leading training school for social workers, giving the neighborhood an opportunity for a happier and richer life, and conducting its work always in the same spirit of democracy and social progress characteristic of its founder. The activities of the house include kindergartens and play rooms for the younger children; social clubs for old and young people; educational classes according to the needs of the neighborhood; a coöperative store; and a maternity centre and clinic, with a visiting physician and with nurses furnished by the Maternity Centre Association. The policy of the settlement is that of the social laboratory where ideas and methods are tested and the results used for the benefit of the community, experimental studies being, however, always subordinated to a constructive local program. Frequently the house has initiated reforms that have later been taken over and developed by the city authorities. One of the first home and school visitors in the city began her work as a resident of Hartley House, and helped work out the plan for visiting teachers since adopted by the Board of Education. Until the city provided summer classes the house offered such extra instruction and maintained three kindergartens, until increased facilities in the public schools of the neighborhood enabled the settlement to discontinue two. The recreational work of the house is not confined to the city, but it provides summer camps for boys and girls and families, the girls' vacation camp, Hartley Farm, at Towaco, New Jersey, being especially important. Under Mrs. Jenkins' guidance, Hartley House has become the centre of social

work and service on the west side, meeting the needs of the neighborhood with up-to-date progressiveness. In this development she was efficiently aided by her daughter, Helen Hartley Geer, whose vital personality inspired all alike, and whose insight into the requirements of the district led Mrs. Jenkins to build at 525 West 47th Street the Hartley Open Stair Tenement. Previous to this, plans for this type of building, which were drawn as a result of Mrs. Jenkins' investigation of housing conditions in the poorer quarters of the city, and which are expected to revolutionize tenement house construction, had been put into effect by Mrs. Jenkins in the upper '60s of the east side and in West 146th Street, and she has since extended her solution of the housing problem for the poor (in the form of single and two family model dwellings) to the Borough of Queens.

For over twenty-two years, Mrs. Jenkins has been especially interested in the problem of Americanization, and has given much thought and time to caring for Slavonic immigrants upon their arrival in this country. She was the sole donor of the Slavonic Immigrant Home at 436 West 23rd Street, New York, which in November, 1909, was opened for the reception of immigrants and for the work of the Slavonic Immigrant Society. The home is Slavonic in architecture, and has been completely furnished, as far as possible, in the racial style, by Mrs. Jenkins, who also pays the salary of the secretary and meets all deficits. Since its opening Croats, Slovenes, Czechs, Slovaks, and Lithuanians have been cared for and it has been at the disposal of the newly arrived, especially unprotected girls, as a stopping place, where clean lodgings and wholesome food could be had, until they should be settled in the new country. During the World War immigration ceased, but the Home offered hospitality to thousands of Slavs returning to Europe as volunteers. The immigrants of Serb origin brought the Serb Federation "Sloga," their national benefit society, to New York in 1909, and established its headquarters in the Slavonic Immigrant Home. It soon became apparent, however, with the rapid growth of the Federation, that larger quarters must be obtained, if the work was not seriously to be hampered. With her accustomed thoughtful generosity, Mrs. Jenkins came to the aid of the organization by giving to the Educational and Benevolent Fund of the Federation a separate house at 443 West 22nd Street. She equipped it with all necessary furniture for the offices, with suitable quarters for employees, with a library, and with a printing plant in the basement for the printing of *Srbobran*, the official organ of the Federation, and its other publications, which are distributed to Serbs throughout the United States. Further to aid this educational work, Mrs. Jenkins created the Serbo-American Ecclesiastical Fund for the assistance of Serb schools and churches in the United States, and for the support of a missionary in the Serbian colonies in American cities. During the Balkan War of 1912, and the World War, the Serbian Home was a clearing house for the Serbian and Montenegrin Red Cross and a point of departure for returning volunteers, of whom there were never less than two hundred, in the winter of 1914–1915, awaiting passage. The Home also assisted the official Serbian missions to the United States and in it was the Serbian Consulate. These activities so overcrowded the Home that, in the summer of 1919, Mrs. Jenkins, as a personal gift, added the next building. The two buildings, remodeled into one, offer ample facilities for the work of the Serbian Federation "Sloga" and of the Consulate General of the Kingdom of the Serbs, Croats, and Slovenes, while its large hall, seating two hundred and fifty persons, is used for the meetings of seven Serbian societies and for fortnightly dances. For the Jan Hus Memorial Bohemian Presbyterian Church at 347–349 East 74th Street, New York, Mrs. Jenkins made possible the erection of one of the most unique and beautiful steeples in the United States, modeled after the steeple on the historic bridge over the Vltava in Prague. She helped in publishing a translation of Bohemian national songs, and is the President of the Advisory Board of the Jan Hus Neighborhood Home. The Reverend Vincent Pisek, pastor of the Jan Hus Church, has said: "There is no name so well known and so deeply respected among the Slavs as that of Mrs. Helen Hartley Jenkins . . . In view of her interest in and love for the Slavs, the National Slavonic Society, the Jan Hus Bohemian Presbyterian Church and other Slavonic societies have made her an honorary member. The reception of Mrs. Jenkins as an honorary member of the National Slavonic Society was a brilliant occasion, which, because of the enthusiasm and love for Mrs. Jenkins manifested by the people, will long live in their memories." Mrs. Jenkins has received many other expressions of gratitude from individuals and organizations for her work among the Slavs, and she has also been decorated by the Kings of Montenegro and Serbia.

Mrs. Jenkins has been called the "fairy godmother" of nursing, a helpful friend of the profession everywhere, and one of its greatest benefactors in America, through her endowment in 1910, of the Department of Nursing and Health at Teachers' College, Columbia University, of which she is a trustee. This department is a reorganization of that of Hospital Economy which was started in 1905 but was unable to develop its work satisfactorily through lack of funds. Mrs. Jenkins placed it on a substantial and permanent foundation, in a position of security, and has constantly upheld and strengthened it by supporting its work and policies. The Department of Nursing and Health is wholly for graduate nurses and its main purposes are "to improve the administration and teaching in schools of nursing by preparing graduate nurses for these special fields, and to aid in the protection of public health by training graduate nurses for all the various forms of public health nursing upon which society is now leaning so heavily." Since its endowment by Mrs. Jenkins its influence has been far reaching, as from all parts of the country come demands for such special workers, for whom hospital training is not in itself sufficient, including leaders and organizers who can awaken public interest and secure support and coöperation for such widespread preventive movements as those for infant welfare, mental hygiene, and the prevention of tuberculosis. In the field of medicine, also, Mrs. Jenkins did inestimable service by founding the New York Polyclinic Hospital, and by endowing the Marcellus Hartley Chair of Materia Medica at New York University. Moreover, she has built the hospital in North Carolina for the Southern Industrial Association, of which she is a Vice-President; and she is a member of the board of the Nursery and Child's Hospital, a director of Stony Wold Tuberculosis Sanatorium, a member of the National Organization for Public Health Nursing, and a member of the educational section and a director of the advisory council of the American Museum of Safety.

In 1916, Mrs. Jenkins was awarded the gold medal of the National Institute of Social Sciences, the presentation being made by President Nicholas Murray Butler of Columbia University, who said:

"It is a special and peculiar pleasure for me to be chosen on behalf of the Institute to make this particular presentation. The recipient of this medal has been my friend from her girlhood, and no one has watched her career with more affectionate interest and with more approval than he who has been asked to make this presentation. She bears a distinguished name. The name of Marcellus Hartley stands high on the roll of honor of the men of affairs in the City of New York, and his daughter has borne and is bearing his name as he would have liked to have her bear it.

"In philanthropic work of large vision and severe practicality, in aiding institutions of learning that have touched her imagination and appealed both to her head and to her heart, in relieving immigrants from Serbia, and in offering a generous and helping hand to the Serbian people in their hour of distress and of need, Helen Hartley Jenkins has distinguished herself as a woman of high purpose, keen intelligence and generous human sympathy. For these traits and for their abundant manifestation she has been selected to receive the gold medal of the Institute, the highest honor which the Institute confers. It is with the greatest possible pleasure that I place this medal in her hand."

In reply Mrs. Jenkins said:

"In thanking you, President Butler, for your gracious speech, and the Institute of Social Sciences for the great and overwhelming honor it has conferred upon me, there is just a word or two I would like to add to those of my profound appreciation.

"This beautiful gold medal was really won for me—not by my own deeds, but by those of my grandfather and my father.

"My grandfather's insight, fifty years ago, in planning that work which the Association for Improving the Condition of the Poor has carried out so successfully, has shown that his ideas were correct. He saw that New York would need relief work, and that the people should be taught to care for themselves. And those ideas were given over to my father, who in becoming one of the pioneers of settlement work created Hartley House. His father, then, had given over to him, just as my father has given over to me and the next generation, the obligation to do for others and to try at least to live unselfish lives.

"The credit, therefore, for those deeds with which you honor me is not mine—it is my father's in every sense of the word; it belongs to his children, and I hope to his grandchildren, who were taught and have been taught that the possession of wealth was a trust, just like any other gift which God bestows—one to be used for the general good."

Mrs. Jenkins is a Vice-President of the National Institute of Social Sciences, which was founded in 1912 under the charter of the

American Social Science Association, and in 1920 she was a member of the Institute's Executive Committee which endorsed and furthered "America's Gift to France" of an heroic statue by Frederick MacMonnies to be placed on the banks of the Marne in commemoration of the valiant stand in 1914 of the French Army, the defenders of civilization, and as a reciprocal gift for the Statue of Liberty, and a lasting expression of that feeling of kinship in democracy which unites the two republics.

During the administration of John Purroy Mitchel as Mayor of New York (1914–1917), he was in almost daily consultation with Mrs. Jenkins in regard to the city charity departments. As a result of these conferences Mrs. Jenkins helped found, in 1916, the Child Placing Bureau, to undertake the placing of sound orphan children in the best possible circumstances for their health and upbringing, and of defectives under conditions that would be a protection to them and to society. No one was better acquainted with the city government at this time than Mrs. Jenkins and to a large group she will always be known as the "Mother of the Mitchel administration." For years Mrs. Jenkins has given personal and sympathetic aid in the rehabilitation of delinquent girls, and has also visited the prisons of the state at frequent intervals. Her knowledge of penal institutions and of the needs of prisoners is thorough and many of her suggestions for improved methods have been adopted. She has always stressed the necessity for the moral, as well as the physical, training of prisoners, and was the first to propose the appointment of psychiatrists on prison staffs. Her deep understanding of penal problems has naturally brought about her appointment to state committees, such as the survey committee named by Governor Smith of New York, of which she is the only woman member. She is also on a committee for the purpose of placing released men and women in the way of honorable employment, and she is a member of the executive committee and chairman of the social hygiene committee of the National Prison Reform Association.

On January 28, 1921, a bill was introduced in the Connecticut State Legislature on behalf of Mrs. Jenkins authorizing the Hartley Trust Foundation with a directorate consisting of Mrs. Jenkins, Miss Grace Jenkins, Governor Lake of Connecticut, and two others, future governors of Connecticut, to be *ex-officio* during their terms of office, a sixth member of the board. The corporation is to have the utmost latitude in the dispensing of the income from a fund, created by Mrs. Jenkins, to aid institutions engaged in charitable, welfare, or educational work of a permanent nature anywhere in the United States.

In addition to the committees and organizations already mentioned, Mrs. Jenkins was formerly a member of the Citizens' Committee of Thirty and a director of the North American Civic League, and she is a member of the Tenement Economic Association, a trustee of the National Conservatory of Music, and a member of many patriotic and hereditary societies, such as the Society of Colonial Dames, the Daughters of the American Revolution, the Daughters of the Cincinnati, the United States Daughters of 1812, the Huguenot Society of America, and the Order of Americans of Armorial Ancestry.

The secret of Mrs. Jenkins' wide influence lies in her tact and industry. Her forceful personality is combined with a breadth of vision and a depth of feeling that make her quick to understand and prompt to aid. These inborn traits have been intensified by her contact with the many classes and conditions of people on whose behalf she has labored. Through knowing the mystical Serbs, she has increased her powers of vision; by her prison work, she has been taught to feel. Her capacity for sympathy, however, does not mean a mere passing sentimental emotion, but an impelling will to creative citizenship.

GEER, HELEN HARTLEY JENKINS (Mrs. Francis Hunt Geer) daughter of Mrs. Helen Hartley Jenkins was born in Morristown, New Jersey, December 29, 1894, and died in New York City, January 20, 1920. As her mother's constant companion she grew up in an environment of inherited civic responsibility, which she developed during her four years at Barnard College, by the intelligent selection of the professors under whom she wished to study in the courses in economics and history. This method, of always selecting the man rather than the course, she followed after her graduation in 1915, when she continued to take special work in economics at the University of California, and at Columbia University, in preparation for the doctorate in philosophy. Bab, as she was always known, was imbued with the joy of life, with the gift of laughter, and with the ability to evoke laughter in others. Her irrepressible spirits and bubbling vitality endeared her to her fellow undergraduates, and made her a recognized leader in all literary, dramatic, and student government affairs of the college. She received all the honors her classmates could bestow upon her, and as class president in her sophomore year and as vice-president of the undergraduates in her senior year, she brought the full power of a many-sided personality to bear upon the successful application among her fellows of the college's ideals. She early gave evidence of a rare literary gift and of dramatic ability of a high order. Her talent of mimicry was especially expressed in the monologues which she wrote and gave in such an inimitable manner that they were literally side-splitting, and she carried everything before her with the charm of her personality and genius. She gave these monologues not only at social gatherings of friends but also frequently in the interests of charity, thereby raising large sums. In her sophomore year, through her influence, the Greek games at Barnard were reorganized, becoming more artistic in color and scenery, and most faithful to Greek tradition. In her junior year she was editor-in-chief of the class publication, *The Barnard Mortarboard*, raising its standard, and putting it for the first time in its history on a sound financial basis, with a substantial balance. The devotion in which her memory is held by her classmates Is shown by the fact that in thirteen months they raised $5000 towards the endowment fund of Barnard, thereby inscribing Helen Hartley Jenkins Geer's name as a founder of the college. This is the first time that such a tribute has been paid a former student.

With all her many youthful activities, she always found time to be an efficient aid to her mother, in the latter's many philanthropies. From her earliest girlhood she took an active part in the work of Hartley House settlement, of which she was later a trustee, founded by her grandfather, named for her great-grandfather, and fostered by her mother. There she threw herself with her youthful and sympathetic enthusiasm into all branches of its work and, while still a young girl, instituted and led the boys' club and the women's club and gave thoughtful and personal supervision to the girls' vacation house, Hartley Farm, now at Towaco, New Jersey. Nowhere were the rare charm of her personality and the force of her character more in evidence then in her relationships with Hartley House. She was always in demand as an entertainer, and she recited her monologues before appreciative audiences who were thereby given a taste of unrestrained fun and elevating joy. During the World War she gave a series of talks of great educational value on the history of European countries, in order to give her audience, composed of representatives from those countries, a background which would interpret to them the situation abroad. During her sophomore year in college she had the vision of what one of her mother's open stair tenements, which the latter had already had constructed on the east side, would mean for the health and general well-being of the families in the neighborhood of Hartley House. From the plans which Bab suggested Mrs. Jenkins built the Hartley Open Stair Tenement at 525 West 47th Street. Bab paid a worker to teach the tenants how to live, and one apartment was set aside as a model object lesson in right furnishing and right living. A health centre was established and also a lunch room which could be patronized as well by outsiders, and where a busy mother could take her pail and bring home nourishing soup for only five cents. She was also a member of the Board of the Florence Crittenden League, her personality never being more vividly expressed than in her association with the unfortunate girls in the League's care, to whom she was from an early age a living power urging them with simplicity to higher ideals. As a member of the Junior League of New York and on its Board of Managers, she built up the settlements committee, now the most successful feature of the League's activities, and established a committee to visit camps and vacation houses. Herein she succeeded in infusing the members of the League with her own sense of responsibility and taught them to make social work a personal matter. Success became inevitable through the magic of her influence. At meetings of the Board she expressed her convictions without fear, and would hold steadfastly to any policy that she had based upon her practical and theoretical knowledge of economics. Although small in stature, her vitality was dynamic and made her a power felt throughout all organizations in which she was interested. Her infinite enthusiasm and courage brought to fruition affairs which an ordinary person would have abandoned as impossible. In recognition of her constructive work in the sphere of social service the Junior League presented in 1921 to Hartley House a memorial to Helen Hartley Geer.

Her marriage to Francis Hunt Geer took place on October 12, 1915, in old St. Paul's Chapel, New York, where the bridegroom's father, the Reverend M. Montague Geer, vicar of the chapel, officiated. They were the parents of two children: Helen Hartley Geer and Francis Geer.

Although so young, Helen Hartley Jenkins Geer had already left a marked impress upon the social welfare work of New York. Her death was a real tragedy, not only to her family and friends, but also to the many who looked up to her for sympathetic aid and understanding, as her qualities of leadership, charm, energy, and vitality fitted her in a unique way to carry on the inheritance of the Hartley line.

PAUL, ALICE, leader in the Woman's Party, daughter of William Mickle and Tacie (Parry) Paul, was born at Moorestown, New Jersey, in 1885. Her earliest American ancestor, Philip Paul, a native of England, located in Gloucester County, New Jersey, November 15, 1685. He was a member of the Council and the House of Representatives of the Province of New Jersey, and a judge of Gloucester County. She is descended, through her mother, from Thomas Stokes, who settled in Burlington County, New Jersey, in June, 1677. He was one of the signers of the Laws and Concessions of West New Jersey. Another maternal ancestor was Captain William Crispin of the British Navy, an uncle of William Penn, who sailed for America, in 1681. He died during the voyage. Captain Crispin had been appointed by William Penn, on September 30th of that year, as Chief Justice of the Provinces ("he be as chief justice to keep ye seal, ye courts and Session"), and as one of the three commissioners to select a site and lay out the City of Philadelphia. He was one of the first purchasers of land in the Province of New Jersey, and when he died his 5,000 acres were confirmed to his children. One notable name in Miss Paul's genealogy is that of John Blackfan, a prominent Quaker leader in the fight for religious freedom in England, who was repeatedly imprisoned on account of his activities. Miss Paul is descended from many other Quaker families who were among the first settlers of Pennsylvania and New Jersey. During nearly every generation members of the family have taken part in the public life of both these states.

Miss Paul's father, William Mickle Paul, died when he was a comparatively young man. He was President of the Burlington County Trust Company, President of the Moorestown National Bank, and a director in various companies. Her grandfather, Judge William Parry, was speaker of the New Jersey House of Representatives for several sessions. He was chairman of the New Jersey Convention at which the Republican Party was launched in the State. Her great-grandfather, Charles Stokes, was a member of the State Convention that drafted the present Constitution of New Jersey; he was also a member of the New Jersey Legislature.

Miss Paul received her early education at a private school, in Moorestown, New Jersey, where she won a scholarship to Swarthmore College. There she was graduated A.B. in 1905. At Swarthmore she had won a scholarship of the College Settlement Association, so immediately after graduation she spent a year (1905–1906) at the New York College Settlement. During that period she was a visitor for the New York Charity Organization Society, the New York Tenement House Commission, and other social agencies. In 1906 she completed the course in the New York School of Social Work. In 1907 she received the degree of Master of Arts from the University of Pennsylvania. About this time she was among the few who won American scholarships at the Woodbrook Settlement for Social Work, at Birmingham, England, where she spent the academic year 1907–1908. During this same period she was an assistant in the Birmingham Charity Organization Society, and the Summer Lane Social Settlement; part of the time, she was connected also with the Cannington Settlement in London. In addition, in order to investigate women's working conditions, she served as a factory hand, in London. In 1908 she was Assistant Secretary of the Dalston Branch of the London Charity Organization Society; a resident at the Christian Social Union Settlement, at Hoxton, London; and Assistant Director at the Peel Institute for Social Work, at Clerkenwell, London. She spent the academic year 1908–1909 as a graduate student in the School of Economics at the University of London.

While in England Miss Paul took an active part in the Woman Suffrage campaign, then in progress. In various parts of England and Scotland from the time she left the University of London in June, 1909, until she sailed for the United States in January, 1910, she lent valuable assistance in many ways. She was imprisoned for fourteen days in the Holloway Jail, in London (July, 1909), for taking part in a suffrage demonstration. In September of the same year, in Dundee, Scotland, she was sentenced to ten days in prison for participating in another suffrage demonstration. In November she was once more imprisoned for a month in Holloway Jail, London, in connection with a further demonstration. She was also arrested, although not imprisoned, four other times during 1909 for her suffrage activities—once for going on a deputation to Parliament, and on other occasions for participating in demonstrations in Norwich, England, and in Glasgow and Berwick, Scotland.

In 1910, upon her return to the United States, Miss Paul entered the graduate school of the University of Pennsylvania, and in 1911 was appointed a Fellow of the University, one of the few women to receive the distinction at that time. In 1912 she was graduated Doctor of Philosophy in Sociology, Economics, and Political Science. Her thesis was *The Legal Position of Women in Pennsylvania*. While she was studying at the University, in 1911, she was a member of the Executive Committee of the Pennsylvania Woman Suffrage Association. In 1912 she became Chairman of the Congressional Committee of the National American Woman Suffrage Association. The following year she and her associates organized the Congressional Union for Woman Suffrage, to finance and assist the work of the Congressional Committee. Miss Paul herself became chairman of the Union. In 1914 the Congressional Union (later known as the Woman's Party) became a separate organization, whose object was to secure a Woman Suffrage Amendment to United States Constitution. Miss Paul was National Chairman of this organization until the campaign finally brought the great woman suffrage victory in 1920. Because of her part in certain demonstrations, in 1917, she was sentenced to seven months in prison in Washington. Five weeks of this term she served, but her "hunger strike" was the cause of her release at the end of that period. She was again imprisoned, in 1918, for ten days, and in 1919 for five days. During the seven and one-half years that marked the campaign of the National Woman's Party for the Federal suffrage amendment, Miss Paul directed activities from Washington, and also gave her personal service in every part of the United States.

After the suffrage victory, when the Woman's Party, in 1921, definitely undertook to remove remaining discriminations against women, Miss Paul became National Vice-President of the Party, and in that capacity has served to the present time.

In 1922 the Washington College of Law conferred upon Miss Paul the degree of LL.B.

THE NATIONAL WOMAN'S PARTY.

The Woman's Party is a national non-partisan organization of women, dedicated to the freedom of women, and open to all women who will work for its cause, rather than for any political party. Its aim is to remove all discriminations against women in public and private life. It seeks to obtain for women equal rights and opportunities with men before the law, in various professions, in industry, in education, in the church, in the home and in our government—in short: to obtain for women a position where they shall be able to direct their own lives, and equally with men to direct the course of our common national life. As a first step in this campaign, the organization is concentrating efforts on the removal of the legal disabilities affecting woman's life, so that there may be no more discrimination against the sex. In addition, Councils are being organized among the different economic and professional groups of the Woman's Party to work for the advancement of women in their particular fields. The Councils are as follows: Actresses, architects, artists, authors, business women, dentists, farmers, government workers, lawyers, home makers, journalists, librarians, ministers, musicians, nurses, osteopaths, physicians, playwrights, political workers, religious workers, scientists, singers, social workers, teachers, and wage earners.

The Woman's Party was organized in 1913, under the name "Congressional Union for Woman Suffrage," as a temporary association to secure the national enfranchisement of women. At that time the campaign for suffrage was proceeding by the slow and laborious state by state method. After an agitation of over 60 years women were enfranchised in only nine states. Suffrage for women was little discussed and in no sense a political question. It had not even reached a vote in Congress for twenty-six years. The Woman's Party demanded immediate and nation-wide suffrage by a federal amendment. It organized the women who were already enfranchised in the nine suffrage states to back this demand by voting against the Party in power as long as that Party blocked the national amendment. It organized deputations to the President and to Congress. These deputations grew larger and more frequent until finally they became a perpetual delegation, in the form of the historic picketing of the White House and of Congress. The question of suffrage was raised from obscurity to a foremost political issue. In 1919 the Administration and Congress capitulated; the suffrage amendment passed Congress and in 1920 the necessary thirty-six states ratified it.

After the winning of suffrage, the Woman's Party at once reorganized (1921) to work for the complete freedom of women in all lines. It was felt that the obtaining of the vote was only a step in the evolution toward the goal to which women's eyes were turned and that as women had stood together for suffrage, so they must stand together until they had opened all gates to women—until every vestige of the subjection of woman had disappeared.

During the first year after the reorganization of the party for its new campaign, permanent headquarters were established in Washington, District of Columbia, to carry on the work for woman's freedom. The historic building opposite the National Capitol, which had been occupied from 1815 to 1819 by Congress, was purchased by the National President of the Woman's Party, Mrs. Oliver H. P. Belmont, and presented as a gift to the association for its permanent home. The Headquarters is designed not only as a national and international center for the carrying out of the program of the organization, but also as a clubhouse where women engaged in any activity for the advancement of women may meet while in Washington—in short, an international embassy for women.

The Headquarters was dedicated May 21, 1922, with impressive ceremonies in which women from all parts of the country participated. Senator Charles Curtis, Chairman of the Rules Committee of the United States Senate; Congressman Simeon Fess, National Chairman of the Republican Congressional Committee, and Senator Thaddeus Carraway, representing the National Democratic Committee, spoke at the dedication, extending in person their good wishes for the new Headquarters. Greetings from the Governors of the various states, from representatives of foreign nations, from women's organizations all over the world, were placed in the cornerstone.

Following the dedication, the remodelling of the Headquarters was undertaken, and the entire expense was borne by Mrs. Belmont. Her gift for this purpose was the largest sum ever given at one time by any individual, during her lifetime, to the cause of women.

The work of the organization is financed principally by membership fees and contributions. A total of over $280,000 has been raised by the National Headquarters since the Equal Rights Campaign began (from March, 1921 to April, 1923).

An exhaustive study of the discriminations against women has been undertaken, as a basis for the campaign for their removal. This investigation is directed by a member of the District of Columbia Bar, who, together with twelve assistants, has made a special study of the law concerning the status of women. In making this investigation, every constitutional provision, every statute, and every court decision bearing upon the position of women is examined. The United States Supreme Court Library, which affords probably the best facilities in the country for such an inquiry, is used for this work. For the first time, when this survey is completed, the exact legal status of women in this country will be definitely known, for the gradual modification of the old common law, varying from state to state, has led to complete confusion as to woman's legal rights.

An entirely new literature in support of the Equal Rights program has been created to replace the suffrage literature used in the earlier activity of the organization. Among the leaflets already prepared, or now in preparation, are those showing the discriminatory laws passed against women in forty-eight states of the Union, and the District of Columbia; in the Federal laws; in citizenship requirements; in Government service; in the diplomatic, consular and foreign trade service; in the professions; in industry; in educational opportunities; in the church; in the enforcement of laws relating to sex offenses; in the wages and salaries paid to women in private and public employment. Pamphlets have also been written concerning the historical background of the Equality campaign and giving information on the development of this movement in other countries.

The attention of the country has been increasingly turned to the Equal Rights question both by a publicity and an organizing campaign. Where at the beginning of the campaign, little was heard or written on the subject, today the people, from one end of the country to the other, are arguing in the press, at their meetings, in the home, for and against "Equality."

As the state legislature convened, the Woman's Party introduces bills for the removal of the disabilities of women in each particular state. One measure, brought in the Wisconsin legislature, passed in its entirety— so that Wisconsin is the only state in the Union, in which there are no legal discriminations against women. Wisconsin thus stands to the new Equal Rights program as Wyoming, the first suffrage state, stood to the suffrage campaign. In the other states various points on the Equality program have been adopted.

The program of the Woman's Party in more detail is given in the Declaration of Principles and the outline of Campaign of the organization, which are here added:

WHEREAS, Women today, although enfranchised, are still in every way subordinate to men before the law, in government, in educational opportunities, in the professions, in the church, in industry, and in the home.

BE IT RESOLVED, That as a part of our campaign to remove all form of the subjection of women, we shall work for the following immediate objects:

That women shall no longer be regarded and shall no longer regard themselves as inferior to men, but the equality of the sexes shall be recognized.

That women shall no longer be the governed half of society, but shall participate equally with men in the direction of life.

That women shall no longer be denied equal educational opportunities with men, but the same opportunities shall be given to both sexes in all schools, colleges, and universities which are supported in any way by public funds.

That women shall no longer be barred from any occupation, but every occupation to men shall be open to women and restrictions upon the hours, conditions and remuneration of labor shall apply alike to both sexes.

That women shall no longer be discriminated against in the legal, the medical, the teaching, or any other profession, but the same opportunities shall be given to women as to men in training for professions and in the practice of these professions.

That women shall no longer be discriminated against in civil and government service, but shall have the same right as men to authority, appointment, advancement and pay in the executive, the legislative, and the judicial branches of the government service.

That women shall no longer be discriminated against in the foreign trade, consular and diplomatic service, but women as well as men shall represent our country in foreign lands.

That women shall no longer receive less pay than men for the same work, but shall receive equal compensation for equal work in public and private employment.

That women shall no longer be barred from the priesthood or ministry, or any position of authority in the church, but equally with men shall participate in ecclesiastical offices and dignities.

That a double moral standard shall no longer exist, but one code shall obtain for both men and women.

That exploitation of the sex of women shall no longer exist, but women shall have the same right to the control of their persons as have men.

That women shall no longer be discriminated against in treatment of sex diseases and in punishment of sex offenses, but men and women shall be treated in the same way for sex diseases and sex offenses.

That women shall no longer be deprived of the right of trial by a jury of their peers, but jury service shall be open to women as to men.

That women shall no longer be discriminated against in inheritance laws, but men and women shall have the same right to inherit property.

That the identity of the wife shall no longer be merged in that of her husband, but the wife shall retain her separate identity after marriage and be able to contract with her husband concerning the marriage relationship.

That a woman shall no longer be required by law or custom to assume the name of her husband upon marriage but shall have the same right as a man to retain her own name after marriage.

That the wife shall no longer be considered as supported by the husband, but their mutual contribution to the family maintenance shall be recognized.

That the headship of the family shall no longer be in the husband alone, but shall be equally in the husband and wife.

That the husband shall no longer own his wife's services, but these shall belong to her alone as in the case of any free person.

That the husband shall no longer own his wife's earnings, but these shall belong to her alone.

That the husband shall no longer own or control his wife's property, but it shall belong to her and be controlled by her alone.

That the husband shall no longer control the joint property of his wife and himself, but the husband and wife shall have equal control of their joint property.

That the husband shall no longer obtain divorce more easily than the wife, but the wife shall have the right to obtain divorce on the same grounds as the husband.

That the husband shall no longer have a greater right to make contracts than the wife, but a wife shall have equal right with her husband to make contracts.

That married women shall no longer be denied the right to choose their own citizenship, but shall have the same independent choice of citizenship as is possessed by their husbands.

That women shall no longer be discriminated against in the economic world because of marriage, but shall have the same treatment in the economic world after marriage as have men.

That the father shall no longer have the paramount right to the care, custody and control of the child, to determine its education and religion, to the guardianship of its estate, and to the control of its services and earnings, but these rights shall be shared equally by the father and mother in the case of all children, whether born within or without the marriage ceremony.

That no form of the Common Law or Civil Law disabilities of women shall any longer exist, but women shall be equal with men before the law.

In short—That women shall no longer be in any form of subjection to man in law to custom, but shall in every way be on an equal plane in rights, as she has always been and will continue to be, in responsibilities and obligations.

The OUTLINE OF THE PLAN OF CAMPAIGN of the organization is as follows:

I.   *National Work.*—Make certain that your United States Senators and your Congressmen give their whole-hearted support and their vote to all Equal Rights legislation before Congress.

II.   *State Work.*—Make certain that your Senators and your Representative in the State Legislature give their whole-hearted support and their vote to all Equal Rights legislation.

III.   *Local Work.*—Make certain that your own locality is at least one spot in the United States where every girl that is born has an equal chance in life with every boy and where, throughout life, there are no handicaps of any kind placed upon women because of their sex.

To this end make certain:

(1) That women are nominated for all elective offices in your local community, your county and your state, and are supported in the elections and are placed equally with men in the offices which control the life of your community.

(2) That women are appointed equally with men to all appointive positions under your local, your county, and your state government.

(3) That the same opportunities are given to girls as to boys in all schools, colleges, and universities in your community which are supported in whole or in part by public funds; that in these educational institutions girls have the same opportunities as boys to study in all departments; that entrance requirements are equal; that the opportunity for trade and vocational training is equal; that opportunity for physical training and for entrance into the athletic life of the institution is equal; that opportunity for obtaining academic honors, scholarships, fellowships, and all other honors is equal.

(4) That in your community, all occupations and professions, whether public or private, are open to women on the same terms as to men; that women equally with men are appointed to the administrative and other positions involving power and high salaries; that women have the same opportunities to advancement in these occupations and professions; that they are paid equally for the same work; that they have equal opportunity to enter the Unions of their trade and to participate in the government of the Unions; that women engaged in business or working at any paid occupations are encouraged and supported; that whenever public money is spent, women receive the appointments, contracts or commissions, equally with men.

(5) That in the churches in your community women have an equal share with men in the governing of the church, and in participation in the ministry and all ecclesiastical offices and dignities.

(6) That in your community the public sentiment supports a single moral and ethical code for men and women, and that all acts which are considered dishonorable or wrong in one sex, are considered the same in the other sex.

(7) That in your community one sex in no way preys upon the other by the white slave trade; by forcing it into prostitution or in any other way; that men and women receive the same examination, quarantine and treatment for sex diseases; that when men and women are punished for sex offenses they are punished in the same way for the same offense.

(8) That in your community married women are not dismissed from government service, the schools, or from private employment because of their marriage.

ANDERSON, ISABEL (Mrs. Larz Anderson), was born in Boston, Massachusetts, March 29, 1876. Her father was the late Commodore George Hamilton Perkins, U. S. N., and her mother, Anna Minot Weld Perkins, a daughter of William Fletcher Weld of Boston. Commodore Perkins' record in the Navy was a brilliant one. He was a graduate of Annapolis, and served in the Civil War with gallantry and distinction as Commander of the *Chickasaw*, one of Admiral Farragut's ironclad monitors, which, in the Battle of Mobile Bay, compelled the supposedly invulnerable ram *Tennessee* to surrender after a desperate fight. He also led the fleet past the forts on the Mississippi River, and landed at New Orleans, where he and Captain Bailey, walking unarmed through a howling mob to the City Hall, demanded the surrender of the city, thereby winning Farragut's eulogy, "the bravest man that ever trod the deck of a ship." A statue of Commodore Perkins by Daniel Chester French stands in the State House grounds in Concord, New Hampshire, his native state, and a replica, in the balcony end of Bancroft

Memorial Hall of the Naval Academy at Annapolis. One of the first modern torpedo boat destroyers of the Navy was named after Commodore Perkins, and a quartermaster's boat in the Army service was named after Mr. Anderson's great-uncle, General Robert Anderson of Fort Sumter fame.

Mrs. Anderson's maternal grandfather, William F. Weld, owner of numberless ships carrying his "black horse" house flag into the Seven Seas and a pioneer railroad builder in the west, laid the foundations of his vast commercial undertakings between the '40s and the '60s of the 19th century and left a large fortune to his family. Through both her parents Mrs. Anderson inherits a long strain of New England ancestry, reaching back, on the one side, to Increase Mather, and on the other, to Joseph Weld, who settled at Roxbury, Massachusetts, in 1633, and received large grants of land. By inheritance, therefore, Mrs. Anderson holds membership in the Society of Colonial Dames and the Daughters of the American Revolution.

Mrs. Anderson passed her childhood in Boston and Newport, and at the old New Hampshire home, her education being imparted by governesses and at Miss Winsor's private school. Later, for a short period, she was enrolled as a student at Boston University. In 1895 she was introduced into society, being also a member of that year's Sewing Circle and the Vincent Club. The next year she was chaperoned on a trip abroad by Mrs. John Elliott, a daughter of Julia Ward Howe, and while traveling in Europe she met Larz Anderson, then the First Secretary of the American Embassy and Chargé d'Affaires, in Rome, and subsequently became engaged to him. Mr. Anderson, who had previously served as Second Secretary of Legation and Embassy in London, belongs to the prominent Cincinnati families of Anderson and Longworth, his grandfather and father, as well as himself, having been graduates of Harvard University. Mr. and Mrs. Anderson were married on June 10, 1897, in the Arlington

Street Church, Boston. They made their honeymoon trip through the West, into the Yellowstone, to Hawaii, to Japan and China, with a yachting cruise through the beautiful Inland Sea. This was followed by many long journeys—a winter in India, where Lady Curzon, an old friend, was Vice-Reine, so that special opportunities were enjoyed; private car trips through Mexico; visits to the mesas, pueblos and cliff dwellings of the Southwest, cruises to Alaska, and yachting trips to the West Indies and South America, and along the coast of England and the fjords of Norway. With a most simple taste, although with such wide opportunities, Mrs. Anderson loved camping, and made venturesome trips into the Canadian Rockies, the Ontario Lakes, the Maine Woods, and the Rocky Mountains. Mr. and Mrs. Anderson have been almost pioneers in houseboating, having been among the first to take advantage of the inside waters that exist between Florida and Maine for cruising in their houseboat.

In 1910 Mr. and Mrs. Anderson accompanied the American Secretary of War, the Honorable J. M. Dickinson, on his official visit to the Philippines, at the time when the Honorable Cameron Forbes was Governor General, and had extraordinary opportunities to study the Islands. The party was received officially by the Emperor of Japan, and at the foot of the Dragon Throne by the Prince Regent on behalf of the baby Emperor of China, and returned home by way of the trans-Siberian railway to be entertained splendidly in Russia. Mrs. Anderson had been received in private audience by the Queen of Italy and also by His Holiness the Pope, and was presented in the Diplomatic Circle at the Court of St. James and had the entrée to the Court Ball and Musicale. Meanwhile she had established her summer home at "Weld" in Brookline, near Boston, where her grandfather had lived, and had embellished the estate with gardens that became famous among the most beautiful in America. In Washington her house was one of the best known, and was filled with collections made during her travels—tapestries, velvets, pictures, jades, Mexican potteries, Philippine weapons. In both houses Mrs. Anderson received distinguished foreigners and compatriots: Presidents, ambassadors, the Imperial Princely Fushimis, cousins of the Emperor of Japan, the Tokugawa descendants of the Shoguns; H.R.H. the Duke of the Abruzzi was a guest for several days; H.R.H. the Prince of Udine; the Duke of Brabant, son of the King of the Belgians; and many royal commissioners and delegates. "Weld" was the only private house in New England that was to be honored by a visit by the King and Queen of the Belgians in 1919, but when the royal couple went into mourning, the plan was changed.

At the time of the Spanish War, Mr. Anderson volunteered and received a commission in the Adjutant-General's Department, acting as Adjutant-General of a Division during the period of hostilities. Mrs. Anderson was among the few women who, at that time, thought of service, and she at once took on many activities, visiting hospitals, personally providing whatever was needed, and looking after the dependent families of soldiers.

When Mr. Anderson was appointed Minister to Belgium in 1911, Mrs. Anderson accompanied him, and was able at once to take her place in diplomatic life, owing to her many associations already made during her residence in Washington, and her travels. Among other services, she established, with great success, a Girls' Student Club for American girls transiently studying in Brussels, as had been done in Paris and London. On Mr. Anderson's promotion to Tokyo as Ambassador, Mrs. Anderson found already prepared a warm welcome and many associations, and she took active part in all the interests of the American Colony, as well as among the Japanese, being already well known from her previous visits, private and semi-official. On her return home she resumed her life in Boston and Washington, social and charitable.

Mrs. Anderson developed her literary talent by publishing in 1908 a book for children called *The Great Sea Horse* in which her experiences in travel and facts in Nature were interwoven with imagination and fairy fancies. This was followed by a series of small *Captain Ginger* stories. Articles for magazines succeeded, and a play called *Everybody* was produced at the Bijou Theatre, Boston. In 1914, at the request of the publisher of the *Spell Series*, Mrs. Anderson wrote *The Spell of Japan*, followed in 1915 by *The Spell of Belgium*, and in 1916 by *The Spell of Hawaii and the Philippine Islands*. In 1917 was published *Odd Corners*, containing personal experiences in out-of-the-way places of the world; and in 1918, on her return from France, she told of her work, and of what she had seen in the Great War, in a book called *Zigzagging*, which was said to be one of the best publications of its kind. Later, in 1920, Mrs. Anderson told of conditions in Washington and war work in *President and Pies*.

Mrs. Anderson has always been greatly interested in politics and active in campaigns. In 1912 she was a member of the Republican Women's Advisory Committee and Chairman of the Women's Massachusetts Republican Committee, organizing rallies and speaking on occasions.

The outbreak of the World War in 1914 meant as much to Mrs. Anderson, as if the United States had entered it at the first, because of her many foreign associations and wide knowledge of conditions abroad. Already a member of the Red Cross Central Committees, she at once took part in relief work, as a member of the original Central Belgian Relief Committee, and in the Organization of the New England Belgian Relief, which had such wonderful success. She was an active member of the Allied Bazaar Relief Committee in Boston, and of the Italian Relief; joined the Women's Training Camp work, and early received a Red Cross diploma. On the entrance of the United States into the War in 1917, she was a Vice-Chairman of the

District of Columbia Red Cross Chapter and was commissioned a Colonel to organize the first experimental unit of a Red Cross Refreshment Corps Canteen. This her energy and executive ability made so successful that it proved a model for similar units throughout the country. When, in the autumn of 1917, the Red Cross determined to establish canteens in France, Mrs. Anderson could not resist the call to go to the front, especially as her work at home had so well prepared her for the work. She sailed in September, 1917, and was at once sent to the Canteen at Epernay, from which she visited Rheims and the front line trenches there. Soon finding, however, that canteen work did not satisfy her desire for active service, she sought a transfer to hospital work at the front, and was militarized into the French Army, and sent to one of the few American units in the French war zone. This was at Cugny, near Saint-Quentin, so soon to be overrun by the Germans. While there, an invitation came from the King and Queen of the Belgians to visit them at their headquarters at La Panne, and as the British were taking over the lines at Cugny, and a vacation was due the workers, Mrs. Anderson went to La Panne and was received and dined with Their Majesties, and given an opportunity to inspect the very front line trenches at Dixmude, Nieuport, and Pervyse. Professor Depage, an old friend from days in Brussels, was head of the Belgian Medical Staff, and suggested that Mrs. Anderson should pass her leave in working at his Ocean Hospital at La Panne, with the result that Mrs. Anderson spent her "vacation" in working in the same room with Her Majesty the Queen. Later she visited Lady Hadfield, a sister of the Honorable George Wickersham, at her hospital at Wimeraux, near the British base at Boulogne. On reporting back to Paris, Mrs. Anderson obtained permission, as she was still on leave, to visit the American front, and going to General Headquarters, dined with General Pershing, an old friend, and with General Edwards, commanding the famous New England Division, and passed on as far as Toul and its hospitals. On returning to Paris, at the moment of the great German drive in 1918, her unit had again been attached to the 3rd French Army at Royallieu, near Compiégne, and Mrs. Anderson remained there nursing until her return home.

Mrs. Anderson has received recognition for general and special work from foreign nations, as well as the Red Cross with bars from the United States. The Emperor of Japan, "in recognition of her meritorious services," conferred on her the Third Class Imperial Order of Merit with the Insignia of the Order of the Sacred Crown. Later she received the Japanese Red Cross Medal and, with "the sanction of the Emperor and Empress," the Order of Merit of the Japanese Red Cross Society. While at the Belgian front, in recognition of her work on behalf of Belgium at home and at the Belgian front in hospitals, Mrs. Anderson was decorated by King Albert with the Medal of Queen Elizabeth with Red Cross; and France awarded her the Croix de Guerre. On her return to Washington in 1918, George Washington University chose her in June as representing American womanhood in the Great War, and conferred on her the honorary degree of Doctor of Letters, in recognition of her writings and "devoted work for those in the service of her country." This is the first instance in the one hundred years of its existence that this University has honored a woman with the literary degree.

HOWE, JULIA WARD (Mrs. Samuel Gridley Howe), daughter of Samuel and Julia (Cutter) Ward, was born in New York City (Marketfield Street, near the Battery), May 27, 1819; died at her home, 241 Beacon Street, Boston, Massachusetts, October 17, 1910. Through her father, a prominent banker of the firm of Prime, Ward and King, she was descended from two Colonial governors; among her forebears were the Cutters, the Marions, the Greens, the Mitchells, the Rays, and the famous Roger Williams himself. From her long line of illustrious ancestors she inherited a large energy and a brilliant intelligence to which she did full justice.

Mrs. Howe was by all means an educated woman in the broadest and most inclusive sense of the term, but she was not a product of the schools. Her vast knowledge and her remarkable culture are attributable principally to her lifelong study and observation. Her daughters quote her own words as the keynote of her unique life: "To learn, to teach, to serve, and to enjoy." Mrs. Howe's accomplishments in the field of education were little short of phenomenal. She was master of at least six languages, and acquired a comprehensive knowledge of music, metaphysics, philosophy, literature, liberal theology, and histrionics. She could act as well as a professional. Moreover, she knew how to preach; she was accomplished as an organizer and leader of great movements, and of the associations which conducted them; and she was a talented exemplar of all the social graces. By no means the least of her accomplishments was her self-control in all the vicissitudes of a long and arduous life, and her art of self-effacement in the truly altruistic service of others. She wrote philosophical expositions on duality of character that aroused admiration even among the transcendentalists; she preached forceful sermons in the Unitarian pulpit; she read Hegel and Kant in the original; she spoke Spanish and Italian, and read and declaimed the ancient Greek; she made extemporaneous addresses to French and Greek notables in their native tongues, and won their highest respect for her adequate linguistic knowledge; and she wrote much poetry of fine feeling and of effective form.

In 1842, Miss Ward first visited the Perkins Institution, South Boston, Massachusetts, where Doctor Samuel Gridley Howe had been Director for nine years. Her special object was to see Laura Bridgman, the blind-deaf phenomenon. Doctor Howe had won worldwide fame by teaching this girl the blind and the deaf-mute alphabet. Helen Keller was later instructed in the same method by Doctor Howe's son-in-law, Michael Anagnos, to the point at which she learned to speak and to read the lips. This first meeting of Miss Ward and Doctor Howe led to their marriage, very shortly afterward. They lived for a short time at the Perkins Institution, but soon established a home of their own in South Boston, Massachusetts. This place, which included many shade trees and a vegetable garden, Mrs. Howe, with typical humorous romanticism, entitled "Green Peace." Mr. and Mrs. Howe were the parents of two sons, Henry Marion, who became a prominent metallurgist; Samuel, who died in infancy; and four daughters, Julia Romana (born in Rome), who married Michael Anagnos; Laura Richards; Florence Hall; and Maude Elliott.

In the intervals of their arduous labors, Mrs. Howe and her husband found time to travel at various times in Europe, where they were received by many people of distinction. While in Rome, in 1843, Mrs. Howe suffered an accident of an unusual nature. While participating in a celebration, her eyes were injured by thrown confetti, which at that time was composed of lime. As a result she was seriously inconvenienced in the pursuit of her studies. Besides traveling in England and on the Continent, Mrs. Howe spent some time in Cuba, and this visit she made the theme of an interesting little book, written in light vein, and entitled, *A Trip to Cuba*. About this same period, she wrote also for newspapers, including the *New York Tribune*.

Soon afterward came the terrible period of the Civil War. To a woman of Julia Ward Howe's sensitive and sympathetic nature, the pathos and the tragedy involved were in the nature of something personally agonizing. Her heart and her soul were stirred even by the prospect of such a conflict, and her famous *Battle Hymn of the Republic* was born of her realization of its actual significance. This poem came to her under remarkable circumstances. In the fall of 1861 she visited Washington on a mission for the Sanitary Commission, which corresponded at that time to the American Red Cross of today. While attending a review of troops in the city she had sung to some of the soldiers the stirring battle song *John Brown's Body*, and a little later John Freeman Clarke asked her why she did not write words of her own to that tune. Mrs. Howe replied that she had considered doing so, but had never definitely set about it. Early the following morning, as she lay half awake waiting for daylight, the poem began to formulate itself in her mind. When she had finished composing it, she rose and hastily wrote the stanzas without even striking a light, for fear of wakening her baby, who was in the room with her. Such hasty composition during the night hours had become a matter of habit, and she used to explain that even she herself could read her writing on such occasions only when the matter itself was fresh in her memory. In this case, the details of the *Battle Hymn of the Republic* had escaped her a few hours later, and had she not taken the precaution to write the verses, the wonderful poem would have been lost to the world. Of the *Battle Hymn* she herself said, soon after composing it, "I like this better than most things I have written." The poem was published at the time in the *Atlantic Monthly*.

This poem will always live, because of its rare beauty and its real appeal to human emotions. It is of more than passing interest to note that it had tremendous popularity, among citizens and soldiers alike, during the World War. But the *Battle Hymn of the Republic* was not the only fine poem that came from Mrs. Howe's pen. *Our Orders*, beginning "Weave no more silk, ye Lyons looms," is an exquisite bit of versification, strong in its emotional and its patriotic inspirational qualities. *Endeavor*, in serious ethical vein, compares well with the great poems of all time. *A Thought for Washing Day* ("The clothes line is a rosary"), compared with the others mentioned, illustrates the wide range of Mrs. Howe's versatility.

Mrs. Howe also accomplished considerable in dramatic writing. She early aspired to the honors of a playwright, and succeeded in writing a play, *The World's Own*, which was highly praised by the managers, and was produced at Wallack's Theatre, New York City, with E. A. Sothern and Matilda Heron in the leading rôles. One critic characterized it as "full of literary merits and dramatic defects." In 1852, Mrs. Howe wrote an elaborate five-act tragedy, modeled after the Greek, and on the basis of the Hippolytus legends. Arrangements were made that E. L. Davenport should produce this play at the Howard Athenaeum, with Edwin Booth and Charlotte Cushing in the cast. For some reason this plan was not consummated, and Mrs. Howe's disappointment was so great that she permanently abandoned playwrighting. However, after Mrs. Howe's death, it was most successfully produced at the Tremont Theatre, with Margaret Anglin in the cast.

Although Mrs. Howe had received a liberal musical education, and was hospitably disposed toward radical departures from the established order in general, it is noteworthy that she was never a votary of the "new music." She had no enthusiasm for Wagner, and her feeling for Brahms amounted to real aversion. She would not consent to attend the Symphony concerts at which such music was introduced. *Tristan and Iseult* Mrs. Howe referred to as "broken china." The new poetry of her time she considered in much the same light. It is rather remarkable that, although Walt Whitman was born at about the same time and place as she, there seems to be no record of their even having made mention of each other.

No biography of Julia Ward Howe would be complete without particular mention of some of the activities of her husband, in which she shared. Samuel Gridley Howe was an ardent reformer, of whom it has been said that he was "always freeing somebody." On one occasion she accompanied him to Crete, upon one of his self-imposed missions, and there she herself became a popular idol. That she was not over-impressed by the honors showered upon her is evidenced by the fact that, upon her return, she composed humorous verses in commemoration of her visit. This is quite typical, for she had the faculty of turning from the sublime to the ridiculous, and while she could write splendid serious verse, she could also produce delightful nonsense rhymes. Mrs. Howe was obliged to accustom herself to her husband's knight-errantry in the interest of reform, for she never knew when his enthusiasm would keep him from home well into the night. Here again her irrepressible wit came into play, and she would compose bedtime verses for the baby, with the father's absence as a theme. But Mrs. Howe seriously sympathized with her husband's reform efforts, and often made a home for the objects of his charity. She was, herself, a true reformer at heart, and consequently her husband's activities struck a sympathetic chord.

The anti-slavery agitation found zealous supporters in both Doctor and Mrs. Howe. When the Civil War came to an end, Mrs. Howe, forcefully impressed by the awful lessons that it taught, conceived the idea of instituting a Crusade of Peace. To that end, she addressed an "appeal to womanhood throughout the world." As a result of her efforts, a congress of women was convened in New York City to promote the cause of international peace, and for this she herself labored until the end of her life. Various other causes, also, received her ardent support —among them, Woman Suffrage. Yet, with all her enthusiasm she was restrained, patient, self-controlled. She was accustomed to visit the State House annually to add her plea for the franchise, and even at the age of eighty-five she made her appearance before the legislative Committee.

Julia Ward Howe, it may be said, wore herself out in the active service of mankind. Her body failed gradually, under the tre-mendous tasks imposed upon it. Her mind, to the time of her death retained that brilliancy and activity which were its leading characteristics throughout a life that will find few parallels. It would seem most fitting that to the very last Julia Ward Howe was enabled to practise that high principle which she advised others to adopt as an inspiration and a motive: to learn, to teach, to serve, and to enjoy.

DAVISON, KATE TRUBEE (Mrs. Henry P. Davison), philanthropist, and organizer and leader of welfare activities, daughter of Frederick and Mary Waterbury (Baldwin) Trubee, was born in Bridgeport, Connecticut, February 2, 1871. Through her father, also of Bridgeport (born April 3, 1845; died, May 29, 1912), she is directly descended from Andris Trubee, a native of Holland, who located in Boston, Massachusetts, during the seventeenth century. Mrs. Davison's mother (born, August 27, 1847), was a direct lineal descendant of one of those Puritans who landed at Plymouth Rock, on the first voyage on the *Mayflower*.

Kate Trubee Davison received her elementary education in private schools and in the public high school, Bridgeport, Connecticut. Later, she spent two years at Miss Salisbury's Seminary, Pittsburgh, Pennsylvania, and one year at Mrs. Life's Seminary, Rye, New York. On April 13, 1893, at the South Congregational Church, Bridgeport, Connecticut, she was married to Henry Pomeroy Davison, banker and philanthropist of New York City (born, Troy, Pennsylvania, June 13, 1867; died, Peacock Point, Long Island, New York, May 6, 1922), son of George Bennett and Henrietta (Pomeroy) Davison. They were the parents of two sons, Frederick Trubee (born, New York City, February 7, 1895), and Henry Pomeroy Davison, Junior (born, Englewood, New Jersey, April 3, 1898), and two daughters, Alice Trubee Davison Gates (born, Englewood, New Jersey, September 6, 1899), and

Frances Pomeroy Davison (born, Englewood, New Jersey, November 11, 1903).

In 1902, Mr. Davison was made Vice-President of the First National Bank of New York City. Later he became a member of the firm of J. P. Morgan and Company, Chairman of the Executive Committee and a Director of the Bankers' Trust Company, and a Director of the American Foreign Securities Company, all of New York City. During the World War he was elected Chairman of the War Council, of the American Red Cross, and served from 1917 to 1919. In May, 1919, in Paris, he was made Chairman of the Governing Board of the World League of Red Cross Societies.

Mrs. Davison has always emphasized the highly important place of the family and the home as constituting the foundation of American civilization at its best, maintaining that the home life of the younger generation will determine what will be the adult's contribution to the community. In her own life she was consistently faithful to this principle, for, as nearly as possible, she planned an ideal home for her children. Her success in social welfare activities has been but the projection, into the community life, of her ideals regarding the family.

Among the first of the enterprises with which Mrs. Davison became associated, was the New York Diet Kitchen, founded more than thirty-five years ago for the purpose of providing proper food for the sick poor. This organization was one of the first to teach mothers the parental care of children. Today, besides this important work at its various centres, it furnishes at cost a high grade of milk for babies and invalids; and, through its staff of trained visiting nurses instructs mothers in the proper care of the home and the scientific feeding of infants. During the influenza epidemic of 1918 these nurses did heroic service among the needy. Mrs. Davison was one of the founders and a member of the Board of Managers of the Cosmopolitan Club, originally for governesses

and secretaries. It was subsequently reorganized as a club for professional women, such as artists, musicians, social service workers, and others.

For three years Mrs. Davison contributed valuable service as one of the Board of Managers of the National Institute of Social Science, whose policies she did much to crystallize and formulate. The membership is composed of those who have made practical contributions to social welfare. At the annual Institute dinner medals are awarded members whose work during the year warrants special recognition. Mrs. Davison is at present serving on the committee which selects the members to be thus decorated. The Institute, promoting and rewarding social service as it does, performs a highly important function in the community. In all of her varied activities Mrs. Davison has constantly watched for opportunities to aid childhood and youth among the poor, although she has by no means confined her efforts to these classes. Her humanitarian efforts have included association, also, with such organizations as the following: the Union Settlement (member of the Board of Managers, and Chairman of the Nursing Committee); Post-Graduate Hospital (Chairman of the Supported Beds Department); New York Throat, Nose, and Lung Hospital (in charge of the Social Service work for three years); Actors' Endowment Fund of America; Orchard House, Glen Cove, New York (Honorary Chairman); and the National Board of the Young Women's Christian Association.

In 1916, before the United States entered the World War, Mrs. Davison was requested to act as President to organize Base Hospital units for the Presbyterian Hospital, and during the summer established three such units. At the same time she was largely instrumental in organizing a Naval Aviation unit, in which were her two sons, Trubee and Harry, some of their fellow-students from Yale University, and others of their friends. They lived at Peacock Point, and daily went to Huntington for their training. The Unit rendered highly meritorious service abroad. During the summer of 1916, Mrs. Davison organized for the girls of Peacock Point a complete First Aid course, which was in charge of a trained nurse from the Presbyterian Hospital. With foresight, energy, and efficiency, she trained the entire community, so that all should be ready to render efficient service of some kind.

During the war period Mrs. Davison became internationally known as a result of her work. In 1917, she was prominent among the organizers of the War Work Council of the National Young Women's Christian Association. The Executive Committee of this Council, of which she was a member, and also Treasurer, from its organization, foresaw many problems that would confront women workers in munitions and other war-time industries. The War Work Council effectively coöperated with the War Camp Community Service in conducting Hostess Houses, and also furnished workers for other organizations. Its activities became world-wide in scope. Shortly before the close of hostilities, the Secretary of War, Mr. Baker, suggested instituting the United War Work Campaign, to include the war workers of all societies doing service here and abroad, with the object of raising a common fund for the successful termination of the War. Mrs. Davison was requested to tour the country for the purpose of effecting coöperation among the women's organizations. This she accomplished with great credit to herself and with marked success for the cause. She succeeded, also, at a time when such a task was especially difficult, owing to the fact that many sections of the country were strictly quarantined on account of the prevalence of influenza.

Mrs. Davison's tact and judgment have perhaps never been more strikingly evidenced than in connection with her Red Cross activities. In her own home county (Nassau County, Long Island, New York), there were so many community chapters and auxiliaries that the work was lacking in efficiency. As County Chairman, Mrs. Davison recognized the seriousness of the situation and she eventually brought about a harmonious merging of these units into the one County Chapter. Having done this, she spared no effort to promote the utmost solidarity and effectiveness within that chapter. The result has been that the Nassau County Chapter has won a well-deserved reputation for achievement. One of the most conspicuous accomplishments, under Mrs. Davison's leadership, has been the centralization of all Red Cross county funds in the treasury of the Nassau County Chapter, where they are readily available to meet the most pressing needs. This arrangement made it possible to carry out, in the public schools, dental service demonstration and public health nursing programs which have set a standard. They have received wide and favorable comment both here and abroad. Mr. and Mrs. Davison's children, during the World War, exhibited the same patriotic spirit as their parents, and served their country well. The elder daughter, Alice, seventeen years old when the United States entered the War, passed government examinations and became an instructor in wireless operation. She was stationed at Huntington, Long Island, New York, where she gave instruction to Navy men, as well as to women who, like herself, wished to serve the country in this capacity. They were the first women employed by the government in this kind of work. Later, the first group was assigned to government duty with the Western Electric Company, the General Electric Company, and the Detroit Telephone and Telegraph Company. Mrs. Davison may well feel that her consistent efforts to make real the ideals of home and family have been amply awarded, as evidenced both in the splendid record of the children, who reflect her influence, and in her own remarkable accomplishments along philanthropic and humanitarian lines.

NATIONAL LEAGUE OF WOMEN VOTERS. When the complete enfranchisement of the women of the United States became a fact, Mrs. Carrie Chapman Catt conceived the idea of a continuing organization of women devoted to the political education of newly-made women voters. At the fiftieth convention of the National American Woman Suffrage Association, held at St. Louis in February, 1919, a league of women voters was organized, as an auxiliary to the National American Woman Suffrage Association. Mrs. Charles H. Brooks, of Kansas, was made chairman and those eligible to membership were the women of the twenty-six states in which women were then permitted to vote in presidential elections. In February, 1920, in connection with the fifty-first and final convention of the National American Woman Suffrage Association in Chicago, the first national congress of the League of Women Voters was held and the organization was made permanent. A board of directors was elected, which subsequently chose as Chairman, Mrs. Maud Wood Park, then Congressional Secretary of the National American Woman Suffrage Association.

In August of that year, the thirty-sixth state ratified the Nineteenth Amendment, and on August 26, 1920, the Secretary of State proclaimed the amendment as part of the Constitution of the United States. The League was now free to become truly national in scope, and in April, 1921, assembled at Cleveland for its second convention, where the By-Laws were so amended as to create the office of President—instead of Chairman—and two Vice-Presidents, and to make these officers elective by the delegates. Seven regional directors, as provided the previous year, were retained. In 1922, the office of Third Vice-President was added—the Board of Directors now consisting of the President, three Vice-Presidents, a Secretary, a Treasurer, and the regional directors—thirteen in all. The regional directors are elected annually by the delegates from their respective regions,

and the general officers are elected for terms of two years each—the President, the Secretary, and the Third Vice-President in the even numbered years, the First and Second Vice-Presidents and the Treasurer in the odd-numbered years.

In April, 1922, a convention was held in Baltimore, and in conjunction with it a Pan-American Conference of women, primarily designed to promote international friendliness. In April, 1923, the fourth annual convention was held at Des Moines, Iowa, when the By-Laws were amended, to cover the extension of the League's activities, which had come as a logical development of the progress of the organization and the needs of the times. As originally stated, the object was to foster education in citizenship and to support needed legislation; as amended, it is to promote education in citizenship, efficiency in government, needed legislation, and international coöperation to prevent war.

Besides the affiliated state Leagues (of which there may be not more than one from each state) and the Leagues of the District of Columbia and Hawaii, two national organizations—the Ladies of the Maccabees and the National Council of Jewish Women—are associate members, and other national organizations "working along similar lines" are eligible to such membership.

The League of Women Voters believes that the enfranchisement of women should bring into the electorate a fresh and vivifying element with a characteristic woman's point of view as its contribution to American public life. It believes that its members should study public questions, not as good citizens only, but as women citizens; that there are matters for which women are peculiarly responsible, and that organization of women is necessary in order to give these matters the emphasis in government which their importance deserves.

These principles do not imply that women voters are expected to operate only through the League. On the contrary, they are urged to act through their political parties, and through social and civic organizations in which men and women work together; but the League exists to give women a common meeting ground for discussion, removed from party bias or organization precedent—an agency through which they can act with other women voters in the interests of those measures for which they see the need most clearly. Although this country is already suffering from over-organization, no other organization exists for this particular purpose; no other organization is designed to take the woman purely as a voter and fit her for her task.

The League of Women Voters is a direct result of the conviction that mere possession of the vote by a large group, hitherto disfranchised, may serve only to complicate present-day problems; that to be effective for the common good, it must be used not only conscientiously, but intelligently. It is the purpose of the League to help the woman citizen acquire the wisdom necessary to use her vote toward constructive social and political ends. With this purpose in view its several departments have been established. As its administrative machinery improves, it becomes increasingly able to carry out the program—education in government and politics, and the creation and maintenance of standards for efficient government and for public welfare.

The League of Women Voters believes that instruction in the duties of citizenship and the principles and machinery of government will eventually become a part of public education for both men and women, but that until such instruction is a recognized and practical part of our educational system, it must be carried on by private agencies. Many institutions and organizations are working to this end, but in order that there may be instruction of women voters on a nation-wide scale, the League has developed a machinery of organization calculated to reach all types of women and a program of citizenship training which has general endorsement.

The League of Women Voters believes that American public life suffers from the indifference of public opinion to government, the gradual decadence of the old American habit of local discussion of public questions, and the change in the character of political parties which has made them agencies of centralized power, rather than instruments for the expression of political principles and policies. It is evident that the machinery of government must be altered, so that it cannot be controlled by powerful and selfish minorities. The League believes that the methods of taking votes, nominating candidates, writing platforms, securing legislation, and administering government must be continually studied and improved. Women can render valuable service by stimulating public opinion and by suggesting the improvement of institutions and parties, because women are not yet bound by partisan precedents or by political habits.

The program of the League provides not only for a study of improved government and of public welfare in government, but it is pledged to that far-reaching international coöperation which is necessary to prevent war. The outcome of the varied educational activities of the League is the formation of standards which become the basis for legislation and the test of law enforcement. These standards are prepared by the national department and standing committee chairmen in consultation with chairmen in the states, reviewed by the national board, and sent out to the state Leagues for study and criticism at least two months in advance of the national convention which finally acts upon them. After adoption by the national and state conventions, they become the active program of the League. Thus the League program evolves from the awakened conscience of the woman voter.

The League's activities are not distinct but interdependent and their purpose is not only to train women for the use of the vote but to get them to use it. In response to the call of its President, embodied in her annual address for 1923, the League is definitely pledged to a crusade to increase the vote in the general election of 1924, by twenty-five per cent over the number recorded in the similar election of 1920.

While the League believes that women are a distinct element in the electorate, it does not believe in a separate woman's party, but that women and men have a common stake in civilization, a common interest in good government, and should form coöperating parts of the body politic.

The League of Women Voters has from its inception urged its members to enroll in political parties. The influence of the average citizen can be made most effective through party organization, since ours is a party form of government. Women as well as men should assume the responsibility of party activity.

The League holds, however, that a citizen's duty is to country first, and to party second; that a party is only a means to an end, and that the end should be kept constantly in view. The women of the League do not believe in giving their consciences into the keeping of political parties, but rather that it is their obligation as party members to help the parties keep pace with enlightened public opinion. In carrying their conscience and intelligence into party counsels, the members of the League aim to make the parties of their choice more efficient organs of government.

The League believes that the activities of the parties do not cover the whole field of civic duty, but that there is a distinct field for other than party organizations whose members will work together, irrespective of party, for certain public objects. It is in the category of such civic organizations that the League of Women Voters belongs. It has so met its responsibilities as to give promise of becoming a strong factor for human betterment through government.

CAMERON, MABEL WARD (Mrs. Charles E. Cameron), author, daughter of Austin Merrils and Delia (Bidwell) Ward, was born in Chicago, Illinois, March 2, 1863, and died in New York, New York, February 22, 1923. Through her father she was descended from Ensign William Ward, one of the Early proprietors of Middletown, Connecticut, whose name appears first in the town records in 1655, and from John Johnson, of Roxbury, Massachusetts (1630), Captain of the Ancient and Honourable Artillery Company: through her mother from John Bidwell, a founder of Hartford, Connecticut (1640), and from Edward Griswold, a settler of Windsor, Connecticut. In every branch of her ancestry she represented English Colonial settlers of New England; and many of her ancestors held public office, as, for example, Secretary Daniel Clarke and Governor Thomas Welles of Connecticut, or took part in the Indian Wars, while seven of them served in the American Revolution.[1]

Mabel Ward inherited her many abilities from her mother, a woman of marked poetic and musical talents and a recognized authority in the genealogical world. She was educated at the Dove Street Cottage Institute, Albany, New York, at Miss Tiffany's School, and the Hartford Female Seminary, Hartford, Connecticut, at Mrs. Sylvanus Reed's School, New York, and by private tutors. She also studied the piano and the guitar, and singing under Mme. De Lande and Signor Errani of New York, who wished to prepare her for the operatic stage. On June 19, 1888, she was married in Hartford to Charles Ernest Cameron, M.D., C.M., M.R.C.S. (Eng), of Montreal, Canada, where their son, Ward Griswold Cameron, was born, April 13, 1889. During her residence there, her interests, as a member of the Montreal Philharmonic Society, continued to be musical; but she was also Chairman for Canada of the Hereditary Order of Descendants of Colonial Governors, of which she was a member, and especially, after 1897, in Boston, Hartford, and New York, she was actively interested in all organizations having as their aim to perpetuate the traditions of the original settlers of the United States. She was a member of the National Society of Founders and Patriots of America, the Ruth Wyllys Chapter of the Society of the Daughters of the American Revolution, the Order of Descendants of Armorial Families, the Foote Family Association, the Chapin Family Association, the Society of Middletown Upper Houses, and the Women's Roosevelt Memorial Association.

Her admiration for the ideals of the Colonial New England woman led her to ally herself with the movement for the enfranchisement of women citizens, and,as a member of the New York State Woman Suffrage Party, she did quiet but efficient work in the 25th Assembly District, and as Captain in the 8th Election District, Lower 10th Assembly District, New York. She was later a member of the Women's National Republican Club,and served on several committees of the Woman's Republican Club of New York, especially on that for the purpose of reporting on the progress of municipal legislation.

During the World War, Mrs. Cameron was a member of the National League for Woman's Service, and served in the Trinity Church, New York, Canteen, and on the St. Agnes (Trinity Parish) Surgical Dressings Committee. She was also a member of the Washington Square, New York, Chapter of the Red Cross Society and of the Sebasco Auxiliary of the Bath (Maine) Chapter, and, after the war, of Soldiers and Sailors of New York.

Mrs. Cameron was the author of many poems of a delicate subjective quality, many of them bearing witness to her close sympathy with the historical traditions and the natural beauties of Connecticut, others indicating an affinity for Japanese modes of expression. *Mind* published her *Laughing Flowers* in its issue for June, 1900, and *A Tragedy of the Wild* in March, 1904. *Fair Maids of Long Ago* appeared in *The Connecticut Magazine* for March-April, 1901; *The Master Craftsman*

(a sonnet on William Morris) in *The Reader* for July, 1903, and *From the Sea at Yule-tide* in *The National Magazine* for December, 1906. *Ariel* printed *Soul Memory* in its May-June number, 1910, *The Ship-Following Ghost* (a Japanese Superstition) in September and *Bubbles* in November, 1910; and *The Peony Maid* (a Japanese Legend) and *Sakasa-Bashira* (a Japanese Fantasy) in February, 1911. Her deep understanding of the Connecticut countrywoman and of the fast disappearing social conditions of the Long Island Sound villages is well illustrated in her serial novel, *A Singer of Southcreek* (*New England Magazine*, January-May, 1907).

Mrs. Cameron was frequently invited to lecture before the societies of which she was a member on two subjects that she had made her specialty, one shell-cameos, the other heraldry for women. She also contributed an article, *Heraldry for Women*, to *Good Housekeeping* for September, 1905, and her paper, *Armorials of our Ancestors*, was reprinted by Charles Collard Adams in his *Middletown Upper Houses*, in 1908, after having been read before the society in the previous year. In 1901 Mrs. Cameron conducted two departments, *Patriotic Societies* and *Historical Notes*, in *The Connecticut Magazine*, and in 1904 was an assistant editor of Volume II of *Chapter Sketches, Connecticut Daughters of the American Revolution—Patriots' Daughters* (Mary Philotheta Root, editor), being also the author of the article in this volume on *Florilla* (*Swetland*) *Pierce*. For *The American Monthly Magazine* (Daughters of the American Revolution) for May, 1906, she edited the biographical articles on Mary P. Root and Ellen Tuttle Lewis and wrote that on Mrs. Collins of Hartford; and in 1909 she prepared (with Katherine E. Conway) *Charles Francis Donnelly: A Memoir* and edited with foreword his *Roma and Other Poems*.

As a contributor to *The National Cyclopaedia of American Biography* and also as a worker for woman suffrage and as a student of the lives of American women of the past,

Mrs. Cameron always felt that the part played by women in the upbuilding of American civilization had been inadequately recognized, and that their records should be gathered in some permanent form so as to be available for historical and educational purposes. Accordingly in 1913 she began to collect material looking forward to *The Biographical Cyclopaedia of American Women* which she actually founded in 1918, in that year incorporating The Halvord Publishing Company, Inc., of New York, for the compiling and publishing of the work. Of this company she was the first President, and to its affairs, as well as to the editing and writing of articles for the Cyclopaedia she gave herself with untiring energy.

Mrs. Cameron was a woman of wide interests and many abilities, a thorough and painstaking student in genealogical and biographical research, a poet of delicacy of perception and expression, broad in her sympathies and unselfishly devoted to her friends and to her family, of authoritative presence in public, and untiringly loyal to any cause or organization with which she allied herself.

[1]See *Lineage Book, Nat. Soc. D. A. R.*, Vol. 5, p. 72, No. 4197, for Delia Bidwell Ward, and Vol. 28, p. 76, No. 27201, for Mabel Ward Cameron; also *History for the Twenty-First Year of the National Society Daughters of Founders and Patriots of America*, p. 41; W. Ferrand Felch: *Who's Who in Genealogy* (1914); Charles Collard Adams: *Middletown Upper Houses*, pp. 109, 605; *Foote Family History and Genealogy* (1907), p. 35; Browning: *Americans of Royal Descent*.

STANTON, ELIZABETH CADY, reformer, was born at Johnstown, New York, November 12, 1815, daughter of Daniel and Margaret (Livingston) Cady. Her father was a judge of the Supreme Court and Court of Appeals of the State of New York, and her mother was a daughter of Colonel Livingstone of Washington's staff. From her mother she inherited the spirit and vivacity which distinguished her long career of public speaking and literary work in behalf of the movement for woman suffrage and other radical reforms of her day. She said of her father that while he was sober and taciturn in manner, his keen sense of justice moved him to modify the somewhat military rule which her mother insisted should prevail in the household.

Elizabeth Cady Stanton owed much in her early girlhood to the friendship and guidance of Reverend Simon Hosack, who was Pastor of the Scotch Presbyterian Church which her family attended in Johnstown. This was a Scotch settlement, in which there prevailed the old feudal ideas regarding women and property. Elizabeth Cady, as a girl, spent much time in her father's office, and there, through the complaints of unhappy dependent women, became well acquainted with the injustice of the common law. Consequently she resolved to do what she could to free her sex from the disabilities under which they were then living. In her childish indignation, thinking that her father and his books were the beginning and the end of the law, she marked obnoxious statutes with a pencil, and proposed to cut them out and thus end them. When she was ten years old, her only brother, who had just been graduated at Union College, died and left her father inconsolable; for, like his neighbors, he believed so firmly in the Blackstonian theory of the headship of the man, that the loss of his only son was a terrible blow to his hopes. Elizabeth, desiring to console her father, resolved to do all that her brother had done. Immediately she began under Doctor Hosack the study of Greek, which she continued at the Academy with such success that she secured one of the two prizes offered for proficiency in that language. With her prize she went at once to her father, expecting that he would praise her as he would have praised his son, but she records pathetically that he merely remarked, "Oh, my child, if you were only a boy." This incident was a bitter disappointment to the ambitious girl, and, mortified by the inequality in the condition and the treatment of boys and girls, she determined to make herself the equal of men in courage and ability. She became proficient in Mathematics, Latin and Greek. On being graduated from the Academy, she was amazed to find that the hope of study at Union College, which she had secretly cherished with the idea of filling her brother's place, could not be carried out. Her chagrin was intensified by her being sent to Mrs. Willard's Girls' Seminary at Troy, New York, where, as she records, she spent "two of the dreariest years" of her life. The next seven years she passed at home, reading widely, and under her father's direction devoting special attention to law. In this way she fitted herself to become the able opponent of oppressive legislation regarding women.

In the spring of 1840 she married Henry Brewster Stanton, already well known as a leader and a lecturer in the anti-slavery movement. Since Mr. Stanton was a delegate to the World's Anti-Slavery Convention to be held in London in June of that same year, they went to London on their wedding trip. Mr. Stanton became Secretary of the Convention. Elizabeth Cady Stanton's indignation was stirred anew by the imputation of inferiority cast upon women by the refusal of the majority of the Convention to admit Mrs. Lucretia Mott and other American women who had been regularly appointed delegates. In Mrs. Mott she met for the first time a liberal-minded thinker of her own sex. The friendship thus begun continued through forty years, and assisted in determining Mrs. Stanton to devote her life and energies to the social, political and moral betterment of women. For six years following her return home she lived in Boston. During this period she made a thorough study of the position of women. As a result, in addition to the woman's rights claimed by Mrs. Mott—remunerative work, property rights after marriage, advanced education, and independent judgment in religion—Mrs. Stanton demanded the removal of woman's civil disabilities by making her political status the same as that of

man. In 1846 she located at Seneca Falls, New York. With Mrs. Mott and others, she issued the call for the first Woman's Rights Convention. It was held at Seneca Falls, July 19 and 20, 1848, and marked the inauguration of the Woman Suffrage movement. Although the object of the Convention was defined to be the discussion of the social, civil, and religious rights of women, no allusion being made to women's political rights, yet in the declaration of sentiments which was prepared as a basis for discussion Mrs. Stanton introduced as the Ninth Resolution a statement that it was "the duty of the women of this country to secure to themselves their sacred right to the elective franchise." Neither her husband—who had prepared for the Convention an abstract of the laws that were unjust regarding the property interests of women—nor Mrs. Mott approved of Mrs. Stanton's demand for the ballot. They argued that it would only bring "ridicule on the cause." Mrs. Stanton persisted, however, and spoke vigorously and eloquently at the first session in defense of the proposal. The resolution was adopted, though not unanimously, by the Convention. This new departure in the movement had few adherents outside the convention. In fact, of those members who signed the Declaration of Sentiments, many later requested to have their names withdrawn. Judge Cady, alarmed at his daughter's radicalism, hastened to her home, where he urged her earnestly, but in vain, not only to forego her convictions but to abandon public life.

From 1848 to the time of the Civil War, Mrs. Stanton devoted herself to the anti-slavery, temperance, education and woman suffrage causes. She was founder and President of the New York Woman's Temperance Society, in its early years, and Chairman of the Woman Suffrage Committee of her state. As early as 1854, she spoke before the New York Legislature in advocacy of a higher status for women. In 1863 she founded the Women's Loyal League, and was elected its

President. The classic address from this society to President Lincoln, signed by Mrs. Stanton, came from her trenchant pen. It is printed in full in the *History of Woman Suffrage*.

In 1866, believing women to be eligible to public office, she offered herself as a candidate for Congress from the Eighth New York District. In her announcement, she said: "Belonging to a disfranchised class, I have no political antecedents to recommend me to your support, but my creed is free speech, free press, free men and free trade—the cardinal points of democracy." She received twenty-four votes. With Susan B. Anthony and Parker Pillsbury she established, and was Editor-in-Chief, of the Woman's Rights journal called *The Revolution*. During the two years of its existence, it was the most vigorous and the most quoted of any suffrage journal ever printed before or since.

The Civil War made the people of the United States think nationally, and leaders of the Woman Suffrage movement naturally adopted still broader lines of thought. The National Woman Suffrage Association was founded in 1869. Mrs. Stanton was its President almost continuously until 1893. At the suggestion of Mrs. Stanton and her co-workers, the Honorable George Julian introduced in Congress, on March 15, 1869, a joint resolution proposing a Sixteenth amendment to the Constitution. It read as follows: "The right of suffrage in the United States shall be based on citizenship, and shall be regulated by Congress; and all citizens of the United States, whether native or naturalized, shall enjoy this right equally, without any distinction or discrimination whatever founded on sex." From 1870 Mrs. Stanton lectured for twelve years throughout the country, eight months each year. She was one of the most popular speakers who ever appeared under the auspices of any lyceum bureau. To her credit is attributed the liberalizing of divorce laws, the opening of higher institutions of learning to women, and

the marked growth in Woman Suffrage sentiment. Throughout this period, Mrs. Stanton was the Samuel Adams of the woman movement, for her pen produced all the "State Papers" issued. She it was who drew up the calls to conventions, the addresses to Legislatures, the appeals to learned bodies, and she it was, also, who made in person, for nearly fifty years, the chief arguments before congressional and legislative committees.

In 1878, the annual convention of the National Woman Suffrage Association was held in Washington, District of Columbia. It had been arranged that Mrs. Isabella Beecher Hooker and Mrs. Lily Devereaux Blake were to conduct the convention, as Mrs. Stanton and Miss Anthony felt they must continue their speaking tours in the West. Mrs. Stanton had urged upon her co-workers the introduction in Congress of a new resolution calling for a suffrage amendment to the National Constitution. Between 1869 and 1878 the efforts of the suffragists had largely consisted of appeals to courts for interpretations in favor of the enfranchisement of women under the Constitution as it stood. After a meeting in St. Louis, about this time, Mrs. Stanton received a telegram saying that it was imperative that she come to the National Capital and carry out her proposals. She immediately went to Washington and, before both the National Woman Suffrage Convention and the Judiciary Committees of Congress, made a plea for a suffrage amendment to the United States Constitution. She persuaded her old friend, Senator Sargent, of California, to introduce the Amendment. This was the first time a suffrage amendment had been introduced, the same in form as the Nineteenth Amendment, adopted in 1920. During the years of reconstruction, she and other suffrage leaders had systematically made every effort to amend the Fourteenth and Fifteenth Amendments when they were under consideration by Congress. Their endeavors to influence this legislation in the interest of women, however, met with no success, so that the changes initiated by Mrs. Stanton in 1869 and 1878 were the first Woman Suffrage amendments *per se.* She never laid claim to having "drawn" these amendments. In 1878, as in the later efforts of the suffragists for a national amendment, the Fifteenth Amendment, securing suffrage for colored men, was copied except that the phrase "race, color, or previous condition of servitude" merely gave place to the word "sex." Although Mrs. Stanton never affirmed that the wording of the suffrage amendment was other than a copy of the Fifteenth Amendment, it may be claimed for Mrs. Stanton that to her is due the credit of first demanding the passage of a Woman Suffrage amendment to the United States Constitution, and of carrying out the practical details of its introduction in Congress.

In 1888 Mrs. Stanton suggested the formation of the International Council of Women. Her suggestion was acted upon, and she presided over the first convention. From 1880 to 1886 she devoted her time to the colossal labor of bringing out the first three volumes of the *History of Woman Suffrage.* Her co-editors were Miss Anthony and Mrs. Gage. This work was followed by *The Woman's Bible,* which caused more newspaper comment than any other work from her pen. In 1897, her reminiscences were published under the title *Eighty Years and More.* During the closing years of her life she was adding to and rewriting these memoirs. This work, together with her *Letters and Diary,* edited by her son, Theodore Stanton, and her daughter, Harriot Stanton Blatch, was published in 1921 by Harper and Brothers. Mrs. Stanton contributed many articles to the *Forum,* the *Arena,* the *Westminster Review,* and the *North American Review.* She was also a constant writer for reform papers and for the daily press. The day she died there appeared in the New York *American* an article which she had written twenty-four hours earlier, and on her writing desk ready for her signature lay open letters to President and Mrs. Roosevelt urging that a recommendation for the consideration of Woman Suffrage be put in the President's then forthcoming message to Congress. It may be said of her that when she died, on October 26, 1902, she was in the full vigor of her powers. Her ready wit and broad nature, her sympathy with the oppressed, her scorn of wrong, her catholicity of spirit, her love of justice and liberty, her intellectual ability, moral courage, and physical energy, together with her unusual opportunities in youth for wide and sound culture, gave Mrs. Stanton a unique place in the history of American women. It may be recalled, in evidence of the universal esteem in which she was held, that all the great national organizations of women united in doing her honor at a meeting in the New York Metropolitan Opera House on the occasion of her eightieth birthday, and that the centenary of her birth was celebrated in New York City, in 1915, at the largest banquet ever held to do honor to the memory of a citizen of the United States.

BLATCH, HARRIOT STANTON, reformer, was born at Seneca Falls, New York, January 20, 1856. Her father, Henry Brewster Stanton, a descendant of Elder William Brewster, the "Mayflower" Pilgrim, was a leader in the anti-slavery movement, and her mother, Elizabeth Cady Stanton called the first convention that made an organized demand for equal suffrage. Mrs. Blatch was graduated A.B. at Vassar College in 1878, with honors in mathematics and membership in Phi Beta Kappa. She continued her studies in Berlin and at the Sorbonne in Paris for another two years, and in 1882, was married in London, England, to William Henry Blatch. They were the parents of Nora Stanton Blatch (born in 1883), a graduate of Cornell University, and the first woman in America to receive the degree of Civil Engineer.

During her twenty years residence in England, Mrs. Blatch was actively connected with the Woman Suffrage Society and the Council of Women Workers, and the Woman's Local Government Committee; was Executive of the English Fabian Society and a member of the Evening Schools Committee of her district. Under the direction of Charles Booth, the statistician, who was then preparing his book, *Village Life in England*, she collected the facts which formed the basis of her thesis, *Conditions of Village Life in England*, which she presented for her master's degree at Vassar College in 1894.

Upon her return to the United States in 1902, Mrs. Blatch continued her work for woman suffrage. In 1908 she founded the Women's Political Union, and became its first President, sixty years after her mother, Elizabeth Cady Stanton, initiated the suffrage movement in the convention at Seneca Falls, New York. In the conduct of the Union Mrs. Blatch introduced political methods for the first time in the history of the American woman suffrage movement, and made systematic efforts to attract the active coöperation of working women. It was under her Presidency that the Women's Political Union originated the practice of holding open-air meetings and street parades. Beginning with a procession of 300 marchers in 1908, the numbers increased year by year, until in 1914, twenty thousand suffragists followed the Women's Political Union in a march on Fifth Avenue, New York.

Mrs. Blatch was a life member of the New York Woman Suffrage Party, a member of the Executive Committee of the Citizens' Union and a National Director of the Woman's Land Army of America. In her relations to labor problems, she has taken the stand that, while conditions for women should be bettered by the extension of the eight-hour law and by improvement in hygienic conditions, such reforms should be applied to all workers, both men and women, and should be urged on humanitarian, not on merely feministic, grounds. In 1920 Mrs. Blatch joined the Socialist Party, becoming one of its national speakers and a regular contributor to labor magazines and newspapers. She has written many articles for *The Westminster Review, The Outlook*, and other magazines; collaborated in *The History of Woman Suffrage;* wrote the introduction to Rembaugh's *Political Status of Woman;* is the author of *Mobilizing Woman Power*, for which President Roosevelt wrote the introduction, and of a *Woman's Point of View* (Woman's Press, 1920). She is co-editor with her brother, Theodore Stanton, of the *Life and Letters of Elizabeth Cady Stanton* (Harper Bros., 1921). She is a member of the Women's University Club, the Civic Club, and the Bill Club of the City of New York.

HEPBURN, EMILY EATON (Mrs. A. Barton Hepburn), daughter of Caleb Curtiss and Susan Allen (Coburn) Eaton, was born at Montpelier, Vermont, September 7, 1865. Her mother was a direct descendant of Edward Colburn, who came to New England, July 17, 1635.

Miss Eaton received her early education in the public school of Montpelier, where she prepared for college, and was graduated B.S. with honors at St. Lawrence University in 1886. Later she pursued post-graduate courses at Barnard College, with botany as her major subject, and was elected to Phi Beta Kappa from the Lambda Chapter. She was married at Montpelier, July 14, 1887, to A. Barton Hepburn (born at Colton, New York, July 24, 1846; died in New York City, January 25, 1922), financier and economist, and for many years President of the Chase National Bank. He was a descendant of Peter Hepburn (born near Glasgow, Scotland), who settled at Stratford, Connecticut, and died there in 1742. Mr. and Mrs. Hepburn were the parents of two daughters: Beulah Eaton, wife of R. M. Emmet, a Lieutenant Commander in the United States Navy, and Cordelia Susan Hepburn, wife of Paul Cushman.

Mrs. Hepburn has shown her interest in

civic, educational, philanthropic and artistic matters, through personal service, and holds office in many organizations. She has never evaded the responsibility thrust upon her, when she has agreed to become financial director or treasurer of women's organizations. Her knowledge of finance has come to her by heredity, as well as through the environment afforded by her marriage. Her development along such lines was also fostered through close association with her uncle, Dorman B. Eaton, the noted Civil Service reformer and philanthropist. He was a native of Vermont but a resident of New York, where he practiced law for many years. He early became unselfishly interested in municipal reform, and, in 1866, drafted the law creating the Metropolitan Board of Health, and, in 1867, the Sanitary Code. In 1878, the first society for promoting civil service reform in the United States was formed at his residence, and he was appointed Chairman of the first Civil Service Commission.

Early in her married life, Mrs. Hepburn became associated with Mrs. Robert Abbe in the work of the City History Club, and has been its President for many years. Among other official positions, she has been Treasurer of the Woman's Roosevelt Memorial Association; President of the Ridgefield Garden Club; Trustee of St. Lawrence University; Director of the Civil Service Reform Association; of the National Navy Club; of the Woman's Pan-Hellenic Association, and of the New York Woman's Phi Beta Kappa Association; President of the New York Alumnae Association of Kappa Kappa Gamma; Chairman of the New York State Committee of the Colonial Dames for the Sulgrave Manor Endowment Fund; Chairman of the Finance Committee of Inwood House; Treasurer of the New York Committee of the American Committee for Devastated France. She is a member of the Ladies' Auxiliary of the Botanical Gardens, the Colonial Dames, Colony, Cosmopolitan, Woman's City and Woman's National Clubs; Metropolitan Mu-

seum of Art, New York Zoölogical Society, Garden Club of America, The MacDowell Club, Art Center, and the International Garden Club. During the World War, Mrs. Hepburn worked untiringly and through various channels, and received the decoration of Officer de L'Instruction Publique from the French Government.

CITY HISTORY CLUB, well called an institution for the molding of "citizens of tomorrow," came into being as the result of the happy thought of two public-spirited citizens.

In the autumn of 1895, a well-known surgeon was walking with his wife through Central Park. Spying the old guns on the little height south of Harlem Mere, and knowing his wife's interest in old New York, he turned to her and asked if she could tell him anything concerning their origin. She confessed her ignorance and both agreed that it would be desirable to investigate, with the idea of marking the relics so that the children of the neighborhood might learn their story.

The couple were Doctor and Mrs. Robert Abbe, and on this spot definite shape was first given to Mrs. Abbe's desire that local history might be taught to the children of New York City, in order that, while learning to revere the old landmarks, they might become more loyal citizens. The two guns have since been suitably mounted and a bronze tablet explaining their history placed on the pedestal.

The City History Club was established in 1896, and incorporated under the laws of the State of New York in 1897. It is approved by the Board of Alderman which has given into its charge the twenty-one remaining milestones in the City limits. It is approved by the University of the State of New York, which recommends it as a "model" for other localities. It is a recognized authority on local history and landmarks. Its Historical Guide is quoted in Baedeker's United States, and in the Encyclopaedia Britannica. It has been awarded medals for its methods of club work at the St. Louis, Milan, Paris and Jamestown Expositions.

Its purpose is to develop a better and more intelligent citizenship through the study of history and traditions of the city, of the lives and deeds of the men who have made the city great, and of the powers and duties of each department of the city and its government.

Thus by arousing an interest in the picturesque history of Manhattan and in the conditions and needs of the City today, the club instils that true kind of patriotism, which is not mere unreasoning emotion excited by flags and drums and catch-words, but an integral part of character. On the principle that we must know a thing before we can love it, it teaches the children to know their city so well that they will not only love it, but will know all about it and be able to think, talk, work and vote intelligently for it.

The Club has been called a "Kindergarten of Citizenship." The boys and girls, under its guidance, are inspired not only with a love for their city, a pride in its past and a faith in its future, but also with a sense of its present short-comings and needs, and a wish to aid in its betterment. The object is, to lay a foundation for sound, vigorous and enlightened citizenship—for that intelligent and unselfish interest in local affairs—which is the necessary basis for intelligent and honest participation in national affairs.

The City History Club celebrates patriotic anniversaries; takes excursions to places of historic and civic interest; gives illustrated lectures in the assemblies of the public schools; publishes leaflets, handbooks and a Guide for the City of New York; gives historical plays and pageants, and, as its main work, maintains for our school children more than thirty clubs in settlements, libraries, Children's Aid Society Buildings and public schools. These clubs have twenty members and meet once each week under the guidance of a trained leader. They are self-governed, with their own elective officers and adapt our ideas to suit their conditions and the traditions of the country from which they came. Each club chooses a name of some person or place connected with the history of the city, such as the Roosevelt Club, or the DeWitt Clinton Club, a custom which at once gives the members suitable ideals. At the end of the year, an exhibition of the work of all the groups is held and banners and pennants awarded to clubs and certificates to individuals for the best grade of work.

The Lecture Bureau is accomplishing another important work. Each year the Club lecturer gives one hundred illustrated lectures entitled "What we owe to Old New York" to the assemblies of the public schools. About 50,000 children are reached each year. These lecture courses are instructive and full of anecdote, and are imbued with an appeal to patriotism. They meet a great need and are enthusiastically received by the principals of the schools.

The City History Club leaves a lasting impression on the minds and hearts of the children, and is of the utmost importance in the development of the civic life of our future citizens.

DE WOLFE, ELSIE ANDERSON, daughter of Doctor Stephen and Georgina (Copeland) De Wolfe, was born in New York, December 20, 1870, and was educated in New York and London, England.

She possessed from childhood a strong dramatic instinct, and as a very young girl played important parts in amateur theatricals. In London she scored a success in *The White Milliner*, at a benefit performance for a church society at the Criterion Theatre, playing before the Prince and Princess of Wales (afterwards King Edward VII and Queen Alexandra). Later, in New York, she appeared in various amateur performances, notably as Gertrude in *The Loan of a Lover*, and as Lady Teazle in *The School for Scandal*. In 1890 she decided to adopt the stage as her profession. To do this she had to overcome prejudices in her family and among friends, for she had been reared in a conservative atmosphere. As time proved, however, she became a striking example of the fact that whenever a woman, who has been most carefully nurtured and protected from the realities of life, elects to assume an independent position in life, she often attains greater success in her chosen calling than those who have been obliged to meet life's problems from their earliest years.

Miss De Wolfe made her professional début under the management of Charles Frohman at Proctor's Theatre, New York, as Fabienne Lecoulteur in Sardou's *Thermidor*, a part which she had studied in Paris under the author's direction. Two seasons on the road followed, during which she played in *Joseph*, *Judge* and *Four-in-Hand*, and later in New York as Rose Reade in *Sister Mary*. She then joined the famous Empire Stock Company, and remained with that popular organization through the years during which it produced many important plays, and reached the height of its fame, with Miss De Wolfe as its leading lady.

In spite, however, of her success with the stock company, her ambition was not satisfied. She aspired to greater triumphs. Consequently, having resigned from the Empire, she formed her own company, and essayed the difficult dual rôle of manager-star. Her success was immediate. Among plays produced by her were many by the brilliant playwright, Clyde Fitch. One of her best-known parts was that of Mrs. Croydon in *The Way of the World*. She also achieved success as Helene in *Catherine*.

In 1903, at the height of her career as a star, Miss De Wolfe retired from the stage and devoted two years to studying the art of interior decorating. Her particular aptitude for this profession had been evidenced while she was stage manager, since the scenery of her plays was noted for the exquisite interiors, the product of her own talent. In 1905 she launched her enterprise and soon became known as the most prominent interior decorator in the United States. She specialized in period furnishings, and these she carried out with the utmost perfection of detail. Her great success has been due, not only to her technical knowledge of her subject, but also to a highly-developed feminine intuition, which while harmonizing line and color, produces rooms that are comfortable and home-like.

At the beginning of the World War in 1914, Miss De Wolfe relinquished all other work, and devoted herself to hospital and Red Cross interests. For many years, together with Miss Anne Morgan and Miss Elizabeth Marbury, she had maintained a residence at Versailles, France, where she spent a portion of each year. In this residence a hospital was established, and there she gained her first experience in nursing the wounded. Miss Morgan, Miss Marbury, and Mrs. Paul Morton were associated in the work. Later, they turned the hospital over to the French Army authorities, for the exclusive use of convalescent soldiers.

In 1916, Miss De Wolfe was transferred to the St. Nicholas Hospital, at Issy-les-Monteneaux, where French wounded were received, and where a specialty was made of the ambrine treatment for those suffering from the frightful burns caused by explosions, liquid fire, poison gas, etc.[1] After spending four months at the St. Nicholas Hospital, Miss De Wolfe became so impressed with the value of the ambrine treatment that she returned to New York, for the express purpose of raising funds to establish dressing stations at the front with ambrine ambulances for first aid. She spent the winter in America, speaking in the large cities of the United States and Canada, and succeeded in raising an ambulance flotilla of twenty-eight cars. Upon returning to France she visited all the hospitals of the American Red Cross, lecturing and demonstrating ambrine.

The Baroness Henri de Rothschild, founder of the Ambrine Mission at Compiégne, then invited Miss De Wolfe to coöperate with her, and her flotilla of ambrine ambulances was attached to this hospital and carried the treatment for first aid right up to the firing line. During the week of March 21, 1918, Compiégne was under constant bombardment. The Germans were advancing rapidly, but Miss De Wolfe refused to leave the hospital, until she had helped to remove all the wounded men.

On March 26th, when Compiégne was evacuated under heavy shell fire, Miss De Wolfe was the last woman to leave the town. For her bravery under fire she was awarded the Croix de Guerre with bronze star. She then became attached to the Château Hospital, dedicated by a wealthy Frenchman to the French Red Cross, for ambrine treatment. This hospital was in the village of Aumont, near Senils, surrounded by three immense barracks, housing French, British and American troops. There Miss De Wolfe worked from the opening of the hospital, and ultimately completed her work at Laon, an advanced dressing station near the front. Throughout the War, she served entirely with the French forces, first with the Third Army Corps, under the command of General Humbert, and later with the Tenth Army Corps, under the command of General Mangin. She is one of the few women who were in the war zone practically all the time. In addition to the Croix de Guerre, she was awarded in 1917 the Médaille des Épidëmies, and in recognition of her three years' service in France, and her remarkable work in caring for the French wounded, which had won the admiration of all the Allied army surgeons, the Surgeon-General of the French Army conferred upon her the Brisques, a medal formed of two gold wings with a red cross in the centre.

¹The healing wax, ambrine, was discovered in 1902 by Doctor Barthe de Sandfort, at that time a surgeon in the French Navy. At first it won scant recognition from the medical profession and, failing this in France, Doctor de Sandfort visited New York with the purpose of introducing his discovery in America. At the outbreak of the war he again endeavored to obtain a hearing in France and finally was given a small room and two patients at the St. Nicholas Hospital, Issy. His success was immediate and so marked that soon a number of rooms and several hundred patients were assigned to him and ultimately the hospital at Issy became recognized as headquarters for the treatment. Ambrine is a compound of resin of amber mixed with paraffin which forms a wax. It is solid when cold, fluid when heated to 140–150° Fahrenheit, and is easily rendered aseptic. When melted it is sprayed over the charred surface and relieves the acute pain instantaneously. It solidifies quickly over the wound and forms a wax glaze, isolating and sterilizing. The addition of cotton preserves the temperature at more than 106° Fahrenheit for many hours. The wax and cotton constitute a non-adhesive shell under which nature does her work of healing undisturbed. This occlusive and adhesive dressing becomes non-adhesive after a short period, thus allowing its removal without pain or hemorrhage and without tearing tissues of new formation. It permits the integral healing of the tissues without scars, without contraction of skin or tendons, and without causing persistent and incurable functional weakness. It is equally efficacious in the treatment of frostbites, a fact which will render this new and simple discovery a real boon to mankind in times of peace. Early in the war the British Admiralty and War Office, recognizing its value, filed large orders for the healing wax.

HOFFMAN, MALVINA CORNELL, sculptor, daughter of Richard and Fidelia Marshall (Lamson) Hoffman, was born in New York City. Her father (born in 1831), a noted English pianist, first came to the United States in 1847 with Jenny Lind, to tour the country under the direction of P. T. Barnum.

Miss Hoffman was educated at Miss Chapin's School and at the Brearley School in New York, and began her art studies at the Art Students' League. After five years' instruction in painting under John Alexander, she entered the studio of Gutzon Borglum, the sculptor, and later worked with Herbert Adams, Max Blondat, Adolph Weinman, and under Auguste Rodin in Paris. Upon her return to the United States she established her studio in New York, but returned to Europe three times for further study. In 1910 she received first honorable mention for sculpture at the Exhibition Internationale in Paris, and exhibited in 1910–1911 at the Paris Salon, in 1909, 1911, and 1912, at the New York Academy, and in 1911 and 1912 at the Philadelphia Academy. In 1914 bronzes by her were shown at the Leicester Galleries, London, and in 1919 bronzes and marbles at Mrs. Harry Payne Whitney's studio in New York. Miss Hoffman's art has the great distinction of a sensitiveness, which depends upon intelligence, as well as feeling, and upon the keen and thorough analysis of the problems to be solved. These have been of great difficulty, as Miss Hoffman has specialized in figures in motion and above all in the dance, the elusive rhythms of rapid movement ordered and controlled. Her group from Bakst's *Ballet Orientale* (1914) is a lesson in the art of tension; the figures, which are those of the Russian dancers, Pavlowa and Novikoff, are Greek in the absence of any slackness of muscle. The same is true of her life-size bronze group, *The Russian Bacchanale*, which was awarded a prize at the National Academy exhibition in 1917, as the most meritorious work of art produced by an American woman. It was presented to France by H. G. Dalton of Cleveland, Ohio, and unveiled in the Luxembourg Museum Gardens, Paris, on September 29, 1919. Miss Hoffman is the first American woman sculptor thus to be represented in the Luxembourg Gardens. Pavlowa and Mordkin posed for this group, and Pavlowa's art finds fitting interpretation in the other bronzes, *Russian Dancers* and *The Pavlowa Gavotte*. In all of these there are no dull poses or meaningless gestures, but only the joyous energy of the dance. The same life animates *The Surprised Faun* (1914) and even *The Fragment*, a torso, the incompleteness of which brings into relief the sculptor's skill in the analysis of muscular activity. The marble *Column of Life* was completed in 1919, as was also the marble *Offrande*, which in February, 1920, received the George D. Widener Memorial Medal in

Philadelphia. Miss Hoffman's portrait busts show her debt to Rodin, although there is never any lack of individual inspiration. Her portrait of her mother shows a beautiful head emerging from a furrowed mountain of marble with crisply modelled features; her head of Mr. Kahn's little son is a careful reading of youthful personality. Other important portraits are those of Frederick Pierce, Boris Anisfeld, the Russian painter, Colonel P. Bunau-Varilla, the French engineer, David Henderson, Director-General of the League of Red Cross Societies; John Muir, the naturalist, and Henry C. Frick. All of these were exhibited in 1919.

Miss Hoffman was the founder and Treasurer of the New York Trouble Bureau, an emergency fund for helping artists, and later was appointed American representative and Treasurer of the War Relief Fund, the Appui aux Artistes de Paris. During the eighteen months of the World War, she worked at the Red Cross headquarters in New York as Director of the Bureaus of Information and Communication with Foreign Countries. In December, 1918, she founded the American Jugo-Slav Relief Committee, which, before January, 1920, sent over $325,000, through Mr. Hoover's American Relief Administration, to help feed the debilitated children of Jugo-Slavia. She went to Paris in May, 1919, to close the activities of the Appui aux Artistes and to assist the final arrangements for opening the Musée Rodin on August 1, 1919.

During August and September she traveled with Miss M. L. Emmet, through Jugo-Slavia and Greece, on a mission for Mr. Hoover and the American Red Cross, collecting photographs and information regarding food distribution and other relief work. She visited many of the Serbian battlefields and farming districts, where she found deplorable conditions, as the women were still under the necessity of doing all the work in the absence of the men. Her experiences in the Balkans appeared in *Travel* for January, 1920, and in

The Survey for March, 1920. In 1912 Miss Hoffman founded the Music League of America, and she is a member of the Institute of Social Sciences and the Three Arts Club.

HOOKER, BLANCHE FERRY (Mrs. Elon Huntington Hooker), daughter of Dexter Mason (1833–1907) and Addie Elizabeth (Miller) Ferry (1841–1906), was born in Detroit, Michigan, July 14, 1871. Through her father, she is descended from Charles Ferry, a native of England, who settled before 1678 in Springfield, Massachusetts. Charles Ferry was baptized in the Walloon Church, in the crypt of Canterbury Cathedral, England. His ancestors were among the Huguenots who fled to England from Picardy in 1566. Through her mother she is a direct descendant of John Miller (born in England, 1609), who settled in Wetherfield, Connecticut, in 1630, and removed to Stamford, Connecticut, in 1642. Blanche Ferry Hooker received her preliminary education at the Liggett School, Detroit, and was graduated in the class of 1894. On January 25, 1901, at Detroit, Michigan, she married Elon Huntington Hooker (born in Rochester, New York, November 23, 1869), civil engineer and electro-chemical manufacturer. They are the parents of four daughters: Barbara Ferry (born, New York City, November 24, 1901); Adelaide Ferry (born, Greenwich, Connecticut, June 10, 1903); Helen Huntington (born, Greenwich, Connecticut, January 1, 1905); and Blanchette Ferry (born, New York City, October 2, 1909). Mrs. Hooker has been actively identified with many civic, philanthropic and educational enterprises, besides making generous financial contributions to these causes. It has been characteristic that her mind and heart have followed with her gifts and that they have been accompanied by the highest type of personal labor. The organizations with which she has been associated have benefited much from her broad point of view, her trained executive mind combined with a rare intuition, and an inherited business ability. In Greenwich, Connecticut, where she has her summer home, Mrs. Hooker in 1910 helped to reorganize and consolidate the various charities of the community. She herself was made President of the new organization, entitled The United Workers. Her interest in politics has found practical expression through her membership in the Board of Governors of the Women's National Republican Club. Mrs. Hooker has always been keenly interested in any movements centering about outdoor life, and was among the first to employ a unit from the Women's Land Army of America. She used the services of this unit on her ancestral farm near Unadilla, New York. Intensely patriotic, she has always believed in the Americanism of Theodore Roosevelt, and as a Director of the Women's Roosevelt Memorial Association she has had an excellent opportunity to express this spirit.

It has perhaps been with educational activities, however, that Mrs. Hooker has been especially associated. In Greenwich she played an important part in a survey that resulted in a widespread improvement of the public schools. She also helped to reorganize the old Greenwich Academy and with Mrs. Elizabeth Milbank Anderson provided a modern school building ideally appointed in every way. Mrs. Hooker strongly favors systematic, scientific training in Civics and Home Economics, and for that reason actively coöperated in the establishment of what is now called the Commonwealth School, in New York City. The Marietta Johnson School of Organic Education, which has a branch in Greenwich, Connecticut, has also held her keen interest. Mrs. Hooker was one of the founders of the Women's University Club, and for several years has served on both the Board of Governors and the House Committee. She has been a loyal and generous alumna of Vassar College, contributing of both time and money to advance the interests of the college. At the time of the Three Million Dollar

Campaign for the Vassar College Endowment Fund, Mrs. Hooker was made Chairman of the Metropolitan District, which, under her leadership, materially surpassed its assigned quota. With her sister, Mrs. Avery Coonley, moreover, she presented to Vassar College the beautiful Alumnae House which adorns the Campus. Together they supervised the construction and furnishing of the entire house. This building is not only a home for visiting alumnae, but it is an important center for various educational projects. Here alumnae and others hold conferences, and here also an opportunity is given visiting foreigners to study the purpose and methods of modern education in an American Woman's College. The Alumnae House is a fitting embodiment of the ideals which are highly practical motives in Mrs. Hooker's useful life.

She is a member of: the Art Alliance of America; the Municipal Art Society; National Arts Club; American Association of University Women; the American University Women's Paris Club; International Association of University Women; Women's University Club; Vassar Club; Greenwich College Club; Public Education Association; Progressive Educational Association; National Kindergarten Association; New York Kindergarten Association; Playground and Recreation Association; Fairhope League of Organic Education; Guild of Needle and Bobbin Crafts; League for Political Education; League of Women Voters; International Woman Suffrage Alliance; National Civic Federation; Women's City Club; Greenwich Social Service; National Women's Party; People's Institute; Republican Neighborhood Association; Women's National Republican Club; Garden Club of America; Greenwich Garden Club; Women's National Golf and Tennis Club; Woodcraft League of America; Women's Roosevelt Memorial Association; Young Women's Christian Association; Adirondack League Club; Colony Club; Daughters of the American Revolution.

COONLEY, QUEENE FERRY (Mrs. Avery Coonley), was born in Detroit, Michigan, April 11, 1874, daughter of Dexter Mason and Addie Elizabeth (Miller) Ferry. Her father (born, 1833; died, 1907), was a descendant of Charles Ferry (died, 1699), who settled at Springfield, Massachusetts, before 1678. Charles Ferry was a descendant of Huguenot refugees, who fled to England, to escape persecution in France in 1586; he was baptized in the Walloon Church in the crypt of Canterbury Cathedral. From him the line of descent runs through his son, Lieutenant John Ferry (born, 1662; died, 1745); his son, John (born, 1687); his son, John (born, 1749); his son, Azariah (born, 1782; died, 1818); and his son, Joseph Northrop (born, 1810; died, 1836); father of Dexter Mason Ferry. Her mother (born, 1841; died, 1906), was descended from John Miller (born, 1609; died, 1664), who settled at Wethersfield, Connecticut, in 1630, and at Stamford, Connecticut, in 1642. Her maternal grandfather, John Budd Miller (born, 1805; died, 1868), was a son of Increase Miller (born, 1779; died, 1848), a grandson of Samuel Miller (born, 1752), and a great-grandson of Increase Miller (born, 1707), who was, in turn, son of Captain Jonathan Miller (born, 1667), and a grandson of John Miller (died, 1702), a son of the Colonist.

Miss Ferry completed her preparatory education in the Liggett School, Detroit, in 1892, and during the next four years was a student at Vassar College, Poughkeepsie, New York. After her graduation, she made an extensive tour abroad, and upon her return to America, entered upon her life work as an active participant in social settlements and in promoting kindergarten education. After her marriage, she only enlarged her activities in these lines, beginning with the opening of a kindergarten in her own home, and continuing by founding a seven-grade school in the village. She was the founder, also, of kindergartens in three villages, near her residence in Illinois, which have developed into centers of social work, coöperating with library and town activities. Her conspicuous work in behalf of education led to her election as a Trustee of Vassar College in 1922, when she was chosen for the honor by the 8,000 alumnae of the institution.

On June 8, 1901, Miss Ferry was married at Unadilla, New York, to Avery Coonley (born in Rochester, New York, October 10, 1870), son of John Clarke and Lydia (Avery) Coonley. Mr. Coonley has been a manufacturer and publisher, and in recent years a member (first for Illinois, later Federal) of the Committee on Publications for Christian Sciences Churches. His mother, a daughter of Benjamin and Susan (Look) Avery, has won wide reputation as a poet and author. Among her best-known works may be mentioned: *Singing Verses for Children; Christmas in Other Lands; Washington and Lincoln; The Melody of Life; The Melody of Childhood* and several cantatas. She is also a constant contributor to periodical literature. Mr. and Mrs. Coonley are the parents of one daughter, Elizabeth Ferry Coonley, who was born in Chicago, Illinois, December 3, 1902.

Mrs. Coonley is a member of the Progressive Education Association, the American Association of University Women, the American Federation of Arts, Washington, District of Columbia; also of the National Women's Party. Her name is enrolled with the Vassar and Cosmopolitan Clubs of New York City, and with the College Women's Club, the Women's City Club, and the Arts and Cleveland Park Clubs, all of Washington.

CATT, CARRIE LANE CHAPMAN, suffragist: In the year 1870, when Susan B. Anthony and Elizabeth Cady Stanton were making their first attempt to get Woman Suffrage written into the Constitution of the United States, and Lucy Stone, and William Lloyd Garrison were pleading with hostile audiences in New England and the Middle West for the same cause, a little girl of eleven years, named Carrie Lane, was playing with her dog about her father's farm in northern Iowa. The nearest neighbors were a mile away, and except for an older brother who worked with their father on the farm, the child had no playmates. She was of a restless and eager disposition, with a hungry and omniverous mind, well grown for her age, fair of hair and grey-blue of eye, with fine features and erect carriage. She read all the books she could get hold of, especially biography and history, and since she was much alone, she acquired the singular habit of reciting aloud to herself and the dog, in order to fix them in her memory, what she had read of the deeds of the great men and women of the past. So vivid was this inner life with her heroes, that one day she was halted in her tracks and very much startled on a deserted country road to hear a Voice, which said to her, "You, too, are going to be called upon to do a great work in the world. But when the time comes, you will not be ready. You do not study hard enough or work hard enough." This was the first and last communication from the other world Carrie Lane ever had, and it is suggestive of the subconscious workings of the mind of a child who was destined to be a leader.

This unusual little girl had an unusual ancestry; people of originality and power. Her father's family came from England to Massachusetts in the early days of the colony, moving thence into Connecticut, and, after the French and Indian War, into Canada. During the Canadian residence, her greatgrandmother conceived herself to be greatly wronged by her husband. Taking what was for those times an almost unheard of resolution, she left him, brought all their children with her across the St. Lawrence into northern New York, cleared a farm near Potsdam, and there made her home. The husband sent a messenger after her, not venturing to go himself, begging her to return. But she would neither go back nor accept any support from him. The son of this determined lady, Carrie Lane's grandfather, was a boy soldier in the Continental Army in the Revolutionary War.

His son, Carrie's father, Lucius Lane, inherited full measure of the adventurous disposition of the family. At the age of nineteen, he caught the gold fever of the early fifties, left the Potsdam farm and journeyed to California by way of the Isthmus of Panama. Three years later, he married and engaged in business at Ripon, Wisconsin. Here Carrie Lane was born, January 9, 1859, the second of three children, and here she lived until the age of seven years. To escape from the confinement of business life, Mr. Lane purchased a farm near Charles City, Iowa, in 1865, and there located with his family. The ancestors of Carrie Lane's mother, Maria Clinton, were among the numerous followers of Roger Williams, when persecution in Massachusetts drove him to found a new colony in Rhode Island. She was a woman of excellent judgment who reared her daughter in habits of thrift, self control and economy.

Carrie attended the "district school" and had completed the High School course at the age of sixteen. Then, although her father thought that she was sufficiently educated, she was determined to proceed further. She taught school a year, in order to earn money for a college course, and at the age of eighteen, entered the sophomore class at Iowa State College. During her college career, she earned all but $100 of her expenses by assisting in the library. She was prominent in student activities, organized a girl's debating society, and was a strong advocate of equal privileges for male and female students. The President of the college was an enthusiast on Herbert Spencer's philosophy, who had all the students read some Spencer, and some students read all Spencer. Carrie Lane took his political economy courses and found herself in the latter group. In later years when she made her first speech in the Capitol at Washington on Woman Suffrage, she quoted Spencer to the House Judiciary Committee. In November, 1880, she was graduated, being twenty one years of age, of a non-conformist type of mind,

accustomed to making her own way, and with a strong ambition to enter the profession of law. This ambition was opposed by her father, who refused financial aid. Nothing daunted by the paternal displeasure, she obtained employment in a law office in Charles City, and spent the greater part of the year 1881 reading law preparatory to entering the State University Law School.

In October, 1881, she was invited to become Principal of the High School in Mason City, and being compelled to earn money to complete her law course, she accepted. In March, 1883, she applied for the position of Superintendent of Schools in Mason City, and although she was the first woman to seek the position, was elected, and served through the year 1884.

In January, 1885, she married Leo Chapman, Editor of the Mason City *Republican*. Her first contact with the woman suffrage movement resulted from reading in this newspaper a notice of the convention of the Iowa Suffrage Association, to be held in Cedar Rapids in October, 1885, at which Lucy Stone was advertised to speak. Moved by instinctive interest in the subject, she went to the convention and met Lucy Stone. The impression made upon her was profound, and on returning to Mason City she organized a suffrage club which remained in active existence until the ratification of the woman suffrage Federal Amendment in 1920. In April, 1886, Mr. Chapman sold the Mason City *Republican*, and removed to San Francisco with the intention of engaging in the newspaper business there, and later sending for his wife to join him. In August of that year, she was notified of his critical illness, and when she reached San Francisco, he was dead.

With stoical resolution, the young widow of twenty-five at once sought means of self support, and obtained a position with a San Francisco trade paper. It was a general utility position, her duties taking her into business offices in the down town section of the city. Again, as in Mason City, she was the first woman to be so engaged, and the astonishment with which the tired business man greeted the apparition of so attractive an agent too frequently took a disagreeable form. It was a grim and bitter experience, and at the end of a year of it, Mrs. Chapman had taken the unalterable resolution of devoting her life to making woman's lot in the business and professional world tolerable. The first thing to do was to enlighten and change public opinion. Accordingly, in August, 1887, she relinquished her position in San Francisco, and began to appear on the lecture platform. At first, she spoke before Teachers' Institutes, and similar gatherings, on educational and general subjects, emphasizing the contribution of women to the advancement of the race. The brilliance of these early addresses soon brought her to the attention of the suffragists, and in 1889, she was invited to speak at the convention of the Iowa Woman Suffrage Association in Oskaloosa. From that time, she has been identified with the suffrage movement, working steadily from the ranks to world leadership.

In 1890, she married George W. Catt, who had been a fellow student at the State University of Iowa. Mr. Catt was a civil engineer, prominent in his profession, with business connections on both Atlantic and Pacific coasts. He was a man of liberal ideas and public spirit, heartily sympathetic with his wife's purpose in life, and throughout the remainder of his life was a generous contributor to the cause which she had embraced. The first two years of their married life were spent in Seattle, after which they made their home successively at Bensonhurst, Long Island, and in New York City.

Mrs. Catt made her first speech at a national suffrage convention in Washington, District of Columbia, in 1890, when she was engaged as organizer, and entered upon her first suffrage campaign the following summer. This was the second South Dakota campaign, and it was a veritable baptism of fire. South

Dakota was a region of vast distances, sparsely inhabited by pioneers, many of them foreign born, who had been reduced by successive droughts to desperate poverty, and who were too deeply engaged in the struggle for existence to care about anything else. Into this dreary waste, invited by politicians who deserted them as soon as they arrived, went Susan B. Anthony and her band of campaign workers. The few local suffragists were divided into factions, without plans or funds. Three political parties were in the field, all hostile to the suffrage amendment. Amid these depressing conditions, the new suffrage organizer entered upon interminable rides in springless wagons over sun-baked prairies, interminable nights on springless beds, meetings at country cross-roads thinly attended by worn-out women, weeks and months of coarse fare, heat, cyclones, and black discouragement. In September, being asked to give an opinion on the prospect of carrying the suffrage amendment in South Dakota, she wrote:

"We have not a ghost of a chance. We are converting women to 'want to vote' by the hundreds, but we are having no appreciable effect on the men. We are appealing to justice for success, when it is selfishness that governs mankind. Ours is a cold, lonesome little movement which will make our hearts ache about November 5th. We need some kind of a political mustard plaster to make things lively."

There follows a brief cold analysis of the situation which foreshadows the great campaign of Mrs. Catt's later career. South Dakota lost the amendment and nearly killed the new organizer, who had typhoid fever following it,—but it made the greatest general the cause ever had. From that time, she aimed to make suffrage a political rather than an ethical issue.

The subsequent ten years, 1890–1900, were passed in unremitting organizing and campaigning in every state of the Union, except Florida. She played a leading part in the three successful campaigns in Colorado (1893), Idaho and Utah (1896). She crossed and recrossed the country, raised money, built up state associations, collected a devoted following who emulated her example and made a memorable speaking tour with Miss Anthony through the southern states in 1895. She was made Chairman of a National Committee on Organization, of which Mary Barrett Hay was Secretary (a working partnership which became permanent), brought into the National American Woman Suffrage Association branches in nearly every state in the Union, mapped out a working policy, largely wrote a series of publications, many of which were used up to the very end of the struggle, and by these activities became known as the brains of the suffrage movement, as Lucy Stone was its concience, Miss Anthony its heart, Mrs. Stanton its attorney, and Miss Shaw its orator.

It was Mrs. Catt, who, in 1894, at the annual suffrage convention, in the face of strong opposition by Miss Anthony urged that the convention meet in other cities throughout the country instead of invariably in Washington. She warned the convention that the West felt unrepresented in the policy of the association. She advocated concentrating for some years on State work instead of Federal. "A Congressman is a green toad on a green tree, a brown toad on a brown tree," she said. "He reflects his constituents. We must find work to secure amendments in the states and have a sufficient number of states to give political prestige to this question. When we have secured enough states to ratify a federal amendment, then and not till then is the time to meet in Washington." As a compromise it was determined to hold the convention on alternate years in Washington, the intervening conventions to be called elsewhere.

In 1896, in presenting her Plan of Work to the Suffrage convention, she said:

"For a whole half century, we have held special suffrage meetings with audiences largely of women. We should now carry our question into every town meeting, caucus or primary, for it is only there that the rank and file of the voters go. They won't come to our meetings. It will be of no more avail in the future than it has been in the past to send appeals to state and national political conventions, so long as they are not backed by petitions from the majority of their voting constituents."

When in 1900, Miss Anthony resigned the Presidency of the National American Woman Suffrage Association, Mrs. Catt was chosen as her successor by the retiring leader. She retained the Presidency four years, during the financial depression following the Spanish-American War, the period being one of peculiarly trying readjustment to new conditions within the organization. New wine was fermenting within the old bottle. To reconcile conflicting opinions and an ever increasing number of strongly marked individualities, to devise fresh methods, above all, to break into the political arena, required rare and skillful leadership. To meet the demands of travel, office work and correspondence, required an iron constitution. To meet the endless calls for public addresses required the genius of persuasion and debate. Mrs. Catt faced every demand successfully. In the midst of these activities, she saw the advantage of linking the suffrage organization in different countries into a world alliance, which would give international prestige and support to the movement. Accordingly in 1902, at her initiative, the first international suffrage conference was called in Washington, and the International Woman Suffrage Alliance was formed. At the first congress of the Alliance in Berlin in 1904, Mrs. Catt was elected President, and at each succeeding biennial congress, she has been unanimously reelected. At the Congress in Geneva, Switzerland, in 1920, the Alliance included thirty-five national branches, representing the women of all the leading races of the world.

In 1904, Mrs. Catt was forced by failing health to retire from the Presidency of the National American Woman Suffrage Association, being succeeded by Dr. Anna Howard Shaw. She left office with a balance of $11,000 in the treasury, no debts, a greatly increased membership, complete files, and a trained corps of workers. This nation-wide working organization had been built up by her initiative and under her direction upon the basis of the two earlier suffrage associations which united in 1890.

From 1904 to 1910, Mrs. Catt's activities were limited by increasing physical disabilities, which culminated in an entire breakdown in the latter year. In 1905, occurred the death of her husband, George W. Catt. In 1907, came the death of her mother. In the midst of these personal sorrows and anxieties, she began to lay the foundations for a suffrage campaign in New York City which was destined to last eleven years, and which finally carried the Empire State for suffrage, thereby winning the most brilliant battle of the long struggle. In 1906, all the suffrage organizations in Greater New York were united in the Interurban Suffrage Council, with headquarters in the Martha Washington Hotel. In 1909, a convention was called in Carnegie Hall, attended by 800 regularly elected delegates from all the boroughs, at which time the Interurban Council took on a regular political structure, and adopted the name, Woman Suffrage Party of New York City. Mrs. Catt was elected Chairman. The idea of political organization for political work was immediately copied in all parts of the country by suffrage forces. Within the next few years, the National American Woman Suffrage Association followed the trail blazed by New York, changed its structures, and became in all but name a party organization for campaign purposes. The advantages of the change as a preparation and exercise in political activities were inestimable, and so keen was the appreciation of the name, Woman Suffrage Party, that one suffrage group in Chicago was incorporated, in order to keep other local groups from having prestige of the name.

In 1908, Mrs. Catt began the circulation of the last national petition to Congress for the submission of a Federal Amendment. The hundreds of thousands of signatures were presented in an impressive demonstration at the Capitol, at the time of the Annual Convention of the National Suffrage Association, 1910. In the summer of 1910, entire cessation from work was imperative, and by the spring of 1911, Mrs. Catt's health was sufficiently improved to permit her to attend the International Woman Suffrage Alliance Congress, held that year in Stockholm, Sweden. Following the congress, she started on a trip around the world, accompanied by Doctor Aletta Jacobs, a prominent suffragist of Holland. This trip was planned as a vacation. It turned out to be a prolonged tour for suffrage propaganda in Egypt, South Africa, India, the Dutch East Indies, Burma, the Philippines, China, Japan and Hawaii. As a result, most of these regions visited became represented in the Alliance at the next meeting. After an absence of a year and a half, Mrs. Catt returned to the United States, landing at San Francisco in November, 1912, just after the election in which Oregon, Arizona and Kansas ratified woman suffrage amendments. Her appearance in New York City was made the occasion of a monster mass-meeting in Carnegie Hall, at which an international pageant of welcome was presented in her honor.

In 1913, the accession of Alaska was almost lost sight of in the stir created by the granting of presidential and partial state suffrage by the Legislature of Illinois. Even more significant of the beginning of the end was the formation in New York, that same year, of the Empire State Campaign Committee, with Mrs. Catt as Chairman. Under her direction, a bill requiring the submission of a suffrage amendment was carried, in the face of vehement opposition, through two successive legislatures, and submitted to the voters, November 2, 1915, when it was defeated by

194,000 out of a total vote of 1,201,000. The magnitude, brilliance and fighting spirit of the New York Campaign were best reflected in the way the suffragists met defeat. On November 4th, two days after election, a mass meeting was called in Cooper Union, New York City, with brass band, flags, cheers and all the accompaniments of victory. Every county in the state was represented, and as fast as pledges could be taken, amid wild enthusiasm, $100,000 were raised for the next campaign, which was voted to begin then and there. Thus out of the ashes of 1915 arose the victorious campaign of 1917.

It was apparent that the progress of the war in Europe at this time had profoundly affected public opinion in regard to the political status of women. Up to this time, the National Suffrage Association had been working along two lines;—to secure a Federal suffrage amendment, and to obtain state action. It was felt now by suffragists throughout the United States that the time had come to make of the National American Woman Suffrage Association a fighting campaign organization which should mass its · main attack on Washington. When in 1915 Doctor Anna Howard Shaw announced her retirement from the Presidency of the association, it was felt that there was but one woman who could create such a fighting body, hold it together and lead it to victory. This was the Chairman of the Empire State Campaign Committee, who in the first flush of defeat had raised $100,000 for the next bout. Accordingly, when the convention of the National American Woman Suffrage Association met in Washington, December, 1915, a deputation representing the unanimous and urgent desire of the delegate body called upon Mrs. Catt and obtained her acceptance, in case she could be released from her office in the New York Campaign Committee. The next day, she was elected, and found herself facing the culminating struggle of her life. At that time, eleven states had granted suffrage by popular vote, Alaska and Illinois by Legisla-

tive enactment, while three-fourths of the states were unenfranchised. It was Mrs. Catt's gigantic task to get a bill through Congress under these unpromising conditions, submitting a suffrage amendment to the United States Constitution to the forty-eight state legislatures, and after that to persuade thirty-six of these state legislatures to ratify the amendment.

In the presidential year, 1916, the first move was to obtain indorsement of woman suffrage as a plank in the major party platforms. It was successful. The next move was to push the bill through Congress, and this meant three years of unparalleled effort throughout the country, among the constituencies, and in Washington, in the assault upon the Capitol. During these years, Mrs. Catt lived on railroad trains and in hotels. She traversed the entire country repeatedly, held endless conferences, ironed out continually arising differences of opinion, interviewed local and national politicians, made speeches and raised money. Her time was divided between Washington and the country at large. During his entire second administration, President Wilson rendered incalculable assistance by appearing before Congress with a special message in behalf of the bill, by advocating it in his general messages, and by making strong personal appeals to influential political leaders. This hearty support was unwavering throughout the congested period of the war, and lasted until Votes for Women was written into the Constitution. While it came from conviction, it was certainly made happier by the President's respect for the leader of the suffrage movement and his appreciation of the political wisdom of her policy. The bill submitting the Suffrage Amendment to the states for ratification finally passed Congress early in the summer of 1919. The campaign then shifted from Washington to the legislatures of forty-eight states. The fourteen months from June 4, 1919, to August 18, 1920, were the most baffling, harrassing, exhausting and momentous of the American suffrage movement. The capacity and resources of the leader met here their supreme test. Three-fourths, thirty-six, of the state legislatures were required to ratify the Amendment. Within ten months thirty-five had ratified. Then came a terrible struggle for the thirty-sixth. Several legislatures rejected the Amendment. Then, after four months of suspense and amid scenes of dramatic excitement, the thirty-sixth—Tennessee—took favorable action during the absence of the die-hard minority, who had run away by night into a neighboring state in a last effort to block a vote by breaking the legislative quorum. During these "bitter-end" weeks, Mrs. Catt was in Nashville, personally directing the local campaign. Tennessee ratified August 18, 1920, and on August 26th, Secretary of State Colby declared the Nineteenth Amendment a part of the Constitution of the United States. Many able, brilliant and devoted men and women contributed to the final victory, but they themselves testify that the indispensable contribution was made by the general in command, and that the two names to be inseparably associated with the Nineteenth Amendment are, Susan B. Anthony who wrote it, and Carrie Chapman Catt who put it through.

No sketch of Doctor Catt's life would be adequate which failed to mention one noteworthy instance in which her fame as a leader brought something besides hard work in its train. A forceful and picturesque lady, who many years before had married Frank Leslie, publisher of *Leslie's Weekly*, rescued the publication from bankruptcy and made it a paying concern. Frank Leslie had died many years before, and she was now known as the Baroness Bazus, a title she claimed by hereditary right. When invited to suffrage gatherings by Mrs. Catt, she invariably came, and when solicited for funds she contributed generously. In 1914, she died, and one day shortly afterwards Mrs. Catt was called from the luncheon table in her home to meet an insistent caller. When she returned to the

dining room, she announced to those present that she had just been informed by the executors of the will that Baroness Bazus had made her the residuary legatee of her estate of $1,600,000. As the legacies to other heirs were small, the major portion of the estate would pass to her. No one was more astounded by this event than the residuary legatee, herself. Prolonged litigation instituted by relatives of Frank Leslie in attempts to break the will, together with other complications, effectually chastened the joy of inheritance. Thus, when making a statement of funds in the Leslie Estate to a business meeting, some years later, Mrs. Catt reflectively prefaced it by a remark that she had sometimes thought the Leslie money was the worst trouble she had ever had. After all expenses had been deducted, the sum actually delivered to her was something less than $1,000,000. To administer this Leslie fund, she formed the Leslie Commission of five well known women identified with various branches of the feminist movement, naturally assuming the chairmanship of the commission herself. The language of the Leslie will was remarkable and emphatic. It stated that the estate was given to Mrs. Catt to use as she thought best for the advancement of the woman suffrage cause. No guarantees were asked, and no restrictions were made. Such assured confidence in a transaction of such magnitude is as rare in this world as it is merited or fortunate. In this case, both giver and receiver were honored and made illustrious by the result. The money came at the time of the greatest need, when the war and the economic collapse following it made if difficult to raise money in volume sufficient to carry through the drive for the Federal Amendment throughout the country, to run the Publishing Bureau, and to maintain headquarters in New York and Washington. The suffrage cause owes a long debt of gratitude to Mrs. Frank Leslie, and to Mrs. Catt, for having unconsciously occasioned her generous deed.

In June, 1921, the Universities of Iowa and

Wyoming conferred upon Mrs. Catt the honorary degree of Doctor of Laws, and later in the same year she delivered the opening course of lectures of the Anna Howard Shaw Foundation in Bryn Mawr College, Pennsylvania.

Her interest, since woman suffrage has been put into effect in the United States, has been divided between two activities,—international disarmament, and organizing sentiment for woman suffrage in the Latin countries throughout the world. Extensive plans toward the latter aim are fully matured, and her support of the disarmament movement has been untiring ever since the conclusion of the war.

Doctor Catt makes her home in winter time in New York City, in summer at her farm, Juniper Ledge, Westchester County, near Ossining, New York. She is in continual demand as a speaker and writer, reads rapidly and insatiably in connection with current events all over the world, is complaisant to every form of literature except love stories and the Congressional Record, an enthusiastic farmer, and delights in the management of her domestic establishment.

Her connection with movements other than woman suffrage is indicated by membership in a number of political reform groups, such as the Honest Ballot Association, the American Proportional Representation League, the American Association for Labor Legislation, the American Academy for Political and Social Science, and the Town Hall Club of New York City. When the United States entered the World War, the National American Woman Suffrage Association was the first woman's organization to be placed at the disposal of the government, and it participated in sending the Women's Overseas Hospital Units to France. Doctor Catt was a member of the National Women's Division of the Council of National Defense, and she was appointed by President Wilson a member of the Chinese Famine Relief Committee. She is a member of the Board of Trustees of the Woodrow Wilson Foundation, the League of Nations Union, the League to Enforce Peace, the Pro-League Independents, the Red Cross, the National Consumers' League, the Women's Trade Union League, and other societies.

Doctor Catt is the last of that remarkable group of women who led the main branch of the suffrage movement in the United States— women of brilliant gifts, unfailing courage, and impassioned moral conviction. She has the typical characteristics of the group:—their originality and independence of mind, persistence of will, singleness of purpose; their eloquence of speech, cheerfulness, saving sense of humor, magnificent freedom from self-pity, sturdy health of spirit. She is differentiated from the group by greater ease and urbanity, a wider range of interests, a scientific habit of mind, a higher capacity to assemble facts, and upon that basis to form a workable program. Because of these distinguishing characteristics, she is frequently called the stateman of the movement. She is at her best in dealing with things on a large scale, with great numbers of people, in drawing heterogeneous detachments together, in-inspiring them with ardor and fusing them into a unified, disciplined, confident attacking force. No small part of her success in such dealings has been due to an impressive and beautiful presence, great personal charm, and unfailing kindness and magnanimity of temper.

Carrie Chapman Catt did not occupy the chief place in the concluding phase of a great social revolution by accident or force of circumstances; but because, when a great situation arose, demanding great leadership, she was the one called by common consent to meet it, and she did not evade the call or shirk the burden of responsibility.

DREXEL, MARY STRETCH IRICK (Mrs. George W. Childs Drexel), the daughter of William H. and Sally S. (Eayre) Irick, was born at her father's country estate, one mile from Vincentown, Burlington County, New Jersey. She was educated at Miss Fannie

Morrow's Private School, Beverly, New Jersey, and Patapsco Institute, Ellicott Mills, Maryland, where she studied for four years under Miss Sarah Randolph and Miss Polly Carter. On November 18, 1891, she was married at Vincentown to George W. Childs Drexel, for ten years Managing Editor of the *Public Ledger*, and during the World War Director of Military Relief, Pennsylvania-Delaware Division of the American Red Cross.

Mrs. Drexel has always devoted much time and energy to practical philanthropy. For twenty-eight years she has employed private visitors for poor families, and the number of these families, under personal supervision, has ranged from fifty to one hundred and seventy-five. During the straitened conditions in the winter of 1914–1915, she organized and furnished funds for a bread-line, where everyone of a thousand men daily received a cup of coffee and a small loaf of bread; she also arranged for bed and breakfast for fifty homeless men daily.

In November, 1914, Mrs. Drexel organized the Pennsylvania Woman's Division for National Preparedness, in which over 11,000 women were enrolled, with chapters in all the important cities of Pennsylvania. The members were trained in modern surgical dressing and in hygiene, first aid, canteen service, motor messenger service, sewing for military purposes, and other activities that might be necessary if the United States should enter the World War.

On April 7, 1917, this organization of 11,000 trained women was turned over to the American Red Cross and every officer in the Woman's Division for National Preparedness was given a position as a Red Cross officer.

The Canteen Department of the Pennsylvania-Delaware Division of the American Red Cross had stations in seventy-three cities and towns, including thirty-seven canteen huts and rest rooms, twenty-nine motor truck stations, with kitchens for the preparation of food, and eleven information booths. The Escort Service of this Department was composed of a group of thirty women, all of whom had had first aid training and some hospital service. They boarded the trains in New York, and were carried through the division or to the towns of the train's destination. The Canteen work in the cities and towns was in charge of 5,371 workers and 3,308 reserve workers, and between September 20, 1917 and November 1, 1919, served 3,870,481 men.

On May 7, 1917, Mrs. Drexel organized the Canteen Service of the Southeastern Pennsylvania Chapter of the American Red Cross, and a few weeks later assumed the office of Divisional Director of the Pennsylvania-Delaware Division Canteen Service. This Canteen Department was composed of seventy-eight auxiliaries and branches, in which 2,700 workers served under fifty-seven captains and fifty-four lieutenants. From September 20, 1917, when activities began, to November 1, 1919, when the Reserve was formed, 2,033,375 men were served. Among the special departments were the Motor Truck Transportation Service which served 30,000 men between January 31, 1918, and June 1, 1919; the Embarkation Service, which, beginning May 6, 1918, served 29,602 men; the Debarkation Service, which, beginning January 28, 1919, served 53,825 men; the Hospital Trains Service, which also provided for wounded men taken from ships, and, beginning in August, 1918, served 156,080 men; the Hospital Train Escort Service, which cared for 26,531 men, beginning December 12, 1918, and the Railroad Station Information Booths which, after November 1, 1918, gave aid and information to 173,242 men. While this work was supported partially by gifts from Red Cross auxiliaries and private individuals to the amount of $68,517.01 the entire expense of the headquarters salaries, offices, and storerooms, together with their full equipment was assumed by George W. Childs Drexel. He donated also the use of the car and the service of the driver for the Canteen Motor Transportation Corps.

The success of this monumental undertaking which has won distinguished praise, is to be attributed to the tireless energy, the practical ability, the unfailing tact, and the sheer genius for organization which Mrs. Drexel exercised with matchless leadership, in her work.

MAXWELL, ANNA CAROLINE, R.N., M.A., daughter of John Eglinton and Diantha Caroline (Brown) Maxwell, was born in Bristol, New York, May 14, 1851. Her father, who was descended from a Maxwell who fought in the battle of Stirling, was born in Scotland, and, after living in Perth and Edinburgh, where he graduated at the University, came to Toronto, Canada, in 1830. Her mother, who was born in Ridgway, Orleans County, New York, August 9, 1821, was a descendant of Thomas Perne, prebendary of Oxford, whose daughter, Rachel Perne, married Edward Rawson. The latter was born in London, England, April 16, 1615, and came in 1634 to Newbury, Massachusetts, where in 1650 he was Secretary of the colony. The line is continued through their son, Grindal Rawson, who married Susanna Wilson; their daughter Rachel Rawson, who married Samuel Wood; their daughter, Priscilla Wood, who married Phineas Davis; their son, Paul Davis, who married Rachel Chapin; and their daughter, Abigail Norcross Davis, who married Jeremiah Brown, the parents of Diantha Caroline (Brown) Maxwell.

Anna Caroline Maxwell received her early education at home and at boarding school and her first training as a nurse in Boston, Massachusetts, where she graduated in nursing from the Boston City Hospital in 1880. In December of that year she went to the Massachusetts General Hospital, Boston, to open the Training School for Nurses and became again its director after her return from England, whither she went in July, 1881, to study training methods. In 1889 she established the Training School for Nurses at St. Luke's Hospital, New York and in 1891 she accepted a call from the Presbyterian Hospital, New York, to establish its Training School for Nurses, at the head of which she remained until 1921. There, efficiency of service was her principal aim, and her institution was known to physicians and nurses of all hospitals as a model of individual care for the patient, her methods being copied and her services sought by other institutions. During the Spanish-American War, Miss Maxwell had leave of absence to act as supervisor of nurses in the Sternberg Hospital at Camp Thomas, Chickamauga Park, Georgia, where, with 160 assistants, she made the nursing of soldiers so efficient that the death rate from typhoid fever was kept down to sixty-seven cases in a thousand. With the outbreak of the World War her services were at once in demand for the organizing of the Presbyterian Unit. She went overseas early in the war to study nursing needs and again after the entrance of the United States to inspect the work of the Presbyterian Unit in France. She herself desired to volunteer as an army nurse, but the Board of Managers of the hospital declined to give her leave as her services were more needed in this country. Nevertheless she was active in Red Cross work and in the movement to obtain military rank for the Army Nurse Corps, and she aided in designing a uniform for army nurses. On her visits overseas she personally inspected more than one hundred army hospitals and brought back a high report of the patriotic service performed by the nurses of this country in spite of the handicap under which they labored in being without rank or other than personal authority. "Their opportunity, however", Miss Maxwell said, "for giving anaesthetics and lending valuable and efficient aid in carrying out the treatment of wounds such as the world has never seen; their satisfaction in the knowledge that they could bring to the soldier in his extremity that atmosphere of home which only a devoted woman can create, are their inestimable reward." Miss Maxwell is a member of many committees and organizations which aim to recruit nurses and make the work more attractive to young women. In 1907 with Amy E. Pope she brought out *Practical Nursing*, which went to a second edition in 1910 and a third edition in 1914. She is a member of the League of Nursing Education, the American Nurses Association, the National Organization for Public Health Nursing, the Cosmopolitan and Woman's City Clubs of New York, and the Haven Country Club of Nyack-on-Hudson, New York. During her forty-five years' devotion to the practice of nursing, Miss Maxwell has come to be honored as one of the most noted members of her profession, whose work has been largely instrumental in raising nursing to its present high professional standard, a fact recognized by Columbia University in awarding her the honorary degree of M.A. in 1917.

PUTNAM, ELIZABETH (Mrs. William Lowell Putnam), daughter of Augustus and Katharine Bigelow (Lawrence) Lowell, was born in Boston, Massachusetts, February 2, 1862. Her father was descended from John Lowell, a native of Bristol, England, who located in Newbury, Massachusetts, in 1636.

Elizabeth Lowell received her education in private schools in Boston. On June 9, 1888, at Brookline, Massachusetts, she married William Lowell Putnam, a lawyer. They are the parents of five children: George, Katharine Lawrence (Mrs. Harvey Hollister Bundy), Roger Lowell, Harriet Lowell, and Augustus Lowell Putnam.

From 1909 to 1914 she was Chairman of the Committee of the Women's Municipal League of Boston. This organization conducted an interesting and helpful experiment in prenatal care, designed to increase the efficiency of the coming generation by obviating those causes of infant feebleness and ill-health that result from lack of scientific supervision before birth. The Committee employed visiting nurses who, in the first year and a half of the work, gave medical and nursing supervision during pregnancy to over six hundred women in Boston and vicinity. Mrs. Putnam prepared a report of this work for the annual meeting of the American Association for the Study and Prevention of Infant Mortality, held in Baltimore, November 9–11, 1910. At the Association's annual meeting, held in Chicago, November 16–18, 1911, Mrs. Putnam discussed the case of the community *versus* midwives and, as a laywoman, emphasized the necessity of preventive medicine for both mother and child. In reporting on the work of her Committee, at the Conference on Infant Hygiene of the Philadelphia Baby Saving Show, in May, 1912, she stressed the spiritual aspects of prenatal care. In September, 1912, the Committee's exhibit in Washington, at the International Congress of Hygiene and Demography, excited much favorable attention. It was afterwards shown in the larger cities of Massachusetts. The work spread, through various agencies, to all the other large cities of the United States and to Canada. It was noticed, also, with commendation in Edinburgh, Scotland, and in New Zealand.

The work that Mrs. Putnam has accomplished has been of inestimable value in educating the people to understand the danger of poorly trained doctors and ignorant midwives, and in reducing the percentage of infant mortality and of ill-born babies. The principal method employed has been to show the mother the rational way to live. Mrs. Putnam has extended her work through many committees and associations. She has been Chairman of the Committee of the Women's Municipal League of Boston on Prenatal and Obstetrical Care. This organization, which continued the earlier work, had its origin in 1914. She has also acted in the following important capacities: Chairman of the Public Health Department of the League from 1912 to 1919; Vice-President of the Household Nursing Association, from 1918 to 1919; member of the Council of the National Child Welfare Association; President of the American Association for the Study and Prevention of Infant Mortality (now the American Association of Child Hygiene) in 1918, and a member of the Executive Committee in 1915, and from 1918 to 1920; and a member of the Executive Committee of the Massachusetts Committee on Child Welfare of the Woman's Council of National Defense. Since 1910 she has been a member of the Executive Committee of the Massachusetts Anti-Suffrage Association; and Chairman of the Relief Department, and a member of the Executive Committee, of the Special Aid Society of American Preparedness.

On July 5, 1917, Mrs. Putnam was commissioned by Brigadier-General E. Leroy Sweetser, acting Adjutant-General of the Commonwealth of Massachusetts, to superintend the compilation of a list of the men going to the World War from that State. Having seen this work well under way, in August, 1917, she turned over her records to the Adjutant-General's Department as a foundation for the Commonwealth's list of the Massachusetts men in the War. On August 29, 1917, she was appointed by the Adjutant-General to take charge of the Department's Information Bureau for soldiers, sailors, and marines. In November, 1917, she was appointed by the Red Cross Casualty Bureau, in Washington and Paris, as its official representative from Massachusetts. She has since had charge of the work of an Intelligence Bureau for foreign-born citizens.

SQUIRE, MARY E., chemist and manufacturer, daughter of Richard and Elizabeth Sloane (Stripp) Squire, was born at Newtown, Long Island, New York, March 13, 1859. Her father, a sea captain (born in Bridgewater, Somersetshire, England), was a son of John Squire, who came of an old family of Somersetshire, and a grandson of Rear Admiral Sir James Bowen, of Ilfracombe, Devon, England. Her mother was a descendant of Sir Matthew Stripp, of Cornwall, England.

Miss Squire received her preliminary edu-
cation at the Newtown Public School, and at St. Joseph's Academy, Flushing, Long Island. Later she attended Northwestern University, where her research work was done, and the Kent College of Law, both in Chicago, Illinois. After teaching for some time in the public schools of Brooklyn, New York, she held the responsible executive position of Business Manager of the Handle Hall Building, Chicago.

This practical business experience and her highly specialized technical training have been substantial factors in her large success with the Allwood Lime Company, Manitowoc, Wisconsin, of which she is the founder, chemist, secretary and general manager. It is in connection with both the technical development and the business management of this enterprise that Miss Squire has won international reputation. With her partner, Doctor Jessie Drew Carpenter, Miss Squire is a pioneer in the practical application of highly specialized geological and chemical knowledge, in connection with quarry and lime-plant operation. For nearly fifteen years she has been actively engaged in a field which today a few of the largest operators are just beginning to cultivate. This fact alone is striking evidence of the initiative, determination, and persistency that go far toward explaining her achievements.

Miss Squire has been engaged in the development of special lime products, which involve larger profits than the ordinary form of lime. As early as 1911 she had become interested in lime and its uses, and expended much time and effort to find a quarry whose geological structure and lime content should compare with those of Germany, whence for two hundred years had come the high-grade lime used in this country. She was fortunate enough to discover just such a quarry at Allwood Siding, near Manitowoc, Wisconsin, the management of which was assumed by her in 1912. She has made of this plant a laboratory for the practice of her broad knowledge, her remarkable ingenuity, and her infinite capacity for work, until now it is unique as a chemical factory for the lime products that have made her name internationally famous. After discovering that the lime in her quarry was of as high quality as the German products (formerly costing from eighty to two hundred dollars a ton laid down on the dock at Hoboken), Miss Squire proceeded, with a thoroughness characteristic of her, to ascertain which kind of stone yielded this high-quality lime. To accomplish this, she spent practically four years, and conducted 240 tests. She made it her purpose, besides finding out the physical appearance and the chemical contents of each stone, to ascertain the kind of fuel best suited for burning it; the best type of kiln in which to produce it; and the most practical and economical kind of returnable container in which the railroads would be willing to transport it.

Miss Squire asserts that one of the secrets of her success lies in the fact that she has been able to teach the company's laborers how to recognize the kind of stone that contains the high-grade lime. "Fifty per cent of the solution of my problem," says Miss Squire, "was due to chemical analysis and geological identification of the stone; and fifty per cent to the burning and ascertaining that certain fuels, or rather, certain sap in the wood fuels will utterly destroy the qualities desired." It is interesting to note that the first day's output was ten pounds, produced with the aid of a poppy-seed grinder. It was in March, 1914, that Miss Squire made the timely discovery of the process of manufacturing steel-finishing lime, formerly made only in Germany. This lime performed a highly important function during the World War, in the finishing of steel balls for ball-bearing cannon carriages, as well as in the finishing of surgical instruments. As early as December, 1915, all of the imported German lime in the United States had been consumed, and it soon became evident that Miss Squire had a great opportunity before her. Because her product

met the most exacting tests, and because her methods were highly effective, and beyond reproach ethically, she was able to fill the existing need satisfactorily, and with great credit to herself. How well her product filled the need from the standpoint of quality may be inferred from the fact that in thirty-two comparative tests of the Allwood and the German lime, the Allwood lime proved the better thirty-one times.

The practical test of actual demand for a lime of the highest possible quality was also successfully met by Miss Squire's product. During the World War the Allwood Lime Company supplied England, Canada, and the entire United States with the finishing lime so essential in the manufacture of munitions, and in the final preparation of surgical instruments. Had the Allies and the United States been unable to obtain this lime, a highly critical situation would have been created. Miss Squire may be credited with having performed a truly patriotic service.

Miss Squire's experiments have also resulted in a *milk of magnesia* lime which has proved extremely valuable in the dairy-products industry. This lime, which is not a preservative, neutralizes excess acid in milk and cream, making it possible for the manufacturers of milk products always to give the consumer absolutely high-grade butter and cheese, without using deleterious materials. Miss Squire made this discovery while she was experimenting, to find a stomach anti-acid, for a prominent physician of Chicago.

Miss Squire is probably the first woman to apply a specialized geological and chemical knowledge to the lime industry. Her great success is largely explained by the principle that she has practised consistently to make something which is the best of its kind, in order that people shall be convinced they cannot do without it. "But," says Miss Squire, "it must honestly be the best." Although Miss Squire and Doctor Carpenter are the sole stockholders and managers of this business, they treat their employees like the members of a family, and it is not surprising that strikes and other labor troubles are unknown at the Allwood plant. In the industry at large, moreover, Miss Squire is widely known for the high ethical standards that she has always maintained. The fame of her American Steel-Finishing Lime, Vienna Polishing Lime, Milk of Magnesia Neutralizing Lime, Horologic and Lustre Lime is due in no small measure to the manner in which she has conducted her business, as well as to the substantial worth of the products themselves.

Miss Squire was a member of the Chicago Woman's Club, from 1894 to 1914. She finds her principal recreation in fishing. It is worthy of special note that she recommends that the lime industry be graded, that producers of both high and low quality lime may always be sure of fair treatment.

TOWN HALL, THE, New York City, the city's outstanding open forum for free discussion, was started by women. Nearly thirty years ago under the leadership of Mrs. Eleanor Butler Sanders, a small group of women who were devoted to the cause of equal suffrage, formed the League for Political Education. Today few of the thousands who attend the lectures and recitals at the New York Town Hall, sponsored by the League for Political Education, are aware that this great forum had a most unusual and picturesque beginning.

In 1894, when the women, who were working valiantly to secure an amendment to the Constitution of the State of New York, met on the eve of the convention, they admitted they were ahead of their time and that women were not sufficiently educated on political matters to use the suffrage, even if it were given to them.

There were present at this history making meeting in the drawing room of Mrs. Henry M. Sanders at 433 Fifth Avenue, Mrs. Sanders, Doctor Mary Putnam Jacobi, physician and pioneer feminist; Mrs. Robert Abbe, formerly Mrs. Courtlandt Palmer, a leader of liberal thought; Lucia Gilbert Runkel, editor and writer whom the late Lawrence Hutton called "the most cultivated woman in America"; Mrs. Ben Ali Haggin and Miss Adele M. Field, who had been a missionary to China.

Shortly after the meeting opened, Doctor Jacobi rose and said: "We have all known from the beginning that we are ahead of our time and that suffrage cannot be granted yet. We know what the answer will be tomorrow when the convention meets at Albany and we know too, that women are not sufficiently educated to use the ballot. I therefore move that this committee be dissolved and that the members organize themselves to establish a League for Political Education for men and women."

And so the League for Political Education came into being. Mrs. Sanders was the mainstay of this group and her death in 1905 was a great loss to the organization. She was so retiring that she would never make a speech or write an article. She would not even preside at a meeting save under great pressure, yet the annals of the League for Political Education are full of stories of her humor, her calm, keen judgment, her views and her ability to think along independent lines. Of all this group, Mrs. Ben Ali Haggin is the only one living today.

The ideal of the early group to inaugurate a forum where people of opposing views could come together and discuss topics of the day has been rigidly adhered to. The first plank in the women's platform was that there must be no arguing for woman suffrage or any other reform without giving the other side an equal chance to talk. It has always remained non-sectarian and non-partisan.

The meetings of the League during the nineties were held in the private parlors of its members. Later they were held in the little assembly room of the Berkeley Lyceum, then in Mendelssohn Hall, the Hudson Theatre, the Engineering Club's Hall, Aeolian Hall and finally Carnegie Hall. Some of the early meetings were so slim in attendance that sixty was esteemed a large audience. It is said that in 1907 when the League first held meetings in the office room of the Berkeley Theatre, it sometimes sent in its office staff to help swell the numbers. Before the audience arrived members of the League set up the camp chairs and then breathed a prayer that the chairs would not collapse and disturb the speaker— to say nothing of those who sat upon them.

During these years with their many migrations from one parlor to another and from one hall to another the members of the League dreamed of one day having an abiding place of their own. It was on January 12, 1921, that the Town Hall at 113–123 West Forty-third Street was formally opened to the people of New York City and the dream of the small group of women leaders in 1894 was fully realized. For the Town Hall, a structure beautiful in itself, was designed to embody for all time a heritage handed down from the Pilgrims, the New England town meeting idea.

Henry W. Taft, chairman of the League for Political Education, in an address at the opening of the Town Hall, declared that there had never been a school for the education of mankind in the principles of civil liberty, the science of government and right living among neighbors which could be compared with the New England town meeting. He asserted that the idea of the New England town meeting was being revived in New York's Town Hall to keep alive the spirit of our ancestors and to help meet the vital, if not epochal crises which modern world conditions are bound to produce.

Today the Town Hall not only has a vital place in New York life, but it has extended its influence to cities all over the country. The great interest in open forums has come largely from such organizations as the League for Political Education. In the interval since its foundation the activities of the League have been extended into a wide field of human knowledge. Public questions and topics of all kinds making the composite of the culture of American civilization are included in its program. Since it was opened three years ago the Town Hall has become one of New York's best known music centers, as well as open forum which has become internationally known.

Although there are many men members of the League for Political Education, women members are still in the majority. Today there are more than 6,000 members of the League, of whom 1,000 are public school teachers. Allied with the League are two organizations which are outgrowths of it, the Economic Club with a membership of more than 1,200 business and professional men and the Civic Forum, which is composed of both men and women members.

In 1901, Robert Erskine Ely, who had been director of the League since 1899, gave up similar work in Cambridge to devote himself to the New York enterprise and became its secretary and director. Miss Mary B. Cleveland became executive secretary of the League in 1907, a position which she still holds and it is due to Miss Evelyn Shulters, membership secretary, that the membership of the League has been brought to its present-day strength.

It was Mrs. William H. Bliss, who by a gift in 1912 started the building fund for the Town Hall. Mrs. Bliss is a member of the board of trustees of the League. Other women members of the board of trustees are: Miss Laura V. Day, Secretary of the Board; Mrs. Henry A. Alexander, Miss Charlotte B. Baker, Miss Mabel Choate, Mrs. Arthur S. Claflin, Mrs. Elgin R. L. Gould, Mrs. Ben Ali Haggin, Mrs. E. H. Harriman, Miss Florence M. Marshall, Mrs. John T. Pratt, Mrs. Ralph L. Shainwald, Mrs. Schuyler N. Warren.

Among the members of the maintenance committee are Mrs. Charles S. Alexander, Mrs. Andrew Carnegie, Mrs. Edward S. Harkness, Mrs. John A. Hartwell, Mrs. Alice

Green Hoffman, Mrs. Frank B. Keech, Mrs. S. H. Kohn, Mrs. J. Pierpont Morgan, Mrs. Henry Morgenthau, Mrs. Charles D. Oppenheim, Mrs. William A. Perry, Mrs. John Kelly Robinson, Mrs. Frank S. Voss and Mrs. Warner W. van Norden.

In all the United States and probably in all the world there is no other civic auditorium that is quite like the Town Hall. This beautiful building is not merely the work of the architects and engineers, the decorators and the distinguished professor who had charge of the perfect accoustics, it shows the careful thought of the women members of the League for Political Education. It is this that makes it distinctive and gives it an atmosphere unlike that of any other civic auditorium . Mrs. John W. Alexander, wife of the distinguished painter, was a prominent member of the committee in charge of the decoration. The comfortable seats, the creamy finish of the walls, the decorations of mulberry and gold with touches of rich blue, the doors that look like French windows, all show an unmistakably feminine touch.

WHITMAN, OLIVE HITCHCOCK (Mrs. Charles Seymour Whitman), daughter of Oliver Nelson and Josephine (Lloyd) Hitchcock, was born in New York City, January 1, 1882. Among her ancestors were Roelofe Martense Schenck and Gerrit Wolferson Kouvenhoven, who came to New Netherlands in 1643. The Kouvenhoven family is traced in the Netherlands back to 1440. Others were the Huguenot, Perrin Thorel, who came to America prior to 1787, and Captain Peter Perrine, who served in the War of the Revolution.

Mrs. Whitman is a graduate of the New York Collegiate Institute. Her marriage to Mr. Whitman took place at the Church of the Ascension, New York, December 22, 1908. They are the parents of Olive Whitman (born in 1910) and Charles Seymour Whitman, Junior (born in 1915). Mr. Whitman (born in Hanover, Connecticut, August 28, 1868),

son of John and Little (Arne) Whitman, has had a distinguished career as lawyer, judge, District Attorney for New York County, 1910–1914, and Governor of New York State from January 1, 1915 to December 31, 1918.

Mrs. Whitman is a member of the Mary Washington Colonial Chapter, New York, of the Daughters of the American Revolution. From 1917 to 1919 she served on the State Board, Daughters of the American Revolution, and is Vice-Chairman of the Americanization Committee, Daughters of the American Revolution. In April, 1920, she was elected Vice-President-General of the National Society, Daughters of the American Revolution, for three years. She is also an honorary member of the Society of New England Women, and a member of the Colonial Dames of the State of New York, the Society of Holland Dames, the Huguenot Society, the Patriotic Women of America, the Colonial Daughters of America, the Washington Headquarters Association, and the Ella Nicholson Chapter (Albany) of the Order of the Eastern Star. She is a member of the Women's Forum of New York, the New York Women's Republican Club, and has served on the Republican Women's State Executive Committee and the Republican County Committee.

She is a member of the Woman's Committee of the First Presbyterian Church, New York, and of the Vacation Association, and is interested in the Infant Welfare Station, the Central Christian Mothers' Union of Albany, the Little Mothers' Aid, the Militia of Mercy, the National Child Labor Committee, the New York State Conference of Mothers, the New York State Committee of Women in Industry, and the Seaside Home for Crippled Children. During the World War she worked in the Liberty Loan campaigns, and aided all war relief organizations, such as the Albany Red Cross Canteen, the Committee for the Protection of French Soldiers, the National Security League, the National Special Aid, the Naval Aeronautic Committee of the

Woman's Naval Service, the Salvation Army War Work Committee, the Young Men's Christian Association War Committee, the Soldiers and Sailors Club, the Stage Women's War Relief, the Woman's Christian Temperance Union, the National League for Woman's Service, the War Camp Community Service, the Woman's Homeopathic Hospital Unit and the Woman's Overseas Hospital.

In December, 1919, Mrs. Whitman was Chairman of the Gift Committee of the New York Community Service Exposition, which collected 8,000 toys for children of the foreign born, and she was on the committee of the Liberty Chorus and Memorial Festival, May 30, 1920. As Chairman of the Reclamation Shop, New York, under the auspices of the National League for Woman's Service, she superintended the clothing and outfitting of over 10,000 soldiers and sailors, who were returning to civil life. All the clothing was donated, and the men were able to pay as little as seventy-five cents for a suit. The shop supported itself and the surplus went to continue the patriotic work of the League.

Mrs. Whitman is a member of the Colony, Cosmopolitan, and Women's City Clubs of New York and the National Republican Club.

VANDERLIP, NARCISSA COX (Mrs. Frank A. Vanderlip), daughter of Charles Epperson and Narcissa (Woods) Cox, was born in Quincy, Illinois. She was educated in public and private schools, and in 1899 entered the University of Chicago, where she was prominent in all student activities. She was a member of the University Dramatic Club and the Esoteric Club, and in 1902 was President of the University of Chicago Young Women's Christian Association. She was also the editor of the *Annual Publication*, and editor-in-chief of the woman's edition of the *Daily Maroon*.

On May 19, 1903, shortly before her graduation with the class of 1903, she was married, in Chicago, to Frank Arthur Vanderlip,

President of the National City Bank of New York. They are the parents of six children: Narcissa, Charlotte Delight, Frank Arthur, Jr., Virginia Jocelyn, Kelvin Cox, and John Mann Vanderlip.

At both her homes, in New York City and at Scarborough-on-Hudson, Westchester County, New York, Mrs. Vanderlip has been identified with many movements for social betterment. As a member of the New York State Woman Suffrage Party she was active in the campaigns of 1916 and 1917, for the extension of the franchise to women in New York. She was Chairman of the 9th Campaign District, which included the counties of Westchester, Rockland, Orange, and Sullivan, and there her vigorous leadership produced highly successful results. In 1918–1919 she was Chairman of the 24th and 25th Congressional Districts of the New York State League of Women Voters, the successor of the New York State Woman Suffrage Party, and in November, 1919, she was elected State Chairman of the League. Although a Republican in politics, Mrs. Vanderlip has kept the League true to its non-partisan platform, and has directed its program to secure protective legislation for women in industry, and to combat reactionary attempts to repeal laws, already passed, for improving the conditions of women and children. Mrs. Vanderlip is Treasurer of the Kennedy Street Settlement, New York, and was the organizer of the Civic Study Club at Ossining, New York. With her husband, she founded, and built, the Scarborough School, which is well known for its definitely constructive ideas.

Mrs. Vanderlip is a member of the Board of Directors of the New York Health Organization, and of that of the New York Girls' Protective Association, of which she is Chairman of the Educational Committee. Constructive and preventive philanthropy interests Mrs. Vanderlip more than palliative measures. The Protective Association seeks to remove the causes which lead girls to conspicuous behavior, and often from that into actual danger. It provides a club house, where girls can enjoy safe freedom; supports two houses, one at 13 East 19th Street and the other at 331 East 69th Street, New York City, where 29,000 girls gather during each year, indoors or in the gardens. Attention is fixed on the girl who has lacked sympathy and opportunity for recreation to such an extent that the desire for happiness or excitement so often results disasterously.

In July, 1919, Mrs. Vanderlip called a conference of Community Councils, the outgrowth of the Council of National Defense, to discuss the question of providing more playgrounds for the thousands of children who have no chance for play under healthful conditions, and to plan community houses where the people, young or old, may create the activities and forms of amusement that they need and enjoy. Mrs. Vanderlip believes that recreation is necessary for grown people, as well as for children, and that the War has proved that the national energy may be best conserved by recreating it through play.

During the World War, Mrs. Vanderlip was Chairman of the War Service Committee of the New York State Woman Suffrage Party and Chairman of the New York Standardized Wartime Dress Committee. She was instrumental in having the Military Census taken by the women of Westchester County, and organized with considerable success local garden and food conservation campaigns before the national program was inaugurated. She established a large dehydrator on her country estate, as an experiment for the county, and was instrumental in organizing the Westchester County Thrift Committee, acting for a time as its Vice-Chairman. She was Chairman of the Women's Committee of the Westchester County Council of National Defense, whose successful Child Welfare Campaign she directed, and in the summer of 1918 she helped establish camps in Westchester and Rockland Counties for the Woman's Land Army of America, in whose work she had been actively interested. In June, 1917,

she had been appointed by Secretary of the Treasury McAdoo to the Federal Women's Liberty Loan Committee; in the subsequent drives she took an active part and in addition was Chairman for the private schools of Westchester County for the United War Work Campaign.

Mrs. Vanderlip is a communicant of the Swedenborgian Church of the New Jerusalem, New York City, and is a teacher in the Sunday School of St. Mary's Episcopal Church, Beechwood, Scarborough. In addition to the organizations already named she is a member of the Colony, Cosmopolitan, and Women's City Clubs of New York, and of the Daughters of the American Revolution.

WHITWELL, GERTRUDE HOWARD (Mrs. Frederick Silsbee Whitwell), daughter of William Henry and Anna Dwight (Whiting) Howard, was born in San Francisco, California. Nathaniel Howard, her first American ancestor, came from Suffolk, England, in 1641, and settled in Dorchester, Massachusetts, where he was made a freeman in 1643. Mrs. Whitwell's grandfather, William Davis Merry Howard, son of Eleazer Howard, who resided on Temple Place in Boston, and was a banker, in the firm of Howard and Merry, removed, in 1838, to San Francisco, and became one of the leading citizens. Within the boundaries of his country estate, the San Mateo Rancho, is contained the part of the area of the present cities of San Mateo and Burlingame, and of the town of Hillsborough. Her mother, Anna Dwight Howard, was descended from Nathaniel Whiting of Boston, England (born in 1627; and died in Dedham, Massachusetts, June 16, 1677), who married Hannah Dwight (born in 1625; died November 4, 1714).

Gertrude Howard was educated in France. She early showed marked ability in music, and studied piano under Paderewski and Breitner. On November 23, 1893, she was married at Emmanuel Church, Boston, Massachusetts, to Frederick Silsbee Whitwell, a counsellor-at-law and trustee. They were the parents of one daughter, Gertrude Howard Whitwell (born February 8, 1896; died November 27, 1908).

For five years Mrs. Whitwell was President of the Vincent Club of Boston, and she has been a member of the Board of Governors and Chairman of the Entertainment Committee of the Chilton Club and a member of the Board of Governors of the Massachusetts Society of the Colonial Dames of America. She is a member of the Boston General Committee of the American Academy at Rome and of the Auxiliary Board of Managers of the Industrial School for Crippled and Deformed Children since the founding of the school. She has also been Chairman of the Ways and Means Committee and a member of the Executive Committee of the Woman's Department of the New England Section of the National Civic Federation.

During the World War, for nearly five years, Mrs. Whitwell was a member of the Executive Committee for Boston of the Lafayette Kits, and also a member of the Executive Committee, and Chairman of the Entertainment Committee, of the American Committee for Devastated France; she was also a member of the Champagne-Argonne Committee. For two years she was a field instructor in the New England Division of the Red Cross and for six months was in charge of the Milton Branch of the Red Cross. She is on the Executive Board of the Polish Relief Committee, and is a member of the Executive Committee of the Girls' City Club and actively interested in the work done at Denison House, Boston.

WHITNEY, GERTRUDE VANDER-BILT (Mrs. Harry Payne Whitney), sculptor, the daughter of Cornelius and Alice Claypoole (Gwynne) Vanderbilt, was born in New York, New York. The Vanderbilt family traces its descent from Jan Aertsen Van der Bilt who came from Friesland, the Netherlands, and settled at Flatbush, Long Island, in 1650.

His son moved in 1715 to New Dorp, Staten Island, and his great-great-grandson, Cornelius Vanderbilt (1794–1877) known as the Commodore, who married his cousin, Sophia Johnson, made his home in the City of New York. While still under twenty he laid the foundation of the great shipping interests centering at New York which made him a power in mercantile and transportation affairs. Shortly before the Civil War he began to transfer his capital from shipping to railroad enterprises, obtaining a controlling interest in the New York, New Haven and Hartford Railroad; and it was his consolidation and expansion of the New York Central and subsidiary lines that made that system the principal carrier between New York and Chicago.

His son, William Henry Vanderbilt (1821–1885), as business manager of his father's railroads, by his economical efficiency further developed the Vanderbilt holdings. As a collector of paintings he encouraged art, and was deeply interested in the success of Vanderbilt University and the College of Physicians and Surgeons, to whose endowments he contributed. To the latter, he and his three brothers presented the Vanderbilt Clinic as a memorial to their father. It is through him that the family is perpetuated, as his brothers left no children. He married Maria Louise Kissam.

Their eldest son, Cornelius Vanderbilt, the father of Gertrude Whitney, was born November 27, 1843, and died September 12, 1901. He continued the family tradition in railroad management as well as in charitable, religious and educational affairs. He was also a patron of art, having not only his own collection of paintings but also presenting to the Metropolitan Museum of Art a noteworthy collection of drawings by the old masters. He married in 1870, Alice Claypoole, daughter of Abraham Evan Gwynne, Esquire, of Cincinnati, Ohio, and Cettie, daughter of Henry Collins Flagg, Mayor of New Haven, Connecticut, 1836–1841. Mr.

Gwynne was the son of Major David Gwynne, U. S. A. (died at his estate, "Fairhope," Jefferson County, Kentucky, August 21, 1849), and Alice Anne Claypoole, daughter of Captain Abraham George Claypoole of Philadelphia and Chillicothe, Ohio, an officer in the Pennsylvania Line, Continental Army, and one of the original members of the Pennsylvania Society of the Cincinnati. The family of Claypoole is of English descent and traceable in direct lines to Edward I, King of England, Ferdinand III, King of Castile and Leon, and to Henry de Bohun, Earl of Hereford and Essex, 1199, one of the twenty-five Magna Charta Barons who were Sureties for that document granted by King John in 1213.

Gertrude Vanderbilt, the eldest daughter of Alice Claypoole Gwynne and Cornelius Vanderbilt, was educated by private tutors and attended Brearley School, New York. On August 25, 1896, she was married at Newport, Rhode Island, to Henry Payne Whitney, Esquire, son of William C. Whitney and nephew of Colonel Oliver Payne. She began the study of sculpture under Henry Andèrson, of New York, and continued with James E. Fraser. Later she entered the Art Student's League and from there went to Paris to study with Andrew O'Connor and Rodin.

While studying, she started the collection of modern American art which has become famous for the foresight and the liberal point of view which it indicates.

Determined to ground herself thoroughly she devoted herself intensively to her art without thought of exhibitions or possible commissions. The intelligence which she brought to her long apprenticeship, during which she evolved the strongly marked native style that has brought her just recognition, was not in vain. It equipped her to carry out in a definite and unified style monumental works. At root an American, her imagination was most appealed to by undertakings which offered her an opportunity to express her native point of view. For the same reason she soon developed a style distinguished, vivid, and American.

In 1908, she won her first recognition in the competition known as the "project of the three arts." This is the prize for the best design made in coöperation by an architect, a mural painter and a sculptor. This special grouping was for an outdoor swimming pool. The general design was by Grosvenor Atterbury; the decorative panels by Hugo Ballin, while Mrs. Whitney's work was the fountain with figure of Pan.

Her model for the Aztec Fountain, now in the Pan-American Building, Washington, District of Columbia, was first shown in 1912. The design is suggested by the art of the original rulers of Mexico. The same year she exhibited a head of a Spanish peasant, an admirable and strong piece of character work, which was bought by the Metropolitan Museum (which also owns the Caryatid).

Her Marble Fountain was awarded the bronze medal for Sculpture, at the San Francisco World's Fair, was purchased by the American Society of Peru and presented to the Peruvian Government. It was erected at Lima in 1924.

In 1914, came the appalling Titanic disaster, when that ill-fated liner was sent to the bottom on her maiden voyage. The women of America organized the Woman's Titanic Memorial Committee to raise funds and erect a statue in Potomac Park, Washington, District of Columbia. The design submitted by Mrs. Whitney won in open competition. The figure is 13 feet high and hewn out of a great rock of granite and commemorates the heroism of the men who raised the dauntless cry "Women and children first!" A replica of the head of this memorial, carved in marble and exhibited in Paris in 1921, was purchased by the French Government for the Luxembourg Museum. The French Government also owns the bronze group entitled "Red Cross," which is in the Musée des Invalides.

During the World War, Mrs. Whitney gave much of her time to relief work of various kinds. In 1914, she established and maintained a hospital for wounded soldiers at Juilly, France, known as "American Ambulance Hospital, B." It was directed by a staff of twenty-five physicians, surgeons and nurses. It was later enlarged and continued for the duration of the war.

At the front she received impressions at first hand which she afterwards expressed in modelling a series of figures for "The Great Adventure of Young Men." Quoting Guy Pene du Bois in his article on Mrs. Whitney's exhibition of war sculpture: "Close she was to the men who were fighting and her vision was developed through sympathy and a realization of their suffering and heroism. In her war sketches her technique has an underlying quality that is mystic. Two large panels were conspicuous details of the Arch of Victory, which was erected at Twenty-fourth Street and Fifth Avenue as part of the formal welcome home of the Twenty-seventh Division, New York's Own, which returned in 1919, after seeing active service overseas. Although, technically speaking, her work on the panelled figures was extremely virile, yet it was notably the vehicle for the expression of deep pity for human suffering, feminine in inspiration, and free from the conventional symbolism that is without mystery."

"The memory of her service overseas was constantly revived when she returned home. She came to her studio from a war canteen, a war relief entertainment, or a war committee. And so she threw 'masses of clay together in the shapes of men,' men who were not merely men but men of war, men enveloped in the chaos of a mad dream, given their character by it."[1]

On Memorial Day, May 1922, there was unveiled in Mitchell Square at 168th Street and Broadway, Washington Heights, New York, the monument to the soldiers, sailors and marines of Upper Manhattan who died in the World War, and provided for by the Washington Heights Memorial Association representing the residents of that and the Inwood sections of the city. The subject of Mrs. Whitney's design, carried out in bronze, symbolizes the combined heroism and humanity of the American warrior. A sailor, wounded and in a drooping posture, is caught in the arms of a stalwart marine, while inclining at one side is the helmeted doughboy, who bends to receive the last words of the dying sailor. This monument received from the New York Society of Architects the 1923 medal for "the most meritorious monument erected during the year."

The equestrian statue to be erected in memory of Buffalo Bill (Colonel William F. Cody) was unveiled at Cody, Wyoming, July 4, 1924.

In 1922, she was also commissioned to make a design for the memorial to the Fourth Division. This memorial is a single figure depicting the ideal American Soldier and is to be erected in Arlington Cemetery, Washington, District of Columbia.

In an article on the exhibition of Mrs. Whitney's work held in Paris, 1922, Mr. Léonce Bénédite, Director of the Luxembourg Museum, wrote: "A glance reveals that the two dominant characteristics of this sculptor's works are the virility of her technique and a marked sense for the decorative in her compositions. It is, therefore, not surprising that this dual quality should lead Mrs. Whitney to express herself monumentally."

When the Paris exhibit was invited to London it was received enthusiastically and one of those who wrote of it, Richard Fletcher, in the London Graphic, said: "These statues are real, poignant, decorative, as only good taste can decorate, and with a tenacious quality which comes from the woman's vision of life and history."

In December, 1922, Gertrude Whitney was requested to present a retrospective exhibition of her work. This was held at the Wildenstein Galleries, New York, and represented twenty years of production. The following works were included:

Titanic Memorial	Duryea Memorial
Washington Heights and Inwood Memorial	
Aztec Fountain	
Arlington Fountain	
"Gassed"	Fourth Division Memorial
"Honorably Discharged"	
Chinoise	
"In the Trenches"	Buffalo Bill
Gray Stone Figure	
Pan	
Boy with Pipes	
"Paganisme"	The Aviator
Bacchante	
Red Cross Group	
Château Thierry	
Colored Soldier	"Orders"
"His Last Charge"	
Jo Davison	
Barbara	
Caryatid	
Wherefore	Monument to a Sculptor
"Home Again"	
"Sighted"	
Colonel X	
Captain S	Refugees
Flora	
Victory Arch Panels	
The Nun	
Portrait Medallion	Doors of El Dorado
Head, Titanic Memorial (Belgian Marble)	
Studies No. 1 and No. 2 Head, Titanic Memorial (Marble)	
Spanish Peasant	American Athlete
Panel from Field House, Lenox	
"His Bunkie",	
Boy with Parrot	The Law
Lieutenant W.	
Stone Head	
Sheilah	Sketch for a War Memorial

The Honorary Degree of Master of Arts was conferred upon her by New York University.

[1] Guy Pene du Bois. An Exhibition of Sculpture by Gertrude V. Whitney, 1919.

LOCKE, BESSIE, daughter of William Henry and Jane M. (Schauler) Locke, was born at Arlington, Massachusetts. Through her father (born Boston, Massachusetts, 1837; died, New York City, 1917), she is descended from Deacon William Locke, a native of London, England (Stepney Parish), who, at the age of six years, in 1634, was brought by his parents to Woburn, Massachusetts. Captain Benjamin Locke, a paternal ancestor, fought in the first battle of the Revolutionary War. Through her mother (born, Arlington, Massachusetts, 1838; died, Brooklyn, New York, 1900), she is descended from William Dodge, a native of England, who located in Salem, Massachusetts in 1629.

Miss Locke has always taken a keen and practical interest in educational matters, particularly those pertaining to juvenile welfare. For some time she was Pastor's Assistant at All Soul's Church, Brooklyn, New York. One of her first connections with kindergarten work was in the capacity of Financial Secretary of the Brooklyn Free Kindergarten Association and the New York Kindergarten Association. Miss Locke performed highly important service as one of the organizers of the National Kindergarten Association, in 1909, and since that time has served efficiently as its Corresponding Secretary. In 1913, as a result of the prominence that she had obtained in this field, she was appointed Chief of the Kindergarten Division of the United States Bureau of Education, Washington, District of Columbia.

Having perceived the great need of more kindergarten facilities in New York City, Miss Locke expended much time and effort to the end that they might be provided. She was highly successful, in securing adequate endowments for four mission kindergartens in Greater New York. She is National Chairman of the Kindergarten Extension of the Congress of Mothers and the Parent Teacher Association; a trustee of the Brooklyn Free

Kindergarten Society; a director of the National Kindergarten Association; and a member of the Board of Directors of the National Council of Women. Miss Locke has been a frequent contributor to newspapers and periodicals on the subject of kindergarten education.

THE NATIONAL KINDERGARTEN ASSOCIATION

The educational value of the early years of childhood is now widely recognized and the kindergarten is acknowledged to be the type of education best suited to the development of very young children.

Frederick Froebel, founder of this system of training, believing that it was too democratic to receive ready acceptance in his own country, looked to America for the consummation of his hopes. He was right, for many of our educational leaders have been warm advocates of his method of furnishing mental, moral, social and physical training for little children, and the kindergarten is now a recognized part of the public school system in every state.

The National Kindergarten Association was incorporated in 1909, for the purpose of promoting the establishment of a sufficient number of kindergartens for all of the 4,500,000 children of kindergarten age in the country, less than 500,000 of whom were then enjoying this educational advantage.

The importance of giving more attention to early training has recently been strongly emphasized by the statement that our criminal classes are costing $3,500,000 a day—and that 507 children committed suicide during the first half of the year 1921, more than double the number who took their lives during the same period in 1920.

In 1913, Doctor P. P. Claxton, United States Commissioner of Education, invited the National Kindergarten Association to coöperate with him in establishing a Kindergarten Division in the Bureau of Education at Washington. This was done, the Association providing a Chief of the Division and several specialists, until July, 1919, when Congress passed a bill which terminated the coöperation between the Bureau of Education and the many organizations which were assisting in its work. However, the affiliation, which lasted for over six years, provided an excellent opportunity for doing important work, which, otherwise, would have been almost impossible of accomplishment.

The lack of accurate information on the various phases of the kindergarten subject indicated the necessity for thorough investigations. The Association and the Bureau of Education, in coöperation, conducted a survey of the schools for training kindergarten teachers, which disclosed a lack of uniformity of ideals and standards. A survey of state laws revealed a serious need for their revision in nearly every state in the Union. A compilation of complete statistics of kindergartens, private, public and mission, gathered for the first time, showed that only one child in nine was receiving this educational advantage, to which every child is entitled in a country advocating equal privileges for all.

The statistics gathered and the information on existing kindergarten legislation were printed and issued in Bulletin form by the Government, as were also the data regarding schools for training kindergarten teachers, the opinions of school superintendents and primary teachers on the practical value of kindergarten education, and excerpts from letters written by persons in charge of charitable institutions which provide this training for their little ones.

Through the generosity of one of its board members, the association sent Miss Elizabeth Harrison, then President of the National Kindergarten College, to Rome, to attend Mme. Montessori's first class for teachers, and the Bureau issued a Bulletin entitled "The Montessori Method and the Kindergarten," written by Miss Harrison, after she had conducted three Montessori classes in Chicago for different types of children.

It was during the affiliation with the Federal Government that field work was started in California, which passed a law in 1913 providing for the establishment of classes upon petition of parents. A Field Secretary of the National Kindergarten Association was appointed a Special Collaborator of the Bureau. The result of her efforts during the first year was fifty six new kindergartens, and to the fall of 1921, she has been instrumental in opening 387 classes in 194 different cities and towns. It is estimated that more than 100,000 children have already enjoyed the advantages of the new classes thus opened on the Pacific Coast, and it is gratifying to consider that every year this number will automatically increase.

The value of legislation in promoting kindergarten extension having been demonstrated in California, special efforts have been made by the Association to have similar laws enacted in the other states of the Union. Because of ignorance and indifference on the part of legislators, many of the attempts have failed, but laws patterned after that of California have been passed in Nevada, Texas, Maine, Arizona, Wisconsin, Kansas and Pennsylvania. Unfortunately, in some of these states it was impossible to secure the legislation until the bills had been so modified as seriously to impair their value. In several instances it was necessary to change the wording from "Must be established upon petition of parents" to "May be established, etc." However, any progressive legislation is considered better than defeat. Three times such bills have been introduced into the New York Legislature without being passed, although they had the endorsement of practically every state organization interested in civic welfare.

In the states where favorable laws have been secured the Association has conducted field work to the extent of its resources. Its efforts have been seriously curtailed by its limited income, for it is dependent solely upon voluntary gifts. But the co-operation of the Federal Bureau of Education, and other organizations, such as the National Council of Women, with its 10,000,000 members, has been of inestimable value in arousing interest in this subject, now recognized as in vital relation to the future welfare of the nation.

Commissioner Claxton had an especially keen sense of the importance of forming right habits of thought and action early in life, and in 1917, in coöperation with the Association, he instituted a service to help parents train their children in their homes. Articles on kindergarten methods were secured from mothers who were formerly kindergarten teachers, and these were issued, upon request, to 3,000 newspapers and magazines having a combined circulation of over 50,000,000. This service has been continued without interruption for four years. The first year's series was printed in bulletin form by the Bureau of Education, 13,500 copies being issued free, and 17,000 copies sold by the Government Printing Office for fifteen cents each. Letters received from mothers prove that this service is meeting a great need. One woman wrote, "Send me your articles and send them quick, and if there is any charge I will gladly pay it. My children have me nearly distracted."

The Association is constantly utilizing every possible means of creating a public demand for kindergartens—through propaganda articles issued to neswpapers and magazines, propaganda leaflets, and correspondence with organizations and individuals who desire information and advice in establishing kindergartens.

The practical value of kindergarten education has been demonstrated beyond question. The task remains to bring about the early establishment of a sufficient number of classes to provide for all of the 4,000,000 children between four and six years of age, who are now being deprived of their rights. This is a difficult enterprise with innumerable obstacles to be surmounted—but a clear vision of the goal ahead and practical methods for accomplishment point to the ultimate achievement of the most far-reaching effort ever made for the ethical and material welfare of the nation.

WOOD, ELIZABETH OGDEN BROWER

(Mrs. Henry A. Wise Wood), was born in New York City in 1873. Her father, John Lefoy Brower, was a member of a family which had lived in New York for over three hundred years. The first of the line was Pieter Clementsen Brower, who was born at Hoorn, The Netherlands, in 1580. He was part owner of the ship *Fortune*, which first sailed to America in 1612, and the States General of Holland gave him extensive trading rights with the New Netherlands in 1614, the year in which he came to New Amsterdam.

The mother of John Lefoy Brower was of the Ogden family which settled in Stamford, Connecticut, in 1641. A year later John Ogden, and his brother Richard, constructed in the fort, by order of Governor Kieft, the first stone church in New York.

John Lefoy Brower has taken an active interest in civic work, and is responsible for many improvements in New York. It was through his efforts that the city now has its splendid traffic system, as it was due to his insistence that, in 1893, the first policeman to regulate vehicular traffic in New York was stationed at 42nd Street and Fifth Avenue. The present system of street signs is also the result of his work.

Mr. Brower married Adelia C. Hartley, the daughter of Robert Milham Hartley, who was born at Cockermouth, Cumberland, England, in 1796 and died in New York in 1881. He was a leading philanthropist in New York, the founder in 1829 of the New York Temperance Society, and, in 1844, of the New York Association for Improving the Condition of the Poor. He was also a supporter of the Presbyterian Hospital, the Workingmen's Home, the Juvenile Asylum, and other charitable institutions. He began the first crusade for pure milk.

He married in 1824 Catharine, the daughter of Reuben Munson, who was fifth in descent from Ensign Samuel Munson (1643–1693), a founder of Wallingford, Connecticut, and a soldier in King Philip's War. His father was Captain Thomas Munson (1612–1783) who settled in New Haven, Connecticut, served with distinction in the Pequot War (1637), was sergeant of the Train Band in 1642, ensign from 1661 to 1664, lieutenant in King Philip's War (1675), and captain in 1676.

Robert M. Hartley was the son of Isaac, who was born in Cockermouth, in 1766, came to America in 1797 with his wife, Isabelle, the daughter of Joseph Johnson of Embledon, England, and died at Perth, New York, in 1851. Isaac's father, Robert Hartley (born at Boughton, England, in 1736; died at Cockermouth in 1803), in 1754 married Martha Smithson, the daughter of Isaac Smithson, and granddaughter of Sir Hugh Smithson, Bart.[1] Robert Hartley was the son of James[2] Hartley of Boughton (1739–1776), whose father was Doctor David Hartley, the psychologist and author of *Observations on Man* (1749). The latter's father was the Reverend David Hartley, vicar of Armley, Yorkshire.

Mrs. Wood was educated by private tutors and attended Miss Peebles' and Miss Thompson's school from 1884 to 1890. In 1891 she was married in New York to Henry Alexander Wise Wood, the inventor and writer. He was born in New York, March 1, 1866, and was the son of Fernando and Alice F. (Mills) Wood. Fernando Wood served as Mayor of New York for several terms, and was a member of Congress for twenty years. Drake Mills, father of Mrs. Fernando Wood, was the second President of the Delaware Lackawanna and Western Railway Company.

Henry A. Wise Wood was awarded by the Franklin Institute in 1908 the Elliott Cresson gold medal for his invention of the autoplate, a machine for automatically making printing plates for newspapers. His inventions have revolutionized the newspaper printing press by doubling its capacity.

He is the author of a volume of poems entitled *Fancies*, published in 1903, and of *The Book of Symbols* (1904), and *Money Hunger* (1908), and of many pamphlets dealing with the war necessities of the nation. He founded the magazine, *Flying*, and was for many years its editor, and was Vice-President of the Aero Club of America.

In 1915 Mr. Wood was a member of the United States Naval Consulting Board, and Chairman of the Conference Committee on National Preparedness founded in 1915. In 1916 he founded the Patriotic Education Society, and was first President of the American Society of Aeronautic Engineers, and in 1919 he founded the League for the Preservation of American Independence, for the purpose of opposing the entrance of the United States into the League of Nations. He is President of the Wood Newspaper Machinery Corporation, and of other corporations.

Mr. and Mrs. Wood are the parents of one daughter, Elizabeth Brower Wood, who in 1916 was married to John Cyrus Distler of Baltimore, Maryland. They have one daughter, Hope Hartley Distler, born in 1918. Mrs. Distler was closely identified with war work in Baltimore, and is Chairman for Baltimore of the Maryland Section of the Woman's Roosevelt Memorial Association.

Mrs. Wood like her husband, has been a strong advocate of national preparedness, and an active participant in national affairs. In 1915, 1916 and 1917 she took an energetic part in the campaign for national defense. With the entrance of the United States into the World War, she assisted in the development of aeronautics, and organized committees to give aid to the military and naval aviators of this country. She also wrote and lectured on national defense and on aeronautics, and published many aeronautical translations from the French.

Convinced that the extension of the franchise to women would merely increase the illiterate and Socialist vote, she opposed such an extension with her pen and on the lecture platform.

Deep sea cruising and photography have been her relaxations from national activities. She was a member of the Navy Red Cross and the National Aeronautic Committee, and is one of the founders and Vice-Presidents of the Woman's Roosevelt Memorial Association. This Association was formed for the purpose of securing Theodore Roosevelt's birthplace at 28 East 20th Street, New York, and of restoring it to become an active centre of Americanization. Mrs. Wood is also Chairman of its National Organization Committee, and has helped rouse interest in this new national institution throughout the world. She is also a member of the Executive Committee of the Woman's Department of the National Civic Federation.

---

[1] This Sir Hugh was father of Sir Hugh Smithson, 1st Duke of Northumberland. The latter's son, Lord Percy, afterwards 2nd Duke of Northumberland, played an active part as a major general on the British side in the American Revolution. His brother, James Smithson, founded, through a bequest of $515,169, the Smithsonian Institute at Washington, D. C.

[2] James Hartley's brother, David Hartley (1729-1813), was the friend of Franklin, an English plenipotentiary to sign the Treaty of Paris between the United States and England in 1783.

WENDELL, EDITH GREENOUGH (Mrs. Barrett Wendell), was born in Swampscott, Massachusetts, August 2, 1859, daughter of William Whitwell Greenough. She is a descendant of Captain William Greenough, and his wife, Catherine Scollay Curtis. Her education was received at Miss Sanger's and Miss Mary Forte's schools in Boston, Massachusetts, and she was married June 1, 1880, at Quincy, Massachusetts, to Barrett Wendell, son of Jacob and Mary Bertodi (Barrett) Wendell. Mr. Wendell was born in Boston, August 23, 1855, and until 1918 was Professor of English at Harvard University. They were

the parents of Barrett Wendell, Jr., Mary
Barrett (Mrs. R. G. A. Van der Wonde),
William Greenough, and Edith Wendell (Mrs.
Charles F. Osborne).

Since 1903, Mrs. Wendell has been President of the Massachusetts Society of Colonial
Dames of America, whose objects are to collect
and preserve manuscripts, traditions, relics,
and mementos of bygone days; to preserve
and restore buildings connected with the
early history of the country; to diffuse
healthful and intelligent information concerning the past; to create a popular interest
in colonial history; to stimulate a spirit of
true patriotism and a genuine love of country;
and to impress upon the young people the
obligation of honoring the memory of those
heroic ancestors whose achievements are
beyond all praise. In addition the society is
engaged in the work of Americanization in all
its phases.

In 1907, Mrs. Wendell was appointed by the
Governor of Massachusetts, State Commissioner to the Jamestown Exposition. From
the beginning of the World War, Mrs.
Wendell served on many war relief committees, including the War Camp Community committees at Camp Devens, Massachusetts; and at Portsmouth, New Hampshire. She was a member, also, of the Boston
Women's Committee for Food Conservation
and the Boston Committee of Public Service,
by appointment of the Mayor of Boston and
served as Vice-Chairman of both. Her most
conspicuous service, however, was with the
Massachusetts Branch of the Special Aid
Society for American Preparedness, of which
she was President from its formation in 1915.
The primary purpose of the society was
expressed in its slogan: "immediate service
without red tape." Its objects are to encourage and promote patriotic education, sentiment, and service among the people and to
aid in the establishment and maintenance of
the national defense.

ALEXANDER, FRANCES GORDON
PADDOCK (Mrs. William Alexander), is
President of the National Special Aid Society,
which was organized in January, 1915, and
incorporated in July, 1916, with Mrs. Charles
Frederick Hoffman as Vice-President and
Mrs. Henry A. Wise Wood as Secretary. Its
object is to mobilize the women throughout
the United States for service to their country,
and, should occasion arise, in the wider needs
of humanity. It is a permanent, non-partisan
body with organized chapters in different
states as centres of local activity. These
chapters stimulate Americanism in such
various lines of study as shall carry out the
aims of the society, coöperating with, and
helping to coördinate, existing workers and
agencies. Its activities include training in
educational, domestic, industrial, hygienic,
and community work, as well as relief in the
event of any great local or national disaster.
The Society has created a volunteer corps of
women, enrolling them by means of service
pledges, and, by a system of cross-indexing,
is ready to call them up in any part of the
country for whatever aid, personal or material,
they can render. It stands also for universal
military training and service as the most
democratic system of defense, and has especially encouraged the Plattsburg Military
Camps and the development of military
aviation. Its patriotic work, moreover, includes the holding of lectures to increase
national loyalty and the formation of classes
in wireless telegraphy, signalling, and swin-
ming, and instruction in the driving of auto-
mobiles, motor-cycles, and motor boats, and
in camp sanitation and cooking.

In the field of relief work the Society has
arranged for the making of surgical supplies
and extra clothing for the military and naval
reserves, the packing of comfort kits for men
in active service, and the listing of hospital
stores for emergencies. It has assisted needy
women by giving them employment in cutting,
sewing, and knitting, and has rendered aid
and service to the sufferers of countries at

war. Again, in the field of industrial preparedness, the Society has provided instruction, under its Department of Home Economics, in thrift and food values, and, under the direction of the United States Department of Agriculture, in scientific gardening, canning, poultry raising, bee farming, and the making of daily products. It maintains a carefully selected library of home economics, and a bureau of information, whose secretary is informed in all matters of service to the housekeeper.

In addition to developing its general program, the Society, during the World War, rendered special aid of great value in several directions. It sent hospital supplies and clothing to Belgium, Russia, Poland, Serbia, the Caucasus, Mesopotamia, Montenegro, France, Italy, and Uganda, much of the sewing being done by unemployed women in New York and some of the knitting by immigrants detained at Ellis Island. In this way the two-fold object of the Society was carried out—work provided for the unemployed at home, and supplies sent to sufferers abroad. In September, 1915, the Society—already definitely representing American women's efficiency in special relief work—inaugurated a general campaign for preparedness, and for adequate national defense, as a safeguard against invasion.

Public meetings, addressed by eminent men of the country, were held weekly at the Society's National Headquarters, and on February 23, 1916, it called, at Carnegie Hall, New York, the first patriotic rally in the city managed by women. At this meeting a large sum of money was raised to train aviators. During the first six months of this year over two hundred women were trained by the Society in New York, under the direction of Red Cross nurses, in home nursing and first aid, and thousands of others were enrolled as active members. With the mobilization of United States troops along the Mexican border, during the crisis of June, 1916, the Society had its first opportunity to show its

resources in an emergency. Under the advice of the highest military authorities, it was able to offer relief to the dependent families of militiamen, and to furnish such supplies, not already provided by the Government, as would add to the comfort and prevent illness of troops along the border. More than two thousand women were employed in making hospital supplies and more than one thousand in sewing, some of them wives of the guardsmen. Canteens were established in entraining stations and thousands of soldiers fed enroute; and a hospital unit was equipped and sent to the border; while by means of the service pledges and cross-indexing, houses that could be used for hospitals, motor cars, horses, personal service and material aid were in readiness for use. The epidemic of infantile paralysis in August, 1916, also gave the Society occasion for immediate service in sending nurses to the homes of afflicted children, providing braces and convalescent treatment, and instructing the children in useful forms of handicraft.

The subject of handicrafts is one in which Mrs. Alexander is deeply interested, and, under the auspices of the National Special Aid Society, she formed the *International Revival of Industrial Art*, to coöperate with artistic people in England and France to provide employment for competent women who can be taught to manufacture textiles, furnitures, embroideries, objets d'art, and a variety of decorative articles, copied from, or based on, the best examples of artistic design to be found in Europe. Thus the highest type of industrial art is preserved and encouraged, the producer and the buyer brought into touch, work of the best quality fostered, the worker's pride in his product stimulated, an appreciation on the part of the public in good workmanship awakened, lost arts among the peasantry of Europe restored, and profitable means of employment introduced to workers in the United States.

Mrs. Alexander's committee has the coöperation of many noted artists and art lovers in America and Europe, a group of these acting as a jury, to pass on the excellence of work offered for sale in the United States. In April, 1920, a preliminary exhibition was arranged by the Vice-President, Mrs. Nina Larrey Duryea, at the Duryea War Relief, New York, and in the fall of 1920 a large permanent exhibition was established. The sure market, offered through the International Revival of Industrial Art, to the peasants of Europe, has helped notably in reconstruction abroad after the World War, and means the preservation from extinction of many special local handicrafts of great beauty and value.

BOARDMAN, MABEL THORP, Red Cross official, was born in Cleveland, Ohio. Her mother, Florence Sheffield Boardman, was the daughter of Joseph Earl Sheffield, of New Haven, Connecticut, founder of the Sheffield Scientific School, of Yale University. Her father, William Jarvis Boardman, was a leading lawyer of Cleveland. He was a grandson of the Honorable Elijah Boardman, United States Senator from Connecticut, and a descendant of Samuel Boreman, of Banbury, Oxfordshire, England, and later of Claydon, who in 1638 settled at Ipswich, Massachusetts, and later at Wethersfield, Connecticut. The earliest known English Boardman ancestor was William Boreman of Banbury who paid taxes in the sixteenth year of the reign of Henry VIII (1525). Through his grandmother, Mr. Boardman was descended from Captain John Mason and William Whiting and also from Governor William Bradford, who with his wife, Alice, the daughter of William Carpenter, went with the Pilgrims to Leyden in 1610 and thence to Plymouth in 1620. Miss Boardman was educated in private schools in Cleveland, Ohio, in New York, and later in Europe. In 1889 her family moved to Washington, District of Columbia, where she has since made her home. Since 1905 she has been a leading official of the American Red Cross

serving as a member of the Executive Council, Chairman of the National Relief Board, and Chairman of the District of Columbia Chapter. It was through her interest and active leadership that the Red Cross was reformed, reorganized and made an agency available, in times of disaster, to the people of the United States and of the world. She directed the activities of the organization after the Messina earthquake, the floods in the Mississippi Valley, and other great natural catastrophes. During the World War she supervised the shipping of surgical dressings to Europe and made many trips of inspection to the battle fronts. As Chairman of the Women's Volunteer Aid of the District of Columbia Chapter, she directed local activities in Washington during the mobilization of troops and during the influenza epidemic of 1917-1918. In 1907 Miss Boardman was United States delegate to the Eighth International Red Cross Conference in London, and again a delegate in 1912 to the Ninth International Red Cross Conference in Washington. She is the author of *Under the Red Cross Flag* (1st edition, 1915; 2d edition, 1917). In recognition of her work for humanity she received the honorary degrees of A.M. at Yale University in 1911 and of LL.D. at Western Reserve University and Smith College. In 1909 she was decorated by the King of Sweden with the King's Order of Merit, by the Italian government with the Gold Civic Crown, and in 1912 by the Emperor of Japan with the Fifth Order of the Crown. She has also received Red Cross decorations from Portugal, Japan, and Serbia, and the medal of the American Institute of Social Sciences. At the third annual mobilization of the uniformed corps of the District of Columbia Chapter, March 16, 1920, she was presented with a testimonial, prepared by Admiral Seaton Schroeder, U. S. N., as follows: "It was your early vision of probable needs that prepared the way, and it was your intuitive insight that guided our steps through the mists of an unknown atmosphere over an untrodden field. Only to those who have striven to carry out your ideals is it given to understand in what degree has successful achievement waited upon your personality." In 1920 President Wilson appointed Miss Boardman to the Board of Commissioners of the District of Columbia. She is a member of the Society of Colonial Dames, the Daughters of the American Revolution, the Congressional Club of Washington, and the Colony Club of New York.

COLE, ANNA RUSSELL (Mrs. E. W. Cole), philanthropist, daughter of Henry F. and Martha (Danforth) Russell, was born in Augusta, Georgia. She is the widow of the distinguished railroad official. At the time of her marriage she was considered the most brilliant and beautiful woman in the South, and was called "the Pride of Georgia." She is now called "the Woman of Yesterday, Today and Tomorrow." Her life is an interesting one from many standpoints, as she has been a patroness of education and social advancement. Her home, Colemere, near Nashville, Tennessee, has always been the scene of many notable functions for men and women of international interest and distinction. She spends her winters in Washington, District of Columbia, where she is the centre of a large circle of literary, artistic, and social personages. It is in her home however that she is best known and beloved. Here she reigns a queen, looking well to the ways of her household. She entertains lavishly, and dispenses a wide hospitality, both at Colemere and in Washington. She is quoted as saying, "The best society is inclusive, and not exclusive." With her husband, she was the founder of the Tennessee Industrial School, in which thousands of girls and boys have been fitted for useful and happy lives. As a memorial to Colonel Cole, Mrs. Cole founded the Cole Lectureship at Vanderbilt University. She also founded the Southern Sociological Congress. Mrs. Cole presented to the city of Augusta, Georgia, a granite monument to four great singers of the South. The monument consists of four columns rising from a tall base and supporting a roof of granite. Inside of the upright columns is a block of granite, bearing on its four sides an inscription to each of the four poets with a thought from the writings of each:

SIDNEY LANIER, 1842–1880
"The Catholic man who has mightily won
God out of knowledge and good out of infinite pain
And sight out of blindness and purity out of stain."

FATHER RYAN, 1842–1880
"To the higher shrine of love divine
My lowly feet have trod.
I want no fame, no other name
Than this—'a priest of God.' "

JAMES R. RANDALL, 1839–1908
"Better the fire upon the roll,
Better the blade, the shot, the bowl,
Than crucifixion of the soul,
Maryland, My Maryland."

PAUL HAYNE, 1830–1886
"Yet would I rather in the outward state
Of song's immortal temple lay me down,
A beggar, basking by thy radiant gate,
Than bow beneath the haughtiest empire's crown."

Mrs. Cole's only son, Whiteford Russell Cole, is President of the Nashville, Chattanooga and St. Louis Railway. Her only daughter, who has inherited her mother's classic beauty, is married to Mr. Dempsey Weaver, a man of social and financial importance.

FREER, ELEANOR EVEREST (Mrs. Archibald E. Freer), composer, was born in Philadelphia, Pennsylvania. She is the daughter of Cornelius and Ellen Amelia (Clark) Everest, both descended from old Connecticut families, the former of Windham, the latter of Farmington. After attendance at private and public schools in Philadelphia, she went in 1883 to Paris, where for three years she was a pupil in vocal music of Mathilde Marchesi, and of Benjamin Godard in diction. Later, in 1902–1907, she studied theory with Bernhard Ziehn in Chicago. On April 25, 1892, she was married at St. George's Church, New York, to Archibald E. Freer of Chicago, and their only child, Eleanor (Mrs. Russell Willson), was born in 1894 in Leipzig, Germany.

Mrs. Freer has composed settings—solos, trios, quartets—to over one hundred and fifty standard and classic lyrics in English, as well as several works for the piano. She advocates vocal music in the vernacular, as necessary to the development of a native music, insisting that, with a proper attention to diction, English words can be made as perfect a vehicle for song as words in a foreign language.

Bernhard Ziehn has said of her song cycle, *Forty-Four Sonnets from the Portuguese*, that it "is a colossal work. So far as my knowledge reaches, I know of nothing that could with justice be placed beside it. It is marvelous enough that such sentiments could be poetically expressed by one person, and more so that another could place these wonderful sonnets in a musical setting, and of the highest order."

During the World War, from 1914 to 1918, Mrs. Freer was engaged in war relief in France with the Red Cross, receiving the Distinguished Service Medal for her services. She was also chairman of the War Relief Club of Chicago and of the Chicago Committee of the French Red Cross and was its official representative in Chicago. In 1918 she was the founder, and has since acted as the treasurer of the Paris "Chicago Hospital" Foundation, a corporation to build in Paris a memorial hospital for general cases, as Illinois' gift to France, which will be thoroughly modern in its equipment and will have special departments for women and children, and for facial and dental surgery and other reparative work. In May, 1921, she founded the "Opera in our Language

Foundation, Inc.," an organization to further in every possible way opera in our language in the United States of America. Affiliated with this, the David Bispham Memorial Fund, Inc., was founded in March, 1922. Mrs. Freer is a member of the League of American Penwomen, the Society for the Promotion of Opera in English, the Fortnightly and Friday Clubs, the Musicians Club of Women, the New York Manuscript Society, etc.

LEIGHT, ANGELINA (Mrs. Edward A. Leight), was born in Chicago, Illinois, September 2, 1875. Her father, Fred Madleuer, of Chicago, was born in Baden, Germany; her mother, Marguerite Blatz, was the daughter of Albert Blatz who came from Bavaria to New York in 1849. Her marriage to Edward A. Leight, who was born in Jersey City, New Jersey, took place in Chicago on May 12, 1892, and they are the parents of Albert Edward Leight, born in Chicago, July 17, 1894.

Mrs. Leight's education, a large part of which was received abroad, gave her a command of languages and developed a strong interest in the arts. She has translated Gustave Kobbé's *Lives of the Great Composers* for the Spanish edition, and she is an active member of the Drama League, the Arts Club, and the Cordon Club of Chicago. Her varied interests are shown by her membership in the Chicago Woman's Club, the Chicago City Club, the Antiquarian Society, the Cercle Français, the Alliance Française, the Friends of China, the Chicago Council on Foreign Relations, and the Woman's Athletic Club.

During the World War she raised large sums for the Red Cross and the Fatherless Children of France by means of concerts and motion picture entertainments at her house, but it was her experience in the various Liberty Loan campaigns that caused Mrs. Irving L. Stern, director of the Advisory Council of the Woman's Department of the Federal Securities Corporation, to appoint her as a member of the Council.

The Federal Securities Corporation was formed after the armistice by the men who had composed the Chicago Liberty Loan Committee and, because of the work done by the women of the city on this committee, they were invited actively to participate. A Woman's Department was formed to give attention to the business of women, assisting them in the selection of safe and secure bonds.

The Department specializes in the education of women in all questions of finance, conducting a monthly class at the Hotel La Salle to which all women are invited without expense or obligation. This class, at which well-known bankers are the speakers, has assumed the form of a civic enterprise and has an average attendance of upwards of a thousand women.

The Advisory Council lends every assistance and protection possible to women investors. Its duties include a monthly meeting with the director to discuss various projects and the best methods for the success of the Department and of sponsoring the monthly classes in finance.

MORRISON, ABBY PUTNAM, radio operator, singer and sportswoman, daughter of David Mitchell and Abby Matilda (Putnam) Morrison, was born in New York City. Her father is a grandson of David Morrison, who came from Aberdeen, Scotland, in 1790, and settled at New Orleans. Through her mother, she traces descent from John Putnam (1589–1662), who came from Buckinghamshire, England, in 1634, and settled at Salem, Massachusetts. Her great-grandfather, General Nathaniel Putnam, was a brother of General Rufus Putnam, of historic fame.

Miss Morrison received her early education in Miss Chapin's School, and the Brearley School in New York City, Miss Vinton's School at Ridgefield, Connecticut, and Miss Porter's School at Farmington, Connecticut. At the outbreak of the World War, Miss Morrison was in Paris, and began to train as a nurse, but returned to New York, and, after a

course at the Young Women's Christian Association, was graduated as a trained attendant. She learned the Morse code through flag signaling at a girl's camp during the summer, and later attended the Marconi School, from which she received a diploma, and, after examination by the United States Government, was licensed as a first-class commercial wireless operator. Meanwhile, she had been enrolled in the United States Navy as a first-class electrician radio, and in November, 1917, she was placed on the reserve list. The Marconi Company was in the Government service during the war, and, as inspector on all the foreign troop transports, Miss Morrison was the only woman to act in that capacity and the only woman enrolled in the Navy. She was also the first woman to act as tester of navy wireless apparatus in the Marconi laboratories.

The following year she organized and was elected President of a league composed of women who had studied and were interested in radio. In November, 1920, Miss Morrison attended the Disarmament Conference at Washington as an onlooker, and was engaged by the Pond Lecture Bureau to give a series of talks on "Behind the Scenes of the Disarmament Conference." In 1921, when Lady Astor attended the Baltimore Convention, Miss Morrison was present as a representative in wireless and personally sent Lady Astor's message to the women of America from Washington to New York by a series of relay wireless stations. In that summer, in the first experiment of broadcasting by radio, she installed and operated a wireless receiving apparatus on the roof of the American Theatre on 42nd Street, to receive for the audience details of the Dempsey-Carpentier fight.

After the Disarmament Conference, the radio craze burst suddenly all over the country, and Miss Morrison was asked to write one of a series of seven books in collaboration with six of the most prominent engineers and scientists in the country. These books were edited by General Squires, Chief of the Signal Corps. While with the Marconi Company she gave private instruction in radio to some of the young aviators, and later was asked to take charge of a class of girls in radio at the Young Women's Christian Association. In May, 1921, she was head of the radio committee at the Society Street Fair for Charity on Park Avenue. At this fair she installed a station for listening-in, and, while the orchestra was playing some miles away, she arranged for the first exhibition of dancing to radio music on an out-of-doors platform by Miss Florence Walton. Since that time Miss Morrison has been active in writing on radio conditions for the American and English newspapers and magazines while experimenting on her own set. Within the past two years, Miss Morrison has resumed the study and practice of music, interrupted by the World War and her keen interest in radio. She has sung many times professionally, both in concert and opera, has met with great success, and still continues her professional career both in America and abroad.

In 1918, she was elected a member of the Institute of Radio Engineers, the only woman ever elected to the Institute. She is also a member of the Junior League of New York, West Side and Forest Hills Tennis Clubs, the Agawamie Club, the Alumnae Association of Miss Chapin's School, the Grosvenor Neighborhood Association, and the Union Music School Settlement.

HOLT, WINIFRED (Mrs. Rufus Graves Mather) sculptor, author, and philanthropist, was born in New York City. Her father, Henry Holt, author and publisher, and son of Dan and Ann E. (Siebold) Holt, was born in Baltimore, Maryland, January 3, 1840, and on June 11, 1863, married Mary Florence West, who died March 7, 1879.

She was educated at the Brearley and other private schools, New York, and studied art in Florence, Italy, and elsewhere in Europe and America. Her principal works in sculpture have been portraits and bas-reliefs, including one of Helen Keller, which has been widely reproduced. She has exhibited at the Architectural League and the National Sculpture Society, New York, and in Florence, Italy, and elsewhere in Europe. She is the founder and honorary secretary of the New York Association for the Blind (1905) and of the Committee for the Prevention of Blindness, the first lay committee founded for this purpose which has become a world-wide movement. She also founded in 1906 the Ticket Bureaux for the Blind in America and Europe.

In 1908 she was a delegate to the International Convention of Workers for the Blind held in Manchester, England. Four years later she was instrumental in the opening of the Emma L. Hardy Memorial Home at Cornwall-on-Hudson, New York, and in 1913 in New York City of the Bourne Workshop for the Blind and the new building for the care and teaching of the blind (known as The Lighthouse), formally opened by President Taft. In the summer of 1914, she was again a delegate to the International Conference of Workers for the Blind, held in London, England, and was the bearer of an autograph letter from President Wilson containing his greetings and those of the American people. While there she was summoned as an expert by the Departmental Committee, appointed by the House of Commons to consider the subject of the blind.

At the same period the National Institute for the Blind in London solicited her permission to issue an edition in Braille of her book, *A Beacon for the Blind, a Short Life of Henry Fawcett, the Blind Postmaster-General of England, for Children Everywhere*, first published in 1911, with an introduction by Lord Bryce. This work has also been translated into French, with an introduction by the Marquis de Vogué, and has been extensively quoted by clergymen and orators.

In June, 1915, she helped to reorganize the

Travailleurs du Sud-Ouest in Bordeaux, France, which became the Phare de Bordeaux, the first Lighthouse for the war blind on the Continent. Later she organized the Phare de France, the French Lighthouse, at 14 rue Daru, Paris, which, with its affiliated French Committees, is incorporated under the French Law. This Lighthouse was formally opened by the President of the French Republic and the American Ambassador, in 1916. Through its efforts the first blind of the A. E. F. were found, relieved and taught, and the first group of American War blind was brought to America with the assistance of one of its teachers, who entered the service of the United States Army, to help the blind at the headquarters of the A. E. F.

For the support of this work among the blinded soldiers, Miss Holt had already formed the Comité Franco-Américain pour les Aveugles de la Guerre in Paris, and the Committee for Men Blinded in Battle, with headquarters in New York. In November, 1916, she returned to New York and spoke there and elsewhere to raise funds for the Phares. She returned to France again in October, 1917, to engage personally in the work of re-education. At the Phare de France blinded soldiers received a thorough training for trades and professions. It had an electric printing press, and issued a magazine and up-to-date books in large editions.

Out-teachers constantly taught in the hospitals, and were summoned, whenever physicians found or feared blindness in any soldier. Miss Holt herself usually attended new cases, especially when the patients had not been told that they were blind, and still had bandages over their eyes. In New York, before the war, she had been called "The Lady of the Lighthouse," and she was now named "la Gardienne de Phare."

At the Phare in Bordeaux men were trained in manual labor. At a third Phare at Sevres they were taught reading, writing, and arithmetic, and were employed by the French Government in the Sevres potteries. There were also two other Phares at Vichy (a club, etc.) and Neuilly-Plaisance. For pupils who had completed the course, follow-up work was undertaken, to see that they were successful in their situations. Many returned to the Phare to help in teaching and entertaining the men in training. Later, in 1919, she went to Italy at the invitation of the Italian Government, and founded a Lighthouse in Rome, Italy, which, by Royal Decree, in 1920, was incorporated as an "Ente Morale."

During four years over $200,000 was raised in the United States for the work of the Phares, and about 900 blind soldiers were re-educated and given the means of self-support, and hundreds of others were aided in hospitals and elsewhere.

On April 10, 1918, she received the Medaille de Reconnaisance, of the highest order, at the request of the President of France. Toward the end of the war she received a Life Saving Medal from Belgium. From May, 1920 to October, 1920 she was in Italy establishing the Rome lighthouse. She received the Gold Medal of the Sanita Pubblica (Health Department) from the Italian Government for her work for the blind. In 1921, while in America, she received the Cross of a Knight of the Legion of Honor from the French Government.

Toward the end of 1921 she went to Poland, at the request of the Polish Government, as their guest, and founded a Lighthouse in Warsaw. In February, 1922, the Headquarters of the Rome Lighthouse was officially opened in its own building by the Queen of Italy and the American Ambassador. In the autumn of the same year she returned to the United States, and, on November 16th, was married to Rufus Graves Mather. At the request of the Board of Directors and the blind the ceremony took place in the Assembly Hall of the New York Association for the Blind, the Bishop of New York officiating, assisted by the Chaplain of Columbia University. In the same month her book, *The Light which Cannot Fail* was published. It consists of stories relating to the blind of several countries, who had been aided by her, and a *Handbook for the Blind and their Friends*. It has received the highest praise from the press, students, experts and others. She is a member of the National Institute of Social Sciences, which bestowed on her its Gold Medal.

HAY, MARY GARRETT, reformer along political, civic and educational lines, daughter of Andrew Jennings and Rebecca C. (Garrett) Hay, was born at Charlestown, Indiana. Her father was a physician, and all his forebears from Colonial days have been professional men, lawyers, clergymen and physicians. Her mother was of a Pennsylvania family of Scotch-Irish ancestry. Doctor Hay was greatly interested in politics, and entertained at his home many of the leading statesmen and politicians of his day. Thus, at a very early age, Miss Hay became accustomed to meet and mingle with people, a talent that has made her a leader since her girlhood.

She was educated in the schools of Charlestown, and subsequently was graduated at "The Western," a college for women at Oxford, Ohio.

Miss Hay was the President of the New York State Federation of Women's Clubs from 1910 to 1912, and of the New York Equal Suffrage League from 1910 to 1918; Chairman of the Woman's Suffrage Party from 1912 to 1920. She was the organizer of the National American Woman Suffrage Association, and for six years its President. When the passing of the Nineteenth Amendment completed the task to which she was so long devoted, and that association became interested in the League for Women Voters, Miss Hay devoted her attention to the work of educating women to become intelligent and independent voters. She realized that this end could be greatly assisted by associating herself with a woman's journal. The medium for this was at hand in the "Woman Citizen," of which she is the Director and Editor. For

four years her work has been almost entirely educational.

Miss Hay was the "father" of the amendment, passed in New York State in 1921, requiring all voters, both men and women, to be able to read and write the English language, thus effectually stopping the voting of illiterate women, who had received the franchise by virtue of their husband's naturalization. The following year she was sponsor for the Federal act requiring separate naturalization for husbands and wives, thus shutting off, at the source, a large number of possible voters who could never become intelligent citizens or competent to realize either the great value of the franchise or to understand even, the fundamentals upon which our government rests.

By "education," Miss Hay does not consider schools and curricula, *per se*, but rather their relation toward women in making them intelligent, efficient and able to work in industrial, business, professional and home-making lines. This education is built largely around the idea of giving to all classes of women opportunity for, and instruction in, the questions of the day, both small and large; in the fundamentals of good citizenship and in the great value of the vote. She teaches that it is the sacred duty of all women to register and to vote independently upon all questions of public policy. Nor does Miss Hay deem it wise to form a separate women's party. She believes that the most lasting reforms can be effected through an alliance with one of the great parties, but urges against too slavish an adherence to party organization candidates. Each candidate should be considered, not only as to party standing, but also as to trained ability requisite for the administration of the office sought. This applies to men as well as to women. In this way the field is opened for the election of trained and intelligent women to places in municipal and other offices for which they are especially equipped.

Miss Hay believes that political reforms can well be accomplished through the intelligent voting of educated women. The step she suggests is to join the local organization of the party chosen, to take an active interest in neighborhood politics and in the selection of that party's candidates. This, she believes, will ultimately result in the choice of candidates of the highest and most desirable class, and cannot fail to have a decidedly marked and beneficial effect upon local, state and federal office holders.

Miss Hay is an active member in many clubs and societies that back the principles for which she has so long fought. She is President of the Women's City Club of New York, and of the Daughters of Indiana; Second Vice-President of the National American Woman Suffrage Association; a member of the Political Study Club, the New Yorkers; the Woman's Press Club of New York City; the Woman's Municipal League; the Woman's Trade Union League; the Mary Murray Chapter of the Daughters of the American Revolution; the Auxiliary of the Salvation Army; the New York City Federation of Women's Clubs. She is also ex-President of the New York State Federation of Women's Clubs, and ex-Director of the General Federation of Women's Clubs.

DARLINGTON, ELLA LOUISE BEARNS (Mrs. James Henry Darlington), daughter of James Sterling and Elizabeth Jane (Cosgrove) Bearns, was born in Brooklyn, New York. Her father, who was for many years President of King's County Savings Institution, Brooklyn, was a son of Henry Bearns, ship-owner, of Haarlem, Holland, a man of unusual education and a highly accomplished navigator, who came to New York about 1800.

Ella Louise Bearns was educated at home by private tutors, and later at Nassau Institute, where she was graduated in 1877. On July 26, 1888, she was married in the Cathedral of the Incarnation, Garden City, Long Island, to the Reverend James Henry Darlington. Theirs was the first marriage celebrated in the cathedral. At that time Doctor Darlington was Rector of Christ Church, Brooklyn, where he continued until his consecration, on April 26, 1905, as First Bishop of Harrisburg, Pennsylvania.

Mrs. Darlington has always ably assisted her husband in his work as priest and bishop, especially in the support of the philanthropic, temperance, and missionary societies of the Church. At the Pan-Anglican Conference in London, July, 1908, her paper, *Mission Study Classes in the United States* was read, the only one written by a woman. Mrs. Darlington was the founder and for seven years President of the Workingwoman's Vacation Society of Brooklyn, New York, which maintained four houses in the country where were sent over thirteen thousand women with children. She has always been interested in the Young Men's and the Young Women's Christian Associations, and has given much time and thought to the work of reformatories and sanatoriums, especially those for crippled children. During the World War she devoted her energies to the work of the American Red Cross.

She is First Vice-President of the Society of Pennsylvania Women, is a member of the Pennsylvania Society of Daughters of the Empire State, and of the Daughters of the American Revolution. She is a member, also, of the Civic Clubs of Harrisburg and of Newport, Rhode Island, where she and Bishop Darlington have their summer home. Among the many church societies in which she is active is the Daughters of the King, and she has served on the Central Committee of Women's Church Work in England. In 1920 she was one of the eight delegates from the United States to the first World's Woman Suffrage Convention at Geneva, Switzerland.

Bishop and Mrs. Darlington are the parents of six children: the Reverend Henry V. B. Darlington, Alfred W. B. Darlington, the Reverend Gilbert S. B. Darlington, Eleanor Townsend Darlington (Mrs. J. Ellis Fisher), Elliott C. B. Darlington, and Kate Brampton Darlington.

DARLINGTON, HANNAH ANNE GOODLIFFE (Mrs. Thomas Darlington), the daughter of James Yarrow and Mary (Topham) Goodliffe, was born at Brampton Manor, Brampton, Huntingtonshire, England, April 1, 1830. Both her parents were members of prominent and wealthy families, and both inherited property. Unfortunate investments, however, diminished their incomes, and the climax of ill fortune was reached in the failure of the private banking firm, with which Mr. Goodliffe had deposited the larger part of his principal. This was the deciding factor which led them to come to America. Accordingly, in the spring of 1832, the family took passage for New York in the ship *Mount Vernon*, and after a voyage of six weeks, arrived in New York. They established their home in Greenwich Village, but eventually removed to Waverly Place, on the north of historic Washington Square, then the most fashionable section of the city.

Mr. Goodliffe became associated with Mr. James Colgate in a successful manufacturing business, and at the same time, pursued his musical activities. He possessed a beautiful singing voice, and was the composer of several popular hymns. As his daughter matured, she also developed a voice of exceptional purity, sweetness, and flexibility, which was cultivated under the best masters of the day. Later, she gave her services in the choir of the Amity Street Baptist Church. She attended Miss Brinkerhoff's private school in New York, later the boarding school of Mrs. York at Tarrytown-on-the-Hudson.

During her stay in Tarrytown, Miss Goodliffe attended Christ Church, sitting in the pew behind Washington Irving, and was intimately acquainted with his nieces and other members of his family. Before her twentieth year, however, she united with the Baptist Church at Fourth Avenue and 13th Street, then under the Pastorate of the Reverend Doctor Cory. On August 1, 1850, she was married in New York, by the Reverend Doctor Patton of the Spring Street Presby-

terian Church, to Thomas Darlington, counsellor-at-law, and son of Peter Darlington, who established one of the first paper mills in the United States, and his wife, Maria Wilde. Mr. Darlington's grandfather was William Darlington of Yorkshire, England, whose ancestral home was "Broomhouse" near Dunse, Scotland.

Soon after their marriage, Mr. and Mrs. Darlington removed to Brooklyn, New York. Here their first children, Alice and Alfred were born and died, and the bell of St. Michael's Episcopal Church, on North 5th Street, Brooklyn, bears their names, with the inscription, "Out of the mouths of babes and sucklings Thou has perfected praise." For a number of years, Mr. and Mrs. Darlington's home was at Ashland Farm, Kingston, New Jersey, and then, for a still longer period, at the corner of High and Court Streets, Newark, New Jersey, but during the last years of their lives, they returned to their old neighborhood, residing at 160 West 12th Street, near Washington Square, New York. In resuming the associations of their early married life, they attended the University Place Presbyterian Church, which Mrs. Darlington had attended, as a bride, on the first Sunday after her marriage, half a century before.

As a girl, Mrs. Darlington had the delicate loveliness so familiar in the miniatures of early Victorian women, and she retained her beauty throughout her life. She was tall of stature and of stately bearing, an ideal gentlewoman, whose quiet dignity and restraint were matched by the low and gentle tone of her voice. Of strong force of character, she never seemed to press her ideas unduly, and yet imperceptibly, but surely, carried out her plans. Her judgment was kindly; she never spoke ill of anyone, and when she could not praise or commend, was silent. Her faith in the power of prayer was unbounded and it was her custom, whenever practicable, to seek to be alone several times a day that she might read her Bible. She thought no sacrifice too great to make for the cause of Christ or for any member of her large family of children, all of whom she brought up as earnest Christians, in the knowledge and fear of the Lord. With her knowledge of French and unusual accomplishments in music, she was also an able guide in their studies. She was active in several missionary societies, and interested in all good causes, aiding them both socially and financially.

Mrs. Darlington died in New York, February 22, 1900, and was buried from the University Place Presbyterian Church, on February 24th. Her husband died May 18, 1903, and was buried from the same church. Their bodies are interred in Woodlawn Cemetery. Mr. and Mrs. Darlington were the parents of eight children: Alice, Alfred, James Henry, Thomas, Jr., Charles Francis, Gustavus Cornelius, Marion Goodliffe and Marguerite (Mrs. J. T. Lippincott).

James Henry Darlington was born in Brooklyn, New York, June 9, 1856. He received the degree of A.B. from New York University in 1877, and A.M. in 1880. In the same year he was graduated at the Princeton Theological Seminary. Later he studied at Princeton University, and was awarded the degree of Ph.D. in 1884. In the meantime, he had been ordained deacon and priest in 1882, and became assistant at Christ Church, Bedford Avenue, Brooklyn, of which he was Rector from 1883 to 1905. During 1896–1898 he was Archdeacon of Brooklyn, and on April 26, 1905, he was consecrated First Bishop of Harrisburg, Pennsylvania. On July 26, 1888, he married Ella Louise Bearns.

Bishop Darlington is a member of the Order of the Cincinnati, is Vice-President of the Sons of the Revolution, and is Chaplain-General of the Huguenot Society. For his services during the World War, he was made an Officer de La Légion d'Honneur, Commander of the order of Léopold II of Belgium, Knight of the Order of St. Sava of Serbia, Grand Commander of the Order of the Crown of Greece, Commander of the Spanish Order of

Queen Isabella, the Catholic, and was awarded the Grand Cross of Italy. He has rendered notable service to the cause of Christian Unity by negotiating in 1920 the Concordat of Intercommunion between the Old Catholic and Anglican Churches, and by arriving at a Preliminary Understanding with the Eastern Orthodox Patriarchate at Constantinople and Athens. He is said by Greek authorities to be the first western prelate invited to sit upon the Œcumenical Throne at Constantinople. In 1920, he was also chosen, with Secretary Root, to dedicate the statue of Abraham Lincoln at Westminster.

Thomas Darlington. Jr., was born in Brooklyn, September 24, 1858. In 1880 he was graduated M.D. at the College of Physicians and Surgeons, New York City, and, after practicing in Newark, New Jersey, in New York City, and as head of the hospital at Bisbee, Arizona, he became, in 1891, Attending Physician of the New York Foundling, the French and the Fordham hospitals, and of the American International Shipping Corporation. From 1904 to 1910 he was Commissioner and President of the New York Board of Health. He was a member of the Committee on Fatigue of the Council of National Defense and is a Major in the Medical Reserve Corps. On June 9, 1886, he married Josephine A. Sargeant, who died in 1890.

Charles Francis Darlington was born in Brooklyn, November 1, 1860. In 1882 he was graduated at Princeton University, and, in 1884, at Columbia Law School, being admitted to the Bar in the same year, and settling in practice in New York City. On January 28, 1903, he married Letitia Craig O'Neill. Since retiring from practice he has given time and means to religious and philanthropic work.

Gustavus Cornelius Darlington was born in 1862 and educated at Princeton University and the Long Island Medical College. He married Kate Annabel Bearns, younger sister of Mrs. James Henry Darlington. He has been an examining physician for New York City, and was in charge of the American Hospital at Vichy during the War.

Marion Goodliffe Darlington is a lecturer and teacher engaged in philanthropic work at the Christian Workers' Home in New York.

Marguerite Darlington married, first, the Reverend Arthur Wilson Wild, late rector at Coatesville, Pennsylvania, and second, Doctor Joseph Thomas Lippincott of Philadelphia.

CRAM, ALICE ESTELLA (Mrs. Daniel Henry Cram), contractor and politican, was born in Boston, Massachusetts, May 16, 1861. Her father, Edward Washington Barry, who was born in Boston, November 28, 1830, was the son of Thomas Jefferson Barry. The latter's father was Edward Barry, a partner of John Hancock. He was born in Boston of Irish parents whose family dates from the early part of the fifteenth century. Mrs. Cram's mother, Sarah Shea, who was born in Boston in 1831, was also of Irish descent. Mrs. Cram received her education in the Norcross Grammar and Girls' High Schools of Boston. Her marriage to Daniel Henry Cram took place in Boston, September 29, 1885, and on February 15, 1890, their only child, Daniel Henry Cram, was born, but lived only one day. Mr. Cram was born in Boston, August 14, 1847, and is the son of Daniel and Mary Ann (Hornsbury) Cram. For five generations his ancestors have been contractors, and he, himself, is a contractor for hoisting machinery and the inventor of Cram's patent derrick. From the beginning of their married life Mrs. Cram was associated in business with her husband. She was co-partner in the construction of the foundations of the Suffolk County Court House, the Boston Public Library, the Horace Mann School, the Beacon Street, Waban, and Wood Island Bridges, Section 5 of the Stony Brook Sewer, the Brookline and Manchester Reservoirs, etc. In 1892 she furnished the machinery for the construction of the Paris Exposition buildings. From 1898 to 1910 she was engaged in business in New York City, renting contractor's machinery. She then returned to Boston where she devoted herself to woman suffrage. She was at one time President of the Players' Equal Suffrage League and is a member of the Massachusetts and Boston League for Women Voters. In 1920 she was the Democratic candidate for the office of Massachusetts State Auditor.

Mrs. Cram is a member of the Professional Woman's League, the Twelfth Night Club, and the Gamut Club, all of New York. She leads an active life, is fond of tennis, enjoys horses and dogs, and drives and takes care of her own automobile.

CALLAN, ESTELLA FOLTS (Mrs. Frank Callan), the daughter of Warner Folts (1830–1918) and Margaret Tanner (1832–1909), was born in Herkimer County, New York. She has been most active and efficient in the organization and development of patriotic societies in Herkimer County and one of the most potent factors in the restoration of the Fort Herkimer church, built in 1757, and the General Nicholas Herkimer homestead, erected in 1764.

Mrs. Callan's ancestors were pioneer settlers of the Mohawk Valley, having come from Philadelphia prior to 1723 and settling upon a grant of land, received from King George I, called "Burnet's Field Patent." Since that time the homestead which Mrs. Callan occupies has been continuously in the family, her children being of the eighth generation on the estate. The present house was built in 1796 by Mrs. Callan's great-grandfather, Major Warner Folts (1776–1837), who journeyed from his home to Sackett's Harbor to render service in the War of 1812. He was also active in church and civil affairs, and in 1823–1824 was a member of the New York State Assembly, making the journeys to and from Albany on horseback. He was the father of Daniel Folts (1747–1793), grandson of Lieutenant Jacob Folts (1711–1808), and great-grandson of Melchert Folts (1676–1759).

Conrad Folts married Anna, daughter of Warner and Lana (Herkimer) Dygert, and a granddaughter of Han Jost Herkimer, Sr. (1695–1775), the founder of the Herkimer family in America.

Han J. Herkimer came to this country from Germany, in 1710, and his family was most important, next to that of Sir William Johnson, in the Mohawk Valley. There, in 1752, with his son Henry, he purchased 2,324 acres of land on the south bank of the Mohawk River. His home, fortified and enclosed within the earthworks of Fort Herkimer, was used as a refuge by the inhabitants of the surrounding country during the French and Indian and the Revolutionary Wars. He was a man of sagacity and ability, and accumulated wealth in lands, chattles and slaves. In 1751 he petitioned Governor Clinton for permission to solicit funds for building a stone church on the site of a log church, built in 1724. The church was completed in 1757, and in 1912 the interior of this venerable edifice was renovated and redecorated by Mrs. Callan, sixth in descent from Han Jost Herkimer.

This venerable patriarch was an early advocate of the cause of American independence, one of the first to contract with the Colonial Government for the forwarding of supplies, and his loyalty and enthusiasm exerted a wide influence throughout the Mohawk Valley. He was the father of thirteen children. Four of his sons were officers in the Revolutionary War, and his son, General Nicholas Herkimer, was the hero of the battle of Oriskany. The home of the General, where he died after the battle, was purchased by the State of New York, in 1915, and given into the custody of the Daughters of the American Revolution, as a public museum. Han Jost Herkimer died August 27, 1775, and is buried, with his wife Catherine, on the north side of the old Fort Herkimer Church, at Fort Herkimer, three miles east of Mohawk, New York.

Mrs. Callan's maternal grandmother,

Nancy Clapsaddle, the wife of Ichabod Tanner, was a daughter of Colonel William Clapsaddle, who was a soldier in both the Revolution and the War of 1812, being only sixteen years of age when first he entered service. His father, Major Enos Clapsaddle[1], was also in the Revolution and fell at the battle of Oriskany. His name is inscribed on the bronze tablet marking the battlefield. Four other lineal ancestors of Mrs. Callan,— Jacob Folts, Conrad Folts, Han Jost Petrie, and John Schultz, all wounded at Oriskany,— also have their names inscribed upon the monument. In all, twenty-two ancestors of Mrs. Callan rendered service, civil and military, during the Revolution.

Ichabod Tanner (1791–1892), who was born in Rhode Island, came with his father, Francis Tanner (1762–1847), his mother, Elizabeth Peterson, and his grandfather, Isaac Tanner (1736–1822), to Herkimer County, New York, in 1796. There Isaac Tanner preempted a thousand acres of land upon which he laid out nine farms for his nine married sons. One of the highest points in Herkimer County has borne the name of Tanner's Hill since that day. Here Ichabod Tanner passed his early years, gathering such education as could be obtained in the country school of the day; then, as a school-teacher, he passed from one district to another. Later he began the study of medicine, and for at least fifteen years was a practicing physician. The arduous nature of this profession, which involved long and fatiguing trips over the country roads, at all hours of the day and night, so discouraged him that he turned his attention to law. He was admitted to the bar, and built up a flourishing practice. Soon after 1862, when over seventy years of age, he purchased land in Wisconsin, where he settled and resided until his death. He owned thousands of acres near Portage City, and there laid out stock farms, and amassed a fortune when past the age of seventy-five. He also passed the bar examination so as to be able to practice law in Wisconsin. He continued in perfect health to the age of one hundred and one, never having used tobacco in any form or having tasted an intoxicating drink.

Isaac Tanner, son of Francis Tanner (1708–1777) and grandson of William Tanner (b. 1660), an early settler of Rhode Island, married, in 1757, Lydia Sherman (d. before 1765), daughter of Benjamin Sherman (c. 1712–1788) and his wife, Mary (b. about 1744). Benjamin Sherman was a son of Thomas Sherman (1658–1719), a grandson of Peleg Sherman, who in 1657 married Elizabeth Lawton, and a great-grandson of Philip Sherman, who was baptized in Dedham, England, February 15, 1610–1611, and who died in Portsmouth, Rhode Island, in 1687. He was descended from Henry Sherman, the elder, of Colchester, Essex, and later of Dedham, England, who was born about 1527 and whose will was dated January 20, 1589. In 1634 Philip Sherman located at Roxbury, Massachusetts, and in 1638 was one of the founders of Portsmouth, Rhode Island. He was also an original proprietor of Aquidneck, Rhode Island, General Recorder of the Colony, and a commissioner and deputy from Portsmouth. He married Sarah Odding, daughter of Mrs. John Porter. Thomas Sherman married, in 1702, Lydia Wilcox, who died in 1727. She was a daughter of Daniel Wilcox, who died in 1702, and who, in 1661, married Elizabeth Cook, daughter of John Cook and Sarah Warren. Her mother was a daughter of Richard Warren, who came to Plymouth on the *Mayflower*, in 1620. John Cook and his father Francis Cook, who married Hester Mahieu, were also passengers on the *Mayflower*, Francis being the seventeenth signer of the Mayflower Compact, and John, the last male survivor of the passengers.

Mrs. Callan's marriage to Frank Demosthenes Callan took place in the old homestead, June 19, 1889. Mr. Callan, who was born in Binghampton, New York, was educated at Cornell University, where he won the Oratorical State Prize in 1882. He combined the practice of law with the real estate business in Chicago, Illinois, where the family lived until his death in 1906. Mrs. Callan has three children: Grace Margaret (Mrs. William Lumsdon Bond), Earl Folts, and Warner Herkimer Callan, all residents of New York City, and two grandchildren; Lydia Sherman and Elizabeth Otis Bond.

In 1908 Mrs. Callan organized the Oliver Hazard Perry Chapter, United States Daughters of 1812, of which she was President until 1920. During this period the official markers of the society were placed over the graves, in thirty-seven different cemeteries of Herkimer County, of 135 soldiers who served during the War of 1812. Mrs. Callan was regent of Mohawk Valley Chapter, Daughters of the American Revolution, Illion, New York, for seven years (1911–1918), and, after five years' retirement, was again appointed Regent in 1922. She directed the marking of seventy-five graves of Revolutionary soldiers. In 1914 she organized the Illion Colony of New England Women of which she is still President (1923). She is also State Regent of the National Society of the Colonial Daughters of America, and a member of the order of Americans of Armorial Ancestry, the Society of Mayflower Descendants of New York State, the Daughters of Founders and Patriots of America, the Colonial Daughters of the Seventeenth Century, the Patriotic Women of America, the New York Historical Society, the Washington Headquarters Association, the Huguenot Society of America, and the New York State Sunday School Association; and she is an honorary member of the Herkimer County Historical Society, an associate member of the B Sharp Musical Club of Utica, New York, and a life member of the Happy Day Club of Richfield Springs, New York. She is also the First Vice-President of the General Nicholas Herkimer Homestead Association. She has served on the Board of Commissioners, with appointments from Governors Smith and Whitman, and has been twice appointed by Governor Miller. She is Lieutenant-Governor of the New York State

Society of Sons and Daughters of the Pilgrims.

Mrs. Callan's enthusiasm, and her deep interest in historical sites, led her to visit and take photographs of many of these historic places in New York State. She has embodied her unique collection of views in a lecture entitled, *Historic Homes and Churches of New York State*, which she has delivered before many patriotic and historical societies; and her paper, *Fort Herkimer Church*, was published in Volume XIV (1915) of *The Proceedings of the New York State Historical Association*.

---

[1] The first building of the Remington Arms Company was erected on the land purchased from the ancestors of Mrs. Callan—the Clapsaddles—and it was a coincidence that Mrs. Callan, the granddaughter of Nancy Clapsaddle, should have, as President of the Oliver Hazard Perry Chapter, United States Daughters of 1812, arranged the program and presided at the unveiling of the bronze tablet placed on a boulder to the memory of Eliphalet Remington who invented the first Remington gun at a forge erected with his own hands.

DAVIS, KATHARINE BEMENT, sociologist, was born in Buffalo, New York, January 15, 1860. Her father, Oscar B. Davis, (born in Lenox, Madison County, New York, 1833; died in Rochester, New York, 1908), was of Welsh descent. His father, Rozzell Davis, came to the Holland Purchase from Connecticut, bought land within the present bounds of Cattaraugus County, and built a log house. His wife, Elvira Allen, was descended from the Vermont family of the name, to which belonged the Revolutionary hero, Ethan Allen, and which dates from early Massachusetts Colonial days. In 1856 Oscar B. Davis married Frances F., daughter of Jeremy and Rhoda (Denison) Bement, of Buffalo. Frances Bement was born in 1839 in Seneca Falls, New York, where her father had lived for many years, being at one time President of the village.

Rhoda Denison Bement was associated with the early group of suffragists and abolitionists. At one time she was manager of one of those "underground stations," whereby slaves were enabled secretly to make their way to the Northern states. When Katharine Davis was three years old her parents moved from Buffalo to Dunkirk, New York, where her father became prominent in village affairs and was President of the Board of Education. He personally supervised his children's studies, and encouraged Katharine to follow the courses in music, especially harmony and thorough base, offered by the summer school of which he was the patron.

In 1877 the family removed to Rochester, New York, where Miss Davis entered the Free Academy. Her studies in chemistry here proved to be the foundation of her life work. She completed her course in 1879, and spent the following year teaching in a country school. Then she returned to Dunkirk, her childhood home, and taught science in the High School. While in Dunkirk, as a member of the Independent Church she came under the influence of Reverend Myron Adams, a man of liberal opinions and high ideals. In 1890, after much study, she entered the Junior Class at Vassar College, Poughkeepsie, New York. Here she enthusiastically took part in the student life, making many friends among both students and professors. At the same time, by passing special examinations, she made up the work of the first two years of the college course. She had planned to make applied or research chemistry her profession; but when the subject brought her to the question of the relation of food to social welfare, she determined to specialize on the chemistry of foods from this point of view. She was elected to Phi Beta Kappa and was graduated in 1892, with honors. Her thesis was entitled *The Missing Term in the Food Problem*.

In 1892–1893, while teaching in the Montague Heights Seminary, Brooklyn, New York, she pursued a post-graduate course in the chemistry of foods at Barnard College, New York. This special preparation helped her to secure an appointment, in the Spring of 1893, as head of the Workingman's Model

Home, an exhibit by the State of New York at the World's Columbian Exposition, Chicago, Illinois. This project had for its purpose to demonstrate whether the requirements as to scientifically chosen foods, determined by means of special study, could be met for a specified amount. In the early autumn of 1893 Miss Davis went to Philadelphia, Pennsylvania, as Head Resident at the St. Mary's Street College Settlement, where she remained for four years. Here her ability as a teacher and her power to kindle ambition in the young found full expression. Broadening ideals taught her that the settlement should aim to heal the mental and social ills of all who come within its influence, and that its work should include the uplift of those who help as well as of those who are helped.

Urged by a desire for further study that should fit her for executive work, Miss Davis resigned in 1897, and entered the University of Chicago as a Fellow in Political Economy. In 1898 she was awarded the European Fellowship of the Woman's Education Association. She studied under Professors Schmoller, Wagner, and Searing at the University of Berlin, and under Professor Philipovitch at the University of Vienna. In preparation for her thesis, which was a comparison of the living conditions of Bohemians in Chicago and in their native country, she was invited to visit the estate of Baron Rueger, where the peasants still preserved many of the customs of feudal times. The Baron was a member of the Bohemian House of Parliament and leader of the Young Czech Party.

In 1899 Doctor Davis returned to the University of Chicago, and in June, 1900, was graduated Doctor of Philosophy *cum laude*. Acting upon the advice of her professors and of Mrs. Josephine Shaw Lowell, who had known her at St. Mary's Settlement, she passed the Civil Service examination at Albany, New York. Immediately afterward she was appointed Superintendent of the New York State Reformatory for Women, about to be opened at Bedford, New York. She was

much attracted by the opportunity to put her own ideas and methods into practice in a new institution. On January 1, 1901, she took up her residence at the Reformatory. The buildings, although they had never been occupied, were not new, and Doctor Davis supervised their alteration and equipment. When preparations had been completed, she engaged an efficient staff, and on May 11, 1901, received the first inmates. During her long term of office she proved her ability to deal with delinquent and defective women and girls. Although often hampered by lack of funds and enabling laws, she introduced methods of vocational training which had never before been tried for women—such as farming, house painting, and making concrete. She also established a laboratory under the auspices of the State Bureau of Social Hygiene. Here girls, upon entering, were examined by specialists in psychology, neuropathology, and sociology.

Doctor Davis knew personally each of the five hundred girls who at any one time were under her charge and always gave them sympathetic, motherly advice and attention. Because of her remarkable executive ability, the institution quickly became known as a model. The results obtained fully justified Doctor Davis's methods. Exact statistics of the work as a whole are not obtainable, for, as Doctor Davis says in her *Study of One Thousand Cases*, "There is nothing quite so difficult to measure in figures as change in character. We can say how many have kept their parole; how many we know have been re-arrested; of how many we know the whereabouts and believe them to be doing well; but the changes in character, the establishment of higher ideals, the doing of more efficient work as the result of the training received, these things can never be measured."

In the winter of 1907, while on a six months' leave of absence, Doctor Davis was in Sicily at the time of the Messina earthquake. Arriving in Syracuse, Sicily, with the first refugees, she began relief work at once, at first as a private citizen, using her own funds, later as a Red Cross agent. She materially helped to stem the tide of demoralization, by putting into practice her gospel of work; and her plan of giving employment to the refugees was followed at Palmero and elsewhere. For her services she received the American Red Cross Medal. Doctor Davis' success at Bedford led the late Mayor Mitchell of New York City to appoint her Commissioner of Correction. She was the first woman to serve in such a capacity. She entered upon her two-year term of office on January 1, 1914, having under her jurisdiction 5,000 prisoners in all the penal and industrial institutions of the city. Her friends felt sure that, in spite of opposition from the press and from old-school politicians, she would perform her duties with credit to herself, great benefit to the city, and honor to women. The abuses in the city prisons were intolerable, but with no sentimentalism Doctor Davis judged the conditions as she found them and set to work to institute reforms. She abolished to a great extent the traffic in habit-forming drugs, and eliminated all officers who accepted bribes, or who were guilty of offenses against the prisoners. She worked especially for the erection of adequate separate buildings for the women prisoners. Her aim was not only to secure decency and cleanliness, but to establish such careful treatment of the individual as would prevent the corruption of first offenders by those already hardened. Doctor Davis definitely announced that her program was to be one of constructive work which should not punish men and women, but should make them over. Her establishment of the Farm School at New Hampton, New York, to replace the Reformatory for male misdemeanants on Hart's Island, opened a door of hope and usefulness for many a despondent boy prisoner. Here, with the honor system in force, boys are taught forestry and farm work, and are given a general training for good citizenship.

Doctor Davis' observation of youthful prisoners of all classes led her to frame the law, passed by the New York State Assembly in 1915, and in effect January 1, 1916, establishing a Parole Commission for New York City. This Committee has power to parole, conditionally release, discharge, retake or re-imprison, without reference to the committing magistrate or judge, any inmate of any workhouse or reformatory under the jurisdiction of the Department of Correction who has been committed under an indeterminate sentence. The Commission may exercise the same power, with the approval of the committing judge, in penitentiary cases.

Doctor Davis was for two years Chairman of the Parole Commission. During 1918 she was Director of the Women's Section of the Social Hygiene Division of the Commission on Training Camp Activities. This organization accomplished much in enlightening the women of the country on matters of social hygiene, by means of pamphlets prepared for women in industry and for club women; lectures; and moving pictures. Immediately after the Armistice, Doctor Davis and Doctor Edith Hale Swift, of Boston, went to Europe as representatives of the War Work Council of the National Young Woman's Christian Association. They visited eleven countries, investigating conditions as to social hygiene work and the part women physicians were playing in the fight against venereal disease. An important part of their mission was to select a number of representative women physicians to attend, as guests of the War Work Council, the International Conference of Women Physicians held in New York City in September and October, 1919.

Since 1919 Doctor Davis, as General Secretary of the Bureau of Social Hygiene, of New York City, has continued her important work. She is a persuasive public speaker, and has often made impressive addresses in prison chapels. She has been a constant supporter of woman suffrage, but never as a state or city official. She holds the honorary degree of LL.D. from Mount Holyoke College

(1912), LL.D. from Western Reserve University (1914), and A.M. from Yale University (1915). She has been second Vice-President of the National American Women's Suffrage Association, and is a member of the Young Republican Club and the Honest Ballot Association. She is a member of the Association of Collegiate Alumnae and since 1918 has been an Alumnae Trustee of Vassar College. She is also a member of the National Civic Federation, the National Prison Labor Association, the Bureau of Social Hygiene; and of the Women's City Club of New York.

DE LAMAR, ALICE ANTOINETTE, was born in New York, New York, April 23, 1895. Her father, Captain Joseph Rafael De Lamar, was a descendant of an ancient French family. His grandfather, a banker in Paris, established a branch of his business in Amsterdam, Holland, which he placed in charge of his son, the father of Joseph De Lamar. The latter was born in Amsterdam in 1848 and was brought up in an atmosphere of culture and refinement. The taste for the good and beautiful established in his youth persisted, and all through his life he was a lover and collector of objects of art. After coming to America Captain De Lamar became identified with large business interests, especially as a developer of mining property on a large scale. He established a home in New York City, with a country house, "Pembroke," at Glen Cove, Long Island. In both houses his rare taste as a connoisseur was evident. His appreciation of art treasures was shown in the noted tapestries, paintings, and sculptures with which he surrounded himself. His interest in research into the cause of disease, and to determine the principles of correct living, was manifested in his will, wherein he bequeathed large sums to Harvard University Medical School, Johns Hopkins University, and the College of Physicians and Surgeons of Columbia University for investigation along these special lines. He married Nellie Virginia, daughter of George and Virginia (Adams) Sands.

Alice Antoinette, Captain and Mrs. De Lamar's only child, spent the early years of her life in Paris, having been taken to France by her parents when only a few months old. In 1902 she returned to America, and was graduated from Miss Spence's school in 1914. In 1915 she was Vice-President of the Spence Alumnae Society when the well-known Orphan Babies' Home was organized by the school alumnae. Upon leaving school she joined the Junior League, but just as she was taking her place among the younger set, especially with those interested in out-door sports, the call for women war workers was sounded and her response was immediate. She first studied wireless at the Marconi school, hoping to be enrolled in the government radio service, but it soon developed that women were not to be admitted to this branch. She then turned to motor driving and joined the National League for Woman's Service, beginning work in April, 1918, as a member of the motor corps. She was already an expert driver and, through taking the course in an automobile school, she became an expert mechanician also. Her work, at first, consisted in driving to the port of embarkation to meet army officers who were taken to nearby camps. She soon became known as one of the coolest and most efficient motor corps drivers in New York, these characteristics being especially shown at the time of the explosion at Perth Amboy, and at the landing of the passengers from the torpedoed steamship *Carolina*. All the motor corps members were assigned to duty on that day, and remained at the pier from early afternoon through the entire night, waiting for the refugees to arrive. Miss De Lamar was one of the most steadfast workers, but after the whole night at the wheel reported for duty as usual at the motor headquarters the next morning. In June, 1918, Miss De Lamar exchanged her khaki for the grey uniform of the Red Cross, transferring to the motor corps of this organization. This corps consisted of about 150 girls and women under the command of Captain Adelaide Baylis. The members were thoroughly drilled in infantry and litter drill, in first aid to the injured, and in mechanics. She was immediately assigned to important duties and served, with rank of corporal, all through the summer, with hard service, during the period of the influenza epidemic and at the time of the Perth Amboy explosion. Another duty to which she was assigned was to meet the ships that brought the thousands of wounded to be taken to the various base hospitals. In November, 1918, Miss De Lamar resigned from the Ambulance Corps, but became a member of the Red Cross Reserve Corps.

FELS, MARY (Mrs. Joseph Fels), daughter of Elias and Fannie (Rothschild) Fels, was born in Sembach, Germany, March 10, 1863. At the age of sixteen she completed the course at the Keokuk, Iowa, High School, and later was a student at St. Mary's Academy, Notre Dame, Indiana, and later at the University of Pennsylvania. She was married at Keokuk, Iowa, on November 16, 1881, to Joseph Fels, a manufacturer of Philadelphia, who died February 22, 1914. Mrs. Fels continues the work begun with her husband before the World War. This work has several phases which converge on the same fundamental purpose of social progress, looking toward the eradication of land monopoly and the readjustment of taxation.

Her activity stands, therefore, in relation to the principles which always inspired Joseph Fels, and which she is interpreting in view of changed conditions. Mr. Fels was both an idealist and a practical business man. He was interested in the application of Jewish ethical ideas to the life of humanity; and prior to the War his reform work was cosmopolitan, rather than nationalistic, because he felt that in this way he could be most faithful to the Jewish world-platform of

justice and peace. The new international situation, involving a reassertion of the Jewish national consciousness, makes it possible for the work going on under the name of Joseph Fels to take a more definite Jewish form while remaining the same in spirit.

Mrs. Fels has made several visits to Palestine since the War, and is deeply interested in promoting the development of Israel's life in connection with the ancient homeland. She is Vice-President of the Bne Benjamin, an organization of the young Jewish farmers of Palestine who share her faith, that the Jewish problem, as such, cannot be solved by the mere physical resettlement of Palestine, unless this movement is linked with a spiritual awakening of Jews and Gentiles alike, both within and without the Holy Land, to the ethical and religious meaning of Israel in world history. Mrs. Fels believes, as did her husband, that one is most Jewish and most Biblical when one interprets the purpose of Israel in terms of cosmopolitan justice. Hence, she holds that the new Jewish nationalism, in order to achieve permanent success, must be controlled by the prophetic vision of service to all mankind. Israel's reassertion in modern life must be based on the spiritual foundations which underlie Israel's greatness.

The Joseph Fels work, as directed by Mrs. Fels since the war, relates to the Jewish reorganization of Palestine; the deeper education of Jews and Gentiles all over the world in the understanding of Israel's history and mission; and the promotion of economic enlightenment in the field of land and tax reform; the various activities being coördinated for the purpose of general human betterment wherein all races and nations may share alike.

MINER, MAUDE E., social worker, daughter of James R. and Mary E. (Newcomb) Miner, was born in Leyden, Massachusetts. Through her father, she is descended from Thomas Minor, (born in Chew Magna, Somersetshire, England, in 1608), who came to America with a company formed by John Winthrop, Sr., on the ship *Arabella*, landing at Salem, Massachusetts, June 14, 1630. Thomas Minor was for a time a resident of Charleston, Massachusetts, where he married Grace Palmer. He aided Governor Winthrop in his relations with the Indians, by formulating official agreements with them and by publishing court orders to the tribes. He mastered their language, and became a recognized authority in Indian affairs. By order of the General Court of Massachusetts he received grants of land in Pequot Colony, now Connecticut, and in 1645, with John Winthrop, Jr. and others, founded New London, Connecticut. He served as a member of the New London court, and also as a military sergeant with power to summon the inhabitants of New London for military training. Later he settled in Stonington, Connecticut, where he received grants of land because of his valuable services in relation to the Indians. He was a public official of the town of Stonington, and served as Treasurer, Recorder, and assistant in the County Court. He was in charge of the County Militia that served upon the occasion of the Indian uprisings.

Miss Miner attended the high school at Greenfield, Massachusettts, from 1893 to 1897. She then entered Smith College, Northampton, Massachusetts, where she was graduated A.B. in 1901. From that time until 1904 she was Professor of Mathematics, and during 1904–1905 Professor of History, at Hood College, Frederick, Maryland. In the summer of 1905 she was connected with the United States Geological Survey at Portland, Oregon. From 1905 to 1907 Miss Miner carried on post-graduate work at Columbia University, New York City, where she was graduated M.A. in 1906. In 1917, having studied while she was carrying on her regular work, she was graduated Ph.D. From 1907 to 1909 Miss Miner was a probation officer in the magistrates' courts of New York City. She has the distinction of having taken the

first civil service examination for probation officer in New York. Since 1908 she has been Secretary of the New York Probation and Protective Association. From 1914 to 1917 she was Chairman of the Girls' Protective League Committee; in 1917 she had charge of the Institute connected with the New York School of Social Work. During 1917–1918, she held the highly important position of Chairman of the Commission on Protective Work for Girls of the War Department Commission on Training Camp Activities, organizing protective work in the cities and towns that were near military or naval camps. In 1918 she was appointed by Governor Whitman a member of the New York State Probation Commission, on which she served until 1919. In the summer of 1919, and again in the spring of 1920, Miss Miner lectured at Teachers' College, Columbia University, on problems of delinquency, and in 1919, also, she was once more in charge of the Institute at the New York School of Social Work. Because of her broad experience, her judgment, and her sympathetic insight, she was made Chairman of the Board of Directors of the National Probation Association, serving during 1919–1920.

Miss Miner is author of *The Slavery of Prostitution* (Macmillan, 1916), which was her thesis submitted in partial fulfillment of the requirements for the degree of Doctor of Philosophy, at Columbia University; and of the following pamphlets: *Reformatory Girls— A Study of Girls Paroled from the New York State Industrial School at Rochester and the House of Refuge on Randall's Island*, (*Charities and the Commons*, February, 1907), her thesis submitted as partial requirement for the degree of Master of Arts, at Columbia University; *Two Weeks in the Night Court* (*The Survey*, May, 1909); *Probation Work in the Magistrates' Courts* (New York Probation and Protective Association, 1909); *Problem of Wayward Girls and Delinquent Women* (Academy of Political Science, 1912); *Social Hygiene* (National Conference of Charities and Correction, 1914); *The Girls' Protective League* (National Conference of Charities and Correction, 1915); *Protective Work for Girls in War Time* (National Conference of Social Work, 1918); *The Policewoman and the Girl Problem* (National Conference of Social Work, 1919); *A Community Program for Protective Work* (National Conference of Social Work, 1920); *Delinquency or Opportunity* (New York City Conference of Charities and Correction, 1920); *The Community's Responsibility for Safeguarding Girls* (published by the Municipal Court of Philadelphia, 1920); and *Annual Reports of the New York Probation and Protective Association* (1909–1920).

Miss Miner is fond of outdoor life—mountain climbing, horseback riding, canoeing, camping, nature study—and believes in making photography a part of it. She enjoys travel, and has twice been in Europe—in the summers of 1902 and 1910. She is a member of the American Institute of Criminal Law and Criminology, the American Prison Association, the Committee on Mental Hygiene of the State Charities Aid Association, and the National Committee for Mental Hygiene; and she is on the Board of Directors of the New York State Committee on Feeble-mindedness. She has served on the board of directors of the National Association for the Provision of the Feeble-minded (1915–1918). She is a member of the National Conference of Social Work; was on its Board of Directors and was Chairman of its Social Hygiene Committee in 1914; and was Chairman of its Sub-committee on Protective Work in 1919 and 1920. In 1920 she was chairman of the committee on delinquency of the New York City Conference of Charities and Correction. She is a member of the Woman's City Club, the Woman's University Club, the Smith College Club, all of New York, and the Smith College Alumnae Association.

PROTECTIVE WORK FOR GIRLS

MAUDE E. MINER, *Secretary*, New York Probation and Protective Association.

The need for increased reformative and protective work for girls was first burned upon my conscience through seeing the long procession of delinquent girls and women pass night after night through the Night Court at Jefferson Market, and through knowing many of these girls by working personally with them as Probation Officer in that court. To provide a home where girls could be cared for, apart from prison cells, when held for investigation or as witnesses in cases pending in the court or when there was no charge against them, and where we could discover individual needs as a basis for helping girls most wisely, Waverley House was established in February, 1908. It was recognized that caring for girls from the courts was a public function, and that a demonstration of the value of such a home should result in a Municipal House of Detention. It was also clearly seen that many girls should be helped without bearing the stigma of arraignment in court. To maintain Waverley House and to carry out a wider program for the protection of youth and the prevention of crime, the New York Probation and Protective Association was organized in May, 1908, and incorporated early the following year. Through the activities of the Association, including Waverley House, Hillcrest Farm, the Mental Clinic, court and investigational work, the Girls' Protective League, and the educational work which has stimulated organizations in other cities, increased protection has come not only to girls in New York City but throughout the country.

WAVERLEY HOUSE

Waverley House is a temporary home where girls remain for a few days or a few weeks while a plan for their future is being determined on the basis of examinations, investigations and understanding of needs. From the first, the distinctive thing about Waverley

House has been the "individual method" of work. This involves knowledge of a girl's mental and physical condition, her home environment, her education, her progress in school and at work, her ambitions and her desires, her temptations and her failures, and the factors that have contributed to her delinquency. The first step is to hear her story, and then to verify it by investigation. A confidential talk with a sympathetic person convinces her that she has found friends. The investigation includes a visit to her home, her school, place of employment, relatives, and to institutions or organizations which have been interested in her. In case the girl lives out of the city, it is necessary to write to her home and, whenever possible, to have an investigation of the home made by a coöperating organization in that city.

The mental examination reveals limitations, possibilities, conflicts, and personality traits and makes it possible for us to know who is feeble-minded, epileptic, psychopathic or otherwise defective, and guides us in placing girls at work, sending them to their homes or securing institutional care or training for them. Many girls who have been found to be feeble-minded have been committed to custodial institutions.

The physical examination is very complete and includes inspection of nose, throat, eyes, ears, heart, lungs, back and pelvic organs, etc. These examinations are a part of the routine of the house and are voluntary; yet girls are always willing and glad to avail themselves of the opportunity of having them. A woman physician is considered essential for this work.

While every effort is being made to understand each girl at Waverley House, the short time she remains there is used to train her in useful work and to stimulate her to better living in the future. The program of class work and household activities keeps girls busy with sewing, cooking, basketry, rug weaving, millinery, knitting, embroidery, bed-making, sweeping, etc. There is also time for recreation, including walks and bus rides, music,

games and moving pictures. Development of the spiritual life is considered the greatest influence in changing character, and special emphasis is placed on this. Girls attend the church of their faith.

After remaining as long as necessary at Waverley House, girls are placed at work for which they are fitted, sent to hospitals for necessary medical care, returned to their homes in New York City or in other cities or states, or sent to institutions or to schools for additional academic, industrial or professional training. When it is advisable to send them to their homes in other cities and parents cannot send money for railroad fares, tickets are provided by the Association. A plan is also made for each girl to be supervised by some organization or individual in the city or town to which she returns. The coöperation of protective organizations, probation officers, churches, or charitable societies is secured in this. Those who remain in or near New York are supervised and befriended by workers of Waverley House and the New York Probation and Protective Association.

At first most of the girls entering Waverley House came from courts, but increasingly Waverley House has reached girls who were in serious moral danger through running away from home and lack of adjustment at home. By caring for them temporarily it has saved them from arraignment in court and detention in prison. Many girls are brought by the Missing Persons' Bureau of the Police Department and Travelers' Aid workers, and others are sent by the District Attorney's office and social organizations in New York and other cities.

When Waverley House was opened, in February, 1908, it occupied the ground floor and basement of a private house, the rent for which was $50 a month. In May, 1908, the Association leased the entire house, and in April, 1911, purchased a six-story house at 38 West 10th Street at a cost of $27,500.

While not more than sixteen or eighteen girls can be cared for at one time at Waverley

House, during a single year approximately 400 girls are given care and study there, and are helped to make their way in the future. From the opening of the home, to October 1, 1919, 3,045 girls have come under its care and supervision.

HILLCREST FARM

The need for giving girls opportunity for training, and for providing for those who could not be adjusted satisfactorily in their own homes or in places of work, led to the opening of Hillcrest Farm as a training school. At first the Association rented property for this purpose, but in 1915 a member of the Girls' Protective League Committee, Mrs. Herbert Scoville, purchased for the Association a 300-acre farm near Twin Lakes, Connecticut.

Girls go to Hillcrest Farm voluntarily and remain six or eight months or less, according to the needs of the individual. There they have opportunity for out-of-door work, such as gardening, harvesting hay and fruit and vegetables, and caring for cows, horses, pigs and chickens. They have training in all kinds of household work and instruction in cooking, laundering, dairying, sewing, arithmetic, reading, writing, English and nature study. From the first assembly in the morning for setting-up exercises, until the evening vesper service of song and prayer, the program is one which takes into account the entire individual and which helps her to make progress physically, mentally, morally and spiritually. Each girl is helped to learn lessons of coöperation, thoroughness, faithfulness, honesty, fair play and team work.

Through the Council meeting and the gatherings of students, girls learn self-government and assume responsibility for the control of the group. When, for the first time, girls consider depriving themselves and others of privileges, they recognize the justice and the importance of discipline and the need for greater self-control.

Girls who have known only city life before, learn to love the free out-of-door life in the open country. They row on the lake, and swim and fish in its waters; they take long hikes to the woods and fields and enjoy the birds and trees and flowers; they revel in the pleasure of the camp fires and the picnics on the summit of a favorite hill.

The Association aims to make Hillcrest Farm an All-Year-School which will eventually give to many more unadjusted girls real opportunity. Such a training school should be maintained as a part of the educational system of the state, reaching those who are in danger of becoming delinquent because of their individual make-up and the dangers in their environment.

MENTAL CLINIC

The value of mental examinations in dealing with girls at Waverley House has been so very great that the Clinic has been opened to others than girls under the care of the New York Probation and Protective Association. As a part of the routine of Waverley House, examinations were given to 1,925 individual girls from 1912 to October 1, 1919. Even before that time many mental examinations had been given to selected girls suspected of being mentally defective. Not only do courts and coöperating social organizations send girls to the Clinic, but personnel workers in industrial organizations have recognized its value and are referring employees for examinations. In helping girls to solve their personal problems and to adjust themselves better at home and at work, the Clinic is doing important service.

The staff of the Clinic consists of a psychiatrist, who is the Director of the Clinic; a psychologist; a field worker; and a stenographer. Doctor Anne Bingham was appointed Psychiatrist and Physician in 1913. Prior to that time, Doctor Frederick Ellis, of the Neurological Institute in New York City, had established the method of examination and had made the mental examinations.

A number of papers and reports containing the results of these examinations have been written as a means of securing increased facilities for the diagnosis and care of the feeble-minded in New York State and wider recognition of the value of mental examinations in understanding and dealing with individuals.

COURT AND INVESTIGATIONAL WORK

The New York Probation and Protective Association has coöperated closely with courts, police, District Attorney, Department of Immigration, and Department of Justice in helping to bring to justice men guilty of abduction, procuring, importing for immoral purposes and interstate traffic. By securing information against these men from young girls who had been wronged by them, by obtaining evidence through investigations, and by caring for the witnesses while these cases were pending in the courts, the Association has aided in the prosecution of a large number of offenders. This work is important in lessening the number of young girls who enter the ranks of prostitution and in preventing stimulation of both demand and supply by these exploiters.

When the Association first helped in the prosecution of men who lived on the earnings of prostitution and who procured girls for prostitution, the only sentence that could be imposed by the court in New York was six months in the workhouse for vagrancy. The utter injustice of this was apparent. Data accumulated by the Association and unsuccessful attempts to bring to justice flagrant offenders helped in 1910 to secure improved laws against men who procure women for prostitution. The first case tried under the new law was one in which an investigator of the Association secured evidence against a man who had compelled a seventeen-year-old Russian girl to solicit on the streets for prostitution and who had taken all her earnings. After conviction, this procurer was sentenced to from ten to seventeen years in prison.

The Association has helped much in the enforcement of the Federal white-slave traffic act passed in 1910, through caring for Federal witnesses and winning the confidence of complainants so that they have been encouraged to tell the truth. Prior to 1910 it had been impossible to convict men guilty of transporting young women from one state to another for prostitution, but the passage of this Act and the vigorous enforcement of it by the Department of Justice have resulted in the apprehension and sentence of many of the most vicious traffickers in vice.

In order to make available to a larger number of social workers and citizens, the New York State and Federal laws which protect girls and women and little children, the New York Probation and Protective Association arranged with Mr. Arthur Spingarn to make a compilation of such laws. The book "Laws Relating to Sex Morality in New York City," embodying the text of these laws and notations showing their interpretation by the courts in important cases, was published in 1916 by the Bureau of Social Hygiene and has been widely distributed.

GIRLS' PROTECTIVE LEAGUE

Two important methods of securing greater protection for girls have been utilized by the Association—one by helping to erect greater safeguards in the community, and another by seeking to develop in girls greater power to protect themselves. The erection of increased safeguards has been carried on under a Protective Bureau, which discovers and helps individual girls in need of protective care and seeks to remedy conditions dangerous to the morals of youth. The educational work by means of which girls are aroused to protect and help each other and of becoming stronger themselves, is being carried on under the name Girls' Service League. As a means of their helping each other more effectively, the League maintains an Employment Exchange and two service clubs, the Girls' Service Club, 138 East 19th Street, and the Yorkville Service Club for Girls, 331 East 68th Street.

The Protective Bureau has a staff consisting

of a Director, six protective workers who are assigned to different districts of the city to do personal work with girls, and protective officers who discover girls in need of care and investigate bad conditions.

The girls under the care of the Bureau come not only through protective officers who go out in the streets and parks and dark corners of the city late at night, but through public schools, settlements, hospitals, churches, neighborhood associations, boarding homes, welfare workers in stores and factories, and social organizations in New York and other cities. Some incorrigible and ungovernable girls are referred by probation officers in courts, when mothers come to complain against their daughters, and it is clear that the girls have committed no offense to bring them under the jurisdiction of the Court. Others are referred for follow-up work by policewomen and by the Missing Persons' Bureau of the Police Department.

Special attention has been given to the runaway girls, and effort has been made to understand the factors responsible for causing them to run away from their homes. In the largest number of instances, there have been quarrels at home due to lack of understanding by foreign mothers of their American-born children, the presence of an unsympathetic stepfather or stepmother in the home, or lack of wisdom on the part of parents in controlling and disciplining their children. Many girls have been told by parents that they could not enter the house if they did not secure a position, or if they returned from a dance hall after the hour of ten o'clock at night. When girls have taken parents at their word and remained away, frequently trouble has followed.

Protective workers help to adjust difficulties in the homes and advise mothers about dealing more wisely with their children. They explain to the parents that they should not take every cent of the girl's wages, leaving nothing for the trifles for which her hearts longs; that fathers should not beat their sixteen-year-old

girls and give them no opportunities for recreation, even if they treated their older children that way in Italy or Russia. Protective workers seek to discover the interests and ambitions of girls under their care and to help them to realize their desires. When feasible, they arrange for them to return to school, to receive training in some special trade, or to take music or art lessons; they refer them to the Employment Exchange of the League for positions, and associate them with neighborhood clubs and wholesome recreational facilities. They bring them again in touch with their churches or parish priests and help to renew the religious influence as a power in their lives. By helping girls at the moment of greatest need, adjusting them more satisfactorily in their homes and places of work, and giving them a different outlook on life, protective workers are doing a vital service, are saving many girls from delinquency, and are making possible for them happier and more useful lives.

Dangerous and immoral conditions in dance halls, moving picture theatres, amusement parks, tenement houses, or places of employment reported by girls or discovered by protective officers, are dealt with promptly by the Bureau. According to the character of the complaint, conditions are reported to the License Commissioner, the Police Department, the District Attorney, the Department of Labor or of Parks, or the Health Department. Reports concerning immoral conditions in parks have resulted in additional lights, improved regulations, and increased police protection; complaints about certain dance halls and amusement places have been responsible for withdrawal of licenses or improved supervision in those places. Complaints about the illegal employment of young girls in factories have not only helped the individual girls but have made employers more watchful about taking other children. Reports of immoral conditions in certain stores and factories have resulted in the dismissal or prosecution of men who were demoralizing young girls, and improvement in the atmosphere of the place. Complaints about conditions in hallways of tenement houses have been responsible for the lighting of halls, the locking of outside doors, and increased vigilance of owners.

Demonstration by protective officers of the value of women with police power working with runaway girls and others, scouting on the streets and in the parks, and supervising young people in amusement places led to the appointment in New York City of official policewomen. Presentation of the necessity of greater centralization and improved methods of dealing with missing girls was responsible for the consolidation of the work in the Bureau of Missing Persons at Police Headquarters, and the order by the Police Commissioner that missing girls should not be arrested and taken to court when located. As the result of this arrangement many missing girls have come to Waverley House, to the Girls' Service Club, or under the care of workers of the Girls' Protective League.

GIRLS' SERVICE LEAGUE

At first the work of girls for the protection and help of other girls was carried on under the name of Girls' Protective League, but it was later given the name Girls' Service League.

Girls may become members of the Girls' Service League by subscribing to the following objects:

To protect girls from moral danger.

To promote moral education.

To encourage right thinking and clean conversation.

To improve conditions of work for girls.

To stimulate faith in the possibilities of life.

The slogan of the League, adopted by the members, is "Girls for Girls." Through the League, girls are seeking to give to others some of the inspiration and opportunities for service which they have received, and which have helped to make their own lives more worth while.

The Central Council of the League consists of two representatives from each unit that has been formed either independently or in girls' clubs, industrial establishments, boarding homes, churches, etc., and meets once each month at the Girls' Service Club. This Council elects the officers of the League, formulates policies, decides upon programs for the work of the year, and chooses speakers for mass meetings. Each unit elects its own officers, chooses its delegates to the Central Council, and is self-supporting. It also decides upon other activities which it will pursue in addition to carrying out the general program of the Service League for the year.

At one meeting each month a topic closely related to the objects of the League is discussed in each unit. A speaker presents the topic in a ten or fifteen-minute talk, and League members join in the free discussion of it. Such topics include standards of work, hours, wages, unemployment, child labor, training for work, methods of increasing efficiency in work, vocational guidance, standards of dress, making budgets, use of leisure time, making vacations worth while, methods of protecting girls, social legislation, importance of right thinking, duties and privileges of citizens, health protection, and child welfare.

As a result of placing upon the girls themselves increased responsibilities for the solution of these problems, they gradually become conscious of their obligation to other girls, to their younger sisters, and to the city and the state. They report girls who are in need of help or bring or send them to the League Club. They tell of conditions which are dangerous in places where they live and work and play, and learn of methods by which such conditions are improved. They do not go out as detectives to discover bad conditions, but they feel a responsibility to help correct those of which they have knowledge.

The Employment Exchange gives vocational guidance to League members and to girls referred by them. This makes it possible for them not only to avoid dangerous places and occupations, but to find the best opportunities. By notifying the Exchange of vacancies in their own places of employment or elsewhere, or of positions which they are leaving, the members have made the Bureau a real exchange. Advice is given to girls about advancing themselves in work and securing necessary training to improve their positions. In order that members may consult the Employment Secretary before making changes in positions, the Exchange has evening conference hours.

Scholarships are provided by the League, to make it possible for ambitious girls to continue their education or to receive vocational training. Some of these scholarships provide tuition and also include payment for board during the period of continued study.

A Loan Fund and a Relief Fund have been established by the League to meet the needs of girls who are temporarily in distress. In periods of industrial depression or of illness, girls with no money to pay for their furnished rooms or for carfares or food have received loans which have carried them over these difficult times.

The Girls' Service Club and the Yorkville Service Club for Girls are centres for the protective and the service work done by League members. At these club houses members hold meetings, report conditions, receive instruction in different kinds of service work, and provide recreational opportunities for younger girls in the neighborhood. Here members rehearse their songs to be sung in hospitals and homes for the aged, they give entertainments and Christmas parties to the poor children in the district, and bring lonely girls living in furnished rooms to informal teas on Sunday afternoons. At the Girls' Service Club there are always vacant beds for young girls who are stranded, who have been driven from their homes or who have not suitable places to stay for the night.

A summer camp maintained by the League provides vacations and week-ends for mem-bers and other girls. Frequently one group of girls pays the board at camp of a girl who has been ill, or who is in special need of a rest. There in the country, many girls learn for the first time to enjoy out-of-door sports, hiking and rowing and swimming, and have their eyes opened to the beauties and wonders of Nature.

Through the Girls' Service League, young women are being enlisted in a great campaign for the making of better women and more useful citizens. Through it they are developing greater powers, higher ideals, and nobler purposes. Through it they are solving one of the most baffling social problems by building up within themselves stronger character as the greatest defense.

EDUCATIONAL WORK

Freeing young girls from wretched lives of vice in the future and giving all girls a better chance for the development of their greatest powers must come through recognition on the part of the great masses of the people of their responsibility for developing and maintaining higher moral standards. This can never come through laws and law enforcement or through fear of disease or of other consequences of vice. Only as each individual assumes personal responsibility for making his own life upright and clean and fine, will the solution of this great problem be found. One means of awakening citizens to their responsibility is increased educational work.

Through many lectures and talks before clubs for men and women, churches, colleges, schools, mothers' meetings, industrial groups, and conferences of organizations, workers of the Association have carried to large numbers of people the message about existing conditions and methods for remedying them. Through articles, pamphlets, reports on the work and a study of one thousand girls published in "The Slavery of Prostitution," results of the work in New York City have been given to the public, and programs have been outlined for protective and preventive work.

The Association has carried its educational campaign to many cities in the United States, and even to other countries, through correspondence, lectures, surveys and workers who have organized the work elsewhere. Several courses for the training of workers have been given, and women who have had experience in the Girls' Protective League or at Waverley House have been called upon to organize similar work in other cities.

During the period of the World War there was great opportunity for the development of the work through the efforts of the Committee on Protective Work for Girls, of the War Department Commission on Training Camp Activities. Almost simultaneously, committees were organized in the cities and towns near the military and naval training camps, temporary homes for girls were established, and protective workers were appointed. Five supervisors in different districts of the country had the responsibility for promoting the work over large areas, and for demonstrating to military and local officials the significance and influence of protective work. The work for girls carried on in camp centres and in other communities during war time has helped to increase the responsibility of those communities for the care of delinquents and for the safeguarding of youth. In many instances permanent organizations have resulted which not only are securing greater protection for youth, but are constantly helping to educate the citizens of those communities concerning their responsibilities for upholding higher moral standards.

Although from year to year, there seems to be little progress in lessening vice, as we look over a period of fourteen years, the advance in society's recognition of its responsibility for abolishing vice and protecting youth is phenomenal. During this time, the public has ceased to condemn the individual girl as the one chiefly to blame, and has recognized its obligation to improve conditions which foster vice, to develop higher moral standards, and to give greater opportunities to youth.

McCORMICK, EDITH ROCKE-FELLER, was born in Cleveland, Ohio, August 31, 1872. She is the daughter of John Davison and Laura Celestia (Spelman) Rockefeller, both of her parents being descendants of colonial families of New England. She was educated by private tutors, specializing in music, languages, literature, and history. As a child of four she reached to the keyboard of the piano and picked and played the melody of *Yankee Doodle* with one finger. Her mother, realizing her precocity and fearing she might play by ear and not be able to read notes, had her begin piano lessons at six years of age. At the age of ten she began to study the 'cello, and at fifteen began to take singing lessons, studying also composition and counterpoint, and took part in the family quartette and trio practice with her brothers and sisters.

After her marriage, on November 26, 1895, to Harold McCormick, son of Cyrus Hall McCormick, she became one of the leaders in the social, literary, and musical circles of Chicago. She was one of the founders of the Artists' Guild and an original guarantor of the Friends of American Art. In 1907 she founded the French School for the study of the French language and literature, and in 1908 she organized and has since been President of the Lovers of Italy, a club designed to encourage the study of the Italian language, art, literature, and history. Outside the Italian Government, she was the principal contributor to the Verdi monument at Parma, Italy. She was made an honorary citizen of Parma, in recognition of this gift, as well as for her generosity in modernizing and redecorating the Teatro Regio for the Verdi centenary opera season in 1913. She also founded and endowed the Edith McCormick Prize at Parma for the best opera written under specified conditions.

In 1909, when Mrs. Rockefeller-McCormick was at her Chicago home, her attention was called to the gradual deterioration of beautiful Ravina Park, and she determined to save this garden spot of the North Shore, and make it unique in its way, as it afterwards became, through her guarantees. Her ambition is to form in Chicago a stock company, which will develop into an organization in the winter time, similar to the Opéra Comique of Paris. She also founded and gave the land for the Chicago Zoological Gardens at Riverside, Cook County, Illinois. This wooded strip of land on the Desplaines River and Salt Creek is a wilderness of hree hundred acres, and will be left in its natural state for the roaming of protected animals, as a part of the forest preserves of the country. It will be modeled after the famous Hagenbeck Gardens in Germany, an expert from Europe being engaged to draft the necessary plans.

Having lived for many years in Europe, where she enjoyed the outdoor concerts and observed the value of music given in the open air, Mrs. Rockefeller-McCormick has had much satisfaction in promoting the Chicago Band Association, formed not only to give concerts in parks, but also in the thickly populated parts of the city. Her interest in music and her conviction that no great city can be complete in its musical life without an organization of men's and women's voices, trained to sing the great oratorios and chorals, has made her a yearly contributor and patroness of the Apollo Club and the Mendelssohn Club. With Mrs. Rockefeller-McCormick, music is a force that she must express, heightened as it has been by its suppression in her very young life as to public performance. As her mother considered the theatre and opera forms of sinful amusement, she was never allowed to attend either of them; but her desire to hear and see art in dramatic form only increased as she became familiar in her study of the beautiful opera arias. Coming to Chicago, where there was no opera, she formed the design of aiding in establishing regular performances. By patronizing the companies who came for short periods, by conferences with leading impresarios, she convinced the people of the necessity of an opera house, and finally, in 1910, had the satisfaction of organizing the Chicago Opera Company. She negotiated by herself the financial business, and secured for Chicago $200,000 worth of stock, which meant that the company was independent of all outside aid. Since then she has been its chief supporter, and has worked indefatigably to make it a success.

In recent years Mrs. Rockefeller-McCormick has passed a large part of her time in Switzerland in study and in supervising the education of her two daughters, Muriel and Mathilde McCormick. After the war she established the Edith McCormick Fund at Zurich to help painters, sculptors, authors, and musicians, who had been impoverished by the Great War. But probably she is destined to be known not primarily as a musician and interested in futhering all arts, but more especially for her research in the field of psychology. Becoming greatly interested in this study, she provided funds in 1914 for translating into English, French, and Russian all the works of Doctor C. C. Jung on analytical psychology. In 1916 she founded and endowed the Psychological Club in Zurich to promote the development of analytical psychology.

Mrs. Rockefeller-McCormick's eldest son, John Rockefeller McCormick, died in 1901 of scarlet fever. In his memory Mr. and Mrs. McCormick founded and endowed the John Rockefeller-McCormick Memorial Institute for Infectious Diseases. Their younger son is Harold McCormick, Jr.

Mrs. Rockefeller-McCormick's culture, intellectural attainments, her spontaneous philanthrophy and humanitarian instincts, manifested both at home and abroad, have made her a conspicuous figure in the world of women. She is a member of the Scribblers (and formerly its President), the Fortnightly, and the Women's Athletic Clubs of Chicago, and the Colony Club and the Club de Vingt of New York.

ROCKEFELLER, LAURA CELESTIA SPELMAN (Mrs. John Davison Rockefeller), was born at Wadsworth, Medina County, Ohio, September 9, 1839. She was a daughter of Harvey Buell and Lucy (Henry) Spelman, and a descendant of Colonial founders of America. Through her father she was of the twenty-first generation from Sir William Espileman, Knight, of an ancient family of England, who lived at the time of the Crusades. His coat-armor, blazoned with plates, is thus described in the terms of Knight erranty: Sable, ten plates between two flanches, argent. Crest: a woodman. Motto: Homo Bulla. Sir William was lord of Brokenhurst in Hampshire, and of Cowsfield, Wiltshire, in the twelfth century. The ancient church at Brokenhurst still stands as when he was Lord of the Manor. Here many of the family in succeeding generations received baptism, and it is within the church that at least ten of the name were buried. Eventually the name was shortened to Spileman, and in America it takes the form Spelman. During the following centuries the family resided in several localities. From one seat at Sudbury they moved, before 1469, to Thaxted, Essex County. This is in the diocese of London, and Thomas Spelman, who is an ancestor in the direct line, bequeathed money for the restoration of the Church of St. John the Baptist. His son, John, removed to Great Baddow, Essex, near Chelmsford; records of the family, the direct ancestors of the American branch, are to be found in the churches of St. Mary, Great Baddow, and St. Mary, Chelmsford. Fifteenth in line from Sir William was Richard, third of that name. He moved to Danbury, Essex, and his burial record, April 16, 1718, is in the register of St. John's Church. His son, Richard Spelman 4th, was baptized in that church, March 7, 1674. He was born in his father's house, "Eve's Corner." He married in England, lost his wife and a child, and set sail for New England in 1700. On shipboard he met Alcey French to whom he was married soon after they

arrived in America. They established their home in the newly settled town of Middletown, Connecticut. Their son, Thomas Spelman, moved to Durham, Connecticut, then to Bedford, afterwards named Granville, Massachusetts. Alcey Spelman, after the death of her husband, made her home with her son, she died and was buried at East Granville. Stephen, son of Thomas, was born at Durham, Connecticut, December 5, 1745, and died at Granville, Massachusetts, December 8, 1800. He married, June 28, 1770, Deborah, daughter of Justus and Deborah (Barlow) Rose, and they were the grandparents of Harvey Buell Spelman.

Laura Celestia Spelman, during her childhood, lived with her parents in several towns in the State of Ohio. The family finally settled at Cleveland, where she received her elementary education in the public schools. She was then sent to a boarding school at Worcester, Massachusetts. Returning to Cleveland, she taught school there for five years. On July 8, 1864, she married John Davison Rockefeller, who was born at Richford, Tioga County, New York, July 8, 1839, son of William Avery and Eliza (Davison) Rockefeller; grandson of Godfrey and Lucy (Avery) Rockefeller; and a descendant of Johann Peter Rockefeller who came from the Rhineland about 1720, landed in Pennsylvania, and settled in Amwell, New Jersey. A monument to this ancestor stands at Larison's Corner in the family burial plot, the land for which was given by Johann Peter himself. He died in 1753. The earliest seat of the family was in France where the name was spelled Roquefeuille.

Mr. and Mrs. John D. Rockefeller first made their home in Cleveland. In 1880 they spent the first of many winters in New York City. In later years they spent much of their time at their beautiful country estate, Pocantico Hills, New York. Soon after their marriage Mrs. Rockefeller transferred her membership from the Congregational to the Baptist Church, of which her husband was a member. Her children were brought up under the rigid rules of the church, in which they carried on much practical work. Her son, John Davison Rockefeller, Jr., is known as a layman who takes an unusual interest in Bible study, and the men's Bible class at the Park Avenue Baptist Church, which he has conducted for many years, is known by reputation all over the world. For more than forty years Mrs. Rockefeller was actively engaged in Sunday School, religious, and philanthropic work, and was seldom absent from the weekly prayer-meeting. She was a devoted mother, and the home environment which she made for her children was happy and healthful. She adhered strictly to the tenets of the Baptist faith—no attendance at theatre or opera, no dancing or card playing, was allowed. Music, however, was part of the home entertainment, and the best of masters were engaged to teach it to her children. Her well-grounded knowledge of history enabled her to appreciate the value of research in family history, and her generosity and enthusiastic encouragement provided the necessary means for exhaustive research in England and America which resulted in the publication of the scholarly book about the Spelmans. Mrs. Rockefeller's character was an inspiration to all who knew her, for in all the relations of life her standards were those of a Christian gentlewoman. Upon the lives of her husband and her children, especially, her influence was profound.

SPELMAN, DEBORAH ROSE (Mrs. Stephen Spelman), daughter of Justus and Deborah (Barlow) Rose, was married on June 28, 1770, to Stephen Spelman. The life record of this couple presents a fine example of practical Christianity, evidenced both in Church activities and in the private life of the home. Stephen Spelman led an exemplary civil life, and loyally answered his country's call at the time of the Revolution.

His wife confronted stirring times, facing, as she did, the perils and self-denials of war,

alone with her family of small children during the period of her husband's service. She rose with fortitude to all emergencies, however, and throughout all her life was an inspiration to womankind. She reared a family of twelve children in the Christian faith, and left behind her the memory of a character that possessed rare beauty. She and her husband were members of the Baptist Church at Granville, Massachusetts. Deborah Rose Spelman died February 5, 1822.

Her son, Samuel Buell Spelman, was born in Granville, and there he taught school when as a young man. With his first wife, Laura Seymour, and a family of small children, he journeyed in a two-horse wagon through New Jersey and Pennsylvania to Ohio, and finally settled at Rootstown. During the War of 1812 he served in defense of the frontier. He was the father of Harvey Buell Spelman, husband of Lucy Henry.

SPELMAN, LUCY HENRY (Mrs. Harvey Buell Spelman), daughter of William and Rachel (Frary) Henry, was born in Blandford, Massachusetts, February 28, 1810. During childhood she located with her parents at Westfield, Medina County, Ohio. She married Harvey Buell Spelman on November 16, 1835. Mr. and Mrs. Spelman lived successively in different towns in Ohio—in Wadsworth, Kent, and Akron—and finally established their home in Cleveland. Here Mr. Spelman became well known, not only as a successful and upright business man, but as a person always having at heart the betterment of his fellows. He was a member of the State Legislature; aided in establishing the first system of graded schools in the state; and served on the Board of Education of Cleveland. His most important work, however, was in connection with the Abolition movement; he was one of those who assisted many runaway slaves to escape to Canada. A school for colored girls, started at the close of the Civil War, in Atlanta, Georgia, was named Spelman Seminary in his honor, and has been maintained largely by his descendants. Eventually he and his wife moved to Brooklyn, New York. He died in New York City on October 20, 1881.

Lucy Henry Spelman was a reformer who shared the advanced views of her husband, and was deeply interested in all the live questions of the day. She had aided Mr. Spelman, while they lived in Cleveland, in the stirring days of the Abolition movement. Upon taking up her residence in Brooklyn she allied herself with the earnest group of women who were behind the temperance movement, than which no force has ever swept over all sections of the country with a greater impetus. The leaders were those women who possessed peculiar qualifications of unwavering conviction, courage, endurance, and power of argument and appeal. Mrs. Spelman was one who possessed these attributes to a marked degree and, although she had always been sheltered in her ideal home environment, when the time came for her to use her special qualifications she did not hesitate to do her part.

The Woman's Temperance Crusade began in 1873, in Washington Court House, Ohio, with the formation of the Woman's Christian Temperance Union. At once the movement spread to almost every state, resulting in a reform which eventually extended around the world. Brooklyn, New York, the "City of Churches," entered upon the work, with zeal. The Woman's Temperance Society was already in existence, and when this body heard of the remarkable results in Western cities, its members immediately began measures aimed to secure for their own city the benefits of the new movement. Under the auspices of the Woman's Temperance Society pledges were circulated, series of prayer meetings were instituted, and mass meetings were held in the churches. The local Woman's Temperance Union, organized in March, 1874, engaged enthusiastically in the work and inaugurated a daily prayer meeting. In response to a call for volunteers, a large number of enthusiasts

agreed to visit the druggists, the licensed grocers, and the saloon keepers. Prayer meetings were held in saloons, many of which were closed through the conversion of the keepers and reopened as temperance restaurants. A reform Club was organized; and the mighty impulse was demonstrated in many spectacular ways. Women, as well as men, were active in all the work. They entered the saloons and held prayer and song meetings. They exhorted upon the streets and in halls. They organized a Crusade March in 1874, and again in 1875. It must be remembered that these women were unused to public life, that they came from quiet homes to make an aggressive fight for what they believed to be right. This Woman's War may well be regarded as the pioneer effort that has resulted in the general Feminist movement which has given to women the right for self-expression in all lines of endeavor. Always Mrs. Spelman was in the forefront of the movement. It is typical of her that she occupied a prominent place in the Temperance procession of women, which took place in Brooklyn for two successive years. She is honored as one whose courage to express her convictions and to battle against odds makes of her a worthy example for womankind. She died at the home of her daughter, Mrs. John D. Rockefeller, in Cleveland, Ohio, September 7, 1897.

SAHLER, HELEN, sculptor, daughter of Reverend D. DuBois and Adeliza Frances (Merriam) Sahler, was born at Carmel, New York. Her father was the great-grandson of Abraham Sahler who, coming from the Palatinate, became a large landowner at Perkiomen, Pennsylvania. His wife, Elizabeth, was a daughter of Louis DuBois of Wicres, French Flanders, who in 1661 located at Hurley, near Kingston, New York. Later he was one of the twelve patentees of New Paltz, New York, where he was a magistrate. He served in the Indian wars. Miss Sahler was educated at private schools in New York City. She has continued her studies in languages and literature, ethics, social problems, and the philosophy of history. She has taken an active interest in various organizations for social reconstruction, such as the League for Industrial Democracy and the Public Forum, Inc., and she labored in behalf of woman suffrage in its unpopular days. Though Miss Sahler has been fond of art, ever since her childhood, she never thought seriously of art as a profession until, to her surprise, the first life-size head that she modelled was accepted at an exhibition of the National Sculpture Society. It was not, however, until a few years afterward that she began studying sculpture, under Enid Yandell, who encouraged her to continue and to enter the Art Students' League. Later she became a pupil of H. A. MacNeil. She has exhibited reliefs, busts, and full-length figures at the National Academy of Design, the National Sculpture Society of New York, the Pennsylvania Academy of Fine Arts, and the Panama-Pacific Exposition (1915). She is perhaps best known for her statues, *The Spirit of Revolt* (1912), *The Dancers* (1916), *The Spain of Columbus' Day* (1917), her *Angel of Light* sundial, and the portrait heads of children. Her etchings have been shown at the International Print Makers' Exhibition and at the Brooklyn and the Chicago Society of Etchers. The spirited action of her figures and of her rendering of child life have been especially praised by critics. Miss Sahler is Secretary of the National Association of Woman Painters and Sculptors, and is a member of the Art Alliance, the Municipal Art Society, the Cosmopolitan, MacDowell and Womens' City Clubs, of New York, and the Lyceum Club, of London, England.

TUTTLE, MABEL CHAUVENET HOLDEN (Mrs. George Montgomery Tuttle), was born is Washington, District of Columbia, November 19, 1873. Her father, Edward Singleton Holden, was of English Colonial descent. Among his early American ancestors were Thomas Royal of Medford, Massachus-

etts, and Humphrey Atherton of Boston, Massachusetts. Atherton, a native of England, settled in America in 1643; he was the first general of the Colonial Army in Boston. Edward Singleton Holden, B.S., of Washington University, was graduated at the United States Military Academy, at West Point. Later he was a director of the Lick Observatory, and was also attached to the Naval Observatory at Washington, District of Columbia. He married Mary Chauvenet, daughter of William Chauvenet, astronomer and mathematician. Their daughter, Mabel Chauvenet Holden, prepared for college at Mary Institute, a department of Washington University, St. Louis, Missouri. She was graduated *cum laude*, in 1893, but instead of entering college she devoted her time to music, especially the study of the piano. Eventually she went to Vienna where, from 1896 until 1898, she was a pupil of Leschetizky. In 1899 she studied with Carreño. During the same year she married Doctor Thomas Story Kirkbride of Philadelphia, who died in July, 1900. They were the parents of Mabel Story Kirkbride, who was born in 1900. In 1906 she was married to Doctor George Montgomery Tuttle of New York. Their daughter, Natalie Chauvenet Tuttle, was born in 1909.

Mrs. Tuttle has been a devoted homemaker, with the training of her children her chief aim and pleasure. Her outside interests have been philanthropy, music, and art. She has engaged in settlement work, especially that connected with the Episcopal Church, of which she is a communicant, and in the development of the church music settlement. She has been interested in the cause of woman suffrage, and in other movements characteristic of the age. During the Great War she gave much time to the relief of Poland and other countries, but the greater proportion of her activities were in behalf of that great organization,

The American Friends of Musicians in France, founded in December, 1917, with Walter Damrosch as President. As Chairman of the Executive Committee, she labored unceasingly to bring financial help to the French musicians and their families who were made destitute by the war. As a musician herself, Mrs. Tuttle had been deeply stirred by accounts of the privations which these artists were undergoing. These accounts came from various sources, but especially in letters from Mme. Nadia Boulanger, the most famous woman organist in France; from M. Charles Widor, the celebrated organist of St. Sulpice, Paris; from Mlle. Ronie, the most famous of French harpists; and from Mr. Blair Fairchild, who became the Paris representative of the Society. Through him the Society kept in touch with the committees organized for the relief of musicians in France, and to him funds were sent with instructions as to their disposal among various committees. This method obviated the necessity of forming a new committee in Paris. The following societies were used as the channels for the American relief: le Comité Franco-Américain du Conservatoire, l'Association Nationale des Anciens Élèves du Conservatoire, la Fraternelle des Artistes, la Petite Caisse des Artistes, and l'Aide Affectueuse aux Musiciens. On January 8, 1918, the first check (for $1,000) was sent to France, and after that date money was sent continuously and in abundance. Every sum collected was forwarded in full, all incidental expenses being met from a fund specially contributed for that purpose. Artists and musical organizations generously and substantially aided the fund, and membership in the society grew rapidly. Branches were established in Boston, San Francisco, Chicago, Philadelphia, Montreal, and many other cities. The need of help became even more pressing during the first period of reconstruction after the Armistice. The return of the musicians to civil life—many of them had been fighting for four years—found them in a state of too great fatigue to permit them to resume the struggle for a livelihood. With stiffened fingers and technique apparently lost, many might have renounced the career which had formerly been their sole aim in life, had it not been for the timely aid sent from America in the name of Art. Many professional musicians were thus enabled to rest and re-educate themselves and gradually resume their normal professional lives. In April, 1919, the remittance of $4,000 to the Conservatory of Music at Rheims was the largest single appropriation made by the Society in its program for the reconstruction of musical France. With courage unabated amid the city's sombre ruins, the people of Rheims decided to reopen the Conservatory which formerly had drawn pupils from all parts of the Continent. Their plea for aid, sent to Mrs. Tuttle, received a prompt response. The four thousand dollars was the sum needed to complete the salaries of the professors and to begin the rebuilding of the edifice. The American Friends of Musicians in France also sent a generous sum to the Conservatoire Nationale of Paris, for its relief work. In conducting the affairs of the Society, Mrs. Tuttle had the assistance of many distinguished Americans, but upon her fell the brunt of the work, and to her devotion is due its success.

Mrs. Tuttle is also the founder of Little Cranberry Island Neighborhood House, Islesford, Maine; a trustee of the Music School Settlement of New York; and a member of the Metropolitan Museum of Art, the American Museum of National History, the Charity Organization Society, the People's Institute, the Equal Franchise Society of New York, the Women's Municipal League, and the Colonial Dames of New York, and of Rhode Island. She is President of Grace Church Trained Nurses' Club, and a member of the Colony Club, the Woman's Cosmopolitan Club, the Thursday Musical Club, and the McDowell Club.

CROSS, GRACE ELLA, physician, was born in Boston, Massachusetts. Her father, Doctor William Plummer Cross, was a descendant of Thomas Cross of Ipswich, England, who with his two brothers came to America in 1635, and settled in Massachusetts. These brothers were direct descendants of Sir Robert Cross to whom arms were granted in recognition of his achievements in the defeat of the Spanish Armada and the burning and overthrow of the Spanish Navy in the Bay of Cadiz in 1602. One of the brothers who settled in America purchased as much land from the Indians as he "could walk around from sunrise to sunset." He accordingly walked down one bank of the Merrimac River half a day, crossed the river, and walked back on the other side for the duration of the day, thereby acquiring some of the best intervale land in the state. On this tract his descendants lived for many years.

Stephen Cross, an ancestor of William Plummer Cross, married Peggy Bowen, sister of Captain Peter Bowen, a famous fighter in the Indian Wars. He was a King's Forrester, and while on a mission in New Hampshire to mark trees to be cut for masts for the King's vessels, he discovered the wonderful water-power of the Winnepesaukee River. On his return to Massachusetts in 1700, he gathered a company composed of his relatives and dependents, and returning to this section of New Hampshire, founded a settlement. He built several mills, among them a pottery and the first jewelry factory in New England. It is said that the first gold beads manufactured in the United States were made here. The maternal grandfather of William Plummer Cross, Deacon Francis Sawyer, was a soldier in the French and Indian and the Revolutionary Wars.

Doctor William Plummer Cross was born in Sanbornton, New Hampshire, July 4, 1816. He was educated in the best schools of his native town and early entered the mill business which was still a family enterprise. At the age of eighteen he joined the State Militia, was immediately made an officer, and proceeded through all the ranks until he became Colonel of the Thirty-eighth New Hampshire Regiment. He early became interested in medicine, and after completing his professional preparation, practiced as an old-school physician, first in Wisconsin, Illinois, and later in Springfield, Massachusetts. Afterward he embraced the principles of homeopathy, and was graduated by the Cleveland Homeopathic Medical College, in 1835. As most of the homeopathic text-books at that time were in German, he acquired a knowledge of that language, and became thoroughly grounded in the teachings of Hahnemann. He practiced later in Nantucket, in the old whaling days, and finally, for forty years, in Boston, Massachusetts. He was always keenly interested in young men, and assisted a number of them in obtaining medical educations. He belonged to all the prominent medical associations of his day and was an Odd Fellow and a Royal Arch Mason. As a man of powerful personality, unusually public-spirited and benevolent, he was popular in his community. He married Ann Forrest, a descendant of William and Dubia Forrest, who came from Londonderry, Ireland, in 1744. William Forrest was of Irish blood and his wife of Scottish ancestry. Their home was in Boston where they lived and died, but eventually some of their children settled in Canterbury, New Hampshire, where the family obtained a grant of land. Here they lived in semi-mediaeval style, having built a fort on a cliff where they were secure from attacks of Indians. During the Revolutionary War, James Forrest, an ancestor of Ann Forrest, commanded the Irish Regiment under the King at the Siege of Boston, while another ancestor, John Forrest, Jr., fought with the Colonial troops.

Both the Cross and Forrest families produced many teachers and physicians. Ann Forrest Cross was primarily a lover of home and her children and interested in domestic concerns, but in later life, which brought greater leisure, she developed the artistic talent which had in earlier days expressed itself in the water-color, crayon-work and delicate embroideries, and became a painter in oils. This work became her chief employment and lent intense enjoyment to the later years of her life. At the age of eighty-five she joined a class in china-painting composed mostly of young women, and continued to exercise her newly acquired art to the age of ninety, when, two years before her death, her eyesight failed. She was a woman of fine appearance, good judgment, and quiet humor, and was an admirable example of a youthful heart dominating the limitations of the years.

Grace Ella Cross was educated in the schools of Boston and under private tutors. She attended the Shurtleff Grammar School, the Baxter Private School, the Bird Private School, the Boston Girls' High School, the Boston Normal School, and the Boston University School of Medicine, where she was graduated M.D. She was further equipped for her work by a post-graduate course in surgery and obstetrics, and special courses in philosophy and English under Harvard College professors, and in sociology under Professor Giddings of Columbia University. At that time she was engaged in medical work at the Morgan Memorial, later the Church of All Nations, where she had charge of one of the large clinics in the dispensary. Her great interest in applied sociology, made her a close student of the various types of people under the care of the Mission. Accordingly she entered, incognita, the night trade-school in the basement of the old Mission, and as she was fond of tools, chose as her point of observation the joining class. There she studied her classmates of many nationalities, and also acquired a good working knowledge of the use of carpenter's tools. Upon receiving her degree, Doctor Cross entered at once upon the practice of her profession. She was very successful from the start and was early recognized as one of the most skillful physicians in

New England. Aside from her private practice she has served in many public positions. For eight years she was physician in the Children's Clinic of the Massachusetts Homeopathic Hospital, and has been connected as a physician with many other organizations. While eminently qualified for the practice of surgery, her broad sympathies have held her to the career of a general practitioner. For eight years she was first assistant to Doctor Frederick Elliott, a prominent surgeon of Boston, who made a specialty of operating in the homes of patients, but since his death has devoted herself to general practice.

Doctor Cross has always been much interested in the work for equal suffrage, and served actively with the National Woman's Party as a member of the State Executive Committee and as a picket. In March, 1919, she was sent as a delegate from Massachusetts to New York, on the occasion of the demonstration of the National Woman's Party, and was one of those who were severely injured during the attack upon the procession by a New York mob.

For ten years Doctor Cross was assistant editor of the *North American Journal of Homeopathy*, and has contributed papers to other medical journals, e.g., *The Tissue Phosphates, The Story of Little Things, Mothers and Daughters, The Climacteric, The Indian Summer, etc.* She has also arranged courses of health lectures and has frequently given talks before women's clubs and girls' classes. But her literary work has not been confined to professional theses. She has been a special writer for the Boston *Globe* and many of her sketches and poems have appeared in various periodicals. She writes in a peculiarly easy, often witty, manner. One of her marked characteristics is the ease with which she thinks in metre and rhyme. In this form it is her habit to jot down the description of any episode or experience, and these narrative poems need no editing. Her love for nature finds expression in many ways. Canoeing is her favorite sport and she spends her long summer holidays exploring the lakes and streams of New England. With a congenial companion, who is also an expert with the paddle, she has made many trips, equipped for camping, travelling through long stretches of solitary water far from hotels and camps, and sleeping in the open under the stars. This is the experience she most loves, and the one that has inspired some of her most beautiful writing. She is an expert photographer and always takes her camera on her trips; securing artistic scenes to illustrate her narratives. The versatility of her character is also expressed through her dramatic talent. She would have been a welcome recruit to the professional stage, and has made a name by her impersonations before clubs in Boston. In Colonial costume as Martha Washington, a style particularly adapted to enhance her natural charm, or made up to represent a character in an old time farce, she is equally convincing. Her ready wit and alert brain respond in an improvised monologue and she has demonstrated this gift before many audiences, dressed to represent a woman from rural New England, and speaking in the native dialect.

Dr. Cross is a member of the Advisory Board and an Associate Editor of *The Biographical Cyclopedia of American Women*. She is a member of the Red Cross, and was active during the war as a member of the Surgical Dressing Committee and as a worker. She is a member of the Family Welfare Foundation, and has held offices in the Massachusetts Homeopathic Medical Society, the Boston Homeopathic Medical Society, the New England Surgical and Gynecological Society, the Twentieth Century Women's Medical Club, the Boston University Women Graduates' Club, the New England Woman's Press Association, and the Mattapannock Woman's Club.

SCUDDER, JANET, sculptor, daughter of William H. and Mary (Sparks) Scudder, was born in Terre Haute, Indiana, October 27, 1874. Her father was a merchant, and was eighth in line from Thomas Scudder, of London, who, with his wife, Mary, settled at Salem, Massachusetts, in 1635.

Miss Scudder was educated at the high school in Terre Haute, and then began studying sculpture under Louis T. Rebisso, at the Cincinnati Art Academy, and continued for three years under Lorado Taft at the Chicago Art Institute. She then went abroad, for study in the academies of Vitti and Colarossi in Paris, finally becoming a pupil of Frederick MacMonnies.

She was awarded a bronze medal by the Columbia Exposition in 1893, for two symbolic figures, one for the Illinois Building and one for the Indiana Building. She received the order for these two subjects while still a student in Chicago. In 1901, eight of her bas-relief portraits were acquired by the State for the Luxembourg Museum in Paris. In 1904, she was awarded a bronze medal for a sun-dial in bronze, which she exhibited at the Louisiana Purchase Exposition in St. Louis. In 1906, a collection of silver portrait bas-reliefs and a bronze, *The Frog Fountain*, were acquired by the Metropolitan Museum of Art, New York City. In 1911, she exhibited in the Paris Salon, and received honorable mention. In 1913, Miss Scudder gave an exhibition of her principal works of art in New York City.

The most important of Miss Scudder's works of sculpture are a seal for the Association of the Bar of New York City; cinerary monument for Daniel Mather Walbridge, at Woodlawn Cemetery, New York; a bronze fountain for the Archbold cottage at Bar Harbor, Maine; a marble sun-dial for Mrs. Warner Leeds, on Long Island; a fountain for the public schools building at Richmond, Indiana; a memorial tablet to Bishop Hare, the great Episcopal missionary bishop to the Indians, placed in the chapel of All Saints School, Sioux Falls, South Dakota, one of the many Indian schools built by this great man;

a fountain, entitled *The Fish Girl*, for Alexander M. Hudnut, Princeton, New Jersey; a fountain for the Honorable Robert Bacon, formerly United States Ambassador to France; a fountain for Mr. John D. Rockefeller, at Pocantico Hills, New York. Miss Scudder is also represented in the Congressional Library, Washington, and in the Indianapolis Museum of Fine Arts. Ten of her works were selected for exhibition at the San Francisco Exposition, for which she received a silver medal in recognition of merit.

During the World War, she was a member of the Overseas Service and was with the Red Cross camp workers in France. She was also one of the four women who organized the Lafayette Fund, and the "Pour les ecrivans Français"—an organized fund for French writers. She is a member of the Colony Club; the Cosmopolitan Club; the Geographical Society; the National Sculptors' Society, and the National Academy. She maintains studios both in New York City and in Paris, France.

Miss Scudder is the first sculptor in America to emphasize the fact that garden work is of more importance than any other form of sculpture, and it is largely due to her efforts that it has gained its present important place in American Art. Although Miss Scudder has attained recognition among the foremost American sculptors, because of her exquisite modeling and highly poetic conceptions, her genius shows at its best in her numerous fountains, the designs of which are ebulliently healthy and playful children; studies of childhood in different attitudes; chubby, elastic and joyous urchins, all precisely in the vein most appropriate to lovely gardens.

PAEFF, BASHKA, sculptor, was born in Minsk, Russia, August 12, 1893, whence her parents, Louis and Fanny (Hirschon) Paeff brought her to Boston, Massachusetts in 1895. As a school girl, her talent for art was quickly shown, and after completing her education at the Boston Girls' High School, she received a diploma as a graduate drawing

teacher from the Massachusetts Normal Art School. She then proceeded to the Boston Museum School of Fine Arts, where her record in the modelling classes was exceptionally brilliant. She was awarded scholarships there, and won in cash all the first prizes for original composition. In her second year she gained the Helen Hamblin Scholarship, accompanied by a hundred dollars extra in cash, hitherto confined to the painting class, and now for the first time awarded to a member of the class in modelling.

After establishing her own studio in Boston, Miss Paeff quickly attained a national reputation by the vitality and truth of her work. Her productions fall into three classes: portrait reliefs, ideal groups in the round, and figures of dogs. The last always seem alive and show a sympathetic comprehension of the animal's character. Of her portrait bas-reliefs, that of Miss Jane Addams, posed at Hull House, Chicago, in 1915, is a work of love for a woman who has been one of Miss Paeff's ideals. The subtlety of the modelling reveals all the refinement and delicacy of the profile and catches the expression of mingled pain, patience, and intelligence that characterizes the forehead and eye, as well as the sensitive mouth and chin. This was exhibited at the Guild of Boston Artists in January, 1917, together with many other successful portrait reliefs, among them those of Miss Helen Morton of Newtonville, Massachusetts, Mr. Arthur Foote, Justice Louis D. Brandeis of the United States Supreme Court, Colonel George Fabyan, Mr. Frank Gardiner Hale, Lieutenant Edward H. Gardiner, Miss Eugenia Gardiner, and others.

Miss Paeff's ability to portray men is well shown in her life size bas-relief of Justice Oliver Wendell Holmes, of the United States Supreme Court, modelled in the summer of 1917 and owned by Mrs. Holmes. The difficult full face pose is well carried out in a dignified, easy, and thoughtful manner, and the modelling of the flesh, with both vigor and sensitiveness. This portrait was shown at the Guild of Boston Artists in March, 1919, where its distinction and fidelity to truth were remarked. The same qualities were apparent in the portraits of the Reverend Francis X. Willmes of St. Louis, Missouri, Lieutenant Curt P. Richter, Doctor Stanley I. Rypins, Grandma Rosenwald, Miss Olga Lesh, Mr. Otto Jaeger of Chicago, and Miss Marv Hemenway of Boston.

In her sculptures in the round Miss Paeff's sense of rhythm and feeling for animation find full expression. In 1916 she completed the model for a bronze sun dial, *Three Children of Light*, for Mr. George B. Douglas of Santa Barbara, California. Here three graceful, nude figures of children, dancing about a vine-entwined pedestal, radiantly symbolize the fleeting hours. While the tradition is Greek, Miss Paeff's conception is distinctive and is carried out with harmony between the rhythmic movement of the lines and the expression on the baby faces. Similar joy in the child as well as great originality in composition appear in the bronze group for Mr. Julius Rosenwald's summer home at Ravinia, Illinois. This is a mother and child, the woman a crouching nude figure guiding a little boy as he approaches a pool with anxious pleasure. This child is a portrait of Mr. Rosenwald's grandson, of whom Miss Paeff had already made a portrait bust. Mother-pride and solicitude are the notes of the young woman's face, while the child expresses excitement and playfulness. The technique is of a high order: simplicity and breadth with no neglect of detail in the modelling and the surfaces alive and firm. *Annushka*, exhibited in 1919, is a portrait bust of much character as is also the marble of J. Macy Willets, Jr., and *A Cloud*, shown in 1917 and 1919, is a graceful and suggestive bit of symbolism. Symbolism of great imaginative power also appears in the sweeping *Wagner's Vision of the Ring of the Niebelung*, owned by Mr. Otto Jaeger, and in *Demon* (1919) in which war is typified in a strongly modelled brutal slinking figure clutching a struggling female.

That the World War stirred Miss Paeff deeply is also evident in her *War Sketch* (1919) and above all in her *Spirit of 1918*. This is a realistic figure of a sailor drummer beating "to quarters." The boy's intelligent face and alert body truly express the enthusiasm and energy of the men in the service. Later sculptures by Miss Paeff are the bronze Boston *Globe* Aviation Trophy (1919), the tablet to Francis Smith, Author of *America*, a bronze statuette of a horse, the James Barr Ames Medal for the Harvard Law School, and the John Warren Memorial Fountain, a drinking fountain presented to Cedarbrook, Maine, by his cousin, Miss Cornelia Warren of Waltham, Massachusetts.

Miss Paeff is a woman of wide sympathies, devoted to all the arts, especially literature and music. She is a member of the Boston Society of Arts and Crafts, the Detroit Society of Arts and Crafts, the Guild of Boston Artists, and the MacDowell Colony, Peterboro, New Hampshire.

LONGMAN, EVELYN BEATRICE, sculptor, daughter of Edwin Henry and Clara Delitia (Adnam) Longman, was born in Winchester, Ohio. She passed her girlhood in Chicago, where she attended the public schools and later, for one year (1897–1898), was a student at Olivet College, Michigan.

From 1898 to 1900 she pursued her art studies under Lorado Taft at the Chicago Art Institute, and was then for three years an assistant in the studio of Daniel Chester French in New York. She has executed many works of sculpture, both architectural and detached, which indicate a genius of high order and a command of technique second to none. Her bronze doors for the Chapel of the United States Naval Academy, Annapolis, and the pair for the Library of Wellesley College, Wellesley, Massachusetts, have earned high praise. Other works are the Allison Monument, Des Moines, Iowa, the sculpture on the Centennial Monument, Chicago, the memorial to General Corbin,

Governor's Island, New York, that to J. S. Kennedy in the United Charities Building, New York, the Ryle Memorial in the Public Library at Paterson, New Jersey, the sculpture on the Foster Mausoleum, Middleburgh, New York, and the figure of the Genius of Telegraphy surmounting the tower of the Western Union Telegraph Building, New York.

Miss Longman's genius has been recognized by silver medals at the St. Louis and the Panama-Pacific Expositions, and by the Julia A. Shaw Memorial Prize awarded her in 1918 by the National Academy of Design. In 1906 she received the honorary degree of Master of Arts from Olivet College.

Miss Longman is a member of the National Academy of Design, of the National Sculpture Society, of the American Numismatic Society, of the American Federation of Arts, of the Archaeological Institute of America, of the Municipal Art Society of New York and of the American Geographical Society.

EBERLE, ABASTENIA ST. LEGER, sculptor, daughter of Harry A. and Clara St. Leger (McGinn) Eberle, was born in Webster City, Iowa, April 6, 1878. Her father (born in Palmyra, Ontario, 1846; died, 1906), was graduated M.D. at McGill University, Montreal, Canada, in 1876. The following year he became a naturalized American citizen. During the Spanish-American War he served as a physician in the American Army. His family, originally from the County Palatine, Germany, located in Lancaster County, Pennsylvania, about 1725; but as subsequent members were Tories, his grandfather, John, and his father, Henry (1795–1876), went to Palmyra, Canada, in 1813, as United Empire Loyalists. All of the family were whitesmiths —highly skilled workers in metals. Miss Eberle's mother was born in Montreal in 1846; She died in 1906. Miss Eberle's grandmother came to Canada in 1836 with her parents who were of Huguenot descent, from Dome Philben Temple More, Tipperary, Ireland.

Until she was twelve years old, Miss Eberle attended various public and private schools, and then studied at the Canton High School, where she completed the course in 1895. She began her studies in modelling at the Y. W. C. A. of Canton, Ohio, but soon afterward entered the Art Students' League, New York City. There she studied under George Grey Barnard and Kenyon Cox. Since 1902 she has conducted her own professional studio in New York City. She has exhibited throughout this country, and specimens of her work are to be seen in the principal art museums of the United States. She received a bronze medal at the St. Louis Exposition in 1904; the Helen Foster Barnett prize at the National Academy of Design, New York City, in 1910; and the bronze medal at the Panama-Pacific Exposition at San Francisco in 1915. She has also exhibited in Paris, Rome, and Venice. Her best known works are The Windy Doorstep, in the Newark Museum, Newark, New Jersey, the Peabody Art Institute, Baltimore, Maryland, the Carnegie Institute, Pittsburgh, Pennsylvania, and the Worcester Art Museum, Worcester, Massachusetts; The Little Mother, in the Chicago Art Institute; Rag Time in the Art Museum, Detroit, Michigan; The White Slave, shown at the Independent Exhibition, New York City, 1912–1913; Girl on Roller Skates, and Mowgli in the Metropolitan Museum of Art, New York City; Salome, purchased by the Italian Art Society, Venice, and by the Twentieth Century Woman's Club of Buffalo, New York; The Lotus Bud, a fountain at the estate of Mrs. L. H. Lapham, New Canaan, Connecticut; and also portraits of Miss Anna Vaughn Hyatt, Mrs. John A. Wyeth, Miss Virginia Thorburn, Master Seeley Newell, and others.

Miss Eberle, in her studies of East Side personalities, evidences a remarkable ability to express in sculpture the subtle individuality that escapes any but the great artist. She is a realist, but not a pessimist. Some of her figures may be drab and unattractive, but they do not arouse a disgust toward humanity.

Her studies of children, with awkwardness turned to grace, invite sympathy rather than pity, and tend to inspire the beholder to practical brotherliness.

BLASHFIELD, EVANGELINE WILBOUR (Mrs. Edwin H.

Blashfield), daughter of Charles Edwin and Charlotte (Beebe) Wilbour, was born September 1, 1858, in Little Compton, Rhode Island, during a summer visit paid by her parents to the homestead which had belonged to her family since the middle of the seventeenth century. She came of Pilgrim stock, a true daughter of the *Mayflower*, related to the Southworths, Churches and Moleyns and was one of the army of people who are proud to claim descent from John Alden and Priscilla.

Despite her lineage, the Puritan strain was not marked in her features or temperament. Somewhere about the year 1900, as she stood looking at portraits in the famous old music school of Bologna, Rossini's music school, the Director, a Churchman and an enthusiast also, remarked: "She cannot be an American." "Americanissima from the beginning," answered her traveling companion, then in reply to questions he admitted that she has had an Arlesian grandmother many times removed. "That's it, that's it," said the priest, "I told you so, she is Latin." At all events, her Latin sympathies were to the fore very early. In her New York home, her childhood memories were of framed photographs of Greek statues, or rather of Greco-Roman copies from the Vatican, and in the School of the Sisters of Saint Mary the Virgin, a High Church Episcopalian School, where she passed several years, the marble divinities were replaced by photographs of the works of Fra Angelico, Lippo Leppi and their circle. Temperament and surroundings thus combined to turn her before almost everything else into a lover of beauty.

When she was still a very little girl her father was engaged in making from the original sheets, as fast as they could be sent to him from Paris, the first English translation of *Les Misérables* of Victor Hugo, followed shortly after by a translation of Renan's *Life of Jesus*. Some of Mrs. Blashfield's most cherished recollections were of having heard Victor Hugo speak in public and of meeting and talking with Renan, a man so extraordinary both in speech and appearance. As her mother, Charlotte Beebe Wilbour, was the first elected President of Sorosis, the daughter frequently met Mrs. Stanton, Susan B. Anthony, and other leaders in the fight for woman's rights.

On July 5, 1881, in Paris, Evangeline Wilbour was married to Edwin Howland Blashfield, a New Yorker by birth and painter by profession. Almost immediately they began their mutual travels in search of subjects, and for the sake of study. They passed many years in France and Italy, visited Greece and spent two winters in Mr. Wilbour's houseboat on the Nile, Mrs. Blashfield, having still a third winter there with her parents. With her husband she wrote articles upon *Nile Life, Castle Life in the Middle Ages, The Paris of the Three Musketeers*, all for *Scribner's Magazine*, also one upon *Stage Setting* for the *Century*. Stories entirely from her own hand followed in the *Atlantic Monthly*. *The Ghoul, and The Education of a Saint* had a very real success, being praised by both friends, editors and public.

Mrs. Blashfield made many visits to Europe, always with her husband, and for her essays and stories she kept her mental background well set with visual memories from her travels. From 1894 to 1897, she collaborated with her husband, and Mr. Albert Allis Hopkins, in editing seventy lives of the Italian painters, selected from *Vasari's Lives*, and published by Charles Scribner's Sons in four volumes. To the text she contributed much critical commentary in the form of footnotes. In 1901 Scribners published her *Masques of Cupid*, a collection which she called "Parlor Plays," including *A Surprise Party, The Lesser Evil, The Honor of the*

Créquy and *In Cleon's Garden*. The scene of the first was New York of today; that of the third was again modern and was laid in the French Provinces; the *Lesser Evil* was suggested by *The Sire de Malétroits Door*, and the motive was used by permission of Mrs. Robert Louis Stevenson. *In Cleon's Garden* was set in Athens in the time of, or rather just after the Syracusan Expedition. In 1901, together with her husband she wrote *Italian Cities*, published in two volumes, again by Charles Scribner's Sons. Four of the chapters, *Ravenna, Siena, In Florence with Romola*, and *The Florentine Artist*, had previously appeared in *Scribner's Magazine*. To these were added other chapters on *Perugia, Assisi, Cortona, Spoleto, Parma, Mantua, Raphael in Rome* and *Florentine Sketches*.

In relation to everything which she wrote, Mrs. Blashfield not only traveled but read widely. Her love of reading began when she was little more than a baby and before she was able to pronounce the words, the sense of which however, she understood sufficiently for profit and entertainment. The French language she understood and read almost as well as English; that is to say she reached for her Larousse, or other French book of reference just about as often as for her Webster's or Century Dictionary. She read Italian also easily, German with difficulty and only for emergency needs. Of Greek she knew nothing, and of Latin little, but before she was eighteen years old her shelves were full of the translations of the classic authors, *Lucian, Marcus Aurelius, Epictetus, Boethius, Plautus* and *Terence* (rather a wide gamut) being particular favorites. She believed greatly in the advantage to a writer, of colloquial language and in Egypt plunged at once into Arabic, but forgot it (as she said) at the end of her three seasons on the Nile.

Although exceptionally devoted to her books and her desk she found time to cultivate her wide circle of friends and acquaintances. She was a charter member of the Colony Club; was faithful to the "Meridian," and, perhaps

most of all, to the Wednesday Afternoon Club. Almost she might have been called the founder of the first Municipal Art Society in America. To William Vanderbilt Allen was due the initial idea of founding a society (in 1893), the dues of which should be applied to the yearly purchase of a work of art for the city of New York. At Mr. Allen's urgent solicitation, she wrote in collaboration with her husband an essay on the advantages of such a society, which was read to an audience in Mr. Allen's studio. Nearly a hundred gentlemen and ladies signed as members. Richard Morris Hunt and Richard Watson Gilder enthusiastically backed the movement, and on that same evening a society was born, which was the first among many kindred societies in most of our large cities. Just before her death in 1915, Mrs. Blashfield was much interested in the erection of a fountain in the Queensborough Market. It was presented to the City of New York by the Municipal Art Society, and bears an inscription with her name, but it has been sadly maltreated by the weather and by chemical action of the material used in laying the mosaic. The fountain was not inaugurated until after her death, and during the long presentation exercises all work ceased by the wish and decision of the market-people in memory of Mrs. Blashfield and the interest which she had shown in them.

Mrs. Blashfield's Egyptian trips had been immediately preceded in 1887 by a summer in Worcestershire, in that picturesque village of Broadway, which Laurence Hutton or Alfred Parsons (it was a mooted point) had discovered, but which Frank Millet had made almost his own and to which he decoyed troops of friends, American, English, and French. The little Worcestershire place with its sixteenth century houses, its Tudor and Stuart memories, its visiting painters, sculptors, writers, musicians and members of Parliament were among Mrs. Blashfield's pleasantest memories.

A three years stay in Europe was ended by a cablegram summons to her husband to come to the Columbian Worlds Fair, and take part in the decoration of the buildings there. In Chicago, just as in Worcestershire, Egypt or Italy, Mrs. Blashfield began many warm friendships; for her eager and intelligent interest in her surroundings vitalized conversation and stimulated her interlocutors. And many of them were interlocutors worth having, for the first years of her married life in New York, from 1881 onward, coincided, in point of date, with the visits of famous artists, dramatic, musical or literary. She met Miss Terry, Irving, Modjeska, the Robertsons, Coquelin, Bernhardt, and with some of them formed lasting friendships. In 1917, again at the hands of the Scribners, appeared her book, *Portraits and Backgrounds*, the title of which showed how much the setting of her essay meant to her. A woman again was at the center and focus of each of her four "Backgrounds." There was Hrotswitha, a tenth century nun, surely the earliest German dramatist; Aphra Behn followed, as the earliest of the English women to earn a living by her pen. Then came Rosalba Carriera, who first made pastel painting popular both at court and with the bourgeoisie. The last of the four essays was a study of that strange victim of circumstances and surroundings, Aissé, Greek slave, adopted daughter in a family of the French noblesse, ornament of salons, zealot in religion, devotee in love, and saint in many ways.

Mrs. Blashfield had a habit of following her heroines about and garnering some of the impressions which they surely must have received from their material surroundings. Thus she went to Gandersheim in the ancient Lower Saxony, now Hanover, to look at least upon the hills and fields which Hrotswitha saw from her convent windows in "the black tenth century." She knew the interior of Rosalba Carriera's little house in Venice, next the Palazzo da Mul, directly opposite to the hotels where the tourists mostly congregate. She

followed also those dominant ladies of the University of Bologna from their studios and classrooms to their tombs in the churches, and she could be reverent while yet holding always in readiness a fund of humor reinforced by an eye keen to detect pretension or disingenuousness. Anyone who happened to travel with her, even for a short time, was sure to note how here, there and almost everywhere, the places visited fitted into some old book or story which she had read, may be as a fourteen-year-old girl. Thus, on the Bodensee, in 1900, where she stopped for the purpose of revising some work, she dropped it all on discovering that at the end of the lake was the setting to *Scheffel's* famous mediaeval romance of *Ekkohard*, and went on instead to visit the place thoroughly.

As she grew older, more and more the events of the great French Revolution filled her mind, and she devoted ten good years to preparation for her study of Manon Phlipon Roland. From the long rows of books upon her shelves she made volumes upon volumes of notes, and she reinforced these by hours in the Bibliothéque Nationale, the Bibliothéque de L'Arsénal, the Astor in New York and the British Museum. Again she followed Madame Roland to her city home in Lyons, her country house in the mountains of the Beaujolais, to Sainte Pélagie and the Conciergerie in Paris, and went to the hiding place of Manon's Girondist friends in the strange little town of Saint Emilion, where the memory of the men of the Gironde will always live, the spirit of the Republic in a city of mediaeval walls and churches. She saw the completion and publication of the first volume of what would have been her *magnum opus*. She had followed the little girl from her chamber (now marked with a tablet) in the house of the Pont Neuf, through school and convent, and as mistress of her father's house, and then of her husband's, when just as the threshold of the Revolution opened wide to the wife of the Minister of the Interior Roland, the author of the book died suddenly of pneumonia only a day after the Armistice of the World's War.

ANDERSON, ELIZABETH PRESTON (Mrs. James Anderson), temperance reformer, was born in Decatur, Indiana, April 27, 1861. Her father, the Reverend Elam Stanton Preston (born near Lynchburg, Virginia, September 29, 1823; died at Valley City, North Dakota, February 27, 1906), was a pioneer minister of the Methodist Episcopal Church in the North Indiana Conference. He was a son of Zenas and Elizabeth (Stanton) Preston, and a grandson of John Preston, eldest son of William Preston, a Quaker, who came in 1713 from Yorkshire, England, to Berks County, Pa. The Reverend Mr. Preston married Maria Shepley (born in Bangor, Maine, April 1, 1830; died in Mishawaka, Indiana, April 24, 1863), who was the eldest daughter of Asher and Sarah (Hill) Shepley. Her grandfather, Captain Benjamin Hill, U. S. A., married Miriam Shaw, and was the son of General James Hill, who married Sarah Hoyt Burleigh in 1774. General Hill first enlisted as a private in the expedition against Crown Point in 1775; was commissioned Lieutenant-Colonel, June 27, 1777; joined the Continental Army under General Gates on September 29th of that year; became Colonel of the Fourth New Hampshire Militia, December 25, 1784, and Brigadier-General, February 13, 1788. He was the member from New Market, New Hampshire, of the Third Provincial Congress, convened at Exeter, New Hampshire, April 25, 1775, and was a leading member of the House of Representatives for the years 1784, 1785, 1786, 1790, 1791, 1792, 1802, and 1805. Together with the Honorable John Langdon, he was the builder of the first United States battleship, the *America*, ordered by Congress, November 9, 1776, which was later transferred to France in compensation for the French ship *Magnifique*, wrecked at the entrance to Boston Harbor.

Elizabeth Preston (Mrs. Anderson) was educated at Fort Wayne College, Indiana, Asbury (now De Pauw) University, Indiana, and the Minnesota State University, where she was a member of Kappa Alpha Theta Sorority. For eight years she taught in the public schools of Indiana and North Dakota, and, in 1889, was made organizer of the North Dakota Women's Christian Temperance Union. The pioneer work of organization occupied her until 1893 when she was elected President, an office she has since held. From 1904 to 1906 she was Assistant Recording Secretary of the National Woman's Christian Temperance Union, and since 1906 she has been Recording Secretary.

As representative of the North Dakota Woman's Christian Temperance Union, Mrs. Anderson has attended all but two sessions of the State Legislature since North Dakota was admitted to the Union and, in addition to her services in helping to retain the state prohibition law and to secure the passage of many other moral laws, she was active prior to the adoption of the Nineteenth Amendment, on behalf of woman suffrage, working through the suffrage departments of the State and National Woman's Christian Temperance Union.

At her request the late Honorable Robert M. Pollock framed the municipal and presidential suffrage bill which she succeeded in putting through both houses of the Legislature in 1917. The North Dakota Woman's Christian Temperance Union, through her efforts, ably supported by the rank and file of the organization, has many reform measures to its credit, among them the laws—raising age of consent for girls to eighteen years; prohibiting the manufacture and sale of Copenhagen snuff and its substitutes; providing for physical education in the public schools; increasing the penalty for Sabbath breaking; prohibiting smoking in public dining rooms, restaurants, cafes and street cars. The organization was also an important factor in securing the law prohibiting impure literature; the repeal of ninety days' divorce law; the laws—prohibiting child labor; providing for juvenile courts; prohibiting Sunday theatres and motion picture shows; and suppressing gambling and immoral houses.

Since equal suffrage has become a fact, Mrs. Anderson has vigorously used the changed situation to further the reforms in which she is interested. In recognition of her services in the cause of temperance, the North Dakota Woman's Christian Temperance Union presented to the State a life-size portrait in oils of Mrs. Anderson, which was accepted by Governor John Burke, and now hangs in the rotunda of the State Capitol at Bismarck.

Mrs. Anderson is a member of the Woman's Home and Foreign Missionary Societies of the Methodist Episcopal Church and of the League of Women voters, and was elected to the National Institute of Social Sciences in 1914. Her marriage to the Reverend James Anderson took place in Tower City, North Dakota, December 11, 1901. He is the son of Alexander and Rachel (McLelland) Anderson of Belfast, Ireland, and was born, September 29, 1863, near Port Hope, Peterborough County, Ontario, Canada. A minister of the Methodist Episcopal Church, he is a member of the North Dakota Conference and has been Superintendent of the Fargo District of that conference since 1915.

By a former marriage the Reverend James Anderson was the father of four children: Fletcher D. Anderson (born at Purple Grove, Ontario, November 24, 1888; killed in action in France, October 5, 1918), who received the Distinguished Service Cross; Annetta May Anderson (born at Purple Grove, Ontario, September 24, 1890; died at Valley City, North Dakota, September 20, 1908); Seward Cuyler Anderson (born at Forman, North Dakota, July 18, 1891), who served two years in France during the World War; and Doctor Howard C. Anderson (born at Forman, North Dakota, August 24, 1892.)

FIELD, SARA BARD, daughter of George Bard and Annie Jenkins (Stevens) Field, was born in Cincinnati, Ohio. Upon the removal of her parents to Detroit, Michigan, she attended the grammar and high schools there. On September 12, 1900, while still a young girl she married Albert Ehrgott, and went with him, after spending some time in extensive travel in Europe and India, to Rangoon, Burma, to serve as a missionary under the auspices of the American Baptist Missionary Union. In Rangoon their son, Albert Field Ehrgott (July 20, 1901–October 12, 1918), was born. Returning to the United States, Mrs. Ehrgott and her family resided for a year in New Haven, Connecticut, where she completed a course in English Literature at Yale University under the late Doctor Lounsbury. Mr. Ehrgott's call to a pastorate in Cleveland, Ohio, made that city their residence for seven years, and here the daughter, Katherine Field Ehrgott (April 11, 1906) was born. In this city, she completed a course in English literature at Western Reserve University. In Cleveland, Mrs. Ehrgott came into close contact with radical, religious, sociological, and economic thought, and definitely threw her life in with movements related to them. This complete change in belief—the awakening from the period of girlhood, with its acceptance of traditional ideas and parental beliefs—made Mrs. Ehrgott's position as the wife of an orthodox minister an impossible one to maintain, with any sincerity or willing service. Upon the removal of the family to Portland, Oregon, Mrs. Ehrgott became a temporary member of the staff of the Portland (Oregon) *Journal*, and in 1910 was sent to Los Angeles to cover the feature work of the McNamara trial, where she originated what was known as dramatic news pictures. Her experience as a newspaper woman was of value to her when, in 1912, for the College Equal Suffrage League, she continued the organization for suffrage in Oregon, begun and carried on for so long by the noble efforts of Abigail Scott Duniway, who was too old for further active service. In her autobiographical work, *Path Breaking*, Mrs. Duniway refers to the work of Mrs. Ehrgott, who contributed, by her hundreds of speeches, to the winning of woman suffrage for Oregon in 1912. She campaigned Nevada for woman suffrage in the successful contest of 1914. In the same year, on November 14th, she procured a divorce from her husband and resumed her maiden name. When the first Woman Voters' Convention was held in San Francisco in September, 1915, during the Panama-Pacific Exposition, Mrs. Field was elected envoy to carry from the Convention to President Wilson a monster petition, demanding national action on the woman suffrage question. She went from San Francisco to Washington by automobile, making speeches in every town, meeting all the governors of states, mayors of cities, and other important officials, and obtaining their endorsement of the national woman suffrage movement. She arrived in Washington in the middle of December, 1915, and headed a deputation of three hundred women who were received by the President. She presented him with the petition, to which were affixed a half million names of voting women, and it was at this hearing that Mr. Wilson first expressed himself favorably in regard to woman suffrage. However, as the Democratic Party failed to keep its pledge to pass the national suffrage amendment, Mrs. Field, during 1916, toured the West as a representative of the National Woman's Party in its campaign against the Democrats. In January, 1917, she was again received by President Wilson, when she carried from San Francisco the resolutions from various groups of Western women passed at memorial services for Inez Milholland Boissevain. In 1918 Mrs. Field conducted the campaign throughout Northern Nevada in behalf of Anne Martin, the first woman to run for the office of United States Senator. Mrs. Field has for many years contributed articles to newspapers, and short stories and poems to magazines. In 1920, under the auspices of the Book Club of California, she published a little book, *The Vintage Festival*, and a collection of her poems appeared in 1922. She is a member of the National Woman's Party, the League for Oppressed Peoples, the American Civil Liberties League, and the Book Club of California.

The Field family, like the Adams family, seem to have an inheritance of brains. Sara Bard Field is an eloquent orator and a brilliant writer. She is a poet, sensitive to nature and to life, and a volume of her poems will soon be published. She knows no class distinctions, and her sweetness and charm are for all members of the human family. She is a cultured, fascinating conversationalist, particularly when the theme is poetry. She is, in the higher sense, very emotional, but her reason tests her emotions. She is passionate for freedom, not only as an emotion, with sympathy for those bound and confined by laws, superstitions, or conventions, but chiefly because she can show, with Socratic logic, that all progressive evolution comes out of freedom and only from freedom. She rejects all bondage of the human soul as well as of the human body, political, social, or religious, and believes that morals also are best in freedom. She is for political freedom for women but believes that it is only a small step. She is above all for the economic and moral freedom of women, and believes a future worth looking forward to can come only out of an honorable free motherhood; by society recognizing that the great vocation of women is motherhood and the education of the future generation. She is for the political freedom of all peoples but recognizes that here also industrial freedom is the larger goal, and she has said from the platform, and on the printed page many times that not till privilege and monopoly are abolished, natural opportunity open to all, and the only class or aristocracy is Nature's aristocracy of soul and intellect, will the full development of the human race be possible. Frail in body, she is absolutely fearless in her convictions.

FRANKENTHAL, TILLIE S. (Mrs. Charles E. Frankenthal), daughter of William and Louise (D'Allamand) Steinhart, was born in San Francisco, California. Her father, who was born in Germany, crossed the continent in 1849 with an ox team to California where he served on the original Vigilante Committee. The daughter was educated at Madam Ziska's Seminary, and in 1888 was married in San Francisco to Charles E. Frankenthal, the son of Emanuel and Kate Frankenthal of Chicago. They were the parents of one daughter, Irma Kate Shivers, born in Chicago.

Mrs. Frankenthal's first ambition was to be a good housekeeper and a good mother. When the World War came it altered the current of her being, as it did that of many thousands of others. She became interested, as all patriots were, in doing something for her country and for humanity.

Her activities were of a major character. She was Chairman of Finance of the Woman's Committee of the Council of National Defense. In this work she raised hundreds of thousands of dollars for various charitable purposes, for the benefit of the soldiers at the front, and the needy ones at home. She organized the entire state of Illinois for this Committee and soon had it operating on the basis of 100 per cent efficiency.

At the close of the war she received the commendation and the praise of the high government officials who came in direct contact with her efforts, and she was awarded the decoration of the Order of Queen Elizabeth by the Queen of the Belgians. She had discovered within herself a tremendous organizing ability which had lain dormant. She looked beyond the horizon of the home, and became interested in finance, especially in that portion of it which relates to women in the world of business. To paraphrase Henry George's expression: "I am for men," Mrs. Frankenthal could adopt the motto: "I am for women." She became connected, in an official position, with a large Chicago bank,

and was instrumental in attracting to the institution a very valuable clientèle among women and men. She later became associated with the Equitable Bond and Mortgage Company as Director of Women's Sales in the Bond Department.

She readily absorbed the intricacies of finance, and her vast fund of financial knowledge she has dispensed freely to thousands of women clients, who come to her office from time to time for advice and information. Mrs. Frankenthal has organized a corps of saleswomen in the bond department of the Equitable Bond and Mortgage Company. This is composed of women who have received some of Mrs. Frankenthal's enthusiasm and inspiration. These women who compose her force of saleswomen are from the representative families of Chicago. With the education in the bond business which they have received from Mrs. Frankenthal they have developed into real bond saleswomen. While this organization is quite young, it has already achieved success, and is destined to lead all organizations of the kind in the country. The course of instruction given by Mrs. Frankenthal is thorough and fundamental, an intensive and valuable education, in finance. She has embodied certain of her ideas in the pamphlet *Bond Quiz*, and she is an authority on the "family budget." She finds time to aid many charitable institutions and organizations in the city, to organize their efforts to raise money, and to finance their plans to aid mankind.

Mrs. Frankenthal has been State Chairman, during a residence in New York, of the Finance Committee of the National League for Woman's Service, and was President of the Children's Benefit League, an organization consisting of fifty-two children's charities. She is on the Board of Directors of the Juvenile Protective League, the Stock Yards Day Nursery, and the Old People's Home; is Vice-President of the Chicago Band Association; and has been a Director of the Illinois Equal Suffrage Association. She was Treasurer of the Republican Women's Campaign during the presidential election of 1921. She is a woman of boundless energy and enthusiasm with an optimism that insures success.

LEAVITT, MARY AUGUSTA, physician, was born in Osaka, Japan, November 3, 1876. Her father, Horace Hall Leavitt (1846–1920), married Mary Augusta Kelly (1853–1914); he was descended from John Leavitt, a native of England, who located in Hingham, Massachusetts, about 1637.

Miss Leavitt was educated in the grammar school in North Andover, the High School in Lawrence, the Latin School in Cambridge, and the High School in Somerville, Massachusetts. In 1895, she entered Wellesley College. After remaining there for two years she entered Mount Holyoke College, where she was graduated A.B. in 1899. That same year she entered the Boston University School of Medicine, where she was graduated M.D. in 1902. She immediately became an interne at the Massachusetts Homeopathic Hospital, and served there for a year and a half.

In 1904, after special graduate work at the Harvard Medical School, she began her professional career, as a general practitioner, in Somerville, Massachusetts. During the same year she was appointed a member of the staff of the Out-Patient Department of the Massachusetts Homeopathic Hospital, in the Gynecological Clinic. In the meantime, she devoted considerable attention to anaesthesia, and in 1907, was appointed official anaesthetist of the Massachusetts Homeopathic Hospital. When, in 1910, she opened an office in Boston, she continued her work in anaesthesia. In 1914, she abandoned general practice, and, with the exception of office work in gynecology specialized in anaesthesia examinations. For three years, also, she taught materia medica in the Boston University School of Medicine, and since 1911 has been Lecturer on Anaesthesia and Clinical Instructor in Anaesthesia to seniors. Doctor Leavitt is a fellow of the American Medical Association, and a member of the Massachusetts Medical Society, the American Institute of Homeopathy, the Massachusetts Homeopathic Medical Society, the American Association of Anaesthetists, the New York Society of Anaesthetists, and the Women's Club of Boston.

SEVERANCE, MARY FRANCES (Mrs. Cordenio A. Severance), author and philanthropist, daughter of General Samuel and Fidelia Holbrook (Faning) Harriman, was born in Somerset, Wisconsin, May 8, 1863. She received her preparatory education at Carleton College, Northfield, Minnesota, and entered Wellesley College, where she was graduated B.S. in 1885. She then carried post-graduate work at the University of Zurich. On June 26, 1887, at Cottage Grove, Minnesota, she married Cordenio A. Severance, a lawyer of St. Paul. Mrs. Severance is Vice-Chairman of the Minnesota Council of National Defense; and Chairman of the St. Paul Council of National Defense; Chairman of the Minnesota Division of the American Red Cross; Chairman of the Ramswey County Child Welfare League; Regent of the St. Paul Chapter of the Daughters of the American Revolution; Chairman of the Minnesota Division of the National League for Women's Service. She is also a member of the Board of the Protestant Orphan Asylum; the Executive Committee of the Roosevelt Memorial Association; the Woman's Welfare League; the Society for the Prevention of Cruelty to Children; the Graduate Council of Wellesley College; the Minnesota Americanization Committee; the St. Paul Institute; the Assembly of St. Paul; and of the Association of Collegiate Alumnae; the College Club Association; the Town and Country, Current Topics, and Schubert Clubs. She is the author of *A Guide to American Citizenship*, a manual for immigrants, and she has collected and edited *The Indian Legends of Minnesota*.

WALLIN, MATHILDA K., physician, the daughter of P. Erik and Maria K. (Hanson) Wallin, was born in Upland, Sweden, July 4, 1858.

She was educated by private tutors and in the public school at home and at the Royal Gymnastic Central Institute of Stockholm. In 1893 she received the degree of M.D. from the Women's Medical College of the New York Infirmary, New York, and has also pursued her medical studies in Berlin and Vienna.

In 1912–1913 she was President of the Women's Medical Association of New York and is now an Attending Surgeon at the New York Orthopaedic Hospital and Dispensary and Attending Orthopaedist at the New York Infirmary for Women and Children.

Doctor Wallin has written for numerous medical publications, and has lectured before the medical societies. She is a member of the New York Academy of Medicine, the American Medical Association, the Medical Women's National Association, the New York State and County Medical Society, the Women's Medical Association, the Woman's Medical Society of New York State, the American Physical Education Association, the American Society for Sanitary and Moral Prophylaxis, the American Physical Education Association, the Swedish Association of Gymnastic Teachers, the Scandinavian-American Association, the Women's University Club of New York, and the New York Federation of Women's Clubs, and as a believer in woman suffrage she has belonged to the Collegiate Equal Suffrage League, the National Woman Suffrage Association, and the Women's National Party.

KERR, HELEN CULVER (Mrs. John Clapperton Kerr), was born at 506 Washington Avenue, Brooklyn, New York, December 10, 1870. Her father, Andrew Roger Culver, was a noted lawyer, noted in legal annals because of his admission to practice before the Supreme Court of the United States at the early age of thirty-four. Her mother, Sarah

Cornelia Gerrodette, was well known for her beauty and her personal charm. From these parents Mrs. Kerr inherited a strong love for books and a keen interest in civic improvement. She received her early education under the direction of private tutors, and spent a large part of her childhood in travel. When at home in Brooklyn, however, she found time to engage in many charities, and was prominent in the debates of the Civitas Club, when that organization was especially active in civics and politics.

On October 1, 1895, she was married, in the house in which she was born, to John Clapperton Kerr, a stock broker of New York. Shortly afterward, she took up her residence in Manhattan, and there became prominently identified with civic work. In coöperation with Mrs. Eugene Grant, she secured the passage of an ordinance which eliminated the worst features of billboard advertising. Many billboards at that time were an offense to the eye and a menace to public morals. Later, when Riverside Park was threatened by railroad encroachments, the Woman's League for the Protection of Riverside Park was organized, at Mrs. Kerr's residence. As Vice-President of the League Mrs. Kerr herself headed the summer campaign which was so largely instrumental in saving the Park. She has also taken part in the civic betterment activities of the Women's City Club, the Women's Municipal League, the Consumers' League, the Parents' League, and the Patriotic Women of America.

When the United States entered the World War, Mrs. Kerr immediately identified herself with the Red Cross; she also gave much time to the Navy League. Working under the supervision of Mr. John H. Lathrop, Red Cross Naval Field Director of the North Atlantic Division, and by authorization of the Fosdick Commission, she arranged for the placing of pianos, victrolas, phonographs, books, athletic equipment, and knitted goods on over five hundred boats and at many camps and hospitals. The Commander of the Armed Guard Detail of the United States Navy, composed of the men who manned the guns on the merchant marine vessels, wrote Mrs. Kerr the following letter of appreciation:

January 3, 1919.
MY DEAR MRS. KERR:

As Commanding Officer of the Armed Guard Detail, New York, and in behalf of the many thousand officers and enlisted men who have been attached to this Command, there is presented to you a loving cup as a remembrance of our esteem.

For many months, it has been our good fortune to have had you interested in the welfare of the personnel of the Armed Guards, with a view of making more pleasant their life while serving afloat as gun crews, radiomen and signalmen on vessels of the United States Merchant Marine.

The result which you accomplished in providing recreation for our personnel in the form of athletic and musical equipment will be appreciated in our hearts through the years to come.

As we reach the parting of our ways, please remember that you have our heartfelt wishes that your future may bring to you the same full measure of happiness that was dispensed by you to the Armed Guards, and it is our hope that you will recall your work among us as one of your pleasing recollections of life.

In grateful remembrance,
Sincerely,
(Signed)   H. H. NORTON,
Commander, U. S. N.,
Commanding.

Another arm of the Navy to claim Mrs. Kerr's interest was the mine-sweeping fleet and their flagship, U. S. S. *Black Hawk*. While engaged in this work, Mrs. Kerr was also Chairman of Recreation for the New York Branch of the Woman's Naval Service, and Chairman of Music for the National Aeronautic Committee.

Mrs. Kerr still further prepared herself for war service by studying wireless, for operation of which she procured the United States Government License in 1917. In February, 1919, since the necessity for recreational work had decreased, Mrs. Kerr entered the Greenhut Hospital, New York City, where she supervised Red Cross supplies and took charge of the Store Room. She remained on duty there until the Hospital closed. Notwithstanding all her many years of active interest in public affairs, Mrs. Kerr is a woman who has never lost her quiet reserve. Mr. and Mrs. Kerr have one child, Helen Culver, wife of Ernest Greene, Jr.

GREENE, HELEN CULVER KERR, (Mrs. Ernest Greene, Jr.), daughter of John Clapperton Kerr, a descendant of John Kerr, of Edinburgh, Scotland, and Helen Culver Kerr, was born in Brooklyn, New York, August 2, 1896. She received her early education with private tutors while traveling in the United States and in Europe, and afterward attended Miss Spence's school, New York City, where she completed the course in 1915. When the United States entered the World War she was made Secretary and Treasurer of the Comforts Committee of the Navy League, Militia of Mercy Unit. For her work with that association during the first six months of the War she was presented with the Navy League ring, and was made a life member. Miss Kerr was also Chairman of the Hospital Garments Committee of Red Cross Unit 205. She organized and financed this work. Miss Kerr had the garments made in the City prison, in various convents, in reformatories, and by church societies, and similar organizations. In her office she supervised the examination, packing, and shipment of the finished garments. In the midst of all this work she had time to take a short course of training at the Post Graduate Hospital, New York City, and during the summer of 1918 did volunteer clerical work at Red Cross Headquarters. Her practical training as a nurse she was able to put to good use during the influenza epidemic of the autum of 1918, when, at an East

Side shelter, with a few friends, she assisted in the nursing and general care of infants and children made orphans by this scourage. She performed her final war service at Debarkation Hospital No. 3. As a Red Cross ward worker, she carried on social work, when this institution was opened; and continued on duty daily until the end of June, 1919. Upon the anniversary of her twenty-first birthday she received from her father the gift of a G. M. C. ambulance, which she presented to the United States Army, and which was one of the few accepted by Surgeon-General Gorgas. At her request, it was shipped as part of the equipment of Base Hospital No. 17 (later No. 3), known as the Harper Hospital of Detroit.

On October 15, 1921, at her parents' country home at New Canaan, Connecticut, Miss Kerr married Ernest Greene, Jr., son of Ernest Greene of New York.

She is a member of the Spence Alumnae, of the Woman's Forum, and is a Junior Member of the Parents' League.

KENNELLY, MARGUERITE AMY, was born in New York City. Her father, Bryan Laurence Kennelly, was a son of William Kennelly, a native of County Tipperary, Ireland, who located in New York City in 1843. His mother was a Nagle of County Cork, of a family allied to that of Edmund Burke, whose mother's maiden name was Nagle. An ancestor, James Nagle, was Secretary for Ireland under James II. Bryan L. Kennelly married, in America, Elizabeth Waterhouse. Her grandfather, Oscar Hoyt, was descended from a colonist of that name who settled in Massachusetts during the seventeenth century.

Miss Kennelly attended Miss Spence's school, in New York City, where she completed the course in May, 1914. Upon the entrance of the United States into the World War Miss Kennelly went to France, and there joined the motor corps of the American Fund for French wounded. In the Spring of 1918,

in Paris, she was detailed to drive a camionette, reporting at the Gare du Nord for the transportation of cases that were being cared for by the Red Cross. In June she was detailed to deliver hospital supplies in or near Paris, and from there, in October, was transferred to Nancy and Lunéville. The following narrative from her pen gives a vivid account of a few of the incidents that occurred during her service:

"The week beginning March 25, 1918, was a busy one for all of us. With the offensive starting and the big Bertha going for all she was worth, the people of Paris just held their breath wondering what was coming next. The atmosphere was indescribably tense. Holy Saturday and Easter Sunday were as still as death. About the middle of the week, the Red Cross asked us (American Fund for French Wounded) if we would help with the clothing and transportation of the refugees. The Gare du Nord, where the refugees arrived from the devastated regions, was one of the busiest places in all Paris those days. As soon as the refugees came off the trains, they were taken down to the cave or cellar of the station, where they were given food first of all, and then clothing. The cave is about the length of a city block, with the canteen and the *vestaire* in one corner and a double row of beds and a long table occupying the remaining space. The place was the scene of many a tragedy; babies were born there, old and young died there, and if the walls could speak they could tell of all the hardships these people suffered. Their courage was wonderful, and I scarcely ever heard them complain. I was detailed to drive a *camionette* for the transportation of the old and sick refugees to hospitals and stations whence they were sent to relatives and friends in the south of France. One of the worst cases I remember was transporting a woman from Arras who had both her legs cut off. She had just come from burying her husband when an obus struck the house and something fell on her, cutting off both legs. From the agony she was in, I gather their flight was made almost immediately after the disaster. This much of the story was told me, between sobs, by her daughter, a girl of about my own age, who had come all the way from Arras with her mother. She said she was the only daughter, and had two brothers at the front. The gendarmes carried the woman out on a stretcher, and laid her at full length in the camion, while her daughter sat in front, beside me. I had to crawl all the way to the station as every little jar caused fresh suffering. Later I carried two old ladies to different stations, one of whom had all her wordly possessions wrapped in a handkerchief. She had never been out of her town before, and felt absolutely lost. She told me what good wages she had earned at home, and how happy and contented she had been, and when I left her at the station she kissed me on both cheeks in true French fashion. Another poor soul, who looked to be about eighty and did not seem to have all her wits about her, I transported the same day. She did not have a person in the world to go to, and I took her to one of our stations where such people were taken care of and sent out to a large camp somewhere south of Paris. All the way over to the station, she kept groaning, 'Oh Mon Dieu, how much further must I go, and what is to become of me!' The saddest case I had was that of a Flemish woman, eighty-two years old, who was put in our charge to take to the Belgian foyer. I say 'our,' because that morning my little French friend, Mlle. D'Envers, came along with me. She had lived in Belgium and spoke some Flemish, fortunately, as this old woman did not speak a word of French. I was afraid she would die before we reached our destination. All her papers of identification were stolen, and the people she lived with had gone off and left her. The English camp came to the rescue and carried her off in a motor. We left her at one of the stations to be sent off to a hospital in the country, and much to her relief a Belgian soldier took charge of her at the station. There were many other very sad

cases, but these were the ones that made the most vivid impressions.

"The middle of June, our counter-offensive started and after that we had very few refugees, so the Fund decided to withdraw the camionette from the Gare du Nord. For a short time I delivered supplies to the different hospitals in Paris and its environs; then in the early part of October I was sent to Nancy and Lunéville to drive for the dispensaries up there. Most of the French doctors in the country towns were militarized, leaving the civilians without any relief in case of illness. At first the A. R. C. took over this work and established dispensaries all through the Toul sector, and when they withdrew the civilian relief the Fund carried on the work with the assistance of the Red Cross doctors. While there were not many cases of serious illness throughout this section of the country, we found that the dispensaries did much for the hygiene and morals of the peasants. They were very fond of the Americans, had great confidence in the doctors, and would do just as they were told. Lunéville was only eight miles from the front, and about three weeks before the Armistice was signed we saw the preparations for the great offensive that was to have started there, had the Germans refused to come to terms. Trainload after trainload of supplies passed through the town, and a steady stream of camions filled the roads on their way to the front lines. We knew that something big was about to happen, but absolute secrecy was maintained by both the soldiers and the officials. It was not until after the eleventh that we learned that the attack would have started the following morning, and Foch, himself would have directed it and made Lunéville his headquarters. On the day of the eleventh, we had a wonderful celebration and went right up to the front line trenches on the shell swept road to Bathlemont, and saw the monument erected to the first American boys who fell in the war, in 1917. As we went along the road we saw the shell holes just freshly made, probably a few days previous. We also saw the graves of our boys, and while we were there skyrockets fell just in front of us; it was a beautiful sight to see the whole country lighted up for miles around. A few days after the Armistice, the first English prisoners drifted through the lines; I say drifted because the prisoners told us that the German guard had run away before delivering them to the French guard, leaving them to shift for themselves without a particle of food or any idea as to where they were going. Many of them got lost in the barbed wire, and others fell by the way. Those that finally reached us were in a dreadful condition; their clothing was in rags, not having been changed since they were taken prisoners in April; their eyes were sunken in their heads; yet in all their misery they marched down the street singing *Keep the Home Fires Burning.*

"Our dispensary was big enough to be used as a small hospital, and we took many of them in for the night. The doctor gave up his clinics and devoted all his time to the prisoners, who were sadly in need of attention. They had had practically nothing to eat but hard bread and barley water, so at first few of them could retain any food. A number of them were brought to the house unconscious, and I remember one man who remained in this condition for three days. They told of the hardships in the German prisons and the cruel treatment of the guards. If any of the German civilians threw them food to eat and they refused to tell who gave it to them, they were starved for thirty-six hours and often whipped, while the civilian who threw the food was imprisoned. We helped the foyer de soldat feed the prisoners and finally the English aviation camp near us heard that they were there and sent two camions full of food for Doctor Percy to distribute to the men. About 1,500 came through in one week, and were sent from Lunéville to a camp in Nancy, and from there straight through to Calais and England."

Upon her return from France in December, 1918, Miss Kennelly joined the Red Cross Motor Corps, and helped in New York City in the transportation of the wounded and the casual officers. Before she devoted all her attention to war services, Miss Kennelly was active in the Parish work of St. Patrick's Cathedral, and for two years was President of the Cathedral Girls' Club.

PUTNAM, RUTH, author, daughter of George Palmer and Victorine (Haven) Putnam, was born in Yonkers, New York, in 1858. She is descended from John Putnam, of Penn, Buckshire, England, who came in 1634 to Plymouth and later settled at Danvers, Massachusetts. She is a sister of George Haven Putnam and John Bishop Putnam (1848–1915), the publishers, of Mary Putnam Jacobi, and of Herbert Putnam. She was educated at home until she was fifteen years of age, attended Miss Anna C. Brackett's school, New York City, for two years, and was then a student at Cornell University, from which she was graduated with the degree of A.B. in 1878. From 1899 to 1909 she was an alumnae trustee of Cornell University. After her graduation she was for a term at Geneva, Switzerland, and also studied at Paris, Oxford, and Leyden Universities. For a year she was at Hanover and Göttingen, Germany, and at intervals has spent many months in France. Miss Putnam's works are mainly historical. She is the author of *William the Silent* (two volumes, 1895) *Annetje Jan's Farm* (1896), *A Mediaeval Princess,* the life of Jacqueline of Bavaria, Countess of Holland, Zeeland and Hainault (1904), *Charles the Bold* (1907), *The Dutch Element in the United States* (1909), *William the Silent* (in the *Hero Series,* 1912), *Alsace and Lorraine* (1915), *The Name of California* (1916), and *Luxemburg and Her Neighbors* (1918). She is also the author of *Half-Moon Papers,* the translator of part of *Block's History of the Netherland People,* and she has written many articles for magazines. The summer of 1919 Miss Putnam spent in the Grand Duchy of Luxemburg, where she had an opportunity to see the structure of a small state, and to watch the efforts of the government to break loose from German influence and to become an independent state albeit there were only 260,000 inhabitants. The result of her observation is embodied in a supplement to *Luxemburg and Her Neighbors*. Miss Putnam is a member of the Women's University Club, New York, the Society of Dutch Letters, Leyden, and the Hispanic Society, New York.

FITZ SIMONS, ELLEN FRENCH (Mrs. Paul Fitz Simons), was born in New York City. Her father, Francis O. French, was graduated at Harvard University in 1857 and studied at the Harvard Law School. In 1865 he was a member of the banking firm of Foote and French, in Boston, Massachusetts. He removed in 1870 to New York where he became the principal owner and a director of the First National Bank. He was a son of the Honorable Benjamin Brown French of Washington, District of Columbia, whose mother was a sister of the Reverend Francis Brown, D.D., president of Dartmouth College.

Benjamin French married Elizabeth, the daughter of the Honorable William M. Richardson, Chief Justice of the Supreme Judicial Court of New Hampshire. She was born in Chester, New Hampshire, and died in Washington.

The French family traces descent from Edward French, one of the founders of Ipswich, Massachusetts, who came from England in 1636. Francis O. French married Ellen Tuck, who was born in Hampton, New Hampshire, April 4, 1838. Her first American ancestor was Robert Tuck, who came from Gorlston, Norfolk, England, in 1636, and, in 1638, was one of the grantees of Hampton, New Hampshire, where he held many town offices. His son, Edward Tuck, was born in England and married Mary, the daughter of Thomas Philbrick. He died April 6, 1652. His son, Deacon John Tuck (1651–1742),

married January 9, 1678, Bethia Hobbs. He owned a large estate with two mills and held town offices. His son, Jonathan Tuck (1697–1781), married Tabitha Towle. He was chosen to succeed his father as church deacon and was twice a member of the General Assembly. He was an influential and well-informed man, distinguished for his geographical knowledge. His son, Jonathan Tuck, Junior (1736–1780), married second, Huldah Moulton. Their son, John Tuck (1780–1847), married Betsy Towle, and their son, Amos Tuck, who was born August 2, 1810, at Parsonsfield, Maine, graduated from Dartmouth College in 1835, thereafter practised law in New Hampshire, and was a member of Congress from New Hampshire for two terms. He married Sarah Anne Nudd and they were the parents of Ellen (Tuck) French.

Ellen French was educated principally in Europe, under private tutors and governesses. She was married, first, in January, 1901, to A. G. Vanderbilt of New York, son of Cornelius Vanderbilt; and they were the parents of one son, William H. Vanderbilt, who was born in New York, November, 1901. She was married, second, in April, 1919, to Lieutenant Paul Fitz Simons, U. S. N., the son of Paul Fitz Simons of South Carolina. In 1920 Lieutenant Fitz Simons was a member of the American Naval Commission which reorganized the Peruvian Navy.

In the autumn of 1916 Mrs. Fitz Simons was one of the organizers, and served as vice-chairman of, the Newport Chapter of the Red Cross, and was the head of its Department of Military and Naval Relief. From the opening of the Young Women's Christian Association Hostess House at the Naval Training Station at Newport, she acted as chairman, a position which brought her into touch with the women enlisted as yeoman and the families of sailors in training at the station. After peace was declared this work was not continued. In 1917 Mr. Daniels, Secretary of the Navy, appointed Mrs. Fitz Simons a member of a committee to act in an advisory capacity to the War Council of the American Red Cross upon navy matters.

Mrs. Fitz Simons is a member of the National Institute of Social Sciences which, in 1919, awarded her its Patriotic Service Medal. She is also a member of the French Institute, the Colony Club, and the Metropolitan Museum of Art, of New York.

BOND, CARRIE JACOBS (Mrs. Frank L. Bond), composer and publisher, daughter of Hannibal and Emma (Davis) Jacobs, was born in Janesville, Wisconsin, August 11, 1863. She was educated in the public schools and high schools, of Janesville, and in Beloit College. On June 12, 1887, she was married at Racine, Wisconsin, to Frank Lewis Bond. For several years the two lived a healthy, vigorous life in the logging camps of northern Wisconsin; but soon after the birth of their only child, Frederick, Doctor Bond died and the young wife was left penniless. She moved to Chicago and there supported herself and her little son by sewing for friends, and doing china painting at odd moments. The women in whose homes she worked heard her singing songs of love and laughter, of sorrow and solace, and were amazed to find that she herself had composed and set them to music, but that none had been published. She had not had a thorough musical education, although she had taken a few music lessons when a young girl and the piano was a pastime to her. But with the appreciative encouragement of friends, the idea developed that people everywhere are the same at heart, and that it is the simple things of life, the things about which she sang, that appeal to rich and poor alike. Her songs expressed her philosophy of life and helped her over hard places. Their inspiration had been found first among the pine, hemlock, and cedar trees, when she lived close to nature in the logging and mining camps, and among people who displayed primitive emotions; then, with her baby in her arms, came the making of lullabies and the songs that have a heart-break in them. *Just*

a Wearyin' for You, Parting, and *Shadows* had been the expression of her emotion at the death of her young husband. Thus she came to believe that her songs would appeal to the home-loving thoughtful American men and women and she began to submit them to publishers. She met, at first, with much discouragement and suffered from misplaced confidence. To one firm she sold eleven songs for $35. The immediate response of the public amazed the publisher. Her popularity increased in England as well as in the United States and music houses were soon eagerly demanding her work. Mrs. Bond, however, became more and more unwilling to deliver the children of her brain and heart into the hands of strangers and in 1901 she established a business for herself as The Bond Shop to publish her own compositions. This "business" consisted at first of one small room, and until her son was old enough to become a partner in the business she was office girl, editor, publisher, and printer's devil. She not only wrote the words and music for songs, but designed and painted the covers as well. The business prospered until in 1921 the Carrie Jacobs–Bond and Son publishing house is one of the largest music publishing houses of the Middle West and is known from Chicago to the Antipodes. The entire plant is most interesting and it is a marvel how one brain could have created such a comprehensive and splendid organization. Mrs. Bond has composed more than six hundred songs, of which *A Perfect Day* is easily the most popular. It is heard in every part of the world where music is played and sung. During the World War Mrs. Bond received many letters from boys "over there" telling her what this song had meant to them,—that it was sung at camp concerts and in hospitals, in the trenches and on the march. Its sales have run into millions of copies. Although Mrs. Bond writes primarily for simple folk, singers of high rank have found her songs among their most successful offerings. Her work has been translated into twenty-six languages and arrangements of them have been made for almost every known instrument including the one-stringed fiddle of the Serbs, and the wailing bagpipes of the Scots. Mrs. Bond's concerts are not in the manner of a professional as her voice is not strictly a singing voice but is more adapted to recitative; but when she talks her songs or half sings them, there is a joyousness or a note of pathos that would have made her famous as an actress. Mrs. Bond spends much of her time in Los Angeles, where she has a house perched against the Hollywood Hills. It is designed to express the ideas and ideals of its owner and she calls it "The End of the Road." Her success, won in the face of hardships and discouragements, points out to beginners with latent genius a road to achievement through faith in self and one's own ideas. Mrs. Bond's gifts are originality and charm and there are few of the common-places of life that she has not made beautiful.

BOOTH, ELIZABETH KNOX (Mrs. Sherman M. Booth), suffragist, daughter of Samuel Gordon and Vena Crutchfield (Young) Knox, was born in Cedar Rapids, Iowa. Her father was the great-grandson of William Knox, Jr., of Fredericksburg, Virginia, and his wife, Susannah Fitzhugh, the former being the son of William Knox of Renfrew, Scotland, who settled in Culpepper County, Virginia, about 1790, where he named his estate Windsor Lodge. After attending the elementary grades in the Cedar Rapids public schools and the preparatory department of Coe College, Cedar Rapids, Elizabeth Knox was graduated from Cedar Rapids High School in 1899. She then entered the academic department of Coe College, where she was a member of the Sinclair Literary Society. She received the degree of Ph.B. in 1903. During the next four years she taught English, two years in the Osage, Iowa, High School, and one each in the Belle-vue, Iowa, High School and the Ida Grove, Iowa, High School. On June 29, 1907, she was married in Grace Episcopal Chapel, Cedar Rapids, to Sherman M. Booth, an

attorney of Glencoe, Illinois. Here she has since made her home. They have three children, Knox, Sherman M., and Elizabeth Booth.

Mrs. Booth is a member of the Woman's Library Club of Glencoe, one of the earliest of women's clubs, and of the Women's College Club of Washington, District of Columbia. In 1912 she organized the Glencoe Equal Suffrage Association and was its first president. At the convention of the Illinois Equal Suffrage Association, held at Galesburg, Illinois, October 1 and 2, 1912, she was elected head of the Legislative Department of the Illinois Equal Suffrage Association for the following year. After inaugurating and perfecting the card-index system of cataloguing legislators, she went to Springfield, Illinois, on January 8, 1913, at the opening of the session of the 48th General Assembly. She remained here throughout every working day of the session. After becoming acquainted with every member of the House and Senate, she catalogued them in the following form:—1. name, residence, business address, 'phone number, occupation; 2. district, party; 3. affiliation—wet or dry, boss, newspaper obligation; 4. religion, type, wife, prominent suffragist in her home district; 5. Suffrage pledge, legislative record, suffrage record; 6. remarks. This card, when completed, told, first, whether the legislator was for or against suffrage, or non-committal. If for, his card either corroborated the fact, or cast suspicion on his promise. If against, his card told whether there was a possibility of converting him. If noncommittal, his card told what chance there might be of winning him to the cause. Those in favor of suffrage were consulted and enlisted to help, while those unalterably opposed, whose cards gave no promise, and whose districts were opposed, were left alone, and thus their antagonism was not aroused. The great bulk of the work was done on the non-committal legislators. The State Suffrage organizations coöperated and completed the organization of suffragists in the State districts, and, wherever it seemed necessary, pressure was brought to bear on a legislator. The cataloguing and organization were accompanied by the strictest watch on legislative procedure, and the bill for presidential and municipal suffrage was piloted through the intricacies of committees, hearings, first, second, and third readings, debates, filibuster, transfer from one house to the other, and, finally, to Governor Dunne's signature. The liquor interests were very active in opposing the measure. The Chicago newspapers became sympathetic and supported the cause. Every possible influence—newspapers, churches, anti-saloon league, all sorts of women's organizations, and prominent individuals—was brought to bear throughout the State, until final victory was achieved when the Governor signed the bill, on June 26, 1913, in the presence of the "Suffrage Lobby" after speeches on both sides. The following winter, 1913–1914, Mrs. Booth spent in Washington, District of Columbia, as a member of the Congressional Committee of the National American Woman Suffrage Association, of which Mrs. Medill McCormick was chairman. Mrs. Booth has since remained at home, occupied with the care of her household at Glencoe, Illinois.

BROWN, OLIVE MARIE McINTOSH (Mrs. Edwin Hewitt Brown), daughter of Henry Payne and Olive Ann (Manfull) McIntosh, was born in Cleveland, Ohio, August 22, 1883. She is descended from Alexander McIntosh, who came to Cleveland from Scotland in 1825. After graduating from Miss Mittleberger's school in Cleveland in 1901, she attended for a year Mrs. Sommers' school in Washington, District of Columbia, and spent another year in Paris, France, as a pupil in Miss Grace Lee Hess' school. On November 6, 1907, she was married in Cleveland to Edwin Hewitt Brown of the General Aluminum and Brass Manufacturing Company of Detroit, Michigan. Mr. and Mrs. Brown have their home at Grosse Pointe, a suburb of Detroit, and are the parents of three children: Olive Anne, Ellanore, and McIntosh. Mrs. Brown has worked actively in support of the charities of the Episcopal Church. She is a director of the Needlework Guild and Secretary of the St. Agnes Home of Detroit, and has been interested in the Children's Free Hospital, the District Nursing Society, and the Grosse Pointe Mutual Aid Society. She is a member of the Detroit Symphony Society, the Detroit Orchestral Association, the Detroit Opera Association, the Morning Music Club, and the Chamber Music Society, and also of the Garden Club of Michigan. During the World War she worked in a Red Cross canteen and served with the rank of Major in the canteen of the Army and Navy Club of Detroit.

BURLINGAME, LILLIAN M., Physician, daughter of Alvah W. Burlingame, whose earliest ancestor came from England to Rhode Island in 1634, and Angeline I. Chichester, was born in Brooklyn, New York. She was educated at Packer Collegiate Institute, Brooklyn, and at the New York Medical College and Hospital for Women, where she received the degree of M.D., with honors, and the senior prize in surgery. For a time she was Visiting Physician at the New York Medical College and Hospital Dispensary, the Memorial Dispensary for Women, and the Eastern District Hospital Dispensary. She was first a lecturer, and afterwards Associate Professor of Gynecology at the New York Medical College and Hospital for Women, an examiner in lunacy, and a lecturer on medical and nursing topics under the New York Board of Education. She is a member of the Alumnae Association of the New York Medical College, the Women's Medical Club of New York, and the Society of New England Women (Colony No. 8, Brooklyn).

CANDEE, HELEN CHURCHILL, author, was born in New York City, October 5, 1868. She is a daughter of Henry Hungerford, a descendant of Benjamin Hungerford, who came from England to Connecticut in 1640, and of Mary E. Churchill, descended from Elder William Brewster, who came to Plymouth on the *Mayflower* in 1620. She was educated in private schools in New Haven and Norwalk, Connecticut, and was married, in Norwalk, to Edward W. Candee. Her travels in America, Europe, and the Far East have been extensive, and she was one of the survivors of the *Titanic* when that ship foundered on April 15, 1912. She has contributed many stories and essays to magazines, is on the editorial staff of *Arts and Decoration*, New York, and is the author of *An Oklahoma Romance* (1900), *Susan Truslow* (1901), *How Women May Earn a Living* (1902), *Styles and Periods in Furniture and Decoration* (1904), *The Tapestry Book* (1910), and *Jacobean Furniture* (1916). For her services in Italy during the World War she was decorated by the Royal Italian Red Cross and she has since been engaged in work on post-war help for ex-service men. She is a member of the Archaeological Society and the National Federation of Arts.

CHANNON, VESTA MILLER WESTOVER (Mrs. Harry Channon), daughter of George Frederic and Elizabeth Quackenbush (Miller) Westover, was born in Oconomowoc, Wisconsin. The Westovers are an old Virginia family. Among her mother's ancestors were John Miller (1644) of Easthampton, Long Island, a founder of Elizabeth, New Jersey; Daniel MacLaren of Edinburgh, Scotland, who came to New York in 1800; and, in the Woodruff family of New Jersey, Judge Thomas Woodruff of Elizabeth, who aided the cause of American independence and who was descended from Thomas Woodrove (1508–1552) through John Woodruffe (1604–1670) of Fordwich, England, a founder in 1639 of Southampton, Long Island. Mrs Channon is a graduate of Grant's Seminary, Chicago, Illinois. She also studied with private tutors in Chicago and New York and has followed special courses at the University of Chicago and at the Sorbonne, Paris. Her marriage to Harry Channon, a merchant of Chicago, took place on August 1, 1893, at St, George's Church, Hanover Square, London. Their son, Henry Channon, 3d, was born in Chicago, March 7, 1897, and, during the World War, served with the American Red Cross in Paris from October, 1917, to October, 1918, acting as buyer for the purchasing department, and, later being attached for several months to the American Embassy in Paris. Mrs. Channon's interests have always been especially in French literature, on which she has written club papers, and from which she has made many translations. In 1905 she founded the French library of the Alliance Française of Chicago, and has since served as chairman of the committee and directrice of the library. In connection with her work she has organized many fêtes for French charities, and in 1907 she was made an Officier d'Académie by the French government. She was chairman of the French booth in the Streets of Paris Fête, Chicago, and of the Red Cross booth in the Bazaar of the Allies, Chicago, in 1917. She spent 1918 in France, occupied with war relief work, chiefly organization and statistics, although it included some immediate personal work among refugees. She also made trips to the devastated districts of France in the interests of the French Red Cross, and, in Chicago, acted as chairman of the French Red Cross Committee, Allied Relief, Women's Division of the Illinois Branch of the Council of National Defense. She was a member of the Woman's War Relief Corps of the American Red Cross. Mrs. Channon is a member of the Chicago Chapter of the Daughters of the American Revolution; the Colonial Daughters of the Seventeenth Century, New York; the Lycéum Club, Paris; and the Chicago Women's, Cordon, Arts, Woman's Athletic, Chicago College, and Chicago Library Clubs of Chicago.

GIBBS, WINIFRED STUART, economist, daughter of George Holman and Catherine Stuart (Karmes) Gibbs, was born in New York City, October 6, 1871. Her father was born in England and came to the United States in 1846. She was educated in the Chicago, Illinois, high schools, under private tutors, and at the University of Rochester, New York, the Rochester Atheneum, and the Mechanics Institute of Rochester from which she received a diploma in 1901. She is a pioneer in applying the principles of home economics to the problems of social science and social economics. In 1906 she founded, and for ten years directed, the home economics work of the New York Association for Improving the Condition of the Poor. As a result of this work, the New York Child Welfare Board fixed certain tentative standards for its widows' pension work. Miss Gibbs instituted the training of students in home economics at Teachers College, Columbia University, to correlate their specialty with social service, and has acted as advisor for similar work in Providence, Rhode Island, Boston, Massachusetts, Chicago, Illinois, St. Louis, Missouri, and elsewhere. In 1909 she was a delegate to the Congress on Home Education at Brussels, Belgium. In June, 1918, the National War Labor Board called her in conference to assist in determining certain facts as to the essentials of living, and in 1919 she was in charge of the nation-wide thrift work of the Federal government, carried on through the States Relation Service of the United States Department of Agriculture. Miss Gibbs is a member of the National Arts Club of New York, the Arts Club of Washington, the American Association for the Advancement of Science, and the American Public Health Association. She is the author of *Lessons in Proper Feeding of the Family*, *Economical Cookery* (1912), *Food for the Invalid and the Convalescent* (1913), and *The Minimum Cost of Living* (1916), and has contributed articles to *The Survey*, *St. Nicholas Magazine*, *The Woman's World*, and other magazines.

GODDARD, EMMA, social service worker, was born in Chicago, Illinois, and is a daughter of Lester O. and Martha E. (Sterling) Goddard. She is a descendant of Francis Cooke, who came to Plymouth, Massachusetts, in 1620 on the *Mayflower*. After being graduated from Miss Masters' school at Dobbs Ferry, New York, Miss Goddard was assistant to Robert Hunter of the Chicago Bureau of Charities, and was a resident at the University of Chicago Settlement under Mary McDowell. For two terms she was President of the Service Club of Chicago which was founded in 1893 for social service and welfare work. Later she moved to Monroe, Michigan, where she is the Secretary and Treasurer of the Gertrude Club, one of eight clubs of the same name doing philanthropic work and assisting organized charities in the state. In 1917 Miss Goddard was appointed by Governor Sleeper to the Michigan State War Board, and she also acted as Vice-Chairman of the Monroe County Liberty Loan Committee. During 1917–1918 she gave public lectures throughout Monroe County for the United States Food Administration. She is a member of the Woman's Athletic Club of Chicago, the Society of Mayflower Descendants, the Society of Colonial Wars, and the Daughters of the American Revolution.

GRAVES, ANGELINE LOESCH (Mrs. Robert Elliott Graves), journalist, daughter of Frank J. and Lydia T. (Richards) Loesch, was born in Chicago, Illinois, January 31, 1875. She was educated in the public schools of Chicago and at the University of Chicago, where she took the degree of A.B. in 1898, continuing the following year as a graduate student in philosophy. On June 30, 1908, she married at Spring Lake, Michigan, Robert Elliott Graves, M.D. From 1906 to 1916 she was assistant and associate editor of *The Public*, Chicago, her interests lying especially in economic, political, and franchise reforms, and in land value taxation. She is a member of the Proportional Representation League of

America, the Women's Trade Union League, the Woman's Peace Party, the Woman's City Club of Chicago, and the Chicago College Club.

HELMER, ELIZABETH BRADWELL (Mrs. Frank A. Helmer), lawyer, daughter of Judge James B. and Myra (Colby) Bradwell was born in Chicago, Illinois, October 20, 1858. Her father was born in England and was brought, at the age of two, to the United States by his parents, who settled near Chicago in 1834. He was a distinguished lawyer of his day, and was especially concerned with the removal of the legal disabilities of women. He presided at the meeting in Cleveland, Ohio, when the National American Woman Suffrage Association was organized. Elizabeth Bradwell was graduated as valedictorian from the Chicago High School in 1876, and entered Northwestern University, where she received the degree of A.B. in 1880, and that of A.M. in 1882. In the latter year she was graduated also from Union College of Law, with the degree of LL.B., the valedictorian and only woman member of the law class of the year. On December 23, 1885, she was married, in Chicago, to Frank A. Helmer, a lawyer, and they are the parents of Mrya Bradwell Helmer, the wife of Doctor James Stuart Pritchard of Battle Creek, Michigan. After 1894, the year of her mother's death, she was associated with her father as assistant editor of the *Chicago Legal News*, the first law journal published west of the Allegheny Mountains, which was founded in 1868 by Mrs. Bradwell. When Judge Bradwell died in 1907, Mrs. Helmer became sole editor of the journal, and has carried it on ever since. In 1893 she was Vice-Chairman of the Woman's Committee, of which her mother was Chairman, on Law Reform and Government of the World's Congress Auxiliary at the Columbian Exposition, and for many years was Chairman of the Fellowship Committee of the Association of Collegiate Alumnae for the awarding of traveling fellowships in European universities. She has written many magazine articles, has edited several volumes of the Illinois Appellate Court reports, and, since 1905, has been the editor of *Hurd's Revised Statutes of Illinois*. With all her legal and editorial duties, she has found time for charitable work, and is the Secretary of the Soldiers' Home in Chicago. She is a member of the American Bar Association, the Illinois State Bar Association, the Association of Collegiate Alumnae, the Daughters of the American Revolution, and the Chicago Woman's, Woman's Athletic, and Twentieth Century Clubs.

REA, EDITH OLIVER (Mrs. Henry R. Rea), daughter of Henry W. and Edith Anne (Cassidy) Oliver, was born in Pittsburgh, Pennsylvania, where her grandfather, Henry W. Oliver, settled in 1842 on his arrival from Ireland. Her education was obtained in the private schools of Miss Fuller and Mrs. Hayward in Pittsburgh, of the Mlles. Charbonnier, and of Miss Brown in New York. On April 23, 1889, she was married in Pittsburgh to Henry R. Rea, Vice-President of the old firm of Robinson-Rea Manufacturing Company. Their children are Edith Anne and Henry Oliver Rea.

On account of poor health, Mrs. Rea was unable to take an active part in War Relief until after the United States entered the World War, but in May, 1917, she financed and helped to manage a very successful Canning Kitchen in Sewickley, Pennsylvania, where she has a country home. Under the direction of a Drexel Institute expert, the ladies of Sewickley furnished vegetables and fruits and canned over six thousand jars, which were all distributed to hospitals in this country, besides one thousand containers of dried vegetables sent to the American Hospital at Neuilly, France. Always an enthusiastic Red Cross supporter, and wishing to concentrate the energy of the women who belonged to the local branch of that organization, Mrs. Rea built a house in the shape of a cross for headquarters in Sewickley. Here all forms of Red Cross work were carried on with excellent results. In October, 1917, Mrs. Rea was appointed Chairman of the first Young Men's Christian Association drive for funds in Pittsburgh, and she was also a member of the Women's Federal Council of the National War Savings Committee and was instrumental in organizing the Pittsburgh branch of the Emergency Aid of Pennsylvania.

Mr. Rea, having offered his services to the Government, became a member of the War Industries Board, and in November, 1917, the family removed to Washington. Mrs. Rea's remarkable executive ability and personality were already known there, and she was at once made Chairman of the Comfort Section of the District of Columbia Chapter of the Red Cross. The work of this particular branch of the service consisted in preparing and providing the comfort kits, which met the daily needs of the men going over-seas. These kits were six-inch by eight-inch khaki bags containing seventeen articles. Thousands of these were shipped to points of embarkation for distribution. The Comfort Section also made hospital bed bags and scrap books. This work grew so rapidly under Mrs. Rea's management that the Comfort Section was moved into headquarters of its own at 1301 Connecticut Avenue, where a corps of volunteer workers was always found.

In May, 1918, when the Red Cross Convalescent House at Walter Reed Hospital, Takoma Park, Washington, was ready for occupancy, Mrs. Rea was appointed Field Director, Department of Military Relief, Potomac Division, to take full charge of everything concerning the Red Cross activities at Walter Reed Hospital, with the rank of Major, directly under the Commanding Officer. One of her first acts was to interest her wide circle of friends. From the inception of the work Mrs. Rea infused her co-workers with her own enthusiasm and quickly surrounded herself with a most efficient band of

women who, like herself, found no task too difficult; and it was no uncommon sight to see the ladies washing windows, scrubbing floors, hanging curtains, and uncrating furniture. The house contained an assembly-room seating over seven hundred and attractively furnished by Mrs Rea, personally, with every means conducive to the comfort and recreation of the convalescents. At one end was a stage solarium, and a billiard and pool room at the other, and, on either side of the stage, were Mrs. Rea's private office and the officers' reading and writing room. The latter was furnished in memory of Mrs. Rea's father, Henry W. Oliver, by Mrs. Oliver, who was ever mindful of the comfort of the men. On the floor above were eight small bedrooms, intended for the use of friends and relatives of the soldiers who might be summoned to the bedside in critical cases. These rooms were decorated and furnished by eight of Mrs. Rea's friends. A completely equipped kitchen and dining-room for the convenience of those living in the house were furnished by the Requisition Club.

For the forty-eight wards to be covered daily, Mrs. Rea appointed three ward visitors, each with three assistants to make the rounds with the articles needed for distribution, which ranged from tooth-paste and stationery to bath-robes and socks. A Red Cross diet kitchen was also included in the plan and special dishes were taken into the wards both morning and afternoon. During very hot weather ice-cream was distributed every afternoon by two Red Cross ladies assigned to this duty. At the Gate House, Red Cross representatives were on duty to issue passes to the house, and strangers, wishing to visit the wards, were provided with a Red Cross escort. A shopping desk was also established for the convenience of the patients, and, as many of them formed the habit of bringing their money to the office for safe keeping, Mrs. Rea became their banker until, with the growth of the business, the Commanding Officer established a patients' bank at the Post.

One of the most difficult problems to solve was that of the bureau of passes and entertainments, demanding unfailing tact and good judgment on the part of Mrs. Rea. Every invitation had to be investigated and passed upon before acceptance. For each man who left the Post permission had to be obtained from his ward surgeon, a pass procured, and transportation furnished, if needed—a heavy task when six or seven hundred men were to be taken to a theatre party in town. Every Tuesday night a dance was given for the patients, and once a week Keith's Circuit sent several acts from their bill, besides inviting one hundred and fifty boys into the city performance on Wednesday afternoons. Nearly every musician of note who visited Washington during 1917–1919 went to Red Cross House, Walter Reed Hospital, and from there into the wards, where a portable organ was used for their accompaniments. Holidays, such as Thanksgiving Day, Christmas, and July 4th, were occasions of special celebrations at the Hospital, with dinners, games, parades, and athletic contests.

After one summer spent at the Hospital, Mrs. Rea saw the need of a swimming pool, and, therefore, gave the Rea Swimming Pool, which was ready for use and turned over to the Post on July 5, 1919. In September, 1919, as matters at home demanded her attention, Mrs. Rea sent in her resignation to take effect on the nineteenth. In a thousand ways she had endeared herself to everyone on the Post from the highest to the lowest. The boys, anxious to show in some way their appreciation, subscribed among themselves ten cents each, to be invested in a loving cup appropriately inscribed, which is one of Mrs. Rea's most cherished possessions.

Although most of Mrs. Rea's work was among the soldiers, she had a thought always for the sailors. Early in the War she turned over her yacht to the Navy for scout service. Her son, Henry Oliver Rea, was an officer in the Navy on board the *Wyoming* with duty in foreign waters for fourteen months. On Christmas following the Armistice, instead of sending gifts to men on the *Wyoming*, Mrs. Rea sent a check so that they might plan their own celebration, and it was unanimously voted to use the money to compile a record of their foreign service so that each man should have a copy. To the Naval Men's Club at Queenstown she gave a soda water fountain, which was greatly appreciated by the men on duty in that vicinity. The National Service School for Girls was another of her varied interests. Girls came to Washington from all over the country to live in tents and take the training that was to fit them for duty wherever called.

For her constructive war relief work, Mrs. Rea was awarded in July, 1918, the Liberty Medal of the National Institute of Social Sciences. She is a member of the National Institute of Social Sciences, the Red Cross, the American Legion, the American Women's Legion of the Great War, the Colony Club of New York, and the Pennsylvania Women's Club.

HOBBS, MARY EVERETT MARSHALL (Mrs. Perry Lynes Hobbs), descendant of many patriots, was born in Cleveland, Ohio, September 20, 1863. Her father, Isaac Holmes Marshall, M.D., who was born in Weathersfield, Ohio, September 17, 1821, and died in Cleveland, Ohio, March 30, 1895, served in the Civil War, and his father William Marshall (1774–1859), was a soldier in the War of 1812. The latter married Rachel McElroy (1780–1871), who planted and tended the crops with the aid of her small children, and rode on horseback all the rough and dangerous way to Pittsburgh, to bring salt to the soldiers of 1812. Both her father, Adam McElroy, and her father-in-law, James Marshall, served in the War of the Revolution. The latter was born in 1745 in County Tyrone, Ireland, where he married Lydia Carson (1754–1830). About 1776 he settled in Lancaster County, Pennsylvania, and later moved to Weathersfield, Ohio, dying there

February 19, 1829. Doctor Isaac Holmes Marshall married Mary Etta Everett[1] (1825–1875), a pioneer Woman's Christian Temperance UnionWorker and in 1869 First President of the Cleveland Good Samaritan Society. She was the daughter of Major Samuel Everett, an officer in the War of 1812, who was born in Pennsylvania in 1793 and died in Cleveland in 1858. On July 14, 1818, he married, at New Berlin, Union County, Pennsylvania, Sarah Pheil (1802–1890), and brought her, a bride of only sixteen years of age, on horseback, to her new home in Liberty, Trumbull County, Ohio. His father, Captain Samuel Everett, fought in the Revolutionary War. He was born about 1760 in Pennsylvania, and died in 1808, at Liberty, Ohio. His wife, Mary Barbara Mosser (1765–1818), was the daughter of Philip Mosser, a Revolutionary soldier from Pennsylvania, whose wife, Barbara, baked bread in her ovens for the hungry soldiers of two New Jersey companies encamped on her farm, on their return from the Whisky Insurrection of 1794. Captain Samuel Everett's father, Thomas Everett, who also served in the early days of the Revolution, died about 1777 in Lynn Township, Northampton County (now Lehigh County), Pennsylvania. It was here at Lynnport that his father, John Everett, received the original Everett grant in 1735, and it was on his property that Fort Everett was built. John Everett married a Holdren, and died before 1772. He was undoubtedly a descendant of the Richard Everett who came in 1634 from Dedham, England, to Dedham, Massachusetts, although the connection has not been established.

Mary Everett Marshall was graduated from the Cleveland Central High School in 1882, and from the School of Art, Cleveland, in 1885. In the same year she won a scholarship of the Cleveland Art Club, where she continued her studies until 1892. On April 6, 1892, she married, in Cleveland, Perry Lynes Hobbs, Ph.D., who was born in Cleveland, September 10, 1861, and died there April 6, 1912. The son of Caleb Secum and Ada Antoinette (Lynes) Hobbs, he traced his ancestry back through his grandfather, Thomas J. Hobbs, Joseph Hobbs, Jr., Joseph Hobbs, Abraham Hobbs, Jr., and Abraham Hobbs, to the latter's grandfather, Thomas Hobbs, of Ipswich, Massachusetts (1657). Doctor Hobbs was a distinguished analytical and consulting chemist, one of the first to specialize as a chemical engineer, and to adapt scientific attainments to industry and commerce. In 1887 he was a student in bacteriology, then almost unknown as a study in the United States, under the famous Doctor Koch, and in 1889 he took his doctorate in philosophy at the University of Berlin. From 1896 to 1912 he was chemist for the Ohio Dairy and Food Commission, and from 1906 to 1910 chemical engineer for the Cowell Portland Cement Plant of California. In 1911 he established, in his own laboratory, the Dairy Ferments Company for the making of a new kind of culture for butter and cheese.

As the descendant of so many patriots in the history of the United States, Mrs. Hobbs has naturally been interested in honoring the memory, and preserving the records, of the founders of American liberty. In 1911 she was a charter member and first Vice-President of the Commodore Perry Chapter, Daughters of 1812, and in that same year she compiled the chapter's first year book, an historic edition, which was placed in the corner-stone of the Perry Memorial Monument at Put-in-Bay, Ohio, July 4, 1913. Again, in 1915, she compiled the first lineage book of the Ohio Society, Daughters of 1812. Her interest in the Daughters of the American Revolution has been as great. She is a member of the Western Reserve Chapter, D. A. R,. and was its registrar in 1921, beginning also in that year the preparation of a valuable set of records of the graves of Revolutionary soldiers in Cuyahoga, Lorain, and Medina Counties, Ohio, and other unpublished data. She had already had experience in this field as an organizer, in 1916, of the Pioneers Memorial

Association for the preservation of the Erie Street Cemetery, Cleveland, and as a member of the Early Settlers' Association of Cuyahoga County. Her research in local and family history has enabled her to make valuable contributions to the genealogical departments of the Boston *Transcript* and the Hartford *Times*, and she is at work on the preparation of genealogies of the Marshall, Everett, and Hobbs families. The connection between a reverent patriotism, and a constructive Americanism for the future, was early apparent to Mrs. Hobbs, and in 1909 she was one of the promoters in establishing a safe and sane Fourth of July. In that same year she was also engaged in the publicity campaign for a Tuberculosis Sanitorium, the first in Cleveland. From 1910 to 1913 she was Chairman of the Executive Board of the Cleveland Council of Women and frequently opened her colonial home on Euclid Avenue for entertainments to raise funds, under the Council's auspices, for philanthropic purposes. In 1910 a series of "Washington Tea Parties" were held there for the benefit of breakfasts for needy children in the public schools. The question of pure and cheaper food continued to occupy Mrs. Hobbs' attention, so that, with the increasing necessity for conservation during the World War, she was prepared in 1916, to demonstrate the possibility of eliminating butter and eggs from breadstuffs, puddings, etc., and the advantage of the so-called "war recipes." Throughout the war she was active in whatever would aid the men in service or those engaged in relief work. In 1917 she prevailed upon the Cleveland stores to regulate hanks of yarn by the quantity needed to knit a pair of socks, and the following year she was chairman of a committee on repairing socks for the men at Camp Sherman until a knitting machine was installed at the camp. Continuing her investigations in the food question, she gave in 1919 a luncheon of canned Army food to demonstrate an additional means of cutting the price of the high cost of living. In 1921 she was elected

Historian of the Cleveland Chapter, War Mothers of America. Early impressed with the necessity of women taking their part in municipal and political affairs, Mrs. Hobbs was a founder in 1913 of the Woman's Civic Association of Cleveland. In 1920 she was a member of the Woman's Harding Club, and helped to organize the Republican Women's League of Cleveland, becoming its president in 1921. She believes that women will exert an influence for good in politics, and is bending her own energies to this end. Other offices which she has held have been those of auditor in 1908-1909 of the Cleveland Sorosis and President in 1911 of the Cleveland Emerson Class, and she is a life member of the Luther Burbank Society and a member of the Tippecanoe and Cinema Clubs of Cleveland, the Interstate Institute, and the Young Women's Christian Association.

Doctor and Mrs. Hobbs are the parents of three children, all born in Cleveland. The eldest, Mary Antoinette Hobbs, was educated at Dana Hall, Wellesley, Massachusetts, and at the National Park Seminary, Washington, District of Columbia. She was active in Red Cross work during the World War and assisted in caring for the soldiers at Newton Hospital, Massachusetts, at the time of the influenza epidemic in 1918. The younger daughter, Katharine Marshall Hobbs, attended Vassar and Wells Colleges. In 1917 and 1918 she was Assistant Director of the Navy League Red Cross, Cleveland, and was reconstruction aid at United States General Hospital No. 3, Colonia, New Jersey, in 1919, and at No. 41, Fox Hills, New York, in 1920. In 1921 she began reconstruction work among the crippled children of Cleveland. The youngest child, Perry Marshall Hobbs, a student at the University of Michigan, was in 1918-1919 a student officer in the aviation branch, United States Navy.

---

[1]Their daughter, Sarah Marshall (Mrs. William M.) Safford, was for years secretary of the Brooklyn Woman's Club and during 1897-1900 delivered many able addresses in London, England, before prom-

inent societies, on American topics, and on literature in general. Their grandson, Maxwell Holmes Marshall, only child of Everett Marshall, served overseas in the World War with the 28th Infantry, 1st Division, Company D, and had the honor of going over the top in the first line in the first American attack at Cantigny, where he was killed in action June 10, 1918.

HOBSON, SARAH MATILDA, physician, daughter of Samuel Decatur and Mary (Sawyer) Hobson, was born in Island Pond, Vermont, September 25, 1861. She is of Colonial stock, her earliest paternal American ancestor, William Hobson, having left Rowley, England, to settle in Rowley, Massachusetts, in 1650. William's father, Henry Hobson, was one of the merchant group in England who helped finance the *Mayflower* expedition. Doctor Hobson's childhood and youth were spent in New England, and here her education was obtained. In 1879 she was graduated from the State Normal School at Salem, Massachusetts; her preparatory course was taken in Vermont Methodist Seminary, Montpelier, Vermont, in 1880–1882; and she was graduated from Boston University with a Ph.B. degree in 1887. Immediately entering the medical department of the same university, she was graduated there in 1890 with the degree of M.D. Her professional life has been spent chiefly in Chicago, Illinois.

That Doctor Hobson is a woman of great energy and efficiency is evidenced in her career, for not only has she been engaged in medical practice but since 1914 she has been an editor of the *Journal of the North American Institute of Homeopathy* and during the last few years, editor-in-chief, a position never before held by a woman. In 1914–1916 she was Secretary of the American Institute of Homeopathy, in 1919 lecturer on social hygiene for the Illinois Department of Health, and also, in the same year, chairman of scholarships of the Vocational Supervision League of Chicago. Doctor Hobson holds membership in the Woman's City Club of Chicago, the Chicago College Club, the Cordon Club, and the After Dinner Club.

She is fond of nature and the out-door life and her favorite recreation is the taking of country hikes.

HOES, ROSE GOUVERNEUR (Mrs. Roswell Randall Hoes), lecturer, daughter of Samuel Laurence Gouveneur, Jr., and his wife, Marian Campbell, and great-granddaughter of James Monroe, fifth President of the United States, was born in Foo Chow, China. Among her ancestors were Isaac Gouverneur, who came from France to New York before 1666; William Hutchinson, Colonial Governor of Massachusetts and Rhode Island from 1640 to 1642; and Peter Palfry, one of the founders of Massachusetts Bay Colony. She was educated at Miss Baer's School, Frederick, Maryland, and in the public schools of Washington, District of Columbia. On December 5, 1888, she married, in Washington, the Rev. Roswell Randall Hoes, chaplain in the United States Navy. Their children were Gouverneur Hoes, 1st Lieutenant, Air Service, U.S.A., Roswell Randall Hoes, Jr., who died in 1901, and Laurence Gouverneur Hoes, private in the U. S. Medical Corps. Mrs. Hoes is founder and President of the Gentlewoman's League and Social and Domestic Agency (the Women's Exchange of Washington), one of the three founders of the Club of Colonial Dames, secretary of the Board of Managers of the Association for Works of Mercy, member of the Executive Council of the Housekeeper's Alliance, and member of the National Society of the Colonial Dames of America. In 1914 she compiled *As I Remember*, a volume of her mother's reminiscences and, in the following year, brought out her *Catalogue of American Historical Costumes, including those of the Mistresses of the White House as shown in the U. S. National Museum*. The collection of costumes here referred to was made by Mrs. Hoes and Mrs. Julian-James. The results attained are not only remarkable, but of great importance, for they have not only brought together many beautiful articles of women's dress and adornment, but also have demonstrated that the United States already has a tradition of costume which is both instructive and full of popular interest. Court costumes worn by distinguished American statesmen, and the uniforms of officers of world-wide fame, have been added to this exhibition, together with a collection of the dress of old-fashioned children, historical laces, fans, jewelry, gloves, slippers and shoes, handkerchiefs, buttons, etc. Many of the dresses in this collection go back to Colonial days, but its most striking feature are the elegant gowns worn on state occasions by the mistresses of the White House from Martha Washington down to Mrs. Taft. Mrs. Hoes since 1916 has been lecturing before some of the largest educational institutions in the country on *American Historical Costumes Worn by the Mistresses of the White House* and *Historic Costumes Worn by Famous American Statesmen*, illustrated by lantern slides made from this collection in the National Museum.

HORSFORD, CORNELIA, archaeologist, daughter of Eben Norton and Phoebe (Gardiner) Horsford, was born in Cambridge, Massachusetts, September 25, 1861. She is descended from William Horsford, who was born in England and in 1633, or earlier, settled in Dorchester, Massachusetts, where he had charge of the fences for the north part of the town, and is otherwise frequently referred to in the records. About 1636 he moved to Windsor, Connecticut, where, in 1652, he was deputy to the General Court, and held other offices. His first wife died in Windsor, August 26, 1641, and he married, second, Jane, the widow of Henry Fowkes. Both returned to England, where he died after 1656 while she died after 1671. John Horsford, William's son by his first wife, accompanied his parents to America and married Phillipa Thrall, November 5, 1657, in Windsor, where he died, August 7, 1683. Their son, Timothy Horsford, was born in Windsor, October 20, 1662, and married, December 5, 1689, Hannah

Palmer, who was born October 30, 1666, and died July 8, 1702. Their son, Daniel Horsford, was born in Windsor, July 5, 1695, married at Hebron, Connecticut, April 6, 1721, Elizabeth Stewart, (died in Williamstown, Massachusetts, in 1783), and died in South Canaan, Connecticut, May 23, 1777. Their son, Captain Daniel Horsford, was born at Hebron, November 8, 1723, was lieutenant of the train band from 1755 and captain from 1765, and died at South Canaan about 1788. About 1748 he married Martha Dibble, who was born December 25, 1719. Their son, Roger Horsford, was born at South Canaan, January 21, 1755, married at South Canaan about 1778 Mary Brown, (born March 15, 1754, and died September 12, 1812), and died at Charlotte, Vermont, August 15, 1818. Their son, Jerediah Horsford, was born at Charlotte, Vermont, March 8, 1791, married at Goshen, Connecticut, September 15, 1816, Cherry Marcia Norton, (born May 31, 1790, and died October 30, 1859) and died at Livonia Station, New York, January 14, 1875. He served at the defense of Burlington in 1812, organized militia in the Genesee Valley, and gained the rank of Colonel after the Battle of Lundy's Lane. From 1814 to 1816 he acted also as a missionary among the Seneca Indians and, later in life, was an assemblyman in the New York State Legislature, and, from 1851 to 1853, a member of Congress. His son, Eben Norton Horsford, Cornelia Horsford's father, was born in Moscow, New York, July 27, 1818, and died in 1893. After being graduated as a civil engineer from Rensselaer Polytechnic Institute in 1838, he was engaged in the New York State Geological Survey. From 1840 to 1844 he taught mathematics and natural sciences at the Albany Female Academy, and then went to Germany to make researches in analytical chemistry. In 1847 he was appointed Rumford professor of applied sciences at Harvard University. His plans for the development of his department led to the formation of the Lawrence Scientific School. After sixteen years in charge of the laboratory of analytical chemistry, he turned to chemical manufactures and became president of the Rumford Chemical Works at Providence, Rhode Island. Among his many discoveries, the most important relate to the preparation of white bread, the restoration of phosphates to milled bran, and the preparation of the medicine acid phosphates. He was especially interested in the development of the science departments at Wellesley College, and was instrumental in having inaugurated there the system of "sabbatical" leaves of absence for professors, and of retiring pensions. Professor Horsford was also engaged, during the later part of his life, in research in the archaeology of the American Indians, and of the early explorations on the north-east coast of the continent. He had a wide acquaintance with Indian languages, and printed the manuscript dictionary of the Moravian missionary, David Zeisberger, in English, German, Iroquois, and Algonquin. Of his publications in this field two are especially notable, one on *The Indian Names of Boston* and one on *The Landfall of John Cabot in 1497 and the Site of Norumbega* which reëstablished the lost location of these places. He married, first, in 1847, Mary L'Hommedieu Gardiner, the author of *Indian Legends and Other Poems* (1855) and of many contributions to the *Knickerbocker Magazine* and other periodicals, and, second, in 1857, her sister, Phoebe Dayton Gardiner, who was born August 13, 1826, and died October 8, 1900. The Gardiner line is traced from Lion Gardiner, who came from Woerden, Holland, July 10, 1635, and was Lord of the Manor of Gardiner's Island, New York, through David Gardiner, John Gardiner, David Gardiner, Abraham Gardiner, Abraham Gardiner, to Samuel Smith Gardiner of Shelter Island, New York, the father of Mary and Phoebe (Gardiner) Horsford.

Cornelia Horsford was educated in private schools in Cambridge and Boston, Massachusetts. Associated with her father in his archaeological researches, she carried on these studies after his death. In 1895 she sent an expedition to Iceland to examine the ruins of the Saga-Time, and during the years, 1895, 1896, and 1897, she arranged for excavations in the British Isles to examine the remains of amphitheatres, forts, etc. She has also directed various investigations into the Norse discovery of America among works of the American Indians. She is the author of *Graves of the Northmen* (1893), *An Inscribed Stone* (1895), *Dwellings of the Saga-Time in Iceland, Greenland, and Vinland* in *The National Geographic Magazine* (1898), *Vinland and its Ruins* in *The Popular Science Monthly* (December, 1899). *Ruins of the Saga-Time*, and many other magazine articles on archaeology. She was formerly a fellow of the American Association for the Advancement of Science, of which her father was a charter member, and is honorary Vice-President of the Viking Club of London, Historian of the Massachusetts Society of Colonial Dames of America, and a member of the National Geographic Society, the Prince Historical Society, the Iceland Antiquarian Society, the Irish Texts Society, the Huguenot Society, the Society of Colonial Lords of Manors, and the Easthampton Garden Club. Her homes are in Cambridge, Massachusetts, and at Shelter Island, New York, where she is President of the Shelter Island Public Library, and where she finds recreation in motoring, boating, gardening, and sketching in water colors.

JACOBS, MARY FRICK (Mrs. Henry Barton Jacobs), daughter of William Frederick and Anne Elizabeth (Swan) Frick, was born in Baltimore, Maryland. Her father was a descendant of Sir George Yeardley who was born in London, England, about 1580 and who, after service in the Low Countries, sailed with Sir Thomas Gates for Virginia in June, 1609, on board the *Deliverance*. The ship, however, was wrecked in the Bermudas and he did not reach Virginia until the following year. On November 18, 1618, he was appointed Governor of Virginia for three years, and was knighted at Newmarket on the 24th of the same month, by James I. In July, 1619, under instructions from the Virginia Company, he summoned the first colonial assembly. In 1626 Charles I reappointed him Governor of Virginia, and he held the reins of government from May 17th until his death on November 10, 1627.

Mary Frick was educated at home by governesses and private tutors. On October 31, 1872, she married, at Baltimore, Robert Garrett, a railroad president and banker, who died, and on April 2, 1902, she married at Baltimore, Henry Barton Jacobs, a physician. All her life Mrs. Jacobs has been an active supporter of many philanthropies and charities, especially those of the Episcopal Church, and has engaged in the work of organizations devoted to civic improvement, while her love of flowers and gardening has led her to ally herself with horticultural and garden societies, especially at her summer home in Newport, Rhode Island. She is the founder of the Robert Garrett Hospital for Children, Baltimore, and a trustee of the Chase Home at Annapolis, Maryland. She is Vice-President of the Bishop Brent Moro Committee and of the Cathedral League of Baltimore and a member of the Girls' Friendly Society. She is also Vice-President of the Women's Civic League, Inc., of Baltimore, and an honorary Vice-President of the Women's Civic League of Catonsville, Maryland, as well as of the Maryland Association Opposed to Women's Suffrage. At Newport she is a member of the Horticultural Society, the Garden Club, the Garden Association, the Improvement Association, and is a member of the Maryland State Horticultural Society. Mrs. Jacobs is a discriminating art collector and a music lover, and belongs to the Art Association of Newport and the Music Club. Her interest in history has made her a member of the Newport Historical Society, and she is Vice-President of Chapter I of the Colonial Dames of America, Baltimore, and a member of the Society of Descendants of Colonial Governors. She is also a member of the Alliance Française of Baltimore and of the Baltimore Contemporary Club and Tudor Club, and of the Casino and the Golf Club at Newport. During the World War she gave her time to the work of the Women's Section of the Maryland League for National Defense and the Women's Committee of Newport Coöperating with the National War Work Council of the Young Women's Christian Association.

CUMMINGS, MARY AUGUSTA MARSTON (Mrs. Robert Fowler Cummings), daughter of Sanford K. and Sarah (Field) Marston, was born at New London, Connecticut. She is descended from Captain William Marston of Yorkshire, England, who came to Salem, Massachusetts, in 1634, through Brackett Marston, who was born at Falmouth, Maine, in 1747 and served in the defense of Portland, Maine, during the War of the Revolution. In all of her lines she is of New England descent. After graduating from Grand Prairie Seminary, Onarga, Illinois, she was married at Onarga, on July 6, 1874, to Robert Fowler Cummings, a grain merchant, who died December 14, 1914. Their children are Lenore, Marion Marston (Mrs. Ralph C. Stevens of Glen Ridge, New Jersey), Austin Benjamin, who died February 11, 1880, Florence (Mrs. Thomas J. Hair of Chicago, Illinois), Irene, who died December 30, 1903, and Marston. Mrs. Cummings is a leader in the patriotic societies of Chicago. She is a member of the Chicago Chapter of the Daughters of the American Revolution and the Illinois Chapter of the Society of Daughters of Founders and Patriots of America and also of the Chicago Women's Club and the Hyde Park Travel Club. For some years she was the Second President General of the National Society of New England Women. Her unfailing tact and courtesy, and her ability as an organizer, have contributed greatly to the growth of this society, which was founded for the purpose of perpetuating the spirit of liberty and steadfast patriotism that animated the women of the New England colonies. During the World War the individual Colonies of the Society, in addition to their regular programme, did practical work in war relief and the encouragement of thrift.

JOHNSON, JULIA MACFARLANE CARSON (Mrs. Richard W. Johnson), educator, daughter of James Clinton and Julia Ann (Macfarlane) Carson, was born in Delmont, Westmoreland County, Pennsylvania, in 1862. Her grandfather, John Carson of Huntingdon, Pennsylvania, who came from the North of Ireland about 1780 and died in 1825, was a graduate of the University of Edinburgh and did much, as a scholar and theologian, by means of lectures and many books and pamphlets, to frame the policies of Pennsylvania in the early days of the Union. He married a daughter of the famous Clinton family, descended from Charles Clinton (1690–1773) of Londonderry, Ireland, who settled in Ulster County, New York, in 1731 and who was the father of General James Clinton and grandfather of De Witt Clinton. James Clinton Carson was also descended from John and Jane (Lancaster) McCarthy who came from Oxford, England, to Washington County, Pennsylvania, about 1750. He took part for many years in the Indian warfare in western Pennsylvania around Fort du Quesne and he and his entire family were for six months prisoners of the Indians. Julia Ann Macfarlane's father was a physician educated at the University of Edinburgh, who died shortly after coming to America early in the nineteenth century. Julia Macfarlane Carson was educated at the high school in Catasauqua, Pennsylvania, and was prepared for college by tutors. She was graduated from Mt. Holyoke College in 1885, and took post-graduate work at the University of Pennsylvania, the University of Cincinnati, and the University of Minnesota, where she received her degree of M.A. After teaching as head of

the Latin department at Coates College, Terre Haute, Indiana, from 1891 to 1894, she was married at Catasauqua, Pennsylvania, February 14, 1894, to General Richard W. Johnson, United States Army, officer and author. Their son, John Macfarlane Johnson, was born January 25, 1895. Since 1897 Mrs. Johnson has been head of the Department of Literature at Macalester College, St. Paul, Minnesota, and from 1897 to 1917 Dean of Women. She has written for various newspapers and magazines and has contributed to the proceedings of the State College Associations of Indiana and Minnesota. She has worked for equal suffrage at Macalester College and throughout the state and has served on the boards of the various suffrage organizations. She has been a member of committees in the St. Paul Welfare League, and is a member of the International Peace Association, the Christian Association, the Association of Collegiate Alumnae, the Mt. Holyoke Alumnae, the Civic League, and the New Century Club.

JORDAN, ELIZABETH, author, daughter of William Francis and Margherita (Garver) Jordan, was born in Milwaukee, Wisconsin. She is descended from Michael Jordan, who came from Cork, Ireland, and settled in Milwaukee about 1834. Her education was obtained at the Convent of Notre Dame, Milwaukee, where she won the Cross of Honor, and later in travel and study abroad. From 1890 to 1900 she was on the editorial staff of the New York *World*, and for three years was assistant editor of the Sunday *World*, in which she published the results of her studies of tenement conditions in New York under the title, *Studies of the Submerged Tenth*. These studies of the poor she later continued in London and Paris. From January 1, 1900, to May, 1913, she was the editor of *Harper's Bazaar*, and from May, 1913, to January, 1918, she was literary advisor to Harper and Brothers. She is the author of *Tales of the City Room, Tales of the Cloister,*

Tales of Destiny, May Iverson—Her Book, Many Kingdoms, May Iverson Tackles Life, May Iverson's Career, Lovers' Knots, The Wings of Youth, and *The Girl in the Mirror.* With Anna Howard Shaw she wrote *The Story of a Pioneer,* and *The Whole Family* in collaboration with William Dean Howells, Henry James, Henry van Dyke, Elizabeth Stuart Phelps, Alice Brown, and others. She has contributed many short stories and essays to English and American magazines and she is the staff editorial writer on a chain of leading American newspapers. Her play, *The Lady from Oklahoma,* was produced in New York by Messrs. Brady and Shubert in 1912–1913. During Mayor Mitchel's administration she was on the Mayor's Committee of Women, New York. She is President of the Gramercy Park Club, Vice-President of the Notre Dame Alumnae Association, and a member of the Big Sisters Association, the New York Committee of the North American Civic League for Immigrants, the Gramercy Neighborhood Association, the Equal Franchise Society, the Author's League of America, the National Institute of Social Sciences, the American Defense Society, the American Red Cross, the National Woman Suffrage Association, the American Committee of Mercy, the American Aero Club, and the Colony, Women's City, and Cosmopolitan Clubs of New York.

KESSLER, CORA PARSONS (Mrs. George A. Kessler), philanthropist, daughter of Erastus and Christine (Pepper) Parsons, was born in Sacramento, California. Her father was descended from Cornet Joseph Parsons, who came from England to Massachusetts in 1650, and built one of the first permanent American residences at Northampton, Massachusetts. She was educated at home and later in the public schools of San Francisco, where she was graduated from the Girls' High School. She married in 1901, in New York City, George Alexander Kessler, the American representative of Messrs. Moët and

Chandon of France. Mr. Kessler was a philanthropist who devoted much of his time and money to the furtherance of the arts and the promotion of science, and when the World War began he engaged in relief and hospital work, turning over to the French government his home in Paris. When the *Lusitania* was torpedoed in 1915 Mr. Kessler was on board and, in gratitude for his escape from drowning, at the suggestion of Mrs. Kessler, he retired from business and dedicated his life to the merciful work of helping the soldiers and sailors of the Allies blinded in the cause of liberty and justice. The problem of thousands of combatants left helpless by the loss of their sight was unprecedented and perplexing. In this emergency Mr. and Mrs. Kessler established the British-French-Belgian Permanent Blind Relief War Fund. To this title, when the United States entered the war, was prefixed the word "American," and later, to cover the Fund's widened activities, which took in the blinded warriors of eight nations, the name was changed definitely to the Permanent Blind Relief War Fund for Soldiers and Sailors of the Allies. Until his death on September 13, 1920, Mr. Kessler was Chairman of the Fund's executive council and Mrs. Kessler was an Honorary Secretary, both devoting their whole time and energy to the Fund's work. They were assisted by many men and women, eminent internationally, who freely gave their services as members of the executive and other controlling committees. Although all available institutions in France had been requisitioned, they were utterly unable adequately to care for the blind, suffering the extreme of physical and mental agony, when Mr. and Mrs. Kessler investigated the situation. They returned to the United States, made known the conditions, and outlined their plan of reconstruction and rehabilitation from which all idea of charity was eliminated, and which was designed to turn these hopeless men into self-reliant, contented members of the community, equipped to support themselves and their families. This work of constructive mercy appealed to the pity and practical sense of the American people who came forward with generous support, and the Fund was established in the spring of 1916 with headquarters in New York and branch offices in Paris. From the beginning of its activities to May, 1919, the Fund raised more than $15,000,000. As need for them developed, five main sections of the Fund were established: the American Section, under the patronage of President Woodrow Wilson; the British Section, under the patronage of King George, Queen Mary, and Queen-Mother Alexandra; the French Section, under the patronage of President Raymond Poincare; the Belgian Section, under the patronage of King Albert and Queen Elizabeth; and the Italian Section, under the patronage of King Victor Emanuel and Queen Elena. The Fund helped the sightless soldiers of eight nations: America, Great Britain, France, Belgium, Italy, Serbia, Rumania, and Portugal, and is to continue this help as long as there is need. In France it established under the administrative direction of the French government and French army authorities the following institutions: the Hostel for Blinded Officers and Soldiers, Chateau de Madrid, Bois de Boulogne, Paris; the Superior and Industrial School for Blinded Officers and Soldiers, Neuilly, where all kinds of professions and trades were taught; the Bookbinding School, Neuilly; the Raw Material Depot, Neuilly, from which upwards of five hundred graduates from institutions for the blind residing in all parts of France were supplied at cost with materials for their trades which otherwise they would have been unable to procure; the Home for Blinded Soldiers and Their Families from the Devastated Regions, La Garenne-Colombes, near Paris; La Roue Braille printing office and library, Paris, which by 1919 had turned out upwards of 9,000 books of instruction and recreation for the benefit of blinded soldiers everywhere; the Home and Training School for Blinded Belgian Soldiers, Port Villez, near Verdun, established at the request

of the Belgian government; the Chateau de la Tour, Rochecorbon, near Tours, and the Brieux estate, near Chartres, placed at the Fund's disposal by its owner. After the signing of the armistice, when it became possible to determine the extent of the conflict's aftermath of suffering, the Fund was able to give up the Chateau de Madrid, the Home at La Garenne-Colombes, the Chateau de la Tour, and the Brieux estate. The other institutions were still maintained. All the inmates were French, with the exception of the Belgians at Port Villez. On leaving the training schools, each pupil was outfitted with the tools, or machinery, and raw materials necessary to give him a good start on his own account in his chosen trade, and his rent was paid for a year. In the case of those unfitted for manual tasks, and who were re-educated to carry on their pre-war professions, their rent also was paid for a year and good situations obtained for them. For soldiers who lost limbs in addition to their sight, the Fund, through the generosity of individual Americans, provided each with $250 yearly for life to round out his small pension. By the same means it purchased for every mutiliated blind soldier a cottage as an assured home for the rest of his days. The number of American blind was few—less than two hundred. They were cared for by the Red Cross Institute for the Blind, to which the Permanent Blind Relief War Fund contributed $100,000. It also rendered aid at the base hospitals at the front by providing appliances and equipment and by sending a member of its staff, himself blind, as an instructor. The British blinded, since the beginning of the war, were cared for at St. Dunstan's, the London estate of Otto H. Kahn, a member of the Permanent Blind Relief War Fund Finance Committee, who placed unreservedly this property at the disposal of Sir Arthur Pearson for the purposes of a training school. The Fund contributed to St. Dunstan's a certain portion of collections each year. In Italy there were eight hundred blinded soldiers to be re-educated and outfitted, and the Fund contributed to the establishment of a training institution there. For Serbia arrangements were made to care for the blinded soldiers at Bizerta, the French naval port in Tunis, and the Fund established training quarters for them at Belgrade under the direction of Miss Margaret S. McFie of the British-Serbian Relief Fund. To Rumania the Fund contributed large sums through Queen Marie for rehabilitation work. Because of its connections throughout the Allied world, King George, in December, 1918, selected the Permanent Blind Relief War Fund as the medium through which to send to the sightless soldiers of the Continental Allies a message of gratitude and encouragement in French Braille in the form of an attractive booklet with embossed portraits of King George and Queen Mary. According to Allied estimate, about 7,000 soldiers, more than half of them French, lost their eyes, and this number was expected to be increased by men who had lost one eye or who had been wounded in the head. As far as the Permanent Blind Relief War Fund was concerned, its duty to those it had undertaken to care for was assured to the very end by the establishment of an After-Care Fund, involving the elements of permanency indicated in the title of the organization. Among the decorations received by Mr. Kessler was that of the Order of Leopold II from the King of the Belgians, and Mrs. Kessler had bestowed upon her the Gold Medal of the Epidemics by the French Government, the Gold Medal of Gratitude by the Italian government, the Commander's Cross of the Order of Maria by the Queen of Rumania, and the Gold Cross of the Kingdom of Serbia by H.R.H. the Prince-Regent Alexander.

BATES, EMMA FRANCES DUNCAN (Mrs. Theodore C. Bates), daughter of Charles and Tryphosa (Lakin) Duncan, was born in North Brookfield, Massachusetts, March 11, 1845. Her birthplace was the old family home, "Aberdeen Hall," so named from the

fact that her father's ancestor, William Duncan, a member of one of Scotland's oldest families, came from Aberdeen in 1700, and settled in Massachusetts. Her mother was a descendant of Revolutionary ancestors in the Lakin line, and, through her mother, Hannah Shipley, of the Shipleys of New York and England.

Emma Frances Duncan was educated at the North Brookfield High School and at the Oread Collegiate Institute, Worcester, Massachusetts. On December 24, 1868, she was married at North Brookfield to Theodore Cornelius Bates of Worcester. They were the parents of one daughter, Tryphosa Bates-Batcheller. Mrs. Bates has always been a public-spirited woman, interested and active in all that has had to do with civic betterment. She has long been a member of the Massachusetts State Committee of the Civil Service Reform Association, of the State Committee of Conservation, and the State Committee on Child Labor, and was formerly State Vice-President of the Woman's Rivers and Harbors Congress.

Mrs. Bates is a member of the National Society of the Daughters of the American Revolution, and for two terms, the full length of time allowed by the Society's constitution, was Vice-President-General for Massachusetts, and, in 1913, was elected Honorary Vice-President-General for life. At the close of her term of office her patriotic labors were recognized by the presentation of a silver loving cup from the members of the Society in Massachusetts, and she was solicited by petitions from chapters throughout the United States to be a candidate for the office of President-General. This, however, she was forced to decline on account of pressure of home duties.

Mrs. Bates is also a member of the Worcester Society of Antiquity and the Society of Antiquity of America, and she has been prominently identified with the Worcester Woman's Club, whose presidency she has had to decline many times on account of her other activities. She is the author of many essays on historical subjects and descriptive of her travels, and has lectured on these topics for the benefit of the various charities in which she is interested.

BATCHELLER, TRYPHOSA BATES (Mrs. Francis Batcheller), author, poet, and musician, daughter of the Honorable Theodore Cornelius and Emma Frances (Duncan) Bates, was born in her grandfather Duncan's house, Aberdeen Hall, North Brookfield, Massachusetts. Her ancestry, through both parents, is exceptional. In the United States the name of Bates is identified with all that is intellectual and literary, and through her great-grandmother, Lucretia Emerson, Mrs. Batcheller is related to the American philosopher, Ralph Waldo Emerson. Her father's family traces its lineage in unbroken line to Sir Gerard Bates (1242), Lord Mayor of London. Originally of Northumberland, the family later removed to the town of Lydd, Kent, England, where was born Sir Thomas Bates, who in 1545 became Lord Mayor of London. In the parish church at Lydd may be seen the brass effigies of Sir Thomas, and of other members of the Bates family, who he buried there, adorned with the coats of arms used by the family in the United States. The first of the name to come to America was Clement Bates, who, in 1636, sailed from England with his wife, five children, and two servants, in the ship *Elizabeth*. He settled at Cohasset, Massachusetts, on land granted to him by the King, and the house then built is still in possession of his descendants. Another forebear, Joshua Bates, brought further credit to the family name by giving, in 1853, $50,000 and later 30,000 volumes toward the establishment of the Boston Public Library and Free Reading Room. It was his original design to establish a library where books could be taken from the shelves, read, and returned, and this idea was carried out in Boston for the first time in

history. The main reading room of the Boston Public Library is called Bates Hall, and the name Bates appears first in the roll of famous names inset in bronze in the pavement of the entrance hall of the building. Mrs. Batcheller's genealogy contains the names of many colonial and revolutionary heroes. Through her paternal grandmother she descends from Major Daniel Fletcher, a gallant officer, who served in the French and Indian Wars, defending the cause of England, and from his son, Captain Jonathan Fletcher, who, though only nineteen years of age, was a Minute Man at the Battle of Lexington. He made an exceptionally fine record, received commission as captain, and served with Washington throughout the entire war. Mrs. Batcheller's father, the Honorable Theodore C. Bates, was for many years one of the most prominent Republicans in the State of Massachusetts. Elected repeatedly to the state senate until he refused reëlection, he declined to become his party's candidate for Governor, and for ten years was Chairman of the Republican State Central Committee. He was known as one of the most philanthropic of the successful business men of Massachusetts, having defrayed the expenses of a college education for many worthy young men of limited means. At a very early age Tryphosa Bates showed marked artistic and literary talent, and was notable for her remarkably retentive memory as early as her third year. Her literary ability was developed very early, and at the age of ten she wrote a series of fairy tales of real merit. She also showed unusual musical ability, and when fourteen years old was already an accomplished violinist and pianist. As she matured, and her beautiful voice developed, much time was given to its cultivation. She has also mastered several modern languages, and speaks fluently French, Spanish, Italian, German, and Russian, and is well grounded in Latin and ancient Greek. As a child she was taught to dance, responding instinctively to her instruction. She prepared for college under private tutors, passed the entrance examinations with honors, and entered Radcliffe College as one of the youngest members of the class of 1899. However, the excellence of her singing attracted so much attention that, on the advice of such prominent critics as Philip Hale, William Apthorp, Louis Elson, and others, she was sent to Paris to study with Mme. Mathilde Marchesi. Three years with this famous teacher were followed by a brilliantly successful début at the Salle Érard, Paris. The critics, both American and European, were unanimous in praising the rare beauty of her voice and the art with which she used it. Massenet, the French composer, was so deeply impressed that he often played her accompaniments, when she sang in concerts in Paris, and Sgambati rendered her the same service when she sang in Rome. Both he and Tosti, as well as Maestro Bustini, composed special music for her. Raffaello Panzani, the critic and conductor, described her voice as "of an eminently sympathetic quality, of a phenomenal extension," and remarked that, "from B flat chest note she can, with the greatest ease, sing F *in alt.*, and the voice is full and even in every register, sweet beyond all expression in melodic songs, strong and forceful in dramatic phrasing." He summarizes her talents thus: "Whether in the 'bel canto' of the Italian classic music, or in the French songs, in English ballads or in the German *lieder*, and also in the great arias of agility, her voice, and her technique remind one of, certainly fully equal, or, better still, really surpass the most celebrated artists of any single kind, light or dramatic, of past times." It is of interest to note that she sings so difficult an aria as the *Queen of the Night* from Mozart's *Magic Flute*, as originally written by him, taking the high F with ease, whereas nearly every other singer attempting it has been obliged to have it transposed several tones lower. Although her conspicuous gifts have been recognized by numerous offers to sing in public concerts, and in opera, Mrs.

Batcheller has appeared only for the benefit of charitable objects.

In 1904 President and Mrs. Roosevelt gave a musical in the White House in her honor, and she had the satisfaction of demonstrating her talent in her native land before sailing to win praise abroad. Her European appearances have been marked by unusual success, and the royal families of every land have received her, not only as a gifted artist, but as an accomplished and beautiful woman. In the same year both she and her husband, Francis Batcheller were presented at the Court of St. James, and since then she has been presented at every court in Europe, and invariably asked to sing at some court function. In England she has enjoyed the constant favor of Dowager Queen Alexandria and has received many expressions of gracious friendliness from Queen Mary. For the generous use of her beautiful voice in behalf of the work of the League of Mercy in England, she was decorated by King George V with the Order of Mercy, an honor that has been awarded to no other American woman. She has been frequently a guest at the royal garden parties at Windsor, and enjoys the friendship of His Grace the Archbishop of Canterbury and Mrs. Davidson, who have entertained her at Lambeth Palace, London.

When in 1905, Mr. and Mrs. Batcheller were presented at the court of Rome, Her Majesty, Queen Margherita, gave a great musical reception in her honor. She also presented her with a diamond pendant, as a token of her admiration of her voice and musical talents, which was accompanied by the following letter:

"Dear Mrs. Batcheller: Her Majesty the Queen Mother charges me to send you herewith this Jewel as a souvenir of the evening passed at the Palace of Queen Margherita, when Her Majesty admired your beautiful voice and really remarkable musical talent. I rejoice with you with all my heart and I beg you to receive, Dear Lady, my distinguished salutations.

MARCHESA DI VILLAMARINA."

Mr. and Mrs. Batcheller were also received in special private audience by His Holiness, Pope Pius X, and later in 1914, had the signal honor of being invited to the coronation of His Holiness, Pope Benedict XV, who also received them in private audience, and gave them his apostolic blessing, year by year.

The cordial reception of Mr. and Mrs. Batcheller by the Italian nobility have afforded her exceptional opportunities to observe the intimate life of court circles, as well as of the Italian people in general. With these advantages she was able to collect material of unusual nature for her books on Italy. These volumes are illustrated with photographs taken by herself, together with autographed portraits personally presented to her. Her first book, entitled *Glimpses of Italian Court Life*, written in the form of letters to her mother and published in 1906, gave the first intimate picture in English of the Italian court and Roman society at the present day. Her Majesty, Queen Elena, accepted the dedication, and gave the young author her autographed photograph for the frontispiece. The volume received the commendation of the American, British and Italian press, and met with so great success that Mrs. Batcheller was moved to plan another, also in the form of letters to her mother.

After another extended visit in Italy, during which she enjoyed even more favorable opportunities to observe the intimate home and social life, she published, in 1911, *Italian Castles and Country Scenes*. Her Majesty, Queen Margherita, accepted the dedication of this volume, and gave her autographed portrait for the frontispiece. His Majesty the King expressed his interest in and approval of the book by also sending his own autographed portrait to be included among its numerous illustrations. Many books, historical and architectural, have been written of the villas of Italy, but this was the first to describe their

present-day occupants and the beautiful and interesting lives of the historic families of Italy. It received much praise from the royal family of Italy, and was more highly commended by the press than even her first book. In point of elegance and simplicity of style, *Le Carnet Mondain* of Rome compared Mrs. Batcheller's letter with those of Madame de Sévigné, a tribute which demonstrated the fact that Mrs. Batcheller had acquired an accepted literary standing.

In 1910 Mrs. Bates-Batcheller was presented at the Imperial Court in Berlin, where she sang, and received many courtesies from the Emperor and Empress, who accepted her books. The following year Mr. and Mrs. Batcheller were presented at the court of Holland, and were received with special attentions by Her Majesty, Queen Wilhelmina, and Her Majesty, the Queen Mother Emma. Later in the same year she was presented at the Court of Austria, then most exclusive in Europe, and was shown unprecedented honors by his Majesty, the Emperor Francis Joseph, who paid her special attention at the court ball and summoned her to a private audience in Schönbrun Castle. She was also invited to the court ball at Budapest, and asked to sing at the Royal Augarten Palace for her Imperial Royal Highness, the Archduchess Maria Josepha, mother of the Emperor Karl.

In the years 1910 and 1911 Mrs. Batcheller made extended tours in Spain. The first was made by automobile with her Royal Highness, the Infanta Eulalia of Spain, aunt of King Alfonso XIII, and proved a long and eventful journey through Spain and Portugal. Mrs. Batcheller and her husband were presented at court in both countries, and the King and Queen and the Queen Mother of Spain not only admired her beautiful voice, but expressed a lively interest in her books on Italy. It was suggested at this time that she write a similar book on Spain. Accordingly, on her second journey in 1911, she completed her preparation of this work, having received every possible facility through the attention of the entire Spanish royal family and her many Spanish friends. The King and Queen accepted the dedication of her volume, and their autographed portraits, together with portraits of many distinguished Spaniards, and views of scenery and Spanish life, taken by the author, are among the illustrations. The book is an account of the motor tour across the Spanish peninsula, and gives almost the only complete picture of modern Spain to be found to the present time. An illuminating account is given of all classes of society, of Spanish art and architecture, and of the country's industrial awakening and present progress. In an interesting way one is shown many side lights on Spanish conditions and new facts are presented in a series of intimate letters concerning Spanish life and society. The narrative includes, also, an account of her brief sojourn in Portugal where she was entertained by King Manoel and his mother, Queen Amélia, who gave a dinner in her honor on the night upon which she was invited to sing at the palace. This volume, which was published in 1913 under the title of *Royal Spain of Today*, has received high commendation from American, English and European reviewers. In addition to her books, short articles and poems by Mrs. Bates-Batcheller have appeared in many periodicals, also papers on scientific subjects and psychical research, and, more recently, on conditions in Italy during and since the War.

Mrs. Bates-Batcheller is an accomplished public speaker, and has delivered addresses and talks before appreciative audiences in several countries and in various languages. Late in 1911, after her return from Spain, she was presented by the Infanta Eulalia to Their Majesties, the King and Queen of the Belgians, at the Royal Palace at Ostende, and later sang for Their Majesties in Brussels. A long motor journey in 1913 took Mr. and Mrs Batcheller across Hungary, Croatia, and Slavonia, and returning through Bavaria, they were the guests at Munich of His Royal Highness,

Prince Henry of Bavaria, and his mother, Her Royal Highness, Princess Arnulfe. At this time a musical reception was given in her honor in the Royal Wittelsbach Palace, and a gold medal was presented to her by His Royal Highness, as a token of his admiration of her voice. In the autum of that year, with the Infanta Eulalia, Mr. and Mrs. Batcheller made an interesting tour of the Scandinavian countries. At Copenhagen they were entertained by Their Majesties, King Christian and Queen Alexandrine, and were received by the Dowager Queen Louise of Denmark. They were also invited to the villa of the Queen Mother Alexandra of England and the Dowager Empress Maria Feodorovna of Russia. At Stockholm they were received in special audience by his Majesty, King Gustaf of Sweden, and invited to lunch at the royal palace with the Crown Prince and Princess. At Bigdo in Norway they were delightfully entertained at luncheon by Their Majesties, King Haakon and Queen Maude. On their return journey they were also entertained by His Royal Highness, the Grand Duke of Hesse-Darmstadt, brother of the late Tsarina of Russia, and there met Their Royal Highnesses, Prince and Princess Henry of Prussia. Mrs. Bates-Batcheller has been privileged to learn the human side of most of the rulers of Europe, while her gifts as a singer and a linguist, her great beauty, and her charming personality have all been factors in her success. She counts the Queen of Rumania among her friends, and has been officially invited to visit in her home.

Always a lover of woman's work and herself an accomplished needlewoman, Mrs. Bates-Batcheller has taken a great interest in the revival of Italian lace-making. She was the first to bring examples of this work to America and arranged for its sale, thus opening a new and fruitful avenue of profitable employment for many Italian women. She is very fond of out-of-door sports, is an excellent horsewoman, a graceful skater, a good tennis player, and a first rate shot.

During the World War, Mrs. Bates-Batcheller was continuously in Italy, where she was active in American and Italian Red Cross work, and by her own efforts established an American fund for Italian mutilated and consumptive soldiers. She sang often in the war hospitals in Italy, giving always her talents for the benefit of the sick and wounded, and in recognition of her services, was awarded the gold medal of Special Merit by the Italian Red Cross at the end of the war. She has also worked under the official patronage of the King and Queen of the Belgians for the Orphanage established by her Majesty, Queen Elizabeth, and named after her daughter, the Princess Marie-José. She has also the patronage and friendship of Her Royal Highness, the duchess of Vendôme, sister of the King of the Belgians. During the war the Princess Marie-José was at school in Florence, and was allowed to visit only in Mrs. Bates-Batcheller's villa in company with her English governess. When it was not possible for the little Belgian Princess to return to her parents, her Christmas holidays also were spent with Mrs. Bates-Batcheller.

Although constantly engaged in war relief during the War, Mrs. Bates-Batcheller did not neglect her chosen charity in England, the League of Mercy, of which she is a Lady Vice-President, nor did she forget her charity work in America, where she has maintained unbroken relations with her various organizations and clubs. She has done excellent work for the National Civic Federation of Woman's Work, of which she is a member, and she was at one time regent of the Abigail Adams Chapter, Daughters of the American Revolution.

Mrs. Batcheller was the first person invited by President and Mrs. Harding, after the inauguration, to sing at the White House. On this occasion President and Mrs. Harding expressed their personal commendation of her work for the children of the devastated regions of Italy, France, and Belgium. Mrs. Bates-Batcheller is a member of the Boston Authors' Club which held a special meeting in her honor

in May, 1921, when she gave an address on *Italian Women*, and at the fourteenth anniversary of the Professional Woman's Club of Boston she sang and spoke on Italian Women in the War. She belongs to the Alliance Française and the Circolo Italiano of Boston, the Authors' League of America, the Radcliffe Union, the Radcliffe Class of '99, the Incorporated Society of Authors of England, the American Woman's Club of London, the Lyceum Club of London, and the Industrie Feminili of Rome, Italy. She is a life member of the American Red Cross Society and of the Societá Dante League of America, a member of the Colonial Dames of Massachusetts, a Lady Vice-President of the League of Mercy, London, and a member of numerous tennis and sporting clubs in America and Europe.

LANG, MARGARET RUTHVEN, composer, daughter of Benjamin Johnson Lang, the distinguished musician, was born in Boston, Massachusetts, November 27, 1867. Mr. Lang was a native of Scotland and was known and honored throughout the musical world. He married Francis Morse Burrage. Mrs. Lang was a charming amateur singer and in this musical household the best of both classic and modern music was constantly studied. Miss Lang began the study of the pianoforte under one of her father's pupils, and continued under his own direction. The deep sympathy that existed between the father and daughter served to develop early her gift for composition. His constant instruction and criticism encouraged her to work indefatigably, and to give to the world no amateurish production. She began writing music when about twelve years old. One of her first compositions was a Quintette of one movement, for strings and pianoforte, written for herself and her little friends. Her later works have fulfilled this early promise, and have constantly increased in interest, in beauty, and in value. Miss Lang also studied violin with Louis Schmidt in Boston; continuing under Drechsler and Abel in Munich during the seasons of 1886 and 1887, and pursued there her studies in fugue and orchestration under Victor Gluth. On returning to America she studied orchestration with George W. Chadwick and with Edward A. MacDowell. Until her father's death in 1909 she was associated with him in all that he undertook, and she herself has written a large number of compositions of various kinds. These include over one hundred and fifty songs, part-songs, piano pieces, and orchestral works. Through all her songs runs one quality, the relation of the music to the thought. She conveys fire and passion, a delicate poetic touch, and an elusive spirit of caprice. Her religious music reveals a disciplined soul and is singularly free from secular influence. The use of the chorale is unique and impressive. Her sense of humor is shown in her *Nonsense Songs* set to the words of Edward Lear. The accompaniments as well as the voice-writing are irresistible for their sustained humor. One of her most characteristic forms of expression is the part-song. She has personally directed and accompanied her own choral works and songs at concerts of various clubs and societies. *The Heavenly Noël*, a Christmas cantata, and *In the Manger*, a carol with chorus, have a wide use. Miss Lang is the first woman to have an orchestral work played by the Boston Symphony Orchestra when Nikisch conducted the performance of her *Dramatic Overture* on April 8, 1893. A critic said of it: "The general character of the work is passionate, with a warmth that seems wholly genuine and unsought; and now and then with more idyllic moments of much beauty; and the orchestration is brilliant." In July and August, 1893, Theodore Thomas conducted two performances and Bendix a third in Chicago of her overture *Witichis*. This was characterized as "music of a refined and lofty standard, noble and pure in conception." These overtures, with a third called *Totila*, are in manuscript, as is a *Ballade* for orchestra, played in Baltimore in 1901, and three arias for solo

voice and orchestra: *Sappho's Prayer to Aphrodite*, for alto, sung for the first time in 1895 in New York; *Armida*, for soprano, given in 1896 at the Boston Symphony Concerts under Emil Paur; and *Phoebus*, for barytone. Miss Lang's work appeals to those who appreciate the best and her new music is welcomed by musicians and music lovers in both the United States and Europe. Miss Lang is a member of the New York Manuscript Society, the Musical Manuscript Society of Boston, the Musical Art Club, the Thursday Morning Musical Club, and the American Music Society.

RUUTZ-REES, JANET EMILY MEUGENS (Mrs. Louis Emile Ruutz-Rees), author, daughter of Joseph and Caroline (Bennett) Meugens, was born in London, England, February 22, 1842. She received her education in private schools in England and Germany. In 1864, she was married to Louis Emile Ruutz-Rees, F.R.G.S. They were the parents of three children: Caroline Ruutz-Rees, Roland Ruutz-Rees, and Thekla Ruutz-Rees Goldmark. In 1882 Mrs. Ruutz-Rees located in New York City, where she was engaged in journalism for some years, and where she has since resided. She is a progressive thinker, believing that woman should play her part in national affairs, and is interested in the philosophy of religion and in Christian mysticism. She is the author of *Life of Horace Vernet*, *Life of Delaroche*, *A Catechism of Rosmini's Philosophy*, *Reflections on the Psalms*, and *The Path to Peace*. She is a member of the American Oriental Society, the Cosmopolitan Club, the Wednesday Afternoon Club, and was the founder of the Kindly Club.

RUUTZ-REES, CAROLINE, educator and author, daughter of Louis Emile and Janet Emily (Meugens) Ruutz-Rees, was born in London, England, August 16, 1865. She was educated in private schools in London, and, after coming to the United States in 1882, continued her studies at Mme. Clement's School, Germantown, Pennsylvania. In 1898-1899 she followed advanced courses in Greek in the Graduate School of Yale University, and was admitted to the degree of L.L.A. at St. Andrew's University, Scotland in 1904. She was again abroad for advanced study in French literature in 1906–1907, at first at Grenoble and later in Paris, where in 1907 she was named Elève Titulaire de l'École des Hautes Études. In 1909 she received the degree of M.A. and in 1910 that of Ph.D. from Columbia University. Miss Ruutz-Rees began her work as a teacher in 1885 in Germantown, Pennsylvania. From 1886 to 1889 she taught at St. John the Baptist's School in New York, and in 1889–1890 at St. Mary's School, Burlington, New Jersey. In 1890 she founded Rosemary Hall at Wallingford, Connecticut, a successful school for girls, of which she has since been headmistress. In 1900 the school was incorporated and permanently established at Greenwich, Connecticut; Miss Ruutz-Rees serving as President and Treasurer of the corporation.

Miss Ruutz-Rees has contributed many articles on French literature to the publication of the Modern Language Association, to Modern Language Notes, the Romanic Review, the Yale Review, and was also a contributor to the Times History of the War. She has written articles on feminism in history, particularly in connection with the French Renaissance. In 1910 the Columbia University Press published her Charles de Sainte-Marthe, A Study in the French Renaissance, which was later translated into French. This work was awarded the Prix Langlois from the French Academy.

Miss Ruutz-Rees worked actively for woman suffrage, and from 1910 was a member of the Executive Committee of the Connecticut Woman Suffrage Association. In 1913–1914 she was a member of the National Board, and Third Vice-President of the National American Woman Suffrage Association, and is now a member for Connecticut of the National Democratic Committee. During the World War, in 1917–1918, she was Chairman of the Woman's Committee of the National and State Councils of Defense, and Chairman for Connecticut of the Y. M. C. A. Overseas Canteen Committee.

Miss Ruutz-Rees is a member of the New England Association of Preparatory Schools, the Headmistresses' Association, the Association of Collegiate Alumnae, the Classical Association of New England, the Archaeological Institute of America, the Modern Language Association, the Société des Études Rabelaisiennes of Paris, the French Institute of New York, the Cércle Rochambeau, the Metropolitan Museum of Art, the Field Club of Greenwich, the Colony, Cosmopolitan and Woman's University Clubs of New York City, and the Albemarle, Ladies', University and International Franchise Clubs of London, England.

MORRISSON, MARY FOULKE (Mrs. James William Morrisson), daughter of William Dudley and Mary Taylor (Reeves) Foulke, was born in Richmond, Indiana, November 14, 1879. Her father was descended from Edward Foulke of Penlynn, Wales, who settled at Gwynned, Pennsylvania, in 1698. During her course at Bryn Mawr College she specialized in chemistry and biology, receiving her degree of A.B. with distinction in those subjects in 1899. On February 7, 1900, she was married in Richmond, Indiana, to James William Morrisson, a wholesale druggist, and they are the parents of five children: Robert (born in 1901), Foulke (born in 1907), Rosemary (born in 1909), Reeves (born in 1913), and James Lord (born in 1917). From 1905 to 1909 Mrs. Morrisson was chairman of the Woman's Civic League of Richmond which conducted a campaign against a corrupt city government that led to a change of administration. Upon her removal to Chicago she continued to take an active interest in social questions and in 1911–1912 was secretary of the Lower North Council of United Charities.

Her work for equal suffrage has been noteworthy. As secretary of the Chicago Equal Suffrage Association from 1911 to 1914, she helped put through the suffrage amendment in Illinois in 1912, and was President of the Association from 1914 to 1919. During this time, she was Chairman of the 21st Ward Civic League which made a house to house canvass of women voters for their first election and carried on a big educational campaign in citizenship. In 1912–1913 she was Recording Secretary of the Illinois Equal Suffrage Association and held the same office in the National American Woman Suffrage Association from 1915 to 1916. During the Republican National Convention in Chicago in 1916, she had much to do with arranging the Suffrage Parade, and she has always given her services freely as a speaker for the cause. At the time of the World War she was one of the original members of the Executive Committee, Council of National Defense for Illinois, and was a speaker for the work of the Committee, for conservation, and in all the Liberty Loan and most of the other war drives. She was also Chicago chairman, for the National American Woman Suffrage Association, of the Women's Overseas Hospitals maintained by the Association in France and raised over $13,000 for their support. She is a member of the Juvenile Protective Association, the Immigrants' Protective League, and the Woman's City Fortnightly, Friday, Casino, Arts, and Bryn Mawr Clubs, and was at one time president of the last.

FOSTER, FAY, composer, was born at Leavenworth, Kansas, daughter of James Hervey and Alice Allen (Monroe) Foster. Through her paternal grandmother, she is a direct descendant of Pocahontas; through her paternal grandfather, of the American composer, Stephen Foster; and through her maternal grandfather, of President James Monroe.

Her musical career may be said to have begun almost in her infancy, for as early as her third year, she was already improvising melodies on the piano, although she had no instruction whatever. At the age of seven, she received her first systematic piano lessons, and, although her general education was not neglected, had so far advanced in the first year as to be thoroughly grounded in harmony and counterpoint. At the age of twelve she had become the conductor of a quartette choir, and played the organ, and at sixteen she completed the course at the Leavenworth High School.

At the age of seventeen she toured the country, as assistant pianist and accompanist, with the William H. Sherwood Concert Company; in the meantime for two years, studying vocal music and piano under William Sherwood at the Sherwood Conservatory of Music, Chicago, and harmony and theory with Frederick Grant Gleason. At nineteen, she was appointed a director of a musical conservatory at Anarga, Illinois. Two years later she went abroad, and for the next twelve years studied, first as a scholarship piano pupil, under Moritz Rosenthal at Vienna, Austria, later at the Munich Conservatory, under Heinrich Schwartz and Sophie Menter. She spent considerable time also in Leipzig, where she was taught technique by Theodore Wiehmeyer, virtuoso under Alfred Reisenauer, and counterpoint, theory and composition under Professor Jadassohn. Later she studied in Cologne, and received voice training in Berlin under Siga Garso and Alexander Heinemann. The next two years she spent in Italy, and was about to make her début in Italian opera, when she fell ill from over work and was forced to rest her voice for two years.

During this period of recuperation, she won, in international competition the prize offered by the German paper, *Die Woche*, of Berlin, for the best new waltz composition. Over 4,200 persons competed, and Miss Foster's waltz, *The Prairie Flower*, received the second prize of 2,000 marks. The waltz was played at a ball in Berlin, over which the German Crown Prince presided, the orchestra being led by Johann Strauss.

Because of the illness of her father, Miss Foster was called back to America in 1911, and settled in New York. In addition to her numerous musical compositions, she has won remarkable success as a voice developer and coach, tutoring numerous opera and concert singers. Miss Foster has written over fifty songs and orchestral and piano pieces, and several operettas, especially for school or club use, and was ably assisted by her mother, who wrote the librettos and lyrics.

Miss Foster was active in War Work, being head of the Foster Unit, which entertained the soldiers at the various camps. She virtually emptied her large library, to send books abroad, and at the holiday seasons always forwarded heavy consignments of delicacies to the "Boys." But her greatest contribution was the stirring song, highly eulogized by Theodore Roosevelt and General Pershing, *The Americans Come;* the great rallying song of the last Liberty Loan Drive. When John McCormack entertained the heroes of the Château-Thierry, this song was the favorite, and he rendered it with the greatest feeling.

Miss Foster is a member of the Musicians' Club of New York, the Authors' League of America and the American Red Cross. In addition to receiving the second prize for her waltz in Berlin, she has won various other honors for her skill in composition, among which may be mentioned: the first prize in contest by Theodore Presser Company of Philadelphia; for the American Song Competition, in New York, in 1914; for the Étude Piano Contest, *Étude de Concert,* 1916; and for the Federation of Women's Clubs, *Women's Chorus,* 1917. Her choruses have been produced by the St. Cecilia Club; Mozart Club (Carl Hahn, Conductor); Tuesday Morning Club, Philadelphia; Lockport Festival Chorus, and the Rubinstein Club.

Among the singers who have rendered Miss Foster's songs are, Eleanora de Cisneros, Sophie Breuslau, Louis Graveure, Mary Jordan, Rafael Diaz, Vera Curtis and Paul Althouse. Her songs include: *Sleep Song; On Dress Parade; The Daughter; Maria Mia; The White Blossoms of the Bog; Sing a Song of Roses; Winter; The Call of the Trail; Springtide of Love; Spinning Wheel Song; If I Were King of Ireland; One Golden Day; Song of the Thistle Drift; Love in Absence; A Nipponese Sword Song; The Red Heart; My Menagerie; Your Kiss At Last; Were I Yon Star; The Maiden; Dusk in June; A Strange Looking Glass; Riverside Drive vs. Avenue A; I'm Glad I Went Over to France; Sunset in a Japanese Garden; The King; In the Carpenter's Shop; Petite Valse de Ballet.*

MOSHER, MARY E., physician, daughter of James and Julia (Murphy) Mosher, was born in Boston, Massachusetts, of New England stock. Her earliest paternal ancestor in this country, Ezekiel Mosher, came from Manchester, England, with his wife, Lydia, and several sons late in the seventeenth century, and settled in the vicinity of Providence, Rhode Island. One son, Daniel, and his family, and another son, John, were massacred by the Indians. Hugh Mosher, of whom Doctor Mosher is a descendant survived. Another ancestor, James Mosher, built the first grist mill in the country, at Newport, Rhode Island, in October, 1761.

Doctor Mosher received her early education in the Boston public schools, and later studied under private tutors. In 1887 she was graduated from the Boston University School of Medicine, and opened an office in Roxbury, Massachusetts, where she has since practised. After five years without a day's vacation, in 1892 she took a trip to Europe, where she studied in the great hospitals in London, Paris, and Vienna. In 1896 she made a second journey across the Atlantic to observe the latest practices in foreign hospitals. In 1900 and 1901 she took further post graduate courses in pediatrics and general pathology at the Harvard Medical School. In addition to her general and professional education, she is widely read, and has acquired a working knowledge of several foreign languages.

No one who knows Doctor Mosher's career will hesitate to say that she is in the best sense a self-made woman, for at the age of twelve years, having just graduated from the grammer school, she lost both parents, and, the family at about the same time suffering financial reverses, it was necessary for the children to become self-supporting. From this early age Doctor Mosher, for the most part, made her own way, always with the end in view of obtaining further education. During her medical course she did nursing in the long vacations and through the term paid for part of her tuition by acting as librarian. A scholarship which she earned was of great assistance, and this she repaid as soon as she was able after starting in practice.

As a physician, Doctor Mosher has enjoyed great success and popularity. She is the typical family physician, feeling not only a professional but also a deep personal interest in her families, many of whom she has cared for and watched in their development into the third generation. She is the true healer, the confidant of joys and sorrows, the sympathetic adviser and devoted friend. Such being her standing in the community, it was with something like consternation that her clientèle learned in the summer of 1898 that she contemplated a journey to the Klondike, then in the second year of the great gold fever. Doctor Mosher, with her sister and a friend, left Boston in March and waited on the west coast until June for a boat to take them up the Yukon River to Dawson, the northernmost inhabited point in the Klondike region. The journey occupied three months, the travellers arriving at their destination in October, 1898. The trip was full of adventure, for an unusually early formation of ice made progress difficult. It was so prolonged that the food supply ran low and the passengers were rationed. The wood used for fuel became exhausted, and at intervals the boat would tie up beside the bank and all hands engaged in chopping and carrying wood to feed the boilers. Arrived in Dawson, Doctor Mosher had a cabin erected which, though it contained only one room, was one of the show residences in the town.

Doctor Mosher, of course, intended to practise her profession, but she found that it was a law that no American should practise in the Klondike, and there was an added prejudice against a woman and a homeopath. With her usual determination, however, Doctor Mosher prevailed upon the authorities to allow her to take the next examination with twenty-seven other candidates. In this examination she passed first in diseases of women and children, but no one was able to pass the entire examination as, some of the questions were so unreasonable as to be practically unanswerable. Doctor Mosher then demanded a second examination, and after much difficulty, and the payment of a second fee of $200, she was given an examination alone. This consisted of a written test from 9 A. M. to 6 P. M., during which time the candidate sat on one soap box and wrote on another, and an oral examination next day from 10 A. M. to 2 P. M. Following this examination Doctor Mosher was allowed to qualify as a practising physician, the only woman practitioner or homeopath in the Klondike.

Doctor Mosher remained in the Klondike for two years, during which time she had many interesting experiences. At one time a serious typhoid epidemic broke out in Dawson and vicinity, and there were many deaths. Doctor Mosher, using Homeopathy in the treatment of these cases, lost no patients. So difficult was it to obtain suitable nursing, that Doctor Mosher had four bunks built in her cabin, and with the aid of her sister and a male nurse she continuously cared for four patients, in addition to her numerous outside cases. One young woman, who had come to Dawson with her husband over the Chilkoot Pass in the first days, died in this epidemic, leaving a baby a few days old. Doctor Mosher, hearing of the case, took the child into her cabin. For six months she cared for it when the glass sometimes registered 60 below zero, and water in a hot water bag would freeze during the night. At the end of this time the grandparents in the Middle West sent for the little girl, and she was taken out on the back of an Indian over the Chilkoot Pass to civilization, the first white child to survive in the Klondike. Doctor Mosher made many photographs during her stay, and these she has utilized in screen pictures to illustrate her lecture on *Pioneer Days in the Klondike*, which she has given many times all over New England.

She belongs to various clubs, in all of which she has held office. She has been twice President of the Twentieth Century Woman's Medical Club, Historian of the Professional Woman's Club, Vice-President of the Boston Homeopathic Medical Society, orator of the Massachusetts Homeopathic Medical Society, Vice-President of the American Institute of Homeopathy, and also in 1920 President of the Massachusetts Surgical and Gyneological Society, the first woman to hold that office.

Doctor Mosher is fond of out-door life and enjoys walking, driving, and swimming. For these she has ample opportunity at her summer residence at Point Independence, Onset, Massachusetts. She is also interested in dramatics, and her talent for acting would easily place her in the professional ranks. In fact, she has had several flattering offers to go on the legitimate stage following her appearance as Sir Oliver in Sheridan's *School for Scandal* at the Plymouth Theatre, Boston. She has a keen sense of humor and, having herself written many skits and humorous poems, often acts as entertainer at some of her clubs, or in the homes of friends. Doctor Mosher is a philanthropist in the truest sense of the word, always ready to extend a helping hand, whether it be to her alma mater, to a popular cause, or through some more obscure channel, to a friend in need.

PULSIFER, ADELAIDE PENNELL (Mrs. Woodbury Pulsifer), daughter of Richard Cobb and Cornelia (Barnes) Pennell, was born in Portland, Maine. Her father was descended from Matthew Hawke, who came from Camden, England, to Hingham, Massachusetts, where he settled August 10, 1638. The first Pennell was Clement, who came to Gloucester, Massachusetts, from Trinity Parish, Jersey, where the family, originating in Normandy, had held positions of importance since the Middle Ages, as is shown by records of the year 1331. Clement Pennell later moved to Falmouth, Maine, where he served in Captain Samuel Skilling's company at the outbreak of the French and Indian War, and held many responsible positions in the community. The line is traced through his son Clement and his grandson Clement to Richard Cobb Pennell. Cornelia Barnes Pennell's ancestors were among the original settlers of Hingham, Massachusetts, the first of the name being Thomas Barnes. During the Revolution his descendant, Cornelius, was one of the "red ink signers" of Continental currency. A grandfather of Cornelia Barnes, Captain Thomas Hersey, who was a descendant of William Hersey of Hingham (1635), led the first military company from Hingham to fortify Dorchester Heights.

When Adelaide Pennell was still a child, her parents moved to Lewiston, Maine, where she received education in music and art, the practice of which has been her accomplishment and enjoyment throughout her life. At the same time she became expert in outdoor sports, especially in the management of spirited horses, in boating, and in tennis and golf. She was married at Lewiston to Woodbury Pulsifer, a physician, and they were the parents of one daughter, Elizabeth, a girl of remarkable character and gifted personality, on whose account they spent much time after 1889 in Washington so that she might attend Mt. Vernon Seminary. In 1902, after the death of their daughter in her twentieth year, Doctor and Mrs. Pulsifer established their home in Washington, although continuing to spend their summers on Casco Bay. From the age of eighteen to the present time, Mrs. Pulsifer has been actively engaged in philanthropic and church work, and has held many offices in local benevolent and literary societies. The civic improvement programme in Lewiston was started with Mrs. Pulsifer as president, and she was one of the founders there of the Ladies' Auxiliary to the Young Men's Christian Association. With twenty-eight other ladies she began the work of the Young Women's Christian Association in Washington and has been a member of its Board of Management from the start and chairman of its Membership Committee, overseeing the successful work that the branch has accomplished during the World War. She has also been active in patriotic work, having been Regent of a Chapter of the Daughters of the American Revolution, State Vice-Regent in Washington, District of Columbia, and Corresponding Secretary General of the National Society. She was one of the charter members of the National Officers' Club, D. A. R., and a charter member of the Women's City Club.

LEARY, JULIA MAY CROFTON (Mrs. George Leary), daughter of John Edward and Anne (Barry) Crofton, and a grandniece of General Garrett Barry (who was killed at the Battle of Bull Run), was born in Newport, Rhode Island. In 1900, in New York City, she married George Leary. They are the parents of one son, George Leary, Jr.

For many years, influenced by the power of her Catholic faith, and by her sympathy for the fallen and misguided, Mrs. Leary has carried on work, in New York City, among the prisoners on Blackwell's Island and with those confined in the Tombs prison, awaiting trial. For this work she prepared herself by a course in penology, under Professor Flagg, at Columbia University. She has found many so-called criminals who needed only to be helped to a better understanding of their own psychology, in order to become good citizens

when released. Through her ability to enter into the thought processes of such individuals, and to talk to them in terms that they could comprehend, Mrs. Leary has been able over and over again to arouse in them the will to right living. Among those confined in the Tombs she often found victims of social injustice—for example, girls whose only offense was that they had fallen into bad company—and Mrs. Leary more than once was able to save a young woman not inherently vicious, but of weak will, from becoming a confirmed member of the criminal class. To do this she has had to bring pressure to bear on the District Attorney's office for a speedy hearing, in order that immediate release, if guilt were not proved, might furnish the opportunity to grow in character in a properly selected environment. The fact that not one of the cases in which Mrs. Leary has interested herself has disappointed her, is testimony to her insight into the causes to blame for arrest, as well as to her own remarkable influence. She established Thursday sewing classes among the women in the Tombs, providing materials, and arranging that the garments become the property of the prisoners, upon release. Mrs. Leary organized a body of paid workers to carry out her methods. During the World War she extended her work to the military prisons, giving particular attention to Governor's Island, New York, where she made arrangements whereby the men might enjoy the recreation of music. She established a fund that made it possible for military prisoners to visit their homes, in cases of emergency, under approved surveillance, and without expense to the Government. In all of these activities she has acted as a sincere friend to those with whom she dealt, sure of her response in making an appeal to the best that was in them.

Mrs. Leary believes little in the force of heredity; much, in the power of environment for good or evil. She claims that the principle involved holds true not only of criminals but also of children, especially backward pupils in the public schools. The correction of defective speech in school children is a matter that has largely occupied her interest, and for a long time she exerted her efforts to persuade the Board of Education, of the City of New York to appoint a director to cope with the problem of defective speech in the city schools. Although she did not succeed in this, she did win the active support of the teachers. Many of them took a special course, given at the Vanderbilt Clinic, which dealt with the nervous problem of defective speech. Mrs. Leary also was the moving factor back of the appropriation for the provision of free or inexpensive luncheons in the schools. She insisted on the importance of this project as contrasted with the possible establishment of elaborate installations for teaching the theory of cooking, which at first was the danger. With Mrs. August Belmont she was a pioneer member of the Educational Dramatic League. This organization undertook to study and correct the faults of children, by a method unique and interesting from a psychological standpoint. That is, in schools and settlements, children, in dramatic entertainments, were assigned to rôles illustrating positive characteristics corrective of their own weaknesses. Mrs. Leary is also interested in the Big Sister movement, the Catholic Girls' Club, and the Army Relief Society. She has been a member of the Political Equality League, is a guarantor of the Civic Forum, and a member of the St. Cecilia Ciub of New York, the International Garden Club, and the Ladies' Athenaeum of London, England.

In 1916 Mrs. Leary purchased a replica of a Chinese monolith, of great value to the student of early Christian missions. The original, a granite block weighing two tons, stands in Sian Fu, Shansi, the ancient capital of China. It is inscribed in old Chinese and Assyrian characters and is a record, made in the eighth century, of the bishops and priests, as well as of missions, of the Nestorian Christians in China of the seventh century. As one of the great historical monuments of the world, it is jealously guarded by the Chinese Government, and was not copied, or even described, until this full-size replica, made of granite from the same quarry as the original, was produced at the direction of a Danish explorer. With much difficulty it was brought to the United States, in 1908, and set up in the Metropolitan Museum of Art, New York City. When Mrs. Leary acquired it, her one thought was to place it where it would have the greatest value to students of Christian history, and accordingly she sent it to Pope Benedict XV, the presentation being made, through Cardinal Falconio, by Monsignor George J. Waring. It now stands in the Lateran Museum, in Rome. As a mark of appreciation for this contribution to historical research, His Holiness, at Easter, 1919, conferred on Mrs. Leary the rank of Lady of the Holy Sepulchre of the First Class, the Catholic decoration most coveted in Europe. The official brief was also signed by Philippus Maria Camassei, Patriarch of Jerusalem, and was accompanied by a signed photograph of the Pope. The late Cardinal Farley, of New York, was the only other person in the United States to attain to the Order of the Holy Sepulchre, and his successor, Archbishop Hayes, gave Mrs. Leary the mitre that Cardinal Farley wore on the occasion of his receiving this honor.

MURRAY, ELLA RUSH (Mrs. William Spencer Murray), was born in Philadelphia, Pennsylvania. Her father, Captain Richard Rush, U. S. N., was a descendant of John Rush, Captain of Horse in Cromwell's army, of whom Cromwell said, "one of my captains, John Rush, than whom I have no better." He was a native of Kent, England, came to America about 1665, and settled in Byberry Township, Pennsylvania. His great-great-grandson, Doctor Benjamin Rush, known as the "father of American medicine," was one of the Signers of the Declaration of Independence. The line is traced through his son,

Richard Rush, who was Minister to England under President Monroe and conducted the negotiations relating to the Monroe Doctrine. His son, James Murray Rush, was the father of Captain Richard Rush. The latter married Ella Mary Day, the daughter of Edgar B. Day, of Catskill, New York, descended from Revolutionary and Colonial stock. Among her ancestors was William Pynchon, Governor of the Connecticut River Colony and founder of Springfield, Massachusetts.

Ella Rush was educated in private schools in Washington, District of Columbia, and Lausanne, Switzerland. She was married at Catskill, New York, September 23, 1905, to William Spencer Murray, a consulting electrical engineer. Mrs. Murray early became interested in the movement for woman suffrage and identified herself with the Congressional Union for Woman Suffrage, later named the National Woman's Party. She is a member of its National Advisory Council and has been an organizer since 1911. She was President of the Anne Arundel County Branch of the Congressional Union for Woman Suffrage of Maryland, President of the Anne Arundel County Branch of the Just Government League of Maryland, President of the Women's Political Union of Connecticut, and President of the Equal Franchise League of New Haven, Connecticut. These all helped to mould public opinion towards the extension of the franchise to women. During the period of the World War, Mrs. Murray was active as a member of the National Red Cross Society, the National Special Aid Society, the Navy League, and the American Defense Society. She is also a member of the National Association for the Advancement of Colored People.

Mr. and Mrs. Murray are the parents of three children: Richard Rush Murray, John Maynadier Murray and William Spencer Murray, Jr.

McCORMICK, RUTH HANNA (Mrs. Medill McCormick), politician, daughter of Senator Marcus Alonzo and Charlotte Augusta (Rhodes) Hanna, was born in Cleveland, Ohio, March 27, 1880. She attended first, the Hathaway Brown School in Cleveland, spent a year at Dobb's Ferry, New York and was for four years at Miss Porter's school at Farmington, Connecticut. Her father, who was the head of many railroads, steamboat lines, and mines, was the first capitalist in the country to recognize labor unions. His predominant wish was to find a means of reconciling capital and labor. He never had a strike among his employees who loved him personally, and always found him helpful and sympathetic. He not only gave his daughter every educational advantage that money could procure but, what was more valuable, put her into personal contact, in his mines, on docks, and on his lake steamers, with laboring people, thus giving her a practical knowledge of the hardships that come to wage earners that few women born to wealth obtain. From the age of fourteen she spent a certain number of months every year studying at first hand these labor conditions. On June 10, 1903, she was married at Cleveland to Joseph Medill McCormick, of Chicago, Illinois, the son of Robert Sanderson and Katharine Van Etta (Medill) McCormick. He was born May 16, 1877; for many years was publisher of the *Chicago Daily Tribune;* in 1912–1914 was Vice-Chairman of the Progressive National Committee; and in 1917 was elected United States Senator from Illinois. They are the parents of Katharine Augusta McCormick and Medill McCormick. Before her marriage Mrs. McCormick was an active worker in the Welfare Department of the National Civic Federation, of which her father was President. Continuing her work after marriage, she organized in 1905 the Woman's Branch of the National Civic Federation. She was particularly interested in women and girls in any work in which they were employed. She therefore supported various civic organizations, to which she devoted all her time while living in Chicago, and became a member of the Woman's Trade Union League, the Consumer's League as a member of its State Board, the American Association for Labor Legislation, and the Women's Club for Civic Improvement in Chicago. In November, 1913, she gave up these interests in order to act as Chairman of the National Congressional Committee of the National American Woman Suffrage Association. With this Association and with the Progressive Party, with which she had become associated in 1912, she worked to educate women politically and arouse them to their responsibilities for civic betterment. During the preparedness campaign which preceded the United States' entrance into the World War, she founded the Woman's Section of the Navy League, in which thousands of women were enlisted. In 1919, when the Republican Party was preparing for the presidential campaign of 1920, Mrs. McCormick was appointed Chairman of the Republican Woman's National Executive Committee. This acted with the Republican National Committee of men, taking part in its councils on terms of perfect equality. Mrs. McCormick's committee selected leading Republican women throughout the country, established in every state a Woman's Republican Executive Committee, and placed in positions of real political power a remarkable body of earnest workers who had been trained as suffragists. Her aim was to bring every Republican woman into the party and to give her an incentive to take part in the campaign through an organization functioning from the National Committee down to the township committee with the minutest detail. She also planned a new line of educational work to teach foreigners to vote, to organize citizenship classes, and to have made proper translations of pamphlets on Americanization and citizenship. Her statement of principles was an admirable combination of idealism and sound politics, and included the declaration that women were going to remove the stigma that hitherto had been attached to politics. Mrs.

McCormick is a tall slender woman of striking appearance. She is an indefatigable worker, of infinite resource, and a ready and convincing speaker. She is a member of the Colony and Woman's City Clubs of New York and the Woman's City Club of Chicago.

LUDLOW, CLARA SOUTHMAYD, scientist, was born in Easton, Pennsylvania, December 26, 1852. Her father, Doctor Jacob Rapelyea Ludlow, who was born November 22, 1824, and died February 11, 1904, was a physician and served as a surgeon in the United States Army throughout the Civil War. He was descended from Thomas Ludlow, of Dinton, Baycliffe, Wiltshire, England, whose son, Gabriel Ludlow, came to New York in 1694. The latter's son was John Ludlow and his grandson was John Richard Ludlow who was the father of Gabriel Ludlow, the father of Doctor Jacob R. Ludlow. Gabriel Ludlow married a daughter of Doctor Jacob Rapelyea (de Rapelje) and his wife, Susan Ditmar. Doctor Jacob R. Ludlow married, November 20, 1850, Ann Mary Hunt, who was born October 28, 1831, and died June 26, 1893. She was the daughter of Henry S. Hunt, who died October 6, 1838, the son of Jonathan Hunt, and of Adah Schenck, who was born May 21, 1793. The latter was descended from Roelof Schenck, who came from Amersfoot, Holland, in 1650, and in 1660 married at Flatbush, Long Island, Netje van Courlenhausen. Their son, Roelof Schenck was born in Pleasantville, New Jersey, April 27, 1697, and married Eugentje van Dorn. Their son, Garret Schenck, born March 21, 1718, married Mary van Sickle. Their son, John Schenck, born May 26, 1750, married Ida Sutphen, and they were the parents of Adah Schenck.

Clara Southmayd Ludlow was educated in private schools, at the Conservatory of Music, Oberlin, Ohio, and at the New England Conservatory of Music, Boston, Massachusetts, from which she was graduated in 1879. For many years she made music her profession, teaching and doing a certain amount of concert work. In 1900 she was graduated with the degree of B.Sc. from the Agricultural and Mechanical College of Mississippi from which she also received the degree of M.Sc. in 1901. In that year she began in Manila, under the authority of the Surgeon General, United States Army, the study of the mosquito in the transmission of disease which has been her specialty ever since. From 1907 to 1909 she was Demonstrator and from 1909 to 1911 Instructor in Histology and Embryology at the George Washington University, Washington, District of Columbia, where in 1908 she was given the degree of Ph.D. in preventive medicine. Her thesis was entitled; *The Mosquito of the Philippine Islands; The Distribution of Certain Species and their Occurrence in Relation to the Incidence of Certain Diseases.* From 1904 to 1910 she was lecturer on mosquitoes and their relation to disease at the Army Medical School, Washington, and she is now entomologist in charge of medical entomology at the Army Medical Museum. Since 1902 Doctor Ludlow has published various papers on her subject and describing new species from the Philippines, Alaska, Panama, Porto Rico, the United States, and Siberia. She is the author of Bulletin No. 4, Surgeon General's Office: *The Disease-Bearing Mosquitoes of North and Central America, the West Indies, and the Philippine Island* (1913). Doctor Ludlow is a Fellow of the American Association for the Advancement of Science, and a member of the American Society of Tropical Medicine, the Washington Biological Club, the Cambridge Entomological Club, the Women's Alliance, the Army Relief, the Women's Army and Navy League, and the Unitarian Church.

LEARNED, ELLIN CRAVEN (Mrs. Frank Learned), writer, is a descendant of Thomas Craven who came from London, England, and settled in New Jersey in 1728. He married Elizabeth Walling of Middletown, New Jersey. Their son, Gershom Craven, married Rebecca Quick, and their son, Tunis Craven, married Hannah, the daughter of Commodore Thomas Tingey, U. S. N. Their son, Captain Tunis Augustus Macdonough Craven, U. S. N., married Marie Louise Stevenson, and they were the parents of Mrs. Learned. Captain Craven's career in the Navy was a distinguished one and his name stands for heroism and self-sacrifice in war. In his honor was named the U. S. S. *Craven,* for which Mrs. Learned was sponsor at its launching at the Norfolk (Virginia) Navy Yard, June 29, 1918. Mrs. Learned was born in New Jersey and was educated in private schools in New York and at the Art Students' League. Her marriage to Mr. Learned took place in Trinity Chapel, New York, April 12, 1893. She is an associate of the Sisterhood of St. Mary and of the Girls' Friendly Society of the Episcopal Church. From 1890 to 1894 and again from 1896 to 1899 she was on the staff of *The Churchman,* and from 1904 to 1905 she was editor of the *Girls' Friendly Magazine.* She has contributed since 1899 to *The Delineator* and since 1907 to *The Ladies' World,* and also to other publications. She is the author of *Ideals for Girls* (1905) and *The Etiquette of New York Today* (1906).

KLINE, FRANCES TALBOT LITTLETON (Mrs. Linus Ward Kline), daughter of Oscar and Alice Marcella (Bernard) Littleton, was born at Farmville, Virginia, January 10, 1869. Her father was descended from William Littleton, who came from England to Virginia about 1700, and the grandfather of her maternal grandmother, Captain John Thomas, sailed with Admiral John Paul Jones on some of his voyages. Miss Littleton graduated from a private school in Petersburg, Virginia, and in 1889 from the State Normal School, Farmville, Virginia. During 1892–1896 she studied chemistry one winter and three summers with Doctor J. W. Mallet of the University of Virginia. She then attended Cornell University where she was a member of

Psi Chapter of Kappa Kappa Gamma Sorority, and where she received the degree of B.S. in 1900. From 1889 to 1892 she taught at Martha Washington College, Abingdon, Virginia, and from 1893 to 1902 she held the position of instructor in chemistry and physics at the State Normal School, Farmville, Virginia. The results of her researches in chemistry were published in her papers, *A Remarkable Molecular Change in a Silver Amalgam* in the *Proceedings* of the Chemical Society of England, a *Note on the Composition of Silver Amalgam*, and *A Method of Determining Starch by Means of the Iodine Reaction* in the *American Chemical Journal*. On January 23, 1903, she was married at Suffolk, Virginia, to Linus Ward Kline, a teacher of Duluth, Minnesota, where she has since resided. She has been for many years a member of the board of directors of the Duluth Young Women's Christian Association and has given much time to the activities of the Methodist Episcopal Church. She has been President of the Duluth Branch of the Association of Collegiate Alumnae and has held other offices and worked on its committees. She is also Vice-President of the Northwest Central Section of the Association of Collegiate Alumnae, and a member of the Ladies' Literature Class, Duluth. During the World War she served as a member of the Duluth Woman's Committee of the Council of National Defense; as a director of the Women's and Girls' Division of the Michigan Circuit, War Camp Community Service; and as director of the Women's and Girls' Division, War Camp Community Service, Dayton, Ohio.

AUSTIN, MARY (Mrs. Stafford W. Austin), author, daughter of George and Savilla (Graham) Hunter, was born in Carlinville, Illinois, September 9, 1868. Her father came to Carlinville as a young man from Rochester, Kent, England, and during the Civil War served as Captain of Company K, 7th Illinois Regiment. Her mother, a woman prominent in social and civic affairs, was descended from Pierre Daggerre, who accompanied Lafayette to this country at the time of the Revolution. In 1888 she was graduated B.S. in Blackburn University, and on May 19, 1891, was married at Bakersfield, California, to Stafford W. Austin, an attorney, who was born in the Hawaiian Islands.

Mrs. Austin spent the first eighteen years of her life in Illinois and the next eighteen principally in the desert regions of southwestern America described in her books. During this second period she acquired that first hand intimacy with aboriginal life for which she is distinguished, making continuous investigations into American Indian life, and the environmental and historical background of the southwestern states. She has also traveled widely in Europe and America.

Since 1905 Mrs. Austin has maintained an apartment in New York and a bungalow at Carmel, California, and has spent occasional long intervals in Europe and in New Mexico. She is widely acquainted with distinguished men both in America and abroad, deriving from them the knowledge of world affairs which has made her essays on political matters among the most important produced by women authors. Her lectures have also brought her wide reputation both in England and the United States. She has appeared before teachers' institutes and universities; and has held an appointment as lecturer on American literature and nature lore at the Los Angeles Normal School. She has also engaged in social research in the southwest for the Carnegie Foundation. During the summer of 1921 she lectured before the Fabian Society in England on *The Background of Anglo-American Relations*.

In addition to her work as a literary artist, Mrs. Austin has been a publicist for all ideas connected with feminism and with matters of community interest; and in 1894–1895 she originated the first community theatre movement. She was the first to make literary translations of American Indian poetry; contributed the chapter on *Aboriginal Litera-*

ture to the *Cambridge History of American Literature* (1919), and is the author of many magazine articles and the following books and plays: *The Land of Little Rain* (1903); *Isidro* (1905); *The Basket Woman* (1906); *The Flock* (1907); *Lost Borders* (1908); *Santa Lucia* (1909); *Christ in Italy* (1910); *The Arrow Maker*, a drama, produced in 1911 at the New Theatre, New York; *Woman of Genius* (1913); *Lovely Lady* (1914); *Fire*, a drama, first played at the Forest Theatre, Carmel, California, 1914; *Love and the Soul Maker* (1915); *The Man Jesus* (1916); *The Man Who Didn't Believe in Christmas*, a play produced in 1917 at the Cohan and Harris Theatre, New York; *The Ford* (1917); *The Trail Book* (1918); *The Young Woman Citizen* (1919); *Outland* (1919); and *Twenty-Six Jayne Street* (1920). Mrs. Austin is a member of the National Arts Club, New York, the Lyceum Club, London, the National Council of Farm City Planning, the Poetry Society, the Wanderers' Club, and the Business and Professional Women's League.

HUTCHINSON, ANNE, came to New England with her husband, William, when she was about forty-three and her husband forty-eight years old, in the ship *Griffin*, landing at Boston, September 18, 1634. She was received into the Boston Church, of which the pastor was the Reverend John Wilson, and the "teacher" John Cotton, on the 2nd of November, some special inquiry being made concerning her views. Her husband had been received on the 26th of October previous. This formality may be regarded as a pledge of citizenship in the Puritan commonwealth, much as naturalization papers are today; so that the date of Anne's adoption into the state, which was then identical with the church, as an American woman is thus fixed.

The English family of William Hutchinson was of Lincolnshire stock, not identical with those of Yorkshire and Nottinghamshire, although it has assumed the same arms. It can be traced to the early part of the sixteenth century in Lincoln, until Edward, the father of William Hutchinson, the immigrant, removed from Lincoln to Alford about 1580. It was there that William Hutchinson resided until his removal to New England with his wife, Anne Marbury (Dryden). Thirteen children were born to them in Alford; three died and were buried there. Ten accompanied their parents to New England; and two were born to them in Boston. As Anne Hutchinson was so distinctly a representative of her sex, her blood inheritance is more important than that which furnishes quarterings to heraldry, granting even that her husband's branch of the Hutchinson name were entitled to the coat which they assumed. Thus the fact that Anne's mother was by birth a Dryden is of essential interest.

The neighborhood of Alford to Boston, England, where the Hutchinsons had often sat under John Cotton at St. Botolph's Church, had created friendly relations with him, and his change of residence doubtless induced them to follow his example. In fact, their eldest son, Edward, then twenty years old, actually accompanied Mr. Cotton on his voyage to Boston.

The Hutchinsons were received with all the cordiality of which the Puritan community was capable. In March, 1635, William Hutchinson and two of his sons, Richard and Francis, became "freemen" of the colony, and, in the following May, William was chosen to represent Boston in the General Court.

Anne Hutchinson took a prominent place in the church and the community almost from the time of her admission, and assumed a position hitherto almost unknown by women, or permitted to them in public affairs. For a considerable time she encountered no difficulty in asserting her views upon religious questions—having passed on the "torch of life" in so wonderful a manner by the duties of maternity—and continued to carry forward in service to her neighbors and to all who were in need of mercy, charity, and sympathy.

She was generous in means, and in those days, when nursing as a distinctive occupation or profession was unknown, her personal devotion in childbirth, and in all kinds of illness, her comfort of the needy, and her consolation to the dying, won her way to the affections of the community. Those who afterwards became her enemies, including Governor Winthrop himself, and the Reverend John Wilson, her implacable opponent, paid tribute to her knowledge of scripture, her wit and wisdom, and her discreet and unfailing charity.

It had been the custom at week-day meetings for the men of the community to discuss the pulpit deliverances of the preceding Sunday. Mistress Hutchinson instituted similar meetings for the women. These grew to have such large attendance, and consequent importance, that, in a community already excited by the controversies which resulted in the banishment of Roger Williams, attention began to be directed to the assemblies at Anne Hutchinson's house. This was increased, perhaps, by the fact that Henry Vane, newly arrived and chosen governor (as well as Mr. Cotton), became advocates, not only of Mistress Hutchinson's methods, but of the special doctrine upon which she insisted, namely, that the works of professors of religion could not be appealed to as justification, without the spiritual gifts of grace. As a result of the personal antagonism which resulted from the severe criticism of their opinions at her meetings, the first warnings were heard of active proceedings against those who listened to Anne Hutchinson's teachings. Governor Vane as a candidate for reëlection was defeated, and returned to England, and while the sentiment in Boston remained less bitter and menacing, the ministers of many towns in Massachusetts were mustered to support measures to be propounded at the General Court against heretical teachings and heretics. Anne Hutchinson's former friends turned against her. Even her old champion, John Cotton, made only a feeble defense, fearing the safety of his own position.

After a two day's trial she was found guilty of heresy and was sentenced to banishment—the sentence to be deferred until the end of the existing winter season—and confined as a prisoner to the care of Mr. Joseph Welde, on the approval of her most bitter enemy, the Roxbury minister. Of this mock trial it has been said: "It was the most shameful proceeding in the annals of Protestantism. Winthrop, a trained lawyer, sat there, grave, stern, convinced beforehand of the culprit's guilt and resolved to banish her from the plantation. As the proceedings came to their predestined conclusion: 'I desire to know whereof I am banished,' said this woman, with the quiet courage of the early martyrs. 'Say no more,' replied Winthrop, 'the court knows whereof, and is satisfied.' Anne Hutchinson bowed her head and placing her hand upon the Bible said: 'The Lord judgeth not as man judgeth. Better to be cast out of the Church than to deny Christ.'"

In the latter part of March, 1638, she was sent from Boston and joined her husband in Rhode Island, where William Hutchinson died at Newport in 1642.

Threats which were made to extend the jurisdiction of the Bay State Colony over the Narragansett country seemed to render the Rhode Island residence an unsafe one for the banished, and several English families having already settled in the New Amsterdam jurisdiction, the Hutchinson family removed thither in the autumn of 1642, and took up their residence in a tract of land purchased near what is now Pelham Bay. It was an unfortunate choice of residence, as the Dutch governor had aroused the enmity of the Indians. In August, 1643, an attack was made on the settlement by savages, who burned Anne Hutchinson's house and slew every person within it, including six of her children, excepting her youngest daughter, who was carried into captivity by the Indians. She was not recovered from the hands of the savages for four years, and had then become one of them, having forgotten her own mother tongue.

The particular conditions of the theological controversy in which Mistress Hutchinson took such a prominent part are interesting today only to the churchman and the historian. The principles which she represented, both in the Bay colony and afterwards in Rhode Island, were woman's freedom of thought and expression, and religious toleration—in her own words, "no person to be accounted delinquent for opinion" in religion or in civil affairs.

In 1911 a bronze tablet to the memory of Mrs. Hutchinson was placed on Split Rock by the Society of Colonial Dames of the State of New York, who recognized that the resting place of this most noted woman of her time was well worthy of such a memorial. The tablet bears the following inscription:

ANNE HUTCHINSON
Banished from the Massachusetts Bay Colony
in 1638
Because of her Devotion to Religious Liberty
This Courageous Woman
Sought Freedom from Persecution
in New Netherland
Near this Rock in 1643 She and her House-
hold were Massacred by Indians

———

This Tablet is placed here by the
Colonial Dames of the State of New York
ANNO DOMINI MCMXL
Virtutes Majorum Filiae Conservant

This tablet was destroyed by some vandal hands and replaced by the original givers, the Colonial Dames of New York.

There has been much confusion in the statements concerning the massacre of the Hutchinson family and as to the exact number of her children. It has been said at one time that all her children were there slaughtered. As appears by the following table, which is believed to be an accurate enumeration, there were only six who were killed there.

1. Edward Hutchinson, baptized at Alford, May 28, 1613; died at Marlborough, Massachusetts, August 19, 1675; married (1) in England October 13, 1636, Catherine Hamby, and (2) Abigail, daughter of widow Alice Vermaes of Salem, Massachusetts.

2. Susanna Hutchinson, baptized September 4, 1614; buried September 8, 1630.

3. Richard Hutchinson, baptized December 8, 1615; admitted to First Church, Boston, Massachusetts, November 9, 1634, and on December 28, 1645, dismissed to Dr. Thomas Goodwin's church in London, where he disappears.

4. Faith Hutchinson, baptized August 14, 1616; died at Boston February 20, 1651/2; married Thomas Savage about 1637.

5. Bridget Hutchinson, baptized January 15, 1618/9; married in 1637 John Sanford, President of Rhode Island in 1653.

6. Francis Hutchinson, baptized December 24, 1620; killed by the Indians with his mother in 1643.

7. Elizabeth Hutchinson, baptized February 17, 1621/2; buried October 4, 1630, at Alford, England.

8. William Hutchinson, baptized June 22, 1623; died early in life.

9. Samuel Hutchinson, baptized December 17, 1624; he had a son, Richard, and was of Portsmouth, Rhode Island.

10. Anne Hutchinson, baptized May 5, 1626; married the Reverend William Collins. Both were killed by the Indians with her mother.

11. Maria (Mary) Hutchinson, baptized February 22, 1627/8; killed by the Indians with her mother.

12. Katherine Hutchinson, baptized February 7, 1629/30; killed by the Indians with her mother.

13. William Hutchinson, baptized September 28, 1631; killed by the Indians with his mother.

14. Susanna Hutchinson, baptized November 15, 1633; married, December 30, 1651, John Cole.

15. Zuryell Hutchinson, baptized in Boston, Massachusetts, January 13, 1636, died early in life.

The testimony of the Reverend James De Normandie given to Anne Hutchinson's character and services was the inspiration for the effort to present an effigy of this notable woman—the noble statue by Cyrus F. Dallin—to the State of Massachusetts, where the installation in the State House might be considered as a symbol of the reparation due by the General Court of today for the injustice and cruelty of its predecessor. In regard to this Doctor De Normandie wrote:

"Anne Hutchinson wielded a power and influence never before nor since equalled by any of her sex in America. Her influence upon the life of women is very marked even at the present day. Their freedom of thought is due to her more than to any other person. She is the spiritual ancestor of every woman's alliance; indeed of every organization in the land for patriotic or social or intellectual or religious conference and improvement—and in all years to come every such assembly should pay homage to the name and the spirit and the gifts and the memory of Anne Hutchinson."

HITCHCOCK, HELEN SANBORN SARGENT (Mrs. Ripley Hitchcock), daughter of Charles Chapin and Mary Elizabeth (Prescott) Sargent, was born in Elizabeth, New Jersey, April 28, 1870. Her father was descended from William Sargent, who came from England to Gloucester, Massachusetts, in 1630, and, in all branches of her ancestry, she descends from members of the Colonial families of Sargent, Dudley, Ellery, Rogers, Leavitt, Swain, Allen, and others, original settlers of New England, who laid the foundations and built the structure of New England and the United States.

Helen Sargent was graduated from Miss Annie Brown's school, in New York, in 1889, and was then a student at the Art Student's League, continuing under private art instruction for many years. On January 7, 1914, she married, in New York (James) Ripley (Wellman) Hitchcock, the son of Doctor Alfred and Aurilla Phebe (Wellman) Hitchcock, who was born in Fitchburg, Massachusetts, July 3, 1857, and died May 4, 1918. He was graduated from Harvard University in 1877, and after experience as a journalist, became literary advisor, first to D. Appleton and Company, and, in 1902, to Harper and Brothers. He was the author and editor of many works on art, history, and biography. By his first wife, Martha Wolcott Hall, whom he married in 1883, and who died September 1, 1903, he was the father of Lieutenant Roger Wolcott Hitchcock, an aviator, who died in action in France, September 2, 1918, and of Ripley Hitchcock, Jr.

Although Helen Sargent Hitchcock studied art for many years, instead of painting for exhibitions, she has given her time to organizing art activities that would benefit other artists, and the art life of the United States. In 1898 she founded the Art Workers' Club for Women and was its president for eleven years. This organization, which has become an important part of the art life of New York women, has for its object the bringing together of artists and models, for the purpose of interest and support. Posing, which hitherto had not been recognized as a profession, has become dignified through the influence of this club. A clubhouse is maintained with a restaurant, library, a bureau for posing engagements, and another for the renting of costumes. During her term as president, Mrs. Hitchcock, because of inquiries made by the artists themselves, learned many of the problems with which the art worker and the art employer in America are confronted. This led her, in April, 1914, to found the Art Alliance of America, of which she is First Vice-President. Upon the entrance of the United States into the World War, in 1917, Mrs. Hitchcock organized the Art War Relief at 661 Fifth Avenue, New York. Besides advancing the artists' work for war needs, there was also formed an auxiliary of the New York County Chapter of the American Red Cross. The committees were composed of women who were members of the following organizations: The Art Alliance of America, the Art Students' League, the Art Workers' Club for Women, the Catherine Lorillard Wolfe Art Club, the Macdowell Club, the American Society of Miniature Painters, the National Arts Club, the National Academy of Design, the National Association of Women Painters and Sculptors, the New York School of Fine and Applied Art, the American Water Color Society, the Pen and Brush Club, the Pratt Institute School of Fine and Applied Art, the School of Applied Design for Women, the Studio Club, the Fine Arts Department of Teachers' College, Columbia University, the Three Arts Club, and the New York Water Color Club. The chief object of the Art War Relief was to bring together artists, art students, and others interested in art, as well as artisans, for the purpose of patriotic service. A committee on reëducation made a survey of the crafts and art industries, which led to the organization of the war service classes, under the Federal Government, to teach art handicraft to young women who then became reconstruction aids in the hospitals for soldiers and sailors. A further activity was coöperation with the committee appointed by the Federal Government in obtaining propaganda posters. The Art War Relief was also active in establishing branches in art schools and art organizations for relief work. Under its initiative, over 550 landscape targets were painted by eminent artists for machine-gun instruction in the training camps. The Art War Relief Bronze Medallion, designed and given by Paul Manship, has become an historic work of art; through its sale funds were raised for relief work. The Book Committee of the Art War Relief raised money for reconstruction work (to establish reading rooms) among the children of the Allies. One in Brussels was opened in September, 1920. Mrs. Hitchcock assisted in organizing the National Committee of One Hundred on Memorial Buildings, of which she was vice-president, to coöperate

with organizations in an effort to assure that such memorials should be worthy tributes to those that fell in the Great War, should express the highest in art, and should promote the welfare of the communities. During the first four months of propaganda, over four hundred towns and cities reported plans for this type of memorial. This committee later amalgamated with the War Camp Community Service. As Vice-President of the American Jugo-Slav Relief, Mrs. Hitchcock assisted in organizing the committee to send, through the Federal Government, clothing and money to these stricken peoples. From the Art Alliance of America developed, in 1920, the Art Center, Inc., of which Mrs. Hitchcock is President. It is organized to advance the decorative and the industrial and graphic arts of America, and includes the following coöperating societies: the Art Alliance of America, the Art Directors' Club, the New York Society of Craftsmen, the Pictorial Photographers of America, the Society of Illustrators, the American Institute of Graphic Arts, and the Stowaways. Its home at 65–67 East 56th Street, New York, was opened November 1, 1921. Here the many galleries and studies will hold exhibitions and conferences, lectures, and various kinds of educational propaganda will be carried on for the benefit of the arts of design, in connection with the every day life of our people. Mrs. Hitchcock is a Vice-President of the National Institute of Social Sciences, a member of the Board of Directors of the Woman's Roosevelt Memorial Association, Inc., in the organization of which she assisted, and a member of the Colonial Dames of the State of New York and of the Cosmopolitan Club of New York City. She is a parishioner of Grace Episcopal Church, New York, and is working to revive the ministry of healing in the churches.

GERSTENBERG, ALICE, playwright, daughter of Erich and Julia (Wieschendorff) Gerstenberg, was born in Chicago, Illinois, where both her parents also were born. Her mother was the daughter of William Wieschendorff, who came to Chicago in 1854 from Hanover, Germany; and her father, who was born in 1858, was the son of Charles Gerstenberg, who came from Paris, France, to Chicago in 1853. He was born in 1829 at Hildesheim, Germany, and was the son of Constantine Gerstenberg of St. Petersburg, Russia. Alice Gerstenberg was educated at the Alcott Public Grammar School, Chicago, where she won the Foster diploma; at the Kirkland Private School, Chicago, where she was valedictorian of her class; and at Bryn Mawr College. Her work as a playwright began in 1908 with the publication of *A Little World*, four college playlets for girls, the first two of which were acted, on March 12, 1908, at the Anna Morgan Studios, Fine Arts Building, Chicago. During the next two years there, followed various sketches which received amateur production by clubs and societies, and, on February 8, 1912, her four-act comedy, *Captain Joe*, was given a professional matinee by the Academy of Dramatic Arts at the Empire Theatre, New York. In the meantime she had been working on her novel, *Unquenched Fire*, which, under the name of "John Gaston," contained a word portrait of David Belasco. This was published in May, 1912, and in the following year was brought out in England. A second novel, *The Conscience of Sarah Platt*, appeared in March, 1915. In the same year, after a successful run at the Fine Arts Theatre, Chicago, her *Alice in Wonderland*, a dramatization of episodes from Lewis Carroll's *Alice in Wonderland* and *Through the Looking Glass*, was put on at the Booth Theatre, New York. The arrangement was charmingly done, with tact, and with a keen appreciation of the values of the original stories. The incidents were so shrewdly chosen and so well presented that admirers of the books without hesitation welcomed the stage appearance of the beloved characters. In the autumn of 1915, the Washington Square Players, at the Bandbox Theatre, New York, gave Miss Gerstenberg's one-act play,

Overtones, a place on their program. This was a delicate fantasy, in which, of the four characters on the stage, two veiled figures represented the alter-egos of the other two. Later produced in vaudeville by Helen Lackaye, *Overtones* was acted in London by Mrs. Lily Langtry in 1917–1918, and was published in the *Drama League Series of Plays*. Other one-act plays by Miss Gerstenberg are *The Pot-Boiler*, a burlesque of the professional playwright, *Beyond, Fourteen, Hearts, Attuned, He Said and She Said, The Buffer, The Unseen, Illuminati in Drama Libre*, all of which, together with *Overtones*, were brought out in book form by Brentano's in 1921. Miss Gerstenberg's work is characterized by a brilliant vein of whimsical humor and a feeling for caricature. She is a member of the Society of Midland Authors, of which she was secretary from 1916 to 1918; the Chicago Equal Suffrage Association; the Little Room Club; the Arts Club, of whose Dramatic Committee she was Chairman from 1918 to 1921; the Chicago Cordon Club; the Women's Athletic Club; the Bryn Mawr College Club, of which she was President in 1919; the Junior League; the Casino Club; the Opera Dance Club of Chicago; and the National Arts Club of New York.

BENTLEY, AUGUSTA ZUG (Mrs. Robert Bentley), was born in Carlisle, Pennsylvania. Her father Jacob T. Zug, was a descendant of Ulric Zug, of Zug, Canton of Zug, Switzerland, who came to Philadelphia on the *James Lordwell*, landing September 27, 1727. He acquired title to 1000 acres of land in Warwick Township, and in 1742 the Penns granted him 1002 additional acres. In the possession of the descendants of Ulric's brother, Peter Zug, who settled near Downingtown, Pennsylvania, is an old family Bible, brought from Switzerland, in which are records showing that the family originally lived in the Palatinate, Germany, and the name was von Zug. The "particle of nobility" *von* was dropped when religious persecutions drove them to Switzerland.

Jacob T. Zug married Annie Eberly, who was descended from Scotch-Irish settlers in Cumberland County, Pennsylvania. Their daughter, Augusta Zug, was educated in private schools, at the Metzger Seminary, Carlisle, and the Girton School, Haverford, Pennsylvania, and she attended lectures at Bryn Mawr College. She was married, at Carlisle, Pennsylvania, October 16, 1895, to Robert Bentley, President of the Ohio Iron and Steel Company, Youngstown, Ohio. They are the parents of Robert Bentley, Jr., Martyn Zug Bentley, and Richard McCurdy Bentley. Mrs. Bentley is active in charitable work, and is President of the Visiting Nurse Association and treasurer of the Young Women's Christian Association of Youngstown. As a Vice-President of the National League for Women's Service, she directed, during the World War, the care of the men in service who passed through Youngstown, and gave much time to the work of the Navy League and the Red Cross. Mrs. Bentley inherits a love for life in the open, and, when at her camp in the Adirondacks, spends much time in the woods.

WAGSTAFF, BLANCHE SHOEMAKER (Mrs. Donald Carr), was born at Larchmont, New York, in 1888. Her father, Henry Francis Shoemaker, banker, of Philadelphia, was a descendant of Peter Shoemaker, a native of Holland, who located in Philadelphia, in 1685. He was one of its first Burgesses and a leading man in the Colony. As a Quaker, he was associated with William Penn who during his visit to Pennsylvania in 1700, preached in Peter Shoemaker's home. Peter's wife, Mercy, was a daughter of Dirck Op den Graeff of Rotterdam. Henry Francis Shoemaker was a pioneer railroad man and the owner of numerous lines. He also organized a large number of corporations in New York and in Western cities, and was a director of many banks, among them the Harriman Bank, the Trust Company of America, and the Chatham and Phoenix Bank. He served in the Civil War with the 27th Pennsylvania

Volunteers. His wife was Blanche, daughter of Colonel James W. Quiggle, LL.D., who was descended from the ancient MacQuiggle family of Scotland. An ancestor served under William of Orange at the Battle of the Boyne. Colonel Quiggle was a State Senator, as well as Deputy Attorney General of Pennsylvania, Consul General at Antwerp, Chargé d'affaires at Brussels, and Special Envoy to General Garibaldi. He married Cordelia Mayer, a descendant of Henri Lemaire, a Huguenot, who fled from Toulouse, France, after the revocation of the Edict of Nantes, in 1685, and came to America.

Mrs. Wagstaff was educated at the Brearley School, New York City, and later made special studies at Miss Spence's School. She continued her work in Greek, Latin, French, psychology, and the applied arts at Columbia University, and there attended lectures by Henri Bergson. In 1906, 1907, and 1911 she visited England, France, and Italy, being presented to the Pope in 1906, and at the Court of King Edward VII of England, in 1907. During a residence in Greece, she attended lectures at the University of Athens, where she specialized in Greek Archaeology. In 1909 she supplemented her already extensive education by work in Italy and at Carthage. She also traveled extensively in the Orient, and in 1911 enjoyed the unique experience of a camping trip in the Sahara. She was deeply impressed by the mysteries of the desert, which she later made the theme of many poems.

At a very early age Mrs. Wagstaff evidenced literary genius. When only seven years of age she began writing verse, and at eleven published a four-page leaflet of original stories and poems. At sixteen her work first appeared in a magazine, and her early poems attracted favorable notice from the English critics George Moore and Arthur Symons. At eighteen she was a Contributing Editor of the *Van Norden Magazine;* and from 1914 to 1919 she was Editor of the *Poetry Journal* published in Boston, a periodical devoted exclusively to verse. During 1916–1918 she wrote book reviews for the *New York Times*. She has also contributed essays and other poems to the *Sun* and *Herald*, of New York, as well as to *Harper's Magazine*, *Smart Set*, and other periodicals in England and in the United States. Many of her songs have been set to music by various composers. In 1917 she was in charge of the Publicity Department of the Second Federal Reserve District for the Liberty Loan. In 1918 she contributed to the *Red Cross Calendar of Verse* and to the Vigilantes, the authors' organization, which, during the World War syndicated essays, verse, and other literary matter.

Mrs. Wagstaff has made many translations of French and Greek verse; her own sociological essays have been translated into French, Spanish, and Danish; and her collections of poetry have been produced in the form of volumes for the blind. Her publications include: *Song of Youth*, poems (1906); *Woven of Dreams* (1908); *Alcestis*, a poetic drama modernized from the Greek of Euripides in pentameter, and staged at the Hudson Theatre, New York City, in 1910; *Atys*, poems (1911); *Eris*, a philosophical poem (1913); *Book of Love*, prose poems (1918); *Narcissus*, poems (1918). Some of her poems appeared in the anthologies: *The Lyric Year*, *Fifes and Drums*, *The Garden of Life*, and *The World and Democracy*, a compendium on the World War (1919). In *Eris* (1913), a dramatized version of the philosophy of Henri Bergson, Mrs. Wagstaff, already known as a gifted youthful poet, fulfilled the promise given by her earlier work. Madison Cawein declared that "no woman poet of the world has done anything like this, in its rhythmical and philosophical beauty." Benjamin de Casseres declared it "the poem of the century." Alexander Harvey, in *Reedy's Mirror*, wrote: "Her genius has so striking an individuality! The interpretation of passion in the light of intellect is achieved by the author. She is rich in poetic triumphs and felicity of epithet. The supreme miracle of

her poetical art is its newness of note. It has the wizardry that tempts to a second perusal. It stimulates like the wine of Homer. Her poetry concerns itself with the great and universal themes. Its essential characteristic is Thought, but the Thought is always beautiful as well as strong." Mrs. Wagstaff's genius places her in the foremost rank among the poets of the nineteenth century. Her work shows a fine intellectual fibre and, above all, is characterized by that delight in beauty for its own sake which is Greek in its spirit.

During the period of the World War, Mrs. Wagstaff gave generously of her time and effort. She was one of the founders of the National League for Women's Service. In conjunction with her work at the headquarters, 257 Madison Avenue, New York City, she organized the General Service Division of twelve hundred volunteers, who gave their services for the various war activities of the City. During 1918–1919 she was associated with the War Camp Community Service at its headquarters, 14 West 40th Street, New York City. She served, also, in a community booth at the club maintained by St. Thomas' Church at 8 West 43rd Street for housing soldiers and sailors. She was active in the drives for the Liberty Loans and the Connecticut Red Cross, and was Chairman of the Society of the Fatherless Children of France, Inc. Mrs. Wagstaff also drove an ambulance, in France, for the American Girls' Aid Unit, with headquarters at Nancy.

Mrs. Wagstaff's permanent residence is in New York City, where she had a studio for many years; her summer home is in Connecticut. She is a member of the Colony, Badminton, and Cameo Clubs, the Sound Beach Golf Club, the Authors' League, the Poetry Society of America, the Pen and Brush Club, the National Association of Women Painters and Sculptors, the Dante League, the Pennsylvania Society, the Huguenot Society, the National League for Women's

Service, and the Vigilantes. Her favorite recreations are music, reading, golf, motoring, and motor-cycling, and she was the first woman motor-cyclist in New York State. She married, first, in New York, April 29, 1907, Alfred Wagstaff, Jr.; they were the parents of one son, Alfred Wagstaff, 3d. She married, second, July 30, 1921, Donald Carr, son of Henry S. Carr, and grandson of General Alexander Shaler, who commanded the 6th Army Corps of the Federal Army during the Civil War. He is a direct descendant of Robert Cushman, organizer of the *Mayflower* Expedition, and of Isaac Allerton, one of the early settlers of New York City. At the outbreak of the World War, Mr. Carr enlisted and served overseas with the 27th Division, United States Army.

KEYES, FRANCES PARKINSON WHEELER (Mrs. Henry Wilder Keyes), author, was born in the former home of President Monroe in Charlottesville, Virginia, July 21, 1885. Her ancestry is notable in that she is descended from seven who fought in the War of the Revolution, and from nine whose services to the American Colonies entitled her to enter the Society of the Colonial Dames of America. John Henry Wheeler, her father, who was born September 5, 1851, was graduated from Harvard University with high honors in 1871; took his degree of Master of Arts there in 1875; and was also admitted to the Massachusetts bar that year. The following year he was a Fellow at Johns Hopkins University; then, the Parker Scholarship being conferred upon him by Harvard, he studied three years in Europe, taking his Ph.D. at Bonn with the highest honors ever given to an American, and was the first American admitted to study Greek manuscripts in the Library of the Vatican. Upon his return, he became first an Instructor at Harvard, then Assistant Professor at Bowdoin College, and, at the age of thirty, Professor of Greek and Head of the Greek Department at the University of Virginia. When he died on

October 10, 1887, at the age of thirty-six, he had already attained the reputation of being one of the half-dozen leading classical scholars in the United States, with a brilliant promise for the future. He wrote for numerous periodicals, usually anonymously. He was the son of the Reverend Melancthon Gilbert Wheeler and Frances Parkinson, and grandson of Zadok Wheeler and Mary Holbrook. Zadok Wheeler was a lawyer of Lanesborough, Massachusetts, and later of Charlotte, Vermont, where he was a representative and a judge. He died in Fort Edward, New York. Mary Holbrook, his wife, was born in Boston, Massachusetts, January 24, 1768. She was the sixth child of Samuel Holbrook, who was baptized at the Old North Church in Boston, May 18, 1729, and died in Roxbury, Massachusetts, July 24, 1784. In 1755 he married Elizabeth, the daughter of Eleazar Williams of Roxbury, by his wife, Sarah, the daughter of Colonel Thomas Tileston of Dorchester. She died in 1809. Samuel Holbrook had a long career as a teacher, beginning in 1745 and being appointed by his brother, Abiah Holbrook, assistant in the latter's school, the South Writing School, which numbered two hundred and fifty pupils. In 1753, he was master of the Writing School in Queen Street and in 1769 he succeeded his brother as master of the South Writing School. In that same year he was one of the Sons of Liberty to dine at the Liberty Tree, and he aided in concealing cannon when General Gage tried to seize the military stores. He was the son of Abiah Holbrook, who was born in Weymouth, Massachusetts, in 1695, and who married Mary Needham at the Old North Church, Boston, October 3, 1717. Abiah Holbrook was the son of Samuel (c.1654–1695) and Lydia Holbrook and grandson of Captain John Holbrook of Weymouth and his wife, Elizabeth Streame. Captain Holbrook was born in 1618–1619 and was prominent in the colony, being a large landholder, a captain in King Philip's War, and frequently a representative. His father, Thomas Holbrook, came with his wife, Jane, and four children, to Weymouth in 1635 on the *Speedwell* from Broadway, Somersetshire, England. John Henry Wheeler married Louise Fuller Johnson, who was born in 1848 and who is descended from William Johnson, who came from Kent, England, in 1634 to Charlestown, Massachusetts, through John Johnson, Thomas Johnson, a writer, David Johnson, and her father, Edward Carleton Johnson.

Francis Parkinson Wheeler was educated at Miss Carroll's and Miss Winsor's schools, Boston, Massachusetts, at Mlle. Dardelle's school, Geneva, Switzerland; and under private tutors in Berlin, Germany. On June 8, 1904, she was married at Newbury, Vermont, to Henry Wilder Keyes, the son of Henry Keyes (1810–1870) and Emma Frances Pierce. Henry Wilder Keyes was born in Newbury, Vermont, May 23, 1862, and was graduated from Harvard University in 1887. For many years a farmer on a large scale at his home at North Haverhill, New Hampshire, he is also connected with extensive banking interests of the state, and has been prominent in Republican politics. From 1917 to 1919 he was Governor of New Hampshire, and since then he has been United States Senator from New Hampshire. Mr. and Mrs. Keyes are the parents of Henry Wilder Keyes, Jr., born at North Haverhill, New Hampshire, March 22, 1905; John Parkinson Keyes, born at North Haverhill, New Hampshire, March 26, 1907; and Francis Keyes, born in Boston, Massachusetts, December, 4, 1912.

Although nurtured in a conservative New England atmosphere, where she had grown up among the traditions of her forebears, Mrs. Keyes has never been bound by it, and early showed her strong individuality. Her ability as a public speaker was foreshadowed at the age of ten, when Senator William Paul Dillingham, then running for the governorship of Vermont, found her campaigning for him from a wagon seat on the countryside. Since her marriage she has been active in politics in connection with her husband's career, frequently speaking in French before the Canadian mill workers of New Hampshire, during the presidential campaign of 1920. During the World War she did extensive Liberty Loan work, and has also engaged in public speaking on behalf of the Sheppard-Towner Maternity and Child Welfare Bill, which passed the United States Senate in December, 1919. Her interest in this bill is but an extension of her dominating principle that motherhood is, for women, the greatest career of all. Mrs. Keyes has written many articles and stories appearing in *The Granite Monthly*, *The Atlantic Monthly* (e. g. *Reflections of a Semi-Bostonian* in the issue for December, 1919), *The Ladies' Home Journal*, *Good Housekeeping*, and other magazines, and she is the author of two novels, *The Old Gray Homestead* (March, 1919), and *The Career of David Noble* (1921). She writes with refreshing humor as well as with tender charm. *The Old Gray Homestead* is a colorful picture of twentieth century rural New England with a practical application of the back-to-the-farm movement, the truthfulness of which is shown by the novel's popularity among rural readers. In recognition of her writings, George Washington University conferred upon Mrs. Keyes the honorary degree of Doctor of Letters, February 22, 1921. She is National Vice-President of the League of American Penwomen; National Vice-President of the Children of the American Revolution; and a member of the National Societies, Daughters of the American Revolution and Colonial Dames of America, and of the Winsor Club of Boston and the Congressional and Colonial Dames Clubs of Washington.

ANGLIN, MARGARET [MARY] (Mrs. Howard Hull), actress, daughter of the Honorable Timothy Warren and Ellen (McTavish) Anglin, was born in Ottawa, Canada, April 3, 1876. Her father was at one time Speaker of the Canadian House of Commons.

Miss Anglin was educated at Loretto Abbey, Toronto, and at the Convent of the Sacred Heart, Montreal. Although she needed great courage to break away from the traditions of her environment and to announce her decision to enter public life in her chosen profession, nevertheless, on completing her studies at the convent, she enrolled as a pupil in the Empire School of Dramatic Acting, New York City. In 1894 she made her professional début in New York in the rôle of Madeline West in *Shenandoah*. In 1895 she joined the company of James O'Neil, and appeared as leading lady in *The Courier of Lyons*, *Virginius*, *Hamlet*, and *Monte Cristo*. In 1897–1898 she acted with E. H. Sothern, and in the season of 1898–1899 she created the part of Roxane in Richard Mansfield's production of *Cyrano de Bergerac*, thereby firmly establishing her reputation. Thereafter she became the popular leading lady of the Empire Theatre Stock Company, where her Mrs. Dane, in *Mrs. Dane's Defense* attracted wide attention, and gave promise of her future success in emotional rôles. This impression was deepened by her performance in *Zira* in 1905–1906 and, with Henry Miller, in *The Great Divide* in 1906–1907.

In 1908 Miss Anglin toured Australia, where she tried out her maturing powers in Shakespearean rôles. Upon her return, after a pleasure trip around the world, she produced *The Awakening of Helena Richie* in New York in 1909 and the *Antigone* of Sophocles in California in 1910, and, as a contrast, a comedy part in *Green Stockings* in New York in 1911. Miss Anglin then became her own manager and played *Twelfth Night*, *As You Like It*, *The Taming of the Shrew*, and *Anthony and Cleopatra*, in western cities, with scenery and costumes designed by Livingston Platt after the newer stage-craft in strong contrast to the traditional settings. She was the stage manager for all the plays as well as the leading player, and brought her large repertoire through Canada back to the East in triumph. In her interpretation of the parts of Viola and Rosalind her differentiation of the two rôles was subtle. She represented Viola with a degree of meekness, and Rosalind, with a gay humor and self-confident poise. Her youthful charm and high spirits were infectious; her beauty enthralled and held the spectators.

During the Panama-Pacific Exposition Miss Anglin presented revivals of the Greek classics at the Theatre of the University of California, where she had been seen already in the Sophoclean dramas *Antigone* and *Electra*. Walter Damrosch composed special music for her performances, which also included the *Medea* of Euripides. She had for a consultant Professor William Dallam Armes of the Department of Literature of the University who made special researches in Greece, where she herself spent some time with the design of acquiring data and atmosphere. In these revivals Miss Anglin proved herself to be a tragedienne of power, with dramatic intensity of expression, previously unknown in her generation, which gave her rank with Rachel and Mrs. Siddons. She held her great audiences spellbound at this time, and also in other cities, where the revivals were repeated, and received great praise from serious students of the drama in every country. In succeeding years she has continued to give plays from the classics at the University of California and has often repeated them in New York and other large cities.

In the annals of the American theatre Miss Anglin will be recorded as one who refused to drift on an easy current of popularity. Her work has been marked by a determination to do something for the theatre itself. She has a record of fine energy and resourceful capacity. Her performances include modern comedy, airy and inconsequential, offset by the loftiest of the old tragedies. She has been associated with the best of living authors, including Mrs. Deland, Henry Arthur Jones, Somerset Maugham, and Emile Moreau, as well as with the finest classic writers. She always supervises the stage settings, devoting much time to detail. In 1920 she returned to New York to open the season in *A Woman of Bronze*, a play in which she had had marked success in the preceding year in Baltimore. Miss Anglin was married in New York, May 8, 1911, to Howard Hull, a well-known writer, and brother of Henry Hull, the actor.

BURKE, KATHLEEN, Colonel, C. B. E. (Mrs. Frederick Forest Peabody), daughter of Thomas Francis and Georgina (Connolly) Burke, was born in London, England, and educated at the University of Oxford and in Paris. During the period of the World War she achieved a record attained by few only of the women whose lives were consecrated to work for the Allies. Her service was extended and diversified, for at different times she was with the British, Italian, Serbian, and American Armies. At the beginning of the War she was sent to Belgium as member of a British Refugee Commission, and worked there during August and September, 1914, until the fall of Antwerp. She escaped from Ostend two days before the arrival of the Germans, and then, proceeding to Serbia, was appointed by the French Government its only woman representative at the front. In May, 1915, she joined the Scottish Women's Hospitals, and, as organizing secretary, visited all the scenes of their activities. She was the first woman at Vimy Ridge with the Canadian troops, and there received the gift of a German flag, captured by a Canadian. She was the only woman permitted to enter the British front lines, and was the first woman to go into Verdun. She remained at Verdun during the great siege, in the summer of 1916, and suffered a wound in the arm. Later in 1916, she came to America to plead the cause of the Scottish Women's Hospitals. Her manner of speaking was direct and forceful, and her audiences were held spellbound by her gift for narration, as she recounted anecdotes of the shocking conditions which she had seen in all the war-ridden lands. In answer to her appeal she received approximately one million five

hundred thousand dollars for her cause. In 1917, when the United States entered the War, she joined the American Red Cross, and made a speaking tour of the country in behalf of its campaign for funds. In 1918 she returned to France, was with the British Army at Ypres, Cambrai, Douai and Lille, and was gassed at Valenciennes. In bitterest terms Miss Burke denounces the Germans for their atrocities committed at the end as well as in the beginning of the war. During their evacuation of Douai they had filled a barracks with three thousand old women and children "for safety," and then gassed them, in order to delay the British, who stopped to nurse these feeble and innocent victims of the Hun. Miss Burke spent the last day of the war with the American troops at Verdun, whither she went on November 9, 1918. She returned to America after the armistice to continue her work for the Scottish Women's Hospitals at their offices in New York. Large sums of money have been administered by her, but her work has been entirely on a voluntary basis, as she has accepted no salary for herself. Miss Burke is fond of outdoor sports, golf and fishing, and is an expert horsewoman. She is the author of *The White Road to Verdun* (1916) and *Little Heroes of France, 1914–1918* (1920). Although she is of British birth, America claims her by adoption. She has been awarded the freedom of the cities of Flint, Michigan, and Fresno, California, and in October, 1918, was named Honorary Colonel of the 138th Field Artillery, United States Army. Also she has been elected a member of the International Brotherhood of Boilermakers, Iron Shipbuilders and Helpers of America, Local No. 6, San Francisco, and has the right of speech in all the Labor Temples of the country. She is a member of the National Chapter, Daughters of the Empire of Canada, and is an Officer de l'Instruction Publique of France. She is a Commander of the Order of the British Empire, a Knight of St. Sava of Serbia, and has been awarded the British Service Medal, the British Victory Medal, the

French Red Cross Medal, the Order of Miseri-
corde of Serbia, the Serbian Cross of Charity,
the Russian Cross of St. George, and the
Greek War Cross. On April 5, 1920, she was
married to Frederick Forest Peabody of Santa
Barbara, California.

UPHAM, ELIZABETH GREENE, (Mrs.
Carl Henry Davis), daughter of Horace A. J.
and Mary (Greene) Upham, was born in
Milwaukee, Wisconsin. She passed her girlhood in Milwaukee and in Kilbourn City, the
summer home of her family. In the picturesque region of the Dells of Wisconsin she
developed a love of nature, and gained knowledge of many of its forms of life. The trees
and flowers became her intimates, and the
birds, moles, snakes, and other creatures of
the wood and river, were subjects of her interested attention. She was reared in a home
where ethics, religion, economics, and the
higher concerns of life were constant themes
of discussion.

Miss Upham was prepared for college in the
Milwaukee-Downer Seminary. She had hardly
begun her college course, when a serious
affection of the eyes compelled her to discontinue most of her studies. However, she
listened at classes and to private reading, and
used her eyes only for laboratory and art work,
whenever possible. By these means she was
able to secure college credits. While in college
she became interested in the teachings of
William Morris and his school, and began the
study of arts and crafts, supplementing her
work in the Kalo Shops in Chicago, the
Thatcher School of Metal Work, Woodstock,
New York, and Commonwealth Art Colony,
Boothbay, Maine. When she regained the
use of her eyes she devoted their service to the
education, through hand-training, of both the
normal and disabled.

In 1912, Elizabeth Upham became an instructor in Applied Arts in Milwaukee-Downer
College and at the end of two years accepted
the position of Director of the Art Department of the same institution.

For years Elizabeth Upham's thought had
been given to the great possibilities of benefit
to the handicapped through hand-training,
her attention being called to it by the years of
limitation in her own experience. It was
largely through her influence that instruction
in these subjects was introduced in the institutions for tubercular and mental patients
in Milwaukee County; later the Legislature
of Wisconsin provided for Occupational Therapy in county sanatorium and state hospitals.

In 1917, Elizabeth Upham received leave of
absence from the College to enable her to
serve her country's needs as a member of the
research division of the Federal Board for
Vocational Education, resigning the Director-
ship of the Art Department, and accepting the
appointment of Professor of Applied Arts in
Milwaukee-Downer College. She was with
the Federal Board for two years, and during
this time prepared reports and wrote many
articles. Her subjects included *Selective
Placement of the Handicapped, Some Principles
of Occupational Therapy, Normalizing the Industrial Cripple, Occupational Therapy and the
Trained Nurse, The Absorption of Handicapped
Labor into Industry, Desirability of Vocational
Education and Direction for Disabled Soldiers,
Ward Occupations in Hospitals* (a pamphlet of
fifty-seven pages), *Training of Teachers for
Occupational Therapy for the Rehabilitation of
Disabled Soldiers and Sailors* (a pamphlet of
seventy-six pages), besides many unsigned
studies and reports of investigation.

In spite of busy years of teaching, research
and government service Elizabeth Upham
never relinquished the purpose to secure a
college education. In June, 1919, after her
return to Milwaukee, she received the degree
of Bachelor of Science conferred by Milwaukee-
Downer College on regular examinations
passed and college work accomplished despite
the limitations, interruptions, and achievements of the previous ten years.

On September 6, 1919, Elizabeth Upham
was married to Carl Henry Davis, M.D.

Mrs. Davis continued her efforts for the disabled in war and in industry, being one of the editors of the Department of Occupational Therapy and Rehabilitation in *The Modern Hospital;* on the Board of Management of the American Occupational Therapy Association; an associate editor of *The Archives of Occupational Therapy,* and Lecturer and Advisor in the Occupational Therapy Training Course in Milwaukee-Downer College.

In the social and club life of her city and state, Mrs. Davis is an active member. She is a member of the Woman's Club of Wisconsin; Chairman of the Publicity and Legislative Committee of the Wisconsin Association of Occupational Therapy; member of the College Club of Washington, District of Columbia; the Milwaukee branch of the American Association of University Women; the Public Health Committee of the City Club of Milwaukee; one of the founders of the Wisconsin Society of Applied Arts; and member of the Junior League of Milwaukee.

Dr. and Mrs. Davis have two sons, Horace Upham and Henry Clinton Davis.

Mrs. Davis' power of accomplishment seems largely to be due to her swift perception, ability to organize, a personality that wins coöperation, and an understanding heart.

BYRNS, ELINOR, lawyer, feminist, and non-resistant pacifist, daughter of Ainsworth Harrison and Eliza (Grover) Byrns, was born in LaFayette, Indiana. Her mother's family came from England to Massachusetts before 1643; her father's family coming several generations later from England to settle in Ohio.

Miss Byrns was educated in the LaFayette High School and the Girls' Classical School of Indianapolis, and was graduated in the University of Chicago and the New York University Law School. In 1907 she was admitted to the New York Bar, and has since practised law in New York City.

She was brought up to believe in woman's rights, her mother, maternal grandmother, and father's sister having been ardent suffragists. In 1908 she became an active suffrage worker, at first with the College Equal Suffrage League, later with the National American Woman Suffrage Association and the Woman Suffrage Party. She held numerous offices, wrote many articles, was for two years in charge of national press work, and in 1917 conducted suffrage schools throughout New York State. Miss Byrns has always been an active pacifist, as a matter of principle, therefore, she resigned from the Woman Suffrage Party, when its officers endorsed participation by the United States in the World War. She continued to work for suffrage as Chairman of the Socialist-Suffrage organization in her district. A socialist since 1909, Miss Byrns joined the Socialist Party in 1917, receiving its nomination for Congress in 1918 and for District Attorney in 1919. Miss Byrns holds that her most important work has been for peace and disarmament. In 1917-1918, she was actively associated with the Women's Peace Party. In 1919 she was elected Chairman of the Women's International League of New York State, and presided at one of the first meetings held to protest against the Peace Treaty, and the failure of the proposed League of Nations to require disarmament. Feeling that peace organizations had failed because their members were united merely by opposition to war, she formed, in October, 1919, a new organization, known as the Women's Peace Society. The members of this society pledge themselves to the belief that human life must be held sacred under all circumstances. They consider it wrong to support or condone war, violence, or bloodshed for any reason whatever. Mrs. Henry Villard, daughter of William Lloyd Garrison, non-resistant as well as abolitionist, became Chairman of this Society, and Miss Byrns, its first Vice-Chairman. In October, 1920, the Women's Peace Society began a campaign for immediate, universal, and complete disarmament. Miss Byrns organized a speaking tour, on which Mrs. Pethick

Lawrence of England and Frau Yella Hertka of Austria, united with American women in demanding world disarmament.

CALLENDER, ESTELLE VICTORIA HUDGINS (Mrs. William Edward Callender), was born in Norfolk, Virginia, April 27, 1873. Through her father, Captain William Edward Hudgins (born in Matthews County, Virginia, April 7, 1838; died in Norfolk, Virginia, July 27, 1920) she is descended from John Hudgins, who came from England to Gloucester County, Virginia, in 1752. John Hudgins' son, Robert (1778–1821), served in the War of 1812. In 1808 he married Susan, daughter of William and Elizabeth Buckner of Gloucester County, Virginia, a great-great-great-grandson of John Buckner, who settled in Gloucester County in 1667 and was a member of the House of Burgesses in 1683, and a descendant of Samuel Matthews, Captain-General and Governor of Virginia (1622–1660). Robert King Hudgins (1812–1903), son of Robert and Susan Hudgins, married, in 1834, Sarah James, daughter of John and Elizabeth (Davenport) White of Matthews County, Virginia. Her father, John White, was a soldier, and her grandfather, William Davenport, a captain in the Revolutionary War. A son of Robert King and Sarah James (White) Hudgins, Captain William Edward Hudgins, married in 1871, Louisa Victoria Stone (born in Philadelphia, Pennsylvania, September 14, 1852; died in Norfolk, Virginia, August 5, 1915), a descendant of Gregory Stone (born in Great Bumbay, Essex, England, April 19, 1592), who came to Massachusetts in 1635 and was made a freeholder in 1636, and of his son, John Stone (born in England; died in Massachusetts in 1672). The line is traced through John's son, Nathaniel (born in England in 1618); Hezikiah (born, 1660); Jesse (born, 1710); Isaac, who served in the War of the Revolution; Jeremy (born, 1769); and Captain E. E. Stone, U. S. N. (born, 1826), who married Leonide de Montalant, and was

the father of Louisa Victoria (Stone) Hudgins. On August 11, 1897, Estelle Victoria Hudgins was married at Norfolk, Virginia, to the Rev. William Edward Callender, a priest of the Protestant Episcopal Church (born in Liverpool, England, December 10, 1866), a son of John Robert and Marian (Kerr) Callender of Edinburgh, Scotland, of the Callenders of Callender. After filling several important rectorships, Reverend W. Callender became, by appointment of the City Council, in 1920, first Port Chaplain of the City of Norfolk, Virginia. Mr. and Mrs. Callender are the parents of Mabel O. Callender (born in Charlotte, North Carolina, April 3, 1899; died June, 1899), Virginia Ormistoun Callender (born in Charlotte, North Carolina, March 4, 1901), Louise de Montalant Callender (born at Mount Pleasant, South Carolina, April 16, 1904) and William Edward Callender, Jr. born in Laurens, South Carolina, February 21, 1908; died March, 1908). Mrs. Callender has accomplished notable constructive work in connection with women's patriotic societies. She was the founder and first regent of the Falls Church Chapter, Daughters of the American Revolution, Falls Church, Virginia, and is the genealogist of the Great Bridge Chapter of Norfolk, Virginia. She is President of the Virginia Society of Daughters of Founders and Patriots of America, and Recording Secretary of the Norfolk Circle, Colonial Dames of America in the State of Virginia. She is a member of the Hereditary Order of the Descendants of Colonial Governors, and was at one time a councillor of the National Genealogical Society of America. Her contributions to genealogical research have been many, the most conspicuous being her *Hudgins Family Genealogy*, compiled in 1912 and published in 1913. During the World War she participated in all the activities of the patriotic societies of which she is a member, and served as a captain in all the Liberty Loan and Red Cross Drives in Norfolk. She was also on the entertainment committee of the War Camp Community

Service of Norfolk, and acted as chaperone at hundreds of entertainments for the officers and men of the United States Service.

CARPENTER, ALICE CAROLINE, organizer, daughter of George Nathaniel and Agnes (Williams) Carpenter, was born in Woodstock, Illinois. Her father, a veteran of the Civil War, was a son of Nathaniel Carpenter, a Justice of the Supreme Court of Vermont, and a great-grandson of Benjamin Carpenter, of Boston, a soldier in the Revolutionary War, and a descendant in the sixth generation of Benjamin Carpenter, who came from England to Massachusetts about 1702. Through her mother, Miss Carpenter is descended from Roger Williams, Founder of Providence, Rhode Island.

Miss Carpenter prepared for Smith College in the private schools of Brookline and Boston, and entered with the class of 1897. After the death of her father in 1895 she traveled abroad for two years. Upon her return she began the study of kindergarten, and entered the kindergarten settlement of Elizabeth Peabody House, in Boston, where she remained for three years, the third year in charge of the settlement. She then studied at Radcliffe and Barnard, specializing in economics. In 1908 she became interested in the suffrage movement and took an active part in Massachusetts, serving as a director of the Massachusetts Woman Suffrage Association. In 1912 she was a delegate to the Progressive Party National Convention, in Chicago, and was a member of the Resolutions Committee. Later, she organized the women of the State of New York for the campaign of the Progressive Party in 1912. After the elections, she became affiliated with the National Committee, speaking and organizing for the Progressive Party throughout the country. In 1916, again she entered the political campaign, as Chairman of the Woman's New York City Committee of the Hughes Alliance.

Miss Carpenter's ability as an organizer was recognized by the business world when she was asked to institute a Woman's Department for the Investment House of Bonbright and Company, Inc. This, the first woman's department of its kind to be established in any investment house, was successfully developed by her in Chicago, Boston, Philadelphia and New York. The Woman's City Club of New York numbers her among its founders and she was its first Secretary and its second Vice-President.

During the World War Miss Carpenter resigned from her business position to devote her whole time to war activities. She was Chairman of the New York City Navy Auxiliary of the Red Cross and a member of its National Advisory Board. She was also Chairman of the New York City Committee of the Woman's Naval Service, and a member of its National Board. In 1918, she was sent abroad by the Red Cross for work in France, arriving just before the Armistice was signed. Upon her return, a few months later, she became identified with reconstruction work, as Chairman of the Employment Committee of the Mayor's Committee of Women on Reconstruction and Relief, and in 1919-1920 was one of the organizers of the reconstruction work for Serbia in the City of New York, being identified with the Serbian Child Welfare Association, as a member of its Executive Committee and as Vice-Chairman of its Trades Committee.

BRADLEY, SUSAN HINCKLEY (Mrs. Leverett Bradley), painter, daughter of Samuel Hinckley and Anne Cutler (Parker) Lyman, was born at Boston, Massachusetts. Somewhat late in life, her father took his maternal grandfather's name, and thereafter was known as Samuel Lyman Hinckley. His first ancestor in this country was Samuel Hinckley, born at Tenterden, Kent, England, who settled at Barnstable, Massachusetts, in 1635.

Mrs. Bradley studied in Rome under Edward Boit, at the Boston Museum of Fine Arts under Frederick Crowninshield, at Dublin, New Hampshire under Abbott Thayer, at the Penn Academy of Fine Arts and in Paris under Simon and Ménard.

In 1879, at Boston, she married the Reverend Leverett Bradley. They were the parents of Leverett Junior, Walter H., Margaret, now Mrs. R. D. Swaim, and Ralph Bradley.

Mrs. Bradley has always been a prolific painter, exhibiting constantly in Boston, New York, Philadelphia and other cities. Her pictures always found a ready sale, and they have been widely scattered. In addition to water color work, Mrs. Bradley possesses an unusual gift for portraiture in charcoal, and these, too, sold promptly and are distributed all over the country.

On the social side, Mrs. Bradley's interests are divided between welfare work and her beloved painting. She is a member of the Chilton Club of Boston, the Woman's City Club of Boston and the Boston Water Color Club, the New York Water Color and the Philadelphia Water Color Club.

During the World War, Mrs. Bradley gave her services to the government by painting large "landscape targets" for the training camps which were of great value for instruction in sighting and range finding.

FROTHINGHAM, EUGENIA BROOKS, author, daughter of Edward and Eugenia (Mifflin), Frothingham, was born in Paris, France, November 17, 1874. On her mother's side she is descended from the Mifflins of Philadelphia and the Crowninshields of Salem. Her ancestor of the latter name and city built and owned *Cleopatra's Barge*, the famous private yacht constructed for the purpose of smuggling Napoleon from St. Helena. Her great-grand-fathei Crowninshield was Secretary of the Navy under Madison. His daughter, Mary Crowninshield, married Doctor Charles Mifflin of Philadelphia, who returned to Massachusetts with her to live in Boston, where their second daughter, Eugenia Mifflin, mother of Eugenia Brooks Frothingham, was born in 1843. There were four other children:

Charles, who died in childhood; Elizabeth, who married Gardiner G. Hammond; Benjamin, who married Sarah Larned of Pittsfield; and George Harrison, who married Jennie Phillips of Salem and was the only one of that family to survive his sister Eugenia. Mary Crowninshield Mifflin, Miss Frothingham's grandmother, was, like the other Crowninshields, powerful, able, and warmhearted. It was owing to her wisdom and self control that the family property was kept intact. The women of both the Crowninshields and the Mifflins were with a few notable exceptions—as, for instance, George Harrison Mifflin of Houghton Mifflin Company—more vivid and compelling than the men. Both families specialized in friends and personal charm, rather than in public service. The Frothinghams, on the contrary, were scholars and public spirited. The first of this line was William Frothingham, who settled in Charlestown, Massachusetts, in 1630, and through marriage they crossed relationship with the families of Adams and Brooks. Traditions of literature, preaching, and public work were in their blood. Miss Frothingham's paternal grandfather was Nathaniel Frothingham, one of the first Unitarian ministers of Massachusetts and a friend of Channing. He married Ann Gorham Brooks and their children were: Thomas Bumstead, Francis Greenwood, Octavius Brooks, a well-known Unitarian clergyman, Edward, Ward Brooks, Ann Brooks, and Ellen. The last never married. Her translations of German literature have been regularly used by Harvard University. She lived her three-score years and ten, dying after having seen many lands and won many friends. Edward married Eugenia Mifflin at Nahant, Massachusetts, August 2, 1870. Their children were: Edward (who died in infancy), Eugenia Brooks, Olga, and Charles Mifflin. Eugenia Mifflin Frothingham was more distinguished by what she was than by what she did. According to Emerson this is the real test of power. None who saw her ever forgot her fascination, vitality, and grace of manner. She was a woman of unique charm which she kept, for men as well as for women, up to the end. Her embroideries will outlive many of those who knew her, and she painted exquisitely on china. But her great love was for animals and for the country. A radiant leader of almost any social gathering she could be induced to attend, she was most happy in an old skirt with a camp stool on her arm, superintending work on her New Hampshire farm. From her mother she inherited a business ability and was wise and controlled in her expenditures and the management of her estates. This New England thrift contrasted oddly with her temperamental impulse. Coming of a long-lived race—her mother and aunts had lived to be well over eighty—she died in her 78th year after a short illness. She never lost her vividness of response to life and that youthfulness in point of view which had always led her to meet progress open-handed, whether it came in the form of new invention, such as the automobile, or new ideas, such as woman suffrage or prohibition.

Eugenia Brooks Frothingham was educated in a Boston private school, until, at the age of fourteen, she went to Europe to study especially languages and music in Paris, Rome and Vienna. In 1901 she published her first novel, *The Turn of the Road*, which won instant popularity and established her reputation for skill and charm in unfolding a romantic love story. This was followed by *The Evasion* in 1907 and in 1911 by *Her Roman Lover*. The author's personal experience of Roman society and her understanding of the subtleties of the Italian temperament lend realism to this clever novel's workmanship. *The Way of the Wind* appeared in 1917 and in 1918 *The Finding of Norah*, a witty and courageous story of Boston, during the months just before America entered the World War. Occasional short stories have also been contributed to magazines. Miss Frothingham, as a member of the Chilton, the Women's City, and the May-

flower Clubs of Boston, and of the Ladies' Athenaeum Club of London, England, has shared in the interests of the women of her class and tastes. Moreover, she has written and lectured for the Massachusetts and the Boston Equal Suffrage Leagues on woman suffrage, and has spoken and written in favor of prohibition. Her work for prohibition has been due to her belief that alcohol is responsible for the greatest part of great evils, such as crime, disease, and poverty. She has always contended that the argument against it—that it violates the rights of man—was so utterly foolish that it was difficult to take intelligent persons seriously when they made this claim. "There has been no advance in the order or morality of mankind that was not obtained by the yielding up of some individual liberty. Civilization could not endure a week but for the ten thousand 'thou shalt not's'" was one of her arguments in this connection. During the World War, Miss Frothingham worked in a naval canteen and a war service shop. She was also treasurer of a small Red Cross unit. But her main activity during this time was in writing and lecturing on the League of Nations. She was on the Speakers' Division of the League of Free Nations and served on the Board of the League of Permanent Peace. In this connection she said in 1919: "I want to see the 'organized friendship of mankind' tried in some such League of Nations as was outlined in the famous Fourteen Points of President Wilson. The thing that so greatly justified the war was the idea that carried so much of the world's youth into those hideous trenches—that they were fighting a war against war. But it seems that our majority opinion is still so myopic that, having destroyed the military machine of Germany, we think ourselves absolved from further effort. The study of European records shows more and more that, while the act of Germany was the occasion of the great war, three hundred years or so of false international idea made the act possible. Under French and Italian diplomacy we are with 'criminal cynicism' digging ourselves into the old diplomatic trenches of 'checks and balances' that neither check nor balance. In the labor parties of different people—including France and England—we find the only organized policies of generous understanding among nations. It is sad that such a hope should be found chiefly among laborites. It would be more sad were it not found at all."

FOX, EMMA AUGUSTA STOWELL (Mrs. Charles Edgar Fox), parliamentarian, daughter of Allen Goff and Caroline (Scott) Stowell, was born in Binghamton, New York. All her ancestors were Puritan settlers of New England. Allen Goff Stowell, who lived from 1819 to 1903, was a descendant of Nathaniel Foote, probably of Shalford, Colchester, England, who came to Watertown, Massachusetts, prior to 1633, and was one of the founders of Wethersfield, Connecticut, where a monument was erected to his memory in 1908. He was born about 1593; married, about 1615, Elizabeth Deming (c. 1595–1683); and died about 1644. His son, Robert Foote, was born in 1627; married Sarah Potter in 1659; and died in 1681. He lived in Wethersfield, Wallingford, and after 1668 in Branford, Connecticut. His son, John Foote, of Branford (born July 24, 1670), married Mary in 1696; and died in 1713. His son, Doctor Thomas Foote, of Branford and Plymouth, Connecticut (born in 1699), married Elizabeth Sutliff, who died November 16, 1789, at the age of 82; and died December 19, 1776. His son, Isaac Foote, of Watertown, Connecticut, and Windsor, New York (born March 15, 1750), married, August 21, 1770, Sarah (March 12, 1751–October, 1815), the daughter of John Selkrigg; and died June, 1834. His daughter, Anna Foote (born July 30, 1772), married, first, Rufus Goff. Their daughter, Mary Goff, married Ebenezer Stowell, and they were the parents of Allen Goff Stowell. Mr. Stowell's wife, Caroline Scott, was born in 1822 and died in 1906. Her first American ancestor was Daniel Warren, who

came from England to Massachusetts in 1628 and whose daughter, Hannah Warren, married David Meads. Their daughter, Hannah Meads, married Ebenezer Locke. Their son, Joshua Locke, married Hannah Read. Their son, Josiah Locke, a captain in the Revolutionary War, married Persis Matthews. Their son, Ira Locke, married Persis Hamilton. The latter was descended from Thomas Woodford who died in this country in 1667 and whose wife was Mary Blott. Their daughter, Mary Woodford, married Isaac Sheldon. Their son, John Sheldon, was born December 5, 1658. He built the old Indian House at Deerfield, Massachusetts, and, on November 5, 1679, married Hannah, the daughter of John Stebbins. She was shot by Indians through a door of the Indian House when Deerfield was sacked February 29, 1704. Their son, Ebenezer Sheldon, married Thankful Barnard. Their daughter, Mercy Sheldon, married David Hoyt. Their daughter, Hannah Hoyt, married Silas Hamilton, and they were the parents of Persis Hamilton, who married Ira Locke. Aceneth Locke, the daughter of Ira and Persis Locke, married Wiley Huntington Scott, and they were the parents of Caroline (Scott) Stowell. Emma Augusta Stowell was educated in private and public schools. For some years she taught, at first in Washington School, Cambridge, Massachusetts, and later in Chicago, where she was head assistant in the Clarke School and afterwards in the North Division High School. On November 8, 1876, she was married at Peoria, Illinois, to Charles Edgar Fox, a merchant of Detroit, Michigan, the son of Henry Hodges and Sarah Ann (Burt) Fox. He was born in Taunton, Massachusetts, in 1847; retired from business in 1912 and died in Detroit in 1918. Mr. and Mrs. Fox were the parents of two children. Maurice Winslow Fox, who was born March 2, 1883, married in 1913, and has three children: Phyllis Rae, Irma Jeannette, and Charles Frederick Fox; and Howard Stowell Fox, who was born October 2, 1889, married in 1916, and has two children: Howard Prentice and Marjorie Stowell Fox. Mrs. Fox has made since 1893 a thorough and scientific study of parliamentary law and has given lectures on this subject in nearly every state of the Union. She has served at many national and state conventions in the capacity of parliamentarian, and has written articles on parliamentary law, which were published in *The Club Woman*, edited by Helen M. Winslow, during 1899 and 1900. They were then recast and appeared in book form in 1902 under the title of *Parliamentary Usage for Women's Clubs*. The book was immediately adopted as a standard by the General Federation of Women's Clubs and is still the parliamentary authority of that organization as well as of hundreds of other national, state, and local societies. In 1914 it was revised and enlarged. In 1899 the Detroit Parliamentary Law Club was organized and Mrs. Fox has been its only President and instructor for the twenty-three years of its existence. She has served on the Board of Education of Detroit, having been elected by the voters of the second ward. For over twenty-five years she has been a trustee of the Women's Hospital and Infants' Home of Detroit, having served as Treasurer and afterwards President of the Board. She has also been President of the Michigan State Federation of Women's Clubs and Recording Secretary and Vice-President of the General Federation of Women's Clubs. She has always been in favor of equal suffrage, not because she claimed that women were wiser or juster than men, but because, to carry out the provisions of the Constitution of the United States, those who are governed by the laws are entitled to have a voice in making the laws. Mrs. Fox is a member of the Daughters of the American Revolution, the Twentieth Century Club of Detroit (of which she was a charter member and at one time President), the Order of the Eastern Star, the League of Women Voters, the Mount Vernon Society of Michigan, the Women's City Club, of Detroit, the Drama League, the Women's Club of the Service Flag, the Michigan Women's Press Association, the Detroit Citizens' League, the Naval Circle of the Grand Army of the Republic, the Detroit Parliamentary Law Club, the Michigan Authors' Association, and Women's National River and Harbors Congress.

FLINT, ANNIE AUSTIN, author, was born in New York City on December 11, 1866. Her father, Austin Flint, M.D., was an eminent physician, the son of Austin Flint, M.D., himself the descendant of three Massachusetts doctors, Joseph, Austin, and Edward Flint. The last named traces back through Thomas and John to the first American ancestor of the name, Thomas Flint, who was born in Matlock, Derbyshire, England, in 1603, and who died in Concord, Massachusetts, October 8, 1653. Miss Flint's mother was Elizabeth Barnum McMaster, a cousin of the historian, John Bach McMaster. Her education was under the direction of governesses and in private schools. From 1893 to 1906 she was assistant editor of *Our Animal Friends*, the official publication of the American Society for the Prevention of Cruelty to Animals. To this she contributed each month unsigned articles, stories, and reports on the Society's activities. She is a member of the Cosmopolitan Club of New York and of the Onteora Club, Onteora-in-the-Catskills. An early story by Miss Flint, *Abraham's Mother*, appeared in *Lippincott's Magazine* and was later reprinted in 1893 in the volume *Ten Notable Stories*. In April, 1897, was brought out her first book, a volume of fairy tales called *Sunbeam Stories and Others*. This was followed in 1903, by another book for children, *A Christmas Stocking*. Both of these were attractively decorated by Mrs. Dora Wheeler Keith. A novel of satire, *A Girl of Ideas*, was published in March, 1903. In 1909 her short story, *Paper Dolls*, was a prize winner in the contest managed by the New York *Herald*. A volume of verses entitled *Vignettes of Onteora* was privately printed in March, 1914, and in

June, 1915, was published her latest novel, a story of alternating personality called *The Breaking Point*.

FRY, EMMA SHERIDAN, educator, daughter of George A. and Emma (Huther) Sheridan, was born in Painsville, Ohio, October 1, 1864. Her father was a Captain in the 88th Illinois Volunteers during the Civil War and was later Collector of the Port of New Orleans and Adjutant General of the State of Louisiana.

Emma Sheridan received her early education in France and was graduated at Hunter College, New York City. While studying for the stage she was a pupil of Steele MacKaye and David Belasco. She took the leading rôles for several seasons at the historic Boston Museum, and for many years was a member of Richard Mansfield's first company, playing leading, and character parts in various comedies. Though she was a young girl at the time, her playing of old Rebecca ably supported Mr. Mansfield's Hyde in *Doctor Jekyll and Mr. Hyde*. She was a member of the company that shared Mansfield's triumph when he appeared as Sir Henry Irving's guest at the Lyceum Theatre, London.

In 1890 Miss Sheridan was married to Alfred Brooks Fry, engineer officer, United States Navy, who served in Cuban waters in the Spanish-American War, as Captain and Engineer Aide, 3rd Naval District, in the Spanish War and in the French and English ports in the World War, 1917–1918. He was naval aide to Theodore Roosevelt during his term as Governor of the State of New York, and has since held office in New York City as Supervising Chief Engineer, of the United States public buildings and Chief of Staff, U. S. N. R., 3rd Naval District. In 1923, Captain Fry was appointed by Governor Smith in command of the New York Naval Militia with the rank of Commodore. Their son, Sheridan Brooks Fry (born in 1894) served in the World War as Ensign and Lieutenant of Aviation, U. S. N.

Emma Sheridan Fry's early stage training and later wide stage experience awakened her interest in the dramatic instinct, related, not to the development of the actor, but to the development of the human being. In 1903 she founded the Children's and Young People's Theatre at the Educational Alliance Building, East Broadway and Jefferson Street, New York. Under the efficient business management of Miss A. Minnie Herts (later Mrs. Heniger), the attention of educators throughout the country was called to the theatre and to Mrs. Fry's work. Her theories fully demonstrated their practical value, not only in the finished verity of the young people's playing but in the cultural, physical, and character development of the players. Plays were arranged by Mrs. Fry to meet the special requirements of the educational development of the young actors. *Little Lord Fauntleroy* and *The Little Princess* by Mrs. Burnet and *Snow White* by Marguerite Merrington were thus adapted, and a special dramatization was made by Mrs. Fry of Mark Twain's *Prince and Pauper*. The *Tempest* and *As You Like It* were also produced.

In 1909 Mrs. Fry withdrew from the Children's Educational Theatre, as it had come to be known, in order to study and experiment, and formulate for other teachers, the laws and principles guiding her own methods. The theatre at the Alliance closed soon after, although a group of young people composed of players from the Educational Alliance, known as "Educational Players," coöperated with Mrs. Fry for some years. These players formed the impetus for establishing the little theatres now so numerous throughout the country. Mrs. Fry, steadfast in her educational intent, finding it impossible to take time to build up an entertainment organization competing for a place in the theatre field, withdrew; although the Educational Players had, meanwhile made themselves known in schools and churches and clubs. Mrs. Fry has also served on Doctor Leipziger's Board of Education Recreation Centre programs. In

1913 Mrs. Fry founded the work of the Educational Dramatic League, initiated by Frederick Howe of the People's Institute. The settlements and schools of New York City were organized by Mrs. Fry in a series of competitive performances of distinguished entertainment value and educational significance, and normal classes were instructed in dramatic methods. Mrs. Fry withdrew from the Educational Dramatic League to conduct a Columbia University extension lecture course and to finish her first book, *Educational Dramatics, a Handbook for Teachers*. She has also prepared a dramatic cast reading arrangement of Shakespeare's *Midsummer Night's Dream*. She is a member of the Pen and Brush Club of New York.

The philosophy of educational dramatics has been set forth by Mrs. Fry as follows: "The dramatic instinct initiates and supports life-processes leading to expression. Expression is the manifestation in outer form of the inner conditions resulting from living. Study of nature in the spontaneous processes of expression leads to the recognition of a sequence of activities: contact, investigation, identification (a double process whereby the object is recognized in its relation to self and the self is realized in its relation to the object), readjustment and recondition, generation of energy, output of impulse and outflow of impulse, causing the body and speech to respond; and in form and movement and aspect voice and speech to become the re-presentation and the agent of the conditioned and adjusted self. This life expression sequence is spontaneous, the body as an instrument of expression taking form automatically and without dictation from consciousness, which finds relief and accomplishes communication by expression, without being aware of dictating the technique of expression. Expression processes are initiated by contact with life experiences or by the dramatic instinct operating to supply contact from the dramatic field. Coöperating with the dramatic instinct contacts may be offered at will and life processes initiated, and thus the self may be exercised in experience and expression related to educational development and to the evolution of the being. An enlightened and scientific knowledge of nature's own process, the spontaneous operations of the dramatic instinct and its regulation to educational purpose are required."

Mrs. Fry's books set forth her own method of applying dramatic principles. She recognizes the dramatic instinct as the agent of evolution and its regulation to be a conscious coöperation with the processes of evolution. The highest art of the theatre recognizes the identity of living and acting, and, inducing life processes, adapts expression to the requirements of the theatre, making the actor a channel for living expression regulated to stage purposes. Educational dramatics develops the human being in relation to himself and his own community, developing the citizen in social, civic, and life relations, making dramatic expression a living experience for the development of the self, and inducing life processes regulated to living purpose. Its purpose is not stage representation, but personal living experience. Inasmuch as evolution is progressive development, and development results from those reactions to environment which we call living, the dramatic instinct is the agent of evolution because it induces the reactions of living. Scientific regulation of the dramatic instinct is the regulation of the evolution of development.

NORTON, MARY BLANCHE, physician and philanthropist, daughter of Frank Upham and Emma (Paul) Norton, was born in Parryville, Pennsylvania, January 23, 1875. She is of the tenth generation in lineal descent from Thomas Norton of Surrey, England, who, with the Reverend Mr. Whitefield, came to Guilford, Connecticut, in 1639; was a signer of the Plantation Covenant of that settlement, and until his death was the town miller and church warden in Mr. Whitefield's church. Thomas Norton owned a large tract of land in the old town of Guilford, where his home lot comprised over two acres on the west side of Crooked Lane, now State Street; he also held seventeen and one-half acres on the "uplands" beyond the town, with one and one-half acres of shore land. His wife was Grace Wells, who belonged to a family prominent in Southern New England, and on Nantucket Island.

One of Thomas Norton's descendants, Aaron Norton, Doctor Norton's great-great-grandfather, founded the City of Akron, Ohio. Another representative of the line was Colonel A. B. Norton, a publisher of Dallas and Mt. Vernon, Texas, who, at the gathering of publishers at the Columbian Exposition, Chicago, in 1893, was welcomed as the oldest living publisher in the United States. A younger brother of the original settler of Guilford, one John Norton, came to this country and settled in Branford, Connecticut, about 1646. These two brothers have had many illustrious descendants, among them being Eli Norton, Solicitor General of the United States Court of Claims, during and after the Civil War; and Professor Charles Eliot Norton, of Harvard University.

By the maternal line, Doctor Norton descends from the famous Peters family, who were among the founders of Philadelphia. Her great-great-grandmother died at the age of 101, and was buried from the house in which she was born and married; in the living-room of this house there stood for over two centuries the table on which the constitution of Philadelphia was written. All the Peters family were professional men and one at least in each generation was a Lutheran minister. The family was originally of German-Swiss descent.

Doctor Norton's father was a railroad man, who early in his married life removed to the far west—for those days—and settled in the frontier town of Eldon, Iowa, largely because it was convenient for his division headquarters. In early life he had been trained to become an ironmaster by his maternal uncle, Thomas McKee, who was one of the wealthiest iron manufacturers of his day in Pennsylvania. Later he turned to railroading, as offering a freer and more adventurous life.

In the little frontier mining and railroading town of Eldon, Doctor Norton received her early education in the public school, supplemented by a fine cultural and musical training from her mother, until she entered Parsons College at Fairfield, Iowa. Here she fell under the influence of two great scholars in the humanities, the President of the College, and the professor of Latin, Albert S. Harkness, then an aged man of wide reputation and great erudition. The influence of these two men led Doctor Norton to become, after receiving the degree of B.S., a teacher, and later, while still very young, the principal of the High School in her home town, Eldon.

As principal, she was brought into constant contact with her pupils, not only in school hours but also in their home life and surroundings. Gradually she derived the conviction that she could do more good to a community if she were to begin on environment. The first step was to organize a library and act as librarian. But when she realized that this was only a part of the work that must be undertaken, she entered upon a course of study, to prepare for real social service work, in Chicago University. For a number of years, she practically gave her services to the poor, living as they live. There could be but one outcome to that close association with want, poverty and disease, and that was to study medicine. Consequently in 1911, Doctor Norton entered Cornell University Medical School, where she was graduated M.D. in 1915. Her work in the Medical School was distinguished, not only for scholarship, but by the evidence she gave to all with whom she came in contact, that she was by temperament richly fitted for the life of service as a physician. Somewhat later Parsons College bestowed upon her the Master's degree.

Doctor Norton's first medical work was with a girls' camp in the Maine woods. Here she cared for the girls physically and spiritually, and also became a well-known figure to all the isolated farmers of that section. Even down to the nearest village she was "their doctor." Her fame spread rapidly during the months of her sojourn, until no one would think of calling the village physician, so long as Doctor Norton was available.

In the next year she entered practice in association with her brother-in-law, Doctor A. E. Fendrick, of Weehawken, New Jersey. A great part of her services was rendered free of charge. She became associated with several women's clinics and, in 1917, started a health campaign under the Women's Municipal League of New York City; this was entirely preventive work, but the exigencies of the war terminated this Committee's undertaking, which had proved really excellent and was progressing with marvelous rapidity. She was, for a time, examining physician on the staff of the Charities Aid Association of New York City.

It was impossible for Doctor Norton to remain an idle bystander, and be merely a physician at home, while there were such pitiful calls for sympathy and help arising from a thousand parts of devastated Europe and Asia Minor. Early in 1919, she joined the Medical Unit of the Near East Relief, and went to Turkey; finally, on a United States destroyer, she reached Trebizond, on the Black Sea, and there remained nearly six months.

Trebizond, just after the armistice, was full of stillness, gloom, and an indefinable fear; a pale ghost of a city against a wall of black hills. The Armenian quarter was a total ruin, and the few Armenians left, were homeless and helpless. Doctor Norton offered her services at once to the Turkish Red Crescent, and the Greek Red Cross, whose physicians were sadly over-worked at the clinics already established, but on almost the first night of her arrival she was stricken with sandfly fever, from which it took several weeks to recover. Meanwhile more refugees kept pouring into the city.

Doctor Norton's first act, after her recovery, was to find a house for her residence and professional headquarters, and she finally located in an old Armenian house which had recently been occupied by Turks. When she was not helping refugees at the clinics and working with the orphans, she scrubbed, calcimined, cleaned and disinfected the vermin-infested walls and floors with phenol and sublimate. Everywhere, on all sides, the atmosphere was drenched with the misery of death in life, of starvation, of the sickness and helplessness of the little children.

As the new personnel arrived from Constantinople, the scope of Doctor Norton's work was vastly increased. To feed, to clothe, to house the homeless people who kept coming in an endless procession was no insignificant task in itself. Some of the women were taught to make over and mend the old clothes from America; others made up garments from new material which finally reached this remote spot. Those who could knit and spin were encouraged to the utmost, because in this way they could free themselves from the stigma of beggary. The boys were set to learn shoemaking and repairing, while the men were put to work on the roads and at cultivating small patches of ground; but, even with all these efforts, the streets were filled with unemployed, hopeless and homeless people. This was the fifth year of their exile, and both men and women looked like beggars.

Every day Doctor Norton went to the clinic, which was a part of a general relief compound where the Red Crescent had established soup kitchens and a clothing supply station. There were literally thousands of Turkish widows and orphans besieging this place, largely because, from being the cheapest place in the world in which to live, it had suddenly become the most expensive. Doctor Norton proved invaluable to the clinic; the orthodox peasant women would not let the men doctors see more of them than the tips of their tongues and their wrists, but by the woman doctor they were anxious to be examined from head to toes, and regarded a stethescope as an instrument of magic. The chief diseases were malaria, syphilis and skin affections. On alternate days Doctor Norton attended the Greek clinic, managed by the Red Cross of Athens, which was inadequately equipped, and was housed in a poorly-furnished, cold room, without apparatus of any kind. Many a Greek woman would walk miles to bring a sick child to the American doctor. These women, serious-minded, splendidly built, and always wearing their entire wardrobes on their persons, layer upon layer, had been beasts of burden for their husbands; and Doctor Norton often found, on examination, that they had literally broken hearts from toil, anxiety, privation, and excessive child-bearing.

On Fridays the Doctor traveled over the mountains to Platana, a village by the sea, where there was a barnlike building for refugees; only food enough for a day or two could be taken on this trip, but great quantities of quinine were provided for these unfortunates, who often were burning with malaria and starvation under their burden of rags. This clinic was attended by the starved and wearied; they had wounds of many kinds, diseased scalps and sore mouths, scabies and blindness.

In the late winter, Doctor Norton was asked to go to Kerasund, to investigate the orphanages—a night's journey from Trebizond, but approachable only by water. Kerasund had long been known as the loveliest city on the Turkish side of the Black Sea; its origin was buried in the myths of the ancient Greeks, but the Kerasund of the post-war days was a city whose streets oozed gloom, and its air was heavy with a palpable hate. The city had a lame mayor who was a combination of tyrant and brigand. He had fought in the Balkan wars, and had returned with a wooden leg, a

hero in the sight of his fellow-townsmen. A former fisherman, Osman Agha, became the chieftain of a tribe of mountain brigands, and had seized the opportunity given by the war to exterminate the Armenians. He was utterly contemptuous of all European governments, and sought only to reinstate the Moslems to their ancient glory and domination. He had but to point his finger to insure absolute obedience. Doctor Norton deemed it wise, early in her stay, to see this Mayor and explain to him that she was there to look after the orphanage, and if possible to set up a public clinic. Osman listened to her, and said he liked America, but he showed honestly that he was an impartial hater of all infidels. Her own personal safety rested solely upon American prestige.

Doctor Norton found the orphanage, which stood directly on the street behind a wooden wall. The interior had no fire save for cooking in the kitchen, and no furniture, except rows of little wooden beds. Thanks to Americans, the children had sufficient clothes and food, but no medical care or instruction. This city was so hostile to the Armenians that all of them had been driven out save these poor orphans. Among them Doctor Norton found some stubborn cases of scabies, and was obliged to treat them in this cold room by the light of a candle, which was also the only source of heat.

But the most important work that Doctor Norton did in Kerasund was among the Greek orphans, not one of whom was a native of the city. They were housed in the basement of a large gray stone school-house, in the upper part of which the more fortunate children received instruction. Save for the attic where they slept, and one room set aside for a hospital, two hundred and ten orphans had no other quarters than the damp cellar and the semi-frozen, muddy yard surrounding the building. Their food was black beans, field corn and hard bread. Many of them had bleeding and ulcerated gums; they had been freed from vermin, but still bore the poisonous marks as well as the scars of torture, syphilis and scabies.

In the cellar Doctor Norton found two rooms full of children sitting up in bed; the rooms, naturally dim, were further darkened by ragged blue curtains. The children's eyes were swollen shut and dripping with pus; she found herself in the midst of an epidemic of acute Egyptian trachoma, beside which there is no worse scourge under heaven. There were no nurses, and only two Greek physicians, an old man worn out by service in the Turkish Army, and a young man just out of the University at Athens. The Athens Red Cross had sent medical supplies but did not dare send doctors and nurses to the hostile city. With two young untrained and trachomatous helpers, Doctor Norton started in to cure and save these two hundred and ten orphans.

With the help of the Greek Bishop, Doctor Norton put some order into the rest of the orphanage, and made arrangements to move the children into a better building, but before she could complete her plans for rehousing them, she herself was stricken with a very virulent type of the disease.

For three weeks this heroic woman remained at Kerasund, in danger of total blindness, and yet unable to go elsewhere. At last a British sloop carried her to Constantinople. But for this means of escape, she would probably have been unable to leave at all, because on that very day, Turkish gendarmes made a "friendly" call at the house. She had been "too much with the Greeks."

When Doctor Norton reached Constantinople, she sought refuge in the American house of the Near East Relief, where she was isolated in the attic, and adequate treatment begun. After months of suffering, confined alone in this attic, she was cured save for partial loss of sight of one eye. Then she began anew her efforts for the relief of the thousands of trachoma sufferers in the Levant. As a result, a hospital was opened in Constantinople capable of caring for about 400

Greek and Armenian orphans. Soon after the opening of this hospital, Doctor Norton was signally honored by King Alexander of Greece, who through his High Commissioner in Constantinople, bestowed upon her the Military Order of King George I, for her distinguished services at Kerasund in Anatolia. She was the first and only woman upon whom this jewel had ever been bestowed, together with its title of Chevalier.

Doctor Norton left for Paris on a furlough shortly after this recognition; and at its expiration expected to return to her hospital in Constantinople. However, she sailed instead, for the United States, to speak throughout the country on behalf of the Near East Relief. Conditions made it possible for Doctor Norton to remain in America, so she determined to resume her practice, specializing on skin diseases, since her experiences in the Levant had demonstrated the crying need for work in this line.

For the past two years, she has been associated with two eminent skin specialists in New York City, and also, during that same period, attached to the staff of the Skin Department of the Vanderbilt Clinic. In addition to this, she has been making a special research as to the findings of the French and German specialists. Doctor Norton's long experience and her investigations in treating disease by physiotherapy have led her to undertake to combine, in a strictly scientific manner, such treatment with special diet, exercise and massage.

EARHART, FRANCES ELIZABETH, librarian, daughter of Joseph and Margaret Jane (Boyd) Earhart, was born in Worthington, Pennsylvania. Her father was descended from John Earhart who came from Prussia to eastern Pennsylvania shortly before the American Revolution. During the Revolutionary War he wintered with Washington at Valley Forge, and fought in the battles of Germantown, the Brandywine, and others. On her mother's side Miss Earhart is a descendant of Captain John Craig and Lieutenant Samuel Craig, officers in the American Revolution, who were early settlers and Indian fighters in western Pennsylvania. Miss Earhart was educated at the Central High School, Duluth, Minnesota; Grove City College, Pennsylvania; the University of Michigan; and the Drexel Institute Library School, Philadelphia, Pennsylvania. From 1903 to 1904 she was a cataloguer in the Buffalo (New York) Public Library, and from 1904 to 1910 chief cataloguer in the Duluth (Minnesota) Public Library. Since 1910 she has been librarian of the latter. She is a member of the American Library Association Council and of its Committee on Work with the Foreign-Born, and of the Council of Direction of the Immigrant Publication Society. During the World War she assisted in all war work campaigns (in which card records were compiled), including those of the Red Cross. In 1917 she was a member of the Executive Committee of the Duluth Soldiers' War Fund. She was a Captain of the Women's Division, Second Liberty Loan, and Secretary of the Women's Division, Third and Fourth Liberty Loans. In October–November, 1918, she was executive of the office staff of the Registration Department of the Minnesota Fire Relief, and in November, 1918, a member of the Executive Committee and Secretary of the Women's Division of the United War Work Campaign. From December, 1918, to March, 1919, she was Assistant Librarian of the American Library Association Hospital Library at United States Debarkation Hospital Number Three, New York City. Miss Earhart is a member of the Duluth Americanization Committee, the Daughters of the American Revolution, the Association of Collegiate Alumnae, the Red Cross, the Women's Council of Duluth, the Saturday Club, the Twentieth Century Club, the Duluth Suffrage Association, and the Duluth Art Association.

RANSOM, ELIZA TAYLOR, M.D., was born in Escott, Ontario, Canada, daughter of William Gowatt and Janet (Ferguson) Taylor. Her father was a descendant of David Hutchinson, who came from England in the Colonial period and settled in Rhode Island. Miss Taylor, attended school for one year in Ontario and then, as her parents had removed to Jefferson County, New York, she attended the country district school in Alexandria Town. She next entered High School at Alexandria Bay, and on completing her work, continued her studies at the State Normal School, Oswego, New York. After graduation she taught in the High School at Alexandria Bay, at the Lyman School for Boys, Boston, and in the public schools of Boston and Brookline, Massachusetts.

Eventually she entered Boston University Medical School where she was graduated with the degree of Doctor of Medicine. She continued her studies in postgraduate work at Johns Hopkins Medical School, Baltimore; the New York Postgraduate Medical School; the New York Polyclinic; and took a course in neurology at the Harvard Medical School, Boston.

She was married at Alexandria Bay, New York, June 28, 1893, to George W. Ransom, Junior, A.M., Principal of Abraham Lincoln School, Boston; they are the parents of two children, Ruth and Eleanor Ransom.

Doctor Ransom located in professional practice in Boston, and has been remarkably successful as a specialist in maternity cases. For ten years she has owned and conducted a thoroughly modern maternity hospital on Bay State Road. Here the methods of the Freiberg Graunen clinic known as "Dammer-Schlaf" or "Twilight-Sleep" are used. With a record of over 1,000 cases the hospital has never had a maternal fatality, and only four infant deaths, and, after dismissal, reports have been received of perfect health existing in all discharged patients, both mothers and babies.

During the World War, Doctor Ransom founded and carried on the work of "The French Baby Fund." She was instrumental in raising large sums of money for this relief work. 35,000 francs were sent to Paris for maternity work and $40,000 were expanded for maternity hospital supplies and infants' clothing. Professor Barr and Mme. Yvonne Sarcey were the distributors in Paris and receipts of goods were acknowledged by the French Minister of War in the name of Doctor Ransom.

As a lecturer on medical subjects relative to women and children and general health topics, Doctor Ransom has established a reputation, and is able to hold the attention of her audience in an interesting and forceful manner. She is the author of medical articles appearing in various professional periodicals.

She holds the Chair of Histology in the Boston University Medical School; is a Medical Examiner for the Equitable Life Assurance Society of New York City; is a member of the National Woman's Medical Association; American Women's Hospital Society; Massachusetts Homeopathic Medical Society; Boston Medical Society; 20th Century Medical Club; Woman's Suffrage Association; Boston Women's City Club; Copley Society of Boston and the Canadian Club.

DURYEA, NINA LARREY, author and war relief worker, daughter of Franklin Waldo and Laura (Bevan) Smith, was born in Boston, Massachusetts. She is a descendant of Urian Oakes, the second President of Harvard College. Her childhood was spent in Boston where she was educated. She later finished her education in Brussels, Belgium, and was presented in society in London under the auspices of the Honorable Mrs. Maxwell-Scott of Abbotsford, Scotland, and her uncle, the Duke of Norfolk. In 1887 she was married at Trinity Chapel, New York, to Chester B. Duryea, the son of Brigadier-General Hiram Duryea of the Duryea Zouaves. They are the parents of one son, Chester B. Duryea, Jr. Mrs. Duryea is the author of *The House of the Seven Gabblers*

(1910), *The Voice Unheard* (1913), *The Sentimental Dragon* (1914), and *The Soul of Fighting France* (1918). When the World War broke out in August, 1914, Mrs. Duryea was in Dinard, near Saint-Malo, France. There she at once engaged in assisting the refugees who poured in from Belgium and Northern France without clothing, food, or hope. The appeal sent by Mrs. Duryea to the United States brought immediate results and she founded the Duryea War Relief (le Secours Duryea) in Dinard. Later, as the work become systematized, and received the official recognition of the French government, its headquarters were moved to Paris and were established at 11 rue Louis le Grand, in rooms lent by the Vicomte de Saint-Seine. In New York an American office was opened as a clearing house for the sixty-nine participating units throughout the United States. The Secours Duryea did work for refugees, for the "réformés" or demobilized wounded, and for destitute French women and children, and, while coöperating with the Red Cross, remained independent for two reasons: because the French government transported its cases direct and quickly from New York to Paris free, and because its work was distinctly for the individual. Up to February, 1915, Mrs. Duryea distributed more than 40,000 articles in the northwest of France, and during the next two years proportionately the same amount was distributed direct through the Clearing House, the Secours National, the Oeuvre des Belges, the Comité des Refugiés du Nord, and through the Queen of the Belgians. Distributions were made, also, to the Dardanelles, Serbia, and Poland. In the summer of 1917 the French government assigned to the Duryea War Relief seventeen ruined villages in the canton of Roye (Somme) to aid. Here members of the staff lived amid the ruins, and distributed to the inhabitants clothing, tools, household utensils, seeds, food, bedding, and clothing. Motor tractor ploughs were sent to sections bereft of man power. Milk was sent to those, especially, wounded soldiers, suffering from tuberculosis, to hospitals, and to babies. Hospitals were also provided with bedding and surgical dressings. Layettes were provided for destitute mothers, usually from those parts of Belgium or France occupied by the Germans. Comfort packages were sent to soldiers and to prisoners in Germany. Special aid was given the réformés, to assist them to a means of earning a living, and to the refugees who arrived in Paris, often without clothing or household supplies. Thirteen days after the armistice, November 11, 1918, Mrs. Duryea was the first civilian to cross the battlefields of the Ardennes and the Argonne, with French motor trucks loaded with supplies. In January, 1919, she returned to America to impress upon the United States the need of continued relief in France during the period of reconstruction. She reported that the Secours Duryea had during the war clothed more than 150,000 war victims and had fed and sheltered many others. For her work Mrs. Duryea has received from France the Legion of Honor and the gold medal of honor; from Belgium the Queen Elizabeth Medal; from Montenegro the Military Medal; from Russia the Order of St. Catherine; and from the National Institute of Social Sciences of which she is a member, the Liberty Service Medal.

DEAN, SUZANNE ELLA WOOD (Mrs. John E. Dean), author and singer, daughter of Doctor Samuel E. and Mary (Stough) Wood, was born in Corona, Ohio, in 1871. Mrs. Wood was the daughter of Doctor Samuel Stough, an eminent physician of Ohio, whose great-grandparents were the Reverend Samuel Stough of Wittenberg, Germany, and the Princess Charlotte Hohenzollern, who came to Maryland at the time of the American Revolution. When S. Ella Wood was a year old, Doctor and Mrs. Wood moved to Chicago, Illinois, where, at the age of six, the daughter entered the Dearborn Seminary. After her graduation she studied abroad, languages, in which she is unusually proficient, and singing. As early as her sixteenth year she sang many of the Italian operas. She is noted for her original and artistic interpretation of Carmen, a rôle especially suited to her talents, for the better understanding of which she spent months in Spain, so that both in acting and costume her characterization of the part is realistic. Her marriage to John E. Dean took place in 1900 at her parents' home, 3924 Michigan Avenue, Chicago. Mrs. Dean has always been interested in the principal clubs in Chicago, and has devoted much of her time and talents to charity. She is a member of the Daughters of the American Revolution, the Colonial Dames, the Loyal Legion, the Woman's City Club, the Antiquarian Society, the Art Institute, the National Security League, the Drama League, the Musicians Club of Women, the Alliance Française, and the Chicago Equal Suffrage League, in whose work she took an active part. She has served also on many committees of the Young Women's Christian Association, and has aided the Refuge and the Humane Society. Her activities also include the arranging for the taking of special moving pictures to be given in hospitals and children's homes. During the World War she spoke and sang for the Liberty Loans and, since, in the interest of various Americanization programs. In April, 1918, she sang the *Marseillaise* and the *Star-Spangled Banner* at Continental Memorial Hall, Washington, before President Wilson and Secretary Daniels and other high officials. For many years Mrs. Dean worked to establish permanent opera in Chicago, and she advocates a subsidized theatre for the encouragement and training of otherwise wasted youthful dramatic and musical talent. Her home has been noted for its musical entertainments at which Gadski, Nordica, Calvé, and other noted artists have sung. She is the author of *A Story a Sofa Told*, *Shibboleth*, *Soldier Sir*, and *Love's Purple*, the last an autobiographical novel which shows a wide knowledge of the social, religious, business, and racing worlds. Mrs. Dean is a sports-woman of great accomplishments, especially in the saddle. Her travels have been wide and she has been presented at the English and German courts. Her frank, generous manner, her knowledge of the world, as well as her talents as a singer have won her distinguished friends in Europe and at home. Since 1908, when her husband and her father died, she has managed her own estate and has been twice around the world.

CURTIS, FRANCES KELLOGG SMALL

(Mrs. Thomas Pelham Curtis), is a daughter of Michael P. and Mary Clarissa (Pratt) Small. The former, a graduate of West Point in 1855, attained the brevet rank of brigadier-general in the United States Army. The latter was a descendant of the *Mayflower* Pilgrims, Richard Warren, Isaac and Mary Allerton, and Francis Cooke. Frances Kellogg Small was born in San Francisco, California, in 1871 and had the usual private school education of the girl of thirty years ago, supplemented by much adventurous traveling in the army life of that day. On August 4, 1893, she was married at Baltimore, Maryland, to Thomas Pelham Curtis, a construction engineer. They have three children: Clarissa Pelham, Thomas J. and H. Pelham. Mr. and Mrs. Curtis have made their home in Boston, Massachusetts, where Mrs. Curtis has been an active worker for woman suffrage. She was the Chief Marshall of the first Massachusetts Suffrage Parade and for three years worked for the Massachusetts Equal Suffrage Association, of whose Executive Board she was a member, as a street speaker, and on the Chautauqua Circuit, throughout the South. As a member of the Americanization Committee of the Boston Equal Suffrage Association, she taught English for two years to Italian women in the North End of Boston, and was leader of Ward II. She was also on the Ways and Means Committee of the Woman Suffrage Party. She is a member of the Massachusetts Society of the Colonial Dames of America and of the Society of Mayflower Descendants. Mrs. Curtis has contributed poems of considerable merit to magazines and newspapers, of which one of the best, *A Boon From Plymouth Town*, is a protest against the neglect of the memory of the Pilgrim mothers.

CORBETT, GAIL SHERMAN (Mrs. Harvey W. Corbett), sculptor, daughter of Frederick Coe and Emma Jane (Ostrander) Sherman, was born in Syracuse, New York. Her father was descended from Philip Sherman of Dedham, Essex, England, who came, in 1633, to Roxbury, Massachusetts, and afterwards, with eighteen others, founded the town of Portsmouth and the Colony of Rhode Island, of which he was the Second Secretary. Mrs. Sherman is a descendant of Michael Dyckman, one of the framers of the New Amsterdam Charter in 1623. Gail Sherman was educated at the Syracuse High School and the Anne Brown School, New York. She began her studies in sculpture at the Art Students' League, New York, under Augustus Saint Gaudens, George DeForest Brush, and others, and was later a student at the École des Beaux Arts in Paris. She was given her first large commission in 1901, and, between then and 1914, when her work was interrupted by the War, she executed many memorial tablets, portrait busts, bas-reliefs, sundials, fountains, and medals. Her work received a medal and mention at the Panama-Pacific Exhibition in San Francisco in 1915. Her best known groups are the Hamilton S. White Memorial, Syracuse, New York (1905), the Kirkpatrick Memorial Fountain, Syracuse (1908), and the bronze doors of the Municipal Building, Springfield, Massachusetts (1913). Miss Sherman was married at Syracuse, June 28, 1905, to Harvey Wiley Corbett, a New York architect. They have two children: Jean and John Maxwell Corbett. During 1915–1917 Mrs. Corbett gave her services to the Woman Suffrage Party, and in 1916–1917 she was Chairman of the Chelsea Branch of the Woman's Municipal League. Mrs.

Corbett is a member of the National Sculpture Society, the American Numismatic Society, the Woman's Municipal League, the New York Women's City Club, and the American Red Cross.

CASWELL, CAROLINE MATILDA, social settlement worker, daughter of Arthur and Sarah (Porter) Caswell, was born in Charlestown, Massachusetts. Among her ancestors were Ezekiel Richardson, who came from Norfolk, England, to Charlestown, in Winthrop's fleet, in 1630; Anthony Morse of Wiltshire, England, who settled in Newbury, Massachusetts, in 1635; and Benjamin Gage, born in Pelham, New Hampshire, August 10, 1740, who was a private in Captain Amos Gage's Company which marched in the Revolution from Pelham, September 29, 1777. Miss Caswell was educated in Charlestown High School. She is best known as the founder and President of the Frances E. Willard Settlement, Boston, Massachusetts. The Settlement is a living monument to her love of humanity and to her tremendous courage and ability in putting her devotion into practice. Miss Caswell has rare gifts and she uses these gifts entirely for others. Perhaps the secret of her charm lies most in the fact that she is so unassuming and so gracious. She is one of those unusual types whom everybody—men, women, and young people love. She has the enviable habit of always finding the best in others, and seems to have almost a magic way of drawing out that best. Her sense of justice is keen, and her understanding and sympathy for people in all walks of life have made her a friend to thousands. Like many who have lived big lives, she has, year in and year out, sacrificed her health, and, never possessing a robust constitution, she has risen wonderfully above weakness and physical pain, to which through life she has been subject. She would not let this deter her from work, and whatever needed to be done she met with, "If it is right and best we must do it." Her fine spirit makes working with her

a pleasure, and her keen sense of humor lightens many a heavy task. As a friend, no one could be more loyal. The way in which the Frances E. Willard Settlement has grown, and the work has developed, proves that Miss Caswell has not alone power of vision, but initiative and splendid business ability. As a public speaker she always commands the closest attention. Her direct method of presenting her subject, and her sympathetic spirit with all that is good, give her the power to impress her hearers with the importance and the truth of all that she has to impart. All this, together with a clear and melodious voice, go to make a public speaker of force and conviction. Miss Caswell's work among the poor of Boston began with the dedication, on November 28, 1894, of three rooms, in a tenement house on Hanover Street, to be used as rest and social rooms for the young women working in the factories in the vicinity. The first Young Women's Home, at 11 Myrtle Street, was dedicated November 16, 1897. This home accommodated sixteen young working women, earning very low salaries, furnished opportunity for a public lunch for women in the lodging houses of the vicinity, and gave two rooms for work among the children of the neighborhood. The following year Miss Caswell organized the Loyal Temperance Legion for boys, and in 1899 she rented a beach house for summer work among working girls. In November, 1901, the Settlement was removed to 24 South Russell Street, Boston, which afforded much better facilities for the growing work, and in the summer a rest house in Dorchester was rented. In 1902 the increasing work among the children necessitated a playground, gymnasium, and special clubrooms. The Frances E. Willard Settlement was incorporated July 7, 1903, with Miss Caswell as President and General Manager, and, with increasing support and endowment, she was able in 1907 to purchase the property at 38–46 Chambers Street, Boston, where have been built the Settlement Clubhouse, for social work in the neighborhood, Phillips Brooks

Hall, for religious and ethical instruction, and Frances E. Willard House, a home for young working women. In the rear is a kindergarten playground and there is also a well-equipped gymnasium for boys. In 1909 property was bought at Bedford, Massachusetts, and here are maintained Llewsac Lodge, an all the year rest home for women, and, nearby, an Industrial Center, for women at the Lodge who need to earn money towards their board. Near Bedford, on the banks of the Shawsheen River, is Nellie Frank Hill Camp, established in 1916, for girls between twelve and twenty years of age belonging to the Settlement clubs and classes. Miss Caswell is a member of the Daughters of the American Revolution, the Consumers' League, the Boston City Federation of Women's Clubs, and many philanthropic organizations. She has devoted a great deal of her life to the interests of the Massachusetts Woman's Christian Temperance Union. During the World War she organized a campaign for raising funds for the war work of the Woman's Christian Temperance Union, securing $55,000 for a field kitchen, an ambulance, the support of French orphans, and reconstruction work.

BROWN, EMILY LYNCH (Mrs. Matthew Wilson Brown), daughter of Geoffrey and Elizabeth (Black) Lynch, was born in Drumin, Ireland, on the Lakes of Killarney, near Killarney, and was brought to Guelph, Canada, by her parents when a small child. Her grandfather, on her mother's side, was an officer in the British Army. His company reinforced Wolfe at the taking of Quebec. Her mother was related to the Herbert family, and her father's family property was at one time part of the estate (on the Lakes of Killarney, famous as the location of Muckross Abbey), owned, for many generations, by the Lords Herbert and, later, by Lord Ardilaum. Geoffrey Lynch, who was an Army officer and a highly educated man, directed his daughter's education, chiefly through tutors, the only way to acquire in the early days, in the part

of Canada where they lived, as thorough an education as she received. About 1857 Emily Lynch was married, in St. Paul, Minnesota, to Matthew Wilson Brown, a contractor of that city. For about thirty years Mrs. Brown was at the head of her own school and kindergarten. The kindergarten system she learned from a pupil of Froebel's and hers was one of the first successfully conducted kindergartens in the United States. Her broad education and natural love of original research work in botany and natural history, and her wide historical education, together with her great love for children, made her school, in the course of time, wonderfully successful, especially in dealing with backward and mentally defective children. She extended a wide charity, and educated at her own expense many children until they were able to become sufficiently independent to go forward successfully in life. She never sought or held office of any kind, but was active in practically all the philanthropic and educational movements in the city of St. Paul in those early days. Many men who were afterward markedly successful in life owed their early start to her training. She was for many years an active participant in the work of Christ Church (Episcopalian), St. Paul, and aided in the establishment of St. Luke's Hospital in that city. She not only donated food in times of necessity but even cared for patients from time to time, when special nursing was required. Her vivid imagination made the stories told her children unusual. Her favorite recreation was the growing of flowers and experimentation in natural history. She died at the age of seventy-eight, the object of widely extended gratitude from people whom she helped, in the course of a long, charitable life of great usefulness.

She left two sons, the Honorable Herbert Wood Brown, formerly State Senator of Montana, Great Falls, Montana, and George Van Ingen Brown, M.D., of Milwaukee, Wisconsin. Doctor Brown is a member and fellow of many surgical and medical societies of the United States and Europe; Fellow of the American College of Surgeons; Lieutenant Colonel, Medical Reserve Corps; Surgeon, United States Public Health Service; Consultant in Oral and Plastic Surgery of the United States Public Health Service at Milwaukee; Plastic Surgeon to the State of Wisconsin General Hospital at the University of Wisconsin, Madison; Consultant, Tacoma Clinic, Tacoma, Washington; and Staff Surgeon of St. Mary's Hospital, Columbia, the Children's Hospital, Milwaukee, the Milwaukee County Hospital, and the Milwaukee County Dispensary. He is the author of *Oral Diseases and Malformations*, a chapter in *Ochsner's Surgical Diagnosis and Treatment*, and other articles published in the medical and surgical journals of the United States and Europe.

GOULD, CORA SMITH (Mrs. George Henry Gould), only daughter of Francis Shubael and Mary Jellett (Duff) Smith, was born in Brooklyn, New York. She received the greater part of her education at the Brooklyn Heights Seminary. About 1876, her family took up their residence in New York City, where she followed her early bent to study painting. Under the tutelage of the artist, Frost Johnson, she accomplished much creditable work.

From her father she inherited a marked ability to write. Early evidence of this talent appeared while she was traveling abroad with her mother. This experience stimulated her imaginative and creative powers, and her correspondence was a keen pleasure to her father. The object of this journey was a visit to her mother's relatives, the Jellett family, in Ireland, whose antecedents had figured prominently for centuries in their country's intellectual and ecclesiastical development. The atmosphere with which she was surrounded was naturally charged with absorbing interest and romance for the impressionable young American.

In 1891, Cora Smith was married to George Henry Gould, a resident of New York City, and a member of the firm of the Heim Leather Belting Company. He was also closely identified with the famous old Seventh Regiment, in which he served as private and officer in Company I for eighteen years. From the birth of their only son, Ormond Valentine Gould, she became a chronicler of child life, and continued the diary of his development, until he had attained manhood. When the United States entered the World War, Ormond enlisted in the Naval Auxiliary Reserve U. S. N., with the rank of Quartermaster (3rd class). On the steamship *Madison* he sailed from New York City to Norfolk, Virginia, and there was transferred to the U. S. S. *Munrio* of the Munson Line. Aboard this vessel he cruised to Cristobal, Panama Canal Zone, running the gauntlet of German submarines; thence to Taltal, South America, and, with a cargo of nitrate for war purposes, returned, by way of San Francisco, to New York City. This trip totaled thirteen thousand miles. His next step was an eight weeks' course in navigation and seamanship at the Pelham Bay Training Station, New York. Shortly afterward Mr. Gould was commissioned Ensign, and entered upon active duty at the Municipal Ferry Terminal, New York City. He was honorably discharged from service at the close of the War.

In 1904, Mrs. Gould published her first book, a compilation from the letters of her aunt, Harriet Frances Behrins, entitled *Reminiscences of California in 1851*. It is an entertaining little story based on facts, and dealing with the experiences of a young married couple in the wilds of the West, following the rush of the gold seekers known as the "Forty-Niners." Her next work, more ambitious, was the editing of her father's poems. This collection, entitled *Gems for All Generations*, she prefaced with a biographical sketch of his life, a rare tribute of a devoted daughter. Inspired by old memories of Litchfield, Connecticut, which she revisited in 1917, after many years of absence, a new story came from

Mrs. Gould's pen, entitled *If a House Could Talk*. This harks back to a happy childhood passed in the old Vaill mansion, the oldest house in the township, built on a former wolf pit in 1744. The tale also embodies an affectionate testimonial to one Julia, who was the attraction in that era. The dedication is full of poetic feeling; the *finis* exhibits a rare quality of expression:—

" 'If a house could talk,' gold mines would suffer in interest, by comparison. The Littérateur would be enriched in such outpouring of comedies and tragedies that even Shakespeare might be outrivalled, and this bit of narrative be quite extinguished by a very antiquated, a very historical, a very well-bred old house, whose voice, mellowed by age and softened by contact with the wisdom and purity of the dwellers therein, I can easily imagine at this '*finis*' offering a benediction on the head of one at least of its devotees, who still lives to remember, and for the dearly beloved that have been called to another Home, I hear it chant:

'Requiem aeternam dona eis, Domine,
Give them eternal rest, O Lord!' "

A copy of this work may be found in the Genealogical Department of the New York Public Library, as well as in the library of the Long Island Historical Society. In 1919 appeared *The Nuisance*, a keenly humorous narrative of a stray dog who established himself as a member of a family, and whose original pranks absorbed all attention.

Mrs. Gould is given to quiet, unostentatious works of benevolence from which she derives genuine pleasure. Her inspiration for all such effort, she claims, are the following lines written by her father:

"We're all at sea; and 'tis our common
duty
To help a fellow-sailor in distress:
Hard gain'd indeed will be that race or
booty
To win which leaves on earth one light
heart less.

"Then let us all, while sailing on life's
ocean,
Blessed by soft gales, beneath kind fortune's star,
Still keep a bright lookout with deep
devotion
For those who in their path less favor'd
are."

At the beginning of the World War, Mrs. Gould personally assumed responsibility for a number of refugees. Among them was a Belgian girl, five years of age, who well repaid the care lavished upon her by her American sponsor. She quickly acquired a knowledge of the English language, and at the age of ten was an accomplished violinist. She inherited her talent from her father, who, prior to the war, was first violin in the Antwerp Opera House, but, after emigrating to America, was driven to street playing by absolute penury in a strange country. Another of Mrs. Gould's protégés was a well-educated young Armenian boy, whom she rescued from poverty. His family, with the exception of a sister, had been massacred by the Turks. To demonstrate his gratitude to Mrs. Gould, he became a naturalized American citizen, and served in France in the American Expeditionary Forces.

The multiplicity of Mrs. Gould's interests, however, has never turned her from her love of family history. In the beginning of the present century she began a collection of family data and relics which is probably as interesting as any in America. Through her mother she is descended from many prominent English and Irish families. Her father's ancestry is traceable to Reverend John Smith (1614) pastor at Barnstable, Massachusetts, who, in deposition made for probate there in 1651, names himself as the only son and heir of Thomas Smith of Brinprittae, Dorsetshire, England. He supposes his age then "to be about thirty-seven it being next May twenty-one years since I came out of England." This Thomas Smith, who married Joan Donn, daughter of Shubael Donn (or Doan) of Dorsetshire, has been traced to Robert Smith of Ipswich, who in 1463 was appointed a justice of the court. The branch of the great family of Smiths descended from him includes some of the prominent families of England, the Edens, Martyns, Waldegraves, and Montcheusis, and dates from the time of William, the Conqueror. John Smith took an active part in the civil life of the colony into which he had come, and in 1663 succeeded Reverend William Sargent as pastor of the Barnstable Church. In 1643 he had married Susanna, daughter of Samuel Hinckley and a sister of Thomas Hinckley, later Governor of Plymouth Colony. Reverend John Smith and his father-in-law became very friendly with the Quakers. Dissensions arose, however, and John Smith resigned his pastorate, and located on Long Island. Here, apparently, he remained but a short time, for we find him recorded in 1666–1667 as one of the incorporators of Woodbridge, New Jersey, with Colonel Daniel Peirce of Newbury, Massachusetts, to whom Governor Carteret had given a grant of land for the settlement of this township. John Smith, after a few years of activity in the affairs of the newly established town, where he was called "John Smith, the millwright," or "mealman," to distinguish him from "John Smith, the Scotchman," returned to Sandwich, Massachusetts, and there became the teacher of the Church. From this office he was retired in 1688, at his own request.

John Smith's eldest son, Samuel (1644–1719/1720), remained in Woodbridge, where in 1692 he married his second wife, Elizabeth Peirce. Their son, Shubael Smith (born in Woodbridge, January 2, 1692), married, March 17, 1716, Prudence Fitz-Randolph, daughter of Samuel, son of Nathaniel Fitz-Randolph, and thus became allied to the prominent family of that name. One of the name later gave part of the land upon which Princeton University now stands, and his gift is commemorated there in the Fitz-Randolph Gates. Shubael Smith was a mariner, plying his trade between the Jersey and Long Island coasts. Hence it was that Huntington, Long Island, became the home of members of his family. Shubael Smith, second, followed in the trade of his father. His son, Moses Rogers Smith, ultimately master of a sailing vessel in the United States Navy in the War of 1812, inherited the same taste for the sea as did his forebears, but possessed a more venturesome spirit, which led him to foreign shores. On one of his visits to the West Indies, he fell in love with Mary Reed, the beautiful daughter of a wealthy and distinguished English family of the Isle of Wight. The young couple eloped, sailing to New York City, where they were married by Bishop Moore in old Trinity Church, in 1798. They made their residence in Division Street, where Francis S. Smith, their fourth son, was born. He became prominent in the literary world of his day as a gifted poet and story writer, and as co-founder, co-partner, and sole editor of the large publishing house of Street and Smith, of New York City. He forged his way to this pinnacle of success from the most humble beginnings, starting as apprentice boy in the office of the New York *Albion*. He worked as a compositor on various newspapers, including the New York *Globe* and the New York *Tribune;* served as an editor on the New York *Dispatch*; and finally established the foundation of lasting success through the medium of the New York *Weekly*, a family story and sketch paper. He himself wrote for the *Weekly* much of the material that made it famous.

The wife of Francis S. Smith, Mary Jellett Duff, daughter of George Campbell and Catharine Maria (Jellett) Duff, was born in Pittsburgh, Pennsylvania, but in her first year came with her parents to New York City. Their home was close by historic Washington Square. She was descended from some of the most distinguished families of England and Ireland. When she was but three years of age, her mother died, and her father's business called him to Newberne, North Carolina, where he and his three children spent the next fourteen years. Mary and her sister, Anna, were educated in the pleasant atmosphere of a private seminary in Newberne, attended by the daughters of the first southern families. Mary's mind developed rapidly. Her father entertained her with family lore and traditions reflecting much glory on her forebears, until the trend of her thoughts began to run quite naturally into old-world grooves. Maps and histories became as fascinating as fairy stories to her imaginative mind. Some time later she returned to New York where she met and married Francis S. Smith. She settled down at the age of seventeen to wifehood and motherhood, although with the maps and histories close by, for occasional recreation. After some years, accompanied by her young daughter, Cora, she went to Dublin to visit her distinguished relatives. Her personal charm and her broad culture won immediate friendship and respect.

Mrs. Smith's mother, Catharine Maria Jellett, daughter of Reverend Matthew and Anna Maria (Sadlier) Jellett, was born in Armagh, Ireland. The Jellett family traces descent from Reverend Mr. Jellett of Durham Cathedral, England, members of whose family followed Cromwell into Ireland and there became largely identified with church and education. Her father (born, 1775; died in Moira, 1823), was Curate of Killaly in the Parish of Geshall, King's County. Her grandfather, Morgan Woodward Jellett (born, 1723), married Brilliana Mason, named from the river Brill in thanksgiving for the rescue of her mother from its depths shortly before the child's birth. The name has been continued in the family to the present day. William Jellett (1632–1717) married, in 1678, Katharine Morgan,.of Moira, County Down, whose father, Captain James Morgan, an aide-de-camp to Oliver Cromwell, was killed at the side of the Lord Protector at the siege of Drogheda. The town land of Tullyard was granted to the daughter, Katharine. She also possessed a portrait of Cromwell and a quaint bloodstone tankard, from which it is said King William, on his way to the Boyne, drank to her health and to his success in the coming battle.

Among Mrs. Smith's near relatives, whom she visited in Dublin, was Reverend Morgan Woodward, her cousin, who was Curate of St. John's, Sligo (1857), Curate of St. Peter's (1864); Canon of Christ Church Cathedral (1880); Rector of St. Peter's (1883); Rural Dean (1888); and a member of many representative committees. Another was John Hewitt Jellett, B.D., who in 1881, upon his appointment, was announced as Provost of Trinity College, Dublin, and served for thirty years, with reputation as one of the best known mathematicians in the United Kingdom. *The Calculus of Variations* and *The Theory of Friction* are two of his principal works.

Mrs. Smith's grandmother, Anna Maria Sadleir, who, on December 5, 1800, was married to Reverend Matthew Jellett, was a descendant of Sir Ralph Sadleir, the last knight banneret of England. His father, Thomas Sadleir, a barrister-at-law, was a son of Charles Sadleir, Cornet of the 13th Light Dragoons, who was taken prisoner at Preston Pans. He was sixth in descent from Sir Ralph Sadleir (1507–1587), who was one of the most important personages of his time. As Lloyd, a writer of the seventeenth century, declares, "For a man, none was more complete." It was while acting as Private Secretary to Thomas Cromwell, Earl of Essex, that he was brought to the notice of Henry VIII, who advanced him to a place in his Privy Council and made him Secretary of State. So highly was he regarded by the King that he was frequently his chosen ambassador to foreign countries on the most important matters of state. In his will the King named him as one of the regents appointed to act during the minority of Edward VI. When Elizabeth ascended the throne,

Sir Ralph again became a member of the Privy Council, and was a representative from Hertfordshire in her first Parliament. He was a party to the treaty of Leith, and in the tenth year of the reign of Elizabeth, was made Chancellor of the Duchy of Lancaster. In 1568 he was one of the tribunal to hear the cause of Mary, Queen of Scots, and later was appointed guardian of her person at Sheffield, where she was imprisoned. In 1584, when she was removed to Tutbury Castle on the borders of Derbyshire, he accompanied her, and was made Governor of the Castle. Sir Ralph returned to Standon Lordship, where he had built a magnificent mansion upon one of the manors bestowed upon him by Henry VIII. There he died, in 1587, possessed of more than twenty manors, and was buried in the parish church. The tradition that with his own hands he seized the standard of Scotland at the battle of Pinkie, near Musselburgh, September 10, 1547, in the thickest of the fight, and for his bravery was made knight banneret on the field of combat, is authenticated by the official record of his knighthood at the time and place named. The standard of Scotland has been placed at his tomb, in Standon Church.

It was at the home of Ralph Sadleir at Standon Lordship that his eldest son, Sir Thomas Sadleir, entertained James VI of Scotland, on his way to London to take the English throne as James I of England. Edward Sadleir, second son of Sir Ralph Sadleir, from whom Anna Maria (Sadleir) Jellett is descended, married Anne Lee, daughter and co-heiress of Sir Richard Lee, the celebrated military engineer, who had the grant of a considerable portion of St. Albans in Hertfordshire. Anne Lee, through both her father and her mother, was descended from most of the governing families of England, so intermarried as to derive descent from the rulers of Europe from the time of Hengot the Saxon (434 A.D.), Alfred the Great, Rhodri Mawr, King of All Wales, Duncan of Scotland, and others with whom are associated facts and traditions of unusual interest. Among all the array of warriors, knights, and nobles, illustrious for feats of valor, the name of Sir Walter Blount (Blunt) stands out prominent. Standard-bearer of King Henry IV, and clad in the King's coat-armor, he fell at the battle of Shrewsbury (1403) while engaged in single combat with the Earl of Douglas. Shakespeare, in his historical play of *King Henry IV*, immortalizes him for his devotion to the King. Hotspur says, as he finds him prone upon the field of battle (Act V, Scene 3, of the First Part of the play):

"A gallant knight he was, his name was Blount (Blunt)." Prior to this (Act IV, Scene 3) Hotspur thus welcomes him as he enters the rebel camp near Shrewsbury, an emissary of the King:

"Welcome, Sir Walter Blunt; and would to God
You were of our determination!
Some of us love you well; and even these some
Envy your great deserving and good name."

Sir Walter Blount (Blunt) married Donna Sanchia de Ayala of the de Ayala family, who were numbered among the Grandees of Ricos Hombres of Spain. Thus to Mrs. Gould derives a royal strain from ancient Castile. The de Ayala family stood in high favor with the royal family, especially with Donna Sanchia, as this extract from a letter to her from the Queen of Castile and Leon illustrates:

"*Por la Regna de Castelia a de Leons a donna Sanchia de Ayala.* I, the Queen of Castile and Lions, send much health to Donna Sanchiamde Ayala as to her I much esteem, and to whom I wish much honor and good fortune . . . God knoweth as well in this as in other things wherein I could help you or do you a favor that I would do it willingly, having a regard to all the services and things which by your letter you send unto me."

To name the distinguished ancestors of Mrs. Gould through so many generations would read somewhat like an abstract from the peerages or landed gentry, but there is a body of men to whom special reference should be made—men from whom it is an honor to claim an unbroken line of descent. These are the barons of power and might who demanded of King John the right of liberty. The great document enforced by these nobles, the Magna Charta, "the great charter of liberties," bears the signatures of William d'Albini, Roger Bigod, Hugh Bigod, Henry de Bohun, Richard de Clare, Gilbert de Clare, John de Lacy, William Malet, Saire de Quinci, Robert de Roos, Geoffrey de Saye, and Robert de Vere, all direct ancestors of Mrs. Gould. Her son, Ormond Valentine Gould, is a life member of the Baronial Order of Runnemede, by right of descent from these barons. Mrs. Gould is a member of the Order of Americans of Royal Descent; the Order of Americans of Armorial Ancestry; and the United States Daughters of 1812.

BOYNTON, HELEN AUGUSTA MASON (Mrs. Henry V. Boynton), one of the three Founders of the National Society of Daughters of Founders and Patriots of America, was born in Cincinnati, Ohio. She is a daughter of Timothy Battelle Mason and of his second wife, Abigail Hall. The latter, who was born in 1800 and died in 1875, was a kinswoman of her husband, being sixth in descent from Robert Mason, the first settler of that name in America, and her husband's ancestor. This Robert Mason was born in England in 1590, and first settled in Roxbury, Massachusetts. He removed to Dedham before November, 1639, and was a member of the Town Council there from 1640 to 1642–1643. His wife died at Roxbury in April, 1637, and he himself died in 1667. Their son, Thomas Mason, about 1650, came with his father to Dedham, as one of its first settlers. He was one of the signers of the Medford Memorial to the General Assembly in 1664 and subscribed towards the building of Harvard College, Cambridge. On April 23, 1653, he married Margery Partridge of Dedham, who was descended from Richard de Pertriche of Wishangen Manor, Gloucestershire, England. Thomas Mason, with two of his sons, was killed during an Indian attack on Medfield in 1676 during King Philip's War. His youngest son, Ebenezer, who was born in 1669, escaped and was the only male to carry on the name. He married on April 25, 1691, Hannah, the daughter of Benjamin Clark of Medfield, and granddaughter of Joseph Clark, a settler of Dedham, and one of the thirteen founders of Medfield. She was born in 1666 and died in 1757. Ebenezer Mason was a quartermaster in 1716, and a representative to the General Assembly in 1730. He died in 1754. His son Thomas, who was born in 1699 and died in 1789, married Mary Arnold (1703–1798), a granddaughter of Doctor Return Johnson, the first physician of Medfield. Their son, Barachias, who was born in 1723 and died in 1795, graduated from Harvard at the age of nineteen. He was a surveyor, and in 1775 made plans (which are still preserved in the town records) for the town of Natick. As he was fifty-three years of age when the Revolution started, his active services were declined, but he gave his grounds for the training of the first company organized in Medfield, and recruited a company of Minute Men. His wife, Love Whitney (1727–1801), the widow of Jonathan Battelle, was the daughter of Mark Whitney of Hopkinton. Her ancestry is illustrious, insomuch as it can be traced to the royal houses of France and England. Their son, Johnson Mason (1767–1856), held many civil offices, and was captain of militia in 1800 and colonel in 1803. His wife, Caty Hartshorn (1768–1852), was a descendant of Henry Adams and Samuel Smith. Johnson and Caty Mason's son, Timothy Battelle Mason, was born in 1801, and died in 1861. His wife, Abigail Hall, was descended from Francis Hall of Henborough, England, whose son

Edward, with his wife, Hester, settled in Braintree, Massachusetts, before 1640. He served in 1645 in the Narragansett expedition, and died in 1670. His son Andrew (1665–1756) married Susanna Capen (1664–1736). Their son, Deacon John Hall (1695–1791), married Hopestill Ockington, who died in 1738. Their son Josiah (1723–1786), who held many responsible positions in his community, and who subscribed to the soldier's pay fund, married Abigail Brown (1728–1775). Their son, Captain Samuel Hall of Newton, Massachusetts (1757–1828), served in Captain Jeremiah Wiswell's company in the Revolution. His wife, Sarah Cheney (1758–1842), was a descendant of the Crusader, Alexander de Hoo, buried at Rhodes, and of Alfred the Great, Charlemagne, and Alexander II of Scotland. Their daughter was Abigail Hall Mason.

Mrs. Boynton has always been interested in historical and genealogical matters and was an active member of the Daughters of the American Revolution. On June 7, 1898, in association with Eugenia Washington and Pella H. Mason, she obtained a charter for the National Society of Daughters of Founders and Patriots of America with the object "to preserve the history of Colonial and Revolutionary times, to inculcate patriotism in the present generation, and in times of war to obtain and forward supplies for field hospitals." The Society had eighteen charter members and Mrs. Boynton served as National President until the General Court held in 1910, when she relinquished her office and served as National Corresponding Secretary *pro tem*, and as National Recording Secretary until 1912. She has also been active on the History, Statute Book, and Printing Committees. During her presidency one of the Society's most important works was the restoration of the chancel of Falls Church, Virginia.

BINGHAM, AMELIA (Mrs. Lloyd M. Bingham), actress, daughter of John and Marie Elizabeth (Hoffman) Swilley, was born at Hicksville, Ohio, in 1869. Her mother was a descendant of Michel Hoffman of Maryland. Her father was born in Holland, whence he came with his father, John Benjamin Swilley, to Hagerstown, Maryland, marrying there and afterwards settling in Ohio. After graduating from Ohio Wesleyan University at Delaware, Ohio, she married Lloyd M. Bingham, a well-known actor, who died in Norway, December 22, 1915, while on the Ford Peace Mission. It was because of her husband's profession that Mrs. Bingham chose a stage career. Her first engagement was with McKee Rankin to tour the Pacific Coast, after which she appeared in *The Struggle for Life* at the People's Theatre, New York. Later she acted in *The Power of Gold* at Niblo's Garden, in *The Village Postmaster* at the 14th Street Theatre, and in *Captain Impudence* at the American Theatre, all in New York. Under Charles Frohman's management, she appeared in *The White Heather* at the Academy of Music, and was leading woman at the Empire Theatre in *His Excellency the Governor*. In 1901 she organized the Amelia Bingham Company and from that time produced her own plays with great success and public favor. Among them were *The Climbers*, *A Modern Magdalen*, *The Frisky Mrs. Johnson*, and *A Modern Lady*. In addition to winning a foremost position on the American stage, Mrs. Bingham has developed her talent for painting in oil and woodcarving. During the World War she was Chairman of the Camp Entertainment Committee of the Stage Women's War Relief, for two years devoting herself to the cheering of the men in the service. Mrs. Bingham is an active supporter of the work of the New York Sunshine Settlement. She has been President of the American Playgoers' Club, Vice-President of the Twelfth Night Club, and is a member of the Ohio Society, the Theatre Club, and the Professional Woman's League. She has always believed that the theatre, as an art, should reflect the highest ideals and not for commercial reasons debase itself to doubtful subjects.

BASSETT, SARA WARE, author, daughter of Charles Warren and Anna Augusta (Haley) Bassett, was born in Newton, Massachusetts. Her father was a descendant of William Bassett who came from England to Plymouth in the *Fortune* in 1621 through his fifth son, Joseph, who settled in Braintree, Massachusetts. Miss Bassett was educated in the public schools of Newton and in 1894 graduated from the Lowell School of Applied Design, then a branch of the Massachusetts Institute of Technology. She received a diploma of honorable mention for designs sent with the latter's exhibit to the World's Fair at Chicago in 1893. Unwilling to accept a designer's position away from home, she turned to teaching and graduated from the Symond's Kindergarten Training School in 1902. Thereafter for twenty years she held a position in the Newton public schools. As English had been her favorite study in high school, she wished to continue this subject, and at once arranged for courses in her spare time at Boston University, where she studied for four years with Professor E. Charlton Black. She constantly practiced writing, at first for the mere love of arranging words, as she had previously arranged colors in her studies in design. She sold some short stories and contributed unsigned articles to the *Youth's Companion*. Self criticism led her to further courses with Professor Charles T. Copeland and Mr. Frank W. C. Hersey at Radcliffe College, where she studied also philosophy under Professors Royce and Palmer. She then returned to Boston University for three year's work under Professor Dallas Lore Sharp. "To those faithful pilots who have guided me upon my course" she dedicated her first novel, *The Taming of Zenas Henry*, an affectionate study of Cape Cod life, published in 1915. She had been in the habit of spending her summers on the Cape and had recognized that, while there were many stories that should be preserved for their local color, other writers had frequently misrepresented the true character of the people. In 1917 followed *The Wayfarers at the Angels* and in 1919 *The Harbor Road*. In these books she shows a delicate humor, set off by a delightful irony that does not disguise her complete and friendly understanding of a cordial, generous, and humorous people. Miss Bassett's long experience as a kindergarten teacher has given her a comprehension of childhood which is reflected in the books she has especially written for young people: *The Story of Lumber* (1912), *The Story of Wool* (1913), *The Story of Leather* (1915), *The Story of Glass* (1916), *The Story of Sugar* (1917), *The Story of Silk* (1918), and *The Story of Porcelain* (1919). In these she has traced in entertaining style the various stages taken in transforming the commodity into the finished product. Miss Bassett is a member of the Boston Women's City Club and the Boston Authors' Club, and an honorary member of the Boston Manuscript Club.

MURRAY, MARGARET POLSON (Mrs. Clark Murray), daughter of William and Margaret (MacLean) Polson, was born in 1844 in Paisley, Scotland, where she received her education, and where she was married, July 20, 1865, to John Clark Murray, who had been appointed in 1862 Professor of Mental and Moral Philosophy at Queen's University, Kingston, Ontario. He was the son of David Murray, Provost of Paisley, and Elizabeth Clark, and was born in Paisley, March 19, 1836. He was a graduate of the Universities of Glasgow, Edinburgh, Heidelberg, and Göttingen, receiving also the honorary degree of LL.D. from Glasgow, and was a Fellow of the Royal Society of Canada. In 1872 he was called to McGill University, Montreal, as Professor of Mental and Moral Philosophy, retiring in 1903, but continuing to add to his many learned publications on philosophy, psychology, and ethics. He died in 1917. Professor and Mrs. Murray were the parents of Alfred Polson Murray (born in 1868), Edith A. Polson Murray (born in 1871), Margaret Polson Murray (born in 1878), Elizabeth Clark Murray (born in 1882), and Grace Polson Murray (born in 1884).

In 1900, when in London during the Boer War, Mrs. Clark Murray founded the Imperial Order of the Daughters of the Empire. The news of the first British reverses, with their casualty lists, was filling everyone with a passionate desire to do something to maintain Imperial traditions, and Mrs. Murray conceived the idea of uniting the women of all parts of the Empire in one great bond. Putting herself quickly in communication with the different sections of Great Britain and its possessions, she found her plan enthusiastically welcomed on all sides. On her return to Canada shortly afterwards, she called a meeting in Montreal which brought an eager response from the whole Dominion. The Constitution, drawn up at that time by Mrs. Murray, is still in force with few alterations, and the Daughters of the Empire have remained, in peace as well as in war, a constructive force in the life of the British peoples. As a war memorial to the men and women who gave their lives in defense of the Empire in the Great War, the Daughters of the Empire have established nine post-graduate scholarships, one for each province annually, to any overseas university, and nine bursaries to Canadian universities, one for each province annually for a period of eighteen years. These are open to sons and daughters of deceased or permanently disabled soldiers, sailors, and aviators. In addition, the Daughters of the Empire are placing in every Canadian school, where children of foreign-born parents are in attendance, an historical library, and they have established a lecture foundation in Canada for the teaching of imperial history. Mrs. Murray also founded a junior organization, the Children of the Empire, and the headquarters of both organizations, originally in Montreal, are now in Toronto. The Imperial Order of the Daughters of the Empire, is also represented in the United States, and Mrs. Murray is an honorary member of the American society as well as an honorary member, representing Canada, of the General Federation of Women's Clubs of the United States. The notable part played by Canadian troops in the Boer War inspired Mrs. Murray to found the Canadian-South African Graves Association, the first organization of women to locate and care for the graves of men fallen in battle. Her work in this field caused her election as honorary member of the Guild of Loyal Women of South Africa. When the Young Women's Christian Association was organized in Canada, Mrs. Murray became its First Secretary, and she has always promoted every form of education and philanthropy. She is an honorary patroness of the Daily Vacation Bible Schools, Montreal Women's Auxiliary, and a member of the Council of the Educational Kinematograph Association of London. Especially has she contributed to a closer understanding on the part of Canadian school children of the meaning of the British Empire by her work as executive Secretary of Imperial Education in the Schools of the Empire, which had its first public inauguration in Montreal on April 27, 1914, when a message of congratulation from Queen Mary was received and read. This work aids in securing imperial outlook, interest, and responsibility in the rising generation by assembling the children with their teachers in the schools twice a month to enjoy a series of lantern slides, with a short description, selected by a system of exchange with England, Scotland, Ireland, Wales, Canada, Australia, New Zealand, India, South Africa, and the islands of the Empire, thus giving an education urgently demanded by the wide separation and the wonderful individual development of the Empire, involving a population of over four hundred millions of square miles. Mrs. Murray is a woman of great physical activity, an indefatigable walker, a musician, and a contributor to magazines. Her articles have appeared in *The Contemporary Review* and the *Nineteenth Century and After*, of London, and she was for some time press correspondent for Montreal, Ottawa, and Washington to *The Week*, Toronto.

IDE, FANNIE OGDEN ("Ruth Ogden") (Mrs. Charles W. Ide), author, daughter of Jonathan and Abigail (Murphy) Ogden, was born in Brooklyn, New York, December 27, 1853. She is descended from John Ogden whose son, Richard, came from England to America, about 1642. She was educated in Brooklyn private schools, and in December, 1875, was married in Brooklyn to Charles W. Ide, a cotton broker, who died in November, 1903. Their only child, Alice Steele Ide, is the wife of Foster Hannaford of Minneapolis, Minnesota. Under her pen-name, *Ruth Ogden*, Mrs. Ide has written juvenile stories that have been favorites with children—*His Little Royal Highness* (1887), *A Loyal Little Red-Coat* (1889), *A Little Queen of Hearts* (1892), *Courage* (1894), *Little Homespun* (1896), *Tattine* (1900), *Loyal Hearts and True* (1900), *Friendship—The Good and Perfect Gift* (1902), and *Little Pierre and Big Peter* (1915). She has also contributed to magazines in prose and verse. She has been intimately connected with the work of the Brooklyn Young Women's Christian Association and with church work along broad lines, and is especially interested in Hampton Institute, Virginia. To educate the public in regard to the training of negroes and Indians in practical good-citizenship, furnished by Hampton Institute, and to help raise money for its support, she was instrumental in organizing the Brooklyn Armstrong Association, now the Hampton Association of Brooklyn, the initial meeting of which took place at her home, and she has been one of its vice-presidents since its organization. The Association, which was originally named after General Samuel Chapman Armstrong (1839–1893), founder in 1868 of Hampton Institute, carries on a campaign of education as to the needs of the Institute, and raises, annually, an average of four thousand dollars in scholarship and general donations. Mrs. Ide is also a member of the Wednesday Afternoon Club of New York and of the Twentieth Century Club of Brooklyn.

CHATFIELD-TAYLOR, ROSE (Mrs. Hobart Chatfield-Taylor), youngest daughter of Senator Charles B. Farwell of Illinois, was born March 9, 1869. She passed her childhood and youth at Lake Forest, Illinois, where she received her education, first at the seminary for girls and afterwards at Lake Forest University. She was married to Mr. Hobart Chatfield-Taylor the day after her graduation in 1889. With a marked clarity of mind she was very proficient in her studies and in her after life was associated with many projects for civic betterment. She was also an advocate of Woman Suffrage. Her principal activities were social and in these her remarkable personality made her supreme. She was in fact a genius in personality, almost faultlessly beautiful and quite faultlessly human and kind. It can be said truthfully that she was the inspiring source of joy and comradeship to all who knew her. When she died in Santa Barbara, California, in 1918, it was said that she was the most regretted of all of her generation. She was an interested spectator of politics and knew many politicians. She was a constant reader of books, and an able critic of her husband's literary work. She was the mother of four children; one daughter and three sons. For all who knew her, she remains a most radiant memory of unfailing optimism, and of unvaryingly excellent and sympathetic assistance to her many friends. In Chicago, her birthplace, it is said that no one can ever take the place which she occupied as the standard bearer of hope and happiness.

DE KOVEN, ANNA FARWELL (Mrs. Reginald de Koven), author, the daughter of Charles B. and Mary Eveline (Smith) Farwell, was born in Chicago, Illinois, November 19, 1860. Her father, who was United States senator from Illinois from 1887 to 1891, was descended from Henry Farwell, recorded as resident at Concord, Massachusetts, in 1635. Henry Farwell came from Devonshire, and the family had four members in Rogers' Rangers in the French and Indian War, while Abraham Farwell fought at Lexington and Henry Farwell served as a captain at the Battle of Bunker Hill. Mary Eveline Farwell, Mrs. de Koven's mother, was a descendant of the Dexter and Angell families of Massachusetts, and, as Treasurer for twenty-five years of the American Board of Commissioners for Foreign Missions, was known as an active worker for the spread of Christianity. Mr. Farwell was the founder of Lake Forest University, where Miss Farwell received the degree of A.B. and was valedictorian of her class. On May 1, 1884, she was married at Lake Forest, Illinois, to Reginald de Koven, the composer and critic, and for six years Mr. and Mrs. de Koven made their home in Chicago. During this period, Mrs. de Kovan was for two years President of the Friday Club and was literary editor of the Chicago Evening Post. In 1889 she translated Pierre Loti's Pêcheur d'Islande (An Iceland Fisherman), published in the Laurel Crown Series of Little Masterpieces of Foreign Authors, which set a standard of excellence in translation. After a year in Vienna, where Mr. de Koven studied orchestration, Mr. and Mrs. de Koven were in London, in 1891, during the production of Robin Hood, the most famous of his operas. On their return to America, they lived for nine years in New York, then in Washington until 1906, when they again made New York their home. Their house was always a rendezvous for noted musicians, as well as for artists, authors, and people prominent in every walk of life. Mrs. de Koven's unfailing charm and broad cultivation, together with her husband's

genius, made her salons as brilliant as any of the most famous of Europe. During this time, Mrs. de Koven wrote many stories and articles for magazines, and in 1894 published her first novel, A Sawdust Doll, which went through many editions in America, England, Australia, and India. By the Waters of Babylon, an historical novel, followed in 1899, and was afterwards dramatized. Before 1906 Mrs. de Koven had been attracted by the character and career of John Paul Jones, and, as a result of extensive research in libraries in England and France, and in that of Harvard University and in the Congressional Library, as well as in private collections and among unpublished papers, she produced, in 1913, her Life and Letters of John Paul Jones, which has been accepted as the authoritative account of the life of America's first great naval commander. In 1916 she wrote The Counts of Gruyère, and has since been a deep student of spiritism. The results of her researches in this field were published in 1920 under the title of A Cloud of Witnesses, a comprehensive volume of great intellectual and emotional appeal. During the World War, Mrs. de Koven was active as a member of the American Red Cross and as a supporter of relief work. She is a member of the Colony Club, and has interested herself in raising the standards of the public schools. Mr. de Koven, to whom music lovers owe a lasting debt of pleasure, died in Chicago, January 16, 1920, while supervising the production of his last opera, Rip Van Winkle. Mr. and Mrs. de Koven were the parents of one child: Ethel Le Roy de Koven, a graduate of Bryn Mawr College, who married H. Kierstede Hudson.

McCULLOCH, CATHERINE GOUGER WAUGH (Mrs. Frank Hathorn McCulloch), lawyer, was born in Ransomville, New York, June 4, 1862. Her father, Abraham Miller Waugh, was a descendant of Abraham Waugh, a native of Northern Ireland, who came to America about 1798 and settled in Pennsylvania. Her mother, Susan (Gouger) Waugh, was descended from a French Huguenot, who fled from persecution in France, remained for awhile in Germany, and about 1734 came to America. After a thorough preparatory education Miss Waugh entered Rockford College, Illinois, from which she received the degrees of B.A. and M.A. She then entered the Law School of Northwestern University from which she was graduated with the degree of LL.B. in 1886, and was admitted to the Illinois Bar the same year. Her marriage to Frank Hathorn McCulloch took place at Rockford, Illinois, May 30, 1890. He was a lawyer with offices in Chicago, and that same year Mrs. McCulloch became his law partner under the firm name of McCulloch and McCulloch. In 1898 she was admitted to the bar of the Supreme Court of the United States. She was the first woman Justice of the Peace in the United States, elected thrice in her home city, Evanston, by men's votes only, for women had no votes for justices in Illinois. Mrs. McCulloch has gained a national reputation as legal advisor for large organizations of women—among them the National and the Illinois Women's Christian Temperance Unions. For twenty-two years she was in charge of the legislative work of the Illinois Suffrage Association, was a First Vice-President and legal advisor of the National Association, and a member of local boards. She took a leading part in the successful passage of the bill which gave women the franchise in Illinois in 1913. Her public work has been largely in the legislatures of various states urging the suffrage for women. Since 1891 bills and resolutions drafted by her have been before every legislature in Illinois. Among those that passed were some resolutions and a bill to raise the age of consent; a bill making mothers joint guardians of their children; a bill granting women presidential, city, and township votes, and the vote on questions of taxes and drainage propositions. Since 1913 the latter has been copied or adapted by ten other states and more states (1919) have the matter pending. In the presidential election of 1916 Mrs. McCulloch was chosen by the Democratic State Convention as one of the presidential electors and received the largest vote of any candidate on the Democratic ticket. In December, 1917 she was appointed by the judges of the Superior Court of Cook County, Illinois, as a Master-in-Chancery. She is the author of *Mr. Lex*, a story; *Bridget's Sisters*, a play, and many short stories, legal pamphlets, and suffrage leaflets. Mrs. McCulloch is an accomplished musician, and her four children have inherited her gift. Various instruments are played by them with the mother acting as accompanist. She also joins them in their outdoor sports, especially in swimming and horseback riding. She is a Congregationalist and deeply interested in Sunday schools and missionary societies, mothers' clubs, the Woman's Christian Temperance Union, and all organizations whose aim is the uplift of humanity. She is an Independent in politics. Mrs. McCulloch is the President of the Illinois Women's Bar Association; Chairman of the Illinois Suffrage Amendment Alliance; member of the Chicago Woman's Club, the Chicago Women's City Club, the Frederick Douglas Center, the Evanston Woman's Club, the Mother's Club, the Woman's Peace Party, and the Political Equality League. During the war she was very active and served on a great many special committees; took part in the various Liberty Loan Drives; and was a member of the Woman's Committee of the Council of National Defense.

Mr. and Mrs. McCulloch are the parents of four children: Captain Hugh Waugh McCulloch, who was with the United States Army of Occupation in Germany; Hathorn Waugh McCulloch; Catherine Waugh McCulloch and Frank Waugh McCulloch.

MARTIN, ANNE HENRIETTA, suffragist and politician, daughter of William O'Hara and Louise (Stadmuller) Martin, was born in Empire City, Nevada, September 30, 1875. Her father was the grandson of Morris

Martin, who came to New York from Ireland about 1820, and of William O'Hara, a Captain in the British Army, who came from Annaghmore, County Sligo, Ireland, to New York with his family about 1815. Miss Martin was educated at the University of Nevada, where she received the degree of B.A. in 1894, and at Leland Stanford Jr. University, where she received the degree of B.A. in 1896 and M.A. in 1897. During her college years Miss Martin took an active part in the social and athletic life of the students. She was elected to Kappa Kappa Gamma and Phi Kappa Phi sororities. In 1892–1894 she was state tennis champion of Nevada and in 1895–1897 tennis champion of Leland Stanford University. Her love of sport has continued and includes golf, horseback riding and tennis. From 1897 to 1901 she was professor of history at the University of Nevada but was given leave of absence to study at Columbia University, and at Chase's Art School, New York, in 1899–1901, and at the Universities of London and Leipzig in 1900–1901. In 1901 she returned to the University of Nevada as lecturer on the history of art until 1903, when she resigned to devote all her time to speaking, writing, and working for woman suffrage. For some years she gave her services to the women of England in association with Mrs. Emmeline Pankhurst in London, where she became a member of the Fabian Society, returning to her home in Reno, Nevada, in 1912. In 1914 she collaborated with Mary Austin on a pamphlet, *Suffrage and Citizenship*, published by the National American Woman Suffrage Association. In the same year, as President of the Nevada Equal Franchise Society, she organized and carried to a successful conclusion on November 3, 1914, the campaign for woman suffrage in Nevada. In 1915 she was appointed the first woman member of the Nevada Educational Survey Commission and served as President of the Nevada Women's Civic League and as a member of the executive committee of the National American Woman Suffrage Association. At the National

Woman's Party's first convention, held in Chicago, Illinois, in June 1916, Miss Martin was elected National Chairman, and in 1917 National Vice-Chairman and member of the national executive committee and Chairman of the national legislative committee. In 1918 she announced herself as Independent candidate for the office of United State Senator from Nevada, the first woman to run for this position. Although defeated, she proved the strength of the movement for equal political rights, as she received approximately 5,000 votes, against 12,000 Democratic, 8,000 Republican, and 700 Socialist. Miss Martin has contributed articles on political and economic subjects to newspapers and magazines, such as: *Our Soldier Settlement Policy in Reconstruction* for October, 1919; *What Women Should Vote For* in *Good Housekeeping* for November 1919; and *The Maternity and Infancy Bill* in *Good Housekeeping* for January, 1920. She is a member of the American Historical Association, the Twentieth-Century Club of Reno, the Lyceum, Ladies' Park and International Franchise Clubs of London, and the National Arts Club of New York.

SWIFT, EDITH HALE, physician, daughter of Frank W. and Alice (Cowell) Hale, was born in Cottage Grove, Minnesota, September 13, 1878. Her father was seventh in line from Edward Rawson, of Gillingham, England, who settled in Newbury, Massachusetts, in 1636–1637. He was the first Secretary of the Colony. The earliest Hale ancestor was John Heald—the change of spelling occurred at a somewhat later date—who came from Berwick-on-Tweed, and settled in Concord in 1635. Her mother's earliest American ancestor was Robert Vose, of England, who settled in Milton about 1640. One ancestor, Mariah Gould, from Groton, served in the War of the Revolution from April 19, 1775, until he was discharged at Peekskill, New York, in 1777.

Doctor Swift was educated in the Boston public schools; received the A.B. degree from Radcliffe College in 1901; M.D. from Johns

Hopkins in 1905; and pursued a post-graduate medical course in Berlin, during 1908–1910.

On November 26, 1907, she was married, in Boston, Massachusetts, to Walter Babcock Swift, a physician (born December 24, 1869, at Geneva, Switzerland), son of Nathaniel H. and Isabella (Babcock) Swift. They are the parents of two children: Barbara (born February 28, 1910, in Berlin, Germany) and Phyllis (born December 14, 1911 in Boston, Massachusetts).

Doctor Swift is a member of the American Medical Association; the Massachusetts Medical Society; the New England Pediatric Society; the New England Women's Medical and the Medical Women's National Association. She is also a member of the College Club, the Women Voter's League, and the Women's Municipal League.

HULING, SARA HAWKS (Mrs. Edward B. Huling), daughter of William Edward and Helen Elizabeth (Brown) Hawks, was born in Bennington, Vermont, January 23, 1872. Four of her great-great-grandfathers,. Major Eleazer Hawks, Captain Hezekiah Armstrong, Lieutenant John Kingsley, and David Haynes, fought in the Battle of Bennington, and her ancestry, reaching back to the founding of New England, makes her eligible to all the patriotic genealogical societies. On her father's side the line is derived from John Hawks, who came from Southampton, England, to Lynn, Massachusetts, in 1636, through Sergeant Eleazer Hawks, Captain Eleazer Hawks, Joshua Hawks, Major Eleazer Hawks, William Hawks, and Alvah Hawks, to William Edward Hawks, who was born January 27, 1832, and died July 29, 1911. On February 2, 1859, he married Helen Elizabeth Brown, who was born March 28, 1834, and who was descended from Peter Brown of London, England, through his grandson, Peter Brown, Deliverance Brown, Samuel Brown, Nehemiah Brown, Samuel Brown, and her father Samuel Hinman Brown.

Sarah Hawks was graduated from the Ben-

nington High School in 1888 and from the Misses Bangs' School, New Haven, Connecticut, in June, 1892. On December 25, 1893, she married in Bennington, Edward Bently Huling of Chicago, Illinois, the western representative of J. and W. Seligman and Company, New York, Bankers and Brokers. He was born in Chicago, May 16, 1870, and is the son of Edward Chase Huling of Shaftsbury, Vermont, and Fanny Peckham Griggs of Lebanon Springs, New York. Mr. and Mrs. Huling are the parents of Katharine Brown Huling (born May 19, 1896), who studied at Miss Porter's School, Farmington, Connecticut, Elizabeth Hinman Huling (born July 8, 1900), a graduate of Vassar College, George Edward Huling (born July 22, 1903; died May 10, 1905), and Sara Frances Hawks Huling (born April 5, 1906).

Mrs. Huling is State President for Vermont of the National Society of Daughters of Founders and Patriots of America. She is a member of the Daughters of the American Revolution, and of the United States Daughters of 1812, of which she is first Vice-President for Vermont; she has been State President for Vermont of the Congress of the Mothers' and Parent-Teachers' Association, is active on the State Board of Charities and in the Woman's Auxiliary of the Young Men's Christian Association, and has been County Director of the Young Men's Christian Association; is Treasurer of the Red Cross, and County Chairman of the Council of National Defense; was County Chairman for the Fourth Liberty and Victory Loans and Chairman of the conservation department of the State Federation of Women's Clubs; and is a member of the Village Improvement Society of Bennington, Vermont, the King's Daughters, and the Welfare Association, the Hospital League, the Fortnightly Club and the Chicago Woman's Club.

MILHAU, ZELLA de, daughter of Edward Leon and Mary (Mannering) de Milhau, was born in New York City, in April, 1870. Her father was a descendant of the ancient French family founded by Bernard Vicomte de Milhau of Rouergue (now Aveyron), France. Comte Henri Jacques de Milhau came from France in 1776 as Royal Commissioner to Louisiana when that was a French province, and his great-grandson settled in Baltimore, giving up his title of Comte and becoming an American citizen in 1813.

After studying at the Art Student's League and privately with Arthur Dow, in New York City, Miss de Milhau continued her studies in etching in Paris and Munich. Favorable attention was attracted by her series of Egyptian etchings, and those of scenes in Canada, in the Rockies, and, on the Long Island Coast. As a sportswoman, Miss de Milhau has been active in driving and riding her own horses and in hunting, but her special interest has been the breeding of sporting dogs. She is the owner of the Pepperidge-Airedale Kennels and is master of the Shinnecock beagles. During the World War she gave her services to the French government, sailing August 7, 1914, on the first ship to carry volunteers, and remaining in France until June 28, 1919. For her work on the French front she received the Croix de Guerre and the gold medal of French Reconnaissance. She is a member of the National Beagle Club, the American Fox-hound Society, the Ladies' Kennel Association of America, the Ramabai Society of Philadelphia, the Meadow Club, the Plastic Club, the Acorn Club of Philadelphia, the Suffolk Hunt Club, the Art Worker's Club, the Art Students' League, the Arts and Crafts Club, and the National Arts Club.

KELLEY, LILLA ELIZABETH, daughter of Samuel and Mary J. (Fitton) Kelley, was born in South Boston, Massachusetts, May 18, 1872. The Kelley family originated in Worcestershire, England. In 1859 Miss Kelley's grandfather, Henry Kelley, came to the United States from Wollaston, England, and landed in New York, but soon afterwards went to Boston. His father was a clergyman, and, on the maternal side, was descended from Robert Bruce. He was literary, artistic, and musical. At one time he was asked to take charge of the music at Worcester Cathedral, but owing to other duties he was obliged to decline the responsibility. He was public spirited and interested in bettering labor conditions. An evidence of this was the fact that upon his departure for America, on August 25, 1859, he was presented with a purse of nineteen sovereigns and an address by the members of the Wordsley Branch of the United Flint Glass Cutters' Society, because of his services in assisting them to gain certain rights and privileges. Miss Kelley received her early education in the Boston public schools and from private teachers, and entered the Emerson College of Oratory, receiving the degree of O.B. in 1890 and that of O.M. in 1891. She has also taken special work at Boston University and was a pupil of Mrs. Erving Winslow, and other private teachers. She is an accomplished elocutionist and platform reader. In 1895–1896 she was teacher of oratory at Tilton Seminary and in 1896–1897 at Wesleyan Academy, Wilbraham, Massachusetts. She has also done miscellaneous writing and special club work. Since 1908 Miss Kelley has been interested in public work of a constructive character, in 1908 as a teacher at the Thompson's Island School for Boys, Boston Harbor, and in 1910 at the School for the Feeble-Minded at Wrentham, Massachusetts. From 1910 to 1917 she was House Officer and Farm Matron at the Lancaster State Industrial School for Juvenile Delinquents at Lancaster, Massachusetts. In these institutions she has helped put into practice the teachings of John Ruskin. Since 1917 she has been a Parole Agent of the Bureau of Corrections at the State House, Boston, Massachusetts. Miss Kelley has varied club affiliations. She is a member of the Woman's Auxiliary of the Civil Service Reform Society, the British Charitable Society, the Massachusetts Forestry Association, the Woman's Alliance (Unitarian), various alumnae associations, and the Presidents'

Club which is composed of ex-club presidents. She is a charter member of the Ruskin Club, Boston, and from 1900 to 1917 held office as its Secretary, Vice-President, and, for eleven years, President. Miss Kelley has published many short stories and poems, but her chief literary work is a book brought out in 1904 entitled *Three Hundred Things That a Bright Girl Can Do*. This work is used by trade schools as a reference book and has the distinction of having been voted as one, out of 3,000 volumes considered, to be added to the young people's department of the libraries of New York State. Miss Kelley is fond of out-door sports, her favorites being rowing, mountain climbing and riding. She adds to her cleverness and versatility a sunny disposition, and she possesses an optimistic philosophy which is a large element of success in her chosen line of work. She considers life "a brave adventure," the experiences of which should be utilized for the purpose of broadening our spheres of usefulness and service and towards the attainment of such an understanding of friendship as shall inspire humanity to realize its highest possibilities.

HASTINGS, CAROLINE ELIZA, physician, daughter of Emery and Mary (Bassett) Hastings, was born in Barre, Massachusetts. She is a descendant of Thomas Hastings, who sailed in the ship *Elizabeth* from Ipswich, England, on April 10, 1634, and settled first in Ipswich, Massachusetts, but later removed to Watertown, where he was sworn freeman on May 6, 1636, and died in 1685.

Caroline Eliza Hastings received her early education in the public schools of Barre, and attended Mt. Holyoke College for one year. From early childhood her desire had been to study medicine, and she had demonstrated in her home an unusual ability to care for the sick. This inborn love may have been an inheritance, as there were physicians on both sides of her family. When she was eighteen years old her attention was called to the opportunities offered by the New England Female Medical College at Boston, which she eventually entered, and from which she was graduated in 1868, with the degree of M.D. Throughout this period her career was opposed by her father, but her mother sympathized with her daughter's ambition. Her college was eventually taken over by Boston University as its Medical School, on a homeopathic basis. To this, after engaging in private practice, she returned for postgraduate work, and in 1872 she was appointed assistant demonstrator. She became, successfully, demonstrator, lecturer, and professor of anatomy. She was remarkably successful as a teacher and her pupils of years ago remember nothing better in their whole course of instruction than Professor Hastings' clear, orderly, and illuminating presentation of the dry details of this difficult subject. In 1894 she completed seven years' service as a member of the Boston School Committee to which she had been appointed by a concurrent vote of the School Committee and the Board of Alderman, taken without her knowledge.

Aside from her practice of medicine, Doctor Hastings's chief interest has been the Talitha Cumi Home, with which she has been connected for fifty years. This is a home for unmarried mothers, which was organized, about 1830, by a group of women. From a small beginning, it has grown to be one of the leading private institutions in Boston. It is situated in a secluded section of Forest Hills with an up-to-date hospital and house equipment, and with beautiful grounds. The name Talitha Cumi signifies, "I say unto thee, Arise." The home is for young girls in their first misfortune, and the belief of the early organizers still prevails, that the young mothers' best chance for future happiness and a restoration of personal dignity lies in the companionship and dependence of the little child. For seven years Doctor Hastings was physician to the home, and then retired in favor of her friend and co-worker, Doctor Julia Morton Plummer.

Doctor Hastings organized, and was first President of, the first Woman's Medical Society in Boston, the Twentieth Century Medical Club, for the purpose of parliamentary as well as scientific study. A fine parliamentarian herself, she believed that women needed training in such technicalities in order that they might have confidence when presenting their views in public. Doctor Hastings is a woman of rare intellect, practical intelligence, and unusual value to her community. Her zeal in assisting women in any way which lay in her power has resulted in benefits to her sex which would be difficult to calculate.

ADAMS, EVANGELINE SMITH (Mrs. George E. Jordan, Jr.), is a descendant of the famous New England Adams family which has given two presidents to the United States, and, through her mother, she is a descendant of Isaac Smith, who made important inventions in locomotive engines, and from whom she seems to have inherited her extraordinary talent for mathematics. Her childhood was strongly influenced by the religious and academic atmosphere of Andover, Massachusetts, then the center of various theological and academic institutions. The Theological Seminary has since been removed to Cambridge, but Phillips and Abbot Academy still claim it as their home. Elizabeth Stuart Phelps (author of *Gates Ajar*) was her Sunday School teacher, and her playmates were the children of the neighboring professors.

Miss Adams' independence and alert personality, even as a very young girl, led Doctor J. Herbert Smith to select her as a student of astrology. Doctor Smith was then Professor of Materia Medica in Boston University, but his profound personal interest was centered in astrology. A reading of Miss Adams' horoscope, together with his personal observation of her, convinced him that, in her character and mental equipment, were qualities which would fit her to elevate astrology to the dignity of an accepted science among modern sciences, and make it again a recognized

influence in the development of mankind. From Doctor Smith, Miss Adams received not only the fruits of his long study, but the priceless gift of his manuscripts and technical library. She also became inculcated with his philosophy and high ambitions for astrology.

For many years, Miss Adams has served the cause with that courage, industry, and intellectuality upon which Doctor Smith counted. She has brought astrology far along the way her beloved teacher indicated, and now is aflame, as he was long ago, to see the still further advance of this ancient science. She is as rapidly as possible withdrawing herself from her insistent clientele of consultants, in order to devote herself to recording her experiences, representing the outpost development of modern astrology, and to compile text-books to inform the public and enlighten teachers to follow in her steps.

Miss Adams is the one astrologer of modern times whose scientific practice of her profession has been upheld by court edict. Judge John H. Freschi's decision in 1914, not only endorsed Miss Adams' professional integrity, but gave legal recognition to this oldest of the sciences. Miss Adams' unique professional significance lies in her ability to relate the accumulated facts and principles of ancient astrology to the problems of modern, up-to-date affairs and people. Her varied experience has greatly developed her native and spontaneous understanding of life and human nature, and her conscientious spirit of inquiry keeps her information abreast of the times, and her devotion to astrology as a human and ever-progressive record of evolution challenges all question. So, like Galilio, experimental philosopher of the sixteenth century, who, in his time, faced judgment upon the integrity of his belief, and under torture at last adjured his "heresies," including the movements of the earth, although his inner spirit still asserted "*E pur se muove*," Miss Adams was sustained, when she faced the challenge of the law and claimed the integrity of astrology. The world has indeed moved, and moved far since the time of Galilio, and Judge Freschi has furthered that progress, which the inquisition so long ago sought to halt.

The very latest discoveries of the modern scientists are often placed before Miss Adams for her investigation and practice, and she is daily enriching the accumulation of her findings of astrology, and bringing to bear upon its ancient edicts the verification of these discoveries. Her clients profit by what they name "The Adams Philosophy," as fully perhaps as they do by the accuracy of her scientific methods concerning the range of astrology and its modern application.

Miss Adams says, "Experience is the supreme teacher." All sciences are predicted upon facts developed in the phenomena of the world, as men have experienced them. The accumulation of the history of specific cases now furnishes the working basis for scientific understanding. As, for example, the physical conformation of the head and body has come to be recognized in criminology as significant of the quality and tendency of the individual types, and with accuracy infers the power of the planets over character development. The horoscope, or chart presenting the planetary influences operating in the life, is calculated by an absolutely mechanical mathematical process. When the process is founded upon accurate information concerning the birth and the relative position and influence of the planets, the resultant findings are accurate. Astrology is never mistaken, though the uninformed or careless astrologer may be. Astrology is not "fortune-hunting" nor fortune-guessing. It is prediction based on the unalterable law of cause and effect. The significance of nature in any phase of expression is to be interpreted by the influences surrounding it. The significance of man's conformation and character as expressed in his living and conduct is to be interpreted by the planetary influences controlling him at the time of his birth. These translate themselves into outer conditions of environment and inner urge of impulse. The science of astrology with mathematical exactness calculates the pressures upon the human being, and the direction, quality and extent of his responses.

COFER, LUISITA LELAND (Mrs. Leland Eggleston Cofer), was born in New York City. Her father, Charles Henry Leland, a direct descendant of John Leland (1512), antiquarian, historian, and linguist of All Souls' College, Oxford, was appointed by King Henry VIII, Royal Antiquary, an office of honor created for him which lapsed with his death. His descendant, Hopestill Leland, born in 1622 in England, was an early colonist of Massachusetts where he settled, 1652, in Sherburne, and was the first paternal ancestor in America of Charles Francis Leland. Another member of the family, distinguished as a scholar, author, and translator of Demosthenes from Greek to Latin, was Doctor Thomas Leland, 1722, of Trinity College, Dublin, Ireland. Charles Henry Leland married Matilda Frothingham of the well-known New England family of that name. Their daughter, Luisita, was educated in schools and by private tutors in New York, and on the Continent. During the impressionable years of early girlhood she spent much time in France and became thoroughly imbued with love for that land, whose language was as familiar to her as her own. Shortly after the outbreak of the Great War, when France was suffering acutely from invasion, Miss Leland became convinced that the best way for her to help was to enlist the sympathies of America in the terrible plight of the little children of France. The condition of these innocent, helpless sufferers was pitiful. She realized that if the old France, forced into this conflict, spending all her energy in the struggle, her young manhood buried on the battlefields, was to give birth to a new France that would be a worthy inheritor of heroic achievements, the young generation of children, alive or to be born must be reared to uphold the traditions of yesterday. Even a short period of neglect brings disastrous results in a child's physical, mental, and moral development; therefore, the need to begin this work was imperative. To meet this emergency a society was formed, through Miss Leland's initiative, which was incorporated in 1915 as *The Fatherless Children of France*, and she was made chairman of the New York Committee. In France, on its honorary, active, and administrative committees, appeared the most distinguished names in the social, political, and intellectual circles of that country. Marshall Joffre gave the undertaking his sympathetic support, as President of the Paris Committee. The work of the Central Board was supplemented by local committees in every town and village, whose business it was to inquire into the circumstances of the orphans in each district, and appoint guardians for them. From the first, it was the policy of the society to leave the children in their own homes, under the care of their mothers, to be brought up in the religion of their parents. Any child under sixteen years of age, living in its own home, whose father had lost his life in the war, and who was certified to be in need, was eligible for help. It was felt that by leaving the child to grow up under the care of its mother in the small town or village, where the memory of the father would be conserved and traditions of valor instilled, the conditions would be far better than if it were placed in an institution. It was estimated, as the war progressed, that there were two million of these war orphans, one million being in actual need. As fast as names were catalogued the lists were sent to Miss Leland's committee in New York, which, in turn, distributed them among local committees whose work consisted in securing adopters or donors. Aid was given at the following rates: ten cents to keep a child one day in its mother's home; $3.00 to keep a child a month; $36.50, a year; and $73.00 two years. Any subscriber of $36.50, after making his pledge and a first payment, was given, upon request, the name and address of the orphan assigned to him, and to the child

was sent the name and address of his, or her, benefactor. It was advised that they correspond, and so keep in personal touch. A letter from the Paris committee also went to the child, or its mother, explaining the friendship of Americans, the amount of help, and the time for which it had been pledged, with instructions to write and thank the American donor. In America all expenses of the committees were paid from voluntary donations for that purpose. There were no salaried officials in the society, and it was the unbroken rule that the entire amount subscribed should go to the children. To understand the full significance of this statement it is only necessary to realize the large sums received by the various branches. At the end of the war, the New York Committee alone had sent to France approximately $1,000,000. The National Executive, which had under it 200 committees throughout the United States, collected approximately $8,000,000. In recognition of this work Miss Leland was, in 1919, awarded the Cross of the Legion of Honor by the French Government, and, by the National Institute of Social Sciences, the Liberty Service Medal. Besides being the chairman of the New York Committee of the *Fatherless Children of France*, Miss Leland was a Vice-President of the National Executive Committee, Chairman of one of the branches of the American Red Cross of which there were nine auxiliaries, and a member of the National League for Women's Service, the American Committee for Devastated France, Edith Wharton's War Charities, French Institute in the United States, the Alliance Française, the Italy-American Society, the National Institute of Social Sciences, the Vacation Association, Women's Department of Civic Federation, and the Colony Club. On November 15, 1919, she married Doctor Leland Eggleston Cofer, Health Officer of the Port of New York.

DAY, ELIZABETH RICHARDS (Mrs. Hilbert F. Day), was born in New Haven, Connecticut, October 1, 1883. Among her ancestors were many of the leading men of the Colonial period in Connecticut, including Governors Robert Treat and Thomas Welles, and General John Lamb and Colonel Jacob Arnold of the Revolutionary Army. Her father, Eugene Lamb Richards, who was born in Brooklyn, New York, December 27, 1837, and who died in 1912, was Professor of Mathematics at Yale University for forty years, and was a descendant of Samuel Richards (1685–1761), who came, about 1705, from Staffordshire, England, to Norwalk, Connecticut. The line is traced through his son, Captain James Richards (1723–1810), his son, Captain James Richards, Jr. (1744–1816), his son, Abraham Richards (1772–1849), and his son, Timothy Pickering Richards (1811–1880), to Eugene Frank Richards. The latter married Julia Lavinia Bacon, who was born in Woodbury, Connecticut, March, 1839, and who died in 1917. She was the daughter of Daniel Bacon, Jr. (1809–1885), the son of Daniel Bacon (1772–1828), the son of Jabez Bacon (1731–1806), the son of Nathaniel Bacon (1696–1769), the son of Andrew Bacon (1666–1723), the son of Nathaniel Bacon, who came to Hartford, Connecticut, in 1639 from Stretton, Rutland County, England, and who died in 1706. Elizabeth Richards (Mrs. Day) attended Miss Willard's school in New Haven and from 1896 to 1898 was a boarding pupil at Rosemary Hall. In 1899 she went to St. Margaret's School at Waterbury, Connecticut, from which she was graduated in 1901. She received, in 1907 her diploma from the Boston School for Social Workers, and thereafter engaged, for a year, in research work on a scholarship from the Russell Sage Foundation. For two years she lived at the South End House Settlement, in Boston, Massachusetts. From 1908 to 1913 she was engaged in organizing the Medical Social Service Department at the Boston Dispensary. During 1913–1914 she collaborated with Miss Mary Richmond on her book, *First Steps in Social Work; a Book for Case Workers*, published by the Russell Sage Foundation. Since then she

has been a trustee of the Boston Dispensary, a member of the Committee of the Permanent Charities Fund, and a member of the Administrative Board of the School for Social Workers, all of Boston. After the explosion of a munitions ship on December 6, 1917, in the harbor of Halifax, Nova Scotia, she went as a representative of the Red Cross to make a survey of the injured people, some 3,334 in number. The purpose of the study was to facilitate the Canadian Government in planning proper vocational and physical care and education for those handicapped by the explosion. Mrs. Day has written articles on medical social service for the National Conference of Social Work and the American Hospital Association. Her marriage to Hilbert Francis Day, M.D., took place at Westover School, Middlebury, Connecticut, January 3, 1914. Doctor Day is the son of William Francis and Lydia Ward (Jenkins) Day and was born in Roxbury, Massachusetts, April 17, 1879. He was graduated from Yale University in 1901 and from the Harvard Medical School in 1905. He then was attached to the staff of the Peter Bent Brigham Hospital, Boston, and is at present a practicing surgeon and obstetrician in Boston. Doctor and Mrs. Day are the parents of: William Francis Day (born December 11, 1914; died December 13, 1915), Richard Ward Day (born August 14, 1916), and Juliana Day (born December 1, 1918). Mrs. Day is a member of the Woman's City Club of Boston, the Mary R. Hillard Society of Westover School, Middlebury, Connecticut, the Stuart Club of Boston, the Graduate Club of the Boston School for Social Workers, and the New England Hospital Social Workers Association. She is interested in dramatics and singing and is fond of out-door sports, especially tennis, swimming, canoeing, and horseback riding.

BOND, MABEL (ANNA JANE) CORNISH (Mrs. Samuel Hazen Bond), was born in Washington, District of Columbia, August

24, 1867. Her father, George Gordon Cornish (September 10, 1834–December 2, 1909), married, in 1857, Ann Araminta Dougherty (February 18, 1839–June 13, 1912). The latter was the daughter of Thomas Dougherty and was one of a large family born on Prince Edward Island whither her father had come from Ireland. She was reared a Roman Catholic but later became a Methodist and was, throughout her life, an active church worker. At the age of sixteen she was apprenticed to a milliner in Bangor, New York, and two years later married Mr. Cornish, a prosperous farmer of the neighborhood. Mr. Cornish was descended from Mr. James Cornish (1612–1698) who came from England and settled at Saybrook, Connecticut, about 1659. In 1662 he married, as his second wife, Mrs. Phebe Brown Larrabee, who died in 1664. Their son, Deacon James Cornish (1663–1740), married, first, Elizabeth Thrall, and second, Hannah Hilliard (1681–1751). His son, Ensign Joseph Cornish (1697–1759), married, first, Mary Eno Humphrey and, second, in 1740, Zerviah Moses. His son, Gabriel Cornish (1758–1841), married, first, Electa Moses and, second, in 1790, Anna Crooks (1775–1869). His son, Alanson Cornish (1800–1872), married in 1831 Lorinda Jane Keeler (1795–1870), and they were the parents of George Gordon Cornish.

Mabel Cornish received her elementary school education in the public schools of Washington, and then attended the Preparatory Department of Vassar College from 1883 to 1885. In the latter year she entered Vassar and received the degree of A.B. in 1889. There followed three years at the Women's Medical College of the New York Infirmary from which she graduated in 1892 with the degree of M.D. During the next year she was Resident Physician at the Babies' Hospital, New York, and from 1893 to 1897 was engaged in private practice in Washington, being also for two years assistant to the Government pathologist, Doctor D. S. Lamb, in the United States Medical Museum and for two

years on the staffs of the Woman's Clinic, Dorothea Dix, and minor institute dispensaries. On November 25, 1897, she was married in Washington to Samuel Hazen Bond, of that city. He is special counsel of the American Surety Company, New York, in charge of the Federal Bond Bureau and was formerly law and bond clerk in charge of surety bonds in the United States Treasury Department. From 1902 to 1907 Mrs. Bond edited and published *The Cattarian*, a magazine in the interest of the long-haired cat. She obtained recognition for the thoroughbred cat and secured its importation to the United States free of duty under the Tariff Act. She also compiled and published *The U. S. Stud Book and Register for Cats*. Furthermore she made a special study of the parasites of cats and her records have proved interesting and useful contributions to the science of genetics. Mrs. Bond was formerly a member of the Medical Association of the District of Columbia, the Vassar Alumnae Association, and the Collegiate Alumnae Association. She is a member of the Washington Humane Society, the National Geographic Society, the Washington Society of Fine Arts, the American Social Hygiene Association, etc. She has traveled widely abroad and finds recreation in gardening and reading.

QUINCY, MARY ADAMS (Mrs. Henry Parker Quincy), was born in Boston, Massachusetts. Her father, Charles Francis Adams, was of the old New England family of that name, members of which have been distinguished from early colonial days by their service to their country, especially as diplomats. The founder of the family in America was Henry Adams, who came from Braintree, England, and was one of the first settlers, in 1632, of Braintree, now Quincy, Massachusetts. The line is traced through his son, Joseph, and his son, John Adams. The latter's son, John Adams, Jr., second President of the United States, married Abigail Smith. Their son, John Quincy Adams, sixth

President of the United States, married Louisa Catherine Johnson, and their son, Charles Francis Adams, married Abigail Brown Brooks. The latter's youngest daughter, Mary, was born in Boston at the family home on Mt. Vernon Street, on historic Beacon Hill, under the shadow of the State House, and her early impressions were gained through an atmosphere of colonial traditions, an inheritance in the household from the earlier period. She was educated in private schools, and by governesses, in Boston, and in the London home of her parents. When in America, her summers were, for the most part, spent at the family estate in Quincy, where for over two hundred years, the family had owned their own estates, passing them on from generation to generation. There, the home of her grandfather, the sixth President, afforded a charming summer playground for herself and brothers and sisters, and there was instilled in her the appreciation and love of nature, which has always been a conspicuous feature of her character. Her love for animals and skill in horsemanship date from these early days. On June 20, 1877, she was married at Quincy to Doctor Henry Parker Quincy, a physician of note, whose home and practice were established in Boston. Through this marriage two of the historic families of Massachusetts became united. Mrs. Quincy, both from her own inherited position, and as the wife of a man of national professional repute, became a power for good as expressed in the traditions of New England. As a member of the Emanuel Protestant Episcopal Church she has always been active in church work. She is public spirited and interested in all movements for reform, including the bettering of city conditions, the welfare of women and girls, especially those who are employed, the care for animals, and the conservation of native birds. She has a clever mind and, as her inheritance indicates, derives from her paternal ancestors, the attributes that lead her to take an interest in public affairs. She has never been before the public,

but her mind has broadened under the genial influence of much time spent in foreign countries, for it has been her custom to go abroad for several months nearly every summer. She is one of the many women who, in the quiet of home life, surrounded by influences that have ripened her intellect, has developed a breadth of thought which should have had a wider field for expression than the confines of home, church, and social organizations. She is very democratic, hospitable, and generous, and broadminded as one would expect of one with her lineage. Before the World War, Mrs. Quincy's vivid imagination was roused with the thought of the need for the United States to prepare, and all the weight of her influence was thrown towards advocating this patriotic necessity. Her war work was done as a member of the National Red Cross, the Navy League of the United States of America, and the Navy Relief Society. She is a member of the National Security League, the Special Aid Society for American Preparedness, the Young Women's Christian Association, the National Consumers' League, the Women's Welfare Department of the Civic Federation, the Women's Municipal League, the Women's Educational and Industrial Society, the United Improvement Association, the American Humane Association, the National Audubon Society, the Bostonian Society, the Quincy Historical Society, the American Geographical Society, the National Geographic Society, the Writers' Press Association, the Mayflower Society, the Society of Colonial Dames of America, the Society of Daughters of Founders and Patriots of America, the Daughters of the American Revolution, the Chilton Club, and the New Riding Club of Boston. Mrs. Quincy's eldest daughter, Dorothy, who is Mrs. Frederic Russell Nourse of Dedham, Massachusetts, was head of the Red Cross work in Dedham during the war. The youngest daughter, Elinor Quincy, Mrs. Claude De Witt Simpson, now of Cathedral, Colorado, was also active in the Boston Red Cross and during the epidemic of influenza in 1918–1919, nursed at Doctor Brooks' Hospital in Boston.

MEYER, ANNIE NATHAN (Mrs. Alfred Meyer), author, daughter of Robert Weeks and Anne Augusta (Florence) Nathan, was born in New York City, February 19, 1867. On February 15, 1887, she was married in New York to Doctor Alfred Meyer, the son of Isaac and Mathilda (Langenbach) Meyer, who was born in New York, June 18, 1854, and who received his degree of A.B. from Columbia University in 1874, and his doctorate in medicine from the College of Physicians and Surgeons of Columbia University in 1877. He is a leading consulting physician of New York, and is attached to the staffs of several consulting hospitals. Doctor and Mrs. Meyer are the parents of one daughter, Margaret Nathan Meyer. Mrs. Meyer was educated entirely by self-directed reading, and prepared herself to take examinations at Columbia University the year before the founding of Barnard College, in 1889. Efforts to gain for young women the advantages of Columbia College had been made at intervals since 1883, when several qualified young women applied for admission to the college, and one, a graduate of the University of Michigan, for admission to the Medical School. A plea on their behalf was made before the Faculty by Mrs. Lillian Devereux Blake, on the ground that the Charter of the college declared that it was "founded for the education of the youth of the City" and that "youth" includes both sexes. President Barnard and several of the faculty favored the admission of women as students, but the Committee on Education decided that any action was inexpedient. In December, 1876, a memorial was presented to the Trustees of Columbia College by Sorosis, a well-known New York woman's club, asking that young women should be admitted to the college classes. The memorial was laid on the table by an unanimous vote. Up to 1879 women were informally admitted to the lectures of

certain professors during regular class hours. This was forbidden in 1879, not because any harm resulted, but because it was discovered that the statutes forbade any but regularly matriculated students to attend lectures. This law had no reference to women, but the Trustees declined to change the letter of the law and the women were excluded. However a course of examination was offered to women by the College, and Annie Nathan Meyer was one of the first to present herself under this rule. Mrs. Meyer was also the first to approach the Trustees with a plan for the founding of an affiliated college for women. Former petitions had asked for co-education, but no one before had suggested the founding of an "annex" as it was called. The petition to the Trustees for official sanction to open Barnard College was based on the article by Mrs. Meyer in *The Nation* of January 21, 1883, which was subsequently placed in the corner stone of the first Barnard College building. For some time Mrs. Meyer had been working to conquer the prejudice against the higher education of women, and with that end in view had edited a series of articles on the subject in the *New York Evening Post*. The new college for women was sanctioned by the Board of Trustees of Columbia College in March, 1889, and the college was chartered by the Regents of the University of the State of New York the following July and formally opened the following October, appropriately named Barnard College in grateful tribute to the late president of Columbia College, a pioneer in his belief in the education of women. Mrs. Meyer not only wrote the memorial to the Trustees, signed the hundreds of signatures to it, interviewed the Trustees personally, but also, herself, raised the greater part of the college's funds during its first four years, and gathered together its first Board of Trustees. For many years Mrs. Meyer was a director of the Aguilar Free Library, since absorbed by the New York Public Library. She has written articles for all the leading magazines of the country. She is the author of *Woman's Work in America* (1891), *Helen Brent, M.D.* (1893), *My Park Book* (1898), *Annys* (1901), *The Dominant Sex* (play 1911), and *The Dreamer* (play 1912). Among her magazine articles have been many on American Art. One, appearing in the *London Studio*, was the first to recognize the high quality of American landscapists. She is a member of the Daughters of the American Revolution, the New York Drama League, the American Federation of Art, the Lyceum Club of London, the Barnard Club, the Adirondack League, the Authors' League of America, the MacDowell Club, the National League of American Pen Women, many war work committees, and is Chairman of the New York Section of the Emergency Committee of the American Home Economics Association.

POTTER, FLORENCE HOLLISTER DANGERFIELD (Mrs. Alexander Potter), lawyer, was born in Auburn, New York, August 14, 1868. Her father, Francis S. Dangerfield, inventor and mechanical engineer (born March 31, 1840; died January 5, 1900), was descended from an English family that has been in this country since about 1650. He married Sarah Hollister (born in Genoa, New York, January 13, 1841; died in Jamestown, Rhode Island, April 20, 1918), a descendant of Lieutenant John Hollister, a native of Somersetshire, England, who located in Wethersfield, Connecticut, in 1642, and later settled at South Glastonbury, Connecticut. The line is traced from his son John, through five generations, Thomas, Charles, Ichabod, Francis, and John Weeks Hollister, to Sarah Hollister Dangerfield. All the women of these families were splendid wives and mothers, women of Puritan stock, possessing integrity, energy, sterling principles, and the courage of true pioneers. Mrs. Potter received her education in the Auburn public schools, and at Cornell University where she won a scholarship. She afterwards studied law at New York University, New York City, where she was graduated LL.B. During one of her years there she was the President of her class, which was composed of ninety-three men and three women. She has since taken special courses of study at various institutions in the United States and abroad, bearing on engineering law and contracts. Mrs. Potter was the second woman admitted to the Bar of the City of New York, and one of her first law engagements was with the City of New York. She has been counsel for the New York Chapter of the Daughters of the American Revolution. She has the distinction of having introduced a suffrage bill in the New York Legislature for the Equal Suffrage Society. On August 12, 1896, in Auburn, New York, she married Alexander Potter (born at Gibraltar, January 18, 1866). He is a consulting civil engineer, specializing in sanitation and hydraulics, and has designed and supervised more than a hundred installations for cities and for private companies in the United States, Mexico, Canada, and the West Indies. Mrs. Potter has been associated with her husband in his engineering work in Mexico, Cuba, Canada, and the United States, assisting him legally, and has conducted cases for him in seven states of the Union and in Mexico. Through her ability in her specialty, she has promoted and developed large water-power plants in Mexico. She has mining and engineering interests there and elsewhere. Mrs. Potter has also worked in behalf of municipal improvements, anti-child-labor and uniform divorce legislation, and the settling of immigrants on farm lands instead of in the large cities.

She was associate editor of the magazine, *City Government*, which was succeeded by *The Municipal Journal*, and has contributed to many publications, both popular and technical. Her wide experience as a traveler has developed a love of exploring wild and strange lands. When at home, in New York City, she finds her recreation in motoring and gardening. Mrs. Potter is a member of the College and University Alumnae Society, the

New York County Bar Association, the Woman's Press Club of New York, the Woman Lawyer's Club, the Society for Prevention of Cruelty to Children, the Society for the Prevention of Cruelty to Animals, and other philanthropic and social organizations.

DAVIS, MIRIAM MADURO PEIXOTTO (Mrs. Michael Marks Davis), daughter of Daniel L. M. and Rachel M. Seixas Peixotto, was born in New York City, February 4, 1842, and died there April 1, 1923. She was survived by her husband, ninety-one years old, six children, fifteen grandchildren and ten great-grandchildren. She was a descendant of a very ancient family, the traditions of which date back in Spain to 1492. The name of the male line was originally Maduro, but upon marriage with a member of the Peixotto family the names were joined, and the latter became the surname of the descendants. In the latter part of the seventeenth century certain members of the family moved to Holland, and the names appear in Amsterdam in the public records. The ancestor of the American branch established himself in Curaçao, West Indies, where Moses Levi Maduro Peixotto was born in 1767. He married and became a very successful merchant, the owner of a fleet of ships. Upon the death of his wife, he traveled, and during a visit to Amsterdam, met and married his second wife, Judith Lopez Zalzedo. They returned to Curaçao, where he continued with success in his business enterprises. In 1807 he sailed for New York on one of his own vessels, landing on June 11th. Eventually, he established the headquarters of his business in New York and became an American citizen. During the latter part of his life he was Rabbi of Congregation Shearith Israel, retaining this office until his death, which occurred in New York in 1828. His eldest son, Doctor Daniel Levy Maduro Peixotto, a physician, scholar, author, and philanthropist, was born in Amsterdam, July 18, 1800, and died in New York in 1843. His early education was obtained in Curaçao,

but, accompanying his father to New York, he entered Columbia College at the age of sixteen, and received his doctorate in medicine in 1819. He was a man of rare attainments, a master of many languages, and a physician who combined skill and erudition. He had a large private practice, and held many offices in the medical world. He was editor of the *New York Medical and Physical Journal*, and an editor of Gregory's Practice, published in 1825-1826. He was President of the New York Medical Society, Secretary of the New York Academy of Medicine in 1825, one of the founders and a Fellow of the College of Physicians and Surgeons of Columbia University, and, later, served as Master in the Masonic order of Washington Lodge No. 21. For a time he was professor and Dean of the Faculty, at Willoughby Medical College, Cleveland, Ohio, but resigned to resume practice in New York City. He married, March 19, 1823, Rachel Mendez Seixas of the ancient family of that name, which originated in Portugal. Abraham Mendez Seixas, his wife, Abigail, and their family removed to London, where the father died in 1738. Their son, Isaac Mendez Seixas, born in Lisbon, Portugal, September 5, 1709, was with his parents in London, and removed to New York in 1738, thus becoming the founder of the family in America. He established a successful mercantile business, and, in 1765, settled in Newport, Rhode Island, where he died November 5, 1781. He married Rachel, the daughter of Moses (also named Raphael) Levy. The latter was born in Spain in 1665, and was the owner of many vessels engaged in trade with North Africa. He settled in New York about 1705 and continued to send his ships to foreign waters, becoming a man of importance and prominent in the early affairs of the city. His daughter, Rachel Seixas, died in New York, May 12, 1797. The line is continued through a son, Lieutenant Benjamin Mendez Seixas, who was born in Newport, Rhode Island, in 1747, and who removed to New York, where he died August

16, 1817. He was a man of distinction, a large property holder, a founder of the New York Stock Exchange, and an officer in the American Revolution. He married Zipporah, the daughter of Hayman and Sloë Levy. Hayman Levy was a wealthy business man, engaged in the fur trade, the first employer of John Jacob Astor. He died in 1789, and his wife, Sloë, died April 5, 1811, at the age of eighty-three. Rachel, the daughter of Lieutenant Benjamin and Zipporah Seixas, was born in 1798 and married Doctor Daniel L. M. Peixotto.

Miriam Peixotto was educated in New York City and was married to Michael Marks Davis on October 17, 1866, by the Reverend Jacques M. Lyons of Congregation Shearith Israel. Five daughters and two sons were born from this union: Constance Davis, born August 8, 1867, married to Benjamin Mordecai; Eva Davis, born September 15, 1868, married to W. Irving Davis; Alice Davis, born August 4, 1870, married to Mortimer M. Menken; Minnie Davis, born September 2, 1872, deceased; Estelle Davis, born January 11, 1875, married to Edwin Goldsmith; Goodman Davis, born June 27, 1876, married to Benveneda Brickner, and Michael M. Davis, born November 19, 1879, married to Janet Hays. Benjamin and Constance (Davis) Mordecai are the parents of Eva, married to Sidney Cardozo (parents of Harold, Constance, Lucile, and Margaret Lieber), Constance, married to Danforth Cardozo (parents of Nancy Cardozo), Kate, married to Clarence Lee (parents of Barbara and Benjamin Lee), and Allan Mordecai Edwin and Estelle (Davis) Goldsmith are the parents of Frances D. and Elizabeth Goldsmith; Goodman and Benveneda (Brickner) Davis are the parents of Walter B. and Richard G. Davis; and Michael M. and Janet (Hays) Davis are the parents of Paul, Burnet, and Michael M. Davis.

Miriam Peixotto Davis devoted the major part of her life to the upbringing of her children, devoting untiring service to their welfare and guiding their education. She celebrated her golden wedding anniversary on October 17, 1916, at the Hotel St. Regis, New York, surrounded by two hundred of her friends, children, grandchildren, and great-grandchildren.

MENKEN, ALICE DAVIS (Mrs. Mortimer M. Menken), social worker, was born in New York City, August 4, 1870. Her father, Michael Marks Davis, was born in Philadelphia, Pennsylvania, June 29, 1832. His father, Goodman Davis, was born in London in 1798 of English parents, and his mother Rebecca (Marks) Davis, was the daughter of Michael Marks, who was born November 11, 1761, at Tower Hill, London, and died in Philadelphia, February 11, 1829. Michael Marks was married at Newport, Rhode Island, October 11, 1786, to Johaveth, the daughter of Moses and Rachel (Mears) Isaacs. The latter was born at Swansey, Massachusetts, June 17, 1767, and died January 17, 1852. Moses Isaacs was the son of Abram Isaacs, who came from England to New York towards the end of the seventeenth century. Michael Marks Davis was married in New York, October 17, 1866, to Miriam M. Peixotto, who is descended from Spanish and Portuguese Sephardic-Jewish families that trace their ancestry to the tenth century in Spain and Portugal, and, were prominent in the seats of learning in those countries.

Mrs. Menken is a member of the Congregation Shearith Israel, New York City, the oldest Jewish congregation in America, established in 1655, among the founders of which were her ancestors. Other ancestors, a century later, took part in the Colonial Wars and the American Revolution. She received her education in New York City, attending Gardner Institute, 607 Fifth Avenue, for nine years, from which she was graduated May 12, 1887, as salutatorian of her class, and where she continued in post-graduate classes in French literature, history, and rhetoric. On October 17, 1893 she was married in New

York City to Mortimer Morange Menken, counsellor-at-law, who was born in New York August 23, 1867. His parents, Jules and Cornelia Menken, were born in the United States of Dutch ancestry. He is a graduate of science and law of the College of the City of New York and Columbia University. Mr. and Mrs. Menken's only child, Harold Davis Menken, was born in New York, January 9, 1895. He was graduated from Horace Mann School in 1911 and from Columbia University in 1914 with the degree of Bachelor of Science. He is a member of the Society of the Sons of the American Revolution. When the United States entered the World War in April, 1917, he at once enlisted in the Navy. He was trained at Pelham Bay Park and Annapolis, receiving his commission as ensign, after which he was placed in command of a submarine chaser in the Gulf of Mexico. At the close of the war he became associated with a large manufacturing concern. On April 23, 1919, he married Harriet Sinton of New York.

In 1890 Mrs. Menken began community service, organizing clubs and classes for the religious instruction of the youth in the settlements of the lower east side of New York, and conducting the relief work of the Sisterhood of the Spanish and Portuguese Synagogue in coöperation with the United Hebrew Charities. She continued this and other forms of philanthropic activity until 1901, when she became President of the Sisterhood, of which, with the exception of three years, she has been president continuously. The Sisterhood's scope of work was enlarged in 1910 to include rescue work for Jewish women arraigned in the city magistrates' courts. When, in that year, the Night Court for women was established, at the request of the judges Mrs. Menken formed a committee to work there for the rescue and uplift of unfortunate women in coöperation with the city probation department. In making a study of community agencies in New York, she found a special need for probation work for girls over sixteen years, and offered her personal service in the field of delinquency, in which activity she has continued uninterruptedly ever since. In order to become acquainted with the various phases of rescue work and methods to meet the problems, Mrs. Menken surveyed conditions relative to courts and institutions in European cities, and has traveled and lectured in the United States, organizing the Big Sister movement in various sections, so as to include rescue and probation work. In 1916 she received, under John Collier, her diploma from the New York Training School for Community Workers, which she entered in order to procure a professional training in social work. Finding that service for the after-care of Jewish women paroled and discharged from penal and correctional institutions in New York City and State was undeveloped, she was appointed Chairman for two years of a committee in the New York Section of the Council of Jewish Women, specializing in the work for delinquent women paroled from the Workhouse and Penitentiary on Blackwell's Island and the State Prison at Auburn, New York. She has since continued this work as Chairman of the Department of Court, Probation, Parole, and After-care in the Central Committeee for Friendly Aid to Jewish Girls, which was organized in 1919 and on April 1st of that year took over the activities of the Probation Committee of the Sisterhood of the Spanish and Portuguese Synagogues. From its formation in 1910, the Committee, with Mrs. Menken as chairman, personally supervised 413 delinquent women who were on probation. The reports published by Mrs. Menken throw valuable light on the causes of delinquency, give statistics of the nationality, age, literacy, and health of the women, and indicate marked success in the reformation of a majority of the probationers. Letters received by the Committee show a deep sense of gratitude on the part of those lifted out of the underworld and a determination to persevere in a life of usefulness. Mrs. Menken frequently visits prisons and reformatories and gives intensive personal service to the unfortunate women paroled or discharged therefrom. She receives hearty coöperation from the Judges, the Department of Correction, and the Parole Commission, as well as from the office of the District Attorney. Prominently identified with correctional homes and institutions of New York City and State, she is on the Board of Directors of the Florence Crittenton League, a shelter for women, and of the Inwood House, a reformatory. She is interested in the New York Training School for Girls at Hudson and in Cedar Knolls School at Hawthorne. In August, 1920, she was appointed by Governor Alfred E. Smith to serve on the Board of Managers of the New York State Reformatory for Women at Bedford Hills.

The problem of meeting the religious, social, and educational needs of the ever increasing number of Sephardic Jews immigrating from Turkey, Greece, Syria, and Arabia, was undertaken by the Sisterhood of the Spanish and Portuguese Synagogue under Mrs. Menken's direction. This work, started in 1903, resulted in the establishment in 1918 of a neighborhood centre at 133 Eldridge Street, New York, in the district where these colonies live. It is the only settlement house in the community where a fully equipped Synagogue is established with a seating capacity for 350 worshippers and where services are held three times every week day, on the Sabbath and on all holy days. The members of the Synagogue are organized into a Brotherhood, through which they receive free medical service and supplies. The educational and recreational facilities include a Talmud Torah, with 190 children on its roll, a kindergarten conducted on the roof garden, and classes in English for adults, both under the Board of Education; classes in sewing and community singing, a library, a gymnasium, and a dance hall. In the summer, children are sent to the country and weekly excursions are given mothers and children to nearby seaside resorts and parks. Clothing is supplied to the destitute, deformed children are taken to the hospital for treat-

ment, and mothers are taught the laws of hygiene and food values. The Americanization work is thorough, as shown by the fact that thirty-one men from the clubs of the Sisterhood served in the World War. In 1918 Mrs. Menken enlisted in the Motor Corps of America for active duty in ambulance and hospital service. She has published articles in *The Survey* on subjects relative to community work, the pamphlets, *In the Shadow of the Underworld*, and *The Rehabilitation of the Morally Handicapped*, and a synopsis of her lecture courses on *Can We Help our Unfortunate Sister and How?* In 1919 she made a survey of correctional institutions dealing with delinquent women for the Committee of Fourteen, of which she is an active member. In coöperation with the Council of Jewish Women she compiled a *Book of Prayer for Jewish Girls* and in 1921 she published a manual, *Meeting the Problems of Maladjusted Youth*. In addition to the organizations already mentioned Mrs. Menken is a member of the Committees on Delinquency and Membership in the Federation of Jewish Philanthropic Societies in New York City, the Jewish Big Sisters, the Jewish Protectory and Aid Society, the Society for the Improved Instruction of Deaf-Mutes, the Women's City Club, and the Society for Political Study, of which she was President from 1911 to 1913. She is Second Vice-President of the Post-Parliament Club, in which she was at one time chairman of the Parliamentary Law Committee; a member of the Speakers Bureau of the Republican County Committee; and a life member of the Knickerbocker Chapter of the Daughters of the American Revolution.

PUTNAM, BRENDA, sculptor, daughter of Herbert and Elizabeth (Munroe) Putnam, was born in Minneapolis, Minnesota, in 1890. Her father, well known as the Librarian of Congress, came of an English family early settled in Salem, Massachusetts. His sister, Doctor Mary Putnam, the wife of Doctor Abraham Jacobi, was the first woman to be admitted as a student in the École de Médecine, Paris.

Miss Putnam was educated in private schools in the United States and abroad. At the age of four she began the study of music, which has always been her principal recreation. For two and a half years she was pianist in the Edith Rubel Trio, which gave chamber concerts in New York, Boston, Washington, Buffalo, and other American cities.

She began the study of art at the age of twelve, and until her twentieth year studied sculpture as part of her school work, as well as at the Boston Museum of Fine Arts under Bela Pratt, and at the Art Students' League, New York, under James Earle Fraser. Since 1910 she has had a studio in New York. She has exhibited at the National Academy of Design, New York; the Academy of Fine Arts, Philadelphia; the International Exposition at Rome (1911); the Architectural League of New York; the Chicago Art Institute, where she received honorable mention (1917) for her fountain, *Water Lily Baby;* the Albright Gallery, Buffalo; and other leading exhibitions. Among her best known works are the marble group *Charmydes* (1915), in the Metropolitan Museum of Art, New York; the fountain *Baby Bird* (1915), owned by the late Jacob Schiff; the marble Memorial Statue to Anne Simon (1917), in the Rock Creek Cemetery, Washington, District of Columbia; the fountain *Playing Children* (1920), in Cleveland, Ohio; the *Thieving Faun*, designed for the garden of the late John F. Dodge of Detroit, Michigan; and the portrait of Sir Johnston Forbes-Robertson, as Hamlet, which was destroyed in the New York Architectural League fire in 1920. Miss Putnam is a member of the American Federation of Arts, and of the National Sculpture Society.

AUBERT, MARION BRAGG, philanthropist, daughter of Caius C. and Eugenia H. (Hofer) Bragg, was born in Cincinnati, Ohio. Her earliest ancestor in this country was James Bragg, who settled in Maine early in the eighteenth century. Her grandfather, Caleb S. Bragg, was the first President of the American Book Company, and to him the school text-book world is greatly indebted. He was the first to develop the idea of printing, at moderate costs, good texts of the classics for school use. Her mother was the daughter of Charles S. Hofer, of distinguished French ancestry.

Mrs. Aubert was educated at Dobbs Ferry and later attended Mme. Beck's school in Paris, France. In 1904, she was married to H. Langdon Laws, son of Harry L. Laws, of Cincinnati. They were the parents of one son, Eugene Langdon Laws (born in 1908). Later, she was married to L. C. Aubert.

Immediately on the outbreak of the World War, Mrs. Aubert, who was then Mrs. Laws, prepared herself for service in France, where, at Auteuil, she founded and maintained, throughout the war, a hospital for little children. It was known as the "Maison des Touts Petits," home for all babies. Before going to France, and while taking a thorough course in nursing, she constantly shipped supplies for this home. After reaching France, she nursed the desperately wounded in the military hospital at Neuilly, Base No. 1. Not only did she nurse and assist at operations in this hospital, but was, for two months, the one nurse for three wards of sixteen men each. She also served as a nurse in the "Home" as well as director. In addition to these two really great undertakings, she helped to start a Rest House for American officers in Paris, under the Red Cross, which was opened on Thanksgiving Day, 1917.

Mrs. Aubert is a member of the Santa Barbara Country Club and also of the Cincinnati Country Club.

EVANS, MARY ELIZABETH, (Mrs. Henry D. Sharpe), daughter of William Edward George and Fanny (Riegel) Evans, was born in Syracuse, New York. Under the name of "Mary Elizabeth" she has the distinction of being one of the youngest successful merchants in the world. She was educated in the public schools of Syracuse.

When she was but fifteen, the family, consisting of Mary Elizabeth, her widowed mother, and three younger children, were thrown on their own resources as a result of the death of her grandfather, Judge Henry Riegel. As the eldest of the children, Mary Elizabeth, without capital or business experience, was confronted with the problem of contributing to the common support. She was already well known as an expert in candy-making and it was suggested that she try to use her talent commercially. She accordingly made a selection of her specialties, packed them attractively, labelled them with her name, and brought them, as samples of what she could do, to a party given by one of her friends. The guests were as pleased with the candies as they were with the little girl's courage. They gave her many orders, and became at once her loyal advertisers. Thus began an enterprise now famous throughout the United States. As the business increased, Mary Elizabeth enlisted the services of her mother and her two sisters, a partnership of four earnest, energetic women, who still constitute the firm of "Mary Elizabeth." The next step was to install a "Help Yourself" booth in the arcade of the University Building in Syracuse, New York. This solved the problem of how to enlarge the selling field without incurring the expense of a shop, which Mary Elizabeth could not as yet afford. Here the candies were put on sale in a small and attractive booth, before which was hung the sign:

"Open these doors,
Take what you will,
Leave cost of goods taken,
Make your change from my till.
Respecting Customers' Honor,
Mary Elizabeth."

The policy thus expressed was maintained in spite of the advice of older persons, and the results justified the young girl's faith in human nature. It was not long before Mary Elizabeth was able to afford a candy shop, which proved a paying venture. From these modest beginnings has grown the large business with headquarters on Fifth Avenue, New York City, and with stores and tea rooms in many other cities. Mary Elizabeth herself is the active head of this enterprise.

During the World War, when Food Administrator Hoover issued his conservation orders, Miss Evans was not satisfied with merely signifying her intention to comply with them. She called upon Mr. Hoover, in Washington, and informed herself in detail regarding his policy. Foods that could be shipped abroad for the use of the Army were to be devoted to that purpose; only those that could not be transported were to be used at home. Conservation in this sense meant the saving of food, not necessarily the saving of money, and did not involve the reduction of business. For instance, beet and cane sugar was reserved for Army Consumption; but sweets might be sold if made without sugar. Miss Evans ingeniously originated many recipes for candy with honey, corn syrup, maple syrup, fruits, and nuts, but without sugar, and these candies were offered whenever possible. Similarly, she devised meatless and wheatless dishes tempting and nourishing for her tea-rooms, while still conforming to the Administration's rulings. As soon as she had worked out methods of conservation for her business, Mary Elizabeth volunteered with the Red Cross for service in France. During 1917–1918 she organized diet kitchens for the American Red Cross and Army Hospitals in Paris and its environs. These centers sometimes prepared special diets for as many as 40,000 men in one day. The magnitude of this work did not prevent Mary Elizabeth from taking an individual interest in the men, and a personal satisfaction in every case of restored health with the aid of her nourishing food. Not only during her service as a Red Cross Worker, but throughout her career, Mary Elizabeth has won the esteem and affection of all who have come in touch with her. She is a cheerful, kindly employer with an enthusiasm that inspires all her workwomen. Mary Elizabeth is the author of *War Time Recipes* (1917) and *My Candy Secrets* (1919). In addition to the Red Cross, she belongs to the St. Cecelia Club. She is fond of horseback riding and other outdoor sports. On June 23, 1920, she married, in New York City, Henry D. Sharpe of Providence, Rhode Island.

LOOMIS, JULIA STIMSON (Mrs. Henry P. Loomis), was born in New York City. Her father, Henry Clark Stimson, was descended from Jeremiah Stimson, a native of England, who located at Dedham, Massachusetts, in the early part of the eighteenth century. Her mother, Julia Maria Atterbury, was descended from a Huguenot family that came to New York after the revocation of the Edict of Nantes. One of her ancestors in this line was Elias Boudinot, President of Congress in 1783, signer of the treaty of peace with Great Britain, and judge of the Supreme Court of New Jersey.

Miss Stimson was educated in private schools in New York. On February 9, 1887, she was married in New York to Henry Patterson Loomis, a physician and a professor of medicine. During the World War Mrs. Loomis was Vice-Chairman of the Tuxedo Park Chapter of the American Red Cross; Chairman and Treasurer of the American Ouvroir which distributed funds for the relief of the orphans of men killed in the French Army and Navy; Vice-President of the American Allies' Coöperative Committee; and founder and a director of the Tuxedo Park Ouvroir for making surgical dressings for the French Army.

She is a member of the Colonial Dames of America, the Colony Club, and the Tuxedo Club. Doctor and Mrs. Loomis are the parents of two sons: Major Alfred Lee Loomis who married Ellen H. Farnsworth, and Henry Stimson Loomis; and one daughter, Julia Atterbury Loomis, who married Captain Landon K. Thorne.

KOHLER, ROSE, sculptor and painter, daughter of the Reverend Kaufman and Johanna (Einhorn) Kohler, was born in Chicago, Illinois, in 1873. Her father, the son of Moritz and Babette Kohler, was born in Fürth, Bavaria, May 10, 1843, and received the degree of Ph.D. from the University of Erlangen in 1867. In 1869 he was called to Beth El Congregation, Detroit, Michigan; became rabbi of the Sinai Congregation, Chicago, in 1871; and from 1879 to 1903 was Minister of Temple Beth El, New York. Since 1903 he has been President of the Hebrew Union College, Cincinnati, Ohio. He has been a leader in Reformed Judaism and a writer of many books and articles on Judaism, ethics, and Biblical criticism, as well as Editor of the Departments of Theology and Philosophy of the *Jewish Encyclopaedia*. In 1870 he married Johanna, daughter of the Reverend Doctor David Einhorn, born in 1848. Doctor Einhorn came from Germany to Baltimore, Maryland, in 1854, and was thereafter a rabbi in Philadelphia and New York.

Miss Kohler was educated in public and private schools in New York and at the Art Academy of Cincinnati, where she has been actively interested in artistic, philanthropic, and educational matters. She was at one time Historian of the Woman's Art Club of Cincinnati, is a member of the Art Committee of the Woman's City Club of Cincinnati, and has been Chairman of the National Committee on Religious Schools of the Council of Jewish Women. Miss Kohler has painted portraits of Mr. L. Rothenberg, Doctor Kohler, Mrs. Kohler, and others, and has executed bas-relief portraits of Doctor Solomon Schechter (1918), and Doctor Kohler (1919). In 1919 she also modelled a pair of book-ends entitled *The Talmudic Scholar*. One of her most notable sculptures is the bas-relief medallion (1920), *The Synagogue*, a symbolic treatment of the idea expressed in the phrase: "My house shall be called a House of Prayer for all people." This sentence is inscribed upon an arch over the dominating central figure of the Synagogue, allegorically presented as a young woman, crowned and with sceptre, and holding the Scroll of the Law in each hand. At the left of the medallion is a group which represents the Congregation. An old man, his head covered and his shoulders wrapped in the praying shawl, announces the new era on the ram's horn. Before him are children with books who symbolize Instruction. To the right is a group expressive of Worship. Behind the youth in an attitude of prayer stands a pulpit on which is the Seven-Branched Candlestick, the symbol of Light. In the background is a priest with hands raised in benediction and a cantor chanting from a scroll. The whole is strong and well-balanced and the countenances of the figures show faith and trust in the future. In addition to the Woman's Art Club and the Woman's City Club, Miss Kohler is a member of the Three Arts Club and the Crafters of Cincinnati.

WHITE, ELIZA MATILDA CHANDLER (Mrs. Stephen Van Culen White), the daughter of Hiram and Juliana (Humiston) Chandler, was born in Marietta, Ohio, May 1, 1831. Her father was a descendant of Captain Miles Standish, who came to Plymouth, Massachusetts, on the *Mayflower* in 1620, and his wife, Barbara. Their son, Alexander, married Sarah, the daughter of John and Priscilla (Mullins) Alden, both *Mayflower* Pilgrims. Elizabeth, the daughter of Alexander and Sarah Standish, married Samuel Delano and their daughter, Elizabeth, was the wife of Joseph Chandler, 3d. Their son, Benjamin Chandler (killed at the Battle of Bennington, Vermont), and his wife, Elizabeth Jeffries, were the parents of Joseph Chandler, who married Patient Mary Andrews, and their son was Hiram Chandler, born in Vermont, September 4, 1797. Juliana Humiston, Hiram

Chandler's wife, was born April 24, 1803. She was descended from Matthias Hitchcock, one of the founders of New Haven, Connecticut, who came from England to Boston, Massachusetts, on the *Susan and Ellen* in 1635. His son, John Hitchcock, married Abigail Merriman. They were the parents of Matthias, who married Thankful Andrews, and the grandparents of Hannah Hitchcock, whose husband was James Humiston of New Haven, Connecticut, the son of Henry Humiston. Jason Humiston, the son of James and Hannah, married Amy Peck, and they were the parents of Juliana, the wife of Hiram Chandler.

Eliza Matilda Chandler was educated at Monticello Seminary, Godfrey, Illinois, and taught school until her marriage on February 24, 1857, at Grafton, Illinois, to Stephen Van Culen White, a lawyer who attained wide prominence in his profession and was during the latter part of his life an influential member of the New York Stock Exchange. Mr. White was born in Chathan County, North Carolina, August 1, 1831, son of Hiram White and his wife, Julia Brewer, who was a descendant of Oliver Cromwell.

During their early married life Mr. and Mrs. White lived in Missouri at a time when the question of slavery was causing much excitement and public feeling. Mrs. White favored the abolition of slavery and strove personally to raise the educational status of the negroes by giving to all whom she could reach lessons in reading. She bravely persisted in her teaching, although at the time, it was a prison offense in Missouri. The pleasure in helping, in a practical way, the downtrodden and the needy characterized Mrs. White's entire life.

After a short period of residence in Des Moines, Iowa, Mr. and Mrs. White moved to Brooklyn, New York, and Mrs. White continued to be among the first to aid any worthy charity. In 1881 she founded the Brooklyn Home for Consumptives, and, assisted by her husband, raised the greater part of its endowment fund of $100,000. At the time of Mrs. White's death in 1907 the institution owned its own spacious grounds and buildings and was caring for more than 110 men, women, and children. Mrs. White's ability to give practical assistance was also evidenced in the many forms of patriotic work in which she engaged. When, in 1858, the Mt. Vernon Ladies' Association of the Union was formed to purchase Mt. Vernon as a national monument, Mrs. White worked for several years to aid in raising the fund. She was the founder of the Fort Greene Chapter (Brooklyn) of the Daughters of the American Revolution, which grew to have a membership of over two hundred, was at the head of the Prison Ship Martyrs Committee of the National Society of the Daughters of the American Revolution, and with the aid of her husband secured an appropriation from New York State and another from the United States government, and received a sufficient sum by private subscriptions, to erect the monument in Fort Greene Park, Brooklyn, New York. She was a member of the Society of Mayflower Descendants, the Colonial Daughters of the Seventeenth Century, and many other patriotic and literary societies. Mr. and Mrs. White were the parents of two children: Jennie Chandler White, wife of Franklin W. Hopkins of Alpine, New Jersey (born in Des Moines, Iowa, March 10, 1860), and Arthur White (born in Brooklyn, New York, August 2, 1865).

WUPPERMANN, JOSEPHINE WRIGHT HANCOX (Mrs. George Wuppermann), manufacturer, daughter of Joseph Wright and Eliza (Hovey) Hancox, was born in Jersey City, New Jersey. Her father was descended from James Hancox, an English merchant of Richmond, Yorkshire, and the owner of several vessels plying between England and America in the seventeenth century. His only son, Edward, commanded one of the vessels which was lost off Block Island in 1689. Edward was so chagrined by this mishap that he allowed his father to believe that he was also lost. After a time spent on Block Island, he settled at Stonington, Connecticut. He married a widow, Mary (Winslow) Hancock, and died in 1755, at the age of eighty-five years. Their son, Edward Hancox, Jr. (born in 1714), married Lucy Cheeseborough, a granddaughter of William Cheeseborough, the first settler of Stonington. Edward died in 1803. Their son, Edward, 3d (born in 1744; died in 1837), married Sarah Sheffield, and their son, Edward, 4th (born in Stonington, in 1772), married Nancy Miner. Edward Hancox, 3d, was the owner of vessels trading with the West Indies, but the War of 1812, which closed the Atlantic ports, ruined him and he emigrated with his family to Central New York, and was drowned in Lake Ontario in 1824. His son, Joseph Wright Hancox, Mrs. Wupperman's father, was born in Stonington, Connecticut, October 30, 1812. Like many of his ancestors, he became a successful ship-owner. Beginning his career in Albany, New York, when only twelve years of age, he prospered, until he was the owner of a line of steamboats on the Hudson River running between New York and Troy, of other lines on the Orinoco and the Japura Rivers in South America, and also of a line of ocean steamers connecting La Guayra and Trinidad. Commodore Hancox, as he was known, broke the monopoly of steamboat traffic on the Hudson River, showing great courage in the face of opposition to his program of just rates. He displayed similar courage during the Civil War, when, in command of one of his own boats, he ran the blockade from Fortress Monroe to New Orleans under charter from the Federal Government. In 1851 he entered politics in New Jersey and was elected a member of the State Legislature, where he was one of the first to advocate prohibition. He married Eliza Hovey at Albany, New York, in April, 1832, and died at Asbury Park, New Jersey, September 12, 1900.

Mrs. Wuppermann was educated at St. Mary's Hall, Burlington, New Jersey, and at Mrs. Hoffman's school in New York City. Thereafter she continued her linguistic studies with a resident governess, learning to speak both French and German fluently. She was married in 1870 at the Church of the Incarnation, New York, to George Wuppermann (born in Bolivar, Venezuela, March 22, 1838; died at Hastings-on-Hudson, New York, June 12, 1915), son of Adolf and Zoyla (Gomez) Wuppermann. Her husband began his business career as a clerk in his father's import and export business in Hamburg, Germany. Later he founded the banking house of J. N. Harriman and Company in Trinidad, and at the same time became General Agent for Doctor J. G. B. Siegert and Sons, manufacturers of Angostura Bitters. In 1878 Mr. Wuppermann established the business in the United States, first under the name of J. W. Hancox, and later as the J. W. Wupperman Angostura Bitters Agency, Inc. Of this corporation Mrs. Wuppermann was President and Treasurer, and her eldest son, A. E. Wuppermann, was Secretary and General Manager. Mrs. Wuppermann's far-sighted policy has gained a wider popularity for this famous medicine.

Always interested in new methods of education, Mrs. Wuppermann early recognized the value of the phonograph as a means of teaching languages, and the Cortina Academy, founded in 1882, of which she was President for several years, gained academic recognition for the excellence of its methods. She also gives personal attention to the management of her real estate in New York City. Mrs. Wuppermann is a member of the Rota Parliamentary Club and the Philharmonic Society, and has always given aid to charities and benevolent activities. She is most interested in the Harlem Young Women's Christian Association, of which she was President for many years.

Mr. and Mrs. Wuppermann were the parents of eleven children, three of whom died in infancy; A. Edward Wuppermann, Eliza Hancox, wife of James Stuart Herrman; Zoyla, wife of Clarence N. Cook; Marguerite, wife of R. W. Smith; Ralph and Frank Wuppermann, who act under the stage name of Morgan; Josephine W. Hancox Wuppermann; and Carlos Siegert Wuppermann. Carlos S. Wuppermann, who was born in New York City, November 29, 1887, and died "in line of duty" at Trier, Germany, April 15, 1919, was educated at Columbia University and the University of Leipsig, and was the author of many poems, plays, and stories of a high order of excellence. His vaudeville sketch, *Laughing Harry*, was produced with success in the winter of 1917. He had already won a name for himself as an actor, but in June, 1917, he enlisted in Base Hospital No. 1, Bellevue Unit, and was sent overseas, being transferred in 1918 at his own request to the Intelligence Department. He did excellent service in France, and was attached to the Army of Occupation at the time of his death.

DRAPER, HELEN FIDELIA HOFFMAN (Mrs. William Kinnicutt Draper), daughter of Richard and Fidelia Marshall (Lamson) Hoffman, was born in New York City in November, 1871. Her father (born in Manchester, England, in May, 1831; died in New York in August, 1909) came from Manchester to New York about 1848. He was the son of Richard Hoffman (born in London in 1803; died in Manchester, in 1891); grandson of Andrew Hoffman (born in 1773; died in Manchester in 1837), and great-grandson of Andrew Hoffman (born in Margate, England, in 1737; died there in 1799). Mrs. Draper's mother, Fidelia Marshall (Lamson) Hoffman, was born in Paris, France, in January, 1849. Her first American ancestor was Samuel Lamson, who came from Durham County, England, to Ipswich, Massachusetts, in 1630. The line is traced through his son, John Lamson (died, 1757); his son John Lamson (1725–1785); his son, Samuel Lamson (1736–1795), of Weston; his son,

John Lamson (born in Weston in 1791; died in Boston, Massachusetts, in 1855); his son, Charles Lamson (born in Boston in 1824; died in New York in 1880), the father of Mrs. Fidelia Lamson Hoffman.

Mrs. Draper was educated in the Comstock and Brearley Schools of New York. Her marriage to William Kinnicutt Draper, M.D., was solemnized in New York, December 28, 1898. Doctor Draper is the son of William Henry and Elizabeth Waldo (Kinnicutt) Draper and was born in New York, February 2, 1863. He received the degree of A.B. from Harvard University in 1885, and that of M.D. from the College of Physicians and Surgeons, New York, in 1888. After a period of study abroad, he began professional practice in New York in 1891, and has been consulting physician to various hospitals.

Mrs. Draper has always been interested in hospitals, in the training of nurses, and in medical social service, and at one time was a member of the New York Public School Board. At the time of the Spanish-American War in 1898, she acted as Secretary of the Red Cross in New York, and, after the reorganization of the American Red Cross in 1905, became Secretary of the New York State Red Cross, and also Secretary of the New York County Chapter, American Red Cross. In 1917 she became Vice-Chairman of the Chapter. During the World War, from May, 1917 to March, 1919, she was Chairman of the National Advisory Committee of Women. In May, 1919, Mrs. Draper was a delegate to the organization meeting of the League of Red Cross Societies in Paris, and in March, 1920, was again a delegate to the first conference of the League held in Geneva. The objects of the League are to encourage and promote in every country in the world the establishment and development of duly authorized Red Cross organizations, and to secure their coöperation; to promote the welfare of mankind by furnishing a medium for bringing within reach of all people the benefits to be derived from present known facts and new contributions to science and medical knowledge and their application; and to furnish a medium for coördinating relief work in case of great national and international calamities. During her visit abroad in 1919 Mrs. Draper inspected the relief and reconstruction work of the Red Cross in Paris and Northern France, and in Belgium, Luxembourg, and Germany. She is a member of the Cosmopolitan Club of New York and of the Board of Directors of the Brearley School.

JOY, HELEN HALL NEWBERRY (Mrs. Henry Bourne Joy), was born in Detroit, Michigan, June 9, 1869. Her father, John Stoughton Newberry (born November 18, 1826; died January 2, 1887) was a member of Congress from 1879 to 1881: her mother was Helen Parmelee Handy (born November 15, 1835; died December 17, 1912).

Helen Hall Newberry was educated in private schools, and on October 11, 1892, was married at Grosse Pointe Farms, Michigan, to Henry Bourne Joy, a manufacturer of Detroit. He is the son of James Frederic and Mary (Bourne) Joy, and was born in Detroit, November 23, 1864. They are the parents of four children: Helen Bourne Joy, (born in Detroit, March 20, 1896) wife of Howard Barker Lee; Marian Handy Joy (born in Detroit, December 16, 1899; died there October 23, 1910); James Frederic Joy (born in Detroit, March 18, 1903; died there November 16, 1906), and Henry Bourne Joy, Junior (born in Grosse Pointe Farms, Michigan, April 8, 1910).

Mrs. Joy is President of the Board of Lady Managers of Grace Hospital, Detroit; First Vice-President of the Woman's Hospital and Infants' Home, Detroit; First Vice-President of the Detroit Branch of the Needlework Guild; Chairman of the Board of Governors of the Helen Newberry Residence, Ann Arbor, Michigan; life member of the Detroit Chapter of the American Red Cross, and Chairman of the Teaching Center Committee during the War; State Chairman of the

Order of Descendants of Colonial Governors; National Councillor, Daughters of Founders and Patriots of America; a member of the Board of the Louisa St. Clair Chapter, Daughters of the American Revolution; the Mayflower Society, the Society of Colonial Dames, the Daughters of 1812, the Society of New England Women, Colonial Daughters of the Seventeenth Century, and the Mary Washington Society; the Society of Arts and Crafts, the Twentieth Century Club, and the Woman's City Club of Detroit; Colony Club of New York, Misquamicut Golf Club, Watch Hill, Rhode Island, and the Watch Hill Yacht Club. She is also Treasurer of the Watch Hill Improvement Society; past President and Treasurer of the Tuesday Musicale Society, and past President and present Treasurer of the Fine Arts Society.

WILLARD, LUVIA MARGARET, physician, daughter of Lockhart Rand and Eleanor (McDermott) Willard, was born in Sawyerville, Quebec, Canada, March 24, 1882. Her father was descended from Major Simon Willard (1605–1676) of Horsmonden, Kent, England, who settled in Cambridge, Massachusetts, in May, 1634. The line is traced through his son Henry, Henry Junior, James, and James Junior, to Longley Willard, who married Deliverance Seaver, a descendant of Robert Seaver, an English settler of Roxbury, Massachusetts, in 1634. Their son, William Willard, married Sabina Rand, a descendant of Robert Rand, who came from England to Charlestown, Massachusetts in 1635. Their son, Lockart Hall Willard, married Margaret McClary, a descendant of James McClary, who settled in New England in the seventeenth century. Their son, Lockhart Rand Willard (born, April 12, 1857; married, April 25, 1881, at Cookshire, Quebec, Canada, Eleanor McDermott (born December 11, 1857; died January 22, 1912), daughter of Martin McDermott, a native of Boyle, County Roscommon, Ireland, who settled at Eaton, Eastern Townships, Canada, in 1838.

He was a descendant of the ancient McDermott family, sometime Lords of Moylurg, Roscommon, a younger branch of the O'Conors, Kings of Connaught.

Doctor Willard was educated at Stanstead Wesleyan College, Stanstead, Quebec, where she received the diploma of Associate in Arts; at McGill Normal School, Montreal, Canada; and at Cornell University Medical College, New York. During her freshman year she was appointed President of all women in the college, and later was a member of the sophomore class society, and Secretary-Treasurer of the medical class. She received the doctorate in Medicine with honor in 1909. After graduation she was Resident Physician for a year at the West Philadelphia (Pennsylvania) Hospital for Women, and for another year at the Long Island College Hospital, Brooklyn, New York. For five years she was in charge of the Tuberculosis Clinics of the New York City Board of Health, and is now Attending Physician to the Chapin Home and to the Jamaica (Long Island) Hospital, of which she is also Secretary-Treasurer.

During the World War, Doctor Willard registered with the Council of National Defense, and was accepted for foreign service with the American Women's hospitals, but the personnel of the unit was cancelled. She is a member of the Alpha Epsilon Iota Fraternity, Cornell University; the Jamaica Woman's Club; the Cornell Women's Club; the Daughters of the American Revolution; the Queens-Nassau Medical Society; the New York State Medical Society; the American Medical Association; the Associated Physicians of Long Island; and the Medical Women's National Association.

ALLEN, MARION BOYD, artist and portrait painter, daughter of Stillman B. and Harriet Smith (Seaward) Allen, was born in Boston on October 23, 1862. Her father was eighth in line from George Allen of Braintree, England, who settled in 1635 at Saugus, Massachusetts.

Marion Allen was educated at Doctor Gannett's school in Boston, and, in 1905, was married, at Boston to William A. Allen, who was born at Sanford, Maine, the son of Emilus and Sarah (Bodwell) Allen.

Mrs. Allen's interests are chiefly centered about her profession, in which she has been very successful, especially as a portrait painter. She is a member of the Copley Society, Boston; the Arts' Club, Washington; the National Arts Club, the National Association of Women Painters and Sculptors, and the Pen and Brush Club, all three of New York City; the Institute Français Aux États-Unis, the Connecticut Academy, and the Buffalo Society of Artists.

During the past few years, Mrs. Allen has painted many portraits, among which are those of Wendell Phillips, Governor Curtis Guild, and Anna Vaughn Hyatt.

The work of Mrs. Allen gained recognition rapidly in various exhibitions—in 1915, she received honorable mention at the Connecticut Academy; in 1919 she was awarded two prizes: the Fellowship Prize, by the Buffalo Society of Artists, and the Popular Prize, by the Newport Art Association; in 1920 she again received two awards: the Hudson Prize, from the Connecticut Academy, and the Medal, Class A, from the Institute Français Aux États-Unis.

NEWCOMB, ELIZABETH WILMOT (Mrs. James Edward Newcomb), philanthropist, daughter of William Allen and Catherine (Borden) Wilmot, was born at Ithaca, New York. The name, which is English, is variously spelled in the records as Wilmot, Wilmote, Wilmarth, and Wilmouth. Benjamin Wilmot, a native of England, with his wife, located in New Haven, Connecticut. He took the oath of fidelity at a court held May 2, 1648; reference is made to him as "old goodman Wilmote." The name appears often in the Colonial records of New Haven, for the family was prominent. By intermarriage in recent years the Wilmots have become allied with the Hitchcock and Bristol families and, through these relationships, have become eligible to certain ancestral societies: notably, the Mayflower Society, the Society of the Colonial Dames of America, and the Society of Daughters of Founders and Patriots of America. The lines are traced through Chauncey Hitchcock who married Sarah Bristol; their daughter, Rebecca Hitchcock, who married Mr. Wilmot; their son, William Allen Wilmot, who married Catherine Borden; to their daughter, Elizabeth Wilmot. Miss Wilmot received her early education in Ithaca, New York, where she attended the public schools as well as Miss Dana's private school.

For many years Miss Wilmot devoted herself to various philanthropic enterprises. On March 23, 1887, she married Doctor James Edward Newcomb, a talented physician who stood at the head of his profession. He was valedictorian of his class at Buckley School; was graduated at Yale in 1880; and ranked among the first ten of his class at the College of Physicians and Surgeons (Columbia University), where he was graduated M.D. in 1883. Having served as interne at Roosevelt Hospital, he entered the Department of Laryngology of that institution. Later he became Laryngologist of Roosevelt Hospital; about the same time he was appointed Professor of Laryngology at the Cornell Medical College, New York City, serving in that capacity until the time of his death on August 27, 1912. For many years he was Secretary of the American Laryngological Association, and he was an active fellow of many other medical organizations, as well as of philanthropic societies. He was also prominent in the field of medical literature. As Editor of *The Transactions of the American Laryngological Association*, of the American edition of Grünwald's *Atlas of the Diseases of the Mouth and Nose*, and, with two other distinguished collaborators, as co-author of one of the best text-books extant on the diseases of the throat and nose, Doctor Newcomb made an enviable reputation. Genial, conscientious, and unselfish, he was a man of rare usefulness and distinction, universally respected and esteemed.

For many years Mrs. Newcomb had been much interested in the welfare of women who earn their own living. It was early brought to her attention that a large proportion of such workers suffered from tuberculosis, but that if they could have proper hygienic conditions, and could gain relief from financial worries they could be cured. In 1900 the woman's Philanthropic organization, the Chi Kappa Club, of which Mrs. Newcomb was President, organized a "rummage sale." The proceeds were to be devoted toward the establishment of a sanitorium for small children, self-supporting girls, and young married women suffering from incipient tuberculosis. The sum of five hundred dollars was raised, and this paid for active and successful propaganda for one year. Early in 1901 a committee of one hundred was organized: the Stony Wold Sanatorium Building Fund Committee, which immediately began to work on behalf of this charity. Mrs. Newcomb was the Chairman. A public meeting was held, contributions were solicited, and the city was canvassed and divided into groups, which later became auxiliaries to the main body. During the first year after organization, each auxiliary contributed six hundred dollars, which fully equipped one room in the sanitorium. Then each auxiliary assumed the support of one occupant. The Sanatorium was incorporated on April 1, 1901, with Mrs. Newcomb as President. In that capacity she has served ever since. From the first, the institution has been non-sectarian. A beautiful property of 1,850 acres on Lake Kushaqua, Franklin County, New York, with an elevation of 1,730 feet, was selected as possessing an ideal climate for the purpose in mind. It was purchased on December 14, 1901. Stony Wold is situated between the Adirondack Division of the New York Central and the Delaware and Hudson railroads. The station on the New York Central is the property of the Sanatorium. Included in the acreage are Buck Pond, on the eastern side; a part of Mountain Pond, on the hill on the western side; and Lake Kushaqua itself, which is about a mile and a half long and three-quarters of a mile wide at its broadest part. This Lake is one of the chain between Saranac Lake and Loon Lake, the outlet of which is the Saranac River, running northward. On September 11, 1902, the cornerstone was laid for the main building, a model edifice built in a half circle so as to admit the best possible light and air. On August 15, 1903, the Sanatorium was formally opened. Owing to Mrs. Newcomb's continual interest and her philanthropic ideals, the organization has kept pace with the most advanced methods. The number of buildings has greatly increased. In 1920 these included, besides the Administrative Building, the following: Stony Wold Hall and Community House; dormitory for patients; store and post office; power house; model cow barn; hay barn; piggery; smoke house; cold storage and ice house; woodworking shop; carpenter shop; paint shop; saw mill; blacksmith shop; incinerator; employees' dormitory; children's schoolhouse and playhouse; five rest shacks; seven cottages; and one industrial settlement house. There is also a schoolhouse. For the children of the employees there is a separate schoolhouse, built by the town of Franklin. The most advanced medical treatment is administered, and women, who through no fault of their own have become ill and dependent, are restored to their positions as breadwinners for their families. An ever increasing number of applications for admission are continually being received at the office of the corporation, 1974 Broadway, New York City. All patients are on probation for the first month. There is a fixed weekly charge for those who are in a position to pay. If in the opinion of the medical director the patients show an improved condition, they are expected to remain at least six months. Very little medical treatment is given, reliance being placed mainly on graduated work and exercise—the amount depends upon the physical condition of the patient. The Trudeau School for Tuberculosis during its summer session holds clinics at Stony Wold. The Sanatorium is placed in Class I, by the State Board of Charities. Whenever, for any reason, an applicant cannot be received she is referred, if possible, to other resources, and a careful supervision is kept of the health of all "ex-patients."

Much of Mrs. Newcomb's success has been due to her ability, through her magnetic personality, to arouse a real and lasting interest in philanthropic enterprises. In addition to being President of Stony Wold Sanatorium, Mrs. Newcomb is a member of the Woman's City Club; the National Society of New England Women; the Chi Kappa Club; the Red Cross Association; the National Association for the Prevention of Tuberculosis; the Association of Tuberculosis Clinics; the Manhattan Day Nursery; the Riverside Day Nursery; the Bethany Day Nursery; the Working Girls' Vacation Society; the Committee on the Prevention of Tuberculosis, of the Charity Organization Society; the Auxiliary to the Gouverneur Tuberculosis Clinics; the Women's Auxiliary of the Salvation Army; the Employment Bureau for the Handicapped; the Theosophical Society; the League for Political Education; the American Museum of Natural History; and the Metropolitan Museum of Art.

LONGFELLOW, JULIA LIVINGSTON DELAFIELD (Mrs. Frederick W. Longfellow), was born at Riverdale-on-Hudson, New York. Her father, Maturin L. Delafield, was descended from John Delafield, who came from London, England, in 1783, and settled in the City of New York. Her mother, Mary C. Livingston, traced descent from the colonial and revolutionary families of Livingston, Beekman, Lewis, Van Rensselaer and Schuyler. Two of her great-great-grandfathers were Chancellor Livingston and General Morgan Lewis.

Mrs. Longfellow received her early education at home through tutors and at private schools in New York. She was married, April 30, 1901, to Frederick W. Longfellow, of New York, and their children are: Julia Delafield, Livingston, and Elizabeth Delafield Longfellow.

Very early in her married life, Mrs. Longfellow began to take an active interest in all matters pertaining to the welfare of the community, and was among the organizers of the Woman's Municipal League of New York, and the City History Club of New York. Since 1893 she has been on various committees of the Red Cross, and on the governing boards of the Serbian Relief Committee, Woman Voters Anti-Suffrage Party, Fatherless Children of France, and Woman's Department National Civic Federation.

She is a member of the Colony Club, Colonial Dames of America, National Civic Federation, Woman's Auxiliary of Cathedral of St. John the Divine, Parents League, Drama League, National Association for Universal Military Training, Pekinese Club, New York Altar Guild, American Rights League, American Constitutional League, National Security Society, Woman's Auxiliary Civil Service Reform, National Special Aid, the Probation League, and the New York Woman's League for Animals. She is also a member of the British War Relief Association, and, during the war, was an active worker attached to the Soldiers and Sailors Unit Number Three of the War Camp Community Service and the 9th Coast Artillery Canteen.

POWELL, CHARLOTTE AGNES, daughter of Christopher H. and Elizabeth (Gillespie) Powell, was born in Boston, Massachusetts, where she has passed her entire life. Her father and mother came to the United States from Queenstown, Ireland, in 1850, having been married just before sailing. The family of Powell came originally from Wales where the name is derived from Ap-hoel or Ap-howell, meaning the son of Howell. Her great grandmother was a sister of Admiral Grace of the British Navy, one of the pioneers in India.

Miss Powell's earlier education consisted of nine years in the elementary schools of Boston, four years in the Girls' High School, and one year in the Boston Normal School. This was supplemented by special courses in dwelling-house construction, household sanitation, interior decorating, etc. She was for some years a teacher in the Boston public schools and a writer on educational subjects, but retired from teaching to enter the profession of building, in which she has had a career both successful and exceptional.

For twenty years, from 1895 to 1915, Miss Powell devoted her entire time and energies to house building, and developed a business acumen which made her a worthy competitor of the most progressive builders. Some idea of the extent of her activities may be obtained from the statement that she has erected and sold nearly two hundred houses, frame and brick dwellings for one, two, or three families. In the course of this work several whole streets were built, and a twelve-acre lot known as "Baker's Field" developed into streets of handsome houses. The financial operations of these enterprises involved the sum of $2,000,000.

Miss Powell has always believed that the making of homes is essentially a woman's field, and that the woman in business for herself has a much better opportunity to succeed, in every sense of the word, than the one who is held in leash by the traditions and prejudices of an employer. She has believed, also, that artistic results are not incompatible with good profits in the market. That the theory is sound is evidenced by the fact that, when a real-estate dealer referred to her as the "Tiffany of builders" the title was never disputed, and that she retired in 1915 with a satisfactory competence.

Since her retirement Miss Powell has spent her time in managing her private interests, and in the work of philanthropic, literary, and social organizations. She is an Ex-President of the Guild of St. Catherine, Ex-President of the Margaret Brent Suffrage Guild, Ex-Secretary of the New England Woman's Press Association, and is a member of the Massachusetts Suffrage Association and of several clubs. She finds recreation in music, art, reading, literary work, and nature study. Miss Powell still dwells upon the humble beginnings of her own success, not in a spirit of boastfulness, but with the desire to encourage other women to go forward with confidence into the business world and there take the place which belongs to them as co-workers with men.

GULLIVER, JULIA HENRIETTA, daughter of John Putnam and Frances Woodbury (Curtis) Gulliver, was born at Norwich, Connecticut, July 30, 1856. Through her father, she is descended from Anthony Gulliver, a native of England, who located in Massachusetts in 1642. Her father's mother was directly descended from John Putnam, of Aston Abbotts, Buck County, England (born about 1580; died in Salem Village, Danvers, Massachusetts, December 30, 1662). This John Putnam was a direct ancestor of General Israel Putnam and of Reverend Daniel Putnam, of Salem, who was graduated from Harvard College in 1717. Through her mother she is descended from the famous Governor Bradford, who founded Plymouth Colony and was for thirty years its Governor. She traces her descent on her mother's side, also, from Captain Thomas Curtis, of Wethersford, Connecticut, who won distinction in the French and Indian wars. Former President Mark Hopkins, of Williams College, Williamstown, Massachusetts, was a member of one of the branches of her family.

Miss Gulliver was graduated A.B. at Smith College in 1879, and after some years returned to pursue post-graduate work. She was graduated Ph.D. in 1888. Two years later she accepted appointment as head of the Department of Philosophy and Biblical Literature at Rockford Seminary, and served in this capacity from 1890 to 1892. She then went abroad, and spent the academic year 1892–1893 in advanced study under Professor Wundt, at the University of Leipzig. Upon her return, in 1893, she was made head of the Department of Philosophy and Biblical Literature at Rockford College.

Having acquired an enviable reputation in the educational world, Miss Gulliver was offered the Presidency of Rockford College, in 1902, and accepted the position, which she has since occupied. At the same institution, she also occupies the Chair of Ethics and Biblical Literature.

In recognition of her accomplishments as an educator, the French Government in 1909 made Miss Gulliver Officier d'Academie. The following year (1910) Smith College conferred upon her the honorary degree of LL.D. Miss Gulliver has contributed articles to various religious and philosophical reviews. She is a member of the American Philosophical Association; North Central Association of Colleges and Secondary Schools; and the Religious Education Association.

BREITUNG, CHARLOTTE KAUFMAN

(Mrs. Edward N. Breitung), philanthropist, is a noted figure in New York on account of her benevolence, as there is practically no charity in the city which she has not assisted. She has spent much time abroad, especially on the continent, where she studied industrial and social service movements. From the breadth of view thus gained she wished to be considered always as the student and helper, while she works for the common good. Although she is a careful student of the public movements in which women take so great a part, she is a firm believer in what may be called indirect philanthropy. Early in her residence in New York she established an unique reputation as the promoter of

artistic uplift in practical and unostentatious ways. She devoted considerable attention to helping young people of talent to secure their education and special training. It was her pleasure to surround herself with young artists, musicians, and writers, and to encourage their dreams and arrange hearings for them with influential people. She was firmly opposed to the idea that talent can best develop under adverse circumstances. On the contrary, she believes in stimulating genius to develop under sympathetic encouragement.

During the World War Mrs. Breitung's services were freely given and in constant demand. She was the first American to send relief supplies to Belgium in 1914, and from that date her activities ramified in many directions. Eventually she gave practically all of her time to war work, and was accounted a highly valuable member of the organization with which she was connected. In 1917 she was appointed by the Mayor of New York a member of the Women's Committee of the League for National Defense. In April of that year she volunteered as captain of a team to help raise, in two weeks, a fund of $100,000 for the League. This work she carried to a successful issue. During the course of the war she gave eight ambulances to the United States Government for use in France, among them one with an X-ray equipment, costing $15,000. At the time France had about two hundred and fifty X-ray ambulances in the field, but the one given by Mrs. Breitung was the first to become the property of the United States Army in France. An ambulance such as this, with its guarantee of quick, effective treatment was an absolute necessity in the work of saving the lives of many wounded men at the front. Mrs. Breitung was quick to realize that this would be a vital way of improving the fighting powers of the army and strengthening its work. The ambulance, the best of its kind that could be made to that date, was inscribed with her name and a statement that it was her gift to the army. On the day before Christmas,

1917, it was presented to General Pershing at his headquarters in France, the American Ambassador making the presentation speech.

Mrs. Breitung was a working member of the Red Cross throughout the course of the War. In the spring of 1918, in the great Red Cross drive, she not only donated large sums of money but was, herself, a serious worker on Mrs. Charles B. Alexander's team. She was also deeply interested in the undertaking of the Navy Auxiliary, No. 205, New York County Chapter of the American Red Cross, when it gave a pageant of allied Nations at the Ritz-Carlton Hotel, under the direction of Ben Ali Haggin. Dramatic stars collaborated with painters in the unique entertainment, the proceeds being devoted to war relief. The American Red Star Animal Relief was a phase of war service which sought to serve the animals of the United States Army as the Red Cross served its men. The Secretary of War authorized the Veterinary Corps to accept animal ambulances for the service. It was resolved, therefore, by those interested to devote the proceeds of the annual horse show, held at Durland's Riding Academy in 1917, to purchase such ambulances. Mrs. Breitung lent her patronage to the occasion, emphasizing her love for all dumb animals, particularly for those forced into the conflict. During the Liberty Loan drives Mrs. Breitung threw herself whole heartedly into the work of the women's committee, to which she gave many hours daily. When campaigning for the third loan she said to a reporter: "These bonds are the means at hand for the War Department to give our men better equipment and more of it; they are the means at hand to equip more men and send them across to increase our fighting strength, and to give us our victory for civilization; they mean everything for the successful conduct of the War." Her forceful arguments, vivacious manner, and magnetic personality brought overwhelming success and the bonds she undertook to sell were placed without difficulty.

During the course of the War Mrs. Breitung promoted seven plays from which $150,000 was raised for soldiers' and sailors' funds. Among them, *Yip Yip Yaphank*, given by soldiers from Camp Upton, was hailed as the best musical play produced in New York in thirty years; *Biff Bang!* with all the impetuosity its name implies, was given in the summer of 1918 by the boys of the Pelham Naval Training Camp. At the premiere Mrs. Breitung had for her guests the members of the station. She purchased the entire seating capacity of the gallery and presented the tickets to Commander Franklin for distribution. The proceeds were used to build a permanent theatre at Pelham. As a financial venture it was a pronounced success, receipts for the week of its production being about $78,000. *Good Luck Sam*, one of the cleverest skits given by men in service, was written and acted by the enlisted men stationed at Camp Merritt. It excelled chiefly by reason of the volume and spirit of its chorus. The proceeds were used to build a community house large enough to accommodate the convalescent troops arriving from overseas and the relatives who should meet them. Through Mrs. Breitung's interest in these events a brilliant list of patrons and patronesses consented to sponsor them, she, alone, assumed the responsibility of providing the necessary finances.

Mrs. Breitung was the founder and a hostess of the Sailors' and Marines' Club and Athletic Field on Riverside Drive, the grounds of which extended from 96th to 102nd Street. They were laid out with tennis courts and baseball diamonds, and a large tent was provided where sailors might sleep. In the clubhouse were many conveniences; pool and billiard tables, writing materials and games, a library with current magazines and daily papers, shower baths, and a canteen. Mrs. Breitung gave personal attention to all the details of management, and so won the affection and esteem of the sailors that special government permission was sought by them to express their appreciation in a gift. This took the form of a vanity case ornamented with diamonds and crystal. Another canteen of which she was the founder was the Michigan Headquarters for soldiers and sailors, the first state club to be started in New York.

Among other war activities Mrs. Breitung was interested in the purchase of musical instruments for the men of the navy; the purchase of athletic equipment for aerial squadrons going over seas; free milk for Italy; free milk for France; relief for blinded soldiers and sailors. Her beautiful house in Versailles, France, whose gardens join those of the Palace, where the Peace negotiations were held, she turned into a hospital for French and American soldiers.

The only child of Mr. and Mrs. Breitung, Juliette, was married in New York, December 11, 1918, to Herbert William Richter.

SHAINWALD, RUTH HART (Mrs. Ralph L. Shainwald), daughter of Samuel and Caroline (Hecht) Hart, was born in Marshall, Michigan. Her father was born in Germany but came in early life to Michigan. Mrs. Shainwald's education was begun in the schools of her native town, and completed by three years in Normal, now Hunter College, New York City.

In 1881 she was married, in New York City, to Ralph L. Shainwald, President of the Standard Paint Company, and a trustee of the Ethical Culture School. Three children were born to them: Maisie Seville, now Mrs. Michael Dreicer; Ralph L. Junior, and Marian.

In a quiet but efficient manner Mrs. Shainwald has accomplished much good work along civic improvement lines, including prison reform. Her interest in the care of mental defectives has been of a highly scientific character, not only in the study of cases, but also in the development of means for vocational education, to render subjects as nearly self-supporting as possible. Her theory in such cases is that in aiding defectives to acquire a vocation, the possibility that they will recruit the criminal class is correspondingly decreased.

Her work in these various phases of social welfare is reflected in the clubs and societies of which she is a member or a director. She is a member of the Women's City Club, Woman's Municipal League, Woman's Conference of the Society for Ethical Culture, and the Municipal Art Society; and a director of the National Child Welfare Association, the Societies Realty Company, the League for Political Education, which erected the Town Hall, New York, and the Society for the Aid of Mental Defectives. She also served on the first Board of Management of the New York Kindergarten Association. Mrs. Shainwald has been long a member of various prison reform associations, and through her continued and untiring efforts, has been largely instrumental in ameliorating existing conditions, and removing many abuses of long standing.

HELMER, NELLIE FITZHUGH (Mrs. Ralph Helmer), social worker, daughter of of Edward Jackson and Mary Eugenia (Armistead) Fitzhugh, was born in Brooklyn, New York. Her father's family dates from the thirteenth century, and one ancestor, Baron Fitzhugh, was among those who forced King John to sign the Magna Charta in 1215. Her mother was descended from William Armistead, who came from England to Virginia in 1635. Another William Armistead was a member of the Revolutionary Committee of Elizabeth City County in 1775.

Nellie Fitzhugh was educated at St. Catherine's Hall and at Packer Institute, Brooklyn, and her marriage to Ralph Helmer, managing director of the Textile Alliance Export Company, Inc., of America, took place in that city on April 8, 1896.

Mrs. Helmer has been strongly interested in the welfare of girls. She organized the Big Sisters of Queensborough, and was its President for three years, resigning on account of ill health to become Honorary President.

The problem of the lonely "hallroom" girl appealed to her as of prime importance, and turned her attention to the work of the New York League of Women Workers, of which she became Secretary and Mrs. Kenneth Muir President. The New York League of Women Workers, with headquarters at 6 East 45th Street, organizes and actively controls evening clubs for women, which are non-sectarian, self-governing, and self-supporting. The aim of the League is to give normal exercise and development to all the best instincts of womanhood, to provide rest, recreation, and recuperation for working girls and women. The movement was founded in 1885 by Miss Grace Dodge, and since that time has grown until it includes twenty-five large clubs in and near New York with a membership of 3,500 girls. There is no idea of charity or "uplift" connected with these clubs. The members have absolute freedom, and engage in such activities and diversions as they prefer. However, the league clubs offer opportunities for recreation and enjoyment with wholesome friends in attractive surroundings; self-expression in singing, dancing, and dramatics; health activities in gymnasium and swimming classes, hikes, and athletic sports; practice in self-government, developing a sense of responsibility, loyalty, and fairness in dealing with others; promotion of industrial harmony by teaching loyalty to the nation, community, and the individual.

The National League, which extends the work of the New York League to other states, provides—educational opportunities, furnishing speakers on civic activities and programs to encourage class work; stimulating interest in art, chorus singing, health, and athletics; legislative protection, seeking the passing of bills bettering the conditions of women workers; and inexpensive vacation facilities in camps and vacation houses. The League's undertakings provide, in reality, a sort of insurance for the club members, in mental as well as physical health, by offering wholesome recreation and congenial companionship to the thousands of girl and women workers, who otherwise would become victims of loneliness.

Mrs. Helmer is also a member of the Women's Board of the Church Charity Foundation, Brooklyn; the Good Citizenship League, Flushing, Long Island; the Sleepy Hollow Chapter of the Daughters of the American Revolution; the King Manor Association, Jamaica, Long Island; the New York Federation of Women's Clubs; and the Woman's City Club, New York.

Mr. and Mrs. Helmer are the parents of three children: Phoebe Armistead Helmer, a student at Bryn Mawr College for two years and, during 1919–1920, a relief worker in France under the Comité Américain pour les Région Dévastés de la France; Ralph Borden Helmer, a graduate of Dartmouth College (1921); and Elizabeth Helmer, a student at Smith College.

WEST, BINA MAY, daughter of Alfred J. and Elizabeth (Conant) West, was born in Columbus, St. Clair County, Michigan. On her mother's side she is a descendant of Roger Conant, first Governor of Massachusetts Bay Colony. She was educated in the Michigan public and normal schools, and was an assistant high school principal from 1888 to 1890. Then she was elected the first woman school examiner in Michigan, as a member of the Board of School Examiners for St. Clair County. About this time, having been deeply impressed by the tragedy in the lives of children who have lost their mothers, she resolved to make it possible for women to obtain, in return for small monthly payments, insurance against sickness or death.

There was at that time no society or company in which a mother could secure protection for her children; few women carried insurance, as such an idea was new. Miss West therefore resigned from the school board, made a thorough study of insurance problems, and exerted the full force of her personality to win converts to her plan of a benefit society.

In 1892, she founded and organized the Woman's Benefit Association of the Ladies of the Maccabees, with a home office at Port Huron, Michigan. Until she had fully demonstrated the feasibility of her plan she paid all expenses out of her own savings. With a generous expenditure of money, time, and energy she optimistically developed the enterprise. To-day the organization is the largest benefit society in the world for women. At a small cost it renders valuable assistance to a large number of women and children. In 1919 more than $10,000,000 was credited on its books, representing the monthly payments of some 188,000 women of fifty-five states and provinces in the United States and Canada. Since the beginning, more than $14,000,000 have been paid out in sick benefits to dependent children and relatives, and not one dollar has ever been lost through dishonesty, bank failures, or poor investments.

In addition to being President of the Woman's Benefit Association, which now occupies its own building in Port Huron, Michigan, Miss West has held office in the Ladies of the Maccabees, as Supreme Record-Keeper from 1892 to 1911, and Supreme Commander from 1911 to 1920. She has been President of the National Fraternal Press Association; and is a member of the Presidents' Association of the National Fraternal Congress; a member of the Executive Board of the Woman's Association of Commerce; Vice-Chairman of the Republican State Central Committee for Michigan; and, under appointment by Governor Sleeper, a member of the Michigan Child Welfare Committee. Since 1895 she has edited the *Ladies' Review* and has written many reports and papers on fraternal beneficiary societies and life insurance principles.

WENTZ, GEORGIE BANYER NICHOLS (Mrs. James Griswold Wentz), daughter of William Banyer and Georgiana (Bulkley) Nichols, was born in Brooklyn, New York. Her father was a descendant of Sergeant

Francis Nicol, who came to this country in 1660 with his uncle, Richard Nicol, afterwards Colonial Governor of New York, and founded the town of Stratford, Connecticut. Among his descendants was David Nichols, great-grandfather of Mrs. Wentz, who served in the American Revolution. Her grandfather was the Reverend Samuel Nichols, a graduate of Yale College and for many years rector of the Episcopal Church at Bedford, New York. He married Susan Nexon Warner, of New York, granddaughter of George Warner whose tablet hangs in St. Paul's Episcopal Church, Broadway and Fulton Streets.

Mrs. Wentz's mother, Georgiana Bulkley, was a descendant of Robert de Bulkeley (ancient spelling Buclough), lord of many manors in Cheshire and Shropshire, England, dating back to the time of King John. She was of the eighth generation in descent from Reverend Peter Bulkeley (born in Odell, Bedfordshire, England, January 31, 1582), a graduate of St. John's College, Cambridge, England, and Rector of the church in Odell where he succeeded his father. He was persecuted as a non-Conformist, and came to this country with his wife, Grace Chetwood, daughter of Sir Richard Chetwood, sailing on the ship *Susan and Ellen* in 1634, and landing at Boston with a large following. Here he determined to cut his way through the wilderness, and founded the town of Concord, Massachusetts, having bought the land in that fertile valley from the Indians, and there built the eleventh church in the colonies, which he served as pastor and leader of his people, until his death some seventeen years later. Reverend Mr. Bulkley's youngest son, Peter, Jr., joined his older sister, who had married the Reverend Mr. Jones, Minister of the church in Fairfield, Connecticut, and there he lived, married and died. All of his descendants lived in Fairfield or Southport.

Mrs. Wentz's great-grandfather was Eleazer Bulkley, who married Mary Ogden, also of Fairfield. He fought in the American Revolution, serving three years in the navy and three years in the army. He afterwards established the firm of E. Bulkley and Sons, in Maiden Lane, New York, which engaged in foreign trade, building and maintaining their own clipper ships for forty years. The youngest of his six sons, all of whom were born, resided and died in Southport, Connecticut, was Charles Bulkley, grandfather of Mrs. Wentz. He married Elizabeth Beers, daughter of Abel Beers and Elizabeth Whitney, and granddaughter of Peter Whitney, all of Southport. Their third daughter was Georgiana Bulkley, mother of Mrs. Wentz. She was born in Southport, educated in the Misses Draper's School for Young Ladies in Hartford, Connecticut, where she completed the course as valedictorian of her class, in June, 1857; was married the following October, made her home in New York, and died there in May, 1908. She was an accomplished woman of strong character and high Christian principles which she implanted in her children, an enthusiastic patriot, of happy disposition, and a devoted mother.

There were three women, Mrs. Wentz declares, who had a great influence on the development of her character and ideals: her grandmother, Bulkley, her mother, Georgiana Bulkley Nichols, and Mrs. Sylvanus Reed, in whose school she completed her education after an attendance of five years. All of these women were fine American types and left an impress on their day and generation. After leaving school, Mrs. Wentz traveled in Europe for two years, and later attended the course in the Woman's Law Class of New York University. In April, 1890, she was married to James Griswold Wentz, of New York, from the old family home in Southport, Connecticut, and they have since lived in New York, with a summer home at Newport, Rhode Island.

Mrs. Wentz has been profoundly interested in the advancement of womankind, and with steadfastness of purpose and enthusiastic endeavor worked for suffrage. She has always sought to awaken the interest of women in the government of our country through the principles of the Republican Party. To this end she has given her untiring efforts, having started her work in 1892, when she arranged mass meetings, secured speakers and entertained them at her home, for the Benjamin Harrison Campaign. In 1894 she became a charter member and First Vice-President of the first Republican club for women in New York, the West End Woman's Republican Club. In 1898 she was one of a group of women who, for six weeks, went through the tenement districts of New York, talking with the women and distributing literature in every apartment for William McKinley; to every succeeding presidential election she has given her personal effort. In 1920, during the Harding campaign, she organized a headquarters for the Woman's Republican Club at 257 Fifth Avenue, where prominent speakers addressed noonday meetings for a month previous to the election, and in Newport, Rhode Island, at the same time she organized a headquarters on Thames Street, with addresses by noted speakers every afternoon.

After suffrage was acquired Mrs. Wentz joined her Republican district organization; she is First Vice-President of that club, and a Captain of her election district for which she makes a house to house canvass. She has been a watcher at the polls, a canvass inspector, a duly elected member of the County Committee, and a delegate to the Republican State Convention at Saratoga in 1920. In October, 1900, she founded the Woman's Republican Club, of New York City, and served as its President from October, 1900, to January, 1908, and again from January, 1911, to the present time. By her earnestness and enthusiasm she carried the club through the years when most women were indifferent to anything political, and now by a broad but conservative policy she seeks, through leading Republican speakers, to bring Republican women voters to a serious sense of their responsibility. In 1905 Mrs. Wentz organized the Woman's Republican Club of Fishkill-on-Hudson which is still a flourishing organization, and in 1919 she organized the Newport County Woman's Republican Club, of Newport, Rhode Island, which soon numbered over 400 members, and still is doing active work.

The desire to raise the status of womanhood has lead Mrs. Wentz into many fields of activity. Her opposition to the cocktail, cigarette and drug habit is well known, and she formed an active committee, of which she was Chairman, against immodesty in women's dress. During the World War she was an active member of the Red Cross, and opened her house at Newport for the entertainment of enlisted sailors from the United States Naval Training Station. In New York, Mrs. Wentz is a member of the alumnae of the Woman's Law Class, New York University; the National Arts Club; the Manhattan Chapter of the Daughters of the American Revolution; Washington Headquarters Association; the Portia Club and the Woman's Republican Club. In Newport, Rhode Island, she was a Vice-President of the Newport Woman's Suffrage League; Charter Member of the Woman's Civic League; Vice-President of the Newport County Woman's Republican Club, and member of the Newport Improvement Association. She is a proposed candidate for the new Department of Public Welfare in Washington, and has the support of leading men in the Republican party in New York State.

The great object in Mrs. Wentz's efforts in the Woman's Republican Club and other Republican clubs organized by her, is to safeguard our Republican form of government and perpetuate the Constitution of the United States through the loyalty and active interest of Republican women voters.

STONER, WINIFRED SACKVILLE (Mrs. James Buchanan Stoner), educator, generally known as "Mother Stoner," is one of the outstanding figures in present-day literary and educational circles in America, and in the world. She has been equally conspicuous and successful in such diverse activities as those of writer, artist, inventor, lecturer, founder of an educational system, war worker, and participant in many philanthropic movements. Her best-known work, perhaps, is her system of "natural education," which, in her own words, aims "to make children healthy, happy, efficient beings through play with a purpose." She modestly ascribes her conspicuous success as a human benefactor to her descent from a "long line of women who loved literature, were poets, dramatists and progressives in their day."

To serve the principles of her educational method, she invented a number of natural education toys, calculated to impart real knowledge to children through their play. Such are her "geom. kiddies," "Lares and Penates," and numerous others, each with a particular purpose attained by its own particular appeal to the childish mind. She has also written many books, principally for the natural education of children: *Evelyn's Adventures, Marcus Curtius, A Boy-Man, My Mother Goose, Titania's History of Rome, Natural Education, Manual of Natural Education, Mother Stoner's Nature Book, Mother Stoner's Song Book, Helpers of Santa Claus, Keeping Facts, Castles in Spain, Success, What I have Seen, Mother Stoner's Nursery Rhymes, Arithmetic Through Play, Geography in Jingles,* and *Memory Helpers.* For the circulation of her books, she founded Mother Stoner, Inc., of which she is the active head, and is constantly occupied with lectures on subjects connected with her educational system, and with duties as an expert in child-training. During 1917–1918, her services were eagerly sought in behalf of soldiers disabled in the World War, and she was appointed Director of Reconstruction Schools established in their behalf.

Mrs. Stoner is Director of the International Association for Natural Education, President of the Natural Education of the United States, and a member of numerous organizations, including the Homemakers' Club, the Little Mothers' Association, the Society of Arts and Sciences, the Association for Universal Education, the League of Women Voters of New York State, the International Esperantist Association, the Women's International Health League, the Art Dress Association, the MacDowell Club, the League of American Pen Women, the Authors' League of America, the Women's Press Club of New York City, and numerous local organizations in several cities.

She was married, at Buffalo, New York, February 3, 1900, to James Buchanan Stoner, M.D., of the United States Public Health Service. They have one child, a daughter, Winifred Sackville Stoner, Jr. (born in Norfolk, Virginia, August 19, 1902), who was married August 7, 1921 to Charles F. de Bruche, of Paris, France. Like her mother, Mrs. de Bruche is a gifted writer and speaker, and is an able assistant in the cause of natural education. Although still young, she has numerous books to her credit, and collaborated with her mother in the *Manual of Natural Education*, published in 1916. She is reputed the youngest person listed in *Who's Who in America*.

An intimate view of the life and activities of Mother Stoner are best had in the following characterization by her friend and co-worker, Haryot Holt Dey:

"Doctor Winifred Sackville Stoner, known to mothers and kiddies all over the world as 'Mother Stoner,' in my opinion is a human dynamo. For many years I have been closely associated with her and I have never seen her show any signs of weariness—never even caught her yawning. She is always alert, ready to do something for someone at any hour of the day or the night. She has demonstrated in her life, just as Napoleon and Edison have proven, that it is not necessary to sleep away one's existence. Mother Stoner feels refreshed after three hours of sleep but when she goes to bed she goes to sleep, 'not to calculate or to think of what is to be done on the coming day.' In the same way she spends very little time eating. One meal each day suffices to give her body machine its proper fuel and judging from the amount of 'pep' that this lady displays she gets more energy from one meal than most people do from three.

"For many years she was a close friend of Doctor Horace Fletcher and she agrees with his belief that it is not so much what people eat as how they eat it. When Mother Stoner eats a meal she wants to eat slowly and to believe that the food is going to be her friend. She likes to eat in an environment of simplicity and beauty and to have her food prepared so that it is most appetizing. No eat and run principle in the life of this energetic woman. 'We are what we eat and drink, also what we breathe and think,' says 'Mother Stoner,' and she certainly demonstrates in her life that the advice she gives comes from experience. One of Columbia's professors recently said of her, 'Doctor Stoner is one educator who proved her own theories in her own life and on her own flesh and blood before she began preaching about them.'

"In thinking of Mother Stoner I see her always with a smile upon her face and 'just ready' to do something. To me she is the loving, energetic mother but the world knows her chiefly as the founder of a so-called system of education by means of which Winifred Sackville Stoner, Jr. was able to pass college entrance examinations at nine years of age and was pronounced by Doctor M. V. O'Shea of the University of Wisconsin 'to know more and to be able to do more at twelve years of age than the average university graduate.'

"Mother Stoner has spent her life in study and research, having some nine tags which she can lawfully attach to her name but she prefers the name of 'Mother' to that of any title. However, her wide range of studies and contact with people of all countries have helped to give her the vision of how the pathway to knowledge may be made a joy instead of drudgery to children. This educator is lawyer, doctor, lecturer, inventor, journalist, expert housekeeper, athlete, author of many books, composer of many songs, a humorist, delightful hostess, but best of all a child lover whom every child loves. And Mother Stoner is not proud of her accomplishments. She is glad to understand the human body from the physician's standpoint so that she may be able to help her beloved 'kiddie-kids.' She loves to engage in all athletic sports because children love these sports. She never puts herself on a pedestal but is one with the kiddies and I have often heard her say that when she reaches her one hundred and fiftieth milestone she expects to be just as young as she is now because she will play with her great-great-great grandchildren. Play-to-a-purpose is the theme of Natural Education and this purposeful play is certainly demonstrated in the home atmosphere of the author of this book that has been translated into many languages. *Self-Control* and *Joy of Service* are the foundation stones of all education according to Mother Stoner and she demonstrates in her own life the power gained by never giving way to tears and fears, or showing anger. The kiddies call her 'Smiling Lady' and they prefer to play with her rather than with children of their own age. Old people love her because she radiates sunshine and makes them forget all their sorrows. And being a jack of all trades she is able to prove herself a master of at least one trade—that of giving sunshine and service to all whom she meets as a World Joyizer."

DEBRUCHÉ, WINIFRED SACKVILLE STONER (Countess de Bruché), daughter of Colonel and Doctor Winifred Sackville Stoner, and known before her marriage at the age of eighteen as Winifred Sackville Stoner, Jr., was born in Norfolk, Virginia, in August, 1902. In her education her mother sought to demonstrate her theory of natural education. In the Stoner home were never heard the words "DON'T" or "MUST." There was no friction between the mother and the child, the teacher and the pupil. The love shown by Winifred for her mother and by the mother for her child was truly great, and their mutual confidence perfect. Mother Stoner showed herself a great mother, with the real mother spirit, in her actions toward Winifred and other young people. And that is the reason that Natural Education, as demonstrated in the life of Winifred Sackville Stoner, has come to stay and to help make children healthier, happier, and more efficient citizens of the coming generation. A happier child than she was never seen, nor a busier one. She was trained from her cradle to keep busy, and to observe the law of order. Her play room was always in order; each of her books and work materials had its own proper place, and was always to be found there. She never worked unless she was interested and that is why work never hurt her.

At five years of age she published her first book, for which she made her own illustrations. Her jingles and short stories have appeared in magazines of every country and she herself appeared in all the courts of Europe, when she was only five years old, lecturing in Esperanto, and striving to help bring peace among all nations through the use of an international medium of communication. At the age of eight years she could speak eight languages and could talk intelligently on current events. Yet she was thoroughly a child. With her bird, Okikusan, trained to sing to the violin when Winifred played, and her pet dog, Bonniebelle, she would romp around the living room of her home, playing with her music teacher for five or ten minutes before settling down to her music lesson. But when once interested in the fairy music there was no trouble in holding her attention. She was willing to practice her scales and to do exercises that are not generally loved by children. With the teacher she took many trips to Music Land, and became acquainted with rhythm, which she called "the synovial fluid of existence." Music has been the greatest factor in the training of this young poet.

At the age of nine she passed college entrance examination successfully and according to the statement made by Doctor M.V. O'Shea of the University of Wisconsin, who has studied this girl from her earliest childhood, she had virtually completed a full curriculum college at the age of twelve. She is the author of fifteen books, the latest being *Jinglelays*, a substitute for "Mother Goose"; is editor of *Mother Stoner's Bulletin*, a pocket book magazine, and is also the inventor of "San-Rhythmics" (a method of graceful exercising while learning interesting facts) as an athlete, she has won prizes for her horsemanship, for fencing, boxing, rowing, swimming, driving, tennis, golf, and skating, the finest developed all-around girl in America, declare those who know her best. Mental exercise from her cradle days has not injured her physically, and to the age of twelve no boy who engaged in any physical contest with this athletic girl came out victor. After the age of twelve Miss Stoner gave up physical bouts with boys but found even keener delight in mental athletics. At the age of sixteen she was lecturing all over the United States in the Lee Keedick Lecture Circuit with such men as Sir Oliver Lodge, John Drinkwater, and other notables. With perfect self possession, she not only gave lectures but answered all questions directed to her after lectures and came out ahead in arguments resulting from open discussion of her ideas concerning education. The mother's claim has always been that Winifred is just a healthy, happy, individual, who has accomplished more than most people of her age because she has always played to a purpose; has found what to do and how to do it; has had a big aim and has been persistent. Those who have met Winifred and heard her talk are convinced that she was born with superior mental as well as physical powers, and has had, therefore, an unusual foundation upon which to build.

PLANTZ, MYRA GOODWIN (Mrs. Samuel Plantz), author, daughter of the Reverend Thomas A. and Content (Craft) Goodwin, was born in Brookville, Indiana, and died in Appleton, Wisconsin. She was descended from Bartholomew Goodwin, who came from England to Virginia, between 1600 and 1625, and was granted by the British Crown an island in the York River, known as Goodwin's Island. The Reverend Thomas A. Goodwin, D.D., a man of great ability and prominence, was editor of the *Indiana American*, which in its day had the largest circulation of any newspaper in Indiana. Later he published the *Indiana Christian Advocate*. He was the author of several books and attained a reputation as an anti-slavery and temperance orator.

Myra Goodwin was educated at the Indianapolis High School and at Mount Vernon Seminary, Washington, District of Columbia, where she completed the course in 1880. During 1881–1882 she taught in a girl's seminary in Indianapolis, and from 1882 to 1884, at De Pauw University. In January, 1885, she joined Frances Willard in the work of the Woman's Christian Temperance Union, and was in the evangelistic department until her marriage at Indianapolis, September 16, 1885, to the Reverend Samuel Plantz, then pastor of a Methodist Episcopal Church in Detroit.

After her marriage she continued her active interest in the Woman's Christian Temperance Union, holding various offices, and was frequently a public speaker before religious organizations and young people's gatherings, such as state and national conventions of the Epworth League and the Woman's Foreign Missionary Society of the Methodist Episcopal Church. Although she shrank from public life, her gifts as a public speaker were too well known to permit of her retirement to inconspicuous departments of service. She was a brilliant conversationalist by reason of her keen wit, her remarkable fund of information, and her quickness of repartee. She also wrote articles on many subjects and was the author of over two hundred poems and more than three hundred short and serial stories. She published three books for young people: *Corner Work* (1892), *A Great Appointment* (1895), and *Why Not?* (1900); and a volume of poems, *Songs for Quiet Hours*, in 1915. She was a member of the Wisconsin State Cabinet of the Young Women's Christian Association, the Daughters of the American Revolution, and the Wednesday Club of Appleton, Wisconsin.

LINDSAY, MARY ANN BATSON (Mrs. William Lindsay), was born at the homestead, Westford Hill, near Westville, Otsego County, New York, October 2, 1839, daughter of Josiah and Ann Batson. Her parents were natives of England, and soon after their marriage came to America and established their home on a farm in Otsego County, New York. They were the parents of eleven children, of whom Mary Ann was the seventh. In the course of her studies in the schools of Westville and Cooperstown, New York, she developed into an unusually bright and diligent scholar. Her home surroundings were helpful, for all the children were carefully trained in industry, as well as in the concentration that educates both mind and body and instils principles of thrift and economy. The children took part in the work of the home. A brother made the family shoes; the girls spun and wove cloth for dressmaking and tailoring; the children helped to make hats; and all shared in the duties of the farm. Mr. and Mrs. Batson were active members of the Baptist Church, and the home atmosphere was devoutly Christian. Family worship was daily practiced, and an upper room in the house was reverently reserved as a place for private devotion, to which the mother often repaired alone or with her children. This early religious training was as much a part of the education of Mary Ann as was the knowledge acquired in the schools which she so eagerly attended.

In 1853, when the precocious girl was four-teen years old, the family moved to another and larger farm in the town of Metomen, near Fairwater, Wisconsin. Even at that early age she became the teacher of the school in her home district, and her four younger brothers and sisters were among her pupils. At the outset her weekly salary was only $1.50, and when she received an increase it was negligible. Yet she saved enough to make it possible later to realize her ambition for a college education, which was begun at the Wisconsin Female College (now Milwaukee-Downer College). Later she studied at Ripon College, and after graduation she resumed teaching. One of her engagements was in the district school near Fox Lake. Following the custom of the day she "boarded round" in the homes of her pupils, and was an occasional visitor in the family of Mrs. Jessie E. Lindsay. The friendship formed between Miss Batson and William Lindsay, terminated in their marriage which took place at the Batson homestead at Metomen, February 16, 1866.

After residing for brief periods at Orinoco, and Rochester, Minnesota, and Fox Lake, Wisconsin, Mr. and Mrs. Lindsay moved, in 1873, to Milwaukee, which became their permanent home. Mrs. Lindsay was essentially a home-maker. Her natural devotion and her desire to be of service were given full expression in her own home. She delighted in her varied household duties, and her life in her own intimate circle possessed rare beauty. This circle spread beyond the confines of her immediate family, to include a large group consisting of the descendants of her nine brothers and sisters who grew to maturity. Mrs. Lindsay inaugurated the custom of holding an annual family reunion. She held the first at her home, in 1885, and arranged for future meetings of the ever widening family circle. Many nieces and nephews remember her with affection, recalling the generosity and the kindly interest that enabled them to enjoy the benefits of higher education and travel.

Mrs. Lindsay was a member of the South Baptist Church of Milwaukee, Wisconsin. Her church meant "home" to her in the widest sense, and she rendered it loyal service. As a leader in the women's societies, and as a teacher of young women in the Sunday School, she was preeminently successful. The Baptist missionary enterprises especially engaged her attention. From her deep interest in the work of her sister, Mrs. Rosina Batson Price, who was a missionary in Burma, and from her exhaustive study of missionary matters in general, Mrs. Lindsay acquired a knowledge of missions that was world wide. In 1892 she was chosen President of the Woman's Baptist Foreign Missionary Society, of Wisconsin. In this capacity she served actively until 1909, when, on account of declining health, she retired. The Society, in recognition of her services, elected her Honorary President for life. In her great desire to help others Mrs. Lindsay always gave generously of her time and her means to various local charitable organizations; with many of which she was associated in an executive capacity. For years she was a director of the Young Women's Christian Association of Milwaukee, and President of the Woman's Auxiliary of the Martha Washington Home. During the latter part of her life Mrs. Lindsay enjoyed with her family the opportunities of travel, not only in the United States, but in Europe, South America, Mexico, and the West Indies. She thus gained a broadened interest and a comprehensive outlook on life. In the course of her travels she formed many friendships which she enjoyed for the rest of her life. Mrs. Lindsay possessed the calmness and serenity, the strength and poise, of a beautiful character rooted in religious conviction. She was a keen student and observer of flowers and plant life, and took pleasure in tending her attractive garden at her summer home, on Oconomowoc Lake. Among her friends she will always be intimately associated with this place. Her winter home was in St. Petersburgh, Florida, and it was there that she died, April 16, 1918. The funeral services were held in the South Baptist Church, Milwaukee, and she is buried in the Lindsay family lot at Forest Hill Cemetery.

Mr. and Mrs. Lindsay were the parents of four sons: William, Harry, James, and Herbert; and three daughters: Annie Margaret, Mary Eva, and Merti.

CHASE, ELIZABETH HOSMER KELLOGG (Mrs. Irving Hall Chase), was born in Waterbury, Connecticut, March 14, 1864. Her father, General Stephen Wright Kellogg, was a descendant of Phillippe Kellogg, who, in 1583, was a resident of Bocking, near Braintree, Essex, England, and in 1585 was living in Great Leigh, Essex, where his son, Martin, was baptized, November 23, 1595. Martin Kellogg was a cloth worker in Great Leigh and in Braintree, where he died in 1671. On October 22, 1621, he married, at St. Michaels, Bishops Stortford, Hertfordshire, Prudence Bird, and their son, Joseph, was baptized at Great Leigh, April 1, 1626.

This Joseph Kellogg, with his wife, Joanna, came to America, and settled at Farmington, Connecticut, some time before 1651. About 1657 he removed to Boston, and in 1659 purchased a home in Roxbury, but sold it in 1661 and settled at Hadley, where he entered into an agreement with the town to keep the ferry between Hadley and Northampton. He was a selectman of the town and Sergeant of the military company in 1663, and was in command of the Hadley troops at the Turner's Falls Fight, May 18, 1676. In 1678 he was appointed Ensign, and later in the same year was commissioned Lieutenant of the foot company, and served until 1692. He died in the winter of 1707–1708. His son, John, was baptized at Farmington on December 29, 1656, and on December 23, 1680, married at Hadley, Sarah (1660–1689), daughter of Samuel and Sarah (Deming) Moody. Their son, Joseph (born November 6, 1685), married, March 15, 1711, Abigail (born July 11, 1688), daughter of Ebenezer and Abigail

(Broughton) Smith. Their son, Jabez (born February 11, 1734) served as a private in Captain Samuel Smith's Company when it went to the relief of Fort William Henry in August, 1757, and in Captain Elijah Smith's Company, Colonel Israel Williams' Regiment, in the expedition against Crown Point in the summer of 1759. In the Revolutionary War he served as corporal at Charlestown, Massachusetts, in 1776, and as Sergeant in 1777. After 1775 his home was in Hanover, New Hampshire, where he died in 1791. He and his wife, Abigail Catlin, were the parents of Julian Kellogg (born in South Hadley, September 27, 1765; died in Shelburne, Massachusetss, August 4, 1813), who married, on February 14, 1788, Molly, daughter of Lieutenant Jacob and Mary (Kellogg) Pool, and a descendant, through her mother, of Lieutenant Joseph Kellogg. Jacob Pool Kellogg, their son (born in Shelburne, February 16, 1793; died October 6, 1843) married, October 20, 1820, Lucy Prescott (born August 4, 1795; died May 25, 1882), daughter of Stephen and Sarah (Prescott) Wright. Their son, Stephen Wright Kellogg, (born in Shelburne, April 5, 1822; died in Waterbury, Connecticut, January 27, 1904) is the father of Mrs. Chase. He entered Amherst College in 1842 and after two years was transferred to Yale, where he was graduated with highest honors in 1846. After a year of teaching he entered the Yale Law School, and after his admission to the bar in June, 1848, practiced his profession in Naugatuck, Connecticut, until 1854. He was then appointed Judge of the New Haven County Court, and was also Judge of Probate for seven years. During 1866–1869 and 1877–1883 he was City Attorney for New Haven. In 1860 he was appointed delegate to the Republican National Convention which nominated Lincoln for the Presidency, and was also delegate to the conventions of 1868 and 1876. During the Civil War he served from 1863 to 1866 as Colonel of the Second Regiment of the Connecticut National Guard, and from 1866 to

1870 as Brigadier General. From 1869 to 1873 he was a member of Congress, and was well known for the practical methods by which he clarified matters in committee. On September 10, 1851, he married Lucia Hosmer Andrews, daughter of Major Andre and Sarah Mehitable (Hosmer) Andrews, and granddaughter of Stephen Titus Hosmer, first Chief Justice of Connecticut; also a descendant through her mother, of Major General Humphrey Atherton, who served in the Colonial Wars, and of Samuel Holden Parsons, who was a Colonel at the Battle of Lexington, and in 1780 was commissioned Major General.

Elizabeth Hosmer Kellogg (Mrs. Chase) was educated at Saint Margaret's School, Waterbury, Connecticut, and at Mrs. Sylvanus Reed's School in New York City. On February 28, 1889, she was married at Waterbury to Irving Hall Chase, President of the Waterbury Clock Company and the Waterbury National Bank. They are the parents of five daughters: Marjorie Starkweather, who married James Rhodes Sheldon, Jr., of Savannah, Georgia; Eleanor Kellogg, who married Charles P. Taft, II, son of Ex-President William Howard Taft; Lucia Hosmer, Elizabeth Irving, and Dorothy Mather Chase. Gifted like her father with a practical mind, Mrs. Chase has always been interested in those philanthropies which minister to health and efficiency. She has supported the Waterbury School of her city. She has been a member of the Society of Mental Hygiene, the Anti-Tuberculosis Association, the Saint Margaret's Graduate Association, and the Army and Navy Young Men's Christian Association. During the World War she was active in relief work. She was Chairman of the Finance Committee of the Waterbury Chapter of the American Red Cross; the Publicity Committee of the Council of National Defense; the Woman's Section of the Waterbury Navy League, the Waterbury Branch of the Fatherless Children of France, and of the Woman's Naval Service,

Inc., of Narragansett Pier, Rhode Island. She is also Treasurer of the Francis Thayer Russell Memorial Fund, and is a member of the Woman's Club of Waterbury, the Waterbury Country Club, the Point Judith Country Club, and the Daughters of the American Revolution. In addition to her home in Waterbury, Mrs. Chase has a summer home, "Miramar," at Narragansett Pier, where her love for out-door sports finds expression in swimming, golf, tennis, and horseback riding.

FRANKLIN, LAURA MERRYMAN (Mrs. Philip A. S. Franklin), was born at "Hayfield," Baltimore County, Maryland. Her father, John Merryman, was fourth in the line of descent from John Merryman (born in Baltimore County, Maryland, 1705) who served as Justice and County Commissioner for Baltimore County, 1753–1754. Her mother was Ann Louisa Gittings, daughter of Elijah Bosley Gittings, who, through his grandmother, Elizabeth Buchanan, was descended from Doctor George Buchanan (born in Scotland, 1698) of the family of Auchontorlis. Doctor Buchanan located in America about 1723, was a citizen of Baltimore, Maryland, and died at Druid Hill, near Baltimore, April 25, 1750. He was one of the commissioners to lay out the town of Baltimore, in 1729; a Justice (or Commissioner) of Peace of Baltimore County, October 13, 1732 to September 5, 1735; Judge of the Quorum for Baltimore County, October 2, 1741, to 1750; and Burgess (Member of Assembly) from the same county, from 1745 to 1750.

Mrs. Franklin received her education at Mrs. Wilson M. Cary's Southern Home School, in Baltimore. On July 18, 1894, at "Hayfield," Maryland, she married Philip A. S. Franklin. They are the parents of two sons, Captain John Merryman Franklin, and Lieutenant Philip A. S. Franklin, Jr., and one daughter, Elizabeth Merryman Franklin. Their eldest son was for nearly a year in France with the 301st Battalion of Heavy Tanks. While there, he was advanced to the

rank of captain and decorated for distinguished service on the Hindenburg Line. Their second son, Philip A. S. Franklin, was Lieutenant of Infantry at Camp Mead, and was attached to the Student Army Training Corps, United States Army. During the war Mrs. Franklin was active in war relief work, and was a Vice-President and a member of the Publicity and Entertainment Committees of the Tank Corps League, which was devoted to the welfare of the Tank Corps, United States Army.

Shortly after her marriage Mrs. Franklin became interested in the New York Home for Homeless Boys, and has been indefatigable in her efforts to promote its usefulness. She is Chairman of the Ladies' Auxiliary of this institution and the only woman on the Board of Directors. The New York Home for Homeless Boys, established in 1899, is free to any homeless boys, irrespective of creed. Its official agents, as well as individuals personally interested, search the parks, bread lines, midnight missions, and courts, in efforts to reach the boy before he becomes a menace to the community. The institution is a home in the best sense of the word. Besides providing clean clothing, three good meals a day, a comfortable bed in which to sleep, and eventually finding suitable employment for the boy, it guides, encourages, and morally strengthens him. The substantial and gratifying results have been due to the faithfulness, sincerity, and efficiency of every individual connected with the institution. It is worthy of note that the officials of the Home, including the Superintendent, literally give their time and their services. They come in contact with many boys from twelve to eighteen years of age who have drifted into New York City, and have received thousands who were homeless, penniless, and miserably clad. In many instances the boys themselves are not responsible for their condition, and a little timely help restores them to a state of independence and self-respect. In 1918, 900 boys were cared for; 23,500 free meals were served; 187 boys were placed in remunerative positions; and 72 were returned to their own homes.

Mrs. Franklin has also devoted much time to the affairs of St. Bartholomew's Kindergarten. She is a member of the Colonial Dames, the International Garden Club, and the National Special Aid Society.

PUTNAM, MARY NICOLL WOODWARD (Mrs. Erastus G. Putnam), was born October 1, 1834, at Ithaca, New York, and died at Elizabeth, New Jersey, November 6, 1923. Her parents, William Amos and Frances Mary (Evertson) Woodward, were both descendants of colonial families of America. Furthermore, as has been stated by genealogists, Mrs. Putnam's ancestral chart is unique in the fact that her descent in every line, through the intermarriage of her ancestors, can be traced to the armorial families of the Old World.

She was married at Keewaydin, Orange County, New York, January 30, 1867, to Erastus Gaylord Putnam (born in Harford, New York, December 23, 1833; died in Elizabeth, New Jersey, October 1, 1915), son of Hamilton and Jeanette (Cleaveland) Putnam. Mr. Putnam spent his life largely in the service of his fellow-men. From 1868 to 1871 he was Business Manager for Cornell University, and resided at Ithaca. Upon resigning from this office he removed in 1872 to Elizabeth, New Jersey, where he passed the remainder of his life. From 1877 to 1887 he served on the City Board of Education, was its President, and was constant in his efforts to furnish the most modern educational methods. It was through him that the High School in Elizabeth was established. From 1888 to 1898 he acted as Health Officer and left a record of marked ability and unwearied devotion.

Mrs. Putnam's father, William Amos Woodward (born in New London, Connecticut, March 21, 1801; died at Keewaydin, New York, September 19, 1883), resided at Ithaca, New York, for many years, and there married, December 4, 1828, Frances Mary Evertson. His father, Amos Woodward (1769–1814), was Deputy-Collector of the port of New London in 1809–1811. He conducted a successful business as a shipper to Europe and the West Indies, and owned his own shipyard where many of his own vessels were built. He married Elizabeth, daughter of Nathan and Elizabeth (Terry) Bailey. Through the Terry family the ancestry is traced to the New England families of Lobdell, Bliss and Eggleston.

Amos Woodward's father, Park Woodward, of Stonington, Connecticut, was during the War of the Revolution, Purchasing Agent for the American Army and a contractor for bridge building. He married his third cousin, Zilpah Park. His father, Thomas Woodward, married at Preston, Connecticut, Dorothy, daughter of Robert and Mary (Rose) Park, granddaughter of Thomas, and great-granddaughter of Sir Robert Park. Sir Robert Park (born in Preston, England, in 1580), the first of the family in America, settled on land owned by him on the Mystic River, Connecticut. He was a friend of Governor John Winthrop, and held many positions of trust in the colonies. Thomas Woodward was fourth in direct descent from Nathaniel Woodward, whose name appears in the colonial records of Boston, Massachusetts, in 1635. He was a descendant of John le Wodeward, ranger of Arden forest early in the fifteenth century, whose grandson, John Wodeward of Solihull, married Petronella de Clinton of Baddesley, of a distinguished and noble family.

William Amos Woodward married Frances Mary Evertson, daughter of Judge George Bloom Evertson and his second wife, Frances Mary Nicoll. Mary Evertson was a granddaughter of Jacob Roeters Evertson (born at South Amboy, New Jersey, in 1734; died in 1807), who located, in 1762, at Amenia, New York, where he had inherited about 1,700 acres of land "laying in the Nine Partners in

Dutchess County, New York." He was elected a Deputy from Dutchess County to the Second Provincial Congress of New York, 1775–1776. He married, Margaret, daughter of George Bloom. The Honorable Nicholas Evertson, Junior (born in New York City, May 24, 1699; died in South Amboy, New Jersey, March 17, 1783), father of Jacob Roeters Evertson, was a Judge of Common Pleas and Quarter Sessions of the Peace, Middlesex County, New Jersey, in 1746, and Justice of the Peace, Monmouth County, New Jersey, in 1747. He married Susanna, daughter of Jacob Roeters. His father, Captain Nicholas Evertson (born December 27, 1659, in Weesp, a suburb of Amsterdam, Holland), married as his second wife, Margaret, daughter of Hendrickse Van Baal (born in Holland in 1636), who was a large landowner in Beverwyck (Albany), and also on the Norman Kill, a Magistrate of Fort Orange, Indian commissioner, and Judge of the Court of Admiralty. His wife, Helena, widow of the Reverend Cornelus Bogardus, was a daughter of Wilhelmus Teller (died, 1701), a merchant of New York, later of Albany, who served at Fort Orange under Governor Kieft, and married as his first wife, Margaret Donckesen, who was the mother of Helena. Nicholas Evertson was Captain of New York troops in an expedition against a French privateer in 1704.

Frances Mary Nicoll, wife of Judge George Bloom Evertson, was a daughter of Doctor Samuel Nicoll. She traced descent from the Reverend William Nicoll, of Islip, Oxfordshire, who married a Woodhall. Their son was John Nicoll; his son, Reverend Matthias Nicoll, a graduate of Oxford University, lived in Plymouth, England; his son, Colonel Matthias Nicoll (born in 1621), a graduate of Cambridge University and a lawyer of the Inner Temple, was appointed Secretary of the Commission "to visit the Colonies and Plantations known as New England." Before leaving England, 1664, he was commissioned Captain of the Military force to take Nieuw Amsterdam from the Dutch and rename it

New York. He held many important positions in the New World, and was the compiler of the "Duke's Laws" that laid the foundation of New York's jurisprudence.

His son, Honorable William Nicoll (born in 1657), son of Colonel Matthias Nicoll, was educated in England for the bar, and first came to America with his father in 1664. He was a member of the Governor's Council, New York, 1691–1698; Attorney General of the Province, 1687; member of the Provincial Assembly from 1701 to 1723, and Speaker of the House for sixteen years. He purchased from the Indians land on Long Island at Islip, long known as Nicoll Manor, and also owned one-half of Shelter Island. He married, in 1693, Anne (Annekin), daughter of Kiliaen Van Rensselaer, the "Great Patroon of Rensselaerswyck." Jeremias was the son of Heer Kiliaen (1580–1646) of that ilk, who was the first Patroon of the Manor of Rensselaerswyck, 1630. The family is of ancient Dutch extraction and, by intermarriage, brought to the Nicoll family the blood of the Van Cortlandts, and other eminent European families, such as those by the name of Van Weely, Lookermans, Schly, Boudinot, Papin, and Bayeux. The son of Honorable William and Anne (Van Rensselaer) Nicoll was Benjamin, who was born at the Nicoll Manor, and inherited it from his father. He married, in 1714, his first cousin, Charity, daughter of Colonel Richard Floyd. Their son, Benjamin Nicoll, Junior, born at Nicoll Manor, Islip, was graduated at Yale College in 1734. He was a lawyer and, successively, incorporator, trustee, and governor of King's College, New York. He married Mary Magdalen, daughter of Honorable Edward Holland, Mayor of the City of New York. Their son, Doctor Samuel Nicoll (1754–1796) was educated as a physician in Edinburgh, Scotland, and Paris, France. From 1792 to 1796 he held the Chair of Chemistry at Columbia College, New York. He married, first, his second cousin, Anne, daughter of Captain Winter Fargie, of the British Army, whose wife was Eve Holland.

Frances Mary, daughter of Doctor Samuel and Anne (Fargie) Nicoll, was born December 17, 1785, at Stratford, Connecticut, and was married, April 13, 1809, to George Bloom Evertson. Their home was in Poughkeepsie, New York, where their daughter, Frances Mary Evertson, was born.

She was a member of the Recreation Association of America; Daughters of the American Revolution of which she founded the Boudinot Chapter, was Regent for ten years and successively state Vice-Regent, State Regent, Vice-President-General, and at the time of her death one of the thirteen Honorary Vice-President-Generals for life; Society of Colonial Dames; Order of the Crown; Huguenot Society of America; Daughters of Holland Dames; Society of Americans of Armorial Ancestry; Society of New England Women; and life member of the New Jersey Historical Society.

GENTH, LILLIAN MATILDA, painter, daughter of Samuel Adam and Matilda Caroline (Rebscher) Genth, was born in Philadelphia, Pennsylvania. She attended the public schools, where she won a fellowship at the Philadelphia School of Design. In 1900 she was awarded the Elkins Scholarship which enabled her to study for a year in Paris under James McNeil Whistler, and to spend three additional years in the galleries of Europe. On her return to Philadelphia the Pennsylvania Academy of Fine Arts awarded her (1904) the Mary Smith Prize. Further recognition followed swiftly and her work has since won many honors, including the Shaw Memorial Prize of the National Academy of Design, New York (1908); the Bronze Medal at the International Exposition of Fine Arts at Buenos Ayres (1910); and the First Hallgarten Prize at the National Academy of Design, New York (1913). Essentially American and also highly individual, Miss Genth's work possesses a strength and sincerity unmarred by the exaggerations of much contemporary art. She has adopted a peculiarly difficult

field—that of the nude figure in landscape; and she has imbued her subjects with spontaneity and imaginative idealism. A noteworthy quality of these canvasses is the luminosity of the sunshine, the delicate beauty of the light. Her technique is firm and direct and her drawing truthful, while the tonality of the colour illustrates her freedom from the bonds of tradition. Notable examples of Miss Genth's works hang in the Carnegie Institute, Pittsburgh, Pennsylvania; the Metropolitan Museum of Art, New York City; the Cremer Collection, Dortsmund, Germany; the National Gallery of Art, Washington, District of Columbia; the Brooklyn (New York) Museum; and in many other galleries throughout the United States. Miss Genth has established her studio in New York, and occupies a foremost position among women artists. She is a Fellow of the Pennsylvania Academy of the Fine Arts, Philadelphia, Pennsylvania; an Associate of the National Academy of Design, New York City; and a member of the American Federation of Arts, Washington, District of Columbia; the National Arts Club, New York City; the Royal Society of Arts, London, England; and the Union Internationale des Beaux Arts et des Lettres, Paris, France.

GILFORD, MARY PENROSE HOOTON (Mrs. Thomas Buchanan Gilford), daughter of Francis Carpenter and Ann (Penrose) Hooton, was born at West Chester, Pennsylvania, October 22, 1881. Through her father, she is descended from Thomas Hooton of Hooton Hall, near Chester, England, who located in Burlington, New Jersey, in 1789, later lived in Philadelphia, and in 1800 settled at West Chester, Chester County, Pennsylvania. She is also a great-great-granddaughter of John Carpenter, a wealthy Quaker of Philadelphia and a descendant of John Hooton (1740–1815), Captain of Light Horse under Lord Cornwallis. Her mother was a great-granddaughter of Thomas Penrose, one of the first proprietors of East New

Jersey, and in 1712 a member of the Common Council of Philadelphia. She was also descended from Clement Plumsted, a member of the Philadelphia Common Council (October 12, 1712); commissioned Justice of the Peace, September 2, 1717, and re-appointed fourteen times during twenty-seven years; Judge of the Court of Common Pleas, Quarter Sessions, and Orphans' Court of Philadelphia County in 1717; and elected Mayor of the City of Philadelphia, October 1, 1723.

Mary Penrose Hopton was educated by private tutors and at Miss Irwin's School in Philadelphia; she also studied for three years in Paris. On January 8, 1902, she married David Trumball Lanman Robinson (died September, 1902); and on October 8, 1908, at West Chester, Pennsylvania, she married Thomas Buchanan Gilford of New York City. She has lived in New York ever since her marriage. During the World War Mrs. Gilford gave her services (1917–1918) to the National Service Club Number 1 (Harvard Unit) and to the Junior War Relief, for which she did Red Cross canteen work. During 1918–1919 once a week, at her home, she furnished entertainment for fifty French sailors and wounded men from the hospitals. Mrs. Gilford is a member of the National Defense League, the American Red Cross, the Philadelphia Country Club, the Acorn Club, of Philadelphia, Pennsylvania, and the Westchester Country Club (New York). She is devoted to outdoor sports, being an expert in golf, riding, driving and motoring.

BIRD, ANNA CHILD (Mrs. Charles Sumner Bird), daughter of Elisha Norwin and Elisabeth Humphrey (Martin) Child, was born in Worcester, Massachusetts, January 13, 1856. Through her father she is descended from John Howland and Francis Cooke, who came on the *Mayflower* to Plymouth, Massachusetts, December 20, 1620, and through her mother, from three other *Mayflower* Pilgrims. All her ancestors arrived in Massachusetts before 1660, with the exception of one branch

that came in 1720; several of her ancestors fought in Colonial and the Revolutionary wars.

She was educated in the public schools and the Oreall Institute, of Worcester, Massachusetts, and at Miss Putnam's School, Boston. On October 19, 1880, she was married, at Worcester, to Charles Sumner Bird, a paper manufacturer of East Walpole, Massachusetts. They are the parents of four children: Francis William; Charles Sumner, Jr.; Edith Harlan; and Joanne Child Bird.

For many years Mrs. Bird was President of the Wednesday Club of East Walpole, and directed its work for civic betterment. She has also been identified with numerous other social and philanthropic organizations, such as the Welfare Nurses' Association, of which she has been President; the Norfolk Agricultural School, being a member of its Council, and Vice-President of its Special Aid Committee. She was also an active worker for woman suffrage and was executive chairman of the Massachusetts Suffrage Association. She is a member of the Chilton and Women's City Clubs of Boston, the Boston City Federation, the Municipal League of Boston, the Daughters of the American Revolution, the Royal Society of Arts, London, and the North British Society, England.

MASON, FANNY PEABODY, war worker, was born in Boston, Massachusetts, daughter of William Powell and Fanny (Peabody) Mason. Her earliest American ancestor, Jonathan Mason, was the owner of a farm of 1000 acres at Walpole, Massachusetts. His wife, Anna Powell, founded the Boston Female Asylum, the first charitable society formed by women in Boston.

Fanny Mason was educated in the private schools of Boston. She has been active in philanthropic and war relief work—had charge, during 1917–1918, of a boy's camp belonging to the Newton Vocational High School; worked for a Committee for the French wounded, employed in making and furnishing Lafayette kits to the French soldiers; and was active in the work of the American Committee for Devastated France.

Miss Mason is associated with numerous civic and philanthropic societies, being a member of the Chilton, Mayflower, and Women's City Clubs, and the Children's Aid Society, the Women's Municipal League (Housing Committee) and the Tuesday Debating Club, all of Boston, and is an Associate of Radcliffe College, Cambridge, Massachusetts.

BISHOP, MARY AGNES DALRYMPLE (Mrs. Frederick Herbert Bishop), daughter of John and Frances Ann (Hewitt) Dalrymple, was born in Springfield, Massachusetts, August 12, 1857. Her grandfather, Samuel Dalrymple, married his first cousin, Anges Dalrymple, both of the Dalrymples of Lochinch, Stranraer, Wigtonshire, Scotland, a family whose head is the Earl of Stair. Her mother, Frances Ann Hewitt, was the daughter of Eli and Mary (Harwood) Hewitt, and a descendant of Peregrine White, son of William and Susan White, the *Mayflower* Pilgrims. Mrs. Bishop was instructed by private tutors. Being an only child, she and her mother, who was still a young woman, became real comrades, and were constantly together. She was unusually precocious, and had learned to read when only four years old. Her talent for singing also developed early, and she was in constant demand as an entertainer. In 1865, she entered the graded school at Grafton, Massachusetts, and on leaving the high school in 1875 was the first girl to complete the classical course. Although offered a scholarship at Wesleyan University, she decided to enter at once her chosen profession as a teacher. She is an accomplished linguist, and throughout her life has continued to study languages with various teachers.

While still a school girl she was editor of the Grafton *Herald;* her stories and poems had been published by the Westborough *Chronotype;* she had contributed botanical articles dealing with the flora of the section to the

Worcester newspapers, and she was local correspondent for the Associated Press. As her writing became more widely known, her work appeared in the *Youth's Companion*, and other journals of nationwide circulation. Later she was honored by the appointment as editor of the *Massachusetts Ploughman* of Boston, then considered the leading agricultural and farm authority, and for several years wrote for it fourteen columns of original matter each week and selected contributed poems and stories for publication, beside doing other editorial work for its eight pages and reporting stenographically the farmers' meetings held under its auspices. Her best work for the Boston *Globe* was the history of Grafton, written on its 250th anniversary. Her marriage to Frederick Herbert Bishop of Wollaston, Massachusetts, Manager of the Universal Winding Company of Boston, took place at Grafton, Massachusetts, September 21, 1889. Although she has no children of her own, she has been a true mother. Mr. Bishop by his first marriage had one son, Francis Herbert Bishop, born July 21, 1886; and four other children, Grace Irene, Walter Howard Oliver, Miriam Nelson, and Virginia, have been taken into the home. Mrs. Bishop has had an unusually fortunate and happy life. Although engaged in many public activities, her chief interest has always been her home where the motherliness of her character has had full scope. Always interested in equal suffrage, she registered with the first women voters. Another reform measure that has long occupied her attention has been the prohibition of the liquor traffic, and she has been active as a member of the Women's Christian Temperance Union. During the World War she was occupied with writing, knitting, and doing other work for the men in service, as a member of the Red Cross and the Hospital Aid Association. She is also a member of the District Nurse Association, the Day Nursery Association, Parents' and Teachers' Association, Women's City Club of Boston, Quincy Woman's Club, Wollaston Woman's Club,

Professional Woman's Club, the Presidents' Club, the Washington American League of Penwomen, the New England Women's Press Association, the New York Women's Press Club, and other organizations.

BORG, MADELEINE (Mrs. Sidney C. Borg), philanthropist, daughter of Julius and Sophie (Walter) Beer, was born in New York City in 1879. Her father, a native of Germany (born in 1832), came to New York in 1849: her mother (born in 1844) was descended from Henry Pike, who came from Holland to New York in 1760.

On November 24, 1899, Madeleine Beer was married to Sidney Cecil Borg, a banker (born in New York in 1875), son of Simon and Cecilia Borg. Their children are Margery Borg (born in 1900) and Dorothy Borg (born in 1903).

Mrs. Borg is prominent in many Jewish philanthropies. She is the President of the Jewish Big Sisters, and is largely responsible for the splendid work of this organization. The Big Sisters are those great-hearted adults whose sympathies are touched by the city child who so seldom gets a "square deal," either in love or guidance, or in wholesome play, and becomes, therefore, defiant and lawless. Since 1912 the Jewish Big Sisters have been active in the field of juvenile delinquency and preventive work, and in the succeeding years there has been a great increase in the number of cases handled, in the individual effort given to each case, and in the success attained.

It is significant that since the Jewish Big Sisters have extended their preventive work there has been a marked decrease in court cases. The Jewish Big Sisters has branches in the Manhattan and Bronx Children's Courts, in the Manhattan and Bronx Domestic Relations Courts and in the Parental Court in the Municipal Building, New York. With over two hundred Big Sisters in actual service, five field workers, and a well developed organization as part of the Federation for Support of Jewish Philanthropic Societies, the Jewish Big Sisters of New York have been facing the problem of furnishing wholesome and attractive recreational activities to the hundreds of Jewish girls coming under their care, when referred by the courts as delinquents, or suggested by interested relatives and friends, or sent by school teachers, employers, or organizations.

As the problem of prevention is of paramount importance, the organization has developed definite principles of method in dealing with the question, mainly, of the establishment of recreational activities. The Good Times Club was organized for the younger children under their supervision, principally the little girls between seven and ten to fourteen years of age. The Anchorage Club, with a summer home at Arverne, Long Island, cares for the older girls. The Big Sisters thus strive to give the little sisters the recreational life of the normal girl; not by placing them apart and organizing specific agencies for them, but by establishing a wholesome club atmosphere, with an open membership, by which their social activities are brought into the normal recreational life of the community.

Mrs. Borg is Chairman of the Board of Directors of the Central Committee; is also head of the Women's Auxiliary of Montefiore Home; is a member of the Women's City Club and the Women's National Republican Club; a Vice-President and Chairman of the Women's Division of the Federation for Support of Jewish Philanthropic Societies. This last society was organized in 1916, as a result of the desire of various Jewish philanthropists in New York to obtain, more efficiency in their drive for funds and to centralize all other efforts.

NATHAN, MAUD (Mrs. Frederick Nathan), daughter of Robert Weeks and Anne Augusta (Florance) Nathan, and sister of Annie Nathan Meyer, was born in New York, October 20, 1862. Her father (1831–1888) was a member of the New York Stock Exchange. His father was Seixas Nathan, son of Simon Nathan, a native of Frome, Somersetshire, England, who located in New York, where his name appeared in the first city directory, dated 1786. Mrs. Nathan's mother was a daughter of William Florance of New Orleans. Mrs. Florance was a daughter of Gershom Mendes Seixas, a distinguished rabbi of New York, who for twenty-eight years served as a trustee of King's College, now Columbia University. His father, Isaac Mendes Seixas, a man of prominence in New York in pre-Revolutionary days, was one of the signers of the Non-Importation Act. Maud Nathan was educated at the Misses Hoffman's private school in West Thirty-eighth Street, New York City, continuing her studies there after Mme de Silva took control. Later she attended the Gardner Institute, on Fifth Avenue, and still later entered the co-educational high school at Green Bay, Wisconsin, where she completed the course, at the age of fourteen, at the head of her class. She continued her studies, under private tutors, giving special attention to voice culture, and spent considerable time in travel, acquiring a speaking knowledge of French and German.

On April 7, 1880, she married her cousin, Frederick Nathan, a member of the New York Stock Exchange. Their wedding tour included England, France, Austria, Germany, Italy, and Switzerland. After an absence of nearly two years, Mrs. Nathan returned to New York well equipped, through study and observation abroad, to carry on practical work in connection with educational and philanthropic movements in the United States. She gained a reputation as a platform speaker for woman suffrage and various philanthropies. In this connection she was the first woman to speak in a Jewish synagogue at the regular Sabbath evening service; and she has addressed the Convention of the Federation of Churches. Mrs. Nathan has been identified with the Consumers' League since its incep-

tion. She is one of the founders and incorporators, and was for many years President, of the New York City League. She has been Chairman of the Committee on Industry of the General Federation of Women's Clubs, a patron of the National Council of Women, and one of the speakers at the Conference of Liberal Religions. In the organization of the Women's Municipal League she rendered valuable assistance; she was one of its first vice-presidents; and she was selected as the one woman speaker to address the mass meeting of the League held at Carnegie Hall, New York.

Mrs. Nathan was the only representative of her sex at a dinner given by people especially interested in the Labor movement, when the close of the nineteenth century was celebrated. She has been a delegate to many international congresses, and has addressed conventions at Geneva and Antwerp, Paris, and Berlin. She spoke to the French and Germans in their own tongues. Mrs. Nathan was one of seven Americans invited to the opening of the Peace Palace at The Hague, and upon that occasion, as a representative of the Daughters of the American Revolution, she presented peace flags which were accepted by the Committee. In 1905 she received from the jury of the Liège International Exposition a diploma and a gold medal for her efficient promotion of the work of the National Consumers' League. She also received a medal from the National Institute of Social Sciences for her work in ameliorating conditions of working girls.

During the World War, in the summer of 1915, Mrs. Nathan once a week entertained a large number of workers who prepared articles for the Surgical Dressings Committee. In 1916 she helped in the Community Kitchen, and once a week during the winter of 1918 she gave out clothing to the French soldiers and sailors and acted as interpreter for them. She was one of the speakers in several of the Liberty Loan campaigns, and also gave her services to the Red Cross Auxiliary (Knollwood Club), the Arts Club Committee, the Manhattan Chapter of the Daughters of the American Revolution, and the Duryea Fund at the Barnard Club. She participated in the great Red Cross parade in New York City.

Mrs. Nathan has been an active figure in several municipal political campaigns, especially as a speaker at mass meetings. She is the Honorary President of the Consumers' League of the City of New York; First Vice-President of the National Consumers' League; Second Vice-President of the New York State Consumers' League; and a member of the Barnard Club, the National Arts Club, the Woman's City Club, the Automobile Club of America, the City Federation of Clubs, the Council of Jewish Women, the Woman's Roosevelt Memorial Association, the Manhattan Chapter of the Daughters of the American Revolution, and a member of the International Lyceum Club of Paris, France. For twenty years Mrs. Nathan wrote the annual report of the Consumers' League. She has written articles for the *Century Magazine*, the *North American Review*, the *World's Work*, for other periodicals and newspapers.

COTTLE, MARION WESTON, lawyer, was born in Buffalo, New York. Her father, Octavius O. Cottle, practiced law for many years in Buffalo, and was one of the best-known probate and real estate attorneys in western New York. His mother, Harriet Biron (Weston) Cottle, was a member of the family of Lord de Weston of England. Her earliest American ancestor, John Weston, settled in Salem, Massachusetts, about 1644, and became an extensive landowner. He was prominent in the affairs of the Colony, and one of those who formulated the principles of Colonial Government. Octavius O. Cottle married Fanny Ford, daughter of Joram and Frances (Ford) Petrie, and a descendant of the Vanderheyden family, Dutch patroons of Troy, New York.

Miss Cottle received her early education at St. Margaret's School, Buffalo, and attended Wellesley College as a special student. In 1904 she received the degree of Batchelor of Laws from New York University, and in 1913 the degree of Master of Laws from Boston University. She was admitted to the New York Bar in 1905, and later, on motion, to the Bar of the United States Supreme Court, and to those of New Hampshire, Massachusetts, Maine, and California. Miss Cottle specializes in probate practice and has had extensive experience as a trial lawyer, mostly in the City of New York. She is an associate editor of the *Women Lawyer's Journal;* lecturer on Domestic Relations at the Washington (District of Columbia) College of Law; lecturer at the Brooklyn Institute of Arts and Sciences, and has toured the United States for the Redpath Chautauqua System. She was always in close touch with the suffrage movement, and many of her talks have been in the nature of a strong appeal for Votes for Women. Miss Cottle is a most convincing speaker, and, unlike many of those who lecture on law, she has the faculty of eliminating dry technical details and of presenting the facts in a most interesting manner. She is considered an authority on the subject of domestic relations and one of her most masterful addresses deals with that subject. In fact, Miss Cottle has been peculiarly successful in making law a popular subject at public gatherings as well as in the college classroom. That she deals with many diverse subjects is shown by the following list giving the titles of some of her most popular lectures: *The World War and its Effect upon the Laws of Nature; The Human Side of the Law; Your Lawyer Friend; Law for Busy Men and Women; Domestic Relations; Woman's Place under the Law; Woman's Status under the United States Constitution; Legal Knowledge as a Safeguard in Business Affairs; The Law of Contracts and its Importance to Women; The Legal Aspects of the Suffrage Movement; Wills and Administration of Estates; The Study of Law as an Element in Mental Training; The Legitimate Place of Legal Training in the College Curriculum; The Possibilities of the Law as a Profession for College Women.*

Miss Cottle is a member of the American Bar Association, the New Hampshire Bar Association, the San Francisco Bar Association, the New York County Lawyers' Association, the Women's Lawyers' Association, the Massachusetts Association of Women Lawyers, the Woman's City Club of New York, the New York Wellesley Club, and the Tau Zeta Epsilon Society of Wellesley College; and is an honorary member of Kappa Beta Pi, the legal honor sorority of the University of California.

SEARS, CLARA ENDICOTT, author, daughter of Knyvet Winthrop and Mary Crowninshield (Peabody) Sears, was born in Boston, Massachusetts, December 16, 1863. Through her father she is descended from John Winthrop (born in Suffolk, England, in 1629), the first governor of Massachusetts, and through her mother from Governor John Endicott, a native of Dorchester, England, who located in America in 1644. In addition to these two, five other ancestors were colonial governors. Clara Endicott Sears was educated in the private schools of Boston, as a representative of one of its oldest families, and became prominent in Boston society.

Throughout her life she has been responsive to the instinct for mysticism that has always characterized the descendants of the Puritans. In 1911 she published *The Power Within*, a series of passages from writers on New Thought, and in 1912, *Selections from Prentice Mulford's Works*. These were extracts from Mr. Mulford's *White Cross Series*, which he had published in Boston, beginning in 1886; they took the form of instructions regarding the application of New Thought to everyday life. About this time Miss Sears built her country home, "The Pergolas," on Prospect Hill near the secluded village of Harvard, Massachusetts, overlooking the Nashua Valley. Here, on a farm of four hundred acres, she interests herself for much of her time in agriculture, horticulture, forestry, and the raising of blooded cattle. She carries on literary pursuits as well, however, finding inspiration in the quiet and peace of a community that has been the scene of significant religious and philosophical experiments. Adjoining Miss Sears' estate lie the house and land called "Fruitlands" where, in 1843, Bronson Alcott and a group of English mystics, supported by Ralph Waldo Emerson, tried to establish what they called a "New Eden." This "Con-sociate Family" was a community somewhat after the order of Brook Farm, but less successful. The house, which dates from about 1717, was falling to pieces when Miss Sears purchased and restored it, with all the original furnishings, as a memorial to the Concord Philosophers. Miss Sears opens the house to the public during the summer months. In 1915 she compiled from letters and diaries *Bronson Alcott's Fruitlands*, an account of this early experiment in applied Socialism. Miss Sears is well able to understand the ideals of the "Con-sociates," but she gives her fullest sympathy and her practical coöperation to the widow of Bronson Alcott in the care of her four small daughters. Besides studying the philosophy of the "Con-sociates," Miss Sears has taken a practical interest in that sect known as the shakers. After spending much time in the old Shaker village near Harvard, interviewing many of their leaders, who placed unpublished material at her disposal, Miss Sears published in 1916, *Gleanings from Old Shaker Journals*, which is both unbiased and illuminating.

On the night of April 6, 1917, at the time Congress was passing the resolution that brought the United States into the World War, Miss Sears wrote her stirring poem, *The Unfurling of the Flag*, which was set to music by John Hopkins Densmore. It was sung in hundreds of churches all over the country, and was used in schools and colleges, in Liberty Loan and Red Cross rallies, by chaplains in the Army and the Navy, and by war relief workers, both in the United States and abroad.

It read as follows:

There's a streak across the sky line
  That is gleaming in the sun,
Watchers from the light-house towers
Signalled it to foreign Powers
  Just as daylight had begun,
      Message thrilling,
      Hopes fulfilling
To those fighting o'er the seas.
"It's the flag we've named Old Glory
That's unfurling to the breeze."

Can you see the flashing emblem
  Of our Country's high ideal?
Keep your lifted eyes upon it
And draw joy and courage from it,
  For it stands for what is real,
      Freedom's calling
      To the falling
From oppression's hard decrees.
It's the flag we've named Old Glory
You see floating in the breeze.

Glorious flag we raise so proudly,
  Stars and stripes, red, white and blue,
You have been the inspiration
Of an ever-growing nation
  Such as this world never knew.
      Peace and Justice,
      Freedom, Progress,
Are the blessings we can seize
When the flag we call Old Glory
Is unfurling to the breeze.

When the cry of battling nations
  Reaches us across the space
Of the wild tumultuous ocean,
Hearts are stirred with deep emotion
  For the saving of the race,
      Peace foregoing,
      Aid bestowing,
      Bugles blowing,
First we drop on bended knees,
Then with shouts our grand Old Glory
We set flaunting to the breeze.

As soon as the United States mobilized its resources Miss Sears became an active worker in the Harvard Red Cross. In response to the Government's appeal for the conservation of food, she organized a club of girls, one of the first of its kind, called the Canning and Evaporating Club of Harvard, Massachusetts. Miss Sears sent to the West for large evaporators, and at once set to work demonstrating the advantage of this method of food conservation for overseas shipment. In this same connection she addressed the Women's Committee of National Defense, at the State House in Boston, taking samples of the produce with her. The Worcester County Farm Bureau became very much interested in this undertaking and sent demonstrators to observe the work of the Club. The canning and evaporating proved to be of such high grade that the entire output was purchased by the 76th Division, American Expeditionary Forces, then stationed at Camp Devens, whence some of the evaporated food was sent to France. The Club took first prize at all of the many competitions that it entered, and received a medal at the Great Eastern States Exhibit, Springfield, Massachusetts. The United States Agricultural Department wrote many letters inquiring about the work. The Department also requested photographs of the Club at work, in order that they might be used by the lecturers who were being sent all over the country to urge the conservation of food. Miss Sears wrote a pamphlet giving an account of the work and of the methods employed, and this was placed by the Agricultural Department in its library at Washington. At the conclusion of the World War Miss Sears received a certificate from the Massachusetts Food Administration commending the work which through her efforts had been accomplished. Photographs of the Club's activities have been included in a text-book which the Agricultural Department is placing in the public schools throughout the country.

The close of hostilities was celebrated by Miss Sears in her *Peace Anthem*, another poem of ringing patriotism. This also was set to music, in 1919, by Mr. Densmore. The War, however, did not diminish Miss Sears' susceptibility to the literary appeal of the Nashua Valley, and in 1918 she published her novel, *The Bell-Ringer*. This is such a legend as would have appealed to Hawthorne; its supernatural elements are delicately treated, and the mysticism of the secluded New Englander is interpreted sympathetically and poetically. Miss Sears also continued her research among the Alcott papers, and in 1919 privately printed a pamphlet on *Three Unpublished Poems of Louisa M. Alcott*. Miss Sears is a member of the Boston Author's Club, the Authors' League of America, the New England Poetry Club, the Chilton and Women's City Clubs of Boston, the American Guernsey Cattle Club, the Society for the Preservation of New England Antiquities, the Massachusetts Society of the Colonial Dames of America, the New England Historic Genealogical Society, and the Massachusetts Society of Mayflower Descendants.

STEPHENS, KATE, author, daughter of Nelson Timothy and Elizabeth Lydia (Rathbone) Stephens, was born in Moravia, New York, February 27, 1853. Her ancestors, native English stock, located during the seventeenth and eighteenth centuries in this country, where New York and the New England States now are situated. Kate Stephens received her early education in the schools of Auburn, New York, and Hartford, Connecticut. She then studied at the University of Kansas, where she was graduated A.B. in 1875, and A.M. in 1878. While pursuing her college course she also received private instruction from tutors, including professors from Harvard University and the University of Berlin. In 1878 she was offered, and accepted, the assistant professorship of Greek and Latin in the University of Kansas. In 1879, a separate chair of Greek having been established, Miss Stephens accepted the professorship of that department, which she held until 1885. Her general experiences in public life, and her special observation of conditions

governing women in private life, led her to a systematic study of the status of women. For the *American Supplement of the Encyclopaedia Britannica*, and for *The Forum, The Atlantic Monthly, The Bookman* and other periodicals, she wrote various articles on this subject, and, several of her later essays she published, individually. As Junior Editor of the *Heart of Oak Books*, she did her first work in compilation. The Senior Editor, Charles Eliot Norton, refers to her work as follows: "I regret that I am not allowed to mention by name one without whose help the books would not have been made, and to whose hand most of the Notes are due." Miss Stephens later became Editor of a number of educational books, individual or in series, which have achieved marked popularity and wide usefulness. Some of these are: the Macmillan *Stories from American History; Johnson's Life of Pope* (1897), *Stories from Old Chronicles* (1909), *Heroes Every Child Should Know* (1907) and *Heroines Every Child Should Know* (1908). In the last one she was co-editor with Hamilton Wright Mabie. In addition, Miss Stephens has edited certain English Classics.

Perhaps there is no better way to convey an accurate idea of Miss Stephens' literary standing, than to quote the reviewers' opinions of the following books, of which she is the author: *American Thumb-Prints: Mettle of Our Men and Women* (1905): "Brilliant and original sketches of American character and institutions . . . a book to read and reread." (*Westminster Review*, London); "The book is pervaded by the idealistic spirit and resonant with hope and faith; it is also clear-sighted, direct and pungent in criticism . . . Miss Stephens is a scholar, but she has lost none of her native wit." (Hamilton Wright Mabie in the *Outlook*). *A Woman's Heart* (1906): "The story of a struggle between the open, philosophic, nineteenth-century mind of the woman, and the form-ridden, acquiescent, medieval mind of the man . . . told with passionate sincerity and fervor of truth." (*Book News*); "The

book is human; it lays bare a human heart."
(Boston *Transcript*); "A book to ponder, for
seldom have nature and ecclesiasticism been
put in clearer antithesis." (*Minneapolis
Journal*). *The Greek Spirit* (1914): "A brilliant and penetrating study of elements and
influences that went to the creation and development of that racial spirit." (New York
Times); "It is splendidly written." (Los
Angles *Times*); "Her account of Orphism and
the mystery religions is particularly to be
commended." (*The Nation*); "C'est un
ouvrage admirable de lucidité et de bon
goût." (*Mercure de France*, Paris). *The Mastering of Mexico* (1916): "These pages give a
new picture of Cortez . . . a human Cortez . . . in democratic council with his
men." (Newark *Advertiser*); "Nothing could
be more admirable than the way in which the
author has held to the quaint language and
spirit of the sixteenth century original."
(New York *Globe*); "Miss Stephens has kept
a very realistic atmosphere in her rendering."
(Boston *Transcript*). *Workfellows in Social
Progression* (1916): "Her arguments are
never prosaic, and she is always delighting
the reader by bringing in some forgotten, or
overlooked, or entirely unfamiliar reference
. . . By a happy knack she keeps her
essays on the level of the concrete . . .
She is a strong believer in the English idea of
liberty, and in the aims and ideals of the
Puritans." (Springfield *Republican*); "A
book for thoughtful people who would take
their humor interwoven with fact, philosophy
and wisdom." (Brooklyn *Eagle*); "Miss
Stephens writes with fascinating brilliancy
and ease." (Baltimore *Sun*). *Life at Laurel
Town; In Anglo-Saxon Kansas* was published
in November, 1920. Miss Stephens is a
member of Theta Sigma Phi and Phi Beta
Kappa; associate founder and the organizer
of certain societies devoted to educational and
patriotic objects; and a member of the Pen
and Brush Club of New York City, as well as
of various college and university alumnae
organizations.

POTTER, FRANCES BOARDMAN
SQUIRE, writer, educator, and lecturer on
feminist, industrial, social, and literary sub-
jects, was born in Elmira, New York, November 12, 1867. Her father, Doctor Truman H.
Squire, eminent physician and surgeon, won
distinction throughout the Civil War as
Surgeon of the 89th New York Volunteer
Infantry, and as Division Field Surgeon in the
Army of the Potomac. He was a personal
friend of General Ulysses S. Grant. Mrs.
Potter's mother was Grace Smith, a native
of Vermont. On her father's side, Mrs.
Potter was ninth in direct descent from
Samuel Squire of Peterborough, England, who
fought in Cromwell's army. George Squire,
son of Samuel, also a native of England
located in Concord, Massachusetts, about
1630. Frances B. S. Potter was eighth in
descent, also on her father's side, from Roger
Williams, Governor of Rhode Island. On
her mother's side, she was fourth in descent
from Major Hezekiah Smith of the 5th
(Hampshire Company) Massachusetts Regiment in the Revolutionary War, who was a
member of the Provincial Congress and of the
Constitutional Convention.

Frances Potter was the youngest of three
children; the others were Charles Squire, a
physician and surgeon in Elmira, New York,
and Caroline Squire Brown. She received her
preliminary schooling in Elmira. Her home
life was guided according to the Puritan traditions of her mother, and enriched also by the
sympathetic companionship of her spiritually-
minded father. In 1883, she entered Elmira
College, the oldest woman's college in the
country, where she was graduated in 1887.
During her school and college life, she was a
leader among her fellows, ardent in her
friendships, and responsive to her instructors.
Possessed of a superb physique, she excelled
in outdoor sports, she also played the banjo
and the violin; had a voice of remarkable
range and quality; taught herself to play the
piano creditably; and managed to be a good
student, as well. In the old halls of Elmira

College tradition still preserves memories of the vivid and gifted girl of the "eighties" who won honors in mathematics, Natural History, and French; sang the hero's part in operettas of her own composing; acted in plays of her own writing; and enthusiastically attended the college dances in the old gymnasium. Her marked and versatile ability was enhanced by her beauty and her charm of manner and bearing. She was graduated A.B. in 1887 and A.M. (in French) in 1888. When her father's death, in 1889, made it necessary for her to support herself and contribute to the family income, she returned to the College as Instructor in French. She also tutored privately and gave singing and violin lessons. The establishment of a summer school of music, in 1890, brought to Elmira a noted New York teacher of singing. Frances became his pupil, and he urged her to study for an operatic career, offering to secure for her a position to sing in a New York church. This would have met the expense of her operatic studies. She was eager to accept the offer, but her mother had the old Puritan aversion to a professional career, and Frances declined the opportunity.

In 1891, she married W. S. Potter of Brooklyn, New York. They traveled for a year through Europe, Egypt, and Palestine. Their eldest child, Agnes Squire Potter, was born in London, England. Within the next four years, three more children were born— Mark Louis, Grace Smith, and Truman Squire. During this period the family resided successively in Brooklyn, New York, Wisconsin, and Minneapolis, Minnesota.

In 1899, domestic circumstances made it necessary for Frances Potter to return to teaching, so she obtained a position as Senior Teacher of English in the East Side High School of Minneapolis, Minnesota. Her success in this profession was immediate and remarkable. The following year she was appointed Instructor in English in the University of Minnesota, in Minneapolis. Students attended her courses in such numbers that in order to accommodate them two large rooms were combined, and even then there was capacity attendance. Frances Potter possessed an unusual gift of teaching, stimulating the mind and the imagination of every student who received her instruction. Besides eloquence and enthusiasm, she had the art of investing every subject with vital meaning and magical beauty. Her wide range of knowledge and interest invested her lectures with an extraordinary richness. She was a musician, writer, investigator of social movements, lover of natural science, woman of the world, mother. It is not to be wondered at that, with this background, she made her courses literally the beginning of a new life for the students. At least twice every year she invited her classes to her home, where she supplemented the subjects of her courses with all the embellishments of musical, pictorial, and dramatic art which her fertile ingenuity could devise.

In 1903 she was made Assistant Professor of English at the University of Minnesota. In 1904, in collaboration with Mary Gray Peck, of the English Department, and Professor Carl Schlenker, of the German Department, she published a play, *Germelshausen*, which was produced by a Minneapolis stock company, and was favorably received in the Twin Cities. In 1905, she published her novel, *The Ballingtons*. This book received widespread attention as "The best presentation in modern fiction of the results of the economic dependence of women." From this time on, Frances Potter's interest in the economic problem underlying social struggles lured her out of the peaceful environment of academic life into the arena of public activity, in connection with political and industrial reform movements.

In the fall of 1905, with her family, she went to England to spend her sabbatical year in study and special research in Cambridge University, working with Professor Walter Skeat and Israel Gollancz. Accompanying her for the same purpose was her friend, Miss

Peck, of the Minnesota University English Department. The close friendship of these two women had begun in Elmira College, where they were fellow-students; it was terminated only by Professor Potter's death. The year which they spent in England was marked by occurrences of historic import. It saw the rise of the militant suffragists, the fall of the Conservative Ministry, the formation of a branch of the Fabian Society in Cambridge University, and other significant events. Professor Potter by invitation addressed many notable gatherings in London, and elsewhere in Great Britain, thus coming in contact with the leaders of the political, industrial, and literary life of the nation. Among these were Professors Skeat and Gollancz, Doctor James Murray of Oxford Dictionary fame, Mr. and Mrs. Philip Snowden, G. Lowes Dickinson, Professor Frederic Maitland, Mrs. Sidgwick and Blanche Clough of Newham College, A. Maude Roydon, May Sinclair, Howard Sturgis, and Henry James.

Professor Potter returned to America in the summer of 1906. One of her first public addresses after her return was made in support of Woman Suffrage, at a hearing before the Minnesota Legislature. She had for some time been intending to aid the Suffrage cause; it was the year in England which brought her intentions to a head, and also clarified her previously vague sympathy with Socialism. From this time on, she was an active Suffragist, and an avowed Socialist of the Fabian, or moderate, school. At this time her brilliancy as a lecturer attracted continually wider attention, and brought an ever increasing number of invitations to speak in all parts of the country. In 1907 she was made full Professor of English at the University of Minnesota. In 1909 she made two special trips to speak on the Pacific Coast— the first to California; the second, to the Convention of the National American Woman Suffrage Association, in Seattle. While she was attending the Convention, strong pressure was brought to bear upon her by Doctor

Anna Howard Shaw, President of the National American Woman Suffrage Association, to accept the position of Corresponding Secretary of the Association. This urgent solicitation, coming as the climax to a number of calls to exchange her university life for a public career, seemed to open the way for her to devote her powers to the service of an immediate and pressing reform. She accepted the offer, and was formally elected by the Convention. Immediately afterward, she sent her resignation to the authorities of Minnesota University, where it caused the greatest surprise and was accepted with genuine regret. When Professor Potter left Minneapolis, in the fall of 1909, she was tendered a farewell banquet, at which speakers prominent in the affairs of the city, the University, and the State paid tribute to her genius and deplored her departure.

Mrs. Potter's official connection with the New York Headquarters of the National American Woman Suffrage Association continued for seven months. Very soon after she assumed office, differences of opinion regarding administrative matters arose between her and Doctor Shaw. The trouble became so acute that it was carried to the Executive Board for settlement. The Board unanimously sustained Mrs. Potter, so she consented to hold office until the next convention met in April, 1910, but she gave notice that at that time she would retire. The entire episode assumed such importance, during the next few years, that it threatened to split the Suffrage Association. The final result was a reorganization along more democratic lines.

One of the delegates to the Convention of the National American Woman Suffrage Association in Washington, District of Columbia, in April, 1910, at which Mrs. Potter retired from the Executive Board, was Mrs. Raymond Robins, President of the National Women's Trade Union League. Mrs. Robins at once invited Mrs. Potter to take up work for the League as Department Editor of *Life and Labor*, the official magazine, and as National Lecturer. Mrs. Potter accepted this offer, moved with her family to Chicago, where the League had its headquarters, and in the late summer of 1910 entered upon her new duties. Simultaneously with taking up industrial work, she assumed the chairmanship of the Committee on Literature and Library Extension of the General Federation of Women's Clubs. Soon afterward she was elected to the staff of the University Lecturers' Association, the first American woman accepted by this international organization. She was also made a member of the regular staff of lecturers of the Brooklyn Institute of Arts and Sciences. During the three years from 1910 to 1913 she was in continual and ever increasing demand as lecturer and writer. Her varied training and mature experience, her striking presence, and her beautiful voice, her kind and catholic disposition toward all men, caused her to be loved and remembered wherever she went. Among her public utterances during this culminating period of her life, three stand out with special significance as illustrating the prophetic character of her thought. The first was the Fourth of July address on *Peace*, delivered in 1912 in Golden Gate Park, San Francisco, to an audience of ten thousand people. This was the first time a woman had ever been selected by the Municipality to appear as the official orator upon such an occasion. The second was her address, *The Declaration of Peace*, on the evening of the same day, delivered before the Biennial Convention of the General Federation of Women's Clubs. Unwearied by her exhausting speech of the afternoon, she spoke for an hour and a half, and so original was her line of thought, so climactic in structure and power, that the great audience was held spellbound. Baroness Von Suttner, who appeared on the same program, declared that Mrs. Potter's speech was the most wonderful she had ever heard on any subject. The third and last of her three greatest speeches was delivered upon the

occasion of her last public appearance, in the Garrick Theatre, Chicago, on Socialist Women's Day, in February, 1913, the subject being, *The Woman Movement and Socialism*. This was only a week before her last illness. She spoke as if inspired, for she was addressing the kind of audience she loved best—keen, critical, unsentimental, but profoundly idealistic. If she could have chosen what her last appearance was to be, she would have been content with this. She died on March 25, 1914.

Even during that year of illness just before her death she courageously continued to do some writing; a spelling book which she compiled was used considerably in public schools throughout the country. Her untimely death was widely lamented, and one of the most striking manifestations of esteem came from the Chicago Women's Trade Union League in the form of a request that her address, *Moses the Strike Leader*, be printed in *Life and Labor* in order that the women in industry might have in permanent form the one of her talks which had meant the most to them.

To sum up the influence of a life so varied and vital as hers in its contacts with her generation, is difficult. It was in her remarkable ability to exert a synthetic and correlating force that she achieved an unusual eminence. She spoke to clubwomen on the labor movement; to industrial women on the intellectual and political movements; to men on the feminist movement. She appealed to every class for a better understanding of every other class. She spoke always persuasively, never antagonistically. She aimed at creating good feeling, at awakening hope, courage and the will to act. Hers was the utterance of a great heart, of a large spiritual faith. She was an ardent advocate of beauty as a factor in popular education; and, to further this relationship, she urged use of The Bible as a literary masterpiece in the curriculum of the schools. No woman of her time was better equipped for the task of promoting coöperation among diverse groups working for human betterment. Her death at the age of forty-seven, when she was at the Zenith of her powers, was a real loss to humanity.

O'DONOHUE, TERESA MARY JEROME, widow of Joseph J. O'Donohue, was at the time of her death, the most prominent figure among women in Catholic charitable circles in the United States. She was born in New York City, February 8, 1838, and died there, January 7, 1918, daughter of Patrick and Mary (Murphy) Riley. Her maternal grandfather, John Murphy, came from Wexford, Ireland, in 1811, and settled in New York. He was the owner of the Bowery Stage Line which ran from the Battery to Fourteenth Street. This business was bequeathed to his son, James Murphy, who, later, sold it and started the Madison Avenue Stage Line, from Wall Street Ferry to 42d Street and Park Avenue.

For many years of her long and useful life Mrs. O'Donohue was looked upon as a national leader in the field of Catholic charity. She was President of the Association of Catholic Charities, Ladies of Charity, from its organization in March, 1902, and witnessed its wonderful growth due mainly to her interest and zeal, from a membership of ten ladies at the beginning, to more than 3,500 who are now engaged in the work.

The Association of Catholic Charities is the ladies' St. Vincent de Paul Society. Its work comprises the supervision of day nurseries, fresh air work, tuberculosis clinics, Big Sisters, hospital visiting, clubs and homes for working girls, auxiliaries to Catholic institutions, and social service in Catholic hospitals and settlements, work among the blind, and parish auxiliaries to the St. Vincent de Paul Conferences. Mrs. O'Donohue was practically the founder in the city of New York, of the Big Sister movement which is a development of the children's court committee of the Association of Catholic Charities. This com-

mittee, appointed by Mrs. O'Donohue in 1902, is still in existence, and is known as the Big Sisters of the Association of Catholic Charities.

The war service activities of the Catholic ladies of New York was inaugurated by Mrs. O'Donohue at her home, on the day following the entrance of the United States into the war. She called together the members of the League of Catholic Women for Civic and Social Reform, an auxiliary of the Association of Catholic Charities, and explained to them the necessity of Catholic women taking up service work for our soldiers and sailors. The result was the establishment of a center at 154 East 38th Street, where Catholic women devoted a great deal of their time to the various phases of war service, and where a Service Club was established for men in uniform. Many branches of this activity were opened in other sections of the city.

It is an interesting fact that Mrs. O'Donohue began her charitable career by working for the welfare of the nation's soldiers and sailors, and the close of her life found her engaged in the self-same unselfish and patriotic endeavor. During the Civil War, shortly after her marriage, and while she lived in the Williamsburg section of Brooklyn, Mrs. O'Donohue organized the Catholic ladies of her neighborhood to work for the Union soldiers and sailors, and they labored just as zealously and just as patriotically as did many thousands of Catholic women during the Great War. For nearly sixty years Mrs. O'Donohue carried on her work of charity, and spent her last days, until incapacitated by a paralytic stroke, in knitting sweaters for the men of our army and navy.

Her charitable activities extended far beyond the boundaries of the archdiocese of New York, and in 1908 she was elected President of the National Federation of Catholic Charities, at the convention held in Richmond, Virginia.

Mrs. O'Donohue received her early education at St. Peter's Academy, New York. She then entered the Academy at Mount St.

Vincent from which she was graduated with high honors. On September 7, 1858 she was married to Joseph J. O'Donohue, one of the most prominent New York merchants of his day, and for two years after her marriage she lived in Williamsburg. The family then removed to New York and Mrs. O'Donohue soon became prominently identified with every Catholic activity of the archdiocese.

Besides being President of the Association of Catholic Charities, and of the National Federation of Catholic Charities, she was also President of the Auxiliary of St. Vincent's Hospital, Vice-President of the House of Calvary, of which His Eminence Cardinal Farley was President; Vice-President of the alumnae of Mount St. Vincent, and, for nine years, President of the Children of Mary of the Sacred Heart Academy. Besides being an unusually efficient organizer and director in charitable affairs, Mrs. O'Donohue took a deep personal interest in the welfare of the poor. In her younger years she made it a habit of personally visiting the poor in their homes, bringing baskets of food to the needy, and doing many acts of personal service that were known only to the members of her own family. Until the Christmas before her death, she visited the Orphan Asylum every Christmas, and personally presented a gift to every child in the institution.

She was one of the founders of the New York Foundling Asylum Auxiliary, and always manifested a motherly interest in the little ones who found a home there. Possessed of wealth, she used her inheritance largely in works of charity. The first check of a new check book was always used for charity, and the first check of a new year was always drawn for the same purpose. Her constant service to the poor and afflicted was a reflex of the kindness and sweetness of her home life, and all visitors, whether of high or low station, were treated alike with a courtesy and kindly welcome that endeared her to all. In 1908 her work in behalf of the poor was recognized in Rome, when Pope Pius X made her a Lady of the Holy Sepulchre. There has been only one other in the United States so honored. Mrs. O'Donohue is survived by three children: Joseph J. O'Donohue, Jr., Mrs. José M. Ferrer, and Miss Teresa R. O'Donohue, who was her mother's close companion and associated with her in all her charitable activities.

CABOT, ELLA LYMAN (Mrs. Richard C. Cabot) educator and author, daughter of Arthur Theodore and Ella (Lowell) Lyman, was born in Boston, Massachusetts. Her father's earliest ancestor was Richard Lyman, a native of Derbyshire, England, who located in York, Maine, about 1630. Among her father's ancestors who rendered distinguished services to their country were Timothy Pickering, of Salem, Massachusetts; Samuel Williams, Secretary of State under Washington; and Theodore Lyman, at one time Mayor of Boston. Her mother's family, the Lowells, included A. Lawrence Lowell, President of Harvard University; Amy Lowell, poet; John Lowell, Judge of the Massachusetts Circuit Court; and James Russell Lowell, poet and essayist.

Ella Lyman Cabot received her early education in private schools of Boston, and later pursued special studies in Radcliffe College, and graduate courses in logic and metaphysics at Harvard, 1900–1904. On October 26, 1894, at Waltham, Massachusetts, she married Doctor Richard C. Cabot (born at Brookline, Massachusetts, May 21, 1868), a graduate of Harvard, and since 1919 Professor of Medicine in the Harvard Medical School. Doctor Cabot has been connected with many of the hospitals and clinics in and about Boston. He has also lectured widely and written profusely upon the subjects of hygiene and medicine as related to the young and to general public welfare.

Mrs. Cabot gives the major portion of her time, outside that required by her family, to teaching ethics and human relations, including child psychology, in a number of private schools. In connection with this work she has published *Everday Ethics*, 1906; *Ethics for Children*, 1910; *Course in Citizenship and Patriotism*, 1914; *Volunteer Help to the Schools*, 1914; and *Our Part in the World*, 1918. She has been a member of the Massachusetts Board of Education since 1905; a Trustee of Radcliffe College since 1904; President of the Woman's Educational Association, 1917–1919; Chairman of the Educaional Department, Woman's Municipal League; a Director of the Garland School of Homemaking; a Director of the College Club of Boston; and a member of the Massachusetts Civic League. She was also for a time President of the Civil Service Reform Auxiliary.

As a recreation, Mrs. Cabot finds an absorbing interest in music and gardening.

GOLDSMITH, ELIZABETH EDWARDS, author, daughter of Allen Thomas and Caroline (Lakey) Goldsmith, was born at Port Gibson, New York. She is descended from Thomas Goldsmith who is mentioned in the records of Southampton, Long Island, as early as 1641. The tradition is that he came to this country from Ireland, and belonged to a branch of the family of which Oliver Goldsmith, the poet, was a member. The family went to Killingworth, Connecticut, about 1682 and later settled in Orange County, New York. In 1790 or 1791 one of the descendants, Thomas Goldsmith, bought half a township from the Phelps and Gorham tract, in what is now Wayne County, New York, but was then a primeval forest. In 1792 he sent his son Thomas to develop the land. This Thomas Goldsmith, in 1812, married Sallie Armstrong Tyler, the widow of Chester Spalding. Upon his death he left the property to his youngest son, Allen Thomas Goldsmith, who was born September 7, 1824, and died November 11, 1894. Caroline Lakey, his wife, was a daughter of Abner Forbes Lakey and Lucy Pomeroy. Her father was a descendant of Matthew Lakey who, in 1726, at the age of sixteen, came on the ship *Eagle* from Londonderry to Boston, and settled in Upton, Massachusetts.

The Lakeys who were strong Protestants, came to Ireland from Scotland in the time of the Stuarts, and Matthew Lakey's father was wounded in the famous siege of Londonderry. Abner Forbes Lakey's father, James Lakey (1757–1827), served in the Revolutionary War and married in 1780 Charlotte, the daughter of Abner Forbes and Phoebe Leach.

Phoebe Forbes (1730–1826) was a woman of strong character; she was fifteen and Abner Forbes, forty years of age, when they married. She was only thirty-seven when her husband died and survived him sixty years. Her three sons served in the War of the Revolution and, hearing that the army was ill clothed and suffering at Valley Forge, she herself sheared the sheep in the dead of winter, wrapped them humanely in old blankets, carded the wool, spun and wove it into cloth, from which she made garments, and sent them to her sons. This indomitable soul killed a rattlesnake with her cane when she was over ninety, and could still spin and read her Bible, when she was gathered to her fathers in her ninety-seventh year.

Caroline Lakey's mother, Lucy Pomeroy, was a descendant of Eltweed Pomeroy, who, with his brother Eldad, came from Devonshire, England, to Dorchester, Massachusetts, in 1633. These brothers were descendants of Sir Ralph de Pomeroy, a companion of William the Conqueror.

Elizabeth Edwards Goldsmith is the sister of Anna Rowena Goldsmith Taylor, and of Kate Goldsmith of Hillcrest, Port Gibson, New York. She was educated at home by governesses, and for a few months attended Wells College. Her early years were devoted mainly to music until over-practice, resulting in a pianist's wrist, put an end to further musical activities. Later, she studied languages and the history of art in Dresden, Germany, and the history of art and symbolism in Florence and Siena, Italy, and

French in Tours, France. She is the author of newspaper and magazine articles and of two books, *Sacred Symbols in Art* (1911), used in the testing of art classes and by travelers visiting the art galleries of Europe, and *Toby, the Story of a Dog* (1913). She is a member of the Daughters of the American Revolution, the Barnard Club, the Pen and Brush Club, the Women's National Book Association, the National Pen League, the International Literary Association, the Drama League, the Woodcraft League, and the New York Society of Art and Archeology.

TAYLOR, ANNA ROWENA GOLD-SMITH (Mrs. William Taylor), educator, daughter of Allen Thomas and Caroline (Lakey) Goldsmith and sister of Elizabeth Edwards Goldsmith was born in Port Gibson, New York, and died at Clifton Springs, New York, August 16, 1921. She was educated at home by governesses, at the Palmyra Classical School, and at Wells College, from which she graduated in 1884. From 1890 to 1896 she was instructor in English and History at All Saints School, Sioux Falls, South Dakota, and at the Wells Preparatory School, Aurora-on-Cayuga, New York, from 1899 to 1901. In the Spring of the latter year, upon the death of the founder and first principal, Sarah Ludlow Yawger, she assumed the direction and management of the school and, by successive steps developing it from Wells School to Wallcourt, Miss Gold-smith's School for Girls, made it widely known. In October, 1913, she was married to William Taylor of Lyons, New York, who died in 1918. She was a member of the Daughters of the American Revolution, the Women's University Club of New York, the Century Club of Rochester, New York, and the Owasco Country Club of Auburn, New York.

RICE, JULIA BARNETT (Mrs. Isaac L. Rice), reformer and philanthropist, daughter of Nathaniel and Annie (Hyneman) Barnett, was born May 2, 1860, in New Orleans, Louisiana, during a temporary residence of her parents in that city. Her father was an English wholesale merchant.

Shortly after her birth the family removed to New York, where Miss Barnett passed her childhood, with occasional visits to her mother's parents in Philadelphia. Her education was broadly classical, including a thorough training in music, since her cherished ambition was to become a skilled pianist. As one of the most accomplished pupils of her future husband, Isaac L. Rice, Miss Barnett had every reason to look forward to a brilliant professional career, but, owing to the misfortune of a paralytic affection of the hands due to overpractice, she was forced to abandon her musical hopes, and though in time she recovered, she was never able again seriously to practice. The ensuing four years were devoted almost entirely to a comprehensive and critical study of French literature. Her desire to qualify for a profession remaining undiminished, however, she entered the Woman's Medical College of the New York Infirmary, now affiliated with Cornell University, and was graduated M.D. in 1885. On December 14th of the same year she was married to Mr. Rice. This marriage was marked by a beautiful harmony of devotion and encouragement of each other's activities. With sympathies, tastes, and intellectual interests in common, Mrs. Rice was aided by her husband in carrying out her many philanthropic plans, while she, by her loving understanding, intelligent appreciation, and undoubting belief in his future, contributed an inestimable element, as he always lovingly recognized, to the development of his remarkable career.

Isaac Leopold Rice was a man of unusual versatility and an ability akin to genius, a type often found during the Renaissance, but, on account of the modern urge to specialization, rarer at the present time. Born February 22, 1850, in Wachenheim, Bavaria, he was brought by his parents, Maier and Fanny

(Sohn) Rice in 1856, to Philadelphia, where he was a pupil in the grammar schools and the Central High School. While still a child he showed so marked a talent for music that he was placed under the tuition of Carl Wolfsohn, and, when only eleven made his first concert appearance as a pianist at the Musical Fund Hall, Philadelphia. The next year he appeared at Irving Hall, New York, and continued thereafter to perform in public, winning high praise from the critics. In 1866, he entered the Conservatoire Nationale in Paris where his already pronounced talent for composition was further developed. During the three years of his residence abroad he completed one concerto for piano and orchestra and outlined two others and a symphony. He also found time to act as musical correspondent to the Philadelphia Evening Bulletin, with letters remarkable for their keenness of perception, their wit and lucidity.

After his return to America in 1869, he determined to devote his energies to teaching, and for that purpose, removed to New York City. There until 1876 he taught continuously, his pupils' concerts helping to confirm his reputation. He planned a *History of Musical Philosophy*, which should coördinate all schools and theories and discuss the function of music, and its relations to the intellectual and moral aspects of life. Most of his ideas found expression in his booklet *What is Music?* which was published in 1875. In this, after reviewing the theories of the ancients and of certain modern philosophers, he set forth his own conception of the part played by music in the universe; that there is a visible nature and an audible nature—visible nature is in space, and is at rest; audible nature is in time and is in motion; they are two aspects of one infinity.

In the following year, 1876, this analogy between time and space was still further clarified in a pamphlet entitled *How the Geometrical Lines have their Counterpart in Music*, in which he argues at some length that the forms of space and the metres of music are merely different expressions of one fundamental idea. In addition to these two suggestive theoretical works, he published in 1876, *The Analysis and Practice of the Scales*, which proved a valuable aid to students of the piano.

In 1876, he completed his second concerto for piano and orchestra, which was highly praised. Shortly afterwards, however, he determined to relinquish his musical career, and to enter the profession of law. In his entrance examination for the Columbia University Law School he showed a command of ancient and modern languages, unusual in a man of his age, and during his course he was the only student able to read Roman Law in the original. Meantime he continued giving music lessons, and read considerably in political science.

In May, 1880, he received the degree of LL.B. *cum laude*, together with two of the three prizes in political science: a hundred-dollar prize for an essay on constitutional history and constitutional law, and one of fifty dollars for an essay on the history of diplomacy and international law. For the next two years he practised law, but had to continue teaching music in order to supplement his income. He pursued his studies in political science and contributed articles to the press on questions of the day. In 1882, he was appointed Lecturer on the Bibliography of History and Political Sciences in the School of Political Sciences of Columbia University and Librarian of the Political Science Library. In that same year he contributed two articles of moment to the *North American Review*. The first, appearing in the January issue, was entitled *A Remedy for Railway Abuses* and advocated nationalization of the railroads, an idea considered radical at the time. *Has Land a Value?* was published in June. In 1883, he founded the Academy of Political Science, and, as its first President, had the satisfaction of seeing it become one of the representative institutions of American thought. In 1883, also, he undertook his first important legal case, as associate counsel and legal advisor for Mr. Hugo Rothschild in the reorganization of the Brooklyn Elevated Railroad Company. In 1885, he organized the law firm of Rice, Friend and Bijur, and at the same time gave evidence of his wide literary interests by starting with his partners the *Franco-American Dramatic Bulletin*, for supplying good translations of contemporary French plays. In 1886, he founded *The Forum*, a monthly review of current opinion. Its first number was dated March, 1886, and, immediately it took its place in the first rank of magazines, because of the impartial character of its articles. For ten years Mr. Rice's public life was occupied in fighting for honest management and the rights of minorities in various railroad organizations. The full story of the rebuilding of the St. Louis and Southwestern Railway; the rescuing of the Texas Pacific from a powerful but unscrupulous syndicate; his action as counsel and director in the Richmond Terminal and Richmond-Danville and Eastern Tennessee Systems, and his restoration to economic health of the Philadelphia and Reading Railroad Company is a long one. These cases were all of peculiar complexity and commanding public importance, and through them he gained, in a few years, both in the United States and in Europe, recognition as one of the foremost exponents of the law and principles governing the conduct of corporate affairs. The results of his experience he made public in an article in *The Forum* (August, 1894), *The Legalized Plunder of Railroad Properties*, which pointed the way to the federal control of interstate commerce, and he was subsequently called into consultation with the committee framing the bill that put his suggestions into effect.

While living in Europe during the years 1891–1893, as representative of the Reading Company, he became strongly interested in the experimental development of the storage battery and recognized its practical value. He organized in 1894 the. Electric Storage Battery Company, and is thus responsible for the first successful application of this inven-

tion to street railways in America. This success encouraged him to devote himself to the new field of applied science. With every visit to Europe he brought back new inventions. In 1897, he introduced the electric automobile, organizing for its manufacture the Electric Vehicle Company, and establishing the first electric cab service in New York City. As a consequence of this enterprise he developed others, some allied or subsidiary, others simply due to his increasing interest in invention, science, and industry. During the ten years from 1897 to 1907, he was an officer or large stockholder in numerous industrial companies.

However, the enterprise which most clearly showed Mr. Rice's business genius and prophetic insight was his sponsoring of the submarine in 1907, when its inventor, James P. Holland, was in danger of bankruptcy through foreclosure by his creditors. After a thorough investigation of the Holland boat, Mr. Rice became convinced of its practical value and future importance, and assumed personally the debt of the Holland Boat Company, and formed the Electric Boat Company to take over its interests. After encountering numerous difficulties in his attempt to raise capital, he finally succeeded in convincing the British Admiralty of the submarine's undoubted utility in war, and the first five boats were built in England by Vickers Sons and Maxim, under Mr. Rice's supervision. Connections were established in Russia and France. Finally, when the European War showed what a powerful weapon the submarine may be, success came with its adoption by all nations as an essential element in modern naval warfare.

Another phase of Mr. Rice's constant mental activity is illustrated by the history of the Rice Gambit. From his youth he had been a chess devotee, and it is said that his first great law case, that of the Brooklyn Railroad Company, came to him as a consequence of the brilliant acumen shown earlier in his life in a game of chess. Certainly he brought to the defense and analysis of his elaboration of the Kieseritzky gambit, first discovered in 1895, the same patience, courage, and intellectual honesty that he brought to law and business. As President of the Triangular College Chess League, whose trophies he provided, of the New York State Chess Association, of several local clubs, and as patron of many others, he constantly encouraged these "athletes of the intellect," as he called them, to see that the game of chess is more than a contest, that it is a work of art. He was the donor of the trophy contested for by the chess teams of the universities of England and America.

Mr. Rice died on November 2, 1915, after an illness of little over a year. The many tributes to his life and works from all parts of the world showed the love and respect in which he was held. Greater recognition would have been his but for his innate modesty that forbade him to look for fame. He had little talent for publicity, and his greatest ambition was working for and with his family. He turned to his wife for the encouragement and help that sustained him through many dark hours, and for the applause when success came; to her he showed sympathetic insight, and the desire that she should develop her own personality with his aid, but in her own way. As a citizen his watchword was honesty in everything and the defense of the rights of the people.

Always interested, as a result of her medical training, in questions of public health, Mrs. Rice began, in 1905, her campaign against unnecessary noises. Her attention was first called to the matter by the continuous blowing of whistles and sirens on tugs and other small vessels in the Hudson River when the boat captains used their whistles for long distance signalling. According to records taken for Mrs. Rice by Columbia law students, the average was about 3,000 blasts per night. The conditions, bad enough along Riverside Drive, were found to be much worse on the other side of the city, where

Bellevue, Flower, and other hospitals, were exposed to similar noises. Letters from the physicians in charge testified to the evil effect of this whistling upon the nervous physical condition of their patients. Although this signalling was not required by either statute or emergency, Mrs. Rice backed by resolutions of the National Board of Steam Navigation and of the American Association of Masters, Mates, and Pilots, appealed in vain to municipal, state and federal authorities. She was informed that there had been no regulation of river noises in the past, that there was no official in the United States with power to determine the size of a boat whistle or manner in which it might be blown, and that the matter came under neither municipal, state nor federal jurisdiction. After a persistent campaign of two years, Congress passed the Bennet Bill enabling the Supervising Inspectors of Steamboats to end unnecessary whistling. This is the only bill ever passed for the purpose of suppressing noise.

With this victory to encourage her, Mrs. Rice proceeded to the abatement of other unnecessary city noises. Under her leadership was formed "The Society for the Suppression of Unnecessary Noise," controlled by two boards, an Advisory Board and a Board of Directors, representing the clergymen, educators, and physicians of New York City. As its first President, Mrs. Rice put into effect her well-considered ideas. These were, primarily, to awaken public sentiment to the absurdity of submitting to unnecessary and confusing city clamor, and, secondly, to aid the inmates of hospitals by decreasing all noise near such buildings. The first appeal to the public was published in the winter of 1906–1907 and was as follows:

The Society for the Suppression of Unnecessary Noise appeals to the public for support. It trusts that it will receive it for the following reasons:

First—It believes that those who contribute so liberally to our hospitals will aid a society whose first efforts will be directed to relieving the intense suffering of our sick poor from the noise-evil. The presence on our Board of Directors of the superintendents of sixteen hospitals speaks eloquently for the need of activity in that direction. The number of hospital patients so represented is over 8,500, their recovery being retarded, rendered difficult, and sometimes altogether prevented by loss of sleep due to unnecessary noise.

Second—It believes that those whose sympathies and efforts are devoted to ameliorating the condition of our congested tenement-house districts will willingly aid a work which will strive to render conditions there more endurable. To the sensitive, noise, even among spacious surroundings, is disturbing; in confined quarters, it is torture.

Third—It believes that those public-spirited men and women who are interested in improving civic conditions in general will help a movement which has for its object the removal of one of the greatest banes of city life, unnecessary noise, which first wrecks health and then is chief torment of illness.

The eagerness with which first steps toward checking the noise-nuisance were greeted by press and public indicated that the time was indeed ripe for an energetic, organized protest against this curse of city life. From the Atlantic to the Pacific there came a hearty response and a general demand for the enactment or reinforcement of ordinance for suppressing useless clamor.

It is needless to say that much noise in a great city is unavoidable, therefore we have not organized an Anti-Noise Society, but one which will confine its efforts to the suppression of unnecessary noises. Some of these are forbidden by statute, others by city ordinance, but in the rush of city life the enforcement of these statutes and ordinances is generally overlooked.

To be on the alert in the suppression of unnecessary noise, to enforce the existing ordinances and laws, to urge the enactment of others when needed, and to act for the Public in all matters of public complaint against noise, our Society has been organized. It will work along broad though conservative lines and is assured of the hearty support and coöperation of the Department of Health.

Once started, a successful campaign was waged throughout the whole United States. Legislative bodies, county councils, boards of health, clubs, and various societies worked for it, and individuals became increasingly enthusiastic. The movement became known all over the world as one of the most revolutionizing reforms of the century, and gained for its founder an international reputation. Marcel Prevost paid her a graceful tribute in the *Paris Figaro* for January 2, 1907, which served to popularize the cause in Europe.

Organizations were started in all the larger countries of Europe, inspired and supervised by the original society in New York.

The Society's first noteworthy achievement was the establishment of quiet zones around hospitals and the erection of "Hospital Street" signs. Convinced, moreover that the Society should make special efforts to curb the unchecked boisterousness of children—in itself one of the most constant sources of distress to hospital patients—and desiring earnestly to awaken in the children a sympathetic recognition of the claim of the sick on their compassion, she formed the Children's Hospital Branch of her society. This grew immediately to the proportion of a small army and, although designed essentially for the relief of the sick, proved of the greatest ethical value to the boys and girls. Hearty endorsement of the plan was received from physicians, clergymen, and educators. One of the most important letters of encouragement came from Commissioner of Health Thomas Darlington, who said:

"I wish to give an unqualified endorsement of your plan to enlist the sympathies of the boys in this city in an effort to obtain quiet in the vicinity of the hospitals. In asking aid of the boys, you are not only rendering a service to humanity and conferring untold benefit upon the sick in the hospitals, but you are encouraging a sense of civic righteousness and responsibility in those who are our potential citizens, and upon whom rests the future government of the city."

Finally the matter was brought before the Board of Education with a request for permission to seek in the public schools the coöperation of the children. Here, too, a prompt commendation was found, and on January 8, 1908, the following resolution was adopted:

Resolved, That the plan proposed by the Society for the Suppression of Unnecessary Noise, as above set forth, be and the same is hereby approved, and that a circular be prepared by the City Superintendent and sent to the principals of the high and elementary schools urging their hearty coöperation in securing on the part of the pupils a sympathetic and helpful interest in the effort to lessen unnecessary noise near hospitals and houses where sickness exists, and that permission be granted to said Society to distribute button-badges to pupils in the public schools who become members of the Children's Hospital Branch of the League.

During the first three weeks after organization Mrs. Rice addressed more than twenty thousand children, all of whom signified their desire to be enrolled as members of the Hospital Branch. The children were asked to write in their own words on blank cards their promise not to disturb the sick in hospitals, and each child was given a badge by the parent society. Mark Twain, himself so fond of children and of whom children were so fond, accepted the Honorary Presidency of the Branch in a letter to Mrs. Rice, which revealed his abundance of sympathy with the movement.

The Society received so much approbation upon the establishment of hospital zones that its President next turned her attention to the question of obtaining quiet zones for schools. In an article in *The Forum* for December, 1911, Mrs. Rice pointed out that this most important feature of school sanitation had been unrecognized hitherto, and that there was urgent need of protecting the young from the injurious effects of outside noise, which by rendering concentration difficult, increased the mental effort required for school tasks, and by preventing free ventilation through enforced closing of the windows, menaced the physical well-being of the child. The Society brought the matter to the attention of the educational and health boards throughout the country and interest in the project of forming the zone was immediate. As for the teachers, their earnestness was most convincing. Many of them said that nothing but the utter impossibility of making themselves heard above the surrounding din could force them to subject their classes and themselves to anything so distressing and so unhygienic as working in unventilated classrooms, and declared that their greatest desire was to obtain even a moderate degree of quiet which would enable them to be heard without shouting and to understand what was being said without following the motions of the lips. It was stated that the effect of continued loud talking on the throat made medical treatment necessary in many cases, and that abnormal conditions of the ears were often due to ear-strain. Probably the most encouraging feature of Mrs. Rice's campaign was the attitude of the foremost educators and health-officers throughout the country.

In her article in *The Forum*, Mrs. Rice also advocated direct ventilation as a safeguard for the health of the child. Of the system of artificial ventilation, she said, "one heard much, and it is an argument which is invariably brought to the fore, when the question of school noises is discussed, the object being to disprove the need of intervention for the sake of the child, since even with closed windows an abundant supply of fresh air is supposed to be possible. It has been proved, however, that ventilating plants, even at the best, are extremely unreliable, a fact well-recognized by many teachers in New York, as well as elsewhere." Because of this, she continued, the most pressing point had never been properly emphasized "for far in importance beyond the pathetic and oft-repeated story of discomfort or rather distress—more serious than the recital of cases of ear-strain or diseased throats—far graver than even the danger to the immature mind of enforced mental concentration amidst constant distractions (a fact today perfectly sensed by none, with the exception of the psychologist and the neurologist), far beyond them all looms up the danger of undermining the health of the child, and of exposing it to the risk of infection through impure and contaminated air."

In 1908, the Society for the Suppression of Unnecessary Noise began through its President an energetic campaign to establish a safe and sane observance of the Fourth of July. The manner of this holiday's celebration had come to inspire veritable terror. Statistics, compiled each year in hospitals and by life insurance companies, indicated that the price paid in accident and death for celebrating the "glorious Fourth" was appalling, and furnished a sad commentary on human folly. Yet patriotic Americans disagreed as to the proper method of celebrating the day. There were those who approved of noisy whistles, explosives, and bell ringing. Others, however, were in accord with Mrs. Rice, when she made her appeal for a dignified celebration unmarred by noise and disorder, with the danger of maiming and death obviated. Her request for an expression of opinion, sent to men of influence throughout the country, met with an immediate response. The words of approval and endorsement were almost invariably accompanied by offers of assistance. Colleges and universities sent her hundreds of signatures to petitions, and forty state governors formed a board of Honorary Vice-Presidents of the Society for the Suppression of Unnecessary Noise. By 1910 many cities had passed protective ordinances, but all of these were merely restrictive, not prohibitive. New York was the first city to pass, February 1, 1910, an ordinance absolutely suitable in tenure and scope.

Over the period of the European War, wealthy men and women often moved out of their homes and turned them over as soldiers' and sailors' clubs. Mrs. Rice decided that she would make hers a canteen, and remain in it as hostess. As it seemed to her that less attention was being paid to French soldiers and sailors than to the men in the American and British service, she determined to conduct her canteen primarily for the comfort of the Gallic allies. She therefore opened at her apartment at 12 East 87th Street, New York, the Cercle Lafayette on September 6, 1918, the anniversary of the birth of the gallant Marquis. From that date, until late in 1919, the club was open every evening of the week and all day on Wednesdays and Saturdays. All guests were served meals and refreshments, entirely without charge, and, in addition were furnished with transportation, cigarettes, and reading matter. From 800 to 1000 cigarettes were provided daily, and flags, cockades, "Nenettes" and "Rintintins" (the worsted mascots of France), with other souvenirs were distributed. Throughout, the attention received by the men was personal, for, as far as possible, Mrs. Rice and her family served their guests. She was assisted by her daughters, the Misses Muriel, Marion, and Marjorie Rice, Mrs. Dorothy Rice Sims, and her daughters-in-law, Mrs. Isaac L. Rice, Jr., and Mrs. Julian Rice. From the time a French soldier, sailor or marine left his ship at the Brooklyn Navy Yard for shore leave, the hospitality of Mrs. Rice and her daughters was at his command, even to the payment of carfares to and from the club. Upon arrival the visitor found every comfort and convenience that could refresh and entertain him, together with homelike surroundings and an easy congenial atmosphere. Greeted by one of the ladies of the family in their native tongue, French visitors first received a tricolour cockade to be pinned to blouse or cap and were then invited to roam at will through the rooms. They might settle themselves at tables to read, play games, chat or listen to music. Young men who were volunteer aids served soft drinks, coffee and cigarettes. At the hour for afternoon tea light refreshments were provided, and later a three or four course dinner was offered to all who cared to remain. Tables were set in the dining room and, if need be, as many as thirty could be placed in the living room, salon, and even the reception hall. The Gothic decorations of the rooms lent an impressive background to the scenes of wholesome diversion after dinner. Dancing, games, letter writing, would occasionally be interrupted by a chorus or by a Breton folksong or a Gascon recitation. In fact, though the ladies were there to be of service, the men entertained themselves. Mrs. Rice extended her hospitality not only beneath her roof but upon it as well as her guests were admitted to a superb roof garden whence there was a wonderful view of the city and surrounding country. Here during the summer of 1919 vaudeville entertainments were given twice a week. With the signing of the Armistice more American soldiers and sailors began to attend the Cercle Lafayette. Their days were Mondays, Tuesdays, Wednesdays and Fridays; and Friday was also especially reserved for the British. However, all nationalities were welcome on all days and the Cercle preserved generally a Gallic atmosphere. The majority of the French were very young, boys of sixteen or eighteen, fresh-faced and clear-eyed, with the light and enthusiasm of youth upon them. To them, often homesick in the city where language and ways were unfamiliar, the Cercle Lafayette soon became home and Mrs. Rice "*ma mere.*" They came as early as three o'clock in the afternoon, generally in charge of a petty officer. There were never less than one hundred of them, and once the number reached one hundred and thirty-eight. A special room was reserved for visitors of rank and Saturday afternoons and evenings were especially set aside for French officers, who frequently came to dine *en famille.* On several occasions Admiral Grout in charge of the Atlantic Division honored the Cercle with his visits, recording in the visitors' book his high appreciation for the wonderful work accomplished by the founder of this, New York's most unique canteen. The Cercle Lafayette was a remarkable personal achievement for humanity and patriotism. As an example of sterling womanhood, of motherhood, and of devotion of one American woman to her sisters across the ocean; as one citizen's tribute of appreciation to France of America's debt of eternal gratitude to her, both in conception and execution, the Cercle will remain forever a monument more enduring than bronze, for it will live in the hearts of hundreds of men, strangers in the land, who found cheer and comfort far from their own firesides at a time when personal encouragement was a need that they felt more keenly than any other. The private assistance given by Mrs. Rice to good work and to humane relief has always been large and in its distribution has brought happier lives and better opportunities to many. She will always be remembered for those qualities of the head that inspired her crusade against unnecessary noise and for those qualities of the heart that led her to devote herself unreservedly to the welfare and entertainment of the soldiers and sailors during and after the war.

Mrs. Rice is the author of *An Effort to Suppress Noise* (*The Forum*, April, June, 1908); *Our Most Abused Sense—The Sense of Hearing* (*The Forum*, April, June, 1907); *The Children's Hospital Branch of the Society for the Suppression of Unnecessary Noise* (*The*

Forum, April, June, 1908); *Our Barbarous Fourth* (*Century Magazine*, June, 1908); *Hoodlumism in Holiday Observance* (*The Forum*); *For a Safe and Sane Fourth* (*The Forum*, March, 1910); *Quiet Zones for Schools* (*The Forum*, December, 1911); and *The Child and the Fourth* (*The Forum*, July, 1913).

To the ideal family life of Mr. and Mrs. Rice was added the blessing of six children. They are: Muriel Rice; Dorothy Rice Sims; Isaac L. Rice, Jr. (born, August 13, 1890, married Beatrice Weil); Marion Rice; Marjorie Rice and Julian Rice (born, October 1, 1893, married Mary Plummer).

FORSYTHE, GRACE C. STRACHAN (Mrs. Timothy J. Forsythe), educator, was born in Buffalo, New York, and died in New York City, July 21, 1922. She was a daughter of Thomas F. and Maria (Byrne) Strachan, who came to New York from Scotland in 1846. Her education was obtained at St. Brigid's School and the State Normal School in Buffalo, and she later took post-graduate work at New York University, and had private lessons in literature, German, French, music, and art. It was as an educator that Miss Strachan earned an international reputation. She began her teaching career in Buffalo at the age of sixteen and, after experience in both the elementary and the high schools there, she accepted in 1893 an offer from Franklin W. Hooper, the President of the Brooklyn Museum of Arts and Sciences, and also a member of the Board of Education, to take a position in Public School 11, Brooklyn, New York. Standing first on a long list of candidates who had taken a competitive examination, Miss Strachan immediately attracted the special notice of the educational authorities. Her success was marked and her promotion rapid. In July, 1900, she was elected to the position which she held for more than twenty years, that of District Superintendent of Schools in New York City.

She was always a prominent member and was usually an officer in the various educational associations, but it was not until 1906 that her greatest work for women teachers began. This was the year of the opening of the campaign for "Equal Pay for Equal Work." The history of the six years' struggle is a long one. Part of it is told in Miss Strachan's *Equal Pay for Equal Work*, published in 1909. As a result of the campaign, the women teachers in the City of New York, on January 1, 1912, began service under a law which included the principles for which they had so long and so strenuously fought: "in the salaries of teachers hereafter appointed, there shall be no discrimination on account of the sex of the teacher." From that time she was a leader in securing an absolutely fair and secure pension law for the teachers of New York City, of a State education law, and of a State salary law, which benefited every woman teacher in the public schools of the State.

Miss Strachan was a member of the Committee on Teachers' Salaries, Tenure, and Pensions of the National Education Association since its organization in 1907. As District Superintendent in charge of Districts 33 and 35, Grace Strachan had 38,000 children and over 1,000 teachers under supervision, and in her district were to be found the best and the most up-to-date expression of all forms of work in elementary schools and Junior High Schools. In these districts were established in Brooklyn the first classes for crippled children, for deaf children, and for anaemic children, and also many classes for the mentally defective.

On April 6, 1917, Miss Strachan was married to Timothy J. Forsythe, an oil operator, the civil ceremony being performed at Fair Haven, Vermont, and the religious at St. Augustine's Church, Brooklyn.

She was the author of many magazine articles and reports on education and was in wide demand as a lecturer. She traveled widely, having visited nearly every state in the Union. She made three trips to Europe, where she observed educational conditions in England, Scotland, Ireland, Holland, Belgium, France, Italy, and Germany. In 1915 she made a trip through the Canadian Rocky Mountains, returning to New York from San Francisco on the Steamship *Finland* through the Panama Canal. She maintained her early interest in music and art, and was a member of the Buffalo Art Club and of the Mozart Society of New York. She belonged to numerous bodies active in civic betterment, the City, State, and National Federation of Women's Clubs, and was a member of the State Democratic League of Women. She also was an active supporter of the Ladies' Aid Association of St. Mary's Hospital, Brooklyn. During the World War she was the organizer and the president of the Teachers' League for National Service, and was a member and a district leader of the Food Administration. In 1914 she was the third president of the Interborough Association of Women Teachers.

LIVERMORE, HENRIETTA J. WELLS (Mrs. Arthur L. Livermore), daughter of Judge Henry Jackson and Maria A. (Goodnow) Wells, was born in San Francisco, California, May 22, 1864. Her father, a resident of Cambridge, Massachusetts, who served for many years as Representative and Senator in the Massachusetts legislature, was descended from Thomas Wells, who came in 1635 from Colechester, Essex, England, to Ipswich, Massachusetts. She was educated at the Harvard Grammar School, Cambridge, and at Wellesley College, where she was a member of the Shakespeare Society and from which she received the degree of A.B. in 1887 and that of A.M. in 1893. On October 21, 1890, she was married at Cambridge to Arthur Leslie Livermore, a New York lawyer, and has since made her home in Yonkers, New York. They are the parents of Henry Wells Livermore and Russell Blake Livermore.

Mrs. Livermore has been president of three college women's organizations in New York City, the Wellesley Club, the New York Association of Collegiate Women, and the Women's University Club, of which she was a founder. She has been active for many years in civic and educational matters, especially the establishment of playgrounds and the promotion of child welfare. For seven years she was president of the Yonkers' Child Study Club and she was chairman of the Educational Committee of the Yonkers' Civic League. The model Fairview Garden School, Yonkers, of which she is president, provides garden plots in summer and a clubhouse in winter for six hundred boys and girls. This work she described in the booklet, *Fairview Garden School*, published by the Russell Sage Foundation, and in magazine articles dealing with the general subject. Finding by experience that women needed the vote (in order to carry on civic work efficiently) Mrs. Livermore interrupted her own activities to help, as a speaker and organizer, in the campaign for equal suffrage. She became a director and Vice-President of the New York State Woman Suffrage Association, and chairman of its Assembly District Committee, which had charge of organizing the assembly districts of the state for a referendum in 1915.

As President of the Yonkers Woman Suffrage Association she brought the membership of that organization up to over three thousand and was later a member of the National Board of the Woman Suffrage Association and chairman of its Literature Committee.

In 1919 she became chairman of the Woman's Executive Committee of the Republican State Executive Committee, her efforts bringing about a large enrollment of women in the Republican Party for the presidential campaign of 1920. She also served as alternate delegate-at-large to the National Republican Convention in Chicago in that year. Her work in politics has throughout been marked by courageous leadership, a sense of fairness, and loyalty to her co-workers and to the cause of Republicanism.

Mrs. Livermore is also president of the Woman's Council of Yonkers, a society to study the full duties of citizenship for women and to attempt to perform them, and she is a member of the Anthropological Society, the Fortnightly Club for the study of history, and the Women's City Club of New York.

SNOW, ELLEN, author and reformer, daughter of Alpheus Franklin and Sara M. (Dean) Snow, was born in Claremont, New Hampshire. Her father, a lawyer of repute, was a descendant of John and Abigail Snow, of Chesterfield, Massachusetts.

Miss Snow has achieved international reputation as an indefatigable worker in behalf of all reforms for the advancement of mankind. She is widely known, also, as a faithful friend to all animals. Even as a very young child, she gave evidence of the unusual powers of perception and analysis that are characteristic of her. Although she enjoyed the activities natural to childhood, she was often pre-occupied with serious problems of life and the universe. In some mysterious way she had even thus early found a key to some of the problems that perplexed her elders. One of her repeated assertions was that she could remember incidents in a pre-natal existence, especially the experience of levitation (floating in the air) as a means of locomotion. To those who understood the child her idiosyncrasies only served to indicate unusual brightness and great promise. Many, however, who had the care of her failed to understand, and therefore sought to repress rather than cultivate her individualities. Consequently, as she grew to womanhood she withdrew into herself and led her life apart, communing with the unseen, or, as she used to express it when she was still a child, retiring "to talk with God."

From early childhood she has had a remarkable command of the English language. Her aspirations to authorship began when she could do no more than print detached letters, and while spelling was for her still in the phonetic stage. While in school she wrote for newspapers, and, as a young woman, received communications from an editor who addressed her "Mr. E. Snow," thinking that the articles he published were written by a man. Soon after leaving school she tired of the conventionalities of a life devoted to society and became interested in various branches of study. She read Buckle, Spencer, Darwin, Huxley, and the works of many philosophers, and made a serious study of the German language. She devoted much time to music, but, having always had a talent for drawing she decided to make art her profession. After studying privately with J. Wells Champney and Alexander Lawrie, she worked all of one winter and spring at the Academy of Design and the Students' League, New York City. She then opened a studio in Hartford, Connecticut, but because of eye-strain was obliged soon after to discontinue work.

Miss Snow keeps constantly in touch with the progressive mental and humanitarian life of to-day. Her correspondence has been extensive, and she has had uncommon opportunities to compare impressions with other thinkers of advanced tendencies. She has employed her ability as a writer to further many reforms, among them those seeking to ensure international peace and the elimination of unnecessary noise in large cities. She is also a strong advocate of cremation, as the only rational and sanitary mode for disposal of the dead. By far her greatest interest, however, and the work that has given her international repute, has been her crusade against cruelty to animals. She has devoted special attention to the anti-vivisection movement. In 1887 she began her active campaign against all forms of horse torture, by making a study of the evolution and use of the check rein. She treated this subject (June 22, 1887) in the first of a series of articles on the horse, which were published in the *Hartford Times* and the *Hartford Daily Courant*. The second article appeared

June 29th, and was followed on July 6th, by an article on the evils resulting from the use of blinders. From this time on, many articles upon these and kindred topics, such as docking and clipping, appeared in the columns of the daily press and in magazines.

At the twelfth annual meeting of the American Humane Association, held in Toronto, Canada, in October, 1888, a paper on the "Check Rein" by Miss Snow was read, and was received with marked approval. This paper, published by the Association as a pamphlet, copiously illustrated, has since been considered a standard and valuable addition to the literature of humane societies. It has had a very wide circulation, and is still in much demand.

Miss Snow's indignation against the use of the check rein was aroused to the point of expression when she saw sleigh races on the thoroughfare in front of her house in Hartford. She coöperated with her neighbor, Rodney Dennis, President of the Connecticut Humane Society, to stop this abuse; and from that time Miss Snow's activities became closely identified with those of Mr. Dennis and his Society. Practically all the annual reports issued by the Society for ten years, from 1888, represented her work. The Connecticut Humane Society was the first organization in the country to take a positive stand against vivisection, and it was Miss Snow who urged the President to oppose this practice. Her home in Hartford may be considered the headquarters from which, for many years, the crusade in America against vivisection was directed, for there she wrote or edited all that the Society has published on the subject. In 1893 a pamphlet *Vivisectors on Vivisection*, compiled by Miss Snow, was published and widely distributed, having first been made a part of the annual report for that year. She has always stood unequivocally for the total abolition of vivisection, and in this respect has found herself in accord with many of the reformers of Europe and America. Miss Snow's intimate friendship with Miss

Frances Power Cobbe, founder of the British Union for the Abolition of Vivisection, had its beginning in their mutual interest in this cause.

Miss Snow possesses an unusually active mind, housed in an extremely fragile body. Her life, therefore, has been a constant battle for physical strength to meet the tasks which she set her brain. During a certain severe illness she had recourse to mental science, and found herself entirely in accord with its fundamental principles. She has always been a student of abstruse subjects, having studied the world religions, and read with appreciation the Indian Vedas. This trend has led naturally to the acceptance of the theory of thought ministration and self-development, but she has not stopped here. Ever since 1899 she has had remarkable psychical experiences; she declares that telepathic communications from spirit friends, and the beautiful and inspiring philosophy expounded by them, have given her unfailing comfort and support. Miss Snow has also given evidence of possessing mediumistic powers, and she is a firm exponent of spirit communication.

Miss Snow has been a voluminous writer. She is the author of many articles, stories, and verses that have appeared in newspapers and periodicals. Among her published works are: *The Treachery of Satan* and *The Check Rein*, 1888; *Vivisectors on Vivisection*, 1893; *Scientized Juveniles*, 1898; *The Conqueror and other Verses*, 1899; *Psychic Experiences* 1902; *A Letter from Heaven*, 1905; *The Evolution of Rose*, 1907; *Animal Immortality*, 1907; *The Confession of Seymour Vane*, 1908; *The Easter of the Soul*, 1909; *The King of the Lord's Highway*, 1909; *Tommy Twistiken's Prayer; Tom's Friend;* and others.

Her paper, *Hell at Close Range*, first published in the *Abolitionist*, London, England, October 15, 1906, and later reprinted in many American papers, has been issued as a leaflet.

Miss Snow is Honorary Correspondent of the British Union for the Abolition of Vivisection, and is Honorary Vice-President of the

International Ethical Society. She is a member of the Vegetarian Society of America, the New England Cremation Society, the Universal Peace Union, the Berkshire Animal Rescue League, and the Jerusalem (Syria) Society for the Prevention of Cruelty to Animals.

THORNE, GERTRUDE L. KEMMERER (Mrs. S. Brinkerhoff Thorne), was born in Upper Lehigh, Pennsylvania. Her father, Mahlon S. Kemmerer, a coal operator, with headquarters at Mauch Chunk, Pennsylvania, carried on an extensive business. He owned mines in Pennsylvania, Wyoming, and Utah, and was largely instrumental in the development of coal mining in all of those states. He married Annie M., daughter of Judge John Leisenring of Mauch Chunk, who was also interested in the promotion of coal mining. Mrs. Thorne's mother was a beautiful, charming and highly intelligent woman. For many years before her marriage she acted as secretary for her father. She died when her daughter was only ten years old, and Gertrude was sent to a private school in Geneva, Switzerland. Upon her return to this country, she attended Miss Pierce's private school at Germantown, Pennsylvania, where she prepared for Bryn Mawr College. In February, 1913, she married S. Brinkerhoff Thorne, a coal operator, and they established their home in New York City.

On November 1, 1918, Mrs. Thorne located in Paris as a volunteer in Red Cross canteen work. She was sent, first, to Is-sur-Tille, and later to a canteen near Dijon, where she remained for three months. The plight of the refugees appealed strongly to her sympathies, and when money was sent to her from the United States for the use of these women and children, she immediately began relief work on their behalf throughout the Département du Nord.

On her first tour of inspection she found that the pitiable condition of these people was largely attributable to malnutrition. Meat was urgently needed, but none was to be had in the Département. Formerly, a staple food had been rabbits, and hardly a farm had been without its hutch. Mrs. Thorne used the $5,000 sent to her from the United States to buy rabbits wherever they could be found. At first she encountered difficulty because of the scarcity of rabbits throughout the Somme Valley, and the high prices demanded. With the aid of the Sous-Préfêt of Paris police, however, she finally obtained a supply at a reasonable rate. She next arranged for their continual distribution to the needy communes at stated intervals, under the supervision of the Red Cross. The mayors of Cambrai, Arras, Douai, Lille, Valenciennes, Roubaix, and other cities, coöperated by proclaiming the rabbits "wards of the State." One peasant woman would hold four rabbits (three females and one male), in trust for nine families, so that any risk of private profit was obviated. As a result of this system a constant source of nourishing food was obtained for about 5,850 families; the warrens were repopulated; and the occupation of caring for the rabbits proved of great benefit to the children of the devastated villages. Upon her return to America, Mrs. Thorne continued to collect and transmit funds for this work.

WARD, MAY ALDEN, author and lecturer, daughter of Prince William and Rebecca (Neal) Alden, was born at Milford Centre, near Columbus, Ohio, March 1, 1853, and died January 14, 1918. Her father was descended from John Alden and Priscilla Mullins, through Captain Jonathan, Andrew, Major Prince, to Andrew Stanford Alden, Mrs. Ward's grandfather. Captain Jonathan Alden married Abigail, daughter of Andrew Hallet, Jr. Andrew Alden, their eldest son, married Lydia Stanford. Major Prince Alden married Mary Fitch, daughter of Adonijah Fitch of Montville, Connecticut, who was a grandson of Reverend James Fitch of Savbrook and Norwich, Connecticut, and his second wife, Priscilla Mason, daughter of

Major John Mason, famous military leader of the Connecticut Colony. A year or two before the beginning of the Revolutionary War, Major Prince Alden and his family removed from Connecticut to Wyoming County, Pennsylvania, where he became a prominent landowner. In 1816 Andrew Stanford Alden, with his wife, Elizabeth Allington and their children, removed from Tioga County, New York, to Ohio. Mrs. Ward's father, Prince William Alden, a merchant and banker (born February 11, 1808; died February 27, 1893), married, in 1844, Rebecca, daughter of Henry Neal of Mechanicsburg, Ohio, and his wife, Catherine, daughter of Isaac Bigelow, of Dummerston, Vermont, and a descendant of John Biglo of Watertown, founder of the Bigelow family of New England. Mrs. Rebecca Neal Alden was born March 11, 1823, and died April 12, 1898. Mr. and Mrs. Alden were the parents of two sons: Henry, who died in childhood; and Reuben, who was killed in the Civil War at the age of sixteen.

From her father, May Alden inherited a taste for history and literature. At a very early age she began to write, contributing articles to the Cincinnati *Commercial* before she was sixteen. She attended Ohio Wesleyan University, Delaware, Ohio, where she was graduated A.B. in 1872. Later she was graduated A.M., and was elected an honorary member of Phi Beta Kappa. After graduation she studied for some years abroad, specializing in French, German, and Italian literature. In June, 1873, she married William G. Ward, since 1898, Professor of English Literature at Emerson College of Oratory, Boston, Massachusetts. Formerly he held the same chair at Syracuse University, and at one time was President of Spokane College.

As a result of her Italian studies Mrs. Ward published her first two books, *Dante: A Sketch of his Life and Works* (1887), and *Petrarch, A Sketch of his Life and Works* (1891). These publications, which are excellent reading, opportunely filled a need for scholarly handbooks in English on these two poets. Her later books are *Old Colony Days* (1897), a study of the Puritans; and *Prophets of the Nineteenth Century* (1900), which includes essays on Carlyle, Ruskin, and Tolstoi, and which has been translated into Japanese.

Mrs. Ward was connected with many clubs. During her residence in Cleveland she was a member of the Ohio Woman's Press Association and was made President of the East Side Conversational Club. While living in Cambridge, Massachusetts, she was for four years President of the Cantabrigia, one of the largest and most active clubs in the country. At the same time Mrs. Ward became a member of the famous New England Women's Club. In this organization she succeeded Julia Ward Howe as President, and was always one of the most efficient members. For two years she was President of the New England Women's Press Association. She was one of the organizers and a charter member of the Authors' Club of Boston; President of the Massachusetts State Federation of Women's Clubs from 1901–1904; and a Vice-President of the General Federation of Women's Clubs, from 1904–1908. In 1904 she founded a club magazine, which became the official organ of the General Federation; she herself was the Editor until 1910. In addition, she has held membership in many philanthropic and educational organizations, as well as in learned societies, such as the Academy of Political and Social Science, the Civil Service Reform Auxiliary, the Association for Labor Legislation, the National Municipal League, the National Child Labor Association, the Massachusetts Woman Suffrage Association, and the Authors' League of America. She was also active on committees of the Boston Music School Settlement, the Woman's City Club of Boston, the Twentieth Century Club, and the Women's Educational and Industrial Union. She was one of the commissioners for Massachusetts at the Louisiana Purchase Exposition in St.

Louis, Missouri, and later at the Portland (Oregon) Exposition. Her social service work on behalf of the industrial schools of the South, in the Consumer's League, and in anti-child-labor movements had won her a place among the most prominent social service workers of the country. As Kate Sanborn has said of her, "In all these offices she has been impartial, well poised, never capricious in manner or opinion. She followed the middle path. As hostess, teacher, author, friend, she was always natural, kindly, thinking of others. And so love, and appreciation, and the truest friendship were given her by all who were so fortunate as to know her and her work."

The principal medium for her life's work, and for the supreme expression of her influence, Mrs. Ward found in her weekly Current Events lectures, to which she devoted herself for more than twenty years. By means of them she gave thousands of women a rare understanding of contemporary history and politics. As has been said by one who benefited from her guidance: "It is wonderful to have invented a profession and led in it. Her clear insight, calm security of judgment, and unfailing courage, have exerted their beneficent influence in these difficult days, bringing poise and patience to many troubled minds. Her work has been larger than she knew, for she had the power to arouse women to think, and to weigh for themselves the meaning of the occurrences of daily life in the greater world of affairs." Such influence as hers could be exerted only by a great personality. As one critic says: "Mrs. Ward possesses a simplicity of manner that only comes with sincerity of purpose, the best breeding, and a backing of desirable ancestry; an executive ability that is never marred by the too frequent accompaniment of a domineering spirit and a desire for control; a straight clear outlook from eyes that hold no secrets; a handclasp that is cordial without being effusive. One is impressed by the apparent ease with which she accomplishes

great tasks. She does not talk of her work, nor take herself too seriously, and is delightfully free from pedantry. What she has done for other women, inspiring a scholarly spirit, giving history and literature in condensed and attractive talks, lifting them above narrow interests, petty jealousies, and the gossipy habit, cannot be told in a brief outline." Mrs. Ward's death occurred suddenly while she was in the midst of her work. She is buried in Mount Auburn Cemetery, Cambridge, Massachusetts.

RIDDLE, THEODATE POPE (Mrs. John Wallace Riddle), known in artistic circles by her maiden name, Theodate Pope, architect of the Theodore Roosevelt Memorial House in New York City, and the Westover School for Girls in Connecticut, is constructing the Pope or Avon School for Boys at Avon, Connecticut, in memory of her parents, the late Mr. and Mrs. Alfred Atmore Pope.

Her father, was born at North Vassalboro, Maine, July 4, 1842, son of Alton and Theodate (Stackpole) Pope. His earliest American ancestor was Joseph Pope, son of Robert Pope, of Yorkshire, England, who came to America in 1634 and settled at Salem, Massachusetts. From him the line of descent is traced through his son Samuel and his wife, Exercise Smith; their son Samuel, second, and his wife, Sarah Estes; their son Robert and his wife, Phebe Leveret; their son Elijah and his wife, Phebe Winslow, and their son John and his wife, Lydia Taber, who were the grandparents of Alfred Atmore Pope.

Mrs. Riddle was a passenger on the last voyage of the *Lusitania*. She herself was rescued, and brought to life after much effort; but her maid and her fellow investigator in psychic research, Professor Edwin W. Friend, were drowned. She is especially fond of children, and having none of her own, has adopted two boys. She married May, 6, 1916, John Wallace Riddle, former American Ambassador to Russia.

Commenting on Mrs. Riddle's plan of her school for boys the New York *Evening Sun* of March 9, 1921, says:

"Architecturally and educationally the Pope School for Boys, for the establishment and management of which Mrs. Riddle has incorporated the Alfred Atmore Pope Foundation (composed of Mrs. Riddle, J. W. Riddle, Mrs. Harris Whittemore, and Henry A. Pope, with Mrs. Riddle as sole managing director as long as she lives), will be unlike any other great preparatory school. It will differ from Groton, St. Paul's and St. Mark's, for instance in giving its students the daily interest of genuine country life in the shape of a little practical farming, forestry, dairying, carpentry and what not, in addition to a full allowance of the highest standard of academic work.

" 'Their minds will work the better for it,' said Mrs. Riddle in discussing her plans. 'It is the old New England idea, for which there is no equivalent nowadays—that healthy interaction of farm and school by which the vitality of the soil enriches the mind, and the training of the brain is aided by the work of the hands. No other method is equal to it. Life nowadays is so artificial, and the present educational method is only too successful in turning out paragons of charming superficiality.'

" 'These practical projects of true country life, to which each pupil will devote a short period—perhaps a couple of hours—every day, will not interfere with the usual pastimes. Indeed, the pastimes at Old Farms will be richer than those of most schools by the addition of trout fishing, for an excellent trout stream runs through the property into the Farmington River, and we will have a trout hatchery on the place. . . .

" 'Each class will be like a committee meeting under parliamentary rules,' she explained, 'A leader will call the class to order, for instance, and call upon one boy to recite something of the lesson of the day. His performance will be picked to pieces by the others, and

creative ideas will be generated by free friction, while the teacher preserves a more or less detached attitude as a sort of umpire.

" 'In a general sense the affairs of the school will be handled by a council, of which possibly one member each may be appointed by the Presidents ex-officio of Yale, Harvard and Cornell Universities, by the Progressive Educational Association, and the National Educational Association, while four will be chosen from parents of boys then attending the school and two from the alumni.

" 'The executive committee of the council will appoint the headmaster, who will nominate a bursar, factor, farm manager and dame. This last will be a highly important functionary, for I am fully alive to the desirability of woman's influence in the diplomatic management of 300 growing lads.

" 'The dame will be chosen for her qualities as a hostess and an executive. She will be responsible for the two women who run the general store, the four matrons in the houses where the younger boys live and for the woman librarian. Moreover, it will be a comfort for mothers to communicate with one of their own sex on such intimate problems as thick underwear and damp shoes.

" 'I believe in strong contrasts. I look forward to seeing our boys enjoy their work in the vegetable garden or the dairy, etc., in rough work clothing, and then in the evening they must dress for dinner. I wish to see them equally at home in the drawing room and the carpenter shop. Widely contrasting experiences enrich life and help a boy to feel at home in any setting.' "

In further commenting on the school, the article adds: "Two unique attractions of the Pope School for Boys will be an art collection and a mastodon. The fossil bones of the latter were discovered on Mrs. Riddle's farm at Farmington, Connecticut, and have been prepared by experts at Yale. The beast is quite an important exhibit, as there was something about it that settled a scientific problem. It will be set up in the crypt under the school cloister. The art collection, which Mrs. Riddle inherited from her father, consists of twenty-five choice examples—Monet, Manet, Degas and Whistler. They will be placed in the school gallery which will also be the music room, and which, with the library beneath, will hang over the bluff looking over 'Sleepy Hollow,' as that part of the valley is designated on old maps."

WILMARTH, MARY J. HAWES (Mrs. Henry M. Wilmarth), daughter of Shubael and Nancy B. (Smith) Hawes, was born at New Bedford, Massachusetts, May 21, 1837; she died at Lake Geneva, Wisconsin, August 28, 1919. Her father was descended from Edmond Hawes of Southampton, England, who located in Yarmouth, Massachusetts, before 1645.

Mrs. Wilmarth received her education at Kimball Union Academy, Meriden, New Hampshire. On May 21, 1861, at Newport, New Hampshire, she married Henry M. Wilmarth who had moved from Newport to Chicago in 1856. Mr. Wilmarth was prominent in the business life of Chicago, where he and Mrs. Wilmarth lived. He was one of the organizers of the First National Bank, and a member of its Board of Directors until he died, in 1885. The first meeting at which Jane Addams explained her plans to found Hull House, as Chicago's first social settlement, was held at Mrs. Wilmarth's home, which stood on one of the lots now occupied by the Congress Hotel. Subsequently, Mrs. Wilmarth became a member of the first Board of Trustees of Hull House. She was also a member of the Board of Trustees of Henry Booth House, of Frederic Douglass Center, and of Rockford College. In 1912 she became a member of the Progressive Party, and, with Miss Jane Addams, served as one of the two delegates-at-large from Illinois to the Progressive National Convention, in Chicago, August, 1912.

Mrs. Wilmarth was active in the Woman Suffrage movement. She helped to organize the Woman's City Club of Chicago, and served as its first President. She was also a Life Member of this club, and after her term as President, was the Honorary President until her death. She was active in the work of the Consumer's League, and for a number of years was President of the Illinois branch. She was three times President of The Fortnightly Club, and a member of the Chicago Woman's, the Woman's Athletic, the Cordon, and the Every Day Clubs, all of Chicago. In 1893 she served as Chairman of the Woman's General Committee of the Educational Congress of the World's Columbian Exposition. Although a member of the First Presbyterian Church of Chicago, she attended Central Church, founded by Professor David Swing in the old Central Music Hall. During the closing years of her life, one of the reforms with which she was keenly sympathetic was the securing of the Saturday half-holiday, during the summer months, for the employees of the department stores. Mrs. Wilmarth is survived by one daughter, Anna Wilmarth, wife of Harold L. Ickes of Chicago.

SIMPSON, JOSEPHINE SARLES (Mrs. David Ferguson Simpson), social worker, daughter of Simeon Benton and Catherine (Lewis) Sarles, was born in Necedah, Wisconsin, February 14, 1862. Her father was a descendant of John Halleck, a native of England, who located on Long Island in 1624.

In 1883 she was graduated Litt.B., *summa cum laude*, at the University of Wisconsin. On January 14, 1886, at Minneapolis, Minnesota, she married David Ferguson Simpson, a lawyer, who for fifteen years was District and Supreme Court Judge in Minnesota. They are the parents of three sons: Donald Sarles, Harold Goodsir, and John Douglas.

Mrs. Simpson has been a member of the State Conservation Commission, appointed by Governor Johnson of Minnesota, and a member of the Pure Water Commission for Minneapolis, appointed by the Mayor. She was head of the Social Survey for Minneapolis; a member of the Woman's National Advisory Committee for the Republican Party in 1920; a member of the Crime Commission appointed by Governor Preus; and Chairman of the Committee on Punishments and Parole, of that Commission. She is an honorary member of the Men's Civic and Commerce Association. From 1893 to 1896 she was Chairman of the Supervisors for Free Kindergartens. From 1913 to 1918 she was President of the Hennepin County Woman Suffrage Association; and she was for some years a member of the National Council of the Woman Suffrage Association. In 1917 she was Chairman of the Woman's Committee of the Council of National Defense, and Chairman of the Organization Committee for Prohibition, for Hennepin County. She is a member of the State Board of the Anti-Saloon League, and head of the Woman's Law Observance League. She is a Charter Member of the Woman's Club of Minneapolis, and a member of the Hostess, Lafayette, Minikada, and Peripatetics Clubs.

WALKER, HARRIET GRANGER HULET (Mrs. Thomas B. Walker), philanthropist and reformer, daughter of Fletcher and Fannie (Granger) Hulet, was born in Brunswick, Ohio, September 10, 1841. Both her parents were born in Berkshire County, Massachusetts, and were descendants of Colonial families of that state. The father of Fletcher Hulet was John Hulet, Jr., of Lee, Massachusetts, who distinguished himself for bravery in the Battle of Bunker Hill, and his grandfather was John Hulet, founder of the first Methodist Church in Berkshire County.

When Harriet Hulet was six years old, her parents moved to Berea, Ohio. She received her early education in the Berea schools, and later studied at Baldwin University. On December 19, 1863, she married Thomas B. Walker, whom she had known since her school days. Mr. Walker was of English ancestry. His father, Platt Bayliss Walker, was a native of New Jersey, and later located in New York City. His mother, Anstis (Barlow) Walker, was a daughter of Thomas Barlow of New York City. Platt B. Walker and his wife located in Xenia, Ohio, where their son, Thomas, was born, February 1, 1840.

The elder Walker died in 1849, while on his way to California. In 1856 Mrs. Walker removed to Berea, Ohio, where there were better educational advantages, and here Thomas attended school. Between the ages of sixteen and nineteen he divided his time between study and work. When he was nineteen he became a traveling salesman. During a business trip he was so favorably impressed with the possibilities of the Western country that in 1862 he settled in Minneapolis, Minnesota. Soon after his arrival there, he joined a Government surveying party; thereafter, over a period of some years, he was engaged in this work for several months at a time. In this way he became acquainted with the Minnesota white pine regions, where he afterward purchased tracts and began the manufacture of lumber.

Mr. Walker's business ventures were attended with such success that he became one of the largest operators in the state. He eventually extended his interests to California, but has retained his residence in Minneapolis, and has always entered heartily into all the progressive movements in that city. It was through his personal efforts that the Minneapolis Business Union was organized, and he was influential in the establishment of the public market which has placed Minneapolis ahead of St. Paul as a distributing center. In his extensive logging and lumber enterprises, in his explorations, Government surveys, and other undertakings, Mr. Walker has employed many thousands of men, but a labor union has never been formed among them. His sympathetic understanding has always established such friendly relations that he has been able to consummate, unhampered by labor troubles, the large business affairs that have brought phenomenal success.

Despite all his preoccupation with big business, Mr. Walker has taken time for the study of science and art, and has always been responsive to the finest things of life. He owns the largest private library in the Northwest; a collection of rare paintings, four hundred of which are hung in the gallery adjacent to his residence; a unique assemblage of pottery and porcelain, jade and crystal, precious stones, and ancient bronzes from China and Japan; and the finest existing collection of necklaces and antique glass. His residence, in the central part of the city, is surrounded by spacious grounds fronting on two streets. The property is unfenced, and is plentifully equipped with benches for the use of the public.

Mr. Walker founded the Minneapolis Public Library, and since its organization has served as President of the Board. He has been one of the principal supporters of the Art School. He has also aided in the upbuilding of the Young Men's Christian Association in the City, the State and the University, and is the Northwestern Member of its International Committee. He is President of the Minnesota Academy of Science, and for many years was Presiding Officer of the Methodist Social Union and Church Extension Society. Owing to his generosity, the thirty Methodist churches in Minneapolis are better equipped, and more sound financially, than the churches of that denomination in any other city in the United States.

Mr. Walker has been an active member of the State Reform School Board, as well as President of the Business Men's Union of Minneapolis, and he is an active member of many local and national scientific, educational, political, and social organizations. He is a thorough student of all questions of the day—social, industrial, and political—and has published numerous articles, as a result of his researches. His book, *The Testimony of the Ages*, has been called the best work on the evidences of Christianity and the after-life that has ever been compiled. It is the product of a lifetime of study. Even during his schooldays, he took special interest in the science of geology, and the discussion of the age of the earth in its relation to the teachings of Christianity. This interest led him to actual work with hammer and chisel, for he was not satisfied with book knowledge alone. He also devoted much time to such collateral subjects as the antiquity of the human race, phrenology, philosophy, and Biblical interpretation.

Mrs. Walker devoted the first twelve years of her married life to her household and the care of her eight children, and throughout her life she considered her home duties paramount. As she found more leisure, however, she gave more and more time to humane and charitable enterprises, many of which she was instrumental in organizing and maintaining. In all that she did she had her husband's admiring support, and was guided and stimulated by his example. At an early age she had united with the Methodist Church, of which her family were members, and, with her husband, became prominently identified with all branches of church work. She was a Charter Member of the Sisterhood of Bethany, an organization whose object was the reformation of erring women. For twenty-three years she was Secretary; then as President, she served this organization until she died. The Sisterhood cares for one hundred and fifty women and children, on an average, every year. Her special interest in this work led her to establish the Children's Home. She was also interested in the Kindergarten Association.

In 1882 Mrs. Walker founded the Northwestern Hospital for Women and Children, and was its President continuously thereafter. It is under the sole management of women directors, and has a training school for nurses, with a staff of women physicians. It owns two of the finest hospital buildings in the Northwest, with accommodations for one hundred patients, and a nurses' home with a housing capacity for sixty. Mrs. Walker was among the first to foster the work of the

Woman's Christian Temperance Union, but after the activities of that organization assumed political significance, she discontinued her association. When, however, the division of the Union took place, Mrs. Walker joined the Non-Partisan Woman's Christian Temperance Union, and resumed her active work. She became Vice-President and State President of non-partisan organizations, in each of which her genius asserted itself. She was also Vice-President of the Minneapolis Young Women's Christian Association. The Newsboys' Home is another institution in connection with which she exerted an active influence.

The question of having a police matron for the City was one that long interested Mrs. Walker. She investigated the work of this office in all the leading cities of the country, and wrote many articles on the subject. Finally she brought together from the Young Women's Christian Association, the Sisterhood of Bethany, and the two branches of the Woman's Christian Temperance Union, a joint committee and induced the Police Commissioner of Minneapolis to create the position and allow the Committee to nominate the matron, upon guaranteeing half her salary annually. For seven years, from 1892 to 1899, Mrs. Walker was President of the Woman's Council, an association comprising all branches of woman's work in the City. This represented seventy organizations, which included all departments of study and work in the fields of education, philanthropy, reform, art, music, literature, and science. To her capable leadership is attributable the substantial growth of this body, which finally became merged with the Federation of Clubs. Mrs. Walker early gave evidence of marked literary ability; even during her school days she was a regular contributor to several periodicals. Throughout her life she employed her literary talents especially on behalf of reform work. She compiled valuable statistics concerning temperance, and at the World's Temperance Conference in Chicago, in 1893,

she delivered a lecture on the Keeley cure for inebriates. Her lectures, written for the Nurses' Training School, Christian Endeavor Society, and Temperance Unions, have been widely quoted and distributed. In brief, Mrs. Walker won national fame as a writer on social and economic subjects. She was a regular contributor to the *Trained Nurses' Magazine* of New York City, and to the *Temperance Tribune*, of whose publication committee she was chairman. During the latter part of her life Mrs. Walker was obliged to institute regular office hours, and to employ a private secretary to aid her in her many private charities, as well as in her public activities. In spite of many outside demands made upon both Mr. and Mrs. Walker, they devoted a large amount of their time to the training and education of their children, often employing methods which, for that period were decidedly advanced. In the spacious yard of their home they built and equipped for their sons a workshop containing a small power plant with lathes, planers, anvils, vices, and all tools necessary for working in iron and wood. There was also in the building a well-appointed gymnasium. Of the eight children born to Mr. and Mrs. Walker, Gilbert M., Fletcher L., Willis J., Clinton L., and Archie D. are associated with their father in the lumber business. A daughter, Julia, is the wife of Ernest F. Smith; a son, Leon B. Walker, died in 1867; and Harriet, wife of the Reverend Frederick C. Holman, died in 1904.

WALLACE, ELIZABETH, educator, daughter of Thomas Freemand and Martha (Torrance) Wallace, was born in Santa Fé de Bogotá, United States of Colombia, in 1866. Her father was descended from Richard Wallace, a native of Glasgow, Scotland, who in 1760 located in Cumberland Valley, Pennsylvania, and later in Westmoreland County, Pennsylvania, where he built the first fort, known as Wallace's Fort. At one time he was captured by the Indians and held for more than a year.

Elizabeth Wallace located in the United States in 1874. In 1886, she was graduated B.S. at Wellesley College, Wellesley, Massachusetts. In 1892 she entered the graduate school of the University of Chicago as a Fellow, and the following year was appointed Reader in Spanish. From 1894 to 1896 she was Dean of Women at Knox College, Galesburg, Illinois. She spent the winter of 1896–1897 in Paris, studying at the Collège de France, and was graduated élève titulaire of the École des Hautes Études. Upon her return to the United States, in 1897, she became Instructor in the Department of Romance Languages at the University of Chicago, where she has remained ever since, as Assistant Professor and Associate Professor of French Literature. From 1893 to 1909 Miss Wallace was also Head of Beecher House at the University, and since 1905 she has acted as Dean of the Junior Colleges. During 1917–1918, on leave of absence, she served overseas with the Rockefeller Mission and the American Red Cross. From the French Government, she received the decoration of Officier d'Académie, and in 1910–1911 she was a Fellow of the International Institute, of Madrid, Spain.

Miss Wallace is a member of the Association of Modern Language Teachers, the Alliance Française, the Society of Midland Authors, and the University of Chicago Settlement League. She also holds membership in the Chicago College, Fortnightly, Little Room, and Cordon Clubs of Chicago. She is the author of South American Republics (1894), La Perfecta Casada (1902), A Garden of Paris (1911), and Mark Twain and the Happy Island (1912).

WINTER, ALICE AMES (Mrs. Thomas Gerald Winter), author, daughter of Reverend Charles Gordon and Julia Frances (Baker) Ames, was born in Albany, New York, November 25, 1865. She received her education at Wellesley College, where she was graduated A.B. in 1886, and A.M. in 1889.

While in college she had the honor of being made a member of the Shakespeare Society. Later she received training at the Philadelphia Academy of Fine Arts. On June 25, 1892, at Boston, Massachusetts, she married Thomas Gerald Winter, a grain merchant of Minneapolis, Minnesota. They are the parents of one son, Charles Gilbert Winter (born, 1893) and one daughter, Edith Ames Winter (born, 1896), wife of Knowlton Lyman Ames.

For two years previous to her marriage, Mrs. Winter was a teacher in Mrs. Quincy Shaw's school in Boston. She has always been actively interested in education and child welfare. Mrs. Winter has been President of the Minneapolis Kindergarten Association, and is a member of the Minnesota Child Labor Committee, the City Playground Commission, and the Visiting Nurse Association. From 1907 to 1913 she was President of the Woman's Club of Minneapolis, and is Vice-President of the General Federation of Women's Clubs; Chairman of the Woman's Committee of the Minnesota Division of the Council of National Defense; a Director of the Woman's Auxiliary of the Minnesota Commission of Public Safety; and a Director of the Minneapolis Chapter of the American Red Cross. She is an honorary member of the Minneapolis Civic and Commerce Association, and a member of the College Woman's and Lafayette Clubs, of Minneapolis. She has contributed numerous articles and stories to magazines, and is the author of two novels, The Prize to the Hardy (1907) and Jewel-Weed (1910). She was the Editor of Charles Gordon Ames—A Spiritual Autobiography (1912).

SETHNESS, HELGA MIDLING (Mrs. Charles O. Sethness), daughter of Julius Anker and Hilda E. (Dunker) Midling, was born in Christiana, Norway, August 27, 1865. During her early years she located in Chicago, Illinois. There she received her education in the public schools, completing the course at the West Division High School. She then studied languages and music at the Chicago Musical College, and later carried on further work in these subjects at Leipzig, Germany. On December 14, 1882, in Chicago, she married Charles Olinus Sethness, a manufacturing chemist. They are the parents of three sons, Charles Henry, Ralph Edward, Walter Douglas, and one daughter, Elva Hilda. In 1906, Mrs. Sethness was an officer of the Klio Association. In 1910, she was on the Executive Committee of Irving Park Sorosis. From 1910 to 1914 she was President of the Aid and Loan Society of Irving Park, Chicago, an association devoted to social and philanthropic service. In 1914 she was appointed a member and a trustee of the Chicago Board of Education, on which she served until 1918. She is Chairman of the Child Welfare and Community Service Committee on School Management in connection with the penny lunch in public schools. During the World War she was a member of the Speakers' Bureau for the Red Cross and Liberty Loan drives. She is also a member of the Political Equality League, the Woman's City Club, the Illinois Athletic Association, the Mothers' Relief Association, and the Drama League.

SEYMOUR, FLORA WARREN SMITH (Mrs. George Steele Seymour), lawyer and editor, was born in Cleveland, Ohio. Through her father, Charles Payne Smith, she is descended from George Smith, who located in Plymouth, Massachusetts, in 1640; and from Stephen Payne—a native of England, who located in Hingham, Massachusetts, in 1638—through his son, Stephen, who fought in King Philip's War. Her mother, Eleanor De Forest Potter, was a descendant of the Potter family that located in Connecticut during the seventeenth century, and of Peter Van Order, who came to New York about 1680.

During Miss Smith's childhood, her parents resided in Washington, District of Columbia. There she attended the Central High School and also George Washington University,

where she was graduated A.B. After several years of business life, six of which were spent in the United States Indian Service, she began her professional studies at the Washington School of Law, where she was graduated LL.B. in 1915. In the following year she received the degree of LL.M. from the Chicago-Kent College of Law.

On July 3, 1915, at Washington, District of Columbia, she married George Steele Seymour, an auditor and lawyer. Since that time she has resided in Chicago, engaged in the practice of her profession. She is Editor of the *College Woman*, Assistant Editor of *The Women Lawyers' Journal*; and for two years was Editor of the *Quarterly* of the legal sorority, Kappa Beta Pi, of which she is a member. In 1921 she published a biographical and historical study of the women of her profession, *Women Lawyers of America*.

Mrs. Seymour is a member of the Women Lawyers' Association of New York, and its Vice-President for Illinois; and is one of the Legislative Committee of the Woman's City Club of Chicago. From 1916 to 1918 she was First Vice-President of the Women of the Empire State. Since 1917 she has been Corresponding Secretary of the National Federation of College Women, and is a member of the Chicago College Club. During the World War she served on the Woman's Committee of the State Council of Defense, and in 1917 and 1919 was a delegate to the National Council of Women.

Mrs. Seymour has written many articles for magazines and finds recreation in book binding. In 1919, with her husband, she organized the Order of Bookfellows, a non-commercial, coöperative association of booklovers, and still continues its business manager. In the first year of its existence it attained a membership of five hundred, located in the various states of the Union, and in a number of foreign countries. It includes many well-known writers, both English and American, as well as many others who are readers, booklovers, and collectors. The purpose of the organization is to produce books by members, and for members, in a non-commercial way, and in the spirit of the booklover; also to further bookish interests generally, and to bring together its members in a spirit of real book-fellowship. Local circles have been formed in a number of different cities, and the great and growing enthusiasm would seem to promise continued success. Every member, upon joining, receives a number, and this number is inscribed in Bookfellow publications, so that each volume becomes the individual property of the member. Each month, except during the summer period, the members receive some "bookly joy." On alternate months this is *The Stepladder*, a unique and independent little journal, edited by Mrs. Seymour, which comments fearlessly on books and publishing problems. It has been highly praised for its pungent and satirical articles. On other months, members receive a section of the *Chronicles of Bagdad*, a book unusual both for its humorous content, and for its unique manner of publication. Sixteen pages are issued at a time, to be held by the members until the book is complete, when it can be bound. This makes an entirely individual volume, of the sort highly valued by the collector. On Christmas, 1919, members received *A Little Book of Bookly Verse*, to which twenty poet-Bookfellows contributed. During the 1919–1920 season three books were published. It is expected that as the membership steadily increases, much more will be accomplished in the future.

BEECKMAN, ELEANOR THOMAS (Mrs. R. Livingston Beeckman), prison reformer and philanthropist, was born at Zanesville, Ohio, January 20, 1878, daughter of General Samuel and Ann Augusta (Porter) Thomas. She was educated by private tutors and attended finishing school; was a member of the Colony Club of New York City and Agawam Hunt Club, Providence, Rhode Island. Mrs. Beeckman was an allround athlete, being a splendid horsewoman, golf and tennis player, a fine swimmer, and one of the first women to drive an automobile. She was intensely interested in philanthropic work, and assisted her husband in prison reform.

She was married October 8, 1902, at Ardsley-on-Hudson, New York, to Robert Beeckman, a stock broker (born in New York City, April 15, 1866), son of Gilbert Livingston and Margaret (Foster) Beeckman. He was Governor of Rhode Island from January 1, 1915 to January 1, 1921, and was a member of the Rhode Island Legislature. During the World War, he was Chairman of the Newport Chapter, American Red Cross, and inspected the Rhode Island troops and the Allied armies at the battle fronts in November and December, 1917. Mrs. Beeckman died suddenly of heart disease at White Sulphur Springs, West Virginia, on December 20, 1920.

STEARNS, LUTIE EUGENIA, lecturer, daughter of Isaac Holden and Catharine (Guild) Stearns, was born in Stoughton, Massachusetts. She is descended from Isaac Stearns, a native of England, who sailed for America with Governor Winthrop in June, 1630, and located in Watertown, Massachusetts. Lutie E. Stearns received her early education in the Milwaukee (Wisconsin) public schools, and was graduated at the Milwaukee State Normal School in 1887. She has always been a wide reader along political, sociological, and literary lines. She taught in the public schools from 1887 to 1889, when she was made Superintendent of the Circulating Department of the Milwaukee Public Library. In this capacity she served for the nine years from 1889 to 1897. At that time she became connected with the Wisconsin Library Commission, for which she acted as Secretary, Library Visitor, and Chief of the Traveling Library Department until 1914. Ever since she formed that connection she has lectured on libraries, before clubs and educational associations and at the libraries of the principal cities of the United States. She has been a member of the Board of Directors of the General Federation of Women's Clubs; Vice-President of the Milwaukee City Club; Chairman of the Library Reference Committee of the Wisconsin Federation of Women's Clubs; and Chairman of the Library Extension Committee of the General Federation of Women's Clubs; and she is President of the Milwaukee Down Town Club; a member of the American Library Association; the American Library Institute; and the Milwaukee State Normal Alumnae Association; and an honorary member of the Kalmia Club and the Milwaukee Social Economics Club. She is Editor of the *Wisconsin Library Commission Handbook* (1896) and *List of Books of Consolation and Interest to Spinsters*, and is the author of *Essentials in Library Administration*, *The Child and the Library*, *Traveling Libraries*, *The Old and New in Education*, and *The Milwaukee School Situation and the Remedy*.

SQUIRES, MARY SMYTH (Mrs. George C. Squires), philanthropist, second daughter of Henry M. and Louise (Gregory) Smyth, was born in San Antonio, Texas. She is descended from Lieutenant George Montague Smyth of the British Navy (who went down on the *Royal George*) through his son, Patrick Smyth, a graduate of Dublin University, who located in Fort Edward, New York, about 1750. On her mother's side she is descended from the Romeyns, of Holland, who located in America early in the seventeenth century; and from the Staffords, of Warwickshire, England, who located in this country early in the eighteenth century. Lieutenant James Stafford was with John Paul Jones on the *Bonhomme Richard* during her famous fight with the *Serapis*. The ship's ensign having gone overboard, in the conflict, Stafford sprang into the water and rescued it. This same flag in now in the Smithsonian Institute in Washington.

Henry M. and Louise Gregory Smyth, who were both natives of Albany, New York, spent their early married life in San Antonio, Texas, where Mr. Smyth had gone in search of health. During the Civil War, as a Union man, he was obliged to seek asylum in Monterey, Mexico. One of Mrs. Squires' earliest recollections is of the journey by carriage, with her beautiful young mother and her sister, from San Antonio to Zacatacas, where her father met them. Jenkins, a freed slave drove them; the journey, through a country infested with Indians, consumed nineteen days. They lived in Monterey for a year, and then located in New Orleans. When the New Orleans *Picayune* printed an account of Mr. Smyth's flight from Texas, everything the family possessed was confiscated and sold by the Confederate Government. Among the effects was Mrs. Smyth's wedding dress, which was bought by a friend, Mrs. Nat Lewis, and later returned to Mrs. Smyth.

In 1867 Mr. Smyth took his family to St. Paul, Minnesota, where his five daughters received their education. Mrs. Squires, having completed her course at the St. Paul High School, enjoyed also the advantages of a thorough musical training. During this period she studied singing under Francis Korbay in New York City. When she was about twenty-two years old, she spent a year in Melbourne, Australia, with her uncle, John Kane Smyth, and also visited the Hawaiian Islands. Since then she has traveled extensively in Europe. On April 29, 1886, she was married in St. Paul, Minnesota, to George Clarke Squires, a lawyer. They are the parents of two sons, Cameron Squires of Portland, Oregon, and George Squires, First Lieutenant in the 17th Aero Squadron, United States Army (killed in action May 18, 1918), and one daughter, Mary Rebecca Squires (Mrs. Mackey Thompson). In 1886, Mrs. Squires started the first large art class ever conducted in St. Paul, under the direction of Mrs. J. C. Burbank. For four years she was Manager of the St. Luke's Hospital Board, and was an active worker in the anti-tuberculosis fight in St. Paul. During the World War she was a member of the women's committee of the National Council of Defense in Minnesota, and was Chairman of the "Red Cross Lane" Salvage Shop in St. Paul. She spoke one hundred times on behalf of the Liberty Loans in St. Paul, Washington, and New York City. She is a member of the St. Paul Chapter of the Daughters of the American Revolution, and for five years she was State Regent for Minnesota. In April, 1917, she was one of four candidates for the office of President-General of the Society. Mrs. Squires was an independent candidate and ran second to Mrs. Guernsey, who was elected. She is also a member of the Society of Colonial Dames, the Welfare League, the Civic League, and was at one time President of the Sibley House Association, Mendota, Minnesota. Mrs. Squires is fond of out-door life; she is a member of the White Bear Yacht Club, and has spent four seasons trout-fishing on the Nipegon River, in Canada.

UELAND, CLARA HAMPSON (Mrs. Andreas Ueland), daughter of Henry and Eliza (Osborn) Hampson, was born in Akron, Ohio, October 10, 1860. Her father was a descendant of Robert Hampson, one of the early English settlers of Pennsylvania. She was educated in the public schools of Akron, Ohio, and of Minneapolis, Minnesota, completing the course at the Minneapolis High School in 1878. On June 19, 1885, at Ada, Minnesota, she married Andreas Ueland, an attorney of Minneapolis. They are the parents of four sons, Sigurd, Arnulf, Rolf, and Torvald, and three daughters, Anne (Mrs. Kenneth Taylor), Elsa, and Brenda (Mrs. Wallace Benedict).

As a result of experience as a teacher in the public schools, Mrs. Ueland has been much interested in the introduction of medical inspection of school children, and in the establishment of courses in industrial art, in Minnesota. She has been a director of the State Art Society; a director of the Minneapolis Associated Charities; Chairman of the Handi-

craft Committee of the Federation of Women's Clubs; Chairman of the Arts and Letters Department of the Woman's Club of Minneapolis, of which she was a charter member; and Chairman of the Finance Committee of the Woman's Welfare League. For four years she was President of the Minnesota Woman Suffrage Association; and a member of the Child Welfare Commission which revised the Minnesota laws relating to children. She is a member of the Daughters of the American Revolution, and an honorary member of the Civic and Commerce Association of Minneapolis.

UPHAM, MARY CORNELIA KELLEY (Mrs. William Henry Upham), was born in Cleveland, Ohio, January 21, 1843, and died at Marshfield, Wisconsin, November 29, 1912. Her father, James Howe Kelley, was a son of Captain John Kelley (born in Virginia about 1760), who served through two enlistments, from 1777 to 1783, in the Revolutionary War. In the War of 1812 he was a Captain in the 1st Ohio (Noel's) Regiment. Six of his family of thirteen children reached maturity. James Howe Kelley and his wife, Emily Chase (Hussey) Kelley, located early in their married life, at Racine, Wisconsin, where they were among the pioneer settlers. Here Mr. Kelley developed his lumber business.

Miss Kelley was educated in the schools of Racine, completed her course at the high school, and subsequently studied medicine with Doctor Duncombe of that city. She obtained a certificate in materia medica, but was married about this time, so that she never made the practice of medicine her profession. Nevertheless she treated many people without remuneration and acquired a considerable reputation. On December 19, 1867, in her father's house, at Racine, Wisconsin, she married Lieutenant William Henry Upham, United States Army. Lieutenant Upham's sister was married at the same time, a double ceremony being performed. Lieutenant Upham, attached to the staff of General Robinson, was stationed with the Fourth United States Artillery at Detroit. A few years later he resigned from the Army, and located with his wife at Kewaunee, Michigan, where he became connected with the lumber firm of Slauson, Grimmer and Company.

In 1872 Mr. and Mrs. Upham removed to Angelica, a new settlement in a clearing between Shewano and Green Bay, at the end of the wagon road. Here Mr. Upham built a shingle mill, and established a lumber business which eventually became the largest in the State. It was here, also, that Mrs. Upham first showed that remarkable courage and initiative which later made her so great an influence for good. As there was no practicing physician within sixteen miles of the settlement, Mrs. Upham, responding to the need, opened an office at her home and ministered to all members of the community. She made no charge for her services. She has the record of never having lost a patient.

As a member of the Presbyterian Church she had always been an ardent church worker. It was natural, therefore, that she should urge the establishment of a church in the new community. Her husband, always in accord with her efforts for the benefit of others, gave the enterprise his support, and soon the people of Angelica had built a small church where Congregational services were held. In 1878 Mr. Upham cleared more ground and built another sawmill, as well as a building to house a general store. His wife, who made for them a comfortable home in three rooms over this store, shared with Mr. Upham the honor of founding the town of Marshfield. The story of her life is inseparably interwoven with that of this town. A few months after settling there, in 1879, she organized the first Presbyterian Church, which has prospered ever since. In Marshfield, as elsewhere, she found that her medical services were in demand, and she continued to meet the need without any thought of recompense.

Within a few years the family removed to a large residence that had been built for them. This became the centre for the many charitable activities, to which Mrs. Upham devoted herself. She had a gift of reaching the inner nature of those with whom she came in contact, and of exerting a great influence for good. She possessed the courage to condemn wrong and champion right, and yet in so doing she aroused no resentment. Moreover, she had the rare faculty of conveying her precepts in such a sympathetic and understanding way that they exerted a lasting influence. Her keen interest in young people led her to organize the Band of Hope, a temperance club, which became strong force in the early days after Marshfield was founded.

Mr. Upham became more and more prominent in public life, and in 1895 was elected Governor of Wisconsin. Mrs. Upham accepted calmly and unostentatiously the honors that her husband's position brought her, and continued her arduous labors in the cause of helpfulness to others. The boys and girls with whom she had to do meant more to her than fame and honor. As a leader and a teacher she fully realized the importance of personally aiding the children of the city that she and her husband had founded, so she continued to give largely of her time.

Mrs. Upham started temperance work for men and women in Wisconsin, and for many years was State President of the Women's Christian Temperance Union. She also accomplished much by way of providing literature for lumber camps. As a writer she was especially successful in stories for children, some of which, as well as her poems, have been published. A thorough student of bird lore, she gave many interesting talks on the subject before women's clubs. She was a member of the Daughters of the American Revolution. Governor and Mrs. Upham were the parents of two daughters, Mrs. Caroline Upham Sawyer and Mrs. Elsie Upham Firning.

SCIDMORE, ELIZA RUHAMAH, author, the daughter of George Bolles and Eliza

Catherine (Sweeney) Scidmore, was born in Madison, Wisconsin, October 14, 1856. She is descended from Thomas Scidmore who came in 1635 from Herefordshire, England, to Boston, Massachusetts, acquiring land which is now Brattle Square. He was a descendant of the Sir James Scudamore of Queen Elizabeth's court, whose armor is now in the Metropolitan Museum, New York, ornamented with architectural motifs taken from Holme Lacy, the Scudamore home since the Knight of Escu d'Amour, mentioned in Spenser's *Faërie Queene* received it as a fief from William of Normandy. Miss Scidmore is the Foreign Secretary of the National Geographic Society and has traveled widely in the Orient and in Alaska. She is the author of *Alaska, the Southern Coast and the Sitkan Archipelago* (1885), *Jinrikisha Days in Japan* (1890), *Guide to Alaska and the Northwest Coast* (1890), *Java, the Garden of the East* (1897), *China, the Long-Lived Empire* (1900), *Winter India* (1903), and *As the Hague Ordains* (1907). She is a member of the Washington Club, the Chevy Chase Club, the Japan Society of London, the Japan Society of New York, and the National Geographic Society.

BARBER, ELSIE YANDELL (Mrs. Donn Barber, daughter of Dr. Lunsford Pitts and Louise Boddie (Elliston) Yandell, was born in Louisville, Kentucky, where she had her early education before entering upon a year's training at the Packer Institute in Brooklyn, New York. Her mother, who was noted as a reformer and philanthropist, established the first free kindergartens and the first schools of reform in Kentucky, and opened the first free babies' hospital in Louisville, in memory of her husband, Dr. Yandell. The latter was the son of Dr. Lunsford Pitts Yandell, Sr., who established the first medical school south of the Mason and Dixon line and wrote a comprehensive history of medicine in the South before the Civil War.

When the plans and program of the National League for Woman's Service were first formulated in February, 1917, Mrs. Barber was appointed National, State, and City Chairman of the Canteen Division. The original idea of canteen service was to fill an emergency by feeding the men at the trains and docks before their departure for camps and overseas. The military forces of the country required the services of a Refreshment Unit, and the New York County Chapter of the American Red Cross with which the National League for Woman's Service coöperated, appointed Mrs. Barber to organize this unit and to recruit the personnel from the volunteers of the National League for Woman's Service. Owing, however, to the fact that thousands of soldiers and sailors who were at camps within accessible distance of New York were daily passing through the city, the plan was conceived of establishing "Service Clubs" in addition to the emergency service. This idea was included in the plans and program of the National League for Woman's Service which coöperated with the War Camp Community Service in the organizing of these Service Clubs. The Service Clubs provided a comfortable and attractive place in which the men could read, write, dance, play billiards, and otherwise amuse themselves, and a canteen where they could purchase food at a nominal price. The canteens in these Service Clubs were under the direct supervision of the Canteen Division of the National League for Woman's Service, and were all self-supporting. There were fourteen National League Canteens in New York City and many others within a short distance of New York. During the war approximately 800,000 men were fed at these canteens. Most of them were near the great terminals of the city and at other important points. In addition to these, several canteens were opened at the request of the Government to serve the staffs of various Governmental Departments, notably the Hudson Street Canteen, which was opened for the Medical Supply Department, and the Wall Street Navy Canteen which was kept open day and night for the staff of the Naval Intelligence Office. All the canteens were for enlisted men, with the exception of the Pershing Club for Officers. Of the ten thousand women who enrolled for service in the Canteen Division, 2500 were assigned to the various canteens. These women prepared the food, served the meals, and furnished the friendly and hospitable atmosphere which contributed so largely to the canteens' success. They were so efficiently trained that they were called upon by many other war organizations, not only for canteen service, but for service in many other capacities, including relief work and entertainments for the men.

Mrs. Barber is the wife of Donn Barber, the architect and editor of *The New York Architect*, to whom she was married in Louisville, Kentucky, November 22, 1899. They have four children: Elizabeth Elliston, Louise Yandell, Elsie Yandell, and Donn Barber, Jr. Mrs. Barber is a member of the Colony Club of New York.

USHER, LEILA, sculptor, was born in Onalaska, Wisconsin. She received her general education in the public schools of La Crosse, Wisconsin, and first studied art in the New York College for the Training of Teachers. There she discovered her talent for sculpture, and continued to study it in Boston and Cambridge, in the studios of George T. Brewster and Henry H. Kitson. Later she worked under the instruction of Augustus St. Gaudens, in the Art Students' League, New York City.

After maintaining a studio for some years in New York, she studied sculpture in the Calarossi studios, Paris; also, from Delacluse she received instruction in drawing. After leaving Paris, she practised her profession in Rome for three winters. During this time she exhibited in the Paris Salon and at the International Art Exposition in Rome, as well as in London and Vienna. She is chiefly known for her portraits of prominent men, bronzes of which are in some of the colleges and universities of the East and South.

Her first work to be publicly shown was a bas-relief of her uncle, Cyrus Woodman, exhibited in the Wisconsin Building at the World's Columbian Exposition, in 1893. Her next exhibit was the bust of a child, which was in the first exhibition of the National Sculpture Society in New York City. Since that time her work has often been seen in the New York and Philadelphia Academies and in various American expositions. Her first portrait to be placed in a public institution was a bas-relief of the famous professor, Francis James Child, of Harvard University, bronzes of which were bought for the Child Memorial Library, and for the Faculty Room at Harvard. A third bronze was purchased for Johns Hopkins University, and plaster casts of this work are at Radcliffe and Bowdoin Colleges. Miss Usher's large bas-relief of Professor Nathaniel Southgate Shaler hangs in the Museum of Natural History in Cambridge, and a bronze replica is owned by Mrs. Shaler. Among other bas-relief portraits of prominent men are those of Josiah Royce, Charles Eliot Norton, Reverend Horatio Stebbins, of San Francisco, Chief Justice Fuller, Robert Underwood Johnson, Blasco Ibáñez, and Major John Wesley Powell, of the United States Geological Survey. The portrait of Major Powell is in the centre of a tablet on the Powell memorial, erected by Congress at the edge of the Grand Canyon, Arizona. A second bronze is on the shaft which marks Major Powell's grave in Arlington Cemetery, Washington, District of Columbia. "I feel that this man was in harmony with the universe," is a tribute that was paid to the memory of Major Powell by one who looked upon this fine sculpture. Another of her large portraits is that of the author, Elijah Kellogg, a graduate of Bowdoin College. This relief has been set in the outside wall of the oldest building at Bowdoin, in commemoration of a strong, unworldly character.

Miss Usher, having no prejudice as to race, color, or creed, conceived the idea in 1902 of modeling Booker T. Washington. In order to study him in the midst of his great work, she went to Tuskegee. The first bronze cast was bought by the friends of Southern education, and presented to Hampton Institute, where Mr. Washington was educated. After his death, a second bronze was purchased for Tuskegee Institute. This portrait was exhibited in the Paris Salon, in 1912, along with a group of small bas-reliefs, including one of Susan B. Anthony.

Miss Usher calls Miss Anthony the most remarkable person it has been her good fortune to portray, and believes that she should rank with Lincoln as one of the greatest of all the advocates of human liberty and justice. She made a life-size head of Miss Anthony, which was purchased for Bryn Mawr College. After Miss Anthony's death another bronze became the property of Rochester University. It was owing to Miss Anthony's efforts that this institution was opened to women. Also in honor of Miss Anthony, Miss Usher struck a medal, a copy of which is owned by the Art Museum of Copenhagen, Denmark. Later she made a bust of the singer, David Bispham at his personal order.

She has made many low reliefs of children, which show all the charm and tenderness characteristic of childhood. During the winter of 1914–1915, when thousands in New York City were unable to secure employment, Miss Usher conceived the idea of modeling types of the various nationalities seen on the streets. She made the busts of eight nationalities, revealing fine faces of the types of men who make their living by the sweat of the brow. In them all she strikingly depicts one marked characteristic—a hungry, hunted look in the eyes.

All of Miss Usher's work evidences a remarkable understanding of character, as well as life, vitality, and individuality. Her portraits catch the spirit of the subject, and constitute an entirely sympathetic interpretation. Miss Usher's enthusiasm for character study led her to specialize in portrait-sculpture. She believes that to make faithful portraits of the men and women who are national leaders, is to contribute to the history of the country.

Miss Usher has always been interested in progressive movements, especially in the economic and political emancipation of women. At the age of nineteen, she was appointed by Susan B. Anthony, President of the first woman suffrage club established in La Crosse, Wisconsin. Thereafter, Miss Usher worked for this cause whenever time permitted, contributing to the *Woman's Journal* of Boston when little over twenty years of age. She was active in the campaign that resulted in a victory for the women of New York State. At this time she addressed many audiences, in New York City, and throughout the State. She also conducted campaign work in Maine, holding meetings in her summer studio, "The Hut of Usher." It was in London, England, that she made her first street speech, and there she met many of the prominent suffragists, with whom she marched in their great processions of 1910 and 1913. It might be said that she was born a suffragist, for her parents, her paternal grandmother, and her aunts were firm believers in the cause.

Miss Usher, through all branches of her family, is of Puritan and Pilgrim descent. The first ancestor was Robert Usher, who located at Stamford, Connecticut, in 1644. Ellis B. Usher, grandfather of Leila Usher, lived in Bar Mills, Maine. For many years he was the most prominent mill-owner on the Saco River. He served with the distinguished body of men who took part in the proceedings of the Maine Constitutional Convention. Ellis B. Usher married Hannah Lane, daughter of Colonel Isaac and Ruth (Merrill) Lane. The Lanes were known as "the fighting family of Buxton"; some of the men served in the French and Indian War, others in the Revolution. The father of Hannah Lane was made a Captain in the War of 1812. Leila Usher's father, Isaac L. Usher, was a well-known newspaper man in Wisconsin. Her mother, Susannah Coffin Woodman Usher, was descended from Edward Woodman, a native of England, who located as one of the first settlers in Newbury, Massachusetts, in 1635. At the age of fifteen, Susannah Usher entered the first normal school in America, established by Horace Mann in 1839. Leila Usher's maternal grandfather was educated in Maine, and became a member of the Maine Bar in 1809. His wife was Susannah Coffin, daughter of Reverend Paul Coffin, a graduate of Harvard College (1759), whose family has a long and noteworthy history.

USHER, REBECCA R., volunteer nurse in the Civil War, was born, August 31, 1821, and died, June 2, 1912, in Bar Mills, Maine, where her father, Ellis B. Usher, had extensive milling and lumber interests. She held membership in the Maine Camp and Hospital Association, formed in Portland in 1862, and was one of the first of its members to go to the front. She was sent to the General Hospital, Chester, Pennsylvania, which was opened in 1862, at the time of the Rennsylvania campaign. Here she took her part in the care of nine hundred patients during the fall and the greater part of the winter of 1862–1863. Every nurse had charge of a ward containing sixty or seventy men; their rations cost fifteen cents a day. In the summer of 1863 this hospital was abandoned, because the front line of action had moved farther south. Miss Usher then went back to Maine for a few months. While there she spent considerable time in setting before the Governor the needs of the Maine soldiers, engaged in the war. Early in the winter of 1864–1865 she again went to the front. At the request of the Maine Camp and Hospital Association she took up her station at City Point, Virginia. Here the Maine Regiment, which suffered heavy casualties, received hospital care. Thousands of soldiers were brought in directly from the battlefield, and nurses, besides carrying on their regular work,

made every effort to entertain the patients with all the cheer and comfort possible. In this situation Miss Usher wrote: "It is very tantalizing to be in the midst of the army and so near the battlefield, yet know so little of what is being done. General Grant lives only a mile from here; yet rumors are so conflicting that we can tell nothing from them."

Miss Usher remained at City Point until Richmond fell. A week after Lee's surrender she wrote home: "Isn't the news of the death of the President terrible? The soldiers are revengeful, and want every rebel hung . . . I have very little anxiety for my country, as Lincoln had so nearly accomplished his work. But my heart is weighed down with grief, personal grief, as if some one very near to me had been called away—and so it will be with the whole people." During the war, she says, she attended a reception given at the White House, filing in with the other nurses to shake the hand of President Lincoln. She had never seen him before, but her faith in him was so great and her sympathy so strong that he seemed to sense them as he met her eyes, and, bending toward her, he said, "How do you do, dear?" as if they had been old friends. This was one of her most cherished memories. This remarkable sympathy of hers was felt by all who knew her. Not only did Miss Usher take up her share of the burden during the war, but the home from which she came was turned into a soldier's forwarding depot for supplies and clothes sent in from that region.

This Usher home, called "The Brick House," was known far and wide for the warm sympathy and hospitality extended to all, whatever their creed or party. A Maine woman, wrote, concerning the Usher family: "Mr. and Mrs. Usher and their children comprised a household which has been almost historic for its wide hospitality, its simplicity, freedom, intelligence, and refinement—a shrine where artists like Ole Bull, Charlotte Cushman, Paul Akers, Harriet Beecher Stowe, and many others, found their lives made sweeter through enthusiastic recognition and appreciation by every member of the family. Their home was open, likewise, with the same liberality to the humble neighbor, the crudest chance acquaintance, and the most radical idealist."

BANNING, MARGARET CULKIN (Mrs. Archibald T. Banning), daughter of William E. and Hannah (Young) Culkin, was born in Buffalo, Minnesota. Her father was a son of Anthony Culkin, a native of Ireland, who located in Oswego, New York, about 1850; and her mother was descended from the Plunkett family, also of Ireland. After four years at the Duluth High School, and one year at the Convent of the Sacred Heart, Rochester, New York, Miss Culkin entered Vassar College, Poughkeepsie, New York, where she was graduated A.B. She then spent a year at the School of Civics and Philanthropy, in Chicago, and until her marriage was professionally engaged in social and philanthropic work. On October 13, 1914, she married Archibald T. Banning, Jr., a corporation lawyer of Duluth, Minnesota. They are the parents of one son, Archibald T. Banning, III, and one daughter, Mary Margaret Banning. During the first years of the World War, Mrs. Banning carried on relief work in London and Holland. Upon her return to Duluth she continued in this and in General Red Cross work. In 1918, she raised $150,000 for the purchase of War Savings Stamps. During the same year she was a member of the Executive Committee of the Duluth branch of the Council of National Defense. She is a member of the Suffrage Association, the Association of Collegiate Alumnae, the Vassar Alumnae Association, and the Drama League of America.

HOLTON, JESSIE MOON (Mrs. Frederick A. Holton), educator, daughter of Clinton A. and Frances (Hawkins) Moon, was born in Ilion, New York, September 16, 1866. On her mother's side she is a descendant of the Brewsters of Massachusetts. She was educated in the grammar school at Newport, New York, and at Fairfield Academy, New York. In 1883 she entered Cornell University, where she studied for one year. After teaching for a year (1884–1885), she returned to Cornell University for a second year of study (1885–1886). She then taught for two years in the Herkimer, New York high school; for three years in the Clinton Liberal Institute, Fort Plain, New York; and for nine years at Mrs. Flint's private school in Washington, District of Columbia.

On July 29, 1891, at Newport, New York, she married Frederick A. Holton (born in Galesburg, Illinois, February 4, 1859), a scientific expert in patent cases. In 1901, Mrs. Holton founded The Holton-Arms School for girls, Washington, District of Columbia, of which she is Principal. She is also instructor in Physiography and in the History of Art. The school has its own buildings, which are well-equipped to meet all the needs of a modern girl's education. Strong emphasis is placed upon the upbuilding of character, as well as upon scholastic excellence. Self-control and a sense of responsibility are inculcated through a system of student government. In the school year 1920–1921 there were 275 pupils and 20 instructors.

BAKER, KATHERINE, Army nurse, daughter of J. Thompson and Margaret Elizabeth (Bordner) Baker, was born in Lewisburg, Pennsylvania, October 4, 1876, and died September 22, 1919. Her father (born April 13, 1847; died December 7, 1919) was a descendant of Wendel Baker, of Union County, Pennsylvania, and her mother is descended from John Bordner of Dauphin County, Pennsylvania. Miss Baker was educated in Bucknell Seminary and Goucher College, Baltimore, Maryland. She then read law, and was admitted to the Pennsylvania Bar. Later she assisted her father in his law office in Lewisburg. In 1904 she located at Wildwood, New Jersey, where she was made a member of the Board of Education. She was a constant contributor to the leading magazines. The *Atlantic Monthly* for February, 1913, contained her *Entertaining the Candidates*, afterwards reprinted in *Atlantic Classics*. She published *The House of Devils* in *Collier's Weekly* (July 19, 1913), and *The Fifty-cent Kind* in the *Atlantic Monthly* (April, 1917). Her last story, *Enjoy the Day*, a leaf from her war experiences, written at Cannes, while she was convalescing from pleuropneumonia, appeared in *Scribner's Magazine* (April, 1919).

In March, 1917, during the crisis of the submarine menace, Miss Baker sailed for France to offer her services as a nurse to the French Government. After training with Doctor Alexis Carrel in his hospital at Compiègne, she was sent to the front, and worked in a tent until late in December, in the bitter winter of 1917. For her sacrifices and her devotion to the soldiers of the 137th Infantry, 3d French Army, she was made a Corporal. Moreover, she was the only woman to be decorated with the Fourragère. Working in snow and mud, without rest, and depriving herself of food and comforts, in order to give them to the wounded, she suffered a breakdown in health and was sent to the South of France. At Cannes she had an attack of pneumonia that nearly proved fatal. The surgeons ordered her to rest for a year, but in about two months, she was at work again. Trains were carrying hundreds of wounded to the rear, where there were few surgeons and nurses, and Miss Baker was soon doing hospital duty fourteen hours a day. The chief surgeons under whom she worked wrote in her *Livret Militaire*, "Perfect nurse from every point of view." She worked with the American Army in the Vosges, where she served in two hospitals, a mile and a half apart. In both of these she acted as interpreter, and in one she had sole charge of a ward. When she had cared for the wounded she would walk in all kinds of weather, to the other hospital, to send messages for the dying, or to bring a priest to console them in their last hours. After the Armistice, Miss Baker returned home broken in health and, after intense suffering, died September 22, 1919, of meningitis contracted, her physicians said, at the front. After her death the French Government conferred upon her the posthumous honor of the Croix de Guerre, with a star. While in France, Miss Baker was appointed a trustee of the Women's College at Rutgers. She was a member of Alpha Phi, the College Club, the Authors' League, and the Art Alliance.

DAVIESS, MARIA THOMPSON, artist and author, daughter of John Burton Thompson and Leonora (Hamilton) Daviess, was born in Harrodsburg, Kentucky. She is fifth in descent, from Joseph Daviess (name then spelled Dovis), who came from the north of Scotland, and settled in Rockbridge County, Virginia, about 1700. Through her paternal grandmother, she traces descent from Colonel William Thompson, who came to America with a body of troops in 1669.

Miss Daviess' grandmother, Maria Thompson Daviess, was a distinguished historian, the first woman member of the Filson Club of Louisville, Kentucky, and a scientific agriculturist on a large "Blue grass farm." She planted the first sorghum seed south of the Ohio River. The members of her family on both sides, belong to the Colonial Dames, the Daughters of American Revolution, and the Daughters of the Confederacy. One of the grandsons of the original Joseph Daviess, Josepth Hamilton Daviess, married a sister of Chief Justice Marshall, and, as United States district Attorney, attempted, though unsuccessfully, to bring Aaron Burr to trial for treason, in 1806. He served as a major under General Harrison at Tippecanoe, where he was killed in 1811, while leading a cavalry charge.

Miss Daviess completed her schooling at Science Hill, Shelbyville, Kentucky, in 1891. During 1891–1892, she pursued a special course in literature at Wellesley College,

Massachusetts, and from 1902 to 1904, studied painting in Paris at the studios of Julien, Delacluse and Vite, Paris. Her work was exhibited in the Paris Salon in 1904–1905, and in 1905 she began painting miniatures and working in art jewelry. Later, she exhibited at the Nashville, Tennessee, Art Club and was awarded the gold medal.

In 1909, Miss Daviess, completed her book, *Miss Salina Sue and the Soap-Box Babies*, and in 1910, *The Road to Providence*. With great regularity, she published at least one book yearly. Some of the most popular are: *Rose of Old Harpeth; The Treasure Babies; The Elected Mother; The Melting of Molly*, which was subsequently dramatized; *Sue Jane; The Tinder Box; Andrew the Glad; Phyllis; Over Paradise Ridge; The Daredevil*, later dramatized; *The Heart's Kingdom; The Golden Bird; Bluegrass and Broadway;* and *The Matrix*.

Miss Daviess' versatility has also been shown in her several plays. In addition to the dramatization of two of her books, she has had two plays successfully produced, *The Purple Slipper* and *The Treasure Hunt*. She has written several photoplays that have been filmed: *Out of a Clear Sky;* and *Little Miss Hoover*, with Marguerite Clarke; and a picturization of her novel, *The Daredevil*, with Gail Kane.

Miss Daviess is a member of the Tennessee Women's Press and Authors' Club; the Nashville Art Association; and in New York City, of the Pen and Brush Club; the Round Table Club; the Centennial Club, and the National Arts Club.

She is also vitally interested in civic betterment work, and is an ardent suffragist, being Vice-President of the Tennessee Suffrage Association. She has been by turn a farmer, a photographer, a sculptor, a miniature painter, a craftsman, a teacher of domestic science, and a writer. She esteems writing above all other vocations.

BLODGETT, DAISY ALBERTINE PECK (Mrs. Delos A. Blodgett), was born in Greenville, Georgia, November 7, 1862. Her father, Professor William Henry Peck, was in all his family lines of English Colonial descent, his ancestors having held office in various towns in Connecticut and serving as military officers in the Colonial Wars and in the War of American Independence. He was the direct descendant of Deacon Paul Peck (born in England in 1608), who came to Boston on the ship *Defense* in 1635, and was one of the party of eighty-four who with the Reverend Thomas Hooker, their pastor, settled in Hartford, Connecticut, in 1636. He was made proprietor "by courtesy of the town," in 1639, his home lot being the present site of the State Library, on Washington Street, near the corner of Capitol Avenue.[1] From the records, he seems to have been one of the leading men of the town; held public offices to the end of his life, and was a deacon of the Congregational Church for many years. He died December 23, 1695, and was buried in what is now the Centre Church burying-ground, where his name appears on the shaft erected to the Founders of the city.

From Deacon Paul Peck and his wife, Martha, the line of descent is traced through their son, Samuel (born, 1647; died, 1696), and his wife, Elizabeth, who resided in West Hartford and died there; through their son, Samuel (born in West Harftord in 1672, settled in Berlin, Connecticut, and died there December 9, 1765), who married, March 6, 1701, Abigail Collier (died, October 28, 1742); through their son, Samuel Peck (born in Kensington, a district of Berlin, Connecticut, January 6, 1701; died in Berlin, August 25, 1784), who married, January 10, 1725, Thankful Winchel (died, January 6, 1762); through their son, Samuel Peck (born in Berlin, May 2, 1734; died there, July 18, 1802), who married, March 3, 1757, his first wife, Ruth Hopkins; through their son, Deacon Samuel Peck (born in Berlin, September 25, 1768; died there, March 19, 1833), who married, November 27, 1794, Polly Maria Upson (born, July 13, 1776; died, December

15, 1853), daughter of Jesse and Hannah (Judd) Upson; through their son, Colonel Samuel Hopkins Peck, (born in Berlin, December 14, 1798; died in New Orleans, Louisiana, September 12, 1862), a wealthy banker of Augusta, Georgia, and New Orleans, and a soldier in the Mexican War, who married (December 25, 1828), his first wife, Mrs. Sarah Holmes De Pate, daughter of Nathaniel Nesbit Holmes of Georgia; and through their son, Professor William Henry Peck (born in Augusta, Georgia, December 30, 1830; died in Jacksonville, Florida, February 4, 1892), who married, October 30, 1854, Mona Blake Kenny, daughter of Bernard Kenny, and granddaughter of Sir Thomas Blake of Menlough Castle, County Galway, Ireland.

William Henry Peck was graduated at Harvard College in 1853, and was appointed Professor of History at the University of Louisiana in 1856. Desiring, however, to make literature his life-work, he became associated with Robert Bonner on the editorial staff of the New York *Ledger*. On the outbreak of the Civil War, he returned to Georgia. He established *The Georgia Weekly* in Atlanta, and was successively President of the Masonic Female College, Greenville (1862), and Professor of Languages in the Le Vert Female College, Tarlberton (1864–1865). From 1868 to the time of his death he devoted himself to his writing, for a time under contract with Robert Bonner, and produced upwards of one hundred novels, besides many short stories contributed to magazines. His novels, which are all distinguished for their force, vivacity, and graphic brilliancy, deal, for the most part, with historical subjects, and show much careful study and scholarly research. The principal titles are: *The Renegade* (1859), *The Conspirators of New Orleans* (1865), *The Phantom* (1866), *The Confederate Flag on the Ocean* (1866), *Maids and Matrons of Virginia* (1867), *The McDonalds: or The Ashes of Southern Homes, a Tale of Sherman's March* (1867), *The Diamond Merchant* (1809),

The Miller of Marseilles (1870), *The Executioner of Venice* (1871), *The Stone-Cutter of Lisbon, a Tale of the Great Earthquake* (1870), *Luke Hammond the Miser* (1871), *Locksmith of Lyons* (1872), *Iron Robert, or the Armourer of Rouen* (1872), *A Romance of Joan of Arc* (1873), *The Tower of Gold, or the Maiden of Seville, a Romance of Pedro the Cruel* (1875), *Icholine Lochran, a Romance of Cornwallis' Capture* (1877), *Irene, or the King's Last Dream* (1876), *Red Butler, or the Warrior of Lake Champlain* (1876), and *Wild Redburn, an Indian Tale* (1877).

William Henty and Mona Peck were the parents of six children: Bertha (Mrs. George Schaefer), M. Beatrice (Mrs. A. E. Dugas), Myrtis (Mrs. Charles Graves Matthews), Mona Byrnina (Mrs. Edward P. Porcher), Daisy Albertine (Mrs. Delos A. Blodgett), and Samuel Henry Peck of Rockledge, Florida.

Daisy Albertine Peck was educated in New York City and Atlanta, Georgia. On June 3, 1893, she was married in New York to Delos Abiel Blodgett. Mr. Blodgett was born in 1825 in Otsego, New York, and died in 1908 in Grand Rapids, Michigan, where he was a successful lumber merchant and President of the Fourth National Bank. Throughout his life he was generously active in public welfare, and, at the time of his death, was arranging to present to Grand Rapids a home for children. Mrs. Blodgett carried out his intentions, under her personal supervision, drawing the first plans herself, and overseeing the furnishing of the home with excellent judgment and taste and great executive ability; and the home was dedicated November 28, 1908, as a memorial to Mr. Blodgett. She was its first President.

In 1910, with her three children, Helen Peck (born July 6, 1895), Delos A. (born November 13, 1896), and Mona Peck (born September 4, 1900), she went to Europe for the purpose of giving them a French education. Her summers were spent at St. Moritz, Switzerland, and her winters at Trouville, France.

After several years abroad, Mrs. Blodgett returned with her children to America, in order that the training given them in Europe might be supplemented by training in lines that would fit them to become useful American citizens. They have creditably satisfied her ambitions. Her son, Delos II, having finished his education, entered business, and married Marion Hilliard of Minneapolis. The elder daughter, Miss Helen Peck, is a graduate of Mt. Vernon Seminary, one of the oldest and best schools of Washington. As a gifted and well educated young lady she has taken her place as one of the social leaders of the younger set of society in the National Capital. Miss Mona Pack Blodgett completed the course at Mt. Vernon Seminary, Mrs. Somers' celebrated school, and was one of the most attractive of the 1919 debutantes of Washington.

Mrs. Blodgett did not go to Washington to devote all her time to social affairs, but has interested herself in many philanthropic and charitable enterprises. During the War she was among those who were untiring in their efforts to promote the best interests and success of every patriotic enterprise. It would have been impossible for her to have accomplished all the work undertaken by her, but for the able assistance of her sister, Mrs. Matthews, a woman of very rare ability, ably seconding Mrs. Blodgett in every undertaking in which she has interested herself. At her beautiful home in Washington, her entertainments are marked by most generous hospitality.

Mrs. Blodgett is a very active member of the Colonial Dames of America and the Daughters of the American Revolution serving on the most important committees in these and other societies. She has displayed fine executive ability and intense activity in the wonderful work which these organizations have undertaken and accomplished. She and her two daughters are accomplished horsewomen, and ride a part of each day.

¹See Porter's *Map of Hartford in 1640*, surveyed and drawn from the records in 1839.

REIGNOLDS, CATHERINE MAY, known as Kate Reignolds (Mrs. Erving Winslow), actress, was born in England, May 16, 1837, a daughter of Captain G. T. and Emma Reignolds. She received her early education at a school near London.

While still a child she came to this country with her mother and two younger sisters, and made her first appearance at John Rice's Theatre in Chicago, in a small part in the popular *Cinderella*. On the same occasion her mother was cast for a singing part far below the true scope of her talents.

"For the sake of encouragement to others," wrote Miss Reignolds in her *Yesterdays with Actors*, "let me say that my novitiate was an utter failure, most awkward, unpromising and uninspired. Any success I afterwards met followed as hopeless a year or two of unremitting effort and struggles as ever a human being spent. Only duty, affection and necessity held me up, my one comfort the hope of being speedily enabled, with my most generous and devoted sisters' help, to release our mother from a thoroughly uncongenial occupation." After the first early struggles and discouragements her rise was rapid, and coming finally to New York, she made her first appearance as Virginia in the *Virginius* of Edwin Forrest. When the centennial of Forrest's birth was celebrated, she wrote an article of reminiscences of her appearances with his company. Her work with Forrest was a mere introductory appeal to the New York public, due to his desire to give the aspirant a chance to satisfy her ambitions, and resulted in an immediate engagement for a summer season in the city, and later in the opportunity to play leading parts at William E. Burton's Chambers Street Theatre.

In John Brougham's revival of *King John* she was seen as Prince Arthur. The notable cast included E. L. Davenport in the title character, William Wheatly as Faulconbridge, and Mrs. E. L. Davenport as Constance. Two years of steadily diminishing receipts necessitated a change of bill, *King John* being followed by the *Pirates of Mississippi* and later by *Tom and Jerry in New York*, in both of which Miss Reignolds had leading parts. For a brief period she played at Laura Keene's Theatre, during its early days, and later was under the management of Ben De Bar in St. Louis and New Orleans, acting in those cities with Matilde Heron, Mrs. John Wood, Jean Davenport Lander, James E. Murdoch, James K. Hackett, and other distinguished players.

While acting in St. Louis, she declined an offer from Barry Sullivan to become leading woman of his company during a tour of the English-speaking world, but accepted an offer to join the company of the Boston Museum, where Mr. E. F. Keach organized one of the best stock companies in the country. Her career here began in August, 1860, and continued for five years, during which she played Desdemona, Juliet, Lydia Languish, Letitia Hardy in *The Belle's Stratagem*, Lady Gay Spanker, Emilie de Lesparre in *The Corsican Brothers*, Peg Woffington, Eily O'Connor in the *Colleen Bawn*, Jeanie Deans in *The Heart of Mid-Lothian*, and other characters in the Boucicault plays, without which no theatrical season was then complete. On June 10, 1865, she took her farewell benefit at the Museum, the bill for the occasion being *Masks and Faces*, in which she acted Peg Woffington, and *The Spirit of the Rhine*. There were kindly farewell speeches and the presentation by a committee of distinguished citizens of a watch and chain.

Later she often gave interesting reminiscences of her days at the Museum, when she entered the stage door from one of the galleries which gave at a touch, but fell back quickly with the force of a ponderous spring. In one of the rooms, where the actors congregated was the sign: "Trifles make perfection," and the members of the company tried to live up to that motto.

The Museum seasons began with a series of old comedies in which, of course, the "leading actress" took the leading part, as well as in all the important productions. She became so identified with the "classic drama," possessing as William Winter said of her "the very spirit of gaiety and sparkling bouyancy," that, after she had left Boston on her starring tour, for three years, she was engaged for several weeks of these productions at each season's commencement. During the five years of the Museum engagement, a few "stars" appeared there, and with the male artists, Miss Reignolds played the opposite rôles.

Miss Reignold's starring tour began at once, after leaving the Boston Museum, at the Broadway Theatre, New York, in *Piccolino*, a translation made for her. Thereafter she starred throughout the country in an extensive repertory, including Shakespeare, the old English comedies, *Griffith Gaunt, Marie Antoinette, Armadale, Richelieu at Sixteen*, and *Nobody's Daughter*. In 1866 she made her first appearance in England at the Princess Theatre, London, and in some of the leading houses throughout the United Kindgom, but her British tour was cut short by injuries received from a fall in the theatre in Exeter, and she returned immediately to this country.

In the fall of 1867 she opened the Boston Theatre with Edmund Falconer in the popular Irish drama of *Innisfallen*. The next time she acted at the Boston Theatre she appeared in *The Shadow of a Crown*, and *Richelieu at Sixteen*, in which she had achieved unusual success. Later she acted at this same theatre with the stock company in *Armadale, Camille, Ingomar, Kathleen Mavourneen*, and *The Angel of Midnight*.

She took no formal farewell of the stage but was for many years prominent as a public reader, especially of the plays of Henrik Ibsen, and as an instructor in the art of acting. She paid a professional visit to London in her later years, and there gained a wide reputation for her reading of Ibsen's *An Enemy of the People* at the Haymarket Theatre. She was instrumental in introducing Ibsen, Sudermann, Bjornson, and other dramatists, to the American public, and in the spring of 1889 gave a series of special matinees at the Columbia Theatre, when *The Pillars of Society*, and others of Ibsen's plays, were acted for the first time in Boston. From Ibsen himself she had special authority to read his plays, of which the first knowledge was, in so many cases, due to her interpretation.

Miss Reignolds wrote two entertaining volumes of reminiscences, and published readings from the old English dramatists. She married Erving Winslow of Boston, on June 20, 1861, and her son, Doctor Charles Edward Amory Winslow, is a well-known biologist and expert in public health, Professor of that department at Yale University. She died at her summer residence in Concord, Massachusetts, July 11, 1911.

COOK, MARGUERITE (Mrs. David C. Cook), born in 1854 in Chicago. Her father, Thomas Murat, was a member of an important French family of that name, long settled in Tallahassee, Florida, where he was born. Her mother, Patience Jane (Evans) Murat (born in 1831), passed her youth in New York City, where she was deeply interested in church work. With her mother, she became a member of John Street Chapel, the first Methodist Episcopal Church in America, where she sang in the choir for years. Her unusual depth of character and sweetness of disposition were accentuated with time. In her last years she lived with her daughter, Mrs. Cook, at Elgin, Illinois, and her loving coöperation made it possible for her daughter to devote much of her time and effort to editorial work and to aid her husband to further his efforts in the establishment of a great educational institution.

Miss Murat completed her education in the Chicago Normal Training School, where the regular courses of study were supplemented by instruction under special teachers. The habits of earnest study acquired in her early years have continued throughout her life.

When only seven years of age, she began teaching contraband negroes who had been brought north, and for years during her childhood, her evenings were spent in this way. Also, before her twentieth year she gave secular instruction to a young men's Bible class. Three of the young men of this class entered what was then known as the Baptist Theological Seminary, and all of them of the class became honorable and honored men, useful and intelligent citizens. Her work with this class was highly commended in a World's Sunday School Convention, convened about that time in Edinburgh.

In 1874 she was married in Chicago to David C. Cook (born in New York in 1852), son of Reverend E. S. Cook, a Methodist minister in New York. Since 1875, she has been continuously and actively engaged with her husband in organizing and establishing the David C. Cook Publishing Company, of which she has been the Secretary since 1881. She has worked side by side with him, helping to build up one of the greatest Sunday-school publishing institutions in the world. For many years, her name has been well known among teachers, and to those interested in instruction of small children. In fact, the development of the younger departments of the modern Sunday-school has in large part been due to her editorial leadership.

Since 1878, Mrs. Cook has edited various books and periodicals; among them may be included the *Sunday-school Lesson Helps*, *The Primary and Beginners Teachers*, *the Comprehensive Teacher and Scholar*, *the Transformation Picture Roll*, and has published many illustrative designs and song books. She has written many miscellaneous educational articles published in magazines and elsewhere.

With all her busy, intellectual life, and care of her own property and business affairs, she has also found time for philanthropic and religious work. For ten years she was an active member of the board of the "Forward Movement Settlement Work." She was

Superintendent of the primary department of the Elgin Methodist Sunday-school for thirty years; was President of a Primary Sunday-school Union for fourteen years and of a local Woman's Foreign Missionary Society for twenty-five years. She was a delegate to the Ecumenical Council at both Boston and Edinburgh. In the denomination of which she is a member, she has been a prominent leader of missionary and young people's work. She was for many years General Secretary of the Young People's Department of the Woman's Foreign Missionary Society of the Methodist Episcopal Church, the largest woman's organization. She and her sons are associate members of old John Street Chapel, in which church her mother was an active worker in her girlhood.

Mrs. Cook was a member for several years of the Chicago Woman's Club. Later she moved to Los Angeles, where she became a charter member and a life member of the Los Angeles Friday Morning Club. She is a life member of the Elgin Woman's Club, and of the National Arts Club of New York City, and a member of the Elgin Every Wednesday Literary Club. She has traveled extensively throughout the world, visiting the best European art galleries, and studying the work of the greatest artists of the lands in which were enacted the scenes of the life of Christ, in order that the wonderful story might be presented in a manner more real and vivid.

She has traversed the United States many times. Her winters are spent with her husband at their home on the Gulf of Mexico, in Florida; their summers, on their estate on a hill overlooking Lake Michigan. Wherever they go their work goes with them.

In addition to strenuous editorial and missionary work, Mrs. Cook has proved herself a successful business woman. Not only has she assisted in managing the publishing company, but has accumulated a competence through wise investments in real estate, beginning with capital she herself had earned. A large part of her earnings have been given away to those who needed help or a start in life.

She has had three sons, two of whom survive. Their lives have been a joy and comfort. Both are in the same line of work as their parents, and are kindly, useful, Christian gentlemen, doing useful service for the world.

Mrs. Cook dearly loves her hosts of friends. As she sits at her desk, she finds comfort and inspiration in gazing into the pictured faces of the wonderful men and women who are and who have been her dear personal friends. Although many have passed on, their presence is very real for her; the room is full of the joy of their presence.

With all her responsibilities, Mrs. Cook has been an ideal wife and mother. She has managed her home, entertained guests, and reared her two sons. In spite of numerous outside activities, she has put her home first, giving several hours each day to the training of her children. Her life has indeed been an active one, but always her motto has been to serve others.

Although now in her seventieth year (1923), she is as alert and active, as mentally efficient, as joyous and ready for fun as many a younger woman. Her friends say of her, "She is just in her prime." The secret of this is an active body, a mind intensely interested in the works of God, and man, and a heart filled with love and sympathy for all, whether good or bad, for she believes that the bad have urgent need of our loving understanding to help them to grow better.

WEIR, IRENE, artist and writer, daughter of Walter and Anne Field (Andrews) Weir, was born at St. Louis, Missouri. Her father, Walter Weir, M.A., was a son of Robert W. Weir, National Academician, who, in 1832 was appointed Professor of Drawing in the Military Academy at West Point. He held this post for forty-two years, and in the Chapel at the Academy, is a large allegorical work, *Peace and War*, ranked as probably his finest production.

The Weir ancestors came originally, from Stirling, Scotland, where they were prominent as magistrates and lawyers. One member of this family, Moses Andrews, served in the Revolution. The night before the Battle of Bunker Hill, in which he fought, he slept with the money bags of the colonial army for his pillow. Other members of the family were prominent in seven colleges: Yale, Dartmouth, Harvard, Hamilton, Cornell, etc. early in the nineteenth century. Miss Weir's grandmother was Tirzah Ann Field of Deerfield, Massachusetts. The Fields were originally Norman French and the name was spelled *de la Feld*.

Miss Weir received her early education at home, in school and, later, in college. She studied and traveled abroad, and attended the Academie in Paris. She took an art course at Yale, where she received the degree of B.F.A. in 1906. She was also a member of the Art Students' League, in New York City.

Since receiving her degree in 1906, Miss Weir has devoted all her time and energy to organizing and directing schools and associations for the development of practical applications of the fine arts. In 1906 she wrote *Greek Painters' Art*, and subsequently many monographs on artists and their work. She has exhibited at the National Association of Women Painters and Sculptors; the Architectural League; the New York Society of Water Color Painters, and the New York Society of Arts and Crafts. She has also served as head of the Art Department of the Summer School at Winthrop College, Rock Hill, South Carolina.

Miss Weir's latest and greatest achievement was the organization of the School of Design and Liberal Arts, at 212 West 59th Street, New York City, of which she is now the Director. The plan of this school is to train students to become designers, painters, craftsmen, camp advisors, and settlement art workers; to prepare them to enter industrial and professional fields with distinction of craftsmanship, and with the spirit of coöpera-

tion and leadership; to work out American ideals in their art. Lectures are given on literature and drama, as well as on the history of art, in order to coördinate imagination and training and to form the basis for "good taste." Drawing and painting from life models are taught daily, also courses in commercial design, dyeing, batik, weaving, embroidery, interior decoration, and, in general, costume and stage designing.

Miss Weir is one of the Directors of the Art Alliance of America; a member of the Lyceum Club of London and of the New York Society of Craftsmen.

ALLEN, ELEANOR WHITNEY, daughter of Thomas and Eleanor Goddard (Whitney) Allen, was born in Ecouen, France, April 18, 1882. Her first American ancestor, Samuel Allen, came from England in 1630, and settled at Northampton, Massachusetts. His grandson, Joseph, who married Elizabeth Parsons, had six sons who fought in the War of the Revolution. One of them, the Reverend Thomas Allen, was known as the "Fighting Parson" of the Battle of Bennington. Her mother's father, Josiah Dwight, Professor of Geology at Harvard, was a direct descendant of John Whitney, of London, England, who settled at Watertown, Massachusetts in 1635.

Miss Allen received her early education in private schools in Boston, and she has since been active in club and welfare work. She was Recording-Secretary, then Vice-President of the Massachusetts League of Girls Clubs; President of the Saturday Morning Club, 1921–1922, and Treasurer of the Girls City Club of Boston, 1918–1922. Until the passage of the Nineteenth Amendment she was active in Anti-suffrage work, and during the World War she worked in the Volunteer Service Bureau and Education Department of the Boston Metropolitan Chapter of the American Red Cross.

Miss Allen was bronze medallist in the Woman's National Golf Championship, 1911; runner-up in the Massachusetts State Championship, 1916; President of the Woman's Golf Association of Boston, 1916–1920; President of the Woman's Eastern Golf Association, 1921–1922; and a member of the Woman's Committee of the United States Golf Association in 1921. She is a member of Chilton, MacDowell, Saturday Morning, and Vincent Clubs, of Boston.

ANDREWS, FANNIE FERN, educational and economic expert, daughter of William Wallace and Anna Maria (Brown) Phillips, was born in Margaretville, Nova Scotia, on September 25, 1867. She was a graduate of the Normal School of Salem, Massachusetts, in 1884, and received the degree of A.B. at Radcliffe College, Cambridge, Massachusetts, in 1902. Afterward, she attended the Harvard Summer School for several terms, and finally spent the years, 1915–1920 at Radcliffe, as a graduate student in International Law. On July 16, 1890, she was married, at Lynn, Massachusetts, to Edwin G. Andrews.

Since her graduation at Radcliffe, Mrs. Andrews has been a leader in educational work of various kinds. In the same year, she began the organization of parents' associations in the Boston schools. She later became Honorary President of the Boston Home and School Association. She lectured at home and abroad, and wrote on educational and international law. During this period she compiled the *Peace Day*, a bulletin for the United States Bureau of Education, issued in 1912. This was followed, in 1913, by *The Promotion of Peace*, another bulletin for the same Bureau. She also wrote *One Hundred Years of Peace with Great Britain*, for the Memorial Day Annual of the Wisconsin State Department of Education.

Mrs. Andrews' really great work for education and peace, began in 1913, when the governments of seventeen states appointed delegates to an International Conference on Education to be held in September, 1914. This conference was called by the Nether-

lands Government, at the suggestion of the United States Government. Meanwhile, the Great War in Europe prevented the holding of the conference, whose fundamental purpose was the creation of an International Bureau of Education. However, much of the preliminary work for this conference had already been done, and Mrs. Andrews had been appointed to represent the United States. In this capacity she had consulted with the Ministers of Education, and other educational authorities, in the principal countries of Europe, concerning the program of the Conference and the functions of an International Bureau of Education. The invitation sent out by the Netherlands had contained a draft c o n v e n t i o n for some such international bureau.

During this interregnum between the outbreak of the World War and the Armistice, Mrs. Andrews resumed her writing. In 1914, appeared *The War—What should be said about it in the Schools?* published by the American School Peace League; *The Freedom of the Seas*, published in 1917, by Martinus Nijhoff at The Hague; *The United States and the World*, and *The World Family*, in *A Course in Citizenship and Patriotism*, in 1918.

In 1919, an appeal was made to the League of Nations Commission of the Peace Conference, sitting in Paris, for the inclusion of an article in the Covenant of the League providing for an International Bureau of Education as a part of the organization of the League. Mrs. Andrews presented this appeal on April 10th, on behalf of the International Council of Women and the Conference of Women Suffragists of the Allied Countries and the United States, meeting as a group in Paris, and composed of delegates representing the United States, England, France, Italy, Roumania and Belgium. The following article was proposed for insertion in the Covenant of the League of Nations: "The High Contracting Parties will endeavor to make the aims and methods of their educational systems consistent with the general principles underlying the League of Nations; and to this end agree to establish as part of the organization of the League a permanent bureau of education." Mrs. Andrews' presentation of the appeal was endorsed by the United States Army Educational Commission, whose headquarters were in Paris, and by various associations from Great Britain, and Ireland, France, Greece, Roumania, China and Jugo-Slavia, who pleaded that wide-spread education in the elements of democratic citizenship are essential to the fulfillment of the League Conventions.

The above article, however, was not inserted in the League Covenant, although several of the members of the League Commission individually expressed their endorsement of the idea, but deemed it wise for the Commission to confine its work to forming the framework of the League of Nations, leaving the details of the organization for future development.

Before Mrs. Andrews left Europe, she wrote a plan for the creation of an International Bureau of Education, which received the endorsement of the French and British educators. Mrs. Andrews gave also several lectures to the soldiers in the camps, under the direction of the Army Educational Commission. The most popular subject in the course was the League of Nations. She deemed it most important that the American officers and soldiers should consider their obligations of citizenship created by the World War. As Mrs. Andrews said: "The Associated Governments at Paris recognized a common citizenship in a democratic world; it is important, that, when the soldiers return home, they should become a force in shaping public opinion, and not only should understand the historical causes of the war and its immediate issues, but also the principles involved in the peace which also they fought to secure."

Mrs. Andrews has written, since the war, several articles on the League of Nations, and a Course in Foreign Relations prepared for Army Educational Commission, Paris, France, in 1919. In her club and society membership, she reflects her lifelong interests. She is Secretary of the National Committee on International Relations; Chairman of the Massachusetts Committee on Pan-American Relations; a member of the National Institute of Social Sciences; the Academy of Political Sciences in the City of New York; the American Academy of Political and Social Science; Council of the National Educational Association; the Association of College Alumnae; the Radcliffe Alumnae Association; the Harvard Teachers' Association; the American Institute of Instruction; the New England Women's Press Association; the Boston League of Women Voters; the League of Free Nations Association; the American Society for Judicial Settlement of International Disputes; the International Guild, affiliated with the *Sorbonne;* the Twentieth Century Club, Boston; the College Club, Paris; a member of the Executive Committee of the Constantinople College Association; of the Advisory Council of the World Peace Foundation; of the League to Enforce Peace; Councilor of the American Civic Association, and Vice-President of the International Peace Bureau, at Berne. Mrs. Andrews is also a corresponding member of the Bureau de Fédérations d'Instituteurs of Paris; and was appointed on the Commission to investigate the subject of Peace from a world standpoint.

CLAXTON, HANNAH JOHNSON (Mrs. Philander P. Claxton), librarian and lecturer, daughter of George L. and Hannah Iredell (Payne) Johnson, was born in Nashville, Tennessee, April 23, 1879. Her father was a direct descendant of Oliver Winslow Johnson, a native of England, who settled in New Hampshire long before the Revolution. One of his descendants removed to Tennessee, in 1800, and there was later joined by another member of the family, Anthony Wayne Johnson. Her earliest American maternal ancestor was George Payne, of England, who settled in Henrico County, Virginia, about 1681. Mrs. Claxton is related to the Winslows of Massachusetts and the Iredells of North Carolina, as well as the Spottswoods and Paynes of Virginia.

She received her education in the public schools of Nashville, the Preparatory School for Vanderbilt University, and by a correspondence course in Chicago University, including several English branches. Following this, she was appointed librarian in the Nashville Public Library and lectured extensively.

On April 23, 1912, she was married to Philander P. Claxton, United States Commissioner of Education (born in Bedford County, Tennessee, September 28, 1862), and son of Josiah Calvin, and Ann Elizabeth (Jones) Claxton. They are the parents of two children: Philander P. Claxton, Jr. (born December 11, 1914), and Mary Hannah Payne Claxton (born July 8, 1919).

Mrs. Claxton has always been prominent in social betterment work, and has ably supplemented the work of her husband who was for many years foremost in educational lines. She was active in creating the public library movement in Nashville, and was for ten years the Head and Director of the Carnegie Library there. During this period she assisted in promoting the Free State Library Commission of Tennessee, and organized the first system in the South whereby books were supplied to the public schools by the public libraries. To her untiring efforts are due many of the rural libraries and rural schools, now found in outlying and isolated spots throughout Tennessee, and the South in general.

Mrs. Claxton is a member of the League of American Pen Women, the Daughters of the American Revolution, Congress Mothers, Federation of Women's Clubs, the Washington Club, National Federation of College Women, Washington College Woman's Club (for "distinguished services rendered") and

the Woman's Committee of the Second Pan-American Scientific Congress.

ROBERTS, SARA WEEKS (Mrs. Ernest William Roberts), daughter of Hiram Bellows and Sarah M. (Burgess) Weeks, was born at St. Albans, Vermont. She is descended from George Weeks, who came to Falmouth, Massachusetts, about 1630. One of his descendants, Thomas Weeks, of Hardwick, Massachusetts, served in the French and Indian War in 1757. His son, Joseph Weeks, who lived to be ninety years of age, was a soldier in the Revolution. He was the father of Joseph Weeks and grandfather of Hiram Bellows Weeks, whose long, useful, and highly respected lives were spent at St. Albans, Vermont.

Through her mother Mrs. Roberts is of Pilgrim ancestry, being descended from Richard Warren, who came to Plymouth on the *Mayflower* in 1620; through her great-great-grandfather, Benjamin Burgess, who served in the Revolution and was a descendant of Thomas Burgess, a settler at Sandwich, Massachusetts, early in the seventeenth century. She was educated in the St. Albans public school and at the Emerson College of Oratory, Boston, Massachusetts, where she followed the regular and post-graduate courses, receiving the degree of A.B. and A.M. On February 2, 1898, she was married at St. Albans to Ernest W. Roberts, a lawyer, who was a member of Congress from 1898 to 1916 and a member of the Naval Committee for sixteen years. They are the parents of Ernest Weeks Roberts, Sara Dean Roberts, John Page Roberts, and Hiram Weeks Roberts (deceased).

Mrs. Roberts was one of the organizers and a former Vice-President of the Consumers' League of Washington, District of Columbia. She has been also President of the National Library for the Blind, Washington, and is now its Honorary Vice-President. She was the second elected President of the Congressional Club, Washington; is a member of the

Executive Board of the Women's Auxiliary Committee of the Pan-American Scientific Congress; is Vice-President of the National Homeopathic Hospital Ladies' Aid and President of the Macdonald Chapter of the National Homeopathic Hospital.

ROBINSON, CORINNE ROOSEVELT (Mrs. Douglas Robinson), poet, daughter of Theodore and Martha (Bulloch) Roosevelt, was born in New York, September 27, 1861. She is eighth in descent from Claes Martenszen van Roosevelt, who came from Holland to New Amsterdam, about 1649. Her brother was Theodore Roosevelt, Twenty-Sixth President of the United States, and their birthplace, 28 East 20th Street, New York City, is now preserved as his Memorial. Her aunt, Miss Anna Bulloch (later Mrs. James King Gracie), guided her early studies. Later she attended Miss Louise Comstock's school until her twelfth year, after which she was trained by private tutors at the home of her parents. On April 29, 1882, she was married to Douglas Robinson, a real estate broker, and later director of the Banker's Trust Company, and a trustee of the Atlantic Mutual Insurance Company and of the John Jacob Astor Estate. They were the parents of four children: Theodore Douglas (born April 28, 1883); Corinne (born July 2, 1886), now Mrs. Joseph W. Alsop; Monroe (born December 19, 1887), and Stewart Robinson (born March 19, 1889).

Mrs. Robinson has always been greatly interested in politics. She worked ardently for the Progressive Party in 1912, for Governor Hughes as Presidential candidate in 1916, for Mayor Mitchel's reëlection as Mayor of New York in 1917, and, in the winter and spring of 1920, for the nomination for President of Major-General Leonard Wood. In the autumn of 1920 she opened her campaign activities in behalf of Mr. Harding, on September 8th, in Portland, Maine, and, until the election in November following, made many speeches, especially on a long tour

in the Middle West. In all her public utterances, which were marked by their direct and forceful appeal to her audiences, she demonstrated that the two great issues before the people were nationalism against internationalism and economy against extravagance.

Mrs. Robinson is a Manager of the Orthopaedic Hospital, the Three Arts Club, and other philanthropic organizations; a member of the Y. W. C. A., the History Club, the Poetry Society of America, the McDowell Club, the Cosmopolitan Club and the Colony Club of New York, and the Essex County Club of New Jersey. She is a life member of the American Red Cross, and showed her interest in its work by forming a chapter at her country home, Henderson House, Herkimer County, New York.

Mrs. Robinson is a writer of verse, her poems first appearing in Scribner's Magazine. At the suggestion of Messrs. Charles Scribner's Sons, all her poems were gathered into a volume, which was published in 1912 under the title of The Call of Brotherhood. Her second volume, One Woman to Another, appeared in 1914. Her third volume, Service and Sacrifice, published in 1919, included Sagamore, her tribute to her brother at the time of his death. The volume is dedicated "To the Memory of my Brother, Theodore Roosevelt, whose Watchwords were Courage and Service, whose Life was a Trumpet Call to Loyalty to America." The poems have a two-fold interest: that which attaches to their intrinsic merit, and that by which they are associated with the memory of the great American.

In the spring of 1921, Charles Scribner's Sons decided to publish the Poems of Corinne Roosevelt Robinson in collected form, namely the three former volumes with the addition of several new poems. In a letter to her, Miss Amy Lowell wrote: "The different rhythms you use are a delight to me and fill me with envy. Your war poems have much of the grand style in them and are like trumpet calls, and your poems to Mr. Roosevelt are very beautiful indeed. It seems to me that I have never read such excellent irony and striking humor as in the *Poetry Society Anthology*. You have a remarkable gift, the touching off of people's characteristics in most excellent and pregnant verses."

Concerning Mrs. Robinson, Professor William Lyon Phelps, of Yale University, in his book, *The Advance of English Poetry*, says: "Mrs. Robinson's poetry comes from a full mind and a full heart. There is the knowledge born of experience, combined with spiritual revelation. She is an excellent illustration of the possibility of living to the uttermost in the crowded avenues of the world without any loss of religious or moral values."

In 1921, Mrs. Robinson published a biography, *My Brother, Theodore Roosevelt*, which gives invaluable information on his character and career.

PALMER, PAULINE (Mrs. Albert E. Palmer), painter, daughter of Nicholas and Franciska (Spangemacher) Lennards, was born in McHenry, Illinois. Her mother was a daughter of John Spangemacher of Dorsten, Germany.

Miss Lennards, after acting for some time as supervisor of drawing in the Chicago public schools, resigned to marry, on May 21, 1891, Albert E. Palmer, M.D., a native of Rochester, New York, who was practising in Chicago. Her career as a painter began with study in the Art Institute, Chicago, which was followed by work abroad, under such masters as Collin, Prinet, Courtois, Lucien Simon, and Richard Miller, in Paris; and in this country under Charles W. Hawthorne in Provincetown, Massachusetts, and New York. While in Paris, Mrs. Palmer won the silver medal at Colorossi's and the bronze medal of the Académie de la Grande Chaumière. She first exhibited at the Omaha Exposition in 1898, and again at the Buffalo Exposition in 1901. Canvasses by her were shown at the Paris Salons of 1903, 1904, 1905, 1906, and 1911, and also in 1911 at the Esposizione delle Belle Arti in Naples. She was awarded the bronze medal at the St. Louis Exposition in 1904, and paintings by her also appeared at the Panama-Pacific Expostion held in 1915 at San Francisco. Other awards have been the Young Fortnightly prize (1907), the Marshall Field prize (1907), the William O. Thompson portrait prize (1914), the Julius Rosenwald purchase prize (1915), honorable mention in the American Painters' Exhibition (1916), all at the Art Institute, Chicago; the Fine Arts Building prize, Chicago, in 1914; honorable mention at the Artists' Guild exhibition in 1915; in 1917 the Clyde Carr prize for her painting, *The Blizzard;* and in 1920 the Edward B. Butler purchase prize for her *In the Sunny South* and the Chicago Society of Artists' silver medal for her *In the Open*.

Mrs. Palmer's work is represented in the permanent collections of the Art Institute, Chicago, the Muncie (Indiana) Art Association, the galleries at Rockford, Illinois, Aurora, Illinois (*A Southern Rose*, 1920), and South Bend, Indiana (*The County Fair*, 1920), in various clubs, and in private collections, such as those of Mme. Schumann-Heink, Frank Logan, E. B. Butler, Homer Stillman, A. Valentine, etc. She served as Vice-President of the Chicago Society of Artists from 1918 to 1919, in which year she was unanimously elected President for 1919–1921, the first woman to hold that office in the thirty-five years of the Society's existence. She is also a director of the Arts Club of Chicago, of which she was a charter member; charter member of the Cordon Club; honorary member of the Lake View Woman's Club; and a member of the Art Service League, the Alumni Association of the Art Institute, the Fine Arts Guild, the Chicago Water Color Club, and the Chicago Woman's Club.

PORTER, ELEANOR HODGMAN (Mrs. John Lyman Porter), author, daughter of Francis Fletcher and Llewella (Woolson) Hodgman, was born in Littleton, New Hampshire, December 19, 1868, and died in

Cambridge, Massachusetts, May 21, 1920. She was of New England ancestry and traced descent from Governor William Bradford of the *Mayflower*. During her youth and young womanhood she showed much musical talent, and was trained as a singer at the New England Conservatory of Music. She sang in concerts and church choirs and was for some years a teacher of music. On May 3, 1892, she was married to John Lyman Porter of Corinth, Vermont. His business was in Chattanooga, Tennessee, whence they moved to Cambridge in 1905.

Although Mrs. Porter had written much verse for private occasions, she did not make writing a profession until 1900, when her first short story was published. From that time she contributed more than two hundred stories to magazines and newspapers, and in 1907, her first novel, *Cross Currents*, was published. This was followed by *The Turn of the Tide* (1908), *The Story of Marco* (1911), *Miss Billy* (1911), *Miss Billy's Decision* (1912), *Pollyanna* (1913), *Miss Billy Married* (1914), *Pollyanna Grows Up* (1915), *Just David* (1916), *The Road to Understanding* (1917), and *Mary Marie* (1920). Mrs. Porter's novels had a wide success because of their optimism and their gospel of gladness, illustrating a love for the good and the generous in human character and a belief in the abiding beauty of life.

STERNER, MARIE (Mrs. Albert Sterner), daughter of Henry and Therese (Sellé) Walther, was born in Brooklyn, New York, on July 7, 1877. She began her education in the Brooklyn public schools at the age of ten, but after a short time was taught by governesses and tutors; for two years, from eleven to thirteen years of age, she attended a boarding school in Frankfort, Germany, and later studied the piano under William Mason and Raphael Joseffy. During this period she became greatly interested in welfare work.

At the age of seventeen, on July 17, 1894, she was married, in Brooklyn, New York, to Albert Sterner, then just beginning to make his reputation as an artist. He was born in London, in 1863, the son of Julius L. and Sarah Sterner. His father was an American and his mother, English. They are the parents of two children: Harold, born in Paris in 1895, and Olivia, born in London in 1905. For several years after her marriage, they lived abroad.

Mrs. Sterner has always been greatly interested in her husband's career and in art generally. After their return to this country, she became associated with M. Knoedler and Company, picture dealers, and remained with them for nearly six years, arranging exhibitions and acting as an expert on modern art. Her activities with this firm were very successful, particularly in the initiative she took in introducing unknown artists and new phases in art. Among the celebrated men she "rediscovered" were Eugene Higgins and Rockwell Kent. She was successful in attracting the attention of collectors and museum directors to their work.

In 1921, Mrs. Sterner organized a society known as Junior Art Patrons of America, of which the late President Harding was the First Honorary President. The underlying purpose of this society is to present in an interesting manner collections of American paintings in all media, sculpture, etchings and lithographs, in New York and other important cities of the country. The main feature of this plan will be the selection of works of art by the child, and in this manner the younger generation will form the habit of studying contemporary art, while still free from all fictitious standards and ephemeral cults.

PARSONS, FANNIE GRISCOM (Mrs. Henry Parsons), educational philanthropist, was born in New York City, September 23, 1850. Her father, John Hoskins Griscom, M.D., was descended from Andrew Griscom, who came from England to Philadelphia,

Pennsylvania in 1680. His patent of four hundred and fifteen acres of land in the colony entitled him to a lot in Philadelphia, on which he built the first brick house, opposite to that of William Penn. Doctor Griscom was the first tenement house reformer in New York City, and his father, John Griscom, LL.D., established the first high school in New York, and the House of Refuge, the first institution for juvenile delinquents. He was President of the first Society for Improving the Condition of the Poor, and was on the first committee for savings banks in New York.

Mrs. Parson's mother, Henrietta Peale, was the fifth daughter of Rembrandt Peale, and granddaughter of Charles Wilson Peale, the famous American artist. The latter's father, Charles Peale, came from England in 1727. His family were of Great Dalby, Rutlandshire, where, from 1650, several were curates of the parish.

Mrs. Parsons was educated in public and private schools of New York, at the Moravian Seminary, Bethlehem, Pennsylvania, and at Doctor Dio Lewis' Seminary, Lexington, Massachusetts. Her marriage to Henry Parsons, a lawyer, took place in New York City, March 5, 1873. They are the parents of Henry Griscom, Henrietta Grace, Bertha (Mrs. Harold H. Bayless), Howard Crosby, John, and Maud Parsons.

Mrs. Parsons was one of the first women appointed on the local school boards of Greater New York, serving from 1902 to 1906. From 1902 to 1909 she was President of the Longacre League, the first parents' organization, with permit from the Board of Education to use school houses for other than school purposes. In 1902 she founded the Children's School Farms of the New York City Park Department, and has since been its Director. Out of this developed the International School Farm League, of which Mrs. Parsons has been President since 1907. It has its headquarters at the Lorillard Mansion, New York Botanical Garden, Bronx Park, New York, and was founded to promote and unify a world-wide interest in children's gardens, by assisting such gardens in suitable parks and vacant lots; by aiding in starting gardens in connection with schools, hospitals, and institutions for children; by urging the employment of teachers especially trained for this work, and by establishing a training school for such teachers; by exhibiting models and pictures of the work, and by conducting a bureau of information on the management of children's gardens. In the seventeen years from 1902 to 1919 the influence of the League reached eleven million people, and in addition to the first Children's School Farm started in 1902 in De Witt Clinton Park, New York, gardens were established at Bellevue Hospital for tuberculous children; in Thomas Jefferson Park, New York; in Corlear's Hook Park, 1913; at School No. 177, Manhattan; at Bernardsville, New Jersey and in London, England, while exhibits were shown at the Jamestown Exposition in 1907, at the International Tuberculosis Exhibits in Washington in 1908 and in New York in 1909, and at other health exhibits.

Since 1918 Mrs. Parsons has been honorary adviser to the Garden School of the New York Botanical Garden, Bronx, and from 1917 to 1919 she was chairman of the War and Victory Garden Committee of the Mayor's Committee of Women. She is the author of various articles and published addresses on children's gardens, and in recognition of her work was awarded the silver medal at the St. Louis Exposition in 1904, the gold medal at the Jamestown Exposition in 1907, a gold medal and honorable mention at the International Tuberculosis Congress, Washington, 1908, and diplomas yearly from 1902 to 1917 from the American Institute.

PAUL, NANETTE BAKER (Mrs. Daniel Paul), lecturer, daughter of William and Jane (Kilgore) Baker, was born in Delaware County, Ohio, March 29, 1866. Her father, who was of an old English family tracing descent from William the Conqueror, came from England to Pittsburgh, Pennsylvania, at the age of ten. Her mother's ancestors lived for many generations in Pennsylvania, several of them serving in the Revolutionary War. On April 11, 1888, she was married at Centerburg, Ohio, to Daniel Paul, a native of Licking County, Ohio, who left farming to enter the Ohio State Senate, afterwards holding various minor offices and later in life becoming a banker.

In 1900 Mrs. Paul was graduated LL.B. at the Washington College of Law, and was admitted to the Bar of the District of Columbia. She has been a member of the faculty of the Washington College of Law, and has lectured widely on parliamentary law, in which she is a specialist. Her textbook, Paul's *Parliamentary Law*, published in 1908, contains original diagrams to illustrate the order of motions. These have been reproduced in large charts for the use of schools, clubs, and classes. Mrs. Paul directs classes in this subject, under the auspices of the Anthony League, and they are a feature of the instruction at the Paul Institute, Washington, of which Mrs. Paul is the founder and president. In addition, the Institute offers advanced courses in citizenship, public speaking, psychology, symbolism, and metaphysics.

In 1912 Mrs. Paul published *The Heart of Blackstone, or Principles of the Common Law*, in which these principles are put into simple, living language, to the end that they may appeal to the average person, and create a new respect for law as such. In his introduction to the book, Justice Thomas H. Anderson, of the Supreme Court of the District of Columbia, says: "The author's rare power of condensation, orderly division of the subjects treated, and their logical development, give special value to this work as a succinct yet comprehensive view of the leading principles and maxims of the common law."

Mrs. Paul has also opened a Biblical Museum of costumes and articles from the Holy Land, collected originally by Madame Lydia Mamreoff Von Finkelstein Mountford, and used by her in her lectures on the life of Christ, for classes studying the Bible from the human standpoint. Mrs. Paul has given lectures on the life of the people of the Holy Land, and on the human side of Bible characters, before many churches and classes, and as a Chautauqua lecturer. She has been an active worker for woman suffrage, and is a charter member of the Anthony League of the District of Columbia, and a member of the Twentieth Century Club and the College Women's Club of Washington, the Woman's Bar Association of the District of Columbia, the League of American Penwomen, the Archaeological Society, and the Progressive Educational Association.

PEIRCE, BERTHA, only daughter of William Frederick and Martha A. (Leonard) Peirce, was born in Roxbury, Massachusetts. Both her parents were descended from the *Mayflower* Pilgrims, and Michael Peirce, the earliest American ancestor of the name, came to America about 1630 and settled in Scituate. The paternal stock is supposed to have originated in Italy from the house of Este through the Este family of Alfonso d'Este, Duke of Ferrara. The earliest American settler, Jeffrey Este, traces his ancestry through a niece of Lord Francis Bacon in England. Miss Peirce's direct line is traced through Mary Este, who was hanged as a witch in Salem, and Benjamin Este of Billerica, Massachusetts, who was killed at Bunker Hill. Another ancestor was George Minot, the originator of the Minot family in America. From a member of this family, Miss Peirce takes her pen-name, "Elizabeth Minot," a name well known in current New England publications.

Miss Peirce was educated in the public schools of Boston: the Gaston Grammar School, the Girls' High School, and the Boston Normal School. Later she pursued special courses in German, French, Italian, and Spanish, all of which she reads, writes, and speaks fluently. Following her graduation in the Boston Normal School, she became a teacher in the Boston public schools, where she is still practising her chosen profession. Her pupils are boys of Junior High School age, and with these she has had rare success. Her method is to set before them a high ideal, and make them understand that she believes in their capacity to attain it. That this method justifies itself is shown by the fact that she is accounted one of the best teachers of her rank in the city.

Miss Peirce is public-spirited, and so far as time will allow, interests herself, and takes part in, work for woman's suffrage, the Red Cross, and the Associated Charities. That she has also artistic and literary tastes is not surprising, when one learns that her grandfather, Joseph M. Peirce, was a portrait painter and a member of the Musical Fund Society (which antedated the Boston Symphony Orchestra), that she is a niece of Madison Obrey, an old-time theatrical performer, and that her father was the author of various plays, the best known of which is *The Fisherman's Hut.* In her childhood days, her family occupied a large mansion-house in Roxbury, and with them lived several aunts and uncles. They were all dramatically inclined, and, together with some friends of similar tastes, organized a Shakespeare Club. Here, in the old drawing-room, were enacted many of the plays of Shakespeare and other dramatic productions. Thus some years of the impressionable period were passed in an atmosphere of romance and imagination, which of necessity must have intensified her inherited dramatic taste. In later life she was closely associated with Mrs. Kate Douglas Wiggin in her summer activities at Quillcote, (creating the part of Mrs. Sargent in Mrs. Wiggin's original production of *The Old Peabody Pew,*) and she has coached many amateur dramatic performances.

Miss Peirce is herself the author of *The Rose of Old Seville,* a volume of plays and poems published in 1904, *The War Lords and Other Patriotic Poems* (1915–1917), a pageant entitled *From the Garden of the Hesperides,* first performed by the Mattapannock Players, November 21, 1919, various published translations of poems from foreign languages and numerous unpublished plays, stories and poems.

While of a scholarly rather than of an athletic type, she is very fond of walking, and her understanding and love of nature manifests itself continually in her poems. Often certain phases of nature are used as backgrounds for passages of especial tenderness and beauty, lending to them their own appropriate atmosphere. Miss Peirce's varied attainments and cheerful personality make her a valued member of several clubs, and her popularity is attested by the fact that she has been a President of the Girls' High School Association, and of the Lady Teachers' Association and was in 1919 Corresponding Secretary of the Mattapannock Woman's Club.

PETERS, FRANCES, was born in New York City. Her father, the Venerable Thomas McClure Peters, D.D., was a descendant of Andrew Peters, born in England in 1634, who settled in Andover, Massachusetts, married Mercy Beamsley of Boston, and died in 1713.

Doctor Thomas McClure Peters was Rector of St. Michael's Church, New York, for fifty years, and first Archdeacon of the diocese of New York. He and his wife, Alice C. (Richmond) Peters, were the parents of ten children. One son, the Reverend J. P. Peters, D.D., was also Rector of St. Michael's Church, a Professor in the Philadelphia Divinity School, and a member of the faculty of the University of Tennessee.

Frances Peters was educated in private schools, specializing in the study of modern languages. She was always an ardent suffragist, and gave much time to the active work of the Woman Suffrage Party. For two years (1914–1916) she was the leader of the (then) 15th (later the 7th) Assembly District, and was urged to run for the office of a vice-

leader of the party for the Borough of Man-
hattan, but was obliged to decline because of
other work. During the period of the World
War, Miss Peters was a member of the Food
Administration, and gave much time to
preparing surgical dressings for the Red
Cross, and in knitting for the Army and Navy
League. In 1917 she helped take the State
Census, working with the suffrage party
under State jurisdiction.

In 1914 Miss Peters inaugurated, and was
made Chairman of the City Beautiful Garden
Movement, with the object of making beauty
spots of the back yards of New York. The
Woman's Municipal League allowed the yard
back of the headquarters, at 46 East 29th
Street, to be used for a first experiment.
Mrs. Frederick Hill, a landscape gardener,
converted the tiny area into a place of beauty.
Gravelled walks, a pergola, and seats with
plants and vines made it a charming retreat.
From the time of this successful development
of her ideas, Miss Peters has conducted a
campaign to arouse New Yorkers to eliminate
all the waste of ill kept, colorless spaces, and
to provide, instead, plots of riotous color,
flowers in spring and summer, evergreens in
winter. To apartment dwellers she has
appealed to establish window boxes, planted
differently for different seasons, to bring
about the maximum of decoration and effect.

In March, 1918, she founded, and became
Chairman of the City Gardens Club, which,
starting with two members, soon became a
large and flourishing organization. Its purpose at first was the transforming of the ugly
back yard into a garden. It shortly added to
this activity the decorating and improving
of all vacant spaces around hospitals, churches,
apartment houses, public buildings, and other
vacant lots. The first public exhibition of
the Club was held in March, 1919, under the
auspices of the New York Horticultural
Society at their Flower Show in the Museum
of Natural History, and, at the suggestion
of Doctor N. L. Britton, Director of the
Horticultural Society, a movement was started

whereby the City Gardens Club distributed
circulars and in other ways sponsored the
planting of trees by individuals in honor of
homecoming soldiers and in memory of those
who will never return. The Department of
Agriculture at Washington supplied the Club
with large quantities of flower and vegetable
seeds which were widely distributed. Among
the organizations that have especially responded to the Club's suggestions are the
New York Historical Society, the Sewanee
Club for Soldiers and Sailors, and the Park
Hospital. The Club has become affiliated
with the National Farm and Garden Association and with the Women's Civic League
of Baltimore through the latter's Home
Garden Committee.

Miss Peters is also Chairman of the 9th
Aldermanic district for the Woman's City
Club, Recording Secretary of the Woman's
League for the Protection of Riverside Park,
and member of the New York Chapter of the
American Red Cross, of the Army and Navy
League, and of the United States Food
Administration.

POLLOCK, HESTER McLEAN, educator,
daughter of John David and Martha (Mc-
Lean) Pollock, and granddaughter of David
Pollock of Ulster County, Ireland, who
settled near Cincinnati, Ohio, in 1821, was
born in St. Paul, Minnesota. After complet-
ing her preparation at the St. Paul Central
High School and Dana Hall, Wellesley,
Massachusetts, she was a student at Wellesley
College for three years. She then returned to
St. Paul, where, for twenty years, she taught
United States history, civics, and economics
in the high schools.

She was the organizer and Director of the
Minnesota State Americanization work and
in this connection published in 1915 a short
history of the state, *Our Minnesota*. In 1919
she was organizer, assistant chairman, and
speaker for the Women's Loan Organization
of the Ninth Federal District, her work on
behalf of the Victory Loan taking her

throughout western Minnesota, Montana, and North Dakota. She has also organized and directed the work of the women's activities, and the educational work of the Ninth Federal Reserve District, and in 1920–1921 she compiled for the United States Treasury Department the education bulletins on thrift work for Minnesota, Wisconsin, Michigan, North Dakota, and South Dakota. She is a life member, the first woman to be admitted, of the Minnesota State Historical Society, a member of the Twin City Historical Association, the Minnesota Educational Association, the St. Paul Ornithological Society, the League of Women Voters, the Business and Professional Women's Club, the College and Woman's Welfare Clubs of St. Paul, and a Director of the Century and Women's City Clubs.

BAKER, CHARLOTTE ALICE, daughter of Doctor Matthew Bridge and Catharine (Catlin) Baker, was born in Springfield, Massachusetts, April 11, 1833, and died in Boston, Massachusetts, May 22, 1909. Doctor Baker's first ancestors in New England were Thomas Baker, a member of Reverend Mr. Eliot's Church in Roxbury, in 1640, and Deacon John Bridge of Cambridge (1632). Her mother was a descendant of Mr. John Catlin (son of John Catlin of Wethersfield, Connecticut), a leading citizen in Branford, Connecticut, and Newark, New Jersey, who located in Deerfield, Massachusetts, when it was permanently settled. Catharine Catlin's mother was descended from Rowland Stebbins (Roxbury, 1634), who was one of the founders of Springfield, Massachusetts.

In the days (1825) when, at Harvard College, a whole "entry" was suspended, if the misdemeanor of one student was not confessed, Matthew Bridge Baker, a Junior from Charlestown, Massachusetts, was "published" with his "entry," and spent some time at Greenfield, Massachusetts. There he met Catharine Catlin, and that he might sooner make her his wife, he left college to begin the

study of medicine. Weak lungs caused Doctor Baker to choose an inland home, and he brought his bride to Springfield where Charlotte Alice was born. Six years later, her father and her brother having died, she and her mother were left alone.

Miss Baker's story of her childhood was printed in *Merry's Museum* (1870) under the title, *The Doctor's Little Girl.* Since she was a delicate child, she did not attend school regularly. During this period, however, a neighborly cabinet-maker gave her valuable instruction in the use of tools. When she was eleven, she spent a year at the Misses Stone's School, in Greenfield, Massachusetts. For board and for tuition in English, Latin, and music her mother had to pay only one hundred and three dollars; and for a summer term of ten weeks at Deerfield Academy, the fee was but three dollars and sixty-four cents. Her reminiscences before an Alumni meeting of the Academy, present an interesting picture of village school life about 1840. She herself writes as follows: "At the age of twelve I was spending the winter with my grandmother in Deerfield * * * I was undisciplined, as far as school training went. A tall and rigid young woman, who seemed to me very old, allowed me to walk back and forth to the Academy with her, and, as I remember, she and I were the only girls that winter * * * An immense and very dirty Franklin stove occupied the middle of the school room without heating it, a leaky stove-pipe dripping puddles of sooty water upon the floor. A red cupboard projecting from the wall almost hid my desk from the teacher * * * Being a stranger and only a girl, I at once became the target for those hard little balls of wet paper, known as spit-balls. I have a painful remembrance that, having been caught in the act of returning a shot, I was kindly but firmly invited to sit on the platform by the teacher, who, at the same time, rapped on a brass-headed nail in his desk-lid, mildly requesting my tormentors to let their attention be concentrated! * * * I remember how mortified I was by my ignorance of elementary arithmetic, as compared with the boys. They repsected me more when they discovered that I could play marbles and "mumble the peg," could steer a sled and drive a horse. I knew my French verbs and I had learned that Calypso could not console herself for the departure of Ulysses though this fact did not take deep hold on my sensibilities. The boys from Wapping, Bloody Brook and Great River drove to school in long, old-fashioned sleighs, tying their horses in the shed of the Orthodox Church. Many a sleigh ride in the milder noonings they gave me, generously allowing me to hold the reins. How hard and cold those old sleigh seats were, low down in the drifts * * * After school in the afternoon, all the boys and girls of both schools who did not have to hurry home 'to do the chores' rushed to the Wilson Hill, improvised sleds of the old-fashioned straight backed chairs, laying them flat on their backs and sitting on the rungs with feet on the inside of the backs. Of course there was no steering such a craft, and when the long backs ran suddenly off the tracks into the high drifts at the side, we pitched head foremost into the snow * * * I took history * * * without digesting it, imbibed a weak solution of natural philosophy * * * Arithmetic was my *bete moire* * * * Had it not been for Calypso and Pious Anneas, who stood me in good stead, I should have been inconsolable. These promoted me to the rank of assistant pupil to- coach younger and duller scholars. As a privilege, we were allowed to take turns in filling the water pitcher, which stood on the window seat behind the teacher's desk. I remember one gorgeous October day, when, irked by confinement in the schoolroom, I took the pitcher over to Mr. Ware's cider-mill opposite, and after riding around on the crank several times and sucking a *quantum sufficit* through a section of pumpkin vine filled my pitcher with cider, returned, and deposited it safely behind Mr. Crittenden, communicating the alluring secret to my

seatmate * * * It was astonishing to see how soon the rumor spread and that pitcher was emptied."

After some months in a school near Boston, she returned to the Deerfield Academy as pupil and assistant-teacher, with the "command of a small room full of youngsters * * * who sat round a big table and kicked each other under it. Mr. Warriner instituted what he called Rhetorical Exercises one evening in the week. Declamations and debates by the boys, compositions and recitations by the girls, a school paper, and a parsing and analysis lesson, by all, in Pope's *Essay on Man.* When he was absent, he entrusted the school to me, which inspired me with confidence in my ability. Thus obliged to criticize the work of others, I learned to criticize my own. I also learned from him never to pretend to knowledge I did not have, but to say to my pupil: 'I do not know, but I will find out'; and then never to fail to meet the question fairly in my class. Such was the foundation of whatever success I have attained in writing and teaching. My school days ended at fifteen, and I began to earn my living."

After living for some time with an aunt in La Salle, Illinois, in 1856, Miss Baker, with her lifelong friend, Miss Susan Minot Lane, of Cambridge, Massachusetts, opened a school in Chicago.

In 1864, the Chicago School was discontinued, in order that Miss Baker might return to her mother in Cambridge, Massachusetts. Then, until she established her Boston school she busied herself with writing. She published book reviews, as well as articles on botany, art, woman's work, and other subjects in newspapers and magazines, but her historical work was more important. Among other papers, she wrote a series for children, which she entitled *Pictures from French and English History.* The year after the Pocumtuck Valley Memorial Association was organized in Deerfield, she read before the Association her paper, *Eunice Williams, the Captive.*

More than a score of times she laid before this organization the results of her careful historical research. In 1897, she printed a volume, containing thirteen papers, entitled *True Stories of New England Captives Carried to Canada during the Old French and Indian Wars*. In the preface, she wrote: "As often as I have read in the annals of the early settlers of New England the pathetic words 'Carried captive to Canada whence they came not back,' I have longed to know the fate of the captives. The wish has become a purpose and I have taken upon myself a mission to open the door for their return." To "open the door" she went several times to Canada searching the official records of Montreal and Quebec, as well as many villages and Indian missions. She was remarkably successful, for she found eighteen Deerfield captives whose fate had been unknown, and many more, also, captured from other towns by Indians. The value of her work was immediately recognized. Francis Parkman, author of the famous "Oregon Trail," quoted Miss Baker, and wrote personally to her: "We are all your debtors." The New York, Cambridge and Montreal Historical Societies solicited her membership. A pupil, writing of Miss Baker's enthusiasm for early New England history, says she recalls being "thrilled and fascinated as if by a fairy tale": another says, "She can make a cobblestone live." Mrs. Mary Hemenway, who had prevented the removal of the Old South Meeting House, Boston, asked Miss Baker to help arouse a patriotic spirit in the children of Boston. Miss Baker, therefore, prepared stories of early American history, which she read in the "Children's Hour," Saturday mornings. These inspired the succeeding courses of lectures along the same lines, and were of influence in the founding of the Old South Historical Society.

As a teacher, Miss Baker did her best work, in character-building. In 1882, the school conducted by her and Miss Lane was moved from Boston to the beautiful home of Mr. and Mrs. Barthold Schlesinger, in Brookline.

During the last decade of her life, Miss Baker was not engaged in regular work. During one vacation she kept a journal, which furnished material later for her attractive little book, *A Summer in the Azores and a Glimpse of Madeira*. Other vacations she spent in the White Mountains, York Harbor, Deerfield, and at Cutt's Island, Kittery Point, where shortly before her death, she built a summer home. But the place that was dearest to her was "Frary House," the oldest and most interesting house in Deerfield, which she rescued from ruin in 1890. She named it for its builder, her ancestor, Samson Frary, who occupied it probably as early as 1683. Ultimately it became the property of the Pocumtuck Valley Memorial Association, to be exhibited as a typical Colonial home.

REID, HELEN ROGERS (Mrs. Ogden Mills Reid), daughter of Benjamin Talbot and Sara Louise (Johnson) Rogers, was born in Appleton, Wisconsin, November 23, 1882. She received her early education in the preparatory schools of her native town; was prepared for college at Grafton Hall, Fond du Lac, Wisconsin, and was graduated at Barnard College, New York, in 1903.

On March 14, 1911, at Racine, Wisconsin, she married Ogden Mills Reid, of New York, the son of Whitelaw and Elizabeth (Mills) Reid, and at that time one of the editors of the *New York Tribune*. They are the parents of Whitelaw Reid (born July 26, 1913) and Elizabeth Reid (born May 9, 1915).

From 1914 to 1918, Mrs. Reid was actively engaged in the New York State Suffrage Campaign, and since 1918 she has been Secretary and Advertising Director of the *New York Tribune*. She is a Trustee of Barnard College; a member of the Women's University Club, the Colony Club, and the Women's City Club of New York, and the League of Advertising Women.

BOSTWICK, HELEN CELIA FORD (Mrs. Jabez A. Bostwick), was born in Cincinnati, Ohio, February 3, 1848, and died in New York City, April 27, 1920, daughter of Smith and Frances (Fox) Ford. The Ford family traces descent from Mathew (Matheu) Ford, sometimes called Martin, a native of England, who lived at Bradford, Essex County, Massachusetts, first appearing in the county records January 25, 1681. He married Lydia, the daughter of John and Lydia (Shatswell) Griffen or Griffing, March 25, 1884[1]. Their son, Matthew Ford, was born at Bradford, April 12, 1691, but the family moved to Topsfield, an adjoining town, where Matthew's boyhood was spent. He went later to Lebanon, Connecticut, returning to Topsfield for his bride, Mary, the daughter of Jacob and Sarah (Wood) Foster, whom he married February 10, 1715–1716. She was born May 13, 1691. In 1724 they removed to Hebron, Connecticut, where they passed the remainder of their lives. That they were prominent in the community is shown by both town and church records. Mr. Ford was the owner of large tracts of land and many cattle. He died in Hebron, October 6, 1769, and his wife died February 16, 1770. They are both buried in the Hebron cemetery.

Mary (Foster) Ford came of an illustrious English family. Her first ancestor in America, Reginald Foster[2], was born in Brunton, England, about 1595. He came to Massachusetts with his wife, Judith, and seven children, settling at Ipswich, Essex County, about 1638. He was a direct descendant of Anacher, Great Forester of Flanders, who died in 837 and whose descendants were the Counts Baldwin of Flanders. His son, Baldwin I, married Princess Judith, the daughter of Charles II (The Bald), King of France, and died at Arras in 877. His son, Baldwin II, married Princess Alfrith, the daughter of Alfred the Great, King of England. The son of Baldwin IV, Sir Richard Forester (Forster or Foster), came to England with his father under William the Conqueror, and received the honor of knighthood after the Battle of Hastings, being then only in his sixteenth year. From him sprang the Foresters of Etherston and Bamborough Castle and of other estates. The family were the principal chieftains of Northumberland, and hereditary governors of Bamborough Castle from the reign of James I to that of George I. Sir Richard's great-great-grandson, Sir John Forster, accompanied Richard I to Palestine, where he was knighted for valor. He was one of the barons, who compelled King John to sign Magna Carta in 1215. His direct descendant, Thomas Forster of Brunton, Esq., by his second wife, Elizabeth, the daughter of William Carr, was the father of Reginald who came to America.

Jacob Ford, the son of Matthew and Mary (Foster) Ford, was born at Hebron, Connecticut, February 9, 1718–1719, and died previous to the date of his father's will in 1763. He married, April 14, 1743, Mary, the daughter of Nathaniel Mann, born June 15, 1723. Their son, Jacob Ford, Jr., was born in Hebron, Connecticut, April 22, 1744, and died in Austerlitz, New York, July 24, 1837. His early life was passed in Hebron, where he married, March 5, 1765, Abigail, daughter of Hosea and Mary (Gilburd) Curtice. With his wife he moved in 1766 to New York State, and acquired land at Austerlitz, Columbia County, then a part of Albany County. He was a successful man and amassed wealth. Besides his home farm consisting of 360 acres, he owned other large tracts on the west side of the Hudson River in the Manor of Rensselaerwyck. He was a member of the Assembly from Albany County from 1781 to 1785. Columbia County was formed in 1786, and he was a member from the new county in 1792. In 1776 and in 1801 he was appointed Justice of the Peace; was Associate Judge of the Court of Common Pleas in 1795, and became First Judge in the following year[3]. He was not only a prominent man in civil life but was active, also, in military affairs. He was commissioned Captain of the Fourth Company, Ninth Regiment, Albany County Militia (Peter Van Ness, Colonel), October 20, 1775; Major of the same regiment, October, 1775; and Lieutenant-Colonel, May 28, 1778. He resigned November 4, 1778[4]. In 1776 he acted under orders from the Committee of Safety, and was especially commended by the Chairman for his activity and spirit. In 1778 he was at Cherry Valley, whence he reported the burning of Springfield in a letter to General Ten Broeck, dated July 18th[5]. Ansyl, son of Colonel Jacob and Abigail (Curtice) Ford, was born June 1, 1772, and died August 2, 1850. He married Esther Fitch (born October 10, 1771; died December 22, 1841), and soon after 1798 removed from Rensselaerville to Franklin, Delaware County, New York. Their son, Fitch Ford (born June 1, 1797; died September 25, 1874) married Abbie Smith (born September 28, 1799; died June 29, 1870). Their son was Smith Ford, the father of Mrs. Bostwick.

Smith Ford lived in Cincinnati, Ohio, whence he directed the extensive cotton and tobacco plantations which he owned in the South. When his business interests were injured by the Civil War, he retired to New York City, living first on Washington Square, later on 47th Street, and finally in Yonkers, New York, where he died. His wife was Frances Fox of Cincinnati, Ohio, daughter of Charles and Mary (Miller) Fox. Her father, born in Bedford, England, in 1796, was admitted to the Bar of Cincinnati in 1823, and practiced his profession continuously from 1823 until his death in 1882. He was appointed to the Bench of the Superior Court of Ohio in 1865.

Helen Celia Ford was educated in Cincinnati and was married to Jabez Abel Bostwick in New York City on December 18, 1866. They were the parents of two daughters, Nellie Bostwick (born April 28, 1868; died January 27, 1906), who married, first, Francis Lee Morrell (died 1893), and, second, Hamilton Wilkes Carey; and Evelyn Bostwick

(Mme. Serge Voronoff) and one son, Albert Carlton Bostwick (born June 2, 1876; died November 11, 1911) who married, June 20, 1898, Mary, daughter of Henry Stokes. Mr. and Mrs. Albert C. Bostwick were the parents of Dorothy Bostwick, Albert C. Bostwick, Jr., Lillian Bostwick, Dunbar Bostwick, and George Herbert Bostwick.

The name Bostwick is of Saxon origin, derived from Botestock Manor, and is variously spelled Bostoc, Bostok, and Bostock. The line is traced to Osmer, owner of the estates of Shipbrook, Davenham, Bostock, and others, in Cheshire, England, as is shown in the Domesday Book (1080). The twenty-first in descent from Osmer was Arthur Bostwick, who was baptized in Tarporley, Cheshire, December 22, 1603. He married, first, Jane, probably a daughter of the Rev. Robert Whittel, rector of St. Helen's Church, Tarporley (1613–1638), and was one of the first seventeen settlers of Stratford, Connecticut, where he occupied one of the original home lots, and was listed as a freeman in 1669. His name often appears in the town records, especially in connection with deeds of land. With him came to America his only son, John Bostwick (baptized in St. Helen's Church, Tarporley, October 18, 1638; died in Stratford prior to December 11, 1688), who married in Stratford, about 1665, Mary, daughter of John and Mary (Carter) Brinsmead (born in Charlestown, Massachusetts, July 24, 1640; died at Stratford before December 28, 1704). John Bostwick inherited his father's entire estate. He also acquired more land from subsequent divisions of the town lots. His son, John Bostwick (born in Stratford, May 4, 1667; died in New Milford) married, about 1687, Abigail, daughter of Joseph and Abigail (Prudden) Walker (born in Stratford, February 17, 1672–1673). He resided first in Derby, Connecticut, and in 1707 was the second settler at New Milford, where he was a man of affairs and a member of various committees. Their son, Joseph Bostwick (born in Stratford in 1695; died in New Milford, September 27, 1756) married, at New Milford July 23, 1724, Rebecca, daughter of Timothy and Rebecca (Turney) Wheeler (born at Stratford, October 31, 1697). He accompanied his father to New Milford, and later was one of the first settlers of the district of the town named Upper Merryall. In October, 1738, he was appointed Lieutenant in the military company of New Milford, and in October, 1743, he was commissioned Captain of the First or North Company. Their son, Joseph Bostwick, Jr. (born in New Milford, August 19, 1728; died at Upper Merryall, November 18, 1808) married at New Milford, February 7, 1750–1751, Betty, daughter of David and Susannah Hurd (born at Stratford, September 26, 1729; died at Upper Merryall, June 17, 1759). Their son, David Bostwick (born at Upper Merryall, April 24, 1752; died at Meredith, New York, June 12, 1818) married at Newtown, Connecticut, Currence Hard (born at Newtown, March 21, 1753; died at Franklin, New York, October 23, 1855). Their son, Abel Bostwick (born in Meredith, New York, March 7, 1797; died at Westfield, Ohio, April 20, 1861) married in Franklin, December 30, 1820, Sallie Fitch (born in Franklin, July 4, 1791; died at Canaan, Ohio, August 29, 1869) of the same family as Esther Fitch, the wife of Ansyl Ford. They were the parents of Jabez Abel Bostwick.

Mr. Bostwick was born in Franklin, New York, September 23, 1830, and was killed in a fire at his summer home at Mamaroneck, New York, August 16, 1892. When he was a boy of ten years of age, his parents removed to Ohio where he passed his early years. His education, which was essentially of a business character, began when he was a clerk in a bank in Covington, Kentucky. Later he engaged in business as a cotton broker, and in 1864 located in New York City. He owned large cotton docks on Staten Island, where also he resided on a beautiful estate until 1877, when he purchased the property at Mamaroneck. When the oil regions of western

Pennsylvania began to be developed as a new source of wealth, Mr. Bostwick became interested in several wells near Franklin, Pennsylvania, and organized the firm of J. A. Bostwick and Company, oil refiners and shippers. In 1872, when John D. Rockefeller formed the Standard Oil Company, Mr. Bostwick aided in its organization and became its first Treasurer, and shortly afterward dissolved his connection with his partner, W. H. Tilford, who also became affiliated with the Standard Oil Company. Thereafter, for many years Mr. Bostwick was the company's chief oil buyer, but in 1885 he retired from the oil business, and in 1886 was elected President of the New York and New England Railroad Company. He held this office until January, 1892. Only two weeks before his death he purchased a seat on the New York Stock Exchange. In all his affairs Mr. Bostwick showed his great ability as a far-seeing organizer. He was of even temperament, striking personality, and great charm, a sound judge of character, so that he became a model for the younger generation of Standard Oil men. He was the friend and adviser of Presidents Grant, Hays and Arthur, and supported Secretary William C. Whitney, in his plans for an enlarged American Navy. He had as well an inventive genius and patented several safety devices such as the Bostwick gate. Mr. Bostwick, whose fortune at the time of his death was estimated at $12,000,000, was always liberal with his wealth, although his gifts were made without ostentation, and many of his benefactions will never be known. He aided generously the charities of the Fifth Avenue Baptist Church, New York, of which he was a member, and built and endowed Emanuel Baptist Church, Suffolk Street, New York. While in Mamaroneck, he aided the Roman Catholic parish and other religious bodies, without regard to denomination. He also materially increased the endowments of Forrest College, North Carolina. Mr. Bostwick believed that education should make one self-reliant by the development of natural talents, that girls should have the same practical training as boys, and that the daughters of the well-to-do should be equipped to earn their own livelihood if necessary. For this reason his elder daughter, Nellie, took a thorough course in dressmaking, and Evelyn, the second child, chose the profession of surgery.

Mrs. Bostwick was essentially the home-maker, devoted to her husband and children, a perfect type of nineteenth century woman-hood. She was interested in the arts and had a notable collection of etchings. Her nature was sweet, charitable, and generous, and she was beloved by all who knew her, or who had experienced her courteous kindness. The members of the police force of New York, especially the traffic policemen of Fifth Avenue, pay a high tribute to her memory, on account of her unfailing concern for their health and welfare. After Mr. Bostwick's death she passed her life in retirement at her home, 800 Fifth Avenue, New York, and during her later years, was a victim of ill health. Nevertheless she maintained her interest in charitable work. Her deeds of benevolence were many, but were performed so secretly that their nature and extent have never been known to the public.

[1] Salem County Records.
[2] Cf. P.
[3] *History of Columbia County*, Vol. 1, p. 53.
[4] Roberts: *New York in the Revolution;* Records, Adjutant General's Office, Albany. His commission as captain and his family Bible, printed in 1712, are owned by Mrs. James Elijah Ford, Buffalo, New York, widow of a great-grandson.
[5] *Public Papers of General Clinton*, Vol. III, p. 555.

VORONOFF, EVELYN, BOSTWICK (Mme. Serge Voronoff), scientist, daughter of Jabez Abel and Helen Celia (Ford) Bostwick, was born on Staten Island, New York, June 7, 1872. She was educated to speak French as well as English, and in 1888 completed the course at Miss Dana's School, Morristown, New Jersey, with honors in literature and arts. As she had always been interested in

surgery, on account of her father's belief in a practical training for girls, and his requirement that his daughters should choose a trade or profession, she followed the course at the old Orthopaedic Hospital, New York, where she laid the foundation for the brilliant work which she has since accomplished as a scientist. Throughout her life she has had her father as an ideal. He trained her mind to be sys-tematic and methodical, and her aim was to be worthy of his name. In 1892 her first marriage took her to England, where she lived until 1912. There she frequently engaged in parish and charitable nursing, and continued her studies at the clinics at King's College, London, to which she was invited by the leading surgeons of the faculty, and also at the Sorbonne, Paris, where she specialized in the arts and at the same time studied singing under Mme. Marchesi.

During the Boer War (1901–1903) she served as a nurse with the British Army, and was decorated with the Military Cross for bravery. After her return to England there ensued a period of social and political activity. She was appointed by the London County Council Inspector of Schools and Hospitals for the Hoxton Division, London, and there organized the Women's Conservative Union. In 1910 she campaigned mid-Derbyshire and in 1911 the Hoxton Division, London, in the interest of Arthur Balfour and contributed articles to London journals and magazines. At this period the militant woman suffrage agitation was at its height, but as a scientist, philoso-pher and practical politician, she declared her opposition to the suffrage movement, and especially to the militant methods. She stressed the physical and nervous difference between man and woman, that man proceeds by logic, woman by intuition; and held that man, because of his greater mental balance, is the one to govern, while woman has her important sphere in education, economics, and the carrying out of good laws.

While in England, she also became identified with the Girl Guides movement, and was herself an active sportswoman. She sailed her yawl *Bona* in yacht races in the Mediterranean, winning the King Edward VII Cup at Cannes in 1911, 1912, and 1913, the Prince of Monaco's Cup the same years, and the Nice Yacht Club's Cup once.

Upon the outbreak of the World War in August, 1914, she offered her services as a nurse to the French government. For a month she was stationed as infirmière supérieure at Val-de-Grâce Military Hospital, Paris, where she performed many minor operations, and after that was on the front in the Vosges, in Champagne, and on the Somme. In 1916 she was appointed head of the nursing staff of the military hospital at the Hotel Majestic, Nice, but broke down from overwork and was blind for four months. Upon her recovery, on February 13, 1917, she was honored by being appointed the only woman on the staff of the Collège de France, with the title of Assistante de Laboratoire. Here she collaborated in the experiments and discoveries of Doctor Serge Voronoff, with whom she was associated for many years in scientific research, and to whom she was married in Paris, July 1, 1919.

Serge Voronoff was born in Voronej, Russia, July 10, 1868, and came to Paris at the age of seventeen. He studied at the Sorbonne, the École de Médecine, and the École des Hautes Études. He was then appointed surgeon to Khedive Abbas-Hilmi of Egypt. In Cairo he was President of the Faculty of Medicine, President of the Académie de Médecine, and Editor of the *Presse Médicale* of Egypt. He also created at his own expense the hospital at Choubrah. For his many services Abbas-Hilmi conferred upon him the cordon of the Legion of Honor affiliated with the Grand Croix of the Medijeh.

In 1910 he returned to France to engage in research work at the Collège de France. In 1914 he became the head of the Russian Hospital at Bordeaux, and, in 1916, was placed in charge of Military Hospital Number 187, devoted to bone and skin grafting. His

health unfortunately failing, he retired for a year, and in 1917 returned to experimental work at the Collège de France, where he is Director of the Laboratory of Experimental Surgery.

There he and Mme. Voronoff perfected the discovery of grafting living tissue in open antiseptic wounds, which usually heal in from twelve days to a month. This method was communicated to the Académie des Sciences, September 1, 1918, in the monograph, *Études sur les bourgeonnements des palies de guerre*. The most important experiments in which Doctor and Mme. Voronoff collaborated had to do with the transplanting of the interstitial gland. These experiments were begun in 1917 and were communicated to the Académie des Sciences on October 8, 1919. They demonstrate that the life of animals so treated is extended, physical and mental vigor reëstablished and maintained, arterio-sclerosis and senile decay prevented, and that the offspring mature rapidly. The book describing these experiments and discoveries is entitled *Vivre* and was translated into English, with the title, *Life*, by Mme. Voronoff, in 1920. The scientific circles in Paris at once recognized the value of these discoveries and in 1920 Doctor and Mme. Voronoff gave demonstrations of their method at the American Hospital, Chicago, Illinois, and at the College of Physicians and Surgeons and the Mt. Sinai Hospital, New York.

Mme. Voronoff was the mother of three children: Marian Barbara Carstairs, the wife of Captain J. de Pret of the British Army, Evelyn Francis, and Francis Francis, Jr. She died in Paris, France, March 3, 1921.

ADLER, HELEN GOLDMARK (Mrs. Felix Adler), philanthropist, daughter of Joseph and Regina (Wehle) Goldmark, was born on Staten Island, New York, September 4, 1859. She was educated at Brooklyn Heights Seminary, Brooklyn, New York, with much additional training at home, in art schools, and by foreign travel.

On May 24, 1880, she was married in New York to Doctor Felix Adler, son of Rabbi Samuel and Henrietta (Frankfurther) Adler, who was born in Alzey, Germany, August 13, 1851. Doctor Adler received the degree of B.A. at Columbia University in 1870, and then studied in Berlin and Heidelburg, where he received the doctorate in philosophy in 1873. From 1874 to 1876 he was Professor of Hebrew and Oriental Literature at Cornell University, and since 1906 has been Professor of Political and Social Ethics at Columbia University. He is the author of many books on social, political, and ethical subjects. In 1876 he established the New York Society for Ethical Culture, and since then has been its regular Sunday lecturer.

Mrs. Adler is the Secretary of the District Nursing Committee of the Ethical Culture Society, which has been the pioneer of all organizations in securing trained nurses for the work of visiting the tenement population of New York City. In 1877, Doctor Adler introduced the English system of district nursing for the poor, adapting it to the conditions of his own city. The Demilt Dispensary in East 23d Street received the services of the first trained nurse, a refined college trained woman, who, in September, 1877, started on her rounds to visit the sick poor in the tenements, serving under the physicians at the dispensary, caring for acute, chronic, contagious, and obstetric cases, and supplementing this work by instructions to the mothers or relatives, by hygienic training, and by relief work when needed in the family. A sewing society, instituted by Doctor Adler among the women of his Society, assisted the nurse in caring for the needy patients, providing supplies of bed linen, clothing, nourishing food, and delicacies for the sick, all of which aided materially in raising the morale of the undernourished and neglected patients. Since 1877 there has been continuously a corps of nurses at work, connected with three dispensaries and supported by Doctor Adler's Society. Shortly afterward, other agencies,

notably the Henry Street Settlement, introduced nurses in other centres, and this led to the marvelous growth of the nursing service in cities and small towns and villages throughout the country.

Mrs. Adler was the organizer of the first committee to provide safe sterilized milk for the babies of the tenements. In 1891 she started, in collaboration with Doctor Koplik, a specialist for babies at the Good Samaritan Dispensary, the service of sterilized milk for the children of the crowded East Side. This was the first milk laboratory in the United States organized for this service. It soon cared for hundreds of cases of sick, underfed, and neglected children, pointing the way to the many organizations of a similar kind whose success in reducing infant mortality in New York has been so marked. This work, the Laboratory Department for Modified Milk for Tenement Babies, was carried on for twenty-five years by Mrs. Adler, and was then taken over by the City of New York.

Mrs. Adler published in 1891 her *Hints on the Study and Observation of Children* and has contributed many articles and translations to periodicals and magazines. She is Secretary of the School of Design and Liberal Arts and herself works in painting, modelling, and craftsmanship. During the World War she served for two years in Canteen and War Work Centre, Number 8, at 33 Central Park West, New York. She is a member of the Women's Municipal League, the Consumer's League, and other educational and philanthropic organizations.

Doctor and Mrs. Adler are the parents of five children: Waldo, Eleanor H., Margaret, Lawrence, and Ruth F. Adler. During the World War the two sons served in the army; Eleanor Adler worked with the War Vocational Board as an organizer of vocational research; Margaret Adler was active as Secretary of the Pennsylvania Land Army of Women; and Ruth F. Adler served for two and a half years in the United States Army, as reconstruction aide in army hospitals.

WHITTON, CHARLOTTE ELIZABETH, sociologist, daughter of John Edward and Elizabeth (Langin) Whitton, was born at Renfrew, Ontario, Canada, March 8, 1896. Her father (born November 22, 1873) is a son of John Heseltine Whitton and his wife, Matilde Carr, of Norwich, England, and grandson of James Thomas Whitton, of Bainbridge, Askrigg, near York, England, who settled about 1830 at what was then known as Whitton's Corners, near Belleville, Ontario. James T. Whitton's wife, Jean Heseltine, of Heseldean, Scotland, introduced the Cheddar cheese industry in Canada, having learned the process in the dairy of her home in Scotland. Previously, only the white-hard Canadian cheese had been made, but as a result of Mrs. Whitton's successful experiments the neighboring settlers adopted the British method. Elizabeth Langin Whitton, Miss Whitton's mother (born in Rochester, New York, June 29, 1871), is the daughter of Michael Langin, of Sligo, Ireland, who married Elizabeth Costello, of Tipperary, Ireland, and settled in the vicinity of Rochester about 1840. The Costellos and the Langins are descended from Spanish and French settlers in Ireland, after the defeat of the Armada and the Battle of the Boyne, respectively.

Charlotte Elizabeth Whitton obtained her early education in the Renfrew public school and at Renfrew Collegiate Institute, where she was graduated with a special medal for distinction and received a scholarship in Queen's University, Kingston, Ontario. In 1917 she received the degree of Master of Arts from Queen's University in English, history, and modern languages, with gold medals in English and in history, and in 1918 she was awarded the Governor-General's medal in education on her pedagogy course in the Department of Education.

She has since been Assistant Secretary to the Social Service Council of Canada, and, in her official capacity, lectures on social work throughout Canada, and carries on special studies and research, particularly along the lines of social education. She has in charge the preparation of investigations and reports, which form the basis of discussion for legislative, or other action, on the problems with which they deal. Besides writing many monthly articles in the sociological magazine, *Social Welfare*, of which she is Associate Editor, she is called upon to speak at various centres, conferences, etc.

Her work is largely educational and takes her to the social welfare activities of Canada and the United States. She also serves, in an advisory capacity, on many consultative and administrative committees on social work in the City of Toronto, as well as in the Province of Ontario, and in some cases in the Dominion of Canada. Among these are the Canadian National Council on Child Welfare, of which she is National Secretary, and the Home and School Council, Toronto. She is a member of the National Conference on Social Work, Cincinnati, Ohio; is National Secretary of the Canadian Women's Press Club, a Central Council member of the Federation for Community Service, and a member of the Toronto Women's Press Club, the Sanctuary Wood Chapter, Imperial Order, Daughters of the Empire, the National Council of Women, the University Women's Club, Toronto, and the Queen's University Alumnae Association. She is also editor of the annual, *Queen's University Alumnae News*. She also contributes articles and sketches to various Canadian periodicals.

Although occupied with her many interests, she is able to indulge her love of sport, both on the ice in winter and in a canoe in summer. Combined with exceptional ability and a retentive memory, Miss Whitton has unlimited energy and accomplishes an almost incredible amount of work. Sympathetic and generous, warm-hearted and unselfish, she is unusually well fitted to take her place among the outstanding women of Canada.

BANGS, EDITH, philanthropist, daughter of George Pemberton and Laura (Pell) Bangs, was born in Cambridge, Massachusetts. Her father was a lineal descendant of Edward Bangs of England who, in 1623, at the age of thirty-two came to New England in the *Ann*, and settled in Eastham, Massachusetts. He was Treasurer of this town for nineteen years, and Deputy to the Colony Council in 1647–1650 and 1663–1664.

Early in the World War Miss Bangs was appointed one of the Vice-Presidents of the National Council, and Chairman of the New England Branch of the American Fund for the French Wounded, an organization with central and subsidiary distributing depots in France, dispensaries, and a volunteer motor corps militarized in the service of the French Army. Although this fund was a national organization, with branch committees throughout the country, more than half of its shipments of supplies to France were made by the New England Branch.

When Miss Bangs was asked to take its Chairmanship, in 1915, there were only a few contributing groups of workers. When the New England Branch closed its work, it had over three hundred and fifty of these groups or branches. At the Boston headquarters, in Boylston Street, war relics, posters, bulletins and other articles formed a valuable means of propoganda, especially in the earlier years of the War.

All the materials required for making relief supplies, such as gauze, flannel, and absorbent cotton, were purchased directly from the mills and factories, and were sold at cost price to all who agreed to return the finished product for shipment to France. These sales of merchandise often totaled $16,000 a month. Work rooms were opened for volunteers on Boylston Street, and an entire house on Beacon Street was given over to cutting and sewing by electric machines, all operated by volunteers. About fourteen to twenty paid workers were employed, principally as bookkeepers and stenographers, but the packing for shipment abroad was done entirely by a corps of men volunteers.

The New England Branch of the American Fund for French Wounded made its first shipment on April 23, 1915, and its last on April 30, 1919. During that period it forwarded 22,530 cases containing supplies valued at $1,852,872, seven delivery motors, one ambulance, and $29,649.76 for the support of the work in France, and for especially designated purposes. A weekly bulletin, compiled from letters received from the workers in France, was issued, which contained information as to the varying needs, and patterns with detailed direction were also supplied. Annual meetings were held, and, at the final gathering, about six hundred members and delegates were present.

Miss Bangs was also Chairman of the Foreign Service Department of the Fund during the latter part of the war, when all communications with the State Department passed through her hands.

In the spring of 1919, the regular work of the American Fund for French Wounded ceased, and it was then proposed to build, equip and endow a children's hospital in the devastated regions of France, in memory of the American soldiers who fell in the war. Thus the American Memorial Hospital, Incorporated, was founded, with headquarters in New York, and Miss Bangs was elected the National Chairman. At the suggestion of the French Government the city of Rheims was selected as the recipient of this gift, which has a $600,000 endowment for its support. The corner stone was laid in May, 1922, by the Honorable Myron T. Herrick, the American ambassador to France, in the presence of a large gathering of French and American friends.

In order to care for the children of Rheims during the years preceding the completion of the permanent building, a temporary hospital was opened in June, 1919, in a ruined hospice, loaned by the city of Rheims. In this building over 1,000 babies were born, and over 50,000 patients were cared for and treated in its wards and dispensary. Under the able direction of Doctor Marie Louise Lefert and Doctor Alicia Flood, of New York, this work has been supported by members and friends of the American Fund for French Wounded, the greater part of its funds having been raised under Miss Bangs' leadership.

In recognition of the great value of her work and in appreciation of the spirit that animated it, the French Government has honored Miss Bangs with two decorations; the gold Médaille d'Honneur and the silver Médaille de la Reconnaissance Française; and also has made her Chevalier de la Légion d'Honneur.

DUER, CAROLINE KING, daughter of James Gore King and Elizabeth Wilson (Meads) Duer, was born in New York City. Her first paternal American ancestor was William Duer, son of John Duer, a member of the British Government in Antigua, who settled in New York about 1770. He had been with Clive in India, and, on the outbreak of the War of the Revolution, joined General Washington's Army, with the rank of Colonel. He married Katherine Alexander, daughter of William Alexander, sixth Earl of Stirling. Katherine Alexander's mother was Sarah Livingston, the daughter of Philip Livingston, Second Lord of Livingston Manor.

Miss Duer was educated at Bishop Doane's School, in Albany, New York.

She has long been a contributor of short stories, poems and essays to *Scribner's*, *Collier's*, *The Century*, *Everybody's*, *Ainslee's*, and other magazines. She wrote *Unconscious Comedians*, a collection of short stories, and, in collaboration with Alice Duer Miller, a *Book of Verses*, that ran through two editions.

Miss Duer went to France in September, 1915, as head of surgical dressings, appliances and apparatus in the hospital founded by Lady Johnstone and Mr. Harold Reckett at Ris Orangis, a village between Paris and Fontainebleau, and remained there for one year under Doctor Joseph Blake. She also worked in Paris for the American Fund for French Wounded.

Returning to this country in the winter of 1916, she went back to France with Miss Anne Morgan early in 1917, accompanying the unit of the American Committee for Devastated France to Blerancourt, the village headquarters given to Miss Morgan by the French Government, and there worked with the Committee during the summer and early autumn. Later, she took a unit from the same society to Soissons for the winter, and remained there until the following spring when the German drive forced the evacuation of that town.

Miss Duer later joined Miss Hackett's English Canteen service in several villages near the front where small clubs were opened for the French soldiers.

HELLMAN, FRANCES (Mrs. Theodore Hellman), philanthropist and writer, daughter of Joseph and Babette (Steinhord) Seligman, was born in New York City, October 4, 1853. Her father, born in Germany, came to this country when he was but twenty years old, and for about forty years was prominent in financial, philanthropic, and educational circles. He founded the firm of J. and W. Seligman and Company, who were the fiscal agents for our Government during the Civil War; and was a close friend of Grant, Harrison and many other great men of that period. He was also one of the founders of the Ethical Culture School.

Mrs. Hellman was educated in New York City, except for four years of study in Germany. On March 7, 1872, she was married, in New York City, to Theodore Hellman, a banker, born in Munich, Germany. They are the parents of three children: Edith, now Mrs. George L. Beer (born in New Orleans, February 24, 1873); Edgar (born in New Orleans, January 15, 1875); and George (born in New York, November 14, 1879).

Mrs. Hellman has translated numerous German and French works into English, among them being Heine's *Lyrics*, Kinkel's

Tanagra, Anatole Levy-Beaulieu's *Israel chez les Nations*, and Jean Gérardy's *Toi et Moi*.

Mrs. Hellman is a member of the Ethical Culture Society, Women's Municipal League, Women's International League for Peace and Freedom, Foreign Policy Association, the Metropolitan Museum of Art, the Charity Organization Society, and the American Red Cross. She is prominent in the community work conducted by the Ethical Culture Society, and also in the Society's Women's Conference.

HENRY, ALICE, editor and lecturer, daughter of Charles Ferguson Henry (died in 1887) and Margaret Walker Henry (died in 1876), was born in Melbourne, Australia. She was educated in private and public schools of Melbourne; is a graduate of its high school and received individual instruction in languages and literature.

For several years she taught in Melbourne, and then joined the staff of the *Argus* and the *Australasian*, Melbourne newspapers, while contributing extensively to the Melbourne and Sydney press. Her specialty was education and the care of the dependent and handicapped child. In 1905 she went to England and Belgium as a representative of the Charities Organization of Melbourne. In the following year she came to the United States as a lecturer on woman suffrage and kindred subjects. In 1907 she joined the National Women's Trade Union League and has worked at its headquarters in Chicago, Illinois, since that time. The League has for its platform: the organization of working women throughout America; equal pay for equal work regardless of sex; the eight-hour day and the forty-four-hour week; a living wage; and full citizenship for women. Until 1910 she was in charge of the editorial and publicity work of the League, and helped to found its organ, *Life and Labor*, of which she was Editor for five years. She also wrote many magazine and newspaper articles.

She is now Secretary and Staff Lecturer of the League's Education Department and gives lectures on women, the bread winners; the living wage; why women should organize; the vote—and after; the International Congress of Working Women, and allied topics. In 1915 she published *The Trade Union Women*, a handbook of the problems of women in industry, and how these are affected by organization. Miss Henry is editor of the book department of *The Suffragist*, the organ of the National Women's Party, and is a member of the Chicago League of Women Voters, the Chicago Women's Trade Union League, the Office Employee's Union of Chicago, the Authors' League of America, the Socialist Party, the American Proportional Representation League, the Fellowship of Reconciliation, and the Young Women's Christian Association.

PATTERSON, ANTOINETTE DE COURSEY (Mrs. T. H. Hoge Patterson), painter and writer, daughter of Samuel Gerald and Eliza Otto (Barclay) De Coursey, was born in Philadelphia, Pennsylvania. Her earliest American ancestor, was Henry De Coursey, of Kinsale, Ireland, who settled in Maryland about 1640.

She was educated at Miss Sanford's School in Philadelphia, later studying and painting in pastels. On September 8, 1896, she married at Portsmouth, New Hampshire, T. H. Hoge Patterson. In recent years Mrs. Patterson has contributed numerous poems to magazines, and in 1913 published *Sonnets and Quatrains*, which was followed in 1914 by *Undine, A Poem*, and in 1916, by *The Son of Merope, and Other Poems*. Her latest work is *The Enchanted Bird, and Other Fairy Stories*.

Mrs. Patterson is a member of the Sedgeley Club and the Philadelphia Art Alliance.

POPE, ABBY LINDEN (Mrs. Albert A. Pope), philanthropist, daughter of George and Matilda (Smallwood) Linden, was born in Newton, Massachusetts.

She was educated in private and public schools in Newton, Massachusetts, graduating, in 1869, at the Newton High School. She was married in Newton, Massachusetts, to Albert Augustus Pope. They were the parents of six children: Albert Linden, Mary Linden, Margaret Roberts, Harold Linden, Charles Linden, and Ralph Linden Pope.

Mrs. Pope's activities, outside her home life, have been principally in behalf of woman suffrage. She has also been prominent in the local Civic Federation. She is a member of the New England Women's Club, the Women's City Club, the Navy League, and the Aero Club.

COOK, LORA MARY HAINES (Mrs. Anthony Wayne Cook), daughter of Lewis Gregg and Sarah Jones (McHoggan) Haines, was born at Lloydsville, Belmont County, Ohio.

Her father (born at Lloydsville, Ohio, April 20, 1842; died at Cambridge, Ohio, July 19, 1920) was a son of Isaac Haines (born 1819; married, 1841; died, October 29, 1906) and Margaret Gregg (born, 1821), a descendant of a long line of Quaker pioneers, prominent in the early history of New Jersey, Virginia and Ohio, and traced his ancestry to Richard and Margaret Haines of Aynhoe of ye Hill, Northamptonshire, England. Because of the civil and religious disabilities imposed upon the Society of Friends in England, Richard Haines sailed for America, with his wife and children, in 1682, but died on the voyage. His son, William Haines (1672–1754), settled, with his brothers, in Northampton Township, Burlington County, New Jersey, where, in 1695, he married Sarah Paine, daughter of John Paine. Their son, Nathaniel, born in the pioneer home in 1706, married, in 1739, Mary Hervey, daughter of John Hervey, at the Burlington Meeting in accordance with the Quaker custom. John Haines, their son (born 1740; died July 20, 1790), married Rachel Austin, in 1768, and served during the War of the Revolution in Captain Mitchell's Company, First New Jersey Regiment. John Haines' son, Nathaniel (1784–1844), married Rachel Engle, in Ohio, in 1807, and became the father of Isaac Haines and the grandfather of Lewis Gregg Haines. The Engles, Austins, and Herveys were all prominent early Quaker settlers in Burlington County, New Jersey, and many of their descendants emigrated to Ohio. There are now (1923) members of the tenth generation of the Engle line still residing in New Jersey. Rachel Engle's father, Abraham Engle, married Patience Gaskell at the Evesham Meeting in 1765. His parents were Robert Engle and Rachel Venicombe (sometimes spelled Vinicum); his mother having been a daughter of William Venicombe and Sarah Stockton (widow of Benjamin Jones), who were married at the Burlingham Monthly Meeting, in 1706–1707. Sarah Stockton was a daughter of Lieutenant Richard Stockton, a native of England, who settled first at Flushing, Long Island, where he was a lieutenant of a horse company in 1665, and of a foot company in 1669. In 1690 he removed to Omeahickon, Springfield Township, New Jersey, where he died in 1705. From him descended Richard Stockton, the signer of the Declaration of Independence.

On her mother's side Mrs. Cook's ancestry is as follows: Sarah Jones (McHoggan) Haines was born at Woodsville, Ohio, March 28, 1840, and died at Cambridge, Ohio, January 25, 1921. She was educated in private schools and entered college at the age of seventeen. In 1864 she was graduated, in the same class with her future husband, Lewis Gregg Haines, at McNeely College, Hopedale, Ohio. She was the daughter of James McHoggan, Jr., (born, Westville, Connecticut, February 3, 1815; died, Moscow, Ohio, November 9, 1892), who married at New Haven, Connecticut, November 8, 1836, Mary Green Meadows (born, Milford, Connecticut, October 16, 1819; died, September 12, 1899). James McHoggan, Jr., was a son of James McHoggan (born at Dumferline, Scotland, 1782; died at

Westville, Connecticut, April 27, 1845), a weaver of cotton and woolen goods and the inventor of several improvements in textile machinery, who married Martha, daughter of Ashbell Lines. Mary Green Meadows, wife of James McHoggan, Jr., had most notable ancestry. She was the daughter of Robert Carter Meadows (born in Liverpool, England in 1780; settled in Connecticut; and lost at sea near Turk's Island in 1827) who married, in New Haven, Connecticut, in 1807, Sarah Jones, daughter of Isaac Jones, who served in the Revolutionary War, and his wife, Mary Pond. Isaac Jones was the son of John Jones, Jr. (1712–1759), and Hannah Bassett (1719–1759), who were married in 1738. They both, died in Durham, Connecticut. John Jones, Jr., was a son of the Reverend John Jones (1667–1718), a graduate of Harvard College, who married Mindwell, daughter of Rowland and Sarah (Whiting) Stebbins. Reverend William Jones was a son of William Jones (born in England in 1624; died at New Haven, Connecticut, in 1705), who was a magistrate of the New Haven Colony in 1602–1603; Deputy Governor in 1664, and again from 1691–1697; Commissioner of the United Colonies, 1664; Member of the Governor's Council, 1665; Assistant to the Governor, 1665–1691, and a Judge of the County Courts in 1695. In 1659 he married his second wife, Hannah Eaton (baptized at St. Stephen's, Coleman Street, London, England, October 6, 1632; died at New Haven, Connecticut, in 1707), daughter of Theophilus Eaton (born at Stoney Stratford, England, in 1590; died at New Haven, January 7, 1657), one of the founders of the Massachusetts Bay Colony, named in the grant of James I, dated March 4, 1628–1629, and came to Boston in 1627. He was assistant to the Governor and Company of the Colony, 1629–1630; one of the founders of the New Haven Colony; Magistrate there, in 1639; signer of the Articles of Confederation of the United Colonies, 1643; in the same year Commissioner of the United

Colonies and first Governor of the New Haven Colony, until his death in 1657. He married, in England, in 1627, Anna Lloyd, widow of Thomas Yale and daughter of the Right Reverend George Lloyd, Bishop of Chester, and his wife, Anne Wilkinson. Bishop Lloyd traced his notable Welsh ancestry to Coel Coedhehawy (295 A.D.), through Rhrodri Mawr (843–877), King of All Wales; through his grandson, Howel Dda (907–948), the great lawgiver of Cambria, whose laws continued in force for four hundred years; through his great-great-grandson, Rhys ap Tewdor Mawr (died, 1098), the founder of the second Royal Welsh Tribe; through his grandson, Rhys ap Gryffydd (died, 1197), representative Sovereign of North Wales; through Gruffudd ay Cynan (died, in 1136, at the age of eighty-two), King of Wales, the last to bear the title; and also to Marchudd ap Cynan, Lord of Brynffenigl in Denbighland, founder of eight noble tribes of North Wales and Powys in the ninth century. Mary Pond, the wife of Isaac Jones, also came of a notable family. Her father was Peter Pond, and her mother, Mary Hubbert (born in Boston, Massachusetts, in 1723; died in Milford, Connecticut, in 1761), daughter of Zachariah Hubbert, who married, May 15, 1722, Mary Hobby (born in the Province House, Boston, February 19, 1702; died, 1730), daughter of Sir Charles Hobby, Knight, son of William and Anne Hobby of Boston. Sir Charles Hobby was knighted by Queen Anne, in 1705, for bravery during the earthquake in 1692 at Jamaica, where he was in command of the sloop *Seaflower*. He was Captain of the Ancient and Honorable Artillery Company of Boston, in 1702–1703, and again 1713–1714; and in 1708, Captain of the Boston Militia. In 1710, he commanded one of two Massachusetts regiments in the expedition against Port Royal and the following year he was Deputy Governor of Annapolis Royal. From 1713 Sir Charles was a Warden of King's Chapel, Boston, serving until his death, which occurred in Boston about 1715.

Mrs. Cook is a college woman. She has specialized in modern languages and music, studying with the best masters both in Boston and Washington. She was married to Anthony Wayne Cook at Cambridge, Ohio, September 15, 1892. Mr. Cook represents the the third generation of his family in the lumber business in Pennsylvania. His father, Anthony Cook, left over eight thousand acres in timber land, remarkable as the only white pine forest standing at present (1923) east of the Allegheny Mountains. Mr. and Mrs. Cook have their summer home, "Waylona," at Cooksburgh, Pennsylvania, a town named for his family, and their winters are spent in Pittsburgh, or in travel. They are the parents of one son, Anthony Wayne Cook, Jr., born in 1897. He attended Shadyside Academy, Pittsburgh, and the Hill School, Pottstown, Pennsylvania, and was graduated in Yale University, in 1919.

Mrs. Cook's pride in her patriotic ancestry naturally led her to take an interest in the new organization of the Daughters of the American Revolution. She joined the Pittsburgh Chapter, her national number being 12,412. In 1899 she resigned from the Pittsburgh Chapter, to organize the Brookville Chapter of Pennsylvania, and from that date served as Regent for fifteen consecutive years, leaving it to accept the office of State Vice-Regent of Pennsylvania, which she held for three years. For four years, Mrs. Cook was State Chairman of the Magazine Committee. During this period she served also as National Chairman of the Insignia Committee, and was an efficient member of several national committees. When, in October 1916, she was elected State Regent of Pennsylvania, Mrs. Cook's real genius as an executive found its proper sphere. It was under her Regency that the D. A. R. war record of the State for a period of one year and eight months showed gifts in money —not including Liberty Bonds—amounting to $319,210.10. In addition to this work, Mrs. Cook organized twenty-one new chapters of the Daughters of the American Revolution

in Pennsylvania. One of these, in Indiana County, has the largest organizing membership (101) in the history of the National Society. During the war, Mrs. Cook was a member of the Executive Board, Pennsylvania Woman's Council of National Defense. In 1920, Mrs. Cook was elected Vice-President General of the National Society, D. A. R., from Pennsylvania to serve for three years. A year later, in 1921, she was unanimously nominated at the Pennsylvania State meeting in Washington, during the time of the Continental Congress, as a candidate for the office of President General, and was elected at the Continental Congress of the National Society, D. A. R., in 1923. This was a spontaneous recognition of her ability as an organizer and presiding officer, her keen judgment and foresight, her honesty of conviction, and her loyalty to the interests of the Society. During all of her patriotic work Mrs. Cook has demonstrated her real ability as a parliamentarian and has made for herself an enviable reputation as a capable presiding officer. Although claimed by social and many other duties, Mrs. Cook is still an eager student of everything that makes for culture. She has kept abreast of the times, and has allowed nothing to interfere with her early love for music and the study of languages.

Mrs. Cook is a member of the Pennsylvania Society of Colonial Dames, the Society of Colonial Governors, the Daughters of Colonial Wars in the Commonwealth of Massachusetts, Daughters of Founders and Patriots, Americans of Armorial Ancestry, and the Mary Washington Memorial Association. She is a member of the Twentieth Century Club of Pittsburgh, and has served as Chairman of its Debate Committee.

COOLIDGE, JENNIE ADELAIDE HOLMES (Mrs. Marshall H. Coolidge), daughter of Byron Martin and Susan Maria (Knowles) Holmes, was born at West Pensaukee, Wisconsin, February 9, 1866. Her father was descended from George Holmes of Nazing, England (died in Roxbury, Massachusetts, December 18, 1645) and his wife, Deborah (born in Roxbury, and died there November 6, 1662); from their son, John Holmes (born in Roxbury in 1643; died May 17, 1676) and his wife, Sarah; from their son, John Holmes (born in Dorchester, Massachusetts, in 1663) and his wife, Elizabeth Gates (born at Marlborough, Massachusetts, in 1671; died in Colchester, Connecticut, in 1726); from their son, Captain John Holmes (born at Stonington, Connecticut, in 1700) and his wife, Mary Harris (born at Montville, Connecticut, in 1702; died at Salisbury, in 1761); from their son, Captain John Holmes (born in Colchester, Connecticut, in 1729) a soldier in the Colonial Wars and in the Revolution, and his wife, Rachel Fellows; from their son, Asa Holmes, also a soldier in the Revolution, and his wife, Elizabeth Painter; and from their son, James Holmes (born in Utica, New York, in 1801) and his wife, Rebecca Pamela Waring, parents of Byron Martin Holmes, Mrs. Coolidge's father (born in 1834), who married, in 1860, Susan Maria Knowles, a descendant of John Knowles (who married Constant Southworth, in 1660) and of John Alden of Plymouth Colony.

Mrs. Coolidge was educated in the public schools of Green Bay and Stevens Point, Wisconsin, and under governesses at home. Her marriage to Marshall Harvey Coolidge, a timber merchant and dealer in iron ore of Minneapolis, Minnesota, took place in Milwaukee, Wisconsin, on June 25, 1883. They are the parents of three sons: Harry Holmes Coolidge (born February 15, 1886); Byron Harvey Coolidge (born August 4, 1888); and Marshall Harvey Coolidge, Jr. (born May 9, 1904). The second son, Byron Harvey Coolidge, served in the World War, being assigned, October 15, 1917, to the 316th Engineers at Camp Lewis, Washington. He arrived at Brest, France, March 4, 1918, and was stationed at Chaumont, Saint-Pierre des Corps, and Bourges, where, in recognition of efficient work, he was promoted to corporal, November 5, 1918, and recommended for the Service Medal.

Mrs. Coolidge was Chairman of "Children's Year" in Minneapolis, under the Council of National Defense, and for this she compiled and illustrated the pamphlet, *Does Your Dollar Go Far or Fast?* She is also the author of *Recreation Plans for the Minneapolis Children's Year Committee*, published in *School Education*, February, 1919, and of *How to Live on $600 Per Year*, printed in 1902 in *Keith's Magazine*. Her lecture, *Patriotic Duties of Women from the Standpoint of the D. A. R.*, was delivered before the Rochester Civic League, February 1, 1921. She has been Corresponding Secretary, Vice-Regent and Regent of Monument Chapter (Minneapolis), Daughters of the American Revolution, State Chairman of the Conservation Committee,, and State Regent of Minnesota, D. A. R. elected to fill a vacancy, May 27, 1920, and reëlected February 24, 1921. From 1899–1904 she was a member of the Clio Club, Minneapolis. She is an active member of the Woman's Club, and was Chairman of the Americanization Committee, and its representative for two years, at the Fifth District Federation. She is also a member of the Society of Daughters of Founders and Patriots of America, the Society of Mayflower Descendants, and of the Minnikanda Club, President of the Parents-Teachers Association of the Kenwood School, and was a national speaker for the Republican Party in 1920.

ROBINSON, JANE MARIE BANCROFT (Mrs. George O. Robinson), historian and philanthropist, daughter of the Reverend George C. and Caroline J. (Orton) Bancroft, was born at West Stockbridge, Massachusetts, December 24, 1847. Her father, born March 20, 1814, came of a family resident at Cape May, New Jersey, for many generations. He was educated for the United States Navy, and received his commission as an officer, but having been converted, he joined the Methodist Episcopal Church, was ordained a minister, and preached for nearly sixty years. His wife, Caroline J. Orton, born at Lake George, New York, June 6, 1832, was a daughter of Lorenzo and Jane (Bogardus) Orton. The Orton family was among the first settlers of Connecticut and Bogardus has been a familiar name from the earliest times in New York.

Miss Bancroft was educated in public and private schools and completed the course at the Emma Willard School, Troy, New York, in 1871. In the following year she was valedictorian of the graduating class at the New York State Normal School (now the New York State College for Teachers), Albany, New York, and in 1877 received the degree of Ph.B. from Syracuse University. From 1877 to 1886 she was Dean of the Woman's College and Professor of French Language and Literature at Northwestern University. During this period she earned from Syracuse University the degree of Ph.M. in 1880, and of Ph.D. in 1884. In 1886 she was appointed the First Fellow in History at Bryn Mawr College, and in 1886-1887 continued her studies at the University of Zürich, Switzerland. In 1887–1888 she was engaged in research work at the Sorbonne, Paris, and was the first woman to be admitted to the École des Hautes Études, as a student in the historical department. Her publications at this time were *The Parliament of Paris and the Other Parliaments of France* (1885), *Deaconesses in Europe and Their Lessons for America* (1888), and later, *The Early History of Deaconess Work in American Methodism.* After her return to the United States in 1888, Miss Bancroft organized the deaconess work of the Woman's Home Missionary Society, and assisted in founding the training schools of the society. In 1890 she arranged meetings in Washington, which led to the establishment of the Lucy Webb Hayes National Training School and the Sibley Hospital.

On May 7, 1891, Miss Bancroft was married to George Orville Robinson, of Detroit, who was born June 14, 1832. His father, Lewis Robinson, was a prominent manufacturer of maps at South Reading, Vermont, and his grandfather, Ebenezer Robinson, was a soldier in the Revolution, and a founder of South Reading. Mr. Robinson was a graduate of the University of Vermont, and throughout his life was a wide reader and close student in various lines. He attained distinction as a lawyer, amassed a competence in many lines of activity, and was honored with high offices, especially in the church in Detroit, and in various philanthropic organizations to which he gave liberally. Mrs. Robinson has commemorated his family in *Ebenezer Robinson, a Soldier of the Revolution* (1898).

Always interested in the work of deaconesses, Mrs. Robinson founded the National Training School at San Francisco in 1900. In 1908 she was elected President of the Woman's Home Missionary Society of the Methodist Episcopal Church, an organization which in 1920 had a membership of over 360,000 and an annual income of over $2,600,000. She continued its President until 1913, and since then has been First Vice-President. In 1908, and again in 1920, she was a lay delegate from Detroit to the General Conference of the Methodist Episcopal Church, and in 1911, to the Ecumenical Conference of Methodism, held in Toronto, Canada. She is a life member of the American Economic Association and of the American Historical Association, and is President of the Western Section of the International Association of Methodist Women. Mrs. Robinson is also a member of the Association of Collegiate Alumnae; Alpha Phi Fraternity; the St. Clair Fishing and Shooting Club of Detroit, Michigan; the Woman's University Club of Los Angeles; and the Shakespeare, Browning and Civic Clubs of Pasadena, California. Mrs. Robinson now resides in Pasadena, California.

MANN, KRISTINE, physician, daughter of Charles Holbrook and Clausine Christiana Riborg (Borchsenius) Mann, was born at Orange, New Jersey, August 29, 1873. She attended Smith College, where she received her degree of A.B. in 1895. In 1900–1901 she was a graduate student and assistant in English at the University of Michigan. She took her master's degree there in 1901 and was then appointed instructor in English at Vassar College where she remained until 1905. From 1905 to 1908 she was instructor in English at Brearley School, New York, and during the last year of her residence there attended lectures in the graduate school of Columbia University. She then entered the Cornell University Medical College and received her doctor's degree in medicine in 1913. The following year she was instructor in the department of physical education at Wellesley College, and in the autumn of 1914 returned to New York to assume the position of director of the hospital established by Messrs. Lord and Taylor for their employees, remaining in charge until 1918. She was also medical director of the Department Store Education Association in New York and started the Health Clinic for Industrial Women, a work supported by private funds that did excellent service for two years, and was only discontinued on account of the War. During part of this time she was a Clinical Assistant at the Cornell University Medical College and in 1917–1918 lecturer on hygiene at Smith College. During the summer session of 1918 Doctor Mann directed the intensive course offered by Mt. Holyoke College to train health officers for the supervision of the health of women workers in munition plants. During the World War she was Director of the Civilian Workers' Branch of the United States Ordnance Department and supervisor of the health of women in the Ordnance Department munition plants. Since the end of the War she has lectured on social hygiene in the colleges and universities of the Southwest under the auspices of the Young Women's Christian Association. As a result of her experience with college and working girls, Doctor Mann is an authority on the physical condition of young American women. She is a member of the American Medical Association and of the Civic Club of New York.

MASON, MARION HOUGHTON (Mrs. Stevens T. Mason), daughter of Alfred Augustus and Caroline (Garlinghouse) Houghton, was born in Buffalo, New York, November 22, 1882. Her mother's family came originally from Holland, where the name was spelled Garlinghuysen. Her father (born March 6, 1851; died October 28, 1892), was a descendant of John Houghton, Jr., who was born in England in 1650, and was brought by his parents to New England the same year. He married Mary Farrar. Their son, Jacob Houghton (1674–1752), married Rebecca Whitcomb. Their son, Jonathan Houghton (1703–1740), was the father of Lieutenant Jonathan Houghton (1737–1829), who married Susanna Moore. Their son, Rufus Houghton (1769–1852), married Abigail Barnard. Their son, Amory Houghton (1813–1882), married Sophronia Oakes, and they were the parents of Alfred Augustus Houghton. Marion Houghton was educated at Miss Baldwin's school, and received the degree of A.B. from Bryn Mawr College in 1906. In 1911 she received the degree of A.M. from Columbia University and the same year the diploma of the New York Graduate School of Philanthropy. On August 8, 1911, she was married at Hartford, Connecticut, to Stevens T. Mason, a lawyer, the son of John T. and Helen (Jackson) Mason, who was born in Baltimore, Maryland, July 3, 1880. They have since made their home in Detroit, Michigan. They are the parents of Helen Houghton Mason, born March 11, 1913; Stevens T. Mason, Jr., born August 22, 1915; and Adelaide Houghton Mason, born January 19, 1918. Mrs. Mason was at one time head worker in the Guild of St. George, Baltimore, and has been a volunteer worker under the

Association of Charities, Detroit. In 1918 she was Secretary, in 1919 Vice-President, and in 1919–1920 President of the Detroit Equal Suffrage League, and President of the League of Women Voters, Detroit, Mrs. Mason has been an agent of the Federal Labor Bureau, and is a teacher in the Americanization work of the Detroit Board of Education. She is a member of the Bryn Mawr Alumnae Association, the League of Women Voters, the Woman's City Club of Detroit, the Detroit Country Club, the Indian Village Club, and the Detroit Fine Arts Society.

VAN NESS, SARAH BOWMAN (Mrs. Joseph Van Ness), of Lexington, Massachusetts, is a representative of two of the most ancient families of England and Wales, the Bowmans and the Powels. Her father, John Bowman, who married Eliza Powel Gittings, was a descendant of the English family of the name. The Bowmans were of the true and original Britons, occupying and owning for centuries the greater part of Cumbria, the beautiful hill district and poets' land of England. The Saxon kings recognized their ownership, and because of their expert use of the bow they were placed in the forefront of the Saxon Army to protect their homes and country. William the Conqueror, because of their dependable character, sturdy physique, knowledge of the country, and skill in bowmanship, chose members of the family for his bodyguard. His life was saved by them in battle, and on the field he dipped his fingers in blood, drawing the simple crossed bows on their shields[1] and bestowing on them and their descendants forever the name of Bowman.[2] Kirkoswald Castle, fifteen miles from Carlisle, built in 1201, held, until its destruction the earliest records of the Bowman family, in the parish church of the village of Kirkoswald the Hethelton branch of the Bowman family still have their pew. The long years of border warfare and disturbance along the marshes of Cumberland and Westmoreland continued to induce the sturdy independence in the Bowmans, seen later in their descendants who settled and built up Watertown and Lexington.

Richard Bowman, born in 1486, moved from Cumberland to Staffordshire and died in 1546. His son, Robert Bowman, married in 1544, at Allston Field Church, Ellen Crychlow, who died in 1590. Their son, Richard Bowman, was baptized in 1546. His son, John Bowman (baptized in Parwick, England, in 1578), married Ann Beresford of Parwick, a daughter of one of the oldest and most honored gentle families in England.[3] Their son, Nathaniel Bowman, was born in 1608. Because of the land tenure troubles of 1615 he sold his property and in 1630 came with his wife, Ann, to America, where he was one of the earliest proprietors of Watertown, Massachusetts. A section of the town was named in his honor.[4] As he was a Cavalier, he would not resign his membership in the Church of England to hold office or to become a freeman, although he did not use his title of "Cavalier Gentleman" until he wrote his will.[5] In 1635 he bought land of Edward Goffee in Cambridge Hills, which since 1713 has been called Lexington. There in 1649 he built the Bowman homestead, which remained an excellent example of early New England architecture until it burned, April 1, 1905. He died in 1682. His son, Francis Bowman (born is Watertown in 1630; died December 16, 1687), married September 26, 1661, Martha Palmer, daughter of Captain John and Martha Sherman and a granddaughter of John Winthrop.[6] Their son, Francis Bowman,[7] who was born in Lexington, September 14, 1662, was known as "ye worshipful Justice." When Lexington was incorporated, March 31, 1713, he was entrusted with the management of the town affairs, and he filled every office in the gift of the people. In 1720 he was appointed by the King as his first "Royal Magistrate" and represented the King personally until his death on December 23, 1744.[8] He married Lydia Stearns, the daughter of Deacon Samuel Stone, a prominent citizen of

Cambridge. Their son, John Bowman, who was born July 14, 1689, and died April 30, 1726, married Mary (Shepard) Stone. Their son, John Bowman, who was born December 5, 1713, and died in 1760, married in 1736, Susanna, the daughter of Captain Joseph and Elizabeth (Bond) Coolidge of Watertown. Their son, Samuel Bowman,[9] who was born November 4, 1749, married Hannah Winthrop, the daughter of Isaac and Mary Davenport.[10] He entered the Revolution as drummer in Captain Parker's Company, rose to the rank of Captain, and served throughout the war until after January 19, 1781.[11] On April 22, 1782, he was commissioned Lieutenant in the First Massachusetts Regiment. He died December 21, 1819. His son, John Bowman, who was born February 11, 1794, frail in health, and who died in 1831, married Lucinda Willard Foster. Directly descended from Reginald Foster,[12] one of the proprietors of Ipswich, Massachusetts, and from Major Simon Willard,[13] one of the proprietors of Cambridge, Massachusetts, in 1634. John Bowman, the son of John and Lucinda Willard (Foster) Bowman, who was born April 16, 1822, and who died in Boston, August 4, 1882, married, August 10, 1848, Eliza Powel, the daughter of George and Sarah (Powel) Gittings of Baltimore, Maryland, born at Sparta, Georgia, October 25, 1823. They were the parents of Sarah Bowman Van Ness. George Gittings was a direct descendant of John Gittings of Baltimore (1659), one of the best educated and most influential men of Maryland, clerk of the Upper House of Burgesses from 1661 to 1669.[14] His earliest English ancestor was Sire John de Giddings of St. Albans, England,[15] a descendant of one of the oldest and most highly-respected families, of Basle, Switzerland.

The genealogy of Sarah (Powel) Gittings is most ancient, being derived from Gwraldeg, King of Garthmadryn (now Brecknock) Wales, who is said to have lived towards the end of the first century.[16] The line is continued through his daughter and sole heiress, Morfydd (Morvytha), who married Teithall (Tathall) ap Annwn Dhu (Antonius Niger), about 260 A.D., and whose son, Teithin (Tydheirn), grandson, Irith y blawd, great-grandson, Teidfallt (Teithphaltim or Teithwalch), and great-great-grandson, Tydor (Tudor or Tewdrig), were all kings of Garthmadryn. The latter's daughter and sole heiress, Marchell (Marcella) married Aulach (Aullech, Afalech, or Olave), buried before the church door at Llanspyddid, the son of Cornach McCarbery (Cormac MacEurbre Gwyddel), King of Ireland. Their son, Brychan Brecheiniog (Brychan Yrth), King of Garthmadryn (since called Brecheiniog or Brecknock), began his reign in 400 and died about 450. His daughter, Gwen (Gwenllian) married Llyr Meryny (Molwynen),[17] lord of Gloucester. Their son, Cradoc Fraich Fra (Caradoc of the Strong Arm), lord of Gloucester, knight of the Dolorous Tower and King Arthur's Round Table, married Tegay Ayruron, daughter and coheiress to King Pelynor. Thence the line is continued through four kings of Ferreg and Brecon, Cawrdaf, Caw ap Cawrdaf, Gloyw, and Hoyw, and thence through Cynvarch ap Hoyw, Cyndeg ap Cynvarch, Teitwalch ap Cyndeg, Tegyd ap Teithwalch, Anharawd ap Tegyd, Gwendy ap Anharawd, Gwungy ap Gwendy, and Hydd Hwgan (Huganus), to Dryffin (Sir Driffin ap Hwgan), who married Crusilla, daughter of Idwal ap Meuric. Their son, Maenarch (Maenyrch), prince of Brecknock, married Elinor (Elen), daughter of Einon ap Selyff, lord of Cwnwd and Cantreff-selyn, who was himself fifteenth in descent from Cradoc Fraich Fra above. Their son, Bleddin ap Maenarch, who lived in the time of William Rufus of England, was the last independent sovereign Brecheiniog. He was slain in battle by Bernard Newmarch, who seized the greater part of his lands, and he was buried by his sons in the abbey of Strata Florida in Cardiganshire.[18] He married Elinor, daughter of Tewdwr Mawr and sister of

Rhys ap Tewdwr, prince of South Wales. Their son, Gwgan (Gwrgan), married Gwenllian, daughter and heiress of Phillip ap Gwys, lord of Gwyston (Wiston), Pembrokeshire. Their son, Trahaern, lord of Llangorse, married Joan, daughter of Bleddin, lord of Cilsant. Their son, Howel, married Gwenllian, daughter of Griffith ap Ivor ap Inon, lord of Sanghenith. Their son, Rhys of Aberllynfni, married Catherine, daughter of Griffith Gwyr of Gower. Their son, Einon Sais, married Joan, daughter of Howel ap Mredith, lord of Miscin. Their son, Einon, married Lettice, daughter of Cadwaladr ap Griffith, lord of Upper Gwent. Their son, Howel Fychan, married Malt, daughter of Llewelyn ap Howelhen. Their son, Llewellyn, the last of the princes of Wales, was slain by the troops of Edward I of England, December 10, 1282. He married Malt (Matilda), the daughter of Jeuan ap Rhys ap Ivor of Elvel. Their son, Howel, married Margaret, daughter of Gwilim Philip Thomas ap Elydr, and was the founder of the family of Powel (ap Howel) of Castle Madoc, Brecknock. Their son, Gwilym dew, married Mary, daughter of Jenkin Richard Jenkin of Aberyscir. Their son, Howel dew, married Maud, daughter of Roger Madoc Richard David. Their son, Gwilym, married Catherine, daughter of John Rees Jenkin of Glyn-nedd. Their son, Howel of Argoed, married Margaret, daughter of William John Havard. Their son, Thomas Powel, Esq., married Sibil, daughter of Sir William Vaughan, Knight. Their son, William Powel, Esq., of Castle Madoc, married Matilda, daughter of Griffith Jeffrey of Glyntawe. This William Powel, according to the inscription on a carved stone over the entrance, rebuilt the present castle in 1588. It replaced a castellated mansion with a keep for prisoners, built in 1045 by Madoc ap Manarche. William Powel's son, Hugh, who died in 1624, married Elizabeth, daughter of Thomas Gwyn of Trecastle. Their second son, Hugh Powel, born about 1555, married for his first wife, Ann, who died in Stratford-on-Avon, in July, 1614.[19] For his second wife, he married, July 10, 1615,[20] Elinor Sadler, who died, aged about eighty years, January 31, 1622. From a memorial tablet above her grave by her pew in Salisbury Cathedral we learn that "This Ellihonor was the wife of Hugh Powell, Esq., High Sheriff of Brecknock in South Wales, and Principal to Thomas Sadler the Elder Esquire of the Body to the King's most excellent Majesty that now is and one of his Highnesse' Justices of the Peace and Quorum within this country who likewise has been register to six reverend and worthy Bishops of the same."[21] William Powel, gentleman, the eldest son of Hugh and Ann, was a subscriber to the London Company that financed the settlement of Jamestown, Virginia, in 1607. He arrived in Jamestown in 1611 and represented the town at the first legislative assembly in America, held at Jamestown in July, 1619, under the Presidency of the Royal Governor, George Yeardley, who brought over laws formulated by Parliament for the government of the colony. William Powel was chairman of the committee to examine these laws and select such as were desirable, the Assembly enacting other laws to replace those that were not fitting.[22] Later, William Powel was appointed Captain in command of the soldiers and fort at Jamestown, and, after an Indian massacre in 1622, in which his kinsman, Nathaniel Powel[23] and family were killed, he pursued the Indians and was himself murdered by them on the Chicahominy River in 1623.[24] As he left no heir in the colony, his property was confiscated by Governor William Berkley at the court held in November, 1643.[25] John Powel, Captain William's youngest son, came to Virginia the following year and at different times brought thirty-eight persons to the colony for whom he received many land grants.[26] His son, John Powel, settled in North Carolina, and died there, January 13, 1709.[27] His eldest son, George Powel, died March 24, 1735.[27] George's third son, Lewis Powel, moved to

Georgia,[28] and his third son, Thompson Powel, married Charlotte Hardy Bridges, a daughter of two of Virginia's earliest and most influential families, originating in Stratford-on-Avon, England. They were the parents of Sarah (Powel) Gittings.

Sarah Bowman (Mrs. Van Ness), was born in Macon, Georgia, November 4, 1859. She received her early education at home under a governess and then entered Winthrop School, Boston, from which she proceeded to Lasell Seminary, Auburndale, Massachusetts. On October 4, 1892, she was married in Boston to Joseph Van Ness, the son of James and Elizabeth (Robb) Van Ness, and a worthy representative of old and honored families of Holland, Scotland, and America. He was born at Andover, Massachusetts, December 13, 1848, and was graduated at the University of Illinois in 1876 and, with honors, at Cornell University in 1878. He was a natural student and a deep thinker, of a kindly and generous nature, aiming to use his talents for the benefit of mankind. In 1883 he wrote as his life's motto: "Not happiness but duty done, is the greatest good that life may bring: even death, and whatever there may be beyond it, can bring no sweeter bliss than comes to him who is conscious of having done his duty to his fellow men." In 1896 he founded the Joseph Van Ness Publishing Company, publishers of *The Shoe and Leather Trade Journal*, and for five years after his death on July 8, 1901, Mrs. Van Ness directed and managed his publishing business.

Mrs. Van Ness is interested in church, philanthropic, and social affairs and in welfare work in state and nation. Her estate, "Fieldstone," East Lexington, Massachusetts, is the site of one of the early Bowman homes, and she has been hostess there of many notable gatherings. In 1913, she entertained the members of the Association of Nathaniel Bowman's Descendants, an organization which she has done much to foster. Her interest in patriotic and historical subjects led her to found, on October 19, 1895, the Lexington

Chapter of the Daughters of the American Revolution, of which she was Regent for eight years. Upon her retirement from office she was made Honorary Regent for life. She is also an honorary member of the Warren and Prescott Chapter, Daughters of the American Revolution, Boston, Massachusetts, and a member of the Massachusetts Daughters of the American Revolution Founders' Society. She is a member of the Society of Daughters of Founders and Patriots of America, by descent from Captain William Powel, of Virginia, and Captain Samuel Bowman, of Massachusetts; the Lexington Historical Society and the Roanoke Memorial Association of North Carolina, and a life member of the Jamestown Society of Virginia, as well as a member of the Council of Vice-Presidents of the National Historical Society of America. She is also a patroness of the Southern Club of Boston and a member of the Outlook Club of Lexington.

---

[1]See illustration of arms: Argent, two bows gules, stringed or, in saltier. (Edmonson: *Herald*, vol. 1; p. 46).

[2]*Homes of Family names;* William Bowman of Alport, England; *Records of Bowmans;* Office of Public Documents, Eng. Arms were granted to other members of the Bowman family in England and Scotland for important services to King and state. Sir William Bowman (1816–1892), the famous ophthalmic surgeon, received a grant from Queen Victoria in 1884.

[3]Beresford: *Beresford of Beresford, Eight Centuries of a Gentle Family*, part iii.

[4]Bond: *History of Watertown*, p. 1083.

[5]The title of "Gentleman" is specifically defined in England as being a man above the rank of yeoman who bears arms and whose family are free-holders. It is to be noted that Carlisle was the last city to hold out for the cavaliers.

[6]*Revised History of Lexington* (1913) vol. ii.

[7]Francis' brother, Joseph Bowman, born May 18, 1674, died April 8, 1762, was an influential man in church and municipal affairs in Lexington; selectman for fifteen years; representative to the General Court six years; first to subscribe money for the purchase of Lexington Common, 1711; captain of Lexington militia, 1717. He married Phebe. (see Gravestone).

[8]Isaac Bowman, younger brother of John, succeeded his father as Royal Magistrate and represented the King until American independence was declared.

While still holding this office he was elected, September 21, 1768, chairman of the committee to "protest against the distressed state of the Province", thus showing his sense of honor and justice to the people. He died July 18, 1785. (see Gravestone).

[9]He selected for his guardian his uncle, Lieutenant John Hoar, husband of Elizabeth Coolidge. His education was in the care of his uncle, the Reverend Jonathan Bowman, for forty-four years pastor of the First Church, Dorchester, Massachusetts, who married Elizabeth Hancock, aunt of Governor John Hancock. (Hudson: *History of Lexington*, pp. 83–88).

[10]Isaac Davenport and his son James were selected by George Washington as his Life Guard. James was presented with a sword for bravery by Lafayette at Yorktown, Virginia, at the time of the surrender of Cornwallis. These men inherited not only the sterling qualities of their ancestor, Orne de Davenport of Warwickshire, England, but also those of their Pilgrim grandmother Warren.

[11]Thirty-four Bowmans served in Massachusetts regiments during the Revolution. Of these Thaddeus Bowman and his family well illustrate the family tradition of patriotism. Thaddeus was the son of Joseph and Phebe Bowman (see note 7). He married, first, December 2, 1736, Sarah Loring, who died December 23, 1747 (Gravestone); and second, February 8, 1753, Sybil Woolson, a widow. He was commissioned Captain of Militia in 1763 and served as such until the outbreak of the war. In 1775 he was elected Chairman of the Lexington Committee of Safety and Correspondence for three years. He was the first to meet the British, April 19, 1775. His name appears on the Roll of Honor in the Archives at Washington of those who furnished money for carrying on the war. He died May 26, 1806, at New Braintree, Massachusetts. Five of his sons served with distinction in the war. One of them, Samuel, born December 2, 1753, was a staff officer of Alexander Hamilton; an original member of the Order of the Cincinnati; and commander of André's guard, by André's request walking arm in arm with him to André's execution. Hamilton Bowman, son of Samuel, after his graduation from West Point, filled important positions under the Government, directing the building of the Treasury and other Government buildings in Washington as well as important forts and defenses of the country, one of his first being Fort Sumter, Charleston, South Carolina. Five Bowman kinsmen were present in Charleston Harbor when the Fort was destroyed in 1864.

[12]See Bostwick, Helen Ford, for Foster line.

[13]Joseph Willard: *Willard Memoir*, p. 338; Pope: *Willard Genealogy*, pp. 1–5. For twenty-two years Major Willard held the highest offices in the gift of the people. He was one of the Governor's Council, a member of the General Court and of the Supreme Judicial Court. He, with Peter Bulkeley, bought Concord from the Indians, whence he was for fifteen years deputy to the General Court. He married, first, Mary Sharpe of Horsmonden, England; second, Elizabeth Dunster, sister of President Henry Dunster of Harvard College; third, Mary Dunster, cousin of President Dunster. His son, the Reverend Samuel Willard was pastor of the Old South Church, Boston, and President of Harvard College from 1701 until his death in 1707.

[14]*Records of Upper House of Burgesses, Maryland.*

[15]*Subsidy Rolls*, 1327. The name is variously spelled: Gittings, Giddings, Giddens, etc.

[16]Sir Joseph Russell Baily, Bart.: *History of Brecknockshire* (revised "Glanusk" edition, 1909), vol. ii, pp. 173, 174, 183, 255.

[17]Son of Myrghion gyl; son of Gornst Galedlon; son of Kenay; son of Ceol, sometime King of Britain. Cf. *Miscellanea Genaelogica et Heraldica*, vol. iv. 3d series, p. 17.

[18]Burke: *Landed Gentry* (1851), vol. ii, p. 1069.

[19]*Burial Records*, Stratford-on-Avon, p. 87. Children by first wife: William, Thomas, and John, born November 4, 1583. (Baptismal Records, Stratford-on-Avon, p. 36).

[20]*Marriage Records*, Stratford-on-Avon, p. 27.

[21]The first sentence of the tablet preceding the one quoted, reads: "A memorial of the truly righteous and religious Elehonor Sadler late of this close of Sarum lineally descended from the ancient and wordhipful family of the Saint Barbes of Ashington in Somersetshire and cousin German to that thrice worthie Lady Walsingham who was mother of the noble Countess of Essex."

[22]*Journal of the House of Burgesses, Virginia*, 1619–1658-1659, p. 6.

[23]Nathaniel Powel married Joyce, daughter of Sir William Tracy of Toddington Castle, Hayles, England. They had one child. He had been elected by vote of the people as Governor of Jamestown until arrival of Yeardley, after which he was one of the Governor's counsellors. He was appointed by King James I to draw the map of Virginia and write an account of the country, its people, climate, and production, and all matters of interest concerning the province. In return, the King granted him a tract of land on the south bank of James River at Powell Creek. The map and history were long ascribed to John Smith until Alexander Brown in his *Genesis of the United States* recognized their true authorship.

[24]L. G. Tyler: *Cradle of the Republic*, pp. 105, 109, 112.

[25]*Virginia State Papers.*

[26]*Virginia State Papers.*

[27]*Chowan County Records.*

[28]*Georgia Records.*

MEYER, LUCY RIDER (Mrs. J. S. Meyer), educator and author, daughter of Richard Dunning and Jane (Child) Rider, was born in New Haven, Vermont. Her father was sixth in descent from Samuel Rider, who married Sarah Bartlett, the daughter of Robert Bartlett and Mary Warren. The latter was the daughter of Richard Warren, who came from Headbury, England, in the *Mayflower*, landing at Plymouth, Massachusetts, December 21, 1620. Jane Child Rider was descended from Samuel Child, a Minute Man at the Battle of Lexington, in 1775, and from John Warren, who came in 1630 to Boston in the *Arabella*, and was private secretary to Governor John Winthrop.

Lucy Rider was graduated from Oberlin College in 1872 with the degree of A.B. and proceeded to the Women's Medical School of Pennsylvania, where she studied from 1873 to 1875, and to the School of Technology, Boston, for technical study in 1877–1878. In 1880 she received her master's degree in arts from Oberlin College and she has also been given the same degree by Cornell College, Mt. Vernon, Iowa. In 1887 she was graduated from the Women's Medical College of Northwestern University with the degree of M.D., and more recently, in 1907, she has taken post-graduate work in the Divinity School of the University of Chicago. On May 23, 1885, she was married in Chicago to J. Shelley Meyer. Their only son, Shelley Rider Meyer, served in France during the World War as sergeant-major in the Division Headquarters of the 86th ("Blackhawk") Division.

In 1885 Doctor Lucy Meyer founded the Chicago Training School for Missions and Social Service, of which she has since been principal and her husband superintendent. The school, which was one of the first of its kind, gives practical training to religious and social workers in coöperation with the Juvenile Protective Association, the United Charities, churches, and other organizations, together with timely courses in home service, immigrant groups, women as citizens, the principles of education, craft work, directed play, physical culture, hygiene and first aid, home economics, the ministry of music and chorus work, and the problems of social, political, and economic reconstruction are discussed. Doctor Meyer was also the founder, in 1887 and 1888, of the Order of Deaconesses in the Methodist Episcopal Church, a group of women absolutely free and voluntary, yet carefully trained and devoting themselves for a period of years, or for life, to religious philanthropy. She has twice been elected a member of the General Conference of the Methodist Episcopal Church, and was a delegate to the Ecumenical Council of Methodism in October, 1911, at Toronto, Canada. She is the editor of the *Deaconess Advocate* and has written many articles and pamphlets on religious and educational subjects, such as *The Fairyland of Chemistry*, as well as the words and music of several songs. Her textbook, *Children's Meetings*, was published in 1885; her *History of Deaconess Work* in 1890, and an educational novel, *Mary North*, in 1902. She is a member of various social service and philanthropic organizations, the Woman's Club of Chicago, and the Political Equality League.

HARRISON, MARY SCOTT LORD, widow of Benjamin Harrison, President of the United States from 1889–1893, was born in Honesdale, Pennsylvania, daughter of Russell Farnum and Elizabeth (Scott) Lord. Her father was Chief Engineer and General Manager of the Delaware and Hudson Canal Company; her mother was a member of the Daughters of the American Revolution. She was educated at Mrs. Moffat's School, Princeton, New Jersey, and was graduated from Elmira College, Elmira, New York.

Mrs. Harrison was an active war worker, serving as Director of the Entertainment Bureau of the Officer's Department of the New York War Camp Community Service, providing amusements for over 1,000 commissioned personnel of the American forces each week. Speaking of her work, Mrs. Harrison said: "We have found officers who were anxious for a taste of the bright lights, and our theatre tickets, opera boxes and concert passes pleased them. Then there were the ones who craved a bit of intimate entertainment which, after all, can be found only in the home. But we were ready and waiting for them, and hundreds have been invited to dinner, week-end parties and motoring trips."

She married, first, on October 22, 1881, at Scranton, Pennsylvania, Walter Erskine Dimmick (died 1882), son of Samuel, E. Dimmick; second, at North Bend, Ohio, April 6, 1896, Benjamin Harrison, ex-President of the United States, son of John Scott Harrison, United States Congressman and grandson of William Henry Harrison, ninth President of the United States. Benjamin Harrison was Colonel of the 70th Indiana Regiment in the Civil War and was appointed Brigadier-General, January 23, 1865. He was elected United States Senator, March 4, 1881, and became twenty-third President of the United States in 1889, serving one term. He died March 13, 1901. General and Mrs. Harrison had one daughter, Elizabeth Harrison, born in Indianapolis, Indiana, in 1897, a lawyer by profession.

WALKER, ELIZABETH HARRISON (Mrs. James Blaine Walker, Jr.), lawyer, was born at Indianapolis, Indiana, February 21, 1897, daughter of Benjamin and Mary Scott (Lord) Harrison. Her great grandfather, William Henry Harrison (1773–1841) was Ninth President of the United States (1841): her father (1833–1901) was Twenty-Third President (1889–1893). Her mother (b. 1858) was an ardent war worker during the World War, and was head of the Entertainment Division of the Officer's Service Department of the New York War Camp Community Service.

Miss Harrison was educated in Tudor Hall, Indianapolis, the Westover School, Middle-

bury, Connecticut, and Miss Conklin's Secretarial School, New York City, and was graduated B.L. at New York University Law School in 1919, and A.B. in the Women's Collegiate Department, Washington Square, New York, in the following year. In 1920, also, she was awarded the degree of Doctor Juris, and was admitted to the Indiana bar.

Miss Harrison was an active war worker throughout the period of American participation in the hostilities of the World War. She aided in drilling the Students' Corps of New York University, and organized numerous war relief units in colleges and schools.

She is a member of the Junior League and the Alpha Omicron Pi Sorority (Nu Chapter), both of New York; of the Daughters of the Cincinnati and the New York University Alumni Association.

Miss Harrison was married, April 6, 1921, to James Blaine Walker, Jr., of New York City, a graduate of Cornell University, who was attached to General Pershing's staff during the World War.

LEARY, ANNIE, philanthropist, daughter of James and Catherine Leary, was born in New York City, where, until her death on April 26, 1919, at the age of eighty-seven, by her many benefactions, she constantly strengthened the work of the Roman Catholic Church. Inheriting a large fortune from her father, who was a prominent merchant of New York, and another from her brother, Arthur Leary, at one time Excise Commissioner of the city, she employed her means to attack the evils that confront unprotected women, especially newly arrived immigrants, and to make effective the ministrations of her Church. As a young woman interested in welfare work, she became aware of the many pitfalls in the path of newcomers from Europe and, therefore, as a refuge for some of these friendless girls, she supported the Irish Immigrants' Home in State Street. In the Italian quarter in the vicinity of Sullivan Street she founded a mission served by Italian priests, who, however unfamiliar with American life, were struggling with small success to extend the work. Realizing that the parents could be reached through the children, Miss Leary established for the latter sewing classes, where they also learned the catechism, frequently taught by Miss Leary herself. As interest grew and numbers increased, Miss Leary purchased an edifice at the corner of Bleecker and Downing Streets which has since become the flourishing parish church of the Madonna of Pompeii. Devoted to the Most Holy Sacrament of the Altar, Miss Leary brought from Canada a chapter of the Order of the Blessed Sacrament, one of whose rules is perpetual adoration, and established them in the Church of Saint Jean Baptiste, where the Fathers have had great success among the French Catholics. Miss Leary also arranged for Sisters of the Order of the Reparation to come to New York from Italy, giving them a house next to the Pius X Art League, supported by her on Charlton Street. Many churches have altars and sacred vessels which are the expression of Miss Leary's faith and generosity. The altar in the chapel of the Convent of the Helpers of the Holy Souls she had brought from France, the home of the order, and every Epiphany she presented it a gift in gold in memory of the gifts of the Magi. The Chapel of the Blessed Sacrament at Bellevue Hospital is Miss Leary's memorial to her brother, Arthur. It is noted for its architecture and for its stained glass windows, especially that of Christ Healing the Sick. Here centres the Arthur Leary Mission, conducted by sisters attached to the hospital, who watch by the sick, provide them with books and various comforts, and see that they have the consolation of the sacraments. This Mission is also maintained on Blackwell's Island, where Miss Leary helped build and support the chapel and where she gave the library and funds for tea and tobacco for the patients. She also devoted much time to the aid of the children on the Island who suffer from tuberculosis, and was led by her experience there

to join, as a vice-president, in the founding of Stony Wold (see Newcomb, Elizabeth Wilmot), the sanatorium for tubercular women and children in the Adirondacks. She was also a vice-president of the Flower Guild, interested especially in its movement to establish small gardens for the children in the poorer quarters of New York, and was connected with many other charities of a practical nature. Miss Leary's many good works brought her recognition from Pope Leo XIII, who on October 11, 1901, conferred on her the papal title of Countess, and one of the first acts of Pope Pius X was to re-confer the title. Countess Leary was a patron of the arts. She loved music and at her houses in New York and Newport, Rhode Island, gave each year a series of afternoon musicals, while she was a constant attendant at the opera. She was the hostess of dignitaries of church and state and her annual dinner on Columbus Day helped initiate that holiday. By her will she left $200,000 to the Archbishop of New York for a sacristy adjoining St. Patrick's Cathedral on Fifth Avenue with the provision that her body eventually be buried in a vault beneath the altar.

TOWNE, ELIZABETH (Mrs. William E. Towne), daughter of John Halsey Jones (born 1832), and Catherine (Osborn) Jones (born 1839), was born in Portland, Oregon, May 11, 1865. She was educated in the public schools of Portland and was married at the age of sixteen to J. Holt Struble. They were the parents of two children, Catherine Elizabeth (Mrs. Edward Lincoln Twing) and Chester Holt Struble. About sixteen years later she moved to Holyoke, Massachusetts, where she was married on May 26, 1900, to William E. Towne, an editor, author, and publisher. He is the son of Salem and Emily (Carpenter) Towne and was born in Walpole, New Hampshire, in 1874.

Mr. and Mrs. Towne became acquainted through their common interest in New Thought, and have devoted a congenial married life to its propagation. For many years Mrs. Towne was a successful healer, but gave up practice to devote herself to writing and lecturing on New Thought. She is the editor of *Nautilus*, a magazine which she founded in 1898, and of which Mr. Towne has been associate editor since 1900. They were joined in 1911 by Chester Holt Struble, as managing editor, and the three are associated in the Elizabeth Towne Corporation, of which Mrs. Towne is President.

Mrs. Towne is the author of many magazine articles and books. Among them are *Joy Philosophy* (1903), *Meals without Meat* (1903), *Practical Methods for Self-Development* (1904), *How to Concentrate* (1904), *How to Grow Success* (1904), *Happiness and Marriage* (1904), *How to Wake the Solar Plexus* (1904), *How to Train Children and Parents* (1904), *You and Your Forces* (1905), *Experiences in Self-Healing* (1905), *The Life Power* (1906), *Your Character* (1909), *Lessons in Living* (1910), *How to Use New Thought in Home Life* (1915). She has lectured on New Thought in all the larger cities and in nearly all the states of the Union.

Mrs. Towne has been since 1915 the Honorary President of the International New Thought Alliance whose headquarters is at Washington, District of Columbia. The ideal of the Alliance is that it is a democracy led by the spirit as a democracy of individuals. In the New Thought centres all have equal rights to the good-will and service of the Alliance which aims to coördinate all individuals and all centres regardless of creed or color, and to serve them all alike in the spirit of truth and love.

Mr. and Mrs. Towne both sat as delegates in the two National Conventions of the Progressive Party, but supported Woodrow Wilson in 1916 and 1920. Mrs. Towne is a Director of the Massachusetts Federation of Women's Clubs, First Vice-President of the Hampden County Women's Club, Chairman of All Holyoke Open Forum which was initiated by the Holyoke Women's Municipal League, and she has been an active worker for woman suffrage. During the World War she was Secretary for Hampden County, Massachusetts, for the Women's Committee of the Council of National Defense.

JOHNSON, CONTENT, painter, daughter of John George and Augusta Adelaide (Hinds) Johnson, was born in Bloomington, Illinois. Her mother was the daughter of Joel and Hannah (Hazard) Hinds. Joel Hinds was descended from original settlers of the town of Hindsburgh, near Rochester, New York; Hannah (Hazard) Hinds came of the Rhode Island family of Hazard. Content Johnson's grandfather, Stuart Hazard, born in Kingston, Rhode Island, located in the Mohawk Valley, New York, where he operated a grist and carding mill. During the War of the Revolution, in which he served as a minute man, the mill was burned by the Indians and he barely escaped the tomahawk and the scalping knife. He removed to Connecticut, but later returned to New York State and settled in Lisle, Broome County, where he died at the age of ninety-six. Stuart Hazard was a cousin of Oliver Hazard Perry, the famous naval hero. His son, Evins Hazard, born in Southington, Connecticut, married Abigail Hawley, of Arlington, Vermont. They were the parents of four sons, Chester, Elisha, David, and Stuart, and of one daughter, Hannah, who married Joel Hinds. Joel and Hannah (Hazard) Hinds were the parents of Margaret Ann (Mrs. Dwight Harwood), Galitza (Mrs. Ridlehuber), and Augusta Adelaide (Mrs. Johnson).

Miss Johnson was named Content Aline after her father's mother, but in signing her canvasses she was accustomed to drop the middle name. She was educated at Miss Jaudon's school in New York. While still very young she studied music (piano) and drawing. Indeed she early showed such talent for music that it seemed as if she might become a musician. During her early girlhood, however, it became apparent that in her career music must give place to painting, in which great genius more and more manifested itself. She attended the Art School at Shinnecock Hills, New York, as well as the New York School of Art, where she was a pupil of William M. Chase. Later, at the Julien Academy, in Paris, she studied for two years under Benjamin Constant and Laurens and Pierre Émile Cornillier, and, with "Mark 1," was awarded the prize for composition.

Upon her return to America, Miss Johnson devoted several years to the intensive study of painting, again under the instruction of William M. Chase. During this period she gradually developed a characteristic style which is marked by many distinguishing qualities. Among these are vivid personality, always strikingly revealed, and an individuality of pictorial imagination that enables the painter to give us compositions of novelty, freshness, and surprise, but without eccentricity or exaggeration. All her work manifests delightfully this vitality and independence of conception, the essential stamp of an artistic gift of the first order. The artist, with intuitive vision, beautifully trained, seems to see straight to the heart of her subject, and to record it with sincerity, truth, and unfailing beauty. Miss Johnson's landscapes, her sunsets, her gardens, her homely village scenes exemplify these traits of forceful originality combined with candour and a pervasive poetic charm. The sunsets, with their deep glowing color convey a haunting sense of solitude and lonely spaces. The *Cornfield in Sunset*, for example, is a masterpiece in tender elegiac mood beautifully felt and portrayed, possessing that subtle combination of reserve strength and delicacy that eludes analysis. Among the rustic scenes, the several versions of *The Oxen Teams*, with driver and cart, have a great depth of tone that helps to convey the wonderfully quiet mood permeating the theme. Miss Johnson's gardens are especially distinguished for an originality of treatment that is entirely lacking in the usual flower pictures. They have all

the natural poetry and gaiety of a sunny garden, in which the rich reds and whites glow and vibrate with life.

In addition to these aesthetic factors, one may always find the master technique of the great artist, the free strong brush-work, always delicately adjusted to the character of the object. Each subject receives an exquisitely appropriate handling in accord with its nature. Miss Johnson's style is as varied as her range of subjects. Her colors show that beautiful freshness which comes only from direct, expert brush-work, the reds and whites being perhaps especially remarkable for subtlety and variety. The drawing and the composition are always of a robust and substantial sort, furnishing a solid framework for the many refinements of treatment which Miss Johnson imposes upon them.

Miss Johnson's portraits, which constitute a very important part of her work, have won for her a place among our finest portrait painters. The mellowness of tone and accuracy of interpretation are reminiscent of the old masters. Her portraits are, as a rule, very deep in key, with a corresponding depth of feeling, and they often evidence a certain Titian-like dignity. That she can also make real such an elusive theme as shy childhood, however, is exemplified in her portrait of two children (exhibited 1923). Her most admired portraits are those of Mrs. Charles Lockwood (of Ann Arbor, Michigan), Mrs. Buell, and Miss May Lyman.

For several seasons Miss Johnson painted scenes in and about the quaint old-world town of Sainte-Anne de Beaupré, near Quebec, and thus becoming familiar with every detail of the home life of the simple Canadian people. Her studio was one of the village houses, and the special study she was enabled to make of her friendly neighbors, while living among them, enabled her to portray the customs of the inhabitants so faithfully that these canvasses are of rare historic interest. In themselves they are marked by an innate beauty which shows the reserve power of the great masters. This is especially apparent in several where oxen, bearing a primitive yoke, are depicted in some wooded by-path. Her interiors reveal the simplicity of color and furnishing that are typical of these homes. She is generous with color—a pink wall, a door of deepest blue, a silver crucifix above a table, a cradle with a woman in picturesque garb spinning near— these are the details that will show to future connoisseurs what was the simple beauty of the life of the people before modernity swept it aside.

Miss Johnson holds frequent "one-man exhibitions" in New York and elsewhere; for example, at the City Club, the Parish House of the Church of the Ascension, the Pen and Brush Club, the Union League Club, the Hotel Majestic, and elsewhere. She has exhibited repeatedly at the National Academy in Chicago, Washington, Philadelphia, and Charleston, and at the International Exhibition in Rome. In 1918 an Art Club was organized in the vicinity of Washington Square, New York, educational in its aims and intended to stimulate an understanding of art. Miss Cecilia Beaux is Honorary Chairman of the Art Committee, of which Miss Johnson is Chairman, and Doctor Christian Brinton assisted in the first exhibition. Miss Johnson is a member of the Society of Painters, the National Institute of Social Sciences, and a Vice-President of the Pen and Brush Club.

STEVENS, DORIS, (Mrs. Dudley Field Malone), was born in Omaha, Nebraska. Her father, Henry Hendebourck Stevens, was a son of Edward and Alice (Broadhurst) Stevens, native of England, who settled in New York City in 1849. Her mother, Caroline (Koopman) Stevens, was born in Utrecht, Holland, in 1856. She was a daughter of Reverend Ralph Koopman who located in America, in 1859, as pastor of the Dutch Reform Church of Paterson, New Jersey.

Miss Stevens received her early education in the public and high schools of Omaha. As a student at Oberlin College, where she was graduated A.B., in 1911, she followed special courses in such subjects as sociology, the woman and labor problems, normal and abnormal psychology, and modern languages. During her college years she was a pupil in piano and voice at the Oberlin Conservatory of Music. After leaving college she was a teacher in private and public grade schools, and taught history and literature in Ohio and Montana. She also tutored preparatory and college students; conducted fresh-air camp work in conjunction with settlement house activities; was piano accompanist for singers and violinists; and made a reputation in dramatic work and as a public speaker. She herself has said that, valuable as she considers her training at Oberlin, it was not to be compared with the practical education received later when she had to solve the problems of life. From the time she left college, she realized keenly, in her teaching as well as in her other work, the professional discrimination against women. Her enthusiasm for the cause of equal suffrage was born of her experience and observation. While still a college student, she met Mrs. Pankhurst and her daughter, Sylvia, and was more impressed by them than by the leaders in the suffrage movement in the United States. They fired her imagination and her emotions. Later, her own experiences convinced her that her feelings on the subject of woman's rights were sound and logical. She undertook her first public work for suffrage during three state campaigns. She soon saw that it was hopeless to waste time on state activities so in January, 1914, she entered the national field. She has been successively organizer, political chairman, legislative chairman, organization chairman, campaign manager, and member of the Executive Committee of the National Woman's Party, formerly the Congressional Union for Woman Suffrage. In her coast-to-coast campaigns she has raised thousands of dollars, addressed hundreds of audiences, and organized numberless committees. In July,

1917, she was sentenced to sixty days in the workhouse for attempting to petition the President, in Washington, for national suffrage for women. After serving three days she was pardoned by the President. Her arrest, trial, and conviction, as well as those of her fellow petitioners, was later declared illegal. In order, however, that their experience might be brought to the attention of the whole country to arouse interest and enthusiasm for the cause of woman suffrage, the "Prison Special" Train carrying Miss Stevens and her party, visited all the principal cities of the United States. Miss Stevens made some of her most forceful speeches at meetings organized to introduce the members of the party to the public, during this trip. Miss Steven's life is devoted to the endeavor to improve the status of women, not only from the political, but also from the social and the economic standpoint. She is the author of the booklet, *The Militant Campaign*, (June, 1919), and the book, *Jailed for Freedom*, (March, 1920). On December 9, 1921, she married Dudley Field Malone, Third Assistant Secretary of State and Collector of the Port of New York, under President Wilson.

HORTON, KATHARINE LORENZ PRATT, (Mrs. John Miller Horton), daughter of Pascal Paoli and Phebe (Lorenz) Pratt, was born in Buffalo, New York. Her father was the founder, and for many years President of the Manufacturers and Traders National Bank of Buffalo, where he was a leading citizen, banker, financier, and philanthropist. Her mother was a native of Pittsburgh, Pennsylvania. Mrs. Horton is also a great-granddaughter of General Samuel Fletcher of Vermont, a famous officer in the Revolution.

Mrs. Horton was educated at the Buffalo Seminary and at the Brooklyn Heights Seminary, Brooklyn, New York. Throughout her life her guiding principles have been those for which her father stood so consistently— good citizenship, patriotism, and philanthrophy—and she has been foremost in every

movement for Americanization grounded on Christian ideals. With her husband, John Miller Horton, she travelled widely and spent several years in Europe, so that her patriotism is based on a sane conception of both Old and New World conditions.

In October, 1901, Mrs. Horton was elected Regent of the Buffalo Chapter of the Daughters of the American Revolution, and has been re-elected unanimously each year since that time. Under her leadership this chapter has more than trebled its membership, until it is the second largest chapter in the National Society, and the largest in New York State, and is honored by having had on its roll the names of four ladies, whose fathers actually served in the Revolution. Mrs. Horton has been indefatigable in sustaining an active interest in the educational work of the chapter. This consists of giving during each winter season three free illustrated lectures weekly on the history of the United States in the Polish and Italian languages, a method of instructing the foreign-born which was originated by the Buffalo Chapter. An additional lecture describing a tour of New York State, as taken by an immigrant, from his landing at Ellis Island to his arrival in Buffalo and at Niagara Falls, was prepared and given by Mrs. Horton, who has also written and delivered several lectures on art and literature and travel talks on Russia, Sweden, Norway, France, Belgium, and Holland, illustrated by views secured during her visits to these countries.

Mrs. Horton, through the chapter, has secured the marking of the graves, in the vicinity of Buffalo, of over one hundred and thirty patriots of the War for Independence. In spite of much discouragement, labor, and expense, the graves and records of all these soldiers were found, and the ceremony of marking them performed with becoming dignity and solemnity, according to a ritual composed by Mrs. Horton.

When the National Society, Daughters of the American Revolution, planned the building of Memorial Continental Hall at Washington, District of Columbia, Mrs. Horton, who was for four years a member of the Committee appointed to execute the plans, recommended that the Buffalo Chapter assist the national organization. This it did with the sum of $1,500, of which $700 was raised at a Colonial entertainment presided over by Mrs. Horton. She also contributed generously, while the chapter presented to the New York State room a bas-relief coat of arms of the State.

In addition to serving on the Memorial Continental Hall Committee, Mrs. Horton has been a member of many other National and State Daughters of the American Revolution committees, such as Franco-American Committee and the Pension Records Committee, of both of which she was Chairman; the American Daughters of the American Revolution Magazine Committee; the Committee to Prevent Desecration of the Flag; the Committee on Real Daughters, and the International Peace and Arbitration Committee, Washington. In 1910 she was Chairman of the New York State Committee on Patriotic Education. The Buffalo Chapter observes Memorial Day by decorating the graves of Revolutionary soldiers with flags and flowers. A commemorative service and ritual, arranged by Mrs. Horton, is held in all the cemeteries where the chapter has placed the bronze markers on the graves and flowers are thrown into the waters of Park Lake in Forest Lawn Cemetery in honor of the sailors of the Navy. Flag Day, June 14th, is also observed by the chapter with suitable ceremonies.

ADAMS, ANNETTE ABBOTT, lawyer, daughter of Hiram B. and Annette Frances (Stubbs) Adams, was born at Prattville, Plumas County, California. She received her education at the Chico State Normal School, where she completed the course in 1897, and at the University of California, where she was graduated B.L. in 1904. From 1907 to 1910 she was Principal of the Modoc County High School at Alturas, California, and then returned to the University of California for further study of law. She received the degree of J.D. in 1912 and was admitted to the bar in May of the same year. In 1913–1914 she was engaged in the general practice of her profession in San Francisco. She was appointed Assistant United States Attorney at San Francisco in October, 1914, and United States Attorney in July, 1918. She is a member of the San Francisco Federation of Women's Clubs and of the San Francisco Center of the California Civic League.

CLERGUE, GERTRUDE ALICE, of Montreal, Canada, was born in Bangor, Maine, and was educated there and at Mlle. Thibault's School in Paris, France. Her father, Joseph Hector Clergue, was born in L'Orient, France, March 20, 1830, and died September 24, 1909, at the residence of his son Francis H. Clergue, at Sault Ste Marie, Ontario, Canada. His father, Jean Clergue, an Ensign in the French Navy, died when his son Joseph was one year of age. Joseph Hector Clergue came to America in 1847 and settled in Bangor, Maine, where most of his life was spent and where June 3, 1852, he married Frances Lombard. Her original ancestor in America on the mother's side was Thomas Lombard, who came to America on the ship *Mary and John* and settled at Barnstable, Massachusetts, May 18, 1631. She is descended from the Colonial Governors—Thomas Hinckley, who was the last Governor of Plymouth Colony, and of Thomas Roberts, Governor of New Hampshire in 1640.

Gertrude Alice Clergue was engaged in war work from the outbreak of the World War in 1914 to its close, receiving in recognition of her services, the decoration of the Médaille de la Reconnaissance Française, from the French Government. She is co-author with her sister, Grace Clergue Harrison, of *Allied Cookery*, published in Montreal and in New York in 1916 and in Paris in 1918—the proceeds of which went to relieve the sufferings of the inhabitants of the devastated districts of France.

She has been Honorary Secretary of l'Aide à la France since its inception, and is a member of the Committee of the Canadian Society for the Prevention of Cruelty to Animals; a member of the Parks and Play Grounds Association; the Society of Decorative Art; the Wolfe and Montcalm Chapter of the Imperial Order of the Daughters of the Empire. She is President of the Women's Press Club of Montreal; an Honorary member of the Shakespeare Club of Bangor, Maine; a member of the Themis Club of Montreal; the Castine (Maine) Golf Club; the Mount Bruno Country Club (Quebec); the Winter Club, Montreal; the Tennis and Badminton Club of Montreal and the Colony Club of New York.

ALDEN, CYNTHIA MAY WESTOVER (Mrs. John Alden), founder and President-General for a quarter of a century of the International Sunshine Society, is a native of Iowa, reared and educated in Colorado; but for thirty-eight years a resident of New York City; church choir leader; customs inspector; secretary for two years to the Commissioner of Street Cleaning of New York City (the first woman ever appointed to a political executive position in New York City); special writer illustrating her own stories with photographs taken by herself; editor of *The Woman's Page* of the *New York Recorder* and of the *New York Tribune*; and active in club life before she brought the Sunshine Society into existence.

She was born in Afton, Iowa, May 31, 1861, daughter of Oliver S. Westover, a mining geologist, and Lucinda (Lewis) Westover. Her mother died when she was a baby, and shortly thereafter Professor Westover removed to Colorado, where silver mining possibilities were being developed, and took his little girl with him. The country was wild. There were few women. Cynthia Westover lived in the open air, learned to swim, to ride, and to shoot straight; learned the calls of different birds, the ways of the prairie dogs, the luring of mountain trout, the habits of the badger, the bear, and the mountain sheep. Later there were schools in some of the mining towns, and she became a student in the Denver High School, fitting herself for a course in the Denver Business College and was graduated B.A. in the first class of the Colorado State University at Boulder.

After a short experience as a teacher in Denver and Boulder she came east. She acquired French by living in a French family, Spanish in a Spanish family and Italian in an Italian family. She practised singing twelve hours a day on difficult church music and became solo soprano in a large church choir of New York City. She passed civil service examinations repeatedly, until one day she received notice that she had been appointed a United States customs inspector. Several important seizures were credited to her. The late Hans S. Beattie was then Surveyor of the Port of New York. When he became Street Cleaning Commissioner he named Miss Westover as Department Secretary. In his absence, leaving Miss Westover at the helm, there was no break in the routine of his office. Three separate strikes of street sweepers were quieted when she talked to the men in Italian.

Standing at the entrance to the City Hall one windy day, she saw a sweeper sweep up the same pile of dirt five times, after it had been scattered as often by the wind. Having decided that such waste of time should be stopped, she made her way to the stables of the Department of Street Cleaning, and there, with the assistance of the Department carpenter, put together an apparatus which soon developed into the useful "dingey," now used by street cleaners in all countries.

To prevent hill horses from being ruptured in hauling loads up the incline at the Department dumps, she invented the first swinging cart, to be operated in connection with a derrick by pulling a string and dropping the load into a scow provided to receive it. Miss Westover received no money benefit from either of these inventions, as she was in the employ of the City, and she made no claim for reward to her ingenuity. However, in 1907, she received an honorable mention from the French Government for inventing the swinging cart.

Collecting material on public questions for the late George William Curtis, editor of *Harper's Weekly* was the first journalistic work done by Miss Westover. After leaving the Street Cleaning Department she kept her pen and camera busy in newspaper work, much of which included the short stories, later gathered into the volume *Bushy*, which appeared in the *New York Recorder*. In 1895, this newspaper put Miss Westover in charge of its Woman's Page, the first attempt ever made to devote an entire page to matters of exclusive interest to women.

On August 15, 1896, Miss Westover was married to John Alden, an editorial writer on the *Recorder*. When the *Recorder* passed out of existance, Mrs. Alden became the head of the Woman's page of the New York *Tribune*, leaving only when the International Sunshine Society was incorporated, in order to devote herself, without salary, or compensation of any form, to the new work. In the meantime, however, she was for ten years editor of a department in the *Ladies' Home Journal*.

The International Sunshine Society was born in the *Recorder* office. It started in the saving of a few of the beautiful chromos which the *Recorder* distributed with its Sunday issue and sending them to farms, ranches and plantations, where children were longing for a bit of color. It developed into a movement to donate anything for which the owner has no immediate use, so that someone else might enjoy it. This continued while Mrs. Alden was on the *Tribune*.

The International Sunshine Society, organized in the parlors of the late Mrs. Joseph Fairchild Knapp in the Hotel Savoy, had its office for more than twenty years at 96 Fifth Avenue, and branches in every state of the Union and several abroad. The central idea, "not sacrifice of what you want yourself, but thoughtfulness to make someone happy with what you do not want," was contagious, and lent itself to a hundred forms of philanthropy. The mother society has never lost this central aim or purpose, but more by accident than design, it was led a number of years ago into the work of making provision for the saving of the bodies and minds of blind babies. It has urged successful legislation on this line in fourteen different states, and conducts a home at Summit, New Jersey, where fifty blind children are cared for. A separately incorporated branch manages another home at 84th Street and 13th Avenue (Dyker Heights), Brooklyn. Both institutions are free from debt, and have a comfortable bank balance.

In 1905, Mrs. Alden received the degree of Master of Literature from Alfred University, Alfred, New York. Besides being the author of many short stories, making quite a feature of *Pictures of Life in the great Metropolis*, under the *nom de plume* of "Kate Kensington," illustrated with photographs taken by herself, she wrote the first history of Greater New York, known as *Manhattan Historic and Artistic; Women's Ways of Earning Money; Bushy, a Story of Child Life in the Far West*, and her famous pamphlet on *The Baby Blind*. Mrs. Alden takes greater pride in her successful work as head of the International Sunshine Society, and her success in efforts to promote the welfare, physical and mental, of the baby blind, than in anything else she has ever attempted.

HIGGINS, KATHARINE CHAPIN (Mrs. Milton P. Higgins), daughter of Aldus M. and Catherine Fisher (Sawin) Chapin, was born in Manchester, New Hampshire, December 11, 1847. Her father (born at Chicopee, Massachusetts, December 27, 1811; died at Worcester, Massachusetts, June 4, 1880), was a descendant of Deacon Samuel Chapin, a native of Paignton, Devonshire, England, whose name appears first in New England in the land records of Roxbury, Massachusetts, in 1631.

This Samuel Chapin was the son of John Chapin of Paignton, and was christened October 8, 1598. He brought to the new world his wife, Cicelly, daughter of Henry Penny of Paignton, whom he married at Paignton, February 9, 1623, and their five children. In 1642 he became one of the founders of the new settlement of Springfield, in Massachusetts, where William Pyncheon had already established himself. He took a prominent part in the town in both civil and religious affairs, was a Deacon of the church and a member of the first board of selectmen, for nine consecutive years.

One of Augustus St. Gaudens' most notable works is the statue erected to the memory of Samuel Chapin, which was unveiled November 24, 1877, in Stearns Park, Court Square, Springfield. There are replicas in the Museum of Fine Arts, Boston, Massachusetts, at City Hall Square, Philadelphia, Pennsylvania, the Louvre, Paris, and the Dresden Gallery. In its title, *The Puritan*, the work assumes a broad significance. It stands for a type of the Puritan character, stern, individual, resolute, vigorous, God-fearing, the pioneer of the new world. The sturdy forceful man strides along on his way to meeting on the Lord's Day with staff and Bible and with face set strongly towards his destination. The figure is of bronze of heroic size, wearing the costume of his day, which lends itself admirably to picturesque treatment, the long plain doublet, roomy breeches, heavy hose, buckled shoes, thick sugar-loaf hat, and the great flowing cloak used by the sculptor to produce an original and unique effect.

Aldus M. Chapin married May 13, 1840, Catherine Fisher Sawin (born at Sherborn, Massachusetts, May 3, 1819; died July 12, 1878), a descendant of Robert Sawin of Boxford, Suffolk, England, whose son, John, was a resident of Watertown, Massachusetts, as shown by the town records, in 1652, and

later of Natick. His son, John, was the first white child born in that town. The line is traced through another son, Thomas, a soldier in King Philip's War: his son, John; his son, Thomas, a captain in the Revolutionary War; his son, Moses, who also served in that war as a corporal; and his son, Bela, who was the father of Catherine Sawin.

Catherine Sawin entered Mt. Holyoke Seminary in 1839, two years after its opening, and thus came under the teaching of its founder, Mary Lyon. In this exceptional environment of scholarship and high ideals the young girl's character broadened and developed. She was trained to become a teacher and eventually was considered the leading woman in educational affairs in Manchester, New Hampshire, where she spent the greater part of her married life. In 1857 she removed with her husband and children to Dubuque, Iowa, where they remained three years, then returning to Manchester.

Katharine Chapin entered school in 1860, and proceeded to Abbot Female Seminary (now Abbot Academy), Andover, Massachusetts, where she completed the course in 1868. She embraced the profession of teaching, and throughout her life has been identified with progress in education. She was married June 15, 1870, at Manchester, New Hampshire, to Milton Prince Higgins, son of Lewis and Susan (Whitney) Higgins. His ancestry was notable, being traced to the *Mayflower* Pilgrims, and in the old country to William the Conqueror. He was born at Standish, Maine, December 7, 1842, and died in Worcester, Massachusetts, March 8, 1912. As a successful manufacturer, the President of the Norton Emery Wheel Company and of the Plunger Elevator Company, he saw the need of technical training in colleges, and was the first to promote commercial trade schools in the United States. For twenty-eight years he was Superintendent of the Washburn Machine Shops at Worcester Polytechnic Institute of which he was a Trustee, and he was Vice-President of the American Society of Mechanical Engineers. Mr. and Mrs. Higgins were the parents of four children: Aldus Chapin Higgins (born in Worcester, Massachusetts, December 7, 1872), Treasurer of the Norton Company and Trustee of the Worcester Polytechnic Institute; John Woodman Higgins (born in Worcester, September 1, 1874), President of the Worcester Pressed Steel Company; Katharine Elizabeth Higgins (born in Worcester, August 6, 1878), married in 1903 to R. Sanford Riley, President of the Riley-Stokes Company; and Olive Chapin Higgins, now Mrs. Lewis I. Prouty.

As a teacher, as the mother of four children, and the grandmother of thirteen, Mrs. Higgins has developed a practical outlook upon the problems of both parents and teachers. This has led her to identify herself with the modern parent-teachers movement. She has served as President of the Massachusetts State Parent-Teachers Association, and has been both Vice-President and President of the National Congress of Mothers and Parent-Teachers Associations. Since 1910 she has made many addresses throughout the country before parent-teacher associations and normal schools on child welfare. Religious education has also occupied her thoughts. She is the Superintendent of the Primary and Junior Departments of the Sunday School and is also the President of the Sunday School Teachers Primary Union of Worcester. Her interest in family history and her ability in research led to her appointment as State Historian for the Massachusetts Daughters of the American Revolution. She is the Regent of the Colonel Timothy Bigelow Chapter, Daughters of the American Revolution, Worcester, Massachusetts, a member of the Worcester Woman's Club, the Worcester Club, the Worcester Tatnuck Country Club, the Abbot Academy Club, and is President of the Woman's Auxiliary of the Worcester County Farm Bureau. In 1920 she was appointed one of ten delegates from the United States to the International Council of Women held in September, in Christiana,

Norway. Mrs. Higgins has written many plays and exercises for the State Sunday School conventions, as well as poems for local occasions. Her most notable published work is the *Higgins Genealogy* (1919), a scholarly volume of over 900 pages.

ANDREW, HARRIET WHITE FISHER, author and manufacturer, was born at Pennline, Crawford County, Pennsylvania, March 31, 1865. Her father, Oscar A. White, was a grandson of Perry Green White, of Syracuse, New York, who removed to Canada in 1857. Her mother, Hannah M. (Fisher) White, was a descendant of Nathan Fisher who settled in Massachusetts in 1700. Another ancestor was John Hinckly, a colonel in the Revolutionary War.

Harriet White's early education was received at the Young Ladies Classical Seminary, Cleveland, Ohio. When fourteen years of age she was sent to Hildesheim, Hanover, Germany, where she continued her studies for four years. She then spent two years in Göttingen under the instruction of Doctor Hiemel Langues. She married, first, July 20, 1898, in London, England, Captain Clark Fisher, Chief Engineer of the United States Navy, who died in Flushing, Long Island, December 31, 1903. She married, second, in New York, April 27, 1912, Silvano Alfredo Andrew, an engineer and lieutenant-commander in the Argentine Navy.

The career of Mrs. Andrew has been one of the most remarkable of any woman in any land. Her chief interest centers in the business which has earned for her the title of "Anvil Queen," and which has made her known as the first and only woman ironmaster in the world. The Eagle Anvil Works, Trenton, New Jersey, of which she is sole proprietor and active head, is the oldest anvil manufactory in America. It was founded in 1843 by Mark Fisher, who invented the method of welding steel on iron and made the first anvil in this country, and has always been known under the firm name of Fisher and

Norris. Mark Fisher's son, Captain Clark Fisher, served in the United States Navy, throughout the Civil War, having been present at the attack on Fort Sumter. He retired from the Navy upon the death of his father, and assumed control of the anvil foundry. During a serious illness, which incapacitated him for several months, the management of the plant devolved upon his young wife, although to that time she had been wholly unfamiliar with business methods. But she was equal to the emergency. Day by day she studied the work of the men and inspected every department of the foundry, gradually mastering all practical details. During this trying period she was forced by conditions contingent upon her husband's illness to change superintendents and meet the workmen to adjust their difficulties. Had she not risen to this emergency the foundry must have closed. After her husband's recovery she continued her interest and, recognizing the fact that in order to hold control of the men, she should know the business from the foundation, she started to work as an apprentice, taking a complete course in every department from that of melting pig iron to bidding for contracts. She learned to chisel the face of an anvil, mold vises, make rail joints and operate the great crane. When at work, she wore a garment similar to a sculptor's smock.

In 1902 her husband died as the result of injuries received in a railroad accident. Mrs. Fisher was very badly hurt at the same time, but ultimately recovered, and took her place as head of the anvil foundry. Due to indomitable courage, perseverance, and wise supervision the factory was enlarged and the business expanded greatly. Indeed, during the three years, 1905–1907, the total income from sales was the largest in the history of the company, and succeeding years have brought increased prosperity. Mrs. Fisher's business acumen was made more than ever manifest when she outbid all competitors for the contract of furnishing anvils and vises for the Panama Canal works. The products of the foundry are to be found in every quarter of the globe and are used by every railroad in the United States. The United States Government has purchased her anvils for its Navy Yards and battleships. Another large volume of business is the export trade with the states of South America, particularly with Brazil and Argentina. The "Eagle" anvils and "Fisher" double screw parallel-leg vises have been in general use since the foundry was established. They are superior to all others on account of the special process used in their manufacture, which was the invention of the original proprietor, Mark Fisher. Under the management of Mrs. Andrew various other types have also been manufactured, some of which have been developed from older patterns to meet present day manufacturing needs, together with those of an entirely new type. In her second husband, Lieutenant Silvano A. Andrew, she has an able coadjutor, whose practical knowledge of engineering has led to the installation of much labor-saving machinery.

One feature that has largely contributed to her success is the tact with which Mrs. Andrew has handled disputes with workmen. Through her knowledge of human nature and her ready fund of wisdom, she has overcome any objections that they might have had to being under the control of a woman. As it is they regard her as a personal friend, a benefactress with no taint of unwelcome philanthropy. Among various plans, which she has developed for their good is a system whereby they might work, if so inclined, on holidays at her farm of 135 acres near Trenton. Here she pays them regular wages for work, and sells them farm produce at much lower than market rates. Through all these years of business success Mrs. Andrew has maintained the conservative attitude of her New England ancestors towards many of the questions of the day, particularly as they affect the status of women and the home. Business activity has not affected her home-making arts, which are displayed conspicuously at her home near

Trenton and in her beautiful "Villa Carlotta" at Urio, Lake Como, Italy.

Mrs. Andrew is an accomplished linguist and well acquainted with the literature of France, Spain, and Germany. She has traveled extensively and has many close friends in the Far East. As an authoress she contributed many short stories to the *North American* under the nom-de-plume of "Mustang." These included *My Four Acre Farm*, *School Life in Germany*, and *Christmas Abroad*. In 1911 appeared her book, *A Woman's World Tour in a Motor*, an account of her trip of more than 23,000 miles by motor car. The directness and naturalness of her style add to the quality of a most interesting narrative which is the reflection of a woman of vigorous personality, dauntless courage, and independence of thought and action.

Mrs. Andrew was the first, and for a number of years the only, woman member of the National Association of Manufacturers. She is a member of the Ohio Daughters Club, New York; the Elna Royal Yacht Club, Como, Italy; the Woman's Republican Club, the Author's Club, and the Professional Women's League, of New York; and a charter member of the Good Citizenship League of Flushing, New York.

CARROLL, CAROLINE MONCURE BENEDICT (Mrs. Mitchell Carroll), daughter of E. D. and Caroline (Doyal) Benedict, was born at Belair Plantation, Parish of Placquemine, Louisinia. On her father's side she is descended from Thomas Benedict, who came in 1637 from Nottinghamshire, England, to Massachusetts Bay, and from James Benedict, (born in January, 1686), who was Justice of the Peace of Ridgefield, Connecticut, deacon of the church, and representative from Ridgefield to the General Assembly of Connecticut. Her earliest maternal ancestor in America was William Randolph, who came from Warwickshire in 1660 and settled on an estate on the James River, about twenty miles south of Richmond, Virginia. He was a

charter trustee of William and Mary College. Miss Benedict was graduated from Lisle (New York) Academy in 1889, and four years later received the degree of A.B. at Wells College. During 1892-1893 she travelled extensively abroad, studying languages and art. On September 6, 1897, she was married, at Lisle, New York, to Alexander Mitchell Carroll, Ph.D., the son of the Reverend Dr. John L. and Sarah G. (Mitchell) Carroll, who was born at Wake Forest, North Carolina, June 2, 1870. Dr. Carroll is Professor of Archaeology and the History of Art at George Washington University, Washington, District of Columbia, and is the author and editor of numerous historical and classical studies. Mrs. Carroll spent the year 1897–1898 in foreign travel, especially in Greece, Sicily, and Italy. She was a student of classical archaeology in Athens and Rome, and in 1914 she made investigations in American archaeology in Colorado and New Mexico. She also attended for five seasons Chautauqua Institution, Chautauqua, New York. Mrs. Carroll is a former President of the Columbian Women, and for many years was a member of the Program Committee of the Washington Club, and of the Hospital Board Committee. She organized the School and Community Association, Cleveland Park School, District of Columbia; organized and was First President of the Cleveland Park Chapter of the Young Women's Christian Association; and is a member of the Educational Committee of the Washington Y.W.C.A. and a member of the Dupont Circle Chapter. For one year she lectured on current events before the Washington Club, and the National Cathedral School, and for two seasons, 1917 and 1918, lectured on American archaeology at the Chautauqua Summer School, Chautauqua, New York. She is a member of the Highlands Auxiliary of the Red Cross; and during 1918 was hostess of the soldiers' circle at the Church of the Covenant. She was a member of the Woman's Committee for the 1st, 2d, 3d, 4th, and 5th Liberty Loans. She is also a member of the Twentieth Century Club, the Washington Arts Club, the Seymour Club, the Calvary Missionary Society, the Washington Society, and the Archaeological Institute of America. In 1916 she published *The Story of Flora Macdonald* and edited and wrote the introductory chapter to a volume on Kashmere. Dr. and Mrs. Carroll are the parents of Mitchell Benedict Carroll, Randolph Fitzhugh Carroll, and Charles M. Carroll. Mitchell B. Carroll entered the Air Service, United States Army, December 1, 1917, and received his commission as second lieutenant June 15, 1918, at the age of nineteen. Randolph F. Carroll enlisted in 1918 at the age of seventeen in the Marine Corps and trained at Paris Island.

FISK, JANETTE (Mrs. Clinton B. Fisk), philanthropist, daughter of Lorenzo Dow and Ruth (Haines) Crippen, was born in Penfield, near Rochester, New York, November 24, 1832. When she was only one year old, her parents moved to Michigan, where, as unselfish pioneers, they did much to settle and beautify the town of Coldwater in Branch County. At the age of eleven Janette Crippen was sent to Leroy Seminary, near Rochester, for a year and a half, but, on account of her mother's delicate health, she was sent to complete her education at Albion Seminary, Albion, Michigan. It was here that she met Clinton B. Fisk, the son of Benjamin Fisk of York, Livingston County, New York, where the former was born December 8, 1828, and on February 20, 1850, she was married to him at Coldwater, Michigan. They were the parents of five children: Harry and Jennie, who died in infancy; Clinton Fisk, who died November 28, 1900; Charles A. Fisk, of Arizona; and Mrs. Mary Fisk Park of New York. Mr. and Mrs. Fisk were in complete sympathy with each other's aims. They had a strong sense of public duty, and in their early married life in Coldwater were active in every movement to build up the town. They were prominent in the Methodist Church,

where Mrs. Fisk presided over the organ and directed the music. On their removal to St. Louis in 1859 they found only a southern Methodist Church, and at once began the organization of a congregation of the Northern connection. The outbreak of the Civil War interrupted this, for Mr. Fisk at once volunteered, was commissioned colonel, and with the 33rd Regiment of Volunteers departed for Pittsburgh Landing. Mrs. Fisk, at home in St. Louis, with a group of friends prepared lint and bandages, and as a representative of the Sanitary Commission secured vacant hotels for the reception of the sick and wounded. She then went to the front and brought back, by steamer to St. Louis, the wounded and dying, for whom she was able to provide many comforts, and to whose families she wrote their last messages. Mrs. Fisk went through the War with her husband, who had received the rank of general, numbering among her friends President Lincoln, and many of the distinguished soldiers of the War, living in a tent and sharing the discomforts of the men to whom she ministered. At the close of the War she found immediate work in assisting General Fisk to establish Fisk University, a school for colored people at Nashville, Tennessee. In this she received generous aid from many influential friends. She took great pride in, and had great ambition for, this institution for the Negro race, and made frequent visits to it. In 1872 General Fisk became interested in business in New York, and for several years he and Mrs. Fisk lived in the Fifth Avenue Hotel, spending their summers at Seabright, New Jersey. In both places they were greatly interested in their church and gave much of their time to its many activities. Mrs. Fisk sympathized fully with General Fisk in his work for temperance, and during the prohibition campaign of 1888 she was his constant companion in lecture tours. After the death of General Fisk in New York, July 9, 1890, she resolved as far as possible to carry on his work. Then came an invitation from the Woman's Home Missionary Society of the Methodist Episcopal Church to become its president. Following her election, she assumed the great responsibility of the office in October, 1893, and, for fifteen years, she held the position of leader, going to all parts of the country as occasion demanded, and four times a year holding her executive meetings in Cincinnati, Ohio. As presiding officer she was noted for her sterling sense of justice, honor, and strict truthfulness, her readiness on the platform, and her quick grasp of every difficult situation. For over twenty years Mrs. Fisk was prominent as an attendant at the Conference for Dependent People, held at Lake Mohonk, New York, and she always had a motherly interest in the young men at the Drew Theological Seminary, Madison, New Jersey. Mrs. Fisk died in New York, January 1, 1912, and was buried on January 4th in Coldwater, Michigan. She was a woman of simplicity and straightforwardness, having great contempt for indirection and ostentation. She delighted in service and gave of herself freely and unselfishly to all the interests that engaged her life.

WARD, FRANCES HENRIETTA WHITE (Mrs. Robert Ellery Ward), was born of a Scotch father and an Irish-English mother, July 31, 1869, in a small village near Detroit, Michigan.

Her father, James Irving White, volunteered at the outbreak of the Civil War. He died a few years after its close as a result of wounds received in battle. Although Mrs. Ward was a sturdy child, at the age of three she was in danger of being permanently crippled by an accident. She was, however, encouraged all through her childhood by a wonderful mother, to overcome every obstacle, and soon was able to compete with her companions in their games and sports, and to equal them all in climbing, skating, swimming, horse-back riding and dancing.

After completing the course in the high school at the age of sixteen, she became a bookkeeper in a large real estate and banking house in a town of about 30,000 inhabitants in Michigan. Here her extraordinary ability came to the notice of the heads of the firm, and at the age of eighteen she was appointed Manager of the properties, including several large office buildings, which she handled with marked success. While in this position her attention was attracted to life insurance, and she decided that this field not only was worth her best endeavor but held great possibilities for the future. Consequently she resigned her position, and created the Women's Department for the Massachusetts Mutual Life Insurance Company for Michigan and Ohio. Her success there was such that the Equitable Life Assurance Society of New York sought her services, and she was made General Agent for Southern Illinois.

During Mrs. Ward's connection with the Equitable, she decided that she would remain in the life insurance business only in a home office, where she could know what is going on, and with this thought in mind she became connected with the National Life Insurance Company, the oldest and largest life insurance company in Chicago, with which she filled the position of Home Office Representative for about eight years.

During the years of her service with the various life insurance companies, Mrs. Ward traveled throughout the United States, earning reputation for the soundness of her business judgment and her willingness to give herself in unstinted service to the interests of any individual or corporation showing integrity, sincerity and honesty of intention.

When the United States entered the World War in 1917, Mrs. Ward resigned as Home Office Representative of the National Life Insurance Company and became active in war work. The day after the Armistice was signed, however, she opened an investment, mortgage and loan office, in order to do her share in aiding the return of normal business conditions in Chicago. She had had such an excellent business training in the insurance field, coming in close contact with the financial affairs on La Salle Street, that the announcement of her enterprise to her business friends brought her immediately a larger volume of business than she could handle alone.

Mrs. Ward financed corporations, working out plans by which they might be reorganized in a way to secure the credit to which they were entitled, under their own policy of administration, and settling them well on their way to success. What she did for corporations she also did for individuals, so there are today many corporations and individuals successful and prosperous wholly because of Mrs. Ward's clear judgment and foresight.

In her business career Mrs. Ward has handled hundreds of thousands of dollars worth of certificates of deposit, without the loss of a single cent to her clients, for she negotiated such paper only from banks, which reputable insurance companies would insure against insolvency.

About 1905 Mrs. Ward, realizing that Chicago's available area for expansion was limited, conceived the idea of a community housing plan, and formed a corporation for this purpose, under the state law of Illinois.

In dealing with many business enterprises Mrs. Ward has found that frequently a woman has actually furnished the brains for the apparently successful man of affairs at the head, and that the woman served in a subordinate and inadequately paid position. To remedy this injustice and to enable women to take jointly, position for which they are fitted, she planned the Women's League Club of Chicago. The objects of this organization were thus formulated: (1) to develop sex loyalty, that women may stand by women as men by men; (2) to foster, protect and promote the ideas, discoveries and inventions of women; (3) to create a center for woman's activities—a real women's building, owned by women, managed by women and filled with women's activities (with a sound financial basis upon which to build this movement); (4) to stand by and promote the principles upon which our Government is founded; (5)

to establish a co-operative basis in governmental and business affairs between men and women; (6) to encourage the companionship between mother and daughter through an auxiliary to be called the Girls' League of Chicago; (7) to provide legal protection for widows through the Women's Legal Department; (8) to ultimately bring together the acknowledged leaders from every line of woman's endeavor, that all may think and act as one for the good of the organization and for all humanity.

Mrs. Ward and her husband, Mr. Robert Ellery Ward, of Minneapolis, were married September 7, 1898, and are the parents of one son, Frederic Ellery Ward, a graduate of Wesleyan University of Bloomington, Illinois.

MUSSEY, ELLEN SPENCER (Mrs. R. Delavan Mussey), lawyer, daughter of Platt R. and Persis (Duty) Spencer, was born in Geneva, Ashtabula County, Ohio, in 1850. Her father, who was the author of *The Spencerian System of Penmanship*, was the son of Caleb Spencer, a soldier of the Revolution, buried at Windham, New York, and was descended from John Spencer, who came from England to Rhode Island between 1635 and 1650 and died in 1684. Both of her mother's grandfathers, Mark Duty and Moses Warren, served in the Revolutionary War.

She was educated at the Geneva (Ohio) High School, Lake Erie College, Ohio, and Rockford College, Illinois, and on June 14, 1871, she was married at Washington, District of Columbia, to Reuben Delavan Mussey, a lawyer. They were the parents of Spencer Mussey and William H. Mussey. During the Civil War R. Delavan Mussey was a Brigadier-General and military secretary to President Johnson. Mrs. Mussey studied law in the office of General Mussey and practised with him until his death in 1892. In 1893 she was admitted to the bar, and is a member of the Bar of the Supreme Court of the District of Columbia, the thirteenth woman to be so admitted, and of the Court of Claims. Of her many cases before the Supreme Court she has never lost one. In 1896 she founded the Washington College of Law, which, in 1899, awarded her the honorary degree of LL.M., and was for seven years its Dean, the only woman dean of a law college. She is now its honorary dean. For twenty-five years she was attorney for the legations of Sweden and Norway and she has been counsel for several national patriotic and labor organizations. She has been the author of bills giving married women in the District of Columbia the right to their own earnings and giving mothers the same right as fathers in the guardianship of their children. She has also been instrumental in gaining legislation for the establishment of free kindergartens, free schools for sub-normal children, juvenile courts, compulsory education, and the Federal Child Bureau. As a member of the Woman Suffrage Association she spoke before the United States Senate Committee in 1910. She is the author of articles on *Marriage and Divorce, Legal Relations of Parent and Child* (*Good Housekeeping Magazine,* November, 1910), *Laws Relating to Women in the Forty-Six States of the Union* (1912), *Laws of Nations Relating to Women* (1912), and *Historic Washington* (*American Monthly Magazine,* April, 1912). For the first six months of 1912 she was the editor of the *American Monthly Magazine.* Mrs. Mussey was one of the founders of the American National Red Cross, was chairman of the women's citizens' committee for the 36th National Encampment, G. A. R., in Washington in 1902, and was formerly Vice-President of the Board of Education, Washington. In September, 1911, she was a delegate to the International Council of Women at Stockholm and she is Chairman of the Committee on the Legal Status of Women of the National Council of Women. She was at one time Vice-President-General of the Daughters of the American Revolution, State Regent of the District of Columbia, D. A. R., and President of the Legion of Loyal Women. She is President of the Women's Bar Association of

the District of Columbia, and a member of the National Geographic Society, an honorary member of the College Women's Club of the District of Columbia, and a member of the Dames of the Loyal Legion and of the Society of Daughters of Founders and Patriots.

LONGSHORE, HANNAH E. MYERS (Mrs. Thomas E. Longshore), physician, daughter of Samuel and Paulina Myers, was born in Sandy Springs, Montgomery County, Maryland, May 30, 1819, and died October 18, 1901, in Philadelphia, Pennsylvania. She was the descendant of the earliest settlers in Pennsylvania, members of the Society of Friends. From them she inherited the heroic courage and spirit of self-denial which led her to overcome the many obstructions she encountered as a pioneer and successful woman physician. But especially was she indebted to the parental influence which stimulated and sustained her in her professional work. Her father, Samuel Myers, a native of Bucks County, Pennsylvania, was a prominent teacher among the Friends. He was a philosophic thinker and his activity in all social and moral reforms gave an aspiring impulse to his children. His interest in education and intellectual development was a strong influence in their lives, and a determining factor in the careers of his daughter Hannah, and her two sisters, all of whom were successful practitioners of medicine. His sympathetic attitude inspired them with the courage and energy to engage in a profession at that time considered an unsuitable one for their sex and in preparing for which they risked forfeiting a reputation for modesty and womanly delicacy. He married Paulina Iden.

Mr. and Mrs. Myers removed from Maryland to Washington, District of Columbia, where their daughter Hannah received the rudiments of her education in a private school. When she was fourteen years old she went with the family to Ohio where they settled on a farm near New Lisbon, Columbiana County. Here, though much engrossed and absorbed in the family welfare and domestic duties, she attended New Lisbon Academy and pursued various branches of scientific study. At night, while the household slept, she worked over her books and acquired much general knowledge especially connected with the subject of health and disease. Her own delicate constitution acting as an incentive to study the fundamental laws of the science of life. In the home right and wrong were the test of values. During the intellectual discussions which took place there, all questions, methods, and duties were settled according to a standard of morality and human advancement, while the conventional or narrow traditional usages and fashions were declared as of no value. The principles of equality were the birthright of Hannah Myers, and it was her custom, while yet a young girl, to walk miles to the meeting houses and schools or any other available gathering place for the country folk and there address them on woman's rights, exhorting the women to develop any talent with which God had endowed them. The sustaining interest of her father, who would call and escort her home, ever spurred her to continue her mission work for her sex.

At the age of twenty-two she married Thomas E. Longshore and went with him to his home near Philadelphia, Pennsylvania. Mr. Longshore was an author and essayist, a radical in social science and religion, whose life was a demonstration of the wisdom and truthfulness of his principles. His progressive ideas, like those of his wife, were far in advance of the time. He was in full sympathy with her thoughts and aspirations, believing absolutely in equal rights for the sexes and willing to coöperate with her in obtaining them. Therefore the wife's environment was a peculiarly fortunate one in which to continue her studies at a period, when the majority of women were cruelly hampered, both at home and outside it, in their pursuit of a professional education. So it was that Mrs. Longshore, in conjunction with her attention to domestic and maternal duties—affairs which she never neglected—continued after marriage her general reading on health and dietetic subjects. Her brother-in-law, Doctor Joseph S. Longshore, was also in advance of his time as he was the earliest champion of the cause of women in medicine. Through him, with others coöperating, the charter of the Female Medical College of Pennsylvania was secured March 11, 1850. The name was changed in 1867 to the Woman's Medical College of Pennsylvania. He served upon the first board of Corporators and upon the first faculty and by so doing subjected himself to persecution and ostracism on the part of his brother practitioners. The house at 627 Arch Street was secured and there the college was established. The attitude of the profession at large was such that in 1859 the Philadelphia County Medical Society passed "resolutions of excommunication against every physician who should teach in the school, every woman who graduated from it, and everybody else who should consult with such teachers." During the years before the opening of the college, Doctor Longshore had encouraged his sister-in-law to use his medical library and under his teaching she prepared for college. When in October, 1850, the doors of the pioneer woman's medical college were opened, Hannah Longshore entered as a member of the first class of students and was graduated with the degree of M.D. in 1851. Her career as a student had been so brilliant that she was at once appointed demonstrator of anatomy at her college. She immediately placed her sign as a doctor in her window. By this act she attained the honor of being the first woman physician in Philadelphia to "hang out her sign." But at the period of doing so it was considered the reverse of an honorable action. The sign was a great curiosity, and street loungers gathered to examine it. Years of persecution followed. Although refined, cultured, and beautiful, of the very type of woman supposed to appeal to the chivalry of men, she was insulted by them and also by the majority of her own sex.

She was even spat upon. Druggists refused to fill her prescriptions, and one took it upon himself to order her home to "look after her house and darn her husband's stockings." Neighbors' children were forbidden by their parents to play with hers, and she was exposed to all the trials, her path beset with every obstacle, that might harass the woman who dared to follow an untried way. But in early life Doctor Longshore had learned to bear persecution, misrepresentation, and criticism without resentment. This discipline of mind and the moral sense to submit silently when resistance could not bring relief had prepared her to meet this storm of adverse public sentiment. With patient, quiet temper, and an irresistible and unconquerable will, following out a deep conscientious conviction, without ostentation, she entered upon her career and continued to practise her profession, her one dominating purpose being to show the world that woman could practise medicine with equal success and profit as man. In 1852 Doctor Longshore conducted a series of five "popular, practical, and fully illustrated" lectures for women. This was undoubtedly the first attempt made by a woman physician to popularize personal and sex hygiene. Nearly three quarters of a century later this pioneer physician had her clear vision vindicated when the National Government, recognizing a fundamental lack, undertook a nation wide campaign of sex education, employing women physicians as the spokesmen. Doctor Longshore soon built up a large and lucrative family practise among women and children extending over a period of forty years of active work. She was always deeply religious, by inheritance and choice a member of the Society of Friends. She believed in overcoming evil with good and in conquering with kindness and love rather than by violence or force. In the government of her household she exercised no other authority than that of kindness, forebearance, and forgiveness. Her appeals were to the honor, honesty, the intelligence, and moral sense of those with whom she had

business dealings, and in her collection of bills for service, she never resorted to the law to enforce a settlement. She was a member and an officer of the Universal Peace Union, and was the author of many articles, reports of cases, etc. appearing in medical journals. As she advanced in age and retired from practice, her intellect remained undimmed, and when she died at the age of eighty-three, she was in full possession of all her faculties. Throughout her career Doctor Longshore was sustained by the loving sympathy of her husband and her two children. Their son, Channing Longshore, was for many years a successful physician, but eventually retired from practice and became a banker. Their daughter, Lucretia (Longshore) Blankenburg, was an ardent worker for equal suffrage and active in other reforms.

DE GOGORZA, EMMA EAMES (Mme. Emilio de Gogorza), opera singer, daughter of Ithamar Bellows and Emma (Hayden) Eames, was born in Shanghai, China, on August 13, 1865. Her father, a lawyer and a graduate of Harvard Law School, was a descendant of Reverend Thomas Cotton, a native of Watley, England, who settled in Cambridge, Massachusetts, in 1680, at the age of twenty-seven years, and of Robert Eames, born in England, who settled at Woburn, Massachusetts, in 1712. Her mother's paternal ancestor was George Headen, of Scottish birth, who settled in Richmond, Maine, prior to the Revolution; Mme. Eames' grandfather, John, of Bath, Maine, changed the spelling of the name to its present form. Her mother's earliest maternal ancestor was Thomas Lennart of Londonderry, Ireland, who settled at Georgetown, Maine, in 1678, and died there in 1756.

Mme. Eames was educated by her mother until her fifteenth year. Her mother, having a singing voice of high quality, early recognized her daughter's genius, and placed her under the instruction of the late Clara Munger, in Boston. Later she was a pupil of Professor John Howard Paine of Harvard University, and also of Wilhelm Gericke, so long famous as Conductor of the Boston Symphony Orchestra. Before Mme. Eames had reached her twenty-first year, she had sung in concerts and churches in Boston. In 1886 she began study in Paris, under the great Marchesi. There her genius attracted the attention of Gounod, the composer, of the operas of *Faust* and *Romeo et Juliette*, who selected her to sing the part of Juliette at the Paris Grand Opera. She made her début on March 13, 1889, singing with the de Reszkes, and awoke the following morning to find herself famous.

Mme. Eames is without doubt the most gifted of American singers; at twenty-four she had beauty, a magnetic personality, charm and a glorious voice. For two years, she sang in Gounod's operas, and at her London début, April 7, 1891, she was highly successful. She is complete mistress of several modern languages, and possesses a high dramatic sense. It was during this first London season that Mme. Eames met and married, on August 1, 1891, Julian Story, a gifted painter, for whom she had sat for a portrait, and from whom she was separated in 1907. For many seasons Mme. Eames sang in London, until she found her strength would not permit her to continue, and still maintain her engagements at the Metropolitan Opera House in New York City.

Mme. Eames sang many times before Queen Victoria, with whom she was a prime favorite. She was summoned frequently to both Windsor and Osborne, and at the Queen's Jubilee in 1897, the Queen herself pinned the Jubilee Medal upon her. King Edward VII was another staunch admirer of her genius, and bestowed many handsome presents upon her. She was also decorated with the Palme Academique of the French Academy.

Mme. Eames' connection with the Metropolitan Opera House of New York began with the restoration of the Italian regime under Abbey, Scheffel and Grau in the winter of 1891. She made her début on December 14th, the opening night, in *Romeo et Juliette*, singing the same part which she had created in her Paris début, and still supported by Jean de Reszke. She sang in nineteen different operas during her long engagement with the Metropolitan. In her first season, beside *Romeo et Juliette*, she sang *Faust, Cavalleria Rusticana* and *Lohengrin*. In the following year she added to her list Micaela in *Carmen, Die Meistersinger* (in Italian) and *La Nozze di Figaro*. In subsequent years she sang Desdemona in Verdi's *Otello;* Mistress Ford in Verdi's *Falstaff*, and Elvira in *Don Giovanni*. For two years she studied abroad, perfecting her rôles in German, returning in 1896 to sing Elizabeth in *Tannhauser;* and Elsa in *Lohengrin*. Later she sang in *Die Meistersinger* and *Die Walkure*, also in German. In 1899 she sang in the first American performance of *Ero e Leandro*, the Italian version of *Zauberflote* in 1900; *Tosca* in 1902; *Iris* in 1907, and of Donna Anna in *Don Giovanni* in 1908.

On February 15, 1909, Mme. Eames permanently retired, after singing Floria Tosca most gloriously at the Metropolitan Opera House, New York City. From that date she lived quietly in Paris, where she married on July 13, 1911, at the Church of St. Pierre de Chaillot, the celebrated barytone, Emilio de Gogorza. On the outbreak of the World War, Mme. Eames returned to her former home at Bath, Maine. She sent abroad for all her belongings, costumes, gifts, letters and decorations. They were packed in a freighter's hold on top of a cargo of wool which caught fire from spontaneous combustion. Everything in the hold was burned, although the fire was extinguished before further damage was done to the ship.

Because of this unfortunate destruction nothing remains to Mme. Eames but the memory of great ovations, of audiences drowning her voice with applause, and of graceful gifts and treasured decorations.

EAVES, LUCILLE. As regards both ancestry and personal experiences Miss Eaves typically represents conditions peculiar to the United States. The chief colonial stocks of the South,—Scotch Irish, English, Scotch, German and Huguenot,—contributed to her heredity. Some of her father's forbears were among the earliest arrivals in Virginia. All of her ancestors located in America before the Revolution; and a number of them served in the Continental army. The restless pioneer spirit kept many of her kindred moving westward until the majority of the latest generation have found homes on the Pacific Coast. A peculiar reinforcement of hereditary tendencies resulted from the frequent intermarriages in the families of the plantation owners of the South.

Since Miss Eaves' maternal grandparents were cousins by both paternal and the maternal lines, her chief hereditary strains are traceable to Charles Rumsey, son of a distinguished officer of Cromwell's army, and David Weir, a Covenanter who was related to several fine old Scotch families. Charles Rumsey, a native of Wales, located in Maryland in 1665; he settled in Cecil County in 1675. His will leaves to his third and youngest son, Edward, the 100-acre plantation known as the "Adventure." Edward, I, married a daughter of the Scotch Douglas family; Edward, II, married Anna Cowman of Virginia; and Edward, III, married Sallie Gill of Pennsylvania. The children of the fourth Edward did not reach maturity, but there are many descendants of his sisters, Anna Cowman and Harriet. Many of the Rumseys were lawyers or physicians. The family, however, has among its prized possessions letters of Washington certifying that James Rumsey, a brother of the third Edward, was the first inventor of the steamboat. David Weir, a native of Antrim County, Ireland, in 1772 located in Chester County, South Carolina, where he acquired a large plantation. John Miller was a member of the party of Scotch-Irish Presbyterians led by the Rev-

erend William Martin. The children of these pioneers intermarried and James Weir, their grandson, born in 1777, located in Kentucky in 1798. His example was followed by his Uncle Samuel Miller and by many others of the South Carolina colonies. These two descendants of Scotch Covenanters married the Rumsey sisters, Anna Cowman and Harriet, who had come to Kentucky from Virginia; their children Edward Rumsey Weir and Harriet Rumsey Miller were Miss Eaves' paternal grandparents.

The family names will suggest the varied heredity which can be claimed by many Americans. Eaves and Ingram were English; Scott, Poague and Wallace were Scotch or Scotch-Irish; Short or Schartz was German. Ancestors bearing these names removed from Roanoke County, Virginia, to Muhlenberg County, Kentucky, between 1800 and 1810. Miss Eaves' father, David William Eaves, was educated as a lawyer. He was graduated Master of Arts at Yale, and continued his education at Heidelberg, where he was graduated Doctor of Philosophy. After the Civil War he married Anna Cowman Weir. They located in Leavensworth, Kansas, where the six children of his first marriage were born. A man of his scholarly tastes was poorly adapted to the turbulent business life of the West. His family experienced alternating periods of prosperity and adversity, while he attempted various business ventures in Kansas, Illinois, Idaho and Oregon.

The family fortunes were at low ebb when Miss Eaves graduated, at the age of seventeen, from the high school of Peoria, Illinois. She taught in the public elementary schools for one year, then served for three years as teacher in the Lapwai (Idaho) Industrial School for the Nez Perces Indians. Her father was Superintendent of this institution at the time. Miss Eaves next taught for a year in the public schools of Portland, Oregon. Some improvement in her father's business outlook at this time made it possible to carry out her ardent desire to continue her education. She entered

Stanford University with the pioneer class, and managed, by close application, to complete her course in three years, at the same time earning a part of her expenses. She used the last dollar of her savings to pay the fee for her B.A. diploma. Shortly after graduation, Miss Eaves accepted a position as teacher of history and civics in the high school at San Diego, California. During the next four years she supplemented her school services with other educational activities in various teachers' organizations and in the University Extension Society. She gave two courses of lectures, and assisted in arranging for other lecture and summer-session courses conducted by University professors. Appreciation of her services moved the authorities to offer her an appointment as Head of the History Department in the newly established State Normal School. Miss Eaves, however, declined the offer, in order to carry on further study. She took her first post-graduate work at Chicago University, where she enrolled during four quarter-terms. She specialized in sociology, but took some courses also in history, economics, and philosophy. An appointment as University Extension lecturer made it possible for her to earn a part of her expenses, by organizing and conducting classes for the study of sociological aspects of American History. She served also as a member of the graduate debating team. The following year she was appointed Instructor in History at Stanford University. Owing to her knowledge of her subject, and her ability as a teacher, her classes grew rapidly. During the second year she was teaching two hundred students, and directing a number of minor historical investigations. Miss Eaves became involved in an "academic freedom" controversy which arose at Stanford at that time, and was one of twenty-five members of the faculty who found it necessary to seek new fields of work.

Her next position was that of Head Resident Worker of the social settlement located at South Park, San Francisco. Mrs. Phoebe

A. Hearst had just furnished this settlement with a fine building and excellent equipment, so that an opportunity was offered for varied social and educational activities. Besides supervising a large number of educational and recreational activities for the people of the neighborhood, Miss Eaves gave special attention to the development of a plan for giving ethical instruction to children by means of stories illustrated with stereopticon pictures. Another of her personal services was the systematic effort to promote a better understanding of the rapidly developing Trade-Union movement.

Miss Eaves was a regular contributor to the local labor paper, and arranged numerous conferences and discussions for persons specially interested in the activities of the San Francisco labor organizations. Workers at the settlement particularly desired to bring about labor legislation. To this end they put forth every effort, and it was through their leadership that California secured its first effective Child Labor law.

After four years of these activities, Miss Eaves attended Columbia University, to continue her study of social, economic and ethical problems. She had expected to take examinations for the degree of Doctor of Philosophy in the Spring of 1906, but when the San Francisco earthquake occurred a few weeks before the appointed date, she returned to assist in the relief of the stricken city. She devoted more than a year to various relief services. The most important of these was the organization of sewing centers where 75,000 warm garments were manufactured by women who volunteered their services as seamstresses. In the fall of 1907 Miss Eaves returned to her interrupted academic work. She was awarded the Flood Fellowship in Economics at the University of California. While studying there Miss Eaves also served as an investigator for the Carnegie Institution. She devoted eighteen months to the preparation of *A History of California Labor Legislation*. This was published by the University of California. In February, 1909, having been appointed Associate Professor of Sociology at the University of Nebraska, she entered upon her active duties there. The following summer she returned to Columbia and passed her Doctor's examinations. At the University Commencement in June, 1910, she was graduated Ph.D. In the summer of 1910, and again during the academic year, 1913–1914, she served as a member of the faculty of the University of California. The syllabus of her course on *Labor Organizations in Great Britain and the United States* was published by the University.

Since September, 1915, Miss Eaves has directed social research for the Women's Educational and Industrial Union, as well as for Simmons College, Boston, Massachusetts, and has also conducted various courses in Sociology at the College. With the assistance of the American Sociological Society, she is now engaged in developing a plan for nation-wide coöperative research dealing with problems of peculiar interest to women. The results of the great variety of social-economic research which she has directed have not been fully published, but the following printed studies are available: *The Food of Working Women in Boston*, published by the Massachusetts Department of Health (Boston, 1917); *War-Time Child Labor in Boston*, published by the National Child Labor Committee (November, 1918); *Training for Store Service, The Vocational Experiences and Training of Juvenile Employees of Retail Department, Dry Goods and Clothing Stores in Boston*, published by The Gorham Press (Boston, 1920); *A Thousand Industrial Accidents Suffered by Massachusetts Children* (published in *The American Child*, Vol. II). In addition to these reports of the results of research, Miss Eaves has published many book reviews and short articles, contributed to the discussions of professional societies.

Miss Eaves is a member of Phi Beta Kappa, the Collegiate Alumnae, the American Sociological Society, the American Economic Association, the Royal Economic Society, the American Association of University Professors, and a number of social-betterment organizations. She has served on important committees of national and state professional societies, and has been an officer or a committee member of many philanthropic and civic organizations.

EINSTEIN, HANNAH BACHMAN (Mrs. William Einstein), philanthropist, daughter of H. S. and Fanny I. (Obermyer) Bachman, was born in New York City. Through her mother, she is a lineal descendant of Isaac Obermaier, who came from Alsace, then a French province, and settled in New York City in 1787.

Mrs. Einstein was educated in New York City; subsequently she pursued special courses in Sociology, Penology and Criminology, in Columbia University; and in 1900 she was graduated at the School of Philanthropy. In 1883, she was married, in New York City, to William Einstein, a woolen manufacturer. They are the parents of one son, William L. Einstein, and one daughter, Marion, now Mme. René Lozé, of Paris, France.

From early life, Mrs. Einstein's interest was largely centered in the problems presented by poverty and economic insufficiency. This interest was augmented by her later studies, until she became recognized as an expert upon the relation between crime of the petty sort, and lowered vitality, due to the impossibility of obtaining a decent living during the years of adolescence. After some study of the conditions, Mrs. Einstein realized that many wrong-doers among the young are the children of widows, who have made every effort to maintain their homes, rather than allow their children to be placed in institutions. On further investigation, she found that the relief granted to those in need, was wholly insufficient for widows with young children.

Through her connection with various relief organizations, she became convinced that these widows needed special help to rear children to become good citizens, and in 1908, with several others, she organized the Widowed Mothers' Fund Association, which, in the succeeding years, granted help to widowed mothers in New York City, amounting to over a million dollars. Before the work had progressed far, however, she realized that private means could never cope with the situation, and that assistance must be obtained from public moneys. For many years, therefore, she labored valiantly in behalf of the movement which finally resulted in the enactment of the Child Welfare Act, Chapter 328, Laws of New York, 1915. This is the act, under which all the work of the Child Welfare Boards in New York City, as well as in New York State, is conducted.

Excellent as are the provisions of the law, Mrs. Einstein recognized that widowed mothers need not only a legislative contrivance for the bestowal of a permanent pension, but also some means of rehabilitation, a public provident financial machinery, whose grants should provide for the first difficult one or two years after the husband's death. If the home were kept together, children would not be sent to hospitals, sanitoriums and other public institutions, save in certain relatively rare instances. In considering the subject Mrs. Einstein always visualized the child and its value to the community. She saw clearly that it rested with the state, in this class of children, to see that they became an asset, rather than a liability. And she saw that it meant, to the mothers, hardship and hard work, which would always be borne gladly because of mother love. That was the factor upon which she counted, and with scarcely a failure. Our public institutions today are overcrowded, but the burden that the State must bear tomorrow, depends largely upon the work being done for and with the children of today—among whom are the mental defectives and the inmates of the almshouses and reformatories of tomorrow. She has often insisted that the wreckage

and waste of human lives might be largely avoided, if communities would only adopt definite programs for the conservation of child-life; that the state's most important asset is the child—for outranking industrial, commercial and scientific discoveries.

Mrs. Einstein declares that the decrease of children in institutions during the past seven years has been more than offset by the increase in the number cared for at public expense under the supervision of Boards of Child Welfare. The preventive work which that form of public relief represents, has the approval of those in public and private life who are well informed on the subject of dependency.

Mrs. Einstein served on the State Commission which investigated the subject of widow's pensions, so-called; she also acted as Chairman of the Committee on Investigation for this commission; her findings revealed many interesting facts regarding the help actually given to widows with children both in New York City and in the State. As one of the original members of the Board of Child Welfare in New York, in 1915, Mrs. Einstein was made Chairman of the Committee of that Board, appointed to pass upon all applications for help. This work is exceedingly arduous, as well as important, because upon its findings depend the moneys to be disbursed, now amounting to over five million dollars annually. Later, Mrs. Einstein became President of this Board, and, in 1919, President of the State Association of Child Welfare Boards.

The state law regarding Boards of Child Welfare, as originally interpreted, required the appointment of such Boards in each county and in the City of New York, but left it to the fiscal authorities of the several localities to grant appropriations at their discretion. This resulted in the failure of a number of up-state counties to grant appropriations to their local boards, as they preferred to leave the widows in the hands of the poormasters of such districts. As President of the State Association of Child Welfare Boards, Mrs. Einstein worked unceasingly to have this condition remedied, with the result, that, in 1920, Governor Miller made mandatory the organization and financing of Child Welfare Boards throughout the state.

Approximately at this time, Mrs. Einstein succeeded in her effort to secure, for the Board of Child Welfare, the coöperation of the State Industrial Commission, with the result that an employment branch was instituted in the offices of the Child Welfare Board in New York City. The value of this employment bureau is incalculable; it serves to keep back of the children after they have passed the age when the Board cares for them financially; it protects young persons from exploitation, and projects its influence over the family many years after the period originally contemplated by the State Act.

During her administration of the affairs of the Child Welfare Board, Mrs. Einstein encountered many cases wherein the widow sorely needed assistance for her children, but was ineligible for such help because her husband had neglected to become a citizen. For a long time Mrs. Einstein labored to secure a new construction of the State Act, but without avail. At present the mother can, if she has been a resident of the country for five years, and of the state for one, obtain her first papers, and, in another two years and ninety days, be granted full citizenship, thus becoming eligible for the Child Welfare Board allowance.

It developed upon Mrs. Einstein to take the first steps in organizing the National Union of Public Child Welfare Officers, of which her co-worker, Miss Sophie Irene Loeb, became the first President. The purposes of the Union are: (1) to promote a national interest in child welfare; (2) to obtain national and state legislation promoting the culture and welfare of the child; and (3) to preserve the unity of family life.

In 1918, Mrs. Einstein was appointed on the Mayor's Committee of Women on National Defense and served as Chairman of the Information Booths Committee; she was also Chairman of the Maintenance Committee of the Woman's Council of National Defense. For several years, she was Vice-President of the New York State Conference of Charities and Correction; on many occasions she has been appointed by the Governor as a delegate to various charity conferences. She has been also Chairman of the Americanization Committee of the New York State Federation of Women's Clubs. Mrs. Einstein is the Honorary President of the Emanuel Sisterhood of Personal Service; she was the founder of the Federation of Sisterhoods, an organization made up of twenty-one smaller organizations, one of which was the Widowed Mothers' Fund Association, of which she was the founder. All these organizations together form the Federation of Jewish Philanthropic Sisters.

FOLKMAR, ELNORA CUDDEBACK (Mrs. Daniel Folkmar), physician, daughter of George and Elizabeth Ellen (Ullrey) Cuddeback, was born in Franklin, Illinois, April 15, 1863. The Cuddeback line is traceable to Jacques Caudebec (Jacob Codebec), a Huguenot, born about 1666 in Caudebec-en-Caux, Normandy, France, where the records of the family are found dating from the year 1,000. Jacques Caudebec, with Peter Gumaer, another Huguenot, located in Maryland about 1685, and shortly afterward settled in New York, where, in 1689, he took the oath of allegiance to King William and Queen Mary. In 1695 he married Margueretta Provost (born, 1673), sister of David Provost, Mayor of New York in 1699–1700, and granddaughter of David William Provost, a Huguenot, and a native of Rouen, France, who located in New York about 1638. Jacques Caudebec secured a patent of land from the Indians in 1697. The large stone house, which he and his sons built, just south of Port Clinton, Orange County, New York, still stands, a firm, substantial, comfortable home. In 1715 he was a member of the first company of Ulster County Militia. His son, William Caudebec (baptized June 24, 1704) was a militiaman in 1738, and a signer of the Revolutionary Pledge in 1775. On April 8, 1733, he married Jemima Eiting (baptized March 17, 1706) a granddaughter of Louis DeBois, who came to America in 1660. Their son, Benjamin Cuddeback (baptized June 21, 1747) in 1767 married Catherine Van Fleet (baptized March 23, 1744). He was a signer of the Revolutionary Pledge, and served as a militiaman in the Revolutionary War under his brother, Captain Abraham Cuddeback. Benjamin's son, Henry Cuddeback (born March 23, 1771) on October 3, 1793, married Esther Gumaer born September 23, 1774) daughter of Jacob Gumaer. Their son, Jacob Gumaer Cuddeback (born March 13, 1799) on February 16, 1833, married his second cousin, Jemima Cuddeback (born October 30, 1805) daughter of Jacob Gumaer Cuddeback (born April 1, 1763) and Blandina Van Etten, granddaughter of Abraham Cuddeback (born October 31, 1738) and niece of Colonel William Abram Cuddeback of the War of 1812. Abraham Cuddeback, a signer of the Revolutionary Pledge and a Captain in the Revolutionary War, a brother of Benjamin Cuddeback, married Esther Gumaer, a granddaughter of Peter Gumaer, who came to America with Jacques Caudebec.

Elnora Cuddeback Folkmar's father, George Cuddeback, son of Jacob G. and Jemima Cuddeback, was born in Pennsylvania, December 10, 1837; married Elizabeth Ellen Ullrey, August 20, 1861; and died in Milwaukee, Wisconsin, December 23, 1906. Elizabeth Ellen Ullrey was born in Indiana, March 2, 1844. Her father was John Ullrey, son of Jacob Ullrey of Shelby County, Ohio; and her mother was Sarah Hoover, daughter of David and Susannah (Weybright) Hoover of the same county. Elizabeth E. Ullrey's parents early moved west, and later settled at Niles, Berrien County, Michigan.

On August 20, 1895, at Janesville, Wisconsin, Elnora Cuddeback married Daniel Folkmar, the son of Michael and Rachel (Anderson) Fulcomer. Daniel Folkmar was born in Rockville, Wisconsin, October 28, 1861. Docteur de l'Université de Paris, and a Docteur des sciences sociales de l'Université Nouvelle de Bruxelles. He is anthropologist and statistician, to the Census Bureau, United States Department of Commerce, Washington.

The record of Elnora Cuddeback Folkmar's education is closely related to the account of her many educational, civic, and professional activities. In 1889 she was graduated in the Normal Department of Alma College, Michigan; and in 1892 was graduated B.S. and M.Ped. at Western Michigan College. She spent five semesters, from 1893 to 1896, at the University of Chicago as a post-graduate student in psychology and natural and social sciences. In 1885 she was graduated Master of Arts in Philosophy at Carthage College, Illinois. During the winter of 1898–1899 she was a post-graduate student in education at the Sorbonne, Paris, and in social sciences at the Collége de France and the Collége des Sciences Sociales. In 1899 she won the certificate of the École d'Anthropologie, a very high honor in scholarship. The following winter she attended the Université Nouvelle of Brussels, Belgium, where she was graduated Docteur des sciences sociales. Her Doctorate thesis, *Education as a Division of Applied Anthropology*, she defended in a course of six lectures before the Faculty and the student body of the University. In 1909, she was graduated M.D. at George Washington University, Washington, District of Columbia.

Doctor Folkmar served her apprenticeship as an educator by teaching for eight years in public schools and one year in a state normal school. Later, for six years, she acted as principal of normal departments in colleges. She was State Institute Lecturer, during the summer months, for eleven years, in Michigan, Illinois, Iowa and Wisconsin. While studying at the Université Nouvelle, in Burssels (1899–1900), she also lectured there on education.

During the course of her medical studies she was for one year (1906–1907) Principal of the Academic Department and Demonstrator of Anatomy at the Wisconsin Medical College (now Marquette University), Milwaukee. While there she organized (1906) the Better Milwaukee Association, which helped to secure an appropriation from the City Council for the purchase of land for several recreation parks near school buildings. Since 1909 Doctor Folkmar has practised medicine in Washington, District of Columbia. She specializes in electrotherapy, reflexotherapy, and other branches in which physical means are employed for the treatment of chronic diseases. She emphasizes the educational duty of the physician, to teach people how to make themselves well and how to stay well. Nor has her own work as an educator ceased. In 1912 she lectured on personal and social sex hygiene for the National Cash Register Company of Dayton, Ohio. In the same year she delivered fifteen lectures on sex education at the Fifteenth International Congress of Hygiene and Demography, held in Washington. The Congress awarded her a diploma of merit for her lantern slides on the subject. Doctor Folkmar has been an active worker in several medical societies. During 1911–1912 she was State Chairman, for the District of Columbia, of the Committee on Public Health Education of the American Medical Association. In 1916, she was Chief of the Medical Corps of the National Service School. From 1909 to 1915 she served as Clinician to the Woman's Clinic, Washington, and for two years (1911–1912) of this period as executive officer and a lecturer in the Educational Department.

In 1913 Doctor Folkmar organized the Woman's Evening Clinic of Washington, and for seven years served as a member of the Board of Directors, Clinician, Lecturer on Health, and Superintendent. The first officers of this organization were Mrs. John Hays Hammond, President; Mrs. Charles E. Hughes, Mrs. Leonard Wood, and Mrs. Richard Wainwright, Vice-Presidents; and Mrs. Julius Lansburgh, Secretary. The purpose of the organization was to provide an evening clinic for wage-earning women, attended by women physicians; and to establish a home for the recuperation of persons below par in health, but not sick enough to be hospital cases. The clinic was unique in many ways. The service was arranged to suit the convenience of the patients—evening hours for wage-earners, and noon hours for housewives. The reception room was furnished as a cheerful living room with potted plants, large easy chairs, and shelves of good books and magazines. A patient says: "It makes you feel almost well just to come here and sit awhile." Although the clinic was supported by the dues of members, it was not free. A small fee was charged, the amount depending upon the margin whereby the patient's income exceeded her necessary expenditures. The average fee paid, for a period of seven years, including over 20,000 visits for consultation, treatment, and medicine, was 30 cents a visit. Thus every patient had the satisfaction of feeling that she had paid her way—that she was not an object of charity. The staff was limited to no one school of medicine; regulars, homeopaths, and eclectics worked harmoniously together to insure the health of women. Besides the usual equipment of instruments for diagnosis and surgery and a well-stocked drug room, the clinic was well equipped for electrical and other physical means of therapy. Emphasis was placed on prevention, on the employment of educational measures for the attainment of health. As an outgrowth of this work, Doctor Folkmar organized the Good Health Club in 1920, and the same year she realized her dream of a home for both the Clinic and the Club. In 1921 the Clinic was reincorporated as the Woman's Welfare Association.

Doctor Folkmar is first Vice-President of the American Association of Medico-Physical

Research; a Fellow of the American Medical Association; second President of the American Electro-therapeutic Association; a charter member of the International Woman's Medical Association and of the Social Hygiene Society of the District of Columbia; a member of the American Genetic Association; the Medical Society of the District of Columbia; the Southern Medical Association; a member of the National Woman's Medical Association; the Central Society of Physical Therapeutists; and the American Social Hygiene Association. She is also a member of the Columbian Women; the League of American Penwomen; Esther Chapter No. 5 of the Order of the Eastern Star; and the Woman's City Club, Washington, District of Columbia.

Doctor Folkmar has writen numerous articles and papers. Prior to 1900 she contributed to educational journals and magazines. During her residence in Milwaukee (1906–1907) she wrote for the city press articles on social and civic betterment; and in 1907 published a series of ten articles on *Life Insurance* in the Milwaukee *Sentinel*. With her husband, Doctor Daniel Folkmar, she is co-author of *A Dictionary of Immigrant Races*, published in 1911 as Volume V of *The Reports of the Immigration Commission*. It was the only one of the forty volumes in this series to appear in a second edition. *The Proceedings of the Central Society of Physical Therapeutists* contained, in 1919, her *Diathermy in the Treatment of Stiff and Painful Joints*. In 1920 these *Proceedings* included her *Diathermy in the Treatment of Sprains, Fractures, Pelvic and Abdominal Adhesions*. Her paper, *Diathermy as a Therapeutic Agent, Especially in the Treatment of Sprains, Fractures, Adhesions, Chronic Stiff and Painful Joints*, read before the thirty-first annual meeting of the *American Electrotherapeutic Association*, was published in *The American Journal of Electrotherapeutics and Radiology* (January, 1921). Her paper on *Medical Diathermy—Definition—Essential Equipment —Fundamental Principles—Technique—Ther-*

apeutic Indications, read before the Tenth Annual Convention of the American Association for Medico-Physical Research in 1921, was published in the *Proceedings* of the Association and also (May and June, 1922), by the *American Physician*.

GANS, BIRD STEIN (Mrs. Howard S. Gans), educator and social worker, daughter of Solomon and Pauline (Bernhard) Stein, was born in Allegheny City, Pennsylvania, May 29, 1868. Her father, a native of Bavaria, (born in June, 1835; died in June, 1902) came with his parents to Baltimore, Maryland, as a very young child: her mother's family came originally from Hamburg, Germany. Her mother was born in New York City.

Miss Stein was educated at Schmidt Institute and the Anne Brown School, New York City; studied law at New York University, and pursued post-graduate courses at Columbia University, Teachers' College, and the School for Social Research. In April, 1888, she was married to Louis Sternberger, and in July 1908, to Howard S. Gans, a lawyer, who was born in Philadelphia, Pennsylvania. Her children are: Marion Stein Gans, and Robert Stein Gans, both born in New York.

Since 1897, Mrs. Gans has been President of the Federation for Child Study, an organization for the development of intelligent parenthood, orginating in the Society for the Study of Child Nature, founded in 1888 at the suggestion of Doctor Felix Adler. The object of the Federation is two-fold, embracing the education of the members in the nature and problems of the child, and practical demonstration of methods. The first, or educational, phase of the work is conducted through lecture courses by leading educators, psychologists, etc., and special conferences at regular intervals. There are also chapter discussions, held by separate groups that meet for the intensive and systematic study of child nature. The work is carried on under the guidance of more experienced members, with a definite program of reading and study to meet individual needs. Ordinarily specific subjects are selected as the work of the season. The writings of recognized authorities upon those subjects are studied, and their views are discussed at the meetings. In addition members are encouraged to discuss their personal problems in the light of the principles developed through this reading and study. Such discussions are in a sense the primary activity of the Federation. They vivify the central idea in Professor Adler's mind—which he imparted to the group of five women whom he called together thirty-five years ago as the nucleus of the Federation—that parenthood is an Art, a Science and a Vocation; that it presents problems capable of being solved only by patient study; that such a study offers the greatest, and, at times, the only hope of sympathetic relations between parent and child. From the chapters have sprung all the other activities, the lecture courses, the visiting mothers, the talks to parents and teachers, the book lists, the school educational experiment committee and the Play Schools. There are now sixty-three active chapters, of which sixteen were organized during the year 1922–1923.

The Summer Play Schools, organized in 1917 under the auspices of the Federation, for the children of the congested districts of New York City, during the public school vacation period, are the direct and concrete result of this study and research. They are held in settlement houses, community buildings, public schools, wherever there are facilities and workers, and each aims to give, to from two to four hundred children, every day from nine to five, nourishing food, medical supervision, and healthful and constructive recreation. This work has the coöperation of the Board of Education, the Board of Health, the Academy of Medicine, the Child Health Organization, and many other civic and philanthropic agencies. It has been endorsed also, by the Department of the Interior of the United States, and the Bureau

of Education has published a pamphlet, *Summer Health and Play School* (1919), setting forth its program and advantages. It is the expressed hope of the Commissioner of Education that the Play Schools may eventually become a public responsibility. A Committee on Play Schools has this work in charge.

Other appropriate committees weave the separate activities of the Federation together, extend the work of the organization as a whole, and make available certain information not easily accessible to the members. Every year *A Selected List of Recent Books for Children* and *A Selected List of Books for Parents* are issued; information concerning schools for children of special requirements is compiled; child legislation is carefully watched, and influence brought to bear to prevent harmful laws and to further good ones: an intensive study is made of the many experiments in education being conducted both at home and abroad; suitable motion picture entertainments are arranged for children and young people, both at public and private places; out of town chapters are organized and supervised; and the message of the Federation is spread through talks to mothers' meetings, Parent and Teacher Associations, and similar bodies. Assistance is also given such agencies as the Public Education Association school visitors. During the year 1923, the Federation published its *Outlines of Child Study*, culled from the minutes of many years of chapter work. It has been received with uniformly favorable comment. The offices of the Federation are at 262 West 76th Street, New York, where a library is maintained. In addition to her work with the Federation, Mrs. Gans has served as Vice-President of the League for the Improvement of Children's Comic Supplements, and as Second Vice-President of the Woman's Conference of the Society for Ethical Culture. For ten years she was a member of the General Committee of the National Board of Review of Motion Pictures, and was the first Chairman of the National

Committee for Better Films. She is a member of the Women's City Club, the Public Education Association, the National Child Labor Committee, the Academy of Political Science, the Federation for Child Study, the Civic Club of New York, the American Ethical Union, the School Art League, the Child Health Organization, the National Conference for Social Work, the Consumers' League, the Progressive Education Association, the American Association for Labor Legislation, the Vocational Education Association, Teachers Union Auxiliary and the Metropolitan Museum of Art.

HOLT, MARSHALL KEYSER (Mrs. Leland Wallace Holt), chemist, miner, and rancher, was born in Alexandria, Kentucky, February 24, 1874. Her father, Marshall J. Keyser, was descended from Benjamin Keyser of Holland, who settled in New Amsterdam (New York) about 1630. Her mother, Mary Margaret Marshall, was a descendant of Thomas Marshall, who came from England to Virginia about 1616, and through Chief Justice John Marshall, was also a great-granddaughter of Sarah Boone, alleged to be the first white woman to set foot on Kentucky soil.

Marshall Keyser (Mrs. Holt) received her early education in the public schools and under private teachers in Alexandria, Kentucky, and was a student at the State Agricultural and Mining College and the Kentucky University, Lexington, Kentucky. Later she attended the Ohio Mechanics Institute at Cincinnati and the Institute of Technology at Munich, Bavaria. From 1895 to 1900 she taught chemistry and German, and then served for two years as a chemist for the West Java Sugar Export Company, in the Island of Java.

On her return to the United States, she was married at Alexandria, Kentucky, March 13, 1903, to Leland Wallace Holt of North Yarmouth, Maine, a lawyer, ranchman, and miner, who died November 10, 1908. From 1908 to 1912 Mrs. Holt was President and Manager of the Holt Land and Cattle Company of Colorado, and President of the New Mexico Iron and Coal Mining Company, and she is still actively engaged in farming, mining, and land development, making her home at San Rafael, Marin County, California. She has written frequently for chemical, mining, and agricultural publications, and from 1910 to 1913 was owner and publisher, and, from 1913 to 1914, Editor of the magazine, *Orchard and Farm*, of San Francisco.

Mrs. Holt has adopted six children, Henry, Richard, Joseph, William, Josephine, and Nathalie Holt, each of whom have taken honors in university work and made successful beginnings in life. She is a member of the Executive Committee of the Farmers' National Congress, of the Executive Council of the International Dry Farming Congress, is the only woman member of the California Country Life Commission, and was formerly a member of the Cosmopolitan Culture Club of Newport, Kentucky. She also has the distinction of membership in the Sonora Valley Yaqui Indian Tribe and the Mescalero-Apache Indian Tribe. Mrs. Holt inherits the active pioneer spirit of a long line of Colonial and Revolutionary warrior ancestors. She has earned her own living as chemist, miner, and rancher, under seven different flags, and has found all willing to give fair returns for honest work.

LAIDLAW, HARRIET BURTON, suffragist, daughter of George Davidson and Alice Davenport (Wright) Burton, was born in Albany, New York, December 1, 1874. She was graduated from the Albany High School and from the New York State Normal College, where she received the degrees of Bachelor and Master of Pedagogy in 1895 and 1896, respectively. She then took special work at Illinois Wesleyan University, receiving the degree there of Ph.B. in 1898. Later, going to New York, she entered Barnard College and obtained the degree of A.B. from Columbia University in 1902. While teaching in a New

York high school, she did post-graduate work at Columbia, and has also taken special courses at the University of Chicago, Harvard, and Oxford, England.

The subject of equal suffrage early engaged the attention of Mrs. Laidlaw, and from girlhood she untiringly worked for it. She was considered a radical, but she was encouraged by the friendship of some of the noted pioneer workers for woman's rights. She made her first speech for suffrage at a parlor meeting in Albany in 1893 and at that date wrote her first newspaper article on the subject. She was active as a page and distributor of literature at the great hearing for the Constitutional Convention in 1894 in Albany. Later, she became Secretary of the College League in New York City and with Mrs. Alice Duer Miller, was largely instrumental in arranging and publishing the first suffrage calendar in 1907. When the Woman Suffrage Party was started in New York she became chairman for the Borough of Manhattan, and she was indefatigable and extremely successful in helping to build up that organization. Her work included that for City, State and Nation. She traveled constantly, making speeches in the interest of her propaganda in all parts of the United States, and she has constantly used her pen as the author of many broadsides, pamphlets, and articles on suffrage for magazines and newspapers. She was a member of the Empire State Campaign Committee, whose special object was to carry the suffrage amendment, and was the first auditor of the National American Woman Suffrage Association. Before the suffrage cause occupied her time to the exclusion of other interests, she was an interested worker in the Women's Municipal League, and in various other organizations including the Municipal Art League; the Child Labor Association, State and National; the Babies' Hospital; the Penny Provident Fund; The Woman's Trade Union; The Plant and Flower Guild; the Vegetarian Society, and was Vice-President of the Pascal Institute of Domestic Science and Secretary of an auxiliary of the Manhattan Trade School for Girls. She served for a number of years as a member of the Vocational Bureau of the Public Education Association. As Secretary of the Progressive State Society she endeavored to arouse the public interest in the plays of Ibsen and other advanced playwrights. Eventually these varied interests gave place to exclusive work for equal suffrage to which Mrs. Laidlaw devoted all her energy.

She is an enthusiastic outdoor woman, and, at her beautiful summer home Hazeldean, Sands Point, Long Island, she spends much time during the season, on the links, or sailing. She is fond of rough camping, and of traveling, and has visited all parts of the United States and many countries of Europe.

Mrs. Laidlaw is a member of the Peace Society, the Woman's University Club, and the Woman's Cosmopolitan Club of New York. She was married at New York, October 25, 1905, to James Lees Laidlaw, a well-known banker and financier. Mr. Laidlaw, an influential public-spirited man, was in full sympathy with his wife in her work for equal suffrage. He was, himself, the President of the Men's National and New York State Leagues for Woman Suffrage. They have one child, Louise Burton Laidlaw.

INDEX

A

B

H

I

J

K

L

Mc

M

N

O

P

Q

R

S

T